HENRY MCBRIDE SERIES IN
MODERNISM AND MODERNITY

YALE UNIVERSITY PRESS

NEW HAVEN & LONDON

Selected Letters of

Rebecca West

Edited, Annotated,
and Introduced by
Bonnie Kime Scott

This book has been published with assistance from the fund for the Henry McBride Series in Modernism and Modernity established by Maximilian Miltzlaff.

Printed in the United States of America.

Library of Congress Cataloging-in-Publication Data
West, Rebecca, Dame, 1892–1983
[Correspondence. Selections]
Selected letters of Rebecca West / edited, annotated, and introduced by
Bonnie Kime Scott.
p.   cm. — (Henry McBride series in modernism and modernity)
Includes bibliographical references (p.   ) and index.
ISBN 0-300-07904-4 (alk. paper)
1. West, Rebecca, Dame, 1892–1983—Correspondence. 2. Women novelists, English—
20th century—Correspondence. 3. Women journalists—Great Britain—Correspondence.
4. Modernism (Literature)—Great Britain. I. Scott, Bonnie Kime, 1944–   . II. Title.
III. Series.
PR6045.E8Z48 1999   828'.91209—dc21   [B]   99-12240

A catalogue record for this book is available from the British Library.

The paper in this book meets the guidelines for permanence and durability of the Committee on Production Guidelines for Book Longevity of the Council on Library Resources.

10 9 8 7 6 5 4 3 2 1

FOR

JANE MARCUS

AND

ALL THE LIONESSES

Contents

Acknowledgments

The people who knew Rebecca West or knew about her have made the process of collecting and editing her letters a delightful collaboration. In some cases, she has set up lasting friendships for me. It says something about the power of her personality and experience that people were so eager to make this project their own.

Members of West's family were most helpful about finding letters and information, and they kept me nourished as I spent long hours poring over their resources. I wish to thank West's niece, Alison Selford, an essential resource on West's genealogy (an interest she blames on the family's Scottish heritage), and West's nephew Norman and his wife Marion Macleod, able stewards with a fine sense of hospitality, who have been helpful in every way imaginable. I have been helped by West's daughters-in-law, Katharine Church and Lily West, and grandchildren, Caroline Duah and Edmund West, and his wife Cheryl (who, I am thankful to say, saved letters in Tupperware containers). Michael Sissons, of Peters Fraser and Dunlop, has been helpful in representing the Estate of Rebecca West, which granted permission for this publication. Among West's friends who shared recollections, some of them making patient and meticulous corrections, are her secretaries Anne McBurney and Diana Stainforth, Merlin Holland, Arthur Schlesinger, Jr., Justin Lowinsky, Madge Garland, A. L. Rowse, Kosara Gavrilovitch, Tony Redd, Michael Denison, Dulcie Gray, and Kit Wright, who perpetuates Rebecca West's fine tradition of hospitality.

I have been greatly helped by the expertise of Jane Marcus, who shared her letters and other documents and her experience editing West; Michael Foot and Jill Craigie; Brian Harrison with his detailed files on suffragettes; Patrick Parrinder, always a resource on Wells and British politics; Kathryn Munday for help on South African identifications; as well as Nigel Nicolson, Michael Holroyd, Brenda Maddox, Samuel Hynes, Faith Evans, Phyllis Hatfield, Jane Gunther, Antony Curtis, Martha Vogeler, Victoria Glendinning, who let me go through the boxes of material she had collected in doing West's first biography, and Carl Rollyson, for incomparable sharing of resources as he worked on his own two books on West. Ann Ardis, Barbara Gates, and Lois Potter gave me critical readings of the introductory material. Deborah Lyall was a great help with typing in the final stages. Susan Abel, my astute manuscript editor at Yale, improved the consistency of the collection, and solved some of its enduring puzzles.

Archivists I couldn't have done without are Vincent Giroud of the Beinecke Rare Book and Manuscript Library at Yale University; Lori Curtis, Melissa Burkart, and Sid Huttner, in Special Collections at the McFarlin Library, University of Tulsa; and Cathy Henderson and Tom Staley at the Harry Ransom Humanities Research Center, University of Texas at Austin. I also thank the following libraries for giving me help and access to letters in their collections and, where appropriate, permission to publish them: the BBC Written Archives Centre, the Mugar Memorial Library of Boston University, the University of Birmingham Library, the British Council Literature Department, the British Library Department of Manuscripts, the Library of Congress Manuscripts Division, the University of Chicago Library, the Columbia University Rare Book and Manuscript Library, the Cornell University Library Division of Manuscript Collections, the Edinburgh University Library, the Morris Library of the University of Delaware, the Houghton Library at Harvard University, Hull Central Library, the University of Illinois at Urbana-Champaign Library, King's College Library of Cambridge University, Lilly Library of Indiana University in Bloomington, the House of Lords Record Office, Library Services (director), University College London, the Pierpont Morgan Library, the New York Public Library Astor, Lenox, and Tilden Foundations, the Princeton University Library, the National Library of Scotland, the Tamiment Institute Library at New York University, the Reading University Library, the University of Sussex Library, the George Arents Research Library for Special Collections of Syracuse University, the library at the University of Warwick, and the Margaret Clapp Library of Wellesley College. Anthony Rota helped me track down the new owner of an important cache of letters.

The University of Delaware enhanced my research through a General University Research Grant, an Arts and Science Project Development Award, a travel award from International Programs and Special Sessions, and summer use on two occasions of the Delaware London Centre, through the good offices of its director, Martin Postle.

Those who contributed to the notes are legion. Among the staff of the University of Delaware Library, I should like to thank Linda Stein, David Landenberg, Patricia Arnott, Leslie Arnott, and Tom Melvin. Helpful among my colleagues at the University of Delaware were Mark Amsler, Stephanie Batcos, John S. Crawford, Julio da Cunha, Karen Gaffney, Laurie Frankel, Jonathan Grossman, David Herman, Kevin Kerrane, Peter Kolchin, William Latham, Thomas Leitch, McKay Jenkins, Lejla Kucukalic, Carlos Plata-Salamon, Lois Potter, Damie Stillman, Ben Yagoda (a special resource on the *New Yorker*), Julian Yates, and Richard Zipser. I also thank Lisa Rollyson for making helpful connections, Martin Brueckner for help on German, and my dentist, Stephen Niemoeller, for help on some troublesome teeth. Edmund T. Rolls transported me to interviews in the English countryside and for a visit to Ibstone, where we were kindly served tea by the staff, thanks to the present owner, Sol Kurzner. Renée and Harlan Bradley helped with accommodations and clippings. Tom Scott was a loyal proofreader. Finally, in addition to the many students who have helped my understanding of West by studying her with me, two deserve special recognition—Jennifer Johnson, who did some of the earliest research into the letters as part of her work for the Summer Humanities Fellowship, and Pat Collier, already an accomplished West critic, who checked my transcriptions for accuracy and made invaluable suggestions as we saw the project to completion.

Introduction

Rebecca West was a prolific correspondent, writing several substantial letters on a typical day, and as many as ten thousand in her long lifetime (1892–1983). The letters display the same inclination toward history, philosophy, psychology, cultural critique, realistic description, and modernist fantasy that made this woman a remarkable writer of fiction, political journalism, literary criticism, and travel narrative. From the time that George Bernard Shaw remarked that "Rebecca West could handle a pen as brilliantly as ever I could and much more savagely," West's politics and her writing have elicited strong, contradictory reactions from writers and scholars alike.[1] The letters are bound to provoke reactions that are just as lively, bringing a deserved renewal of attention to West as a defining intellect of the twentieth century.

West deliberately fashions her own biography through letters; in them she challenges rival accounts of her groundbreaking professional career, her frustrating love life, and her troubling family relations. She offers many versions of her parents. West needed particularly to come to terms with her father, Charles Fairfield, and with what she is reluctant to call his desertion of the family when she was eight years old. She struggles along into old age with the criticisms of her elder, talented, but authoritarian physician-sister, Letitia Fairfield. Her decade-long love affair with H. G. Wells (1913–1923) presents enduring problems. Their letters help the two to shape a feline love-fantasy, in the face of Wells's regular retreats to his wife Jane Wells and of West's unplanned pregnancy. After separating, Wells and West argue over educating and rearing their son, Anthony West, and later she battles with Anthony's versions of their shared story. In correspondence to a set of loyal confidants, West mulls over various later love affairs, including failed ones with Lord Maxwell Beaverbrook and Judge Francis Biddle, as well as the problems encountered in her long-term marriage to Henry Andrews.

West also sets down her own version of the literary movements and writers of her day, including in the older generation Arnold Bennett, George Bernard Shaw, H. G. Wells, and Ford Madox Ford, and among her contemporaries, Ezra Pound, James Joyce, and T. S. Eliot. Throughout her career, in the letters as well as her essays and reviews, West puts women writers and editors on the map—to mention a few from the long list, Dora Marsden, Emma Goldman, Bryher, Irita Van Doren, G. B. Stern, Fanny Hurst, Eleanor Wylie, and Dorothy Thompson. She takes us into the inner circle at the *New Yorker* immediately after World War II, when she offered her first spy reportage to its editor Harold Ross. She takes us along on challenging assignments, for example, showing how hard it is to get a good story on royalty for the *Evening Standard,* and notes the problems of transatlantic syndication. West defends her most controversial writing, including her accounts of American congressional investigative committees established to combat communism in the McCarthy era.

When West wants to make known her version of a troublesome incident, she repeats whole blocks of material to numerous correspondents. This obsessive pattern is particularly pronounced in accounts concerning her struggles to separate from Wells and obtain an adequate financial settlement for herself and their son. Disputes over Anthony's autobiographical and biographical efforts are the most frequently and tumultuously rendered. West has left explanations several pages in length to accompany some of his letters to her, all preserved in the West archive in the Beinecke Rare Book and Manuscript Library at Yale University. When such biographers as Victoria Glendinning and Gordon Ray appear, they receive long summaries of events, signed as a letter might be, to guide their writing. West liked to believe that, in dealing with personal and professional problems, she was logical and could secure the endorsement of reasonable people. Her letters eased the solitary decision making that characterized much of her life.

In his biography of his father, Anthony described his mother's letters as "riveting mixtures of wit, acute observation, sharply intelligent commentary and a wild paranoia." Perhaps blinded by his own biased sampling, he predicted mistakenly: "Their strangeness, and the cruelty of many of the caricatures of her contemporaries that they contain, as well as the freedom with which they approach the truth, make it seem highly unlikely that her executors will make them generally available for a long time to come" (A. West, 1984) 58.

More problematic for today's readers is the occasional inclusion in West's letters of derogatory ethnic, racial, and sexual attitudes and labels. She uses *Wop* and *Jew ape,* as if the terms come naturally, when writing in 1948 to Henry of an unpleasant experience. Homosexuals are repeatedly referred to as pansies. She records ambivalent opinions of Oscar Wilde for decades. That she mentions homosexual liaisons as a regular element in her accounts of communist spy cases suggests that she shared and promoted a belief, common in the McCarthy era, that the two were associated. She writes about Jewish women friends such as Fanny Hurst and of the African-American actor Paul Robeson as exotics. Countering these patterns, she writes of Harlem with flair and enjoyment. She shows affection for gay men, beginning with Reginald Turner, whom she addresses as "Uncle Reggie." West reports her attraction to a series of Jewish men, gives evidence of enduring, close friendships with Jewish women such as G. B. Stern, and makes early and sustained efforts to help fugitives of the Holocaust, Slavs as well as Jews.

West offers fresh interpretations of the well-known figures who surrounded her (in addition to the figures already cited, John Gunther, Virginia and Leonard Woolf, Harold Nicolson, D. H. Lawrence, Sinclair Lewis, Alexander Woollcott, Charlie Chaplin, Eleanor Roosevelt, Harold Macmillan, and Arthur Schlesinger, Jr.). In her later years, she generously assists biographers of other writers with lengthy recollections, replete with amusing incidents and physical details. Ever the journalist, she delights in making a scoop, whether it be news of a former lover or of a Soviet spy plot. She both investigates and generates political intrigues. West gives friends living abroad periodic assessments of the British government's performance in times of crisis. Some letters are vibrant travelogues, observant variously of such matters as native clothing, crafts, landscapes, employment, conventions of gender, festivals, and history. She helpfully identifies the nature of her local informants and her most valuable source books. In going on at length about her discomforts, West may give detailed information on the transportation system of a distant place, or its health remedies. Her love of the Riviera and the American Middle West take form first in the letters. Descriptions that later appeared in her exceptional work on Yugoslavia, *Black Lamb and Grey Falcon,* or her essays on South Africa receive their first formulation in letters written to friends and family members.

Rebecca West played a vibrant role in nine decades of history and made the most of her place in them, as the letters show in new ways. She addressed Fabian socialism, the suffrage movement, the domestic side of two world wars, women's entry into the scientific and literary professions, the emergence of literary modernism out of Edwardian realism, America in the Roaring Twenties, the rise and trials of fascism, the plight of refugees, communism, cold war espionage, lynching trials, apartheid, and second-wave feminism.

She tests our ideas of political affiliation by identifying herself to J. B. Priestley as the "last liberal left" (22 June 1955, University of Texas at Austin), despite her increasing conservatism and writing that convinced many that she favored Senator McCarthy's methods in rooting out communism.

Some of the letters reveal surprising material. West was an astute financial planner. She stuck to a negative reading of Britain's support of Tito and argued to the end the merits of his rival, Draza Mihailovitch. West entered competitively into the family obsession with their family tree. She gossiped at length about the royal family—for example, reporting on an early encounter with Mrs. Simpson and the Prince of Wales and on the course of their romance. The letters give enough information about her health problems and their treatment to engage a medical historian. While they reveal a great deal about the writing and reception of her published work, the letters also set forth her hopes for projects that never materialized—additional travel books on America, Mexico, and South Africa, and a study tentatively titled "Second Thoughts on Feminism." Until her death, she suppressed publication of *Sunflower*, the novel inspired by her relationship with Lord Beaverbrook, though she discusses its progress for years in the letters. On balance, she comes out relatively well, as a concerned woman who strove for the understanding of her discontented son. Her caring extended to the grandchildren within reach, and to younger people such as Merlin Holland and Norman Macleod, who compensated for the remoteness of her immediate family.

Members of West's generation, born a decade or two before the turn of the twentieth century, were probably the last great letter writers, having both the habit of regular writing and the willingness to express themselves at length. West's letters have value beyond their obvious biographical interest because they frequently address the concerns of the century she so avidly occupied. She consistently finds and sorts out remarkable information. Her letters entertain, with representations of character that are often as lively and as piercingly witty as Virginia Woolf's. Her correspondence with her literary colleagues and agents helps illuminate the economics of publishing, without falling into the self-serving quality that characterizes much of James Joyce's much more narrowly focused correspondence. She displays, rather, the concern for others' work that is one of the finest qualities of the letters of D. H. Lawrence.

West takes an interest in the letters of other writers, though she rarely reviewed collections. In a 1932 review of D. H. Lawrence's letters, West is pleased to find that "the irascibility and suspicion which have been over-emphasised in some accounts of him were more than balanced by serenity and good sense." She also admires the "exquisite landscapes" of his letters and their "revelation of how spontaneous in him was his sense of beauty in nature."[2] In her exchange with Vyvyan Holland over the publication of the letters of his father, Oscar Wilde, she argues against expurgation of their homosexual content, despite family concern about his image and about the potential effect on Wilde's grandson. She discusses Gordon Ray's editing of the Wells-Shaw correspondence before turning him loose on her own collection of Wells's letters.

The trope of the letter served West at various stages of her writing career. At its start, when she was literary editor at the *New Freewoman* (1913), West was required to respond to letters to the editor, in the process defending and often extending her essays and reviews. Letters were her principal form of contribution to a later feminist periodical, *Time and Tide.* The *Bookman* titled her columns for 1929–1930 "A London Letter" and (when she ventured to the Continent) "A Letter from Abroad." This format allowed her to expand beyond reviewing lists of books to include events and cultural observations.

West reveals herself in many moods and states of mind—girlish mischief, extreme fatigue, rapture over the beauty of places or fine food, and ultra confidence in her pronouncements on literature, politics, and persons. She repeatedly expresses suspicion of malice in others, including the Deity, and on rare occasions expresses that emotion herself. Yet the letters also display long-term devotion to friends and feminist solidarity. West can be extremely funny, as when she describes a hospital where she had an operation for a fibroid tumor as the invention of Edgar Allan Poe and Ambrose Bierce. Alexander Woollcott took to reading her letters aloud at Washington dinners and reported that she had Felix Frankfurter and Archibald MacLeish rolling on the floor (11 November 1939, Yale University). As a gifted and witty raconteur, she was able to craft original comparisons and move toward unexpected, yet (one realizes) carefully orchestrated conclusions. As in her essays, West favors whatever sustains the life force, and dreads evil with a firm conviction of its existence and its deadliness.

West's secretary in the 1940s, Anne Charles McBurney, recalls West at her vast, disorderly, horseshoe-shaped desk, sequestered on the second floor of Ibstone House. West describes the desk as an "early eighteenth century wine table." Eventually, owing to excessive age or the burden of her papers, it "suddenly split across in two places" (letter to Gordon Ray, 2 August 1972, Pierpont Morgan Library). At her desk, West would be rifling through brimming baskets of letters received, exclaiming, "Oh, God! Oh, God," at intervals, when a desired paper failed to surface. That same exclamation marks numerous letters to the intimates admissible during her moments of domestic or professional mayhem. Her last secretary, Diana Stainforth, found West fun to work with—often more eager to chat than to get to her letters. In Stainforth's memory, West is seated beneath a beautiful circular window in Kingston House, her final abode. She occupies a high-backed, vinyl-covered wing chair, with tables arranged around her, and wears a favorite turquoise dressing gown. She might dictate letters while lying in bed. In her prime, West also frequently wrote from ships bound to or from America, wiring in a publishing emergency to A. D. Peters or George Bye, her agents on either side of the Atlantic. In Philadelphia on an oppressive summer day, she admitted to McBurney, "I have written most of this in a bra and pants—but now those have gone" (1948, private collection).

Although there is no typical Rebecca West letter, some general conventions obtain. West often begins with an apology for the delay that includes a description of what family responsibility, illness, or travel has prevented her from corresponding. Early in a letter, she is likely to pick up on a theme of common interest, or respond to the recent experiences of her correspondent. When she is obsessed with a problem—some assault on her professional reputation, or the problematic behavior of a family member—almost any topic will lead into that concern. Her sentences are apt to be ponderous, with a complex phrase for each of many intersecting or additive forces to the situation described. Dashes work to string out the sentence, and the verb often comes as a delayed gratification. Seeming to like the repetition of proper names, West uses pronouns sparsely. It is not unusual for her to supply her own notes, marked with a cross or an asterisk; afterthoughts run along the sides of letters, or follow her signature.

West usually signed her letters simply "Rebecca," sometimes abbreviated *R* or *RW.* She had taken the name Rebecca West from Ibsen's heroine in *Rosmersholm* when she started writing for the *New Freewoman* in 1912. To many of her Fairfield relatives she remained Cicily, her spelling of her given name, Cicely Fairfield. She was Auntie C. to the offspring of Winifred, the middle sister in the family. The youngest of three daughters, West signed her early letters to her eldest sister, Lettie, with "Baby." A childish misunderstanding of the spelling of *antelope* won her the name Anne in the family; she furnished the names Frisk and Podge for her sisters, and regularly used Podge or Podgers in letters to Winifred. Many of West's intimate names derived from an imaginary bestiary, with a premium placed on "pussingers," or cats. Most famously, she was "Panther" to Wells's "Jaguar"—a feline pair regularly commemorated in his love letters to her. As a small boy, Anthony was encouraged to call her Aunty Panther. For a time, Anthony chose to go by the Miltonian name Comus, which enters the letters as well. At the height of the relationship with her grandson, Edmund, and his first wife, Vita (which declined with their divorce), they received letters that closed with her line drawing of a cat's posterior. West and her husband, Henry Andrews, selected "Ric" for him and "Rac" for her, names taken from dogs that appeared in a French comic strip; she tended to use "Rac" with her grandchildren. "Simpkin" was a signature saved for confidants, when West was some years into her marriage, and she was "Lady Mary" to Pamela Frankau. The distinguished justice Francis Biddle called her "my dearest Rat" and "my dragon lady" in his love letters (letter to West, 29 August 1946, Yale University). Hers to him appear not to have survived.

Most of her letters are imprinted with her current address, or that of the hotel where she was staying. West's small, consistently neat handwriting is, even into her old age, relatively easy to decipher. One dealer (Bernard Rota) has used compactness as a selling point for her letters—there is often a great deal to the page. Dating is a more difficult matter. With the exception of business correspondence, which is carefully dated, West supplies the day of the month sometimes, but rarely the year. Except in her letters on Yugoslavs, she generally omits accent marks in foreign languages. The University of Tulsa archive reveals that before sending letters of emotional importance, West frequently drafted fragments in notebooks or at the typewriter. Letters not sent have survived in the archives, and a few appear in this selection. With family and close friends, West sends letters slashed with crossed-out words, many of which are worth showing because they may betray emotion, or the perfecting of her impressions.

West began to develop a strategic plan for the disposition of her correspondence around 1955, when she was shocked by what she took to be her own portrait in her son's novel, *Heritage*. An invaluable collection of biographical evidence existed in letters she had received from H. G. Wells before, after, and during their famous ten-year liaison. Yale became the repository for her letters, by a process explained in a 1973 letter to an old friend, the author Beverley Nichols:

> I kept all H. G.'s letters, which amounted to 800. I think I would have destroyed them before I died, but when Anthony began to act peculiarly and wrote that awful book, I gave them to Yale University, who put them in the Beinecke. I would have given them to the British Museum but they replied to my letter offering them with a printed form asking me to send a specimen letter so that the Trustees could judge whether they wished to accept them.[3] The Beinecke then followed up by asking me to send them all my papers, past and current, which I have been doing ever since. (Typescript letter [June or July 1973], private collection)

She represented Yale's interest in her papers to G. B. Stern, as follows: "This is not a tribute, I regret to say, I mean the buying of my letters, to the greatness of the Panther, but they are taking over all my papers, bank books, solicitors' files, after I am dead, as an effort at historical research—since it is most difficult to reconstruct how people actually lived from day to day" (11 September 1960, Stern Collection, Boston University). The Yale archive is far from complete. Papers left at her death were sold by West's estate to the University of Tulsa in Oklahoma. Numerous letters are still in private hands. A major collection was sold while this edition was in progress.

In several cases, West's letters were deliberately destroyed. She reports that Wells disposed of nearly all of her letters to him, with the exception of a few in an envelope that escaped his attention. Some of these remaining ones were sacrificed by Anthony West, who claimed to be protecting her from judgments that she was too materialistic, though she suspected more sinister motives. Letters from the years of West's deepest infatuation with Lord Beaverbrook were also destroyed by their recipient. West wrote to Pamela Frankau and G. B. Stern in an effort to secure more letters for Yale and was disappointed to find large gaps in the correspondence they had preserved. In justifying herself, Stern expressed a wish to protect Lettie from reading her sister's negative comments.

West, too, limited the collection. Her letters disclose that she tore up some letters at the time she sent the bulk of them to Yale. In the draft of a letter to Wells's daughter-in-law Marjorie, West assured her: "I have weeded out these letters carefully and there are none which are not charming and delightful and the best of H. G., except for some irritable ones which are also amusing. And those I am annotating so that they will do nobody any harm" (14 February 1950, University of Tulsa).

West controlled access to the letters she did deposit at Yale. The basic plan was to deny use of them to all but those persons she designated, until after the deaths of both herself and her son. This "blanket veto on inspection of any of all this except by persons authorized by" her was "according to custom," or so she explained to Beverley Nichols. She approved of Gordon Ray, who was given access to the letters as Wells's biographer and subsequently produced a narrative of their relationship, *H. G. Wells and Rebecca West* (1974), written in frequent consultation with West, who barred him from speaking with Anthony. Ray deferred also to the feelings of Wells's son Gip, particularly in regard to Jane Wells, who figured as a villain in many of West's accounts. West imposed some censorship on Ray. She instructed him to remove any references in the letters that were damaging to survivors, including Lettie, whom she wanted to shield from knowledge of Wells's negative assessments of her. The Ray volume evoked a response from Anthony, and in turn one from West to him. Ray's book has also had the unfortunate effect of reducing her presence in the forthcoming four-volume edition of Wells's letters. Its editor, David C. Smith, prints only a very small number of Wells's letters to West. He justifies this near-exclusion by citing the existence of Ray's volume, even though the book really only weaves extracts from the letters into Ray's own narrative on the relationship of West and Wells.

In selecting from West's letters available to me, I have endeavored to include a wide range of her acquaintances, as either recipients or subjects of letters, and substantive references to the full canon of her writing. I am striving for a balanced record of her character, which could easily be sweetened or soured in the selection. I have to some extent protected the living from intrusion and defamation. There are now plenty of the dead to bear the main burden of her satire. The selection will complement the two existing biographies by Victoria Glendinning and Carl Rollyson and will, I hope, serve to encourage additional critical and biographical projects.

Annotating Rebecca West is a challenging business because she was active for so long, traveled so widely, and participated in so many circles of writers and political figures. To read her letters in an informed way is to receive an education in the culture of the twentieth century.

[1] For Shaw's letter, see the plate in *The Young Rebecca* following p. 198. The significance of her ten-year liaison with H. G. Wells has been argued back and forth. Their son, the author Anthony West, played his mother's principal antagonist, Fay Weldon staged a fantasy re-enactment, and West's first biographer, Victoria Glendinning, in conversation with me, said that she was overcome by the sadness of it all. West horrified William Carlos Williams with her lack of reverence for James Joyce's *Ulysses,* though Austin Briggs and I have been fascinated equally by the nature of Williams's attack and by what it missed of West's insightful contextual criticism. The extent and significance of West's feminism has been debated: One set of writers, including Samuel Hynes and Gordon Ray, exempts her from that designation; another, led off by Jane Marcus in her collection *The Young Rebecca,* reconnects West to her feminist and socialist roots (see Scott, *Gender of Modernism,* 562). Some feminist critics see unusual and disconcerting elements in West's feminism. Moira Ferguson, for example, discusses the combination of feminism with recurrent Manichaeanism in West's work, and Sue Thomas expresses disappointment over West's turning from materialist feminism to more essentialist feminism. West's antinomies were part of what attracted her first bibliographer, Evelyn Hutchinson, to her, whereas I have detected an attempt to break through binaries in her work (*Refiguring Modernism,* vol. 2: 125–30). Critics disagree over what genre elicited her best, or what her falling outside standard genres did to her reputation. Samuel Hynes, Jane Marcus, Gloria Fromm, Margaret Stetz, and her most recent biographer, Carl Rollyson, all make vastly different selections of her greatest successes.

[2] West discusses Lawrence's letters in a review involving numerous other works, most of them by T. S. Eliot, hence the title of her review-essay, "What Is Mr. T. S. Eliot's Authority as a Critic?"

[3] The British Library has retained relevant correspondence between its staff and West. Although the library's response came in the form of two letters from the staff, not as printed forms, as West states, the letters were mechanical and uninviting—form letters, in effect.

1892   21 December Cicely Isabel (she later spells this Cicily), is born to
Charles and Isabella Fairfield. Joins two sisters, Letitia (Lettie,
b. 1885) and Winifred (Winnie, b. 1887), at 28 Burlington Road,
Westbourne Park, London.

1894   Family settles at 21 Streatham Place off Brixton Hill, South
London (described in *Family Memories*).

1900   The family moves to the home at 9 Hermitage Road, Richmond-
on-Thames, Southwest London (described in *1900*).

1901   Charles Fairfield leaves the family and travels first to Sierra Leone.

1902   Cicily moves with mother and sisters to Edinburgh, settling at
2 Hope Park Square, Buccleuch Place, Edinburgh.
Develops mild tuberculosis.

1906   Studies at George Watson's Ladies' College.
Charles Fairfield dies, alone in Liverpool boardinghouse.

1907   Her first publication appears, a letter to the editor in *The
Scotsman*.
Is active in suffrage movement around Edinburgh.

1910   Stays briefly with her aunt Sophie and uncle Arthur Fairfield in
Golders Green.
Studies at Academy of Dramatic Art, London.
Family settles in April at Fairliehope, Chatham Close, Hampstead
Garden Suburb.

1911   As author for the *Freewoman,* Fairfield takes "Rebecca West" as
pen name.
Reviews H. G. Wells's novel *Marriage*.

1912   Works for Fabian Summer School. Writes reviews for *Everyman*.
Meets Wells.

1913   Joins staff of the *New Freewoman*. Writes for the *Clarion*.
In May, travels to Paris and Spain with her mother.
She and Wells become lovers.

1914   In March, moves to Brig-y-don, Victoria Avenue, Hunstanton, for
duration of pregnancy.
4 August, Anthony Panther West is born.
Mother and child move to "Quinbury," Alderton, Royston Park
Road, Hatch End, in East Hertfordshire.

1916   *Henry James* is published.
1917   Shares rooms at 51 Claverton Street, Pimlico, London, with Wells
        during London visits.
        Moves to Southcliffe, Leigh-on-Sea.
        Experiences German bombing raids.
        In August, Winifred marries Norman Macleod.
        In October, Anthony is boarded at a Montessori School in
        London.
1918   *The Return of the Soldier* is published.
1919   West moves to 36 Queen's Gate Terrace, South Kensington,
        London.
1920   In November, begins three-month visit to Capri, staying with
        Compton and Faith Mackenzie. Has Italian holiday with Wells.
        Meets D. H. Lawrence near Florence.
1921   In August, Isabella Fairfield dies.
        "Notes on Novels" series for *New Statesman* begins.
1922   *The Judge* published. West is a guest at Garsington.
        Takes Spanish holiday with Wells, who is ill.
1923   Hedwig Gatternigg attempts suicide in Wells's flat.
        West breaks with Wells.
        Makes first trip to United States. Visits New York, New England,
        Chicago, Utah, and California on a lecture tour that extends into
        1924.
        Liaison with Lord Beaverbrook founders.
1924   Meets John Gunther in Chicago, Charlie Chaplin in California.
        New friends include Fannie Hurst, Alexander Woollcott, Irita Van
        Doren and Walter White.
        In April, returns early, as Anthony misses her.
        In autumn, facilitates Emma Goldman's visit to London.
1925   Spends the summer at Diano Marina, Italy.
        Has love affair with John Gunther.
1926   In January, makes U.S. trip.
        Spends spring holiday with Anthony at Diano Marina.
        Carries on adoption disputes with Wells. Anthony is withdrawn
        from St. Piran's, begins school at the Hall, Hampstead.
        West becomes a regular on the French Riviera, at Antibes.

Makes autumn voyage to United States.

Begins reviews for *Herald Tribune Books*.

Has affair with Steven Martin, California banker.

Ghost-writes *War Nurse*.

1927 Makes U.S. visit in April. Steven Martin dies.

Undergoes psychoanalysis in Florence, with Mary Wilshire.

Works on *Sunflower*.

Stays on Riviera at Frifri Palace, near Agay.

Late December, moves to 80 Onslow Gardens, SW 7

1928 In March and September, visits Paris.

Anthony is placed in Norfolk sanatorium—tuberculosis is suspected.

In July, *The Strange Necessity* is published.

Anthony enters Stowe school.

Lions and Lambs is published with her commentary on David Low cartoons.

October–November, West visits United States.

1929 *Harriet Hume* is published.

Summers at Villa Mysto, in Agay, on French Riviera.

1930 *War Nurse* (unsigned) is published.

Summers at Villa Mysto.

D. H. Lawrence is published. West sends money to Frieda Lawrence.

1 November, marries Henry Andrews. They honeymoon in Genoa.

1931 Moves to 15 Orchard Court, Portman Square, London.

In August, ectopic pregnancy is aborted at Swiss clinic.

Ending in Earnest is published (her essays from the *Bookman*).

1932 Anthony is analyzed by Hans Sachs; he goes to America.

1933 *St Augustine* and *A Letter to a Grandfather* are published.

1934 In January, West visits Switzerland.

In September, has operation in London Clinic.

1935 Makes U.S. visit for first time since marriage, stopping in Washington, D.C.

Travels for British Council to Scandinavia, Latvia, and Finland.

The Harsh Voice is published.

1936   Makes British Council trip to Yugoslavia, Bulgaria, and Greece.
The Thinking Reed is published.
In October, Anthony marries Katharine (Kitty) Church.

1937   West makes second trip to Yugoslavia, with Henry.
Is awarded the Order of Saint Sava.

1938   Makes third trip to Yugoslavia.

1939   Summers at Old Possingworth Manor, Blackboys, near Uckfield,
Sussex. Visits with Leonard and Virginia Woolf.
Begins involvement with war refugees.

1940   In January, falls ill with jaundice.

1941   Has operation for fibroids in maternity hospital.
Purchases Ibstone House.
Black Lamb and Grey Falcon is published.
First grandchild, Caroline (Caro) is born to Anthony and Kitty
West.
Anthony runs a farm with a "Panther herd" of Guernsey cattle.

1942   West thinks of writing a history of England. Prepares to take war
casualties at Ibstone House.

1943   Britain backs Tito, to her disgust.
Edmund (Em) is born to Anthony and Kitty West.

1944   Wells is suspected to have cancer.
Anthony plans to leave Kitty.

1945   Rebecca West begins her association with Harold Ross at the *New
Yorker* with report on Joyce trial.

1946   Attends and reports on Nuremberg war tribunal.
Has affair with Francis Biddle.
13 August Wells dies.
Friendship with Charles Curran, features editor of the *Evening
Standard,* begins.
Friendship with Evelyn and Mary Hutchinson begins.

1947   Visits Greenville, North Carolina, to report on lynching trial for
the *New Yorker.*
Visits Germany.
The Meaning of Treason is published.
In November, has *Time* suppress paragraph on her life with Wells.

1948   June–July, reports on Republican, Democratic, and Progressive
        Party presidential conventions in United States. Visits Dorothy
        Thompson in Vermont.
        British Institute for Political Research is formed (with West on its
        board) to combat communism.
        Anthony begins Wells's biography.

1949   In June, Rebecca travels throughout Germany with Dorothy
        Thompson and Henry.
        Awarded CBE (Companion of the British Empire).

1950   German travel with Henry leads to articles "Greenhouse with
        Cyclamens."
        Anthony's emigration to the United States causes dispute over
        Wells's papers, which are controlled by Marjorie Wells.

1951   Rebecca West writes on communist spy Klaus Fuchs.
        Visits Chartres at Easter.
        6 December, Ross dies.
        Pig farming begins at Ibstone.

1952   West studies role of Whittaker Chambers in Alger Hiss trial.
        Collaborates with Roberto Rossellini on film of Colette's *Duo*.
        Anthony and Kitty West divorce.

1953   West's articles on U.S. Congress investigative committees
        published in London *Sunday Times*, reprinted in *U.S. News and
        World Report*, arouse controversy over McCarthyism.
        In December, Anthony marries Lily Emmet.

1954   Oppenheimer case is tried.
        West works on behalf of Gavrilovitch family.

1955   In spring, travels in Spain.
        In October, Anthony West's *Heritage* is published.
        Rebecca West's *Train of Powder* is published.

1956   *The Fountain Overflows* is published.

1957   Delivers Terry Lectures at Yale University.
        A Preliminary List of the Writings of Rebecca West, ed. G. Evelyn
        Hutchinson, appears.
        West is awarded the French Legion of Honor.
        In July, stays in Venice, suffering from phlebitis.

Spends Christmas in France.

The Court and the Castle (based on Yale lectures) is published.

1959   West is named DBE (Dame Commander of the Order of the British Empire).

1960   January–March, visits South Africa for *Sunday Times* series "In the Cauldron of Africa."

In May, Winifred Macleod dies.

West visits Madrid for Velázquez exhibition.

Solicits letters for collection at Yale.

Henry has operation for deafness.

1961   In January Dorothy Thompson dies.

In February, lawsuit over South African articles is decided against West.

Sophie is born to Anthony and Lily West.

Rebecca West testifies against censorship of D. H. Lawrence's *Lady Chatterley's Lover.*

1962   In January, visits New York and Barbados.

Forms friendship with Diana Trilling.

In June, experiences gall bladder problems.

1963   Reports on Profumo case.

The Vassall Affair is published.

1964   *The New Meaning of Treason* is published.

Writes on Christine Keeler–Profumo affair and Kennedy assassination.

In April, has gall bladder operation.

Adam is born to Anthony and Lily West.

1965   May–June, visits New York.

1966   *The Birds Fall Down* is published.

In autumn, visits Mexico City, Philadelphia, and Washington, D.C., with Henry.

1967   Visits Mexico.

1968   3 November, Henry Andrews dies.

1969   Moves to final residence, 48 Kingston House North, Prince's Gate, SW 7.

Makes second visit to Mexico City.

1971   In spring, visits Merlin Holland in Lebanon.
       In September, visits Ireland with Lettie.
1972   Advises Mackenzies on Wells biography.
       Anthony West returns to England.
1973   Rebecca West grants Gordon Ray access to her papers.
1974   Gordon Ray's *H. G. Wells and Rebecca West* is published.
       Anthony West reviews Ray in *Harper's*.
1975   Rebecca West has operation for removal of cataracts.
1976   In December, commemorates death of Milan Gavrilovitch.
1977   *Rebecca West: A Celebration* is published.
1978   In February, sister Lettie dies.
       BBC films *The Birds Fall Down*.
       Great-grandson Kwabena Barnabas Panther Duah and great-
       granddaughter Vanessa West are born.
1979   In March, infant Barnabas dies.
1981   Film version of *The Return of the Soldier* is produced.
       Her granddaughter Sophie visits.
1982   *The Young Rebecca, 1911–1917,* is published.
       1900 is published.
       The publication of Leslie Garis's article in the *New York Times
       Magazine* greatly upscts West.
1983   15 March, West dies.
1984   Anthony West's *H. G. Wells: Aspects of a Life* appears.
1985   *Cousin Rosamund* is published.
1986   University of Tulsa buys the West papers in her possession at the
       time of her death.
       Sunflower is published.
       Harold Orel's *The Literary Achievement of Rebecca West* is published.
1987   *Family Memories* is published.
       Victoria Glendinning's *Rebecca West: A Life* is published.
       27 December, Anthony West dies.
1992   *The Only Poet* is published.
1995   Carl Rollyson's *Rebecca West: A Saga of the Century* is published.
1996   February–April, *The Return of the Soldier* is produced as a drama
       in London.

Plantagenet Kings

:

Anthony Denny (Henry VIII favorite) = Joan Champernown

:

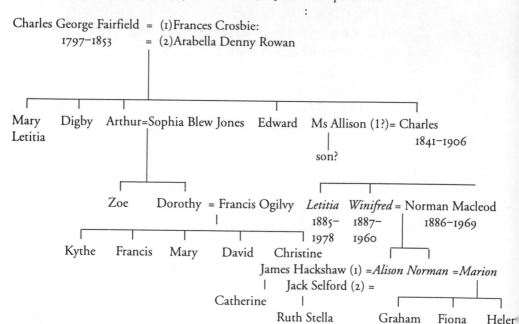

Charles George Fairfield = (1)Frances Crosbie:
1797–1853   = (2)Arabella Denny Rowan

Mary   Digby   Arthur=Sophia Blew Jones   Edward   Ms Allison (1?)= Charles
Letitia | 1841–1906
                                                                son?

        Zoe   Dorothy = Francis Ogilvy   *Letitia*   *Winifred* = Norman Macleod
                            | 1885–   1887–   1886–1969
Kythe   Francis   Mary   David   Christine   1978   1960
                                            James Hackshaw (1) =*Alison Norman* =*Marion*
                                                    | Jack Selford (2) =
                            Catherine |
                                        Ruth Stella   Graham   Fiona   Helen

Names of recipients of letters in the collection are in italics.

Family Tree

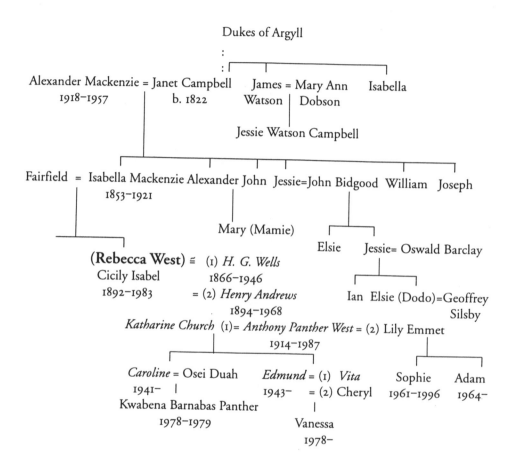

Dukes of Argyll

Alexander Mackenzie = Janet Campbell   James = Mary Ann   Isabella
1918–1957   b. 1822   Watson │ Dobson

Jessie Watson Campbell

Fairfield = Isabella Mackenzie Alexander John Jessie=John Bidgood William Joseph
1853–1921

Mary (Mamie)

Elsie   Jessie= Oswald Barclay

(Rebecca West) ≅ (1) *H. G. Wells*
Cicily Isabel   1866–1946
1892–1983   = (2) *Henry Andrews*   Ian Elsie (Dodo)=Geoffrey
                      1894–1968   Silsby

Katharine Church (1)= *Anthony Panther West* = (2) Lily Emmet
                          1914–1987

Caroline = Osei Duah   *Edmund* = (1) *Vita*   Sophie   Adam
1941– │   1943– = (2) Cheryl   1961–1996   1964–
Kwabena Barnabas Panther   │
1978–1979   Vanessa
                                1978–

Biographical Sketches

Andrews, Henry (1894–1968), husband of Rebecca West (m. 1930). Henry was born in Burma to parents who identified themselves as British. His father was in the import-export business, and the family spent considerable time in Hamburg, Germany. Henry attended Oxford but failed to obtain a degree because of difficulty with examinations. Caught in Germany by World War I, he was interned for the duration. Henry worked for the international banking firm Schroders until the mid-1930s, after which he worked for war ministries and on behalf of refugees. He helped manage the farm operation at Ibstone, had a passion for art and architecture, and spoke seven languages.

Arling, Emanie [Sachs during her first marriage] (d. 1981), American writer for *Smart Set* and the *New York Times*. Her works include the novels *Talk* (1924) and *Red Damask* (1927), *"The Terrible Siren": Victoria Woodhull* (1928), and *A Pot with Feeling: Flower Paintings* (1960). She and West shared confidences from 1923 onward, and West's *Ending in Earnest* (1931) is dedicated to her.

Astor, Viscountess Nancy Witcher Langhorne (1879–1964), American-born millionaire and hostess at the grand estate of Cliveden, married to the second William Waldorf Astor. She was the first woman M.P. to take a seat in the House of Commons (1919). Her circle, portrayed in *Remains of the Day*, favored appeasing the fascists in the 1930s.

Beaverbrook, William Maxwell Aitken, Lord (1879–1964), Canadian-born industrialist, newspaper owner and editor, head of various British war ministries in both world wars. West's hopes for a lasting love affair with him, following her breakup with Wells, were dashed at a New York rendezvous in December 1923.

Bennett, Arnold (1867–1931), English novelist, editor, playwright, and critic for Beaverbrook's *Evening Standard*. His best known works are set in the potteries of Staffordshire, where he was born. He depicts obscure lives realistically but affectionately. His novels include *Anna of the Five Towns* (1902), *The Old Wives Tale* (1908), and the Clayhanger trilogy. West had few positive things to say about his literary politics.

Bye, George Thurman (1887–1957), American literary agent for Rebecca West from the 1920s through the 1940s, when A. D. Peters began to handle her accounts on both sides of the Atlantic. Among Bye's other clients were Alexander Woollcott, Charles Lindbergh, and Eleanor Roosevelt.

Cape, Herbert Jonathan (1879–1960), West's English publisher. He opened his own company in 1921. His list included works by Sinclair Lewis and Ernest Hemingway.

Chaplin, Sir Charles Spencer (1889–1977), English-born movie actor, director, writer, and producer, best known in the role of the little tramp of silent film. Chaplin made a return visit from Hollywood to London in 1921, and renewed the relationship with West on her first visit to California in 1923.

Curran, Charles (1903–1972), English editor and politician, described by West as a soul mate. They met in 1947 when he was features editor at the *Evening Standard*. He was elected Conservative Party M.P. for Uxbridge in 1964. Curran fended off an intimate relationship with her. To Anne McBurney she described his Greys Inn flat as "very bare, everything subordinated to the marvellous library, all the finest books on political science and modern history, and exquisitely arranged. . . . One could feel he sat there and dreaded what was outside" (2 December 1972, private collection).

Duah, Caroline West (1941–), West's older granddaughter, born to Kitty and Anthony. Educated at Oxford, she married a native of Ghana. West was proud of her artwork and her beauty.

Fairfield, Josephine Letitia Denny, "Lettie" (1885–1978), the eldest of the three Fairfield daughters—nearly eight years Rebecca's senior. Like Rebecca, Lettie was a member of the Women's Social and Political Union (WSPU) and the Fabian Society. She was a Catholic convert. Lettie received her M.D. degree from Edinburgh University and School of Medicine for Women in 1911. While serving as house surgeon at the Jewish Hospital in Manchester (1908–1909) and as resident officer at Children's Hospital, Nottingham (1909–1910), she lived away from the family. After the family returned to London, she joined the London County Council as an assistant medical officer in 1912, rising to senior medical officer in 1930. As a lieutenant colonel in the Royal Air Force during World War I, she supervised the corps of women doctors in the WRAFS. After the war, she became one of the first women to be called to the bar. In 1920, she was the educational commissioner for the National Council for Combatting Venereal Diseases (NCCVD), touring the West Indies under the auspices of the Colonial Office. She was the author of a study on epilepsy, did research on genealogy and witchcraft, and like Rebecca, delighted in reading crime fiction.

Flanner, Janet (1892–1978), American journalist best known for her "Letter from Paris," signed "Genêt," a column published in the *New Yorker* from 1925 on, for nearly fifty years; she wrote from London during World War II. Her column discussed politics, the arts, publishing, and the work of expatriate American women.

Ford Madox Ford (1873–1939), British novelist and editor whose works include *The Good Soldier* (1915) and the tetralogy *Parade's End* (1924–1928). He edited both the *English Review* and (from Paris) the *transatlantic review*. Ford shared a household with Violet Hunt at Camden Hill and was a close friend of H. G. Wells and a collaborator of Joseph Conrad.

Frankau, Pamela (1908–1967), English novelist, journalist, and autobiographer who spent summers in the late 1920s with Rebecca and Anthony West on the French Riviera. She both worshipped and feared West and became Anthony's confidant. West's depiction of Frankau and her liaison with Humbert Wolfe in "The Addict" compromised their friendship. Frankau retaliated with *The Devil We Know* (1939), and a parodic piece, *A Letter from R*b*cc* W*st* (1986), published years after West's death. Frankau's other works include *The Marriage of Harlequin* (1927), *Jezebel* (1937), *A Democrat Dies* (1939)—on fascism, *Slaves of the Lamp* (1965), and *Pen to Paper: A Novelist's Notebook* (1961). Several of her stories were aired on television.

Gawthorpe, Mary (1881–1960?), schoolteacher, leader in the early Labour Party and Fabian groups around her native Leeds, and suffragist, imprisoned in Holloway. Through her speeches on the northern circuit of the WSPU, she became Letitia Fairfield's friend and West's mentor. Gawthorpe helped edit the WSPU journal, *Votes for Women*, and assisted in the founding of the *Freewoman*.

Goldman, Emma (1869–1940), a Lithuanian-born immigrant who arrived in the United States in 1885, Goldman founded and edited the anarchist journal *Mother Earth* and reviewed socially conscious dramas. Jailed for conspiracy to obstruct the selective service law, she was deported in 1919. Her subsequent visit to Russia left her disenchanted with Bolshevist

Communism—to West's satisfaction. West tried to set her up as a lecturer in London and gave a celebrity dinner in her honor (1924).

Gunther, John (1901–1970), American journalist whose lively style and careful research is shown in a series of "Inside" books: *Inside Europe* (1936), *Inside Asia* (1939), *Inside Latin America* (1941), *Inside U.S.A.* (1947), *Inside Africa* (1955), *Inside Russia Today* (1958), and *Inside Europe Today* (1961). He became first a lover and then a lifelong friend of West.

Harrod, Sir Roy (1900–1978), British economist who applied the "multiplier concept" to foreign trade; biographer of his mentor, Maynard Keynes. He was a friend of Henry Andrews from his Oxford days and a lecturer in Economics at Oxford.

Hodges, Margaret, Cambridge graduate who served as West's secretary during World War II, typing the many drafts of *Black Lamb and Grey Falcon* while living at Ibstone. She became a lifelong friend, and West was her daughter Ann's godmother.

Holland, Merlin (1945–), English journalist and writer, the son of Thelma and Vyvyan Holland. West and a group of friends she rallied helped to finance his education, and he became an important late correspondent for West. He worked for an English company based in Beirut (1969–1974) before returning to England to work in publishing. He is the author of *The Wilde Album* (1997).

Holland, Vyvyan (1886–1967), English author, editor, and translator, the son of Oscar Wilde. After his first wife died in a freak accident (1918), he led a lively existence that included West as an intimate. He married Thelma Besant (1943). Holland kept West's framed photograph, which was autographed as follows:

> To Vyvyan Holland
>   who is no gentleman
> From Rebecca West—who is no lady
> These very qualities having been the basis
> of an affectionate friendship lasting over 40
> years.

Holland's pictorial biography of Wilde (1960) was dedicated to Rebecca West.

Hueffer, Ford Madox—See Ford Madox Ford.

Hunt, Violet (1866–1942), suffragist and novelist whose works show a concern with women's sexuality. Her home, which she shared with Ford Madox Ford from 1908 to 1918, was an artistic center, where West and Wells visited and young writers (*les jeunes*) received encouragement.

Hurst, Fannie (1889–1968), Jewish American author. She was the highest-earning U.S. writer of fiction in the 1920s and 1930s. Hurst began her career with short stories, collected in *Just Around the Corner* (1914). Her novels included *Star-Dust* (1921), *Lummox* (1923), *Back Street* (1931), and *Imitation of Life* (1933). All offer sympathetic studies of women. She wrote the scripts for film versions of several of her works.

Hutchinson, [George] Evelyn (1903–1991), and Margaret Hutchinson. Evelyn Hutchinson, a zoologist and professor of biology at Yale University, was introduced to West's writing by his wife Margaret. He wrote of West in "The Dome," in *The Itinerant Ivory Tower* (1953), and compiled a bibliography of West's works (1976). The Hutchinsons were responsible for the establishment of the Rebecca West Collection at Yale University's Beinecke Rare Book and Manuscript Library. West's letters to them are so long and comprehensive, repeating what is stated elsewhere, that only a modest selection can be offered here.

Lawrence, D. H. (David Herbert) (1885–1930). West met the controversial author of *Sons and Lovers, The Rainbow,* and *Women in Love* outside Florence in 1921. She popularized his writing through her criticism and wrote an elegy for him, *D. H. Lawrence* (1930). West received a letter from Lawrence (15 April 1929) that praised her as "a real good squaw for scalps" and encouraged her to write more about him. She remained a defender of Lawrence at the trial of *Lady Chatterley's Lover.*

Lewis, Sinclair (1895–1951), American novelist whose novels offer satirical realist treatments of the Middle West. Among his best-known works are *Main Street* (1920), *Babbitt* (1923), which was reviewed appreciatively by West, and *Elmer Gantry* (1927). Grace Hegger was his first wife. West met Lewis in 1923. He received the Nobel Prize for Literature in 1930.

Lowinsky, Ruth (d. 1958), one of West's closest friends. She was a vital, direct woman, fond of entertaining at her London home in Kensington Square and at Stoneway in Gloucestershire. She wrote cookbooks, and according to her son, Justin (an economist who serves as one of West's executors), never quarreled with Rebecca West.

Lynd, Sylvia (1888–1952), English poet and prose writer, educated at the Slade School of Art and the Academy of Dramatic Art. Her collection of prose pieces *The Thrush and the Jay,* which West comments upon, was published in 1916. She married *Daily News* editor and essayist Robert Lynd in 1909 and was an important early confidante of West's.

McBurney, Anne Charles (1918–), educated at St. Mary's School, McBurney served for five years in the Women's Auxiliary Air Force during World War II. She was West's secretary at Ibstone House from 1946 until she married the prehistorian Charles McBurney in 1953. She received particularly good letters from West concerning her travels and reporting assignments.

McCarthy, Joseph Raymond (1908–1957), Republican senator from Wisconsin. The term *McCarthyism* describes his ruthless and often groundless investigative practices. Coming close on the heels of the conviction of Alger Hiss on spy charges, McCarthy's exaggerated claims of Communist infiltration into the U.S. Government, first made in a speech at Wheeling, West Virginia, had great impact. He rose to become the chair of both the Senate Committee on Government Operations and its Permanent Subcommittee on Investigations (1953). McCarthy was censured by the Senate in December 1954.

Macleod, Norman (1926–), West's nephew, the son of her sister Winifred. A chemical engineer, he spent much of his career at Edinburgh University. Macleod developed a close relationship with his aunt and became her chief heir.

Macleod, Winifred Fairfield—"Winnie" or "Podge" (1887–1960), the middle one of the three Fairfield sisters. Rebecca considered her her "muse." Winifred was educated at Cheltenham Ladies' College, where she specialized in history, and at Maria Grey College in London, where she trained as a teacher. Like her sisters, she became involved in Fabianism and the suffragist movement. She taught in a boys' preparatory school before marrying Norman Macleod in 1917.

Macmillan, [Maurice] Harold (1882–1986), Scottish publisher and statesman who served as chancellor of the Exchequer before becoming prime minister (1957–1963) at the time of the Suez Canal crisis. The Vassall spy case (1962) and the Profumo scandal (1963) led to his resignation.

Marcus, Jane, American feminist scholar and critic, a professor at the City University of New York (CUNY) Graduate Center. She persuaded West of the importance of her early feminist writings and went on to collect and edit *The Young Rebecca*. Marcus also has to her credit several books on Virginia Woolf.

Marsden, Dora (1882–1960), editor of the *Freewoman* (founded in 1911), which was revived as the *New Freewoman* (1913) and later named the *Egoist*. Marsden was a militant member of the WSPU but later renounced its agenda for a broader social program and "individualist" ideology. Two essays by West describe Marsden and her primary sponsor, Harriet Shaw Weaver: "The Freewoman" (1926) and "Spinster to the Rescue" (1970). Marsden's leading articles and her book *The Definition of a Godhead* (1928) tend toward a feminist philosophy.

Mansfield, Katherine (1888–1923), New Zealand-born short-story writer whose stories were first published in the *New Age*. Her major works include *In a German Pension* (1911), *Prelude* (1918), and "The Garden Party" (1922), all of which take on sexual themes. After her untimely death from tuberculosis, her husband, John Middleton Murry, edited and published additional works by her.

Maugham, William Somerset (1874–1965), English novelist, playwright, and short-story writer. He traveled widely, often with his companion and secretary Gerald Haxton, and settled in the South of France in 1928. Maugham's straightforward prose features cosmopolitan characters and settings. He is best known for the novels *Of Human Bondage* (1915), *The Moon and Sixpence* (1919), and *Cakes and Ale* (1930), and for his enduring short stories.

Melville, Sara Tugander (Sally), secretary to Bonar Law, leader of the Conservative Party. West met Melville during her early days with Wells and found in her a confidante.

Middleton Murry, John (1889–1957), English critic and editor of a series of modernist magazines (*Rhythm, Athenaeum,* the *Adelphi*), friend of D. H. Lawrence, and husband of Katherine Mansfield.

Mihailovitch, Draza (1893–1946), leader of Serbian Chetnik guerrilla force against the German occupation of Yugoslavia. He was also opposed to Tito's Communist forces, which defeated and executed him. West would write the introduction to David Martin's *Ally Betrayed,* a book vindicating Mihailovitch.

Morrell, Lady Ottoline (1873–1938), hostess of Garsington Manor near

Oxford and memoirist. She was particularly supportive of D. H. Lawrence and Aldous Huxley, and she was the lover of Augustus John and Bertrand Russell. T. S. Eliot, Virginia Woolf, Lytton Strachey, and Katherine Mansfield were among her friends.

Nicolson, Sir Harold George (1886–1968), member of the British Foreign Office who served in Madrid, Constantinople, Tehran (where he was born), and Berlin (1909–1929), and Labour M.P. (1935–1945). The author of essays, biography, and literary studies, he wrote for Beaverbrook's *Evening Standard,* starting in 1930. Husband of Vita Sackville-West. Rebecca West encountered him on her Balkan travels and remained a friend.

Nin, Anaïs (1903–1977), French diarist, critic, and novelist, trained as a psychoanalyst. She wrote a study of D. H. Lawrence, a preface for Henry Miller's *Tropic of Cancer,* and *The Novel of the Future* (1968). Her experiment with the "continuous novel" grew into *Cities of the Interior* (1961) and *Seduction of the Minotaur* (1961). Her diaries, dating back to 1931, began to appear in 1966. In the volume titled *Fire,* she quotes West's remarks concerning a lover, despite West's protest that Nin is inaccurate. She was married to Hugh P. Guiler, an artist, film-maker, and banker.

Peters, A. D. (August Detlaf) (1892–1973), German-born English literary agent. He worked briefly as a literary critic before establishing his own firm (1923). West moved to him from Pinker and became one of the first of his long roster of distinguished clients. He was both an advocate and a friend.

Ratcliffe, S. K. (1868–1958), English journalist, member of the Fabian Society, and champion of liberal causes who befriended the Fairfields when they resettled in London. He freelanced for the *Daily News,* the *Manchester Guardian,* the *Nation,* the *New Statesman,* the *New Republic,* and *Herald Tribune Books.* Ratcliffe lectured regularly in the United States (1914–1939) and lived there during much of World War II. Hogarth Press published his study *The Roots of Violence* (1934).

Ray, Gordon N. (1915–1986), American academic, director of the Guggenheim Foundation, and trustee of the J. P. Morgan Library. Ray was given access to West's correspondence with Wells in order to assemble *H. G. Wells and Rebecca West* (1974). He also wrote *The Illustrator and the Book in England from 1790 to 1914* (1976).

Robeson, Paul (1898–1976), African-American singer, actor, and activist. He was an All-American football player and trained in the law. Robeson appeared in the Provincetown Players' productions of Eugene O'Neill's *All God's Chillun Got Wings* (1924) and *The Emperor Jones* (1924) and gave a memorable rendition of "Ol' Man River" in *Showboat*. The Robesons' move to London (1928) and visit to the Soviet Union aroused suspicions that they had communist sympathies.

Ross, Harold Wallace (1892–1951), founding editor of the *New Yorker*, to which he brought many of the greatest journalistic talents of his age, including Rebecca West, E. B. White, James Thurber (West disliked Thurber's biography of Ross), and Janet Flanner. The outwardly gruff Coloradan was both driven and sensitive. During World War I, Ross went to France to edit the *Stars and Stripes* for the American troops. He was a key figure at the Algonquin Round Table. West dedicated to Ross *The Meaning of Treason,* which reprinted her earliest work for the *New Yorker.*

Schlesinger, Arthur M., Jr. (1917–), American historian whose writings on American history include two Pulitzer Prize winners, *The Age of Jackson* (1946) and *A Thousand Days* (1966), on the presidency of John F. Kennedy. Also of note are *The Age of Roosevelt* and *The Imperial Presidency*. Schlesinger's second wife is Alexandra Emmet, the sister of Lily Emmet West, Anthony West's second wife.

Selford, Alison Flora (1920–), daughter of Winifred Macleod and niece of Rebecca West who writes under her maiden name, Alison Macleod. West was outraged by her membership in the Communist Party, which Selford left in 1957. *The Death of Uncle Joe* (1997) is an account of her communist experiences. She is also the author of a play, *Dear Augustine,* produced at the Royal Court (1958). Her novels are *The Heretics* (1965), *The Trusted Servant* (1967), *No Need of the Sun* (1969–published as *City of Light* in the United States), *The Muscovite* (1971), *The Jesuit* (1972—published as *Prisoner of the Queen* in the United States), and *The Portingale* (1976). Selford reports that West became increasingly friendly near the end of her life toward her niece, and though they still argued furiously, they enjoyed many outings together.

Sinclair, May (1863–1946), English novelist, feminist, and suffragist interested in psychoanalysis who was instrumental in the careers of younger writers, including Ezra Pound. Her works include *The Tree of Heaven* (1917) and *Mary Olivier* (1919). She may have influenced West.

Stern, G. B. (Gladys Bertha—Mrs. Holdsworth, 1890–1973), English novelist who studied with West at the Academy of Dramatic Art and became one of her closest friends. She is best known for a multivolume account of the Raconitz family, which draws on her Jewish heritage. The first volume, *Tents of Israel* (1924), was staged as *The Matriarch* (1929). Stern wrote on Robert Louis Stevenson and, with Sheila Kaye-Smith, on Jane Austen. Her friendship with West endured until Stern died.

Thompson, Dorothy (1894–1961), American journalist who served as a foreign correspondent in Berlin and Vienna during the 1920s, becoming known for the column "On the Record." She was married to Sinclair Lewis (1928–1942). Among her books is *I Saw Hitler*. West considered her a soul mate.

Tito, Josip Broz (1892–1980), leader of the Communist Party in Yugoslavia beginning in 1937, leader of Partisan guerrilla forces during World War II, and dictator of Yugoslavia from 1945 until his death. He gained the support of Britain (1946) and became president (1953–1980). Tito maintained a degree of independence from the Soviet Union and in consequence was expelled from Cominform in 1948.

Turner, Reginald (1869–1938), curator of the Palazzo Horne in Florence, journalist, and wit. Once a friend of Oscar Wilde and Max Beerbohm, he was reputedly the illegitimate son of the first Lord Burnham. He was an elderly member of an expatriate homosexual circle when West struck up a friendship with him.

Van Doren, Irita (1891–1966), American editor for the *Nation* (1919). As editor of the *New York Herald Tribune Sunday Literary Supplement* (1926–1963) she commissioned West's work and soon became a friend. She was married to Carl Van Doren, and she aided him in his research after their marriage (1912).

Vinaver, Stanislav (1890–194?), poet and chief of the Yugoslav Press Bureau who conducted parts of West's tours of Yugoslavia. West based the fictional character Constantine in *Black Lamb and Grey Falcon* on him. West often spells his first name Stanislaus.

Walpole, Hugh Seymour (1884–1941), relatively traditional novelist on the fringes of Bloomsbury. West considered him influential in critical circles, and corresponded with him regarding negative reviews she had published on his works.

Wells, Amy Catherine Robbins, renamed "Jane" by H. G. Wells (d. 1927). Wells's second wife (m. 1895). She tolerated his affairs, served as his hostess, and assisted him with his writing.

Wells, Frank R. (1903–?), younger son of Jane and H. G. Wells.

Wells, G. P. (George Philip), "Gip" or "Gyp" (1901–1985), biologist, the older son of Jane and H. G. Wells.

Wells, H. G. (Herbert George), "Jaguar" to West (1866–1946), English novelist, historian, and social thinker whose writing was often freighted with ideas for social amelioration. He made major contributions to the genres of utopian fiction and science fiction and is best remembered for his scientific romances, starting with *The Time Machine* (1895) and including *The Island of Doctor Moreau* (1896) and *The War of the Worlds* (1898). His novels on social subjects include *Love and Mr Lewisham* (1900), *Kipps* (1905), and *Tono-Bungay* (1909). The son of the housekeeper of the stately home of Uppark in Sussex, after being apprenticed to a draper, he taught at Midhurst Grammar School before winning a scholarship to study science in South Kensington under Thomas Henry Huxley. In 1903 he joined the Fabian Society but then left under the shadow of his adulterous affair with Amber Reeves. Wells gave spirited support to the national effort during World War I, and in later years he envisioned a world government. His *Short History of the World* (1922) found a wide audience. *Experiment in Autobiography* (1934) gives his own account. He was West's lover (1913–1923) and the father of Anthony West.

Wells, Marjorie, H. G. Wells's daughter-in-law, who married Gip in 1927. As H. G.'s literary assistant in his final years, she took responsibility for his papers after his death.

West, Anthony Panther, "Comus" (1914–1987), novelist and critic, the son of West and H. G. Wells. His early endeavors included painting, dairy farming, and working for the BBC. Anthony moved to the United States in 1950, where he wrote for the *New Yorker*. A serious breach with his mother ensued when his autobiographical novel *Heritage* (1955) was published. His other works include *Another Kind, Mortal Wounds,* and *David Rees, Among Others*. His final work was *H. G. Wells: Aspects of a Life,* which includes a concerted attack on his mother.

West, Edmund, "Em" (1943–), West's older grandson, born to Kitty and Anthony. Edmund became a physician. West admired his first wife, Vita.

[West], Katharine Church ("Kitty") (1910–), English painter, the first wife of Anthony West and mother of West's eldest two grandchildren, Caroline and Edmund.

Wilde, Oscar (1854–1900), Dublin-born aestheticist, author of essays, fairy stories, fiction (*The Picture of Dorian Gray*), and plays (*Lady Windermere's Fan, The Importance of Being Earnest*). He was imprisoned (*The Ballad of Reading Gaol*, 1898) for homosexuality in 1895 and died bankrupt and exiled in Paris. His apologia is given in *De Profundis* (1905). West's main reason for writing about him in the letters was her friendship with his son, Vyvyan Holland.

Woolf, Leonard Sidney (1880–1969), English writer, Fabian socialist, and editor of the *Nation*. After his time in the colonial service in Ceylon he married Virginia Woolf (1913). His writing includes two novels, essays on topics such as the Co-operative Movement and the League of Nations, and a multivolume autobiography. The Woolfs' Hogarth Press published West's "Letter to a Grandfather" (1933).

Woolf, Virginia Stephen (1882–1941). West wrote appreciative reviews of this eminent woman writer's central feminist book, *A Room of One's Own* (1929), and of the novels *Orlando* (1928) and *The Waves* (1933). Woolf's major works also include *Mrs Dalloway* (1925) and *To the Lighthouse* (1927). The two women met in 1932 and exchanged visits, but West never considered her a "twin soul." West is mentioned in *A Room of One's Own* for her brash feminist pronouncement that men are "snobs." In her letters, Woolf both defends West and critiques her lifestyle.

Woollcott, Alexander (1887–1943), American playwright, actor, and drama critic for the *World* and the *New York Times*. His essays are collected in *While Rome Burns* (1934), and his personality has left a mark on a comedy by George S. Kaufman and Moss Hart, *The Man Who Came to Dinner* (1939), in which Woollcott acted. He was one of West's earliest American friends, and by the late 1920s he had earned the warm salutation "Dear Alexander Woollycoat" and her "pet lamb" epithet.

Note on Editing Conventions

The letters are arranged more or less chronologically in parts that mark six phases in the life of Rebecca West. Preceding the letters in each part is a further brief introduction. Wherever possible, entire letters have been included. Passages from related letters are often quoted in the notes. Additional quotations embellish the introductions to each part.

Identifications of frequently cited persons are provided in the "Biographical Sketches," and are signaled by a bold citation in the index.

Words that cannot be deciphered are indicated in square brackets, thus: [probable letters?].

Uncertain transcriptions are indicated in this way: [probable words?].

Words crossed out by West are printed in ⟨angle brackets⟩, with an x for each word if undecipherable.

Words inserted above the line by West are supplied in {curly brackets}.

Book and journal titles are printed *in italics,* although West rarely underlined them.

Dates of letters follow the address from which the letter was sent (where available). My own dating of letters, based on notes made by recipients, on postmarks, or on internal evidence appears in square brackets [late 1948].

West's own spellings (and misspellings) of names and so on are retained in the letters but are corrected in the notes.

West frequently makes her own, perfectly adequate identifications, and in such cases I have refrained from supplying notes.

PART ONE *1907–1923*

Panther with a Pen

THIS EARLIEST GROUP OF LETTERS BEGINS PRECOCIOUSLY WITH A LETTER to the editor of the *Scotsman,* published when Rebecca West was fourteen. The sequence continues through her decade of intimacy with H. G. Wells. Recorded here are her initiation to public life, through participation in the suffrage movement as well as the Fabian Society, her entry into the writing profession via the *Freewoman* and the *Clarion,* and her struggles to keep a literary career going alongside the challenges of attending to a lover and a son.

The correspondence first locates West as a schoolgirl in Edinburgh, where the female members of the family settled in 1902 after her father, Charles Fairfield, left them indefinitely for a brief, unsuccessful venture in Sierra Leone. In 1960, West declined an invitation from Edinburgh to speak about her old headmistress at George Watson's Ladies' College, where she had been a scholarship student. She offered, by way of explanation, an early literary exploit:

> There were in the class in which my best friend, Flora Duncan, and I found ourselves when we were about fourteen, some silly girls who liked to go to Blackford Hill and be picked up by students. Flora and I thought this was silly and dangerous, and we wrote some derisive verses of the most innocent nature which we circulated. . . . Miss Ainslie came into possession of them and read us a lecture before our class which would have [been] justified if we had introduced *La Vie Parisienne* or some similar publication to the halls of George Watson's. (Letter to Miss Fleming, 1 December 1960, Yale University)

West goes on to say, "I think I would have gone on to the University if it hadn't been for her, and I have always felt the lack of a University education as a real handicap."

By April 1910, West had made her move to London, where she settled with her mother and sisters in the house they named Fairliehope. She reports on her rough entry into Academy of Dramatic Arts: "I have passed into the A. D. A. all right—under difficulties. I fainted in the Tube going up, at Baker St. . . . Three very nice women came and looked after me, and one asked, 'Are you going to meet anyone who'll look after you, a sister?' 'No,' I muttered piteously 'A Theatrical manager!' and closed my eyes. I then heard a whisper—'Poor child—an actress! I'll pay for the brandy!' " (letter to Letitia Fairfield, 18 April 1910, Indiana University, Bloomington).

In the balance of these letters, we find West at a series of addresses of dwellings chosen jointly with H. G. Wells, who became her lover in 1913 and who was the father of her son, Anthony West, born in August 1914, just as World War I was breaking out. "Jaguar" is her pet name for Wells in these letters, and "Panther" his salutation for her. "Panther," which also became their son's middle name, remained a preferred signature for her intimate letters. Important correspondents are her eldest sister Letitia Fairfield, addressed at first childishly as "Cow," Dora Marsden, editor of the *Freewoman,* S. K. Ratcliffe, a Fabian journalist who befriended the family during their early days in London, and G. B. Shaw. There is a gap in the letters around the time of Anthony's birth.

With these letters, West takes us into the melee of police action during suffrage demonstrations. We experience the home front during World War I, when bombs fell close enough to kill the family cat. West remarks on her intentions with her first books and struggles with manipulative literary agents. We hear of the pleasures and trials of her decade with Wells. Troubled by such events as a woman's attempted suicide in his flat (which West helped to cover up), and what she considered increasingly erratic and demanding behavior on his part, it was she who ended the affair. We meet their son Anthony, seen as both a treasure and a distraction from her work.

West's talents for drama, humor, and parody of herself and others develop early. She takes on Cockney accents and devises pet names. She poses and amuses, already balancing the historical with the personal and the philosophical. She spends the check for her first novel on "the most expensive hat I have ever bought in my life," offering characteristic justifications:

> The hat was a direct consequence of the Italian disaster. All these war horrors instead of making me ascetic make me turn furiously to sensuous delights. Such a pleasure to think that if all the world's gone wrong that hat at least is right. And after {and during} air raids I don't pray or speculate on the World State but drench myself in scent and eat chocolates. Perhaps it's only a reaction against an unusually abstinent life—I've never had any amusing trimmings to life—but I think there is an impulse to reassure oneself that life's worth living by simple pleasures. (Letter to Sylvia Lynd, Thursday 1917, Boston University)

To: The Editor of the *Scotsman*   16 October 1907

Sir,—I was very much interested in the letter signed "Mater" in this morning's issue, as it seems to reflect no inconsiderable part of feminine opinion. The writer is not very clear as to her opening point. She denounces the N. W. S. P. U. [National Women's Social and Political Union] as unpatriotic on the declaration of war on the Liberal Government, independent of their divers personal political creeds. And why? Because it is the duty of women to support our Constitution against all revolutionary efforts; to, in short, defend the nation from Socialism. I for one cannot follow "Mater" here. How are we to fulfil the aforenamed duties by supporting the party that has been Socialism's truest friend, that has been its most devoted fosterer; that has, in fact, already commenced an active campaign against an integral part of our Constitution—the Lords?

Also, I do not think that "Mater" realises the profound national effects of the subjection of women on the nation. If she considers the position of women in the industrial field, if she thinks of the Cradley Heath chainmakers and the whitelead workers, surely she should realise it is a question affecting the Empire itself.[1] While women have to endure such squalid physical agony to gain their daily bread, while children are born sightless and distorted, already tainted with the lead poisoning, it is not only the duty of every woman, but of every patriot to press this question before all others and immediately. For not only is the sex degradation implied in manhood suffrage dangerously near, but we are threatened by a Legal Prevention of Married Women's Factory Employment Act—a magnificent measure, but without the guarantee of a legal share of a husband's wages falling to the wife. Heaven knows what that will mean!

It is obviously incumbent on every one whose eyes are open not only to the sufferings of women, but to the well-being of the nation, to accept the call to action of the N. W. S. P. U., and to thank the noble women who are giving not only their time and labour, but not a little of their own private interests, to this great cause.—I am, &c.

CICILY ISABEL FAIRFIELD

[1] Published in the *Scotsman*, 16 October 1907, 9. In her letter of 14 October, "Mater" had complained of the "pro-Boerism of the Liberal Women's Clubs" and wished that "men would discuss politics with women, and thus naturally women would take a more Imperial view." West shifts her gaze on empire to a view of the working class at home.

To: Letitia Fairfield   24 Buccleuch Place, Edinburgh
                                          [late December 1908]

Dear Cow,

Thank you so very much for your present, you naughty old Cow! I have been so very busy and dissipated of late that I have delayed writing. We have had a very fine time—last Wednesday Miss Moloney and Louisa Walker spoke for the Men's League—I think Miss Moloney is one of the loveliest creatures I ever saw. She spoke very well indeed, but has an astonishing faculty for saying the first-thing that comes into her head—e.g. "Think of the cumbrousness of Irish divorce laws! Why, *a relative of my own* had to go to the House of Lords to get rid of a man who wasn't worth staying in the room with!" The audience reeled but adored her!

On Thursday I went to a supperparty at Mrs Easson's to meet Miss Moloney. She was simply delighted to hear of Miss Gawthorpe's disturbing influence on Writston. She is a very witty speaker and really rather logical in spite of her wild tendency to say the most unexpected thing possible. Her looks carry her every where—she has such pretty brown hair and blue eyes and a marvellously perfect mouth. The occasion was the inauguration of the Votes for Women Club—a secret militant society for men and women. We come into active service first on Jan. 5th, when Haldane comes.[1] We are to have a big protest meeting outside.

While we were at Mrs Easson's a funny little man came in—the husband of one of the W. F. L. [Women's Freedom League] London organisers, named Holloway. He left the Civil Service on account of having delivered a political speech not long ago, and is now on the stage. He was in the King's Theatre panto, so he invited {Nelly[2] and I} ⟨me⟩ to go round to the rehearsal on Friday morning. It was very interesting. The King's Theatre is lovely "behind," and the dear old wardrobe mistress took us to her bosom and showed us all the dresses. The company—which was very kind to us—was most bushossy[3]—mostly highly respectable Jews. The girls, altho' some were popular panto beauties, were all very plain—Nelly and I were about the best looking there. We were only admitted because the manager, Davis, who used to be a Gilbert & Sullivan man, is a keen Suffragist. Mr. Holloway is a dear little Cockney, who talks about nothing but his wife, his daughter and womans Suffrage.

On Monday I shopped until I flopped, and went to the Paterson Concert.

Bushos[4] told you about the meeting at the Mound. Nelly was very captivating and "fluttered." The crowd "licked its lips." The dear dainty little Scotts spoke too with Morag Burn Murdoch,[5] Miss Chapman,[6] and Cecilia Haig.[7] The Scotts are magnificent workers but have not the slightest sense of humour. They said to me very solemnly: "Could you not come to prison with us in July, Miss Fairfield? It would be so *nice* and *homelike* if we could all go together!" They are very keen on Nelly and us going to E. Fife then. They were there last holidays.

I hope you will like the *Shropshire Lad*.[8] Do read "Bring in the nameless grave to throw"—"Loveliest of Trees"—"Look not in my eyes for fear!"

I am glad Pat Woodlock[9] got off so easily, though it was obviously a police conspiracy.

I am so sad when I think of a lonely Cow on Christmas Day—hasn't anyone offered to house the Cow for the day? I hope you will have your turkey and plum pudding, anyway.[10]

Lily is tired, so will write tomorrow.[11] Please write me Mary G's [Gawthorpe's] address.

I am so glad you are better. Anyone would get ill if that gas stove is still raising Cain in the sitting room!

With best wishes for the New Year. May 1909 bring votes for Women!

Your loving baby

West, R., MSS   manuscript
Indiana University, Bloomington, Indiana

[1] Richard Burdon Haldane (1856–1928), a liberal Scottish statesman and Fabian. He served as British secretary of state for war (1905–1912), and was instrumental in the founding of the London School of Economics.

[2] Nelly Porter, a friend who had studied with Lettie. After her marriage she went to live in the Outer Hebrides.

[3] Bushossy, having the qualities of a bushos, or bus horse, an overworked and underfed animal used to pull buses before they were motorized.

[4] The Fairfield girls applied the term *Bushos* to their teachers, and teasingly here to Winnie, who had joined that profession.

[5] Morag Burn Murdoch (d. 1929), sculptor, artist, and early member of the WSPU. In its obituary, the *Women's Leader and the Common Cause* (8 February 1929) called her "a true democrat and a great favourite" with "the man on the street."

[6] Adeline M. Chapman signed a letter (4 August 1916) to Prime Minister Asquith on behalf of the New Constitutional Society for Women's Suffrage.

⁷ Haig died (December 1911) of injuries sustained at Caxton Hall on 18 November—Black Friday.

⁸ Collection of verses (1896) by English poet and classicist A. E. Housman (1859–1935).

⁹ Called the Liverpool Suffragette, she was sentenced to three months in prison in March 1909.

¹⁰ Letitia Fairfield was working at the Jewish Hospital in Manchester, where she made contact with members of the WSPU.

¹¹ Lily was a nickname for their mother, Isabella Fairfield.

To: Letitia Fairfield   34 Park Parade
                                                         Whitley[1]
                                                         [1909]

Dear Cow!

I am sorry I couldn't write before but I have been busy all the time ever since I left you. We had a splendid meeting at Harrogate[2]—both Christabel[3] & Lovey Mary[4] were at their very best. Zena and Phyllis Dare were among our most enthusiastic listeners. I believe there was a splendid profit but of course don't know. We missed ⟨both⟩{each} other at the station but from Stockton to Newcastle we travelled together. I thought Christabel was very decent indeed, not at all sarcastic.

As for Newcastle I have been very busy—helping at meetings all Wednesday. That morning at the dinnerhour in an engineering and railway works district Mary talked the little Shortt[5] down completely. On Thursday I stood outside the poll at Forsyth Rd and shouted "Keep the Liberal out!"[6] I turned three votes on the doorstep, anyway. But the Liberal women are ghastly! They stood on the other side of the gate and shouted insults at us the whole time. I had five large Liberal ladies bearing down on me calling me a hooligan and a silly fool and other pretty names. One Liberal man tried to shake me and hurt me, much to their delight; but the police man settled all that. However one Suffragette, Mrs Brown of New Castle,[7] was knocked down and trampled on by a member of the Woman's Liberal Federation. They tried to make me stop shouting "Keep the Liberal out" but of course it was no good. I kept on from 10 till 8! Of course I got my meals all right. Everybody was very nice except the Liberal women—who have a repertoire of vituperation that I cannot believe to be equalled anywhere. They looked exactly like comic postcard Suffragettes. The police were quite all right, so I was always safe. The police warned me not to go up to hear the poll unless I was with plenty of friends, as the women would scratch my eyes out![8] I knew Renwick was in. Shortt is a more attractive man, and was followed about by bevies of adoring damsels. He lost a good many workmen's votes on account of a motor he sent round the town—full of his children, with a huge placard "Vote for Daddy!" They couldn't stand that. A great number of working men voted for woman's Suffrage—spoiled their papers or voted Socialist, in most cases, I am told. I haven't seen an analysis of the votes yet; as I didn't go up.

I was agreeably surprised with Mrs Martel.[9] She's a dear old soul in spite of the hair, and takes the crowd tremendously. Of the prisoners only Elsie Howie[10] and Vera Wentworth[11] are anything like first-rate speakers. Vera W. is a little terror—rather a handsome girl. Miss Hamilton Scott and Miss Higgins are very good too.

We had some very queer experiences. Miss Agston received an invitation to "The Girls of Gottenburg" outside the poll. I was selling p[ost].c[ard].s at one of our largest meetings when a wild eyes [sic] individual rushed up and thrust half a sovereign in florins into my hand and said "That is for your picture post card, madame!" I blushed and declined the compliment, and rushed away. Outside the poll one of the Liberal agents addressed me thusly—"Stop shouting, my dear, and come and have some tea in town!" I didn't! It reminded me of little Archietect [sic]. To whom I send my love.[12]

I suppose you will have seen Lovey Mary by now. I lost track of her in Newcastle. How the crowd adored her! But Mrs Pankhurst[13] has a wonderful hold on them. Mr. Shortt spoke to me, by the way. He has plenty of push, but solid intellectual talent, I should think.

I have thoroughly enjoyed myself all this month, and wish I was going back to play with my Cow in cheerful Cheetham.[14] Isn't it dreadful to be left with neither little dawg nor baby?[15]

I am too tired to write anymore, and I don't think I have much more to say. I am writing to Darwin.

Your affectionate
Baby

West, R., MSS.   manuscript
Indiana University, Bloomington

---

[1] Probably Whitley Bay, a seaside resort east of Newcastle-upon-Tyne in northern England.

[2] Spa town north of Leeds in Yorkshire, where WSPU members were trying to establish a branch. Rebecca West accompanied Mary Gawthorpe on this propaganda tour.

[3] Christabel Pankhurst (1880–1958), eldest daughter of Emmeline, and founding member of the WSPU. Known for charismatic speeches, one of which is parodied in *The Judge* (60).

[4] Pet name for Mary Gawthorpe.

[5] Edward Shortt (1862–1935), English Liberal M.P. (1910–1922). He was more interested in problems of Irish Home Rule than in suffrage. Liberals had generally placed other reforms, such as taxation and welfare, ahead of suffrage—hence the protest.

[6] See West's letter to the *Scotsman,* 16 October 1907, where she defends the split between the NWSPU and the Liberal Party.

[7] Margaret Brown's arrest was reported in *Votes for Women* (25 November 1910), which cited her for by-election work, and for having all her daughters in the WSPU and her husband in the Men's Political Union.

[8] West gave Lettie an even more dramatic account of the Leith Gaiety meeting in a letter written from Edinburgh (5 December 1909, Lilly Library, Indiana University, Bloomington):

Leith is very friendly and the crowd was very sympathetic. First Miss Hudson addressed the crowd and led them against the doors. The police drove ⟨them⟩ {her} into a wynd [Scots: narrow alley] but the crowd got her out again. A working man lifted her up in his arms, and she called on the crowd to push her in, and they got her right to the doors. The police beat her back and struck her again and again in the face. Then two plain clothes men arrested her and one kept hitting her across the windpipe, so she gripped him by the throat until he promised not to do it again. In a minute the crowd rescued her, and she led them back to the doors and was arrested again. Again she was rescued and this time the police led a baton charge. It was a disgusting sight—one man had his head cut open from ear to ear, and several people were covered with blood. Everyone was so dismayed that she was rearrested and taken away quite quietly. The people were fearfully impressed by the fact that she held the purple, white, and green flag high above her head the whole time. Then Nurse Elsie Brown (staff-nurse of Dr. Haulton's nursing home, kept by Miss M'Farlane) broke Leith P. O. windows, and we had a big Protest Meeting, hurried back to the office with news, and helped to get tea.

[9] Mrs. Martel, a prominent Australian suffragist who served as a chairman at the 1908 Hyde Park meeting.

[10] Elsie Howey (1884–?), a speaker at the Hyde Park meeting. She led the Fourth Women's Parliament on horseback on 29 June 1909 when they petitioned Prime Minister Asquith. She was imprisoned and forcibly fed (1910), as reported by Constance Lytton.

[11] Vera Wentworth, imprisoned member of the WSPU (1907).

[12] Presumably a friend of Lettie's. West's early manuscript *Adela* ends with the protagonist's meeting an attractive architect.

[13] Emmeline Pankhurst (1858–1928), founder, with daughters Christabel and Sylvia, of the WSPU. She was frequently imprisoned for militant suffragist activities and was a highly effective speaker. She desisted from suffrage activities to support the war effort during World War I and stood for Parliament as a Conservative in 1926.

[14] Town near Manchester in northern England.

[15] Nicknames for the younger sisters, Winifred and herself.

To: Letitia Fairfield

24 Buccleuch Place
Edinburgh
20 March 1910

My dear Cow,

We are so sorry to hear that you are run down again! It will be good to be nearer you so that we can inspect you at more frequent intervals.[1] It's very unfair that a fine Cow like you should be weakly.

I expect you have heard as much as we have about Fairliehope Cottage—I hope you like the name. If you don't you ought to be ashamed of yourself, because it is a most beautiful William Morris[2] word and the name of a wonderful old farm on the Pentlands looking over towards the Clyde. Podge [Winifred Macleod] is planning out a garden—herbaceous borders, rose-poles, and such like. Mother's only stipulation is that there must be wall-flowers, and I demand a lilac bush and almond tree, so she has a free hand.

The great event of this week was Lovey Mary's [Gawthorpe's] visit on Thursday. I had to stay in on Thursday afternoon, as it is the day the house is to be seen and Cousin Jessie[3] "doesn't like to be left alone with strangers in the house," but I went on Thursday evening to the Oddfellow's Hall. She called me on the platform afterwards and we had a talk. She looked well though tired, and had on the nummiest green silk gown you ever saw! The audience was very much taken with her—particularly when she turned up her snubby little nose. She sent her love to you—and hoped to see me at the Actresses' Franchise League meeting she is having in April. She was in one of her naughty, gurglesome moods, and bounced on her chair and waved her hands about in her funniest way. I couldn't understand half she said. She was always jumping about; giving a dramatic representation of a dialogue be-tween an Anti and a Adult Suffragist: and whisking round to me with confidential information—all rather confusing! Something about the "New Age"—and that she was going to live in London when we got the vote—she always came back to that with a purport I couldn't quite catch. For once I wished that her conversational style was a little less fragmentary. But she had great, great ch'm!

Yesterday Flora, Ada and I went a 15 mile walk. We trained to Balerno, walked along the Old Lanark Road and crossed over Carnwath Moor by Harperrig Reservoir, and climbed up to the pass between the East & West Cairn Hills. This is the Cauldstaneslap—the one in *The Weir of Hermi-*

ston[4]—a most awful wilderness of bare moors—1300 ft above sea level. We had to go rather out of our way, as we couldn't walk in the snow, which lay pretty thick on the mountains. The hills are about 2,000 ft, and in wild shapes. We walked for six miles without seeing a house, and in the whole 15 miles only met 2 people. When we got to West Linton—which is a lovely place, in the prettiest part of Peebleshire,—we found that the benevolent railway company insisted on us leaving at 4.45 or not at all till 8 o'clock. So— as the station is 2 miles from the village—we couldn't have tea. For 1/6 the N. B. R. gave us 2 hrs of travelling including half an hour's repose at a station, dropped, for some reason, beside a couple of cottages. No stuffing anywhere, and we'd wolfed all our sandwiches among the mountains! The dear child did wonders when it returned to the bosom of its fambly [*sic*]! The bother is that my left leg is quite lame today. I don't know if its possible, but I feel as if that burn had affected it. It's been queer ever since.

Cousin Jessy is slowly driving the family to acute mania. The old thing, which came back from the Scarlet Babylon quite perky, is driven into being quite shocking. Both Podgers and I want to punish fussiness by a blow on the head, but we do very well.

Although Nelly [Porter] has not heard about her engagement all her friends have been invited to a "farewell tea" on Thursday—very Nelly-like! She is very keen to go to London and wants me to introduce her to an actor—her ambition is to "go up the river—on Sunday—with an actor." Talk about Miss Porter's heart attacks!

Your loving
Baby

West, R., MSS   manuscript
Indiana University, Bloomington

[1] By this time, the family was planning a move to London. Lettie was working at Children's Hospital in Nottingham.

[2] William Morris (1834–1896), Pre-Raphaelite poet, founder of the Arts and Crafts Movement, essayist, and author of socialist fantasies.

[3] Janet Watson Campbell, called Jessie, the daughter of West's maternal grandmother's older brother, James.

[4] Novel by Robert Louis Stevenson, left unfinished at his death but published 1896.

To: Dora Marsden   Fairliehope
                                    Chatham Close
                                    Hampstead Garden Suburb, N.W.
                                    [June 1912]

Dear Miss Marsden—

I opened your letter in trepidation, fearing that you were coming after me with a gun for that mad article on "Elsie Lundtner."[1] (As it is I still live in terror of that serious minded person, Miss Gallichan, who thinks Karen Michaelis the greatest living author). But it was pure kindness! Very welcome, too. I was told last week that my article on "Minor Poets" was "better than a dog-fight"! So I needed consolation.

I am glad you are better. I am now. My trouble was both tragic and ludicrous, but it's over now. Still my life is in a tangle just now. Entirely my own fault.

You wonderful person—you not only write those wonderful front-pagers, but you inspire other people to write wonderfully. Miss Willcocks has never before done anything so fine as "The Function of Passion." And it's your lead she's following.

The *Daily Herald* has seduced me into editing their Woman's Page. They are tired of baby-clothes they say, and want "non-Gospel" talks to women. I fear this means trials for sedition, so I may not long be free.

Everyone behaves beautifully at the Freewoman Discussion[2] Circle—it's like being in Church—except Miss Robinson,[3] Mr Weston,[4] and myself. Barbara Low[5] has spoken very seriously to me about it. So you know what you come back to.

I am glad you want to have a talk ⟨to⟩ {with} me. It's true we see each other very rarely. I shall be in town more regularly now, so we will certainly be able to see each other some day. But don't come back till you're quite well. We would rather "the Leaders" stayed away than came back in a damaged condition!

                                    Yours very sincerely,
                                    Rebecca West

Dora Marsden Collection   manuscript
Princeton University

[1] West published a review of Karin Michaelis's *Elsie Lindtner* in the *Freewoman* (13 June 1912).

[2] Discussion Circles were an outreach program of the *Freewoman.*

[3] Rona Robinson, another suffragette and *Freewoman* collaborator, educated in science.

[4] Selwyn Weston, regular contributor to the *Freewoman,* where he expressed anarchist, socialist views on literature and sexual emancipation. He reputedly embezzled funds from the Freewoman's Discussion Circle. In 1965 he wrote West regretting that he hadn't consoled her better when she was a "waif" of eighteen, betrayed in love (3 December 1965, Yale University).

[5] Barbara Low, secretary of the Freewoman Discussion Circles, a lay analyst, and a friend of D. H. Lawrence. Author of *Psycho-Analysis: A Brief Account of Freudian Theory* (1920) and translator of Anna Freud. A member of the *New Freewoman* staff and an occasional contributor, Low told Mrs. Fairfield (apparently inaccurately) that Rebecca was having an affair with Selwyn Weston. She wrote to West much later concerning efforts to get Freud and Anna Freud to England in the Hitler era (1937, Yale University).

To: Harold Rubinstein[1]

Fairliehope,
Chatham Close
Hampstead Garden Suburb, N.W.
[28 August 1912]

Dear H. F. Rubinstein—

I STOLE your *Freewoman!* St John Ervine[2] was clamouring for a sight of it, and I wanted to see where they had decapitated Strindberg—so we simply stole it![3] I expected to hear from you, somehow, and knew your address would turn up,[4] somehow, so I didn't feel guilty, somehow! I send its fellow by this post, and implore your forgiveness! Don't give me away to Stephen Swift!

Having exhausted my exclamation marks I can now calmly thank you for your photographs. A candid friend said of them, this afternoon, "You know, you are extraordinary like a monkey, Rebecca ⟨and⟩{but} not often so like a good tempered monkey as you do in these!" They are jolly good photographs. I had lunch with Hart at Eustace Miles'[5] today, and told him that he looked like Lord Byron in all of them. He took the compliment quite as a matter of course! Which was very disappointing to me.

Our second week at Barrow House was quite jolly. We spent most of our time on the lake with F. E. Green (I wish you had met him—he is the nicest old pet) and Slattery.[6] We had a riotous time on the last night rowing over to a meeting at Keswick in the tub, with Mr Mills crouched in the bow under a life-belt, shouting entreaties to "hug the shore" at the top of his Boston

(Mass) voice. He refused to row back with us and walked home with Miss Simpson at hand to administer spiritual consolation.

There were some quite nice new arrivals. St John Ervine, the Irish playwright, and his pretty wife. A schoolmistress who had flaming golden hair, was six feet tall, and could swim two miles down the lake and never turn ⟨the⟩ {a} hair—We were very sorry to part from good old Leicester. One night he gave Slattery, Miss Hall, my sister and I an impressive lecture against rashly adventuring in the stormy seas of matrimony. (I have often wondered whether Miss Marsden would sack me if I got legally married).

I am reading rather an interesting book of short stories—*Pride of War* by Gustaf Janson—about the Turco-Italian war.[7] You, as a self-centred person {Compliment intended.}[8] will understand me when I say that it is only now, for the first time, that I have realised the existence of such a war! Sound the populace of Bellaggio on the subject, and tell me how they feel about it. I am reviewing this for the *English Review.* Yesterday afternoon the *E. R.*[9] sent me two long novels—*Humpty-Dumpty* by Daniel Chaucer (who is really, I perceive, Ford Madox Hueffer) and an Indian novel, commanding that the reviews should arrive by midnight! I did it—God and the authors forgive me! But today I have a woolly head because of it.

Your article is now with the Editor. Pre-conjugal it is. Your Wagner extracts are being well fed and looked after. Of course I don't mind your giving me charge of your "English affairs." I should certainly do the same to you—this sentence is ambiguous—what I mean is, I should certainly give you "little chores" to do should the occasion arise!

Forgive great haste and exhaustion!

Yours sincerely
"R. W."—Cicily Fairfield

Rebecca West Collection   manuscript
Yale University

[1] Harold F. Rubinstein, young solicitor who frequented both the Fabian Summer School and the Freewoman Discussion Circle.

[2] St. John Greer Ervine (1883–1971), Irish playwright and novelist. Born in Belfast, he settled in England and became a critic for the *Morning Post* and the *Observer.* His works include a study of G. B. Shaw.

[3] West published a two-part review of Strindberg's *The Confessions of a Fool* and *Plays,*

"Strindberg—The English Gentleman," *Freewoman* 2 (14 and 22 August 1912). August Strindberg (1849–1912), Swedish playwright, novelist, and poet. *Miss Julie* (1888) is the best known of his naturalistic plays depicting the war between the sexes. His later, more surrealistic works anticipated Expressionism.

[4] Her letter is addressed to him in Bellagio, Italy.

[5] Hugh Hart, a businessman friend. Eustace Miles (1868–1948), English author of self-help books on economic and physical well-being.

[6] Barrow House, near Keswick was the site of the Fabian Summer School. Rubinstein had attended the first week. Green, the lecturer for the second week, heading out for a late-night drink, had pocketed the front door key, to the distress of the management. The next day "Slattery and I ruined his reputation by keeping him out on the lake long after the hour of the discussion he should have opened" (letter to Rubinstein, 16 August 1912, Yale University).

[7] Gustaf Janson (1866–1913), Swedish author whose *Pride of War* was published in 1912.

[8] West's note in lower margin.

[9] *English Review*, periodical first edited by Ford Madox Hueffer (Ford). Her brief, unsigned reviews of *The New Humpty-Dumpty* and *The Anglo-Indians* by Alice Perrin appeared in vol. 12 (September); her review of Janson in vol. 12 (October). West wrote another review of *The New Humpty-Dumpty* for the *Freewoman* (26 September 1912).

To: Ford Madox Ford (Hueffer)   Fabian Summer School
                                                 Barrow House
                                                 near Keswick
                                                 Sunday night [1912]

Dear Mr Hueffer,

   I am remembering your dinnerparty with passion in this dreadful place— I concentrate on it in the middle of lectures on the Decentralisation of Labour till I feel a little happier. It is curious about Miss Sinclair's sealed air. Don't you think that ever so many distinguished women with degrees and things ⟨have⟩ {give} that shut effect? Perhaps it is an effect of the Puritanism of women. Most men have so much more to repent that they must be amusing to justify their existence. Thank you so much for asking me.

                                        Yours sincerely,
                                        Rebecca West

Cornell University   manuscript

To: Harold Rubinstein

Fairliehope
Chatham Close
Hampstead Garden Suburb, N.W.
[2 October 1912]

Dear Mr Rubinstein—

No, no, no, I must not! I should love to go to the concert with you, but I am overburdened with work. I have to prepare a lecture for the Ethical Society in addition to my ordinary work.

As you prophesied H. G. Wells wrote to me and asked me to go and see him. I went. He is living in the rectory on Lady Warwick's estate at Easton—near Dunmow in Essex.[1] I found him one of the most interesting men I have ever met. He talked straight on from 1.15 till 6.30 with immense vitality and a kind of hunger for ideas. His wife is charming but a little effaced. Next time I see you I must tell you what he said.

I do regret that concert! {Not the one I went to—which I loved, but the one I cannot go to.}[2]

Yours sincerely,
Cicily—Fairfield—
Rebecca—West

Rebecca West Collection   manuscript
Yale University

[1] Easton Glebe, Wells's country home from 1912 to 1927, when his wife died.
[2] West's note in lower margin. In the margin of a letter mailed to Rubinstein on 24 October 1912 (Yale University), West also reported meeting Violent Hunt and Ford Madox Ford (Hueffer).

To: Dora Marsden and Grace Jardine[1]

Fairliehope
Chatham Close
Hampstead Garden Suburb, N.W.
[November 1912]

My Dear Dora and Grace,

I have been too weary to write for months. I went to Bournemouth at the beginning of November and stayed with a maiden aunt who drove me melancholy mad.[2] It is a ghastly place. Crumbly cliffs and a hinterland of suburban red brick slums, interspersed with patches of waste ground where unemployed bathing machines hold protest meetings. When I got free of it I got ill again, but, thank the Lord! my sister [Letitia] has prodded me over and found the physical basis of my nervous disturbance. I'm being treated for it and I shall be much better in future. I hope you're better. The letter which I read to the Discussion Circle sounded as though you felt the calm was doing you good. I must have read your letter with deep expression for subsequently Miss Macdonald rose from her seat and congratulated me on my lovely voice, and kissed me. There is an epidemic of kissing in the Freewoman Discussion Circle. Since you left London I have been kissed by

Miss Macdonald

Stella Brown,[3]

Barbara Low,

Helena Kingscote Greenlaw,

Miss Gallichan

and

A lady in deep mourning with an interest in Eugenics who gives away leaflets on Proportional Representation. In spite of these distractions I have been working quite hard. I turn out 2000 words for the *Clarion*[4] most weeks, for which service A. M. Thompson has given me a panegyric in this week's issue which makes me blush to think of. He alludes to me as "almost a child in years," which is not likely to send up my price in Fleet St. However they pay me decently and thus I keep body and soul together.

The *Chicago Evening Post* devoted its leader to a general consideration of my beauty, intelligence, and review of *Marriage,* on Oct. 30.[5] That was the letter you forwarded to me with the Association for Woman Suffrage envelope. They do seem to love us in America. But, as they have refused to allow [Mylius?] to enter, I shouldn't think we would pass Ellis Island. But I hope there is some chance of the *Freewoman* reviving here. I can't collect any subscribers, for all the people I know either took it in before or are too poor or abhor it. Oh, if only I were a millionaire! But, as it is, if you would send me a form of appeal for subscribers, I would type copies and send them to all the people I can possibly think of. I would have offered to do this before, but I have been so busy. I am sending back a book I borrowed from you ages ago, and apologise for not doing so before. I can't even think of a reasonable excuse! May I buy you a copy of *The Great State*,[6] which I also have? I don't know how much it cost, as it is reticent on the point, so name your price. I thought you might be willing to sell in view of your stern remarks on the subject. That reminds me. Wells expatiated at length the other day on your sweetness and brilliance.[7] I think he misses the *Freewoman* very much and appreciates you better now he has to do without you. Rather a quaint thing happened the other day in connection with him. I told him that I was working on an article about him and was not quite sure about certain facts. He wrote back telling me to send him the proofs at a certain address in Switzerland by a certain date. I wrote and told him I couldn't manage it in the time. The next thing was that one morning when I was in my bath my mother knocked on the door and said "There's a telegram for you." I told her to read it to me. There was a long pause and then she read, icily, "No hurry about the artichoke. Wells." She has also disapproved of the acquaintance and this "chops and tomato sauce" message was the last straw. Of course it should have been "article," not "artichoke." I must say I like Wells. He hasn't made love to me and it is fun watching his quick mind splashing about in the infinite. Do you want me to send you *Marriage?* I've finished all my reviews. I thought I'd ask you before sending it, in case you had seen it already.

The Discussion Circle is quaint. That dandy of cranks, D'Auvergne, is always jumping up demanding that we should all be kind to illegitimate children, as if we all made a habit of seeking out illegitimate infants and insulting them.[8] And there is the funniest person, a Swede called Hugo Dick, who plays a continual card game: he produces tickets for demonstrations of cosmogonous [euryhthmic] dancing and presses them into your hand, dealing them all round the Circle. Stella Browne sends me horoscopes occasionally. I am to "form a union with an American" and "not wear Chinese curios." So the path of life is clear before me.

I must go and post this. I hope you're better and that your work goes on well. With love to you both,

Yours ever,

Rebecca West

Dora Marsden Collection   manuscript
Princeton University

[1] Marsden's most constant companion, besides her mother. She was a staff member of the *Freewoman* and its successors.

[2] Jessie Watson Campbell, who taught French at a boarding school, Helsington Towers, in Bournemouth, on the south central coast of England in Dorset.

[3] Stella Browne (1882–1955), socialist feminist, influenced by Havelock Ellis. She fought for contraception, wrote in favor of auto-eroticism in the *Freewoman,* and founded the Abortion Law Reform Association (1936).

[4] The *Clarion* (1891–1935), socialist newspaper edited by Robert Blatchford, to which West contributed numerous articles (1912–1913), many of them anthologized in Jane Marcus, ed., *The Young Rebecca.* Marcus provides a useful introduction to the *Clarion* and related labor organizations (pp. 89–92).

[5] Published in the *Freewoman* (19 September 1912; rpt. *The Young Rebecca* 64–69), West's review of H. G. Wells's 1912 novel identified him as "the old maid among novelists." This unflattering criticism also got his attention. By the time she wrote this letter, Wells had already made her acquaintance.

[6] *The Great State: Essays in Construction,* ed. Frances Evelyn (Maynard) Greville, Countess of Warwick, H. G. Wells, and George Robert Stirling Taylor (1912). Utopian or socially ameliorative essays. Wells and Roger Fry were among the contributors.

[7] Wells provided a testimonial to the *Freewoman* which was published in an ad to promote the *New Freewoman.*

[8] Edmund B. D'Auvergne, author for the *Freewoman.* He argued that marriage gave men a commercial advantage in controlling women's bodies.

To: H. G. Wells[1]

Fairliehope
Chatham Close
Hampstead Garden Suburb, N.W.
[circa March 1913]

Dear H. G.,

During the next few days I shall either put a bullet through my head or commit something more shattering to myself than death. At any rate I shall be quite a different person. I refuse to be cheated out of my deathbed scene.

I don't understand why you wanted me three months ago and don't want me now. I wish I knew why that were so. It's something I can't understand, something I despise. And the worst of it is that if I despise you I rage because you stand between me and peace. Of course you're quite right. I haven't anything to give you. You have only a passion for excitement and for comfort. You don't want any more excitement and I do not give people comfort. I never nurse them except when they're very ill. I carry this to excess. On reflection I can imagine that the occasion on which my mother found me most helpful to live with was when I helped her out of a burning house.

I always knew that you would hurt me to death some day, but I hoped to choose the time and place. You've always been unconsciously hostile to me and I have tried to conciliate you by hacking away at my love for you, cutting it down to the little thing that was the most you wanted. I am always at a loss when I meet hostility, because I can love and I can do practically nothing else. I was the wrong sort of person for you to have to do with. You want a world of people falling over each other like puppies, people to quarrel and play with, people who rage and ache instead of people who burn. You can't conceive a person resenting the humiliation of an emotional failure so much that they twice tried to kill themselves: that seems silly to you. I can't conceive of a person who runs about lighting bonfires and yet nourishes a dislike of flame: that seems silly to me.

You've literally ruined me. I'm burned down to my foundations. I may build myself again or I may not. You say obsessions are curable. ⟨But they're not not for⟩{They are.} But people like me ⟨who⟩ swing themselves from one passion to another, and if they miss smash down somewhere where there aren't any passions at all but only bare boards and sawdust. You have done for me utterly. You know it. That's why you are trying to persuade yourself that I am a coarse, sprawling, boneless creature, and so it doesn't matter. When you said, "You've been talking unwisely, Rebecca," you said it with a certain brightness: you felt that you had really caught me at it. I don't think you're right about this. But I know you will derive immense satisfaction from thinking of me as an unbalanced young female who flopped about in your drawing-room in an unnecessary heart-attack.

That is a subtle flattery. But I hate you when you try to cheapen ⟨me to myself⟩{the things I did honestly and cleanly}. You did it once before when you wrote to me of "your—much more precious than you imagine it to be—self." That suggests that I projected a weekend at the Brighton Metropole with Horatio Bottomley.[2] Whereas I had written to say that I loved you. You did it again on Friday when you said that what I wanted was some decent fun and that my mind had been, not exactly corrupted, but excited, by people who talked in an ugly way about things that are really beautiful. That was a vile thing to say. You once found my willingness to love you a beautiful and courageous thing. I still think it was. Your spinsterishness makes you feel that a woman desperately and hopelessly in love with a man is an indecent. . . .

Rebecca West Papers   manuscript
Yale University

[1] Wells's love affair with West was one of many he conducted as his second wife Jane continued to serve as an efficient literary secretary. This letter is unsigned and incomplete and probably was not sent. Wells's reference, in a subsequent letter, to images of burning suggests that he received a similar letter. He tried to break off the relationship in mid-1913, when he went abroad with Elizabeth von Arnim.

[2] Horatio William Bottomley (1860–1933), M.P., journalist for the *Sunday Pictorial*, and financial speculator with an aptitude for elaborate, fraudulent schemes.

To: Harold Rubinstein   Quinbury
                                                         Braughing
                                                         Ware, Herts
                                                         [22 October 1914]

Dear Mr Rubinstein,
    G. Harold Rubinstein!.
    You might have waited till Shaw was dead! Now the poor thing will have to know the ineffable grief of being superannuated. Indeed I don't ask "Who is Alan Dale?"[1] Everybody however remotely connected with the stage has heard of him—he is the most bitter and brutal writer America has to show. So you see whom you have conquered! I have settled here till April or May of next year—when I have anybody amoosing [sic] down you must come too. I'm just better but am not very fit.[2] As a new course of treatment I'm trying to get sent out to the front as a war correspondent. I have high hopes!
                                        Yours ever,
                                            Rebecca West

Rebecca West Collection   manuscript
Yale University

[1] Alan Dale (1861–1928), English-born American dramatist and "smart style" critic for Hearst's *Cosmopolitan,* highly respected in his day.
[2] West is evidently keeping the birth of Anthony (4 August 1914) a secret.

To: Mrs Townshend[1]

Brig y don.
Victoria Avenue
Hunstanton:[2]
[1915]

Dear Mrs Townshend.

Would you mind posting the enclosed? It would be a kindly service.

I've had such a gloomy week. H. G. [Wells] came back from Ireland on Friday with his knee sprained for the second time in a month and went back to Easton on Saturday and sprained it a third time. So the poor dear ⟨is⟩ {has been} packed in plaster of paris ever since. While I have sorrowed from afar—alone too, as my friend didn't turn up last week-end. However she is coming this week-end and I will receive the damaged polygamist back on Monday.

I have just seen about *Blast* in the *Times Literary Supplement.*[3] It is described as a Manifesto of the Vorticists. Am I a Vorticist? I am sure it can't be good for Anthony if I am.

Yours affectionately,
Rebecca

H. G. Wells Collection   manuscript
Boston University

[1] Carrie Townshend had since December 1913 provided a meeting place for Wells and West in her London home.

[2] Town on the Norfolk coast.

[3] Periodical promoting the avant-garde Vorticist aesthetic, edited by Wyndham Lewis. West's "Indissoluable Matrimony" appeared in the first of its two numbers (1914–1915).

To: Sylvia Lynd

Alderton
Royston Park Road
Hatch End
[autumn 1915]

Dear Mrs Lynd,

You wrote to me months ago but I have been living in such amazing atmospheres that even if a neuralgic blindness had not fallen on me I could not have written to a sane human being. First I was requisitioned by Lord

Kitchener[1] to cook for eleven men who were billeted in an empty house near me at Braughing. My steaks became so popular that the eleven men became attached to me and were a permanent feature of my front garden. This was not good for work, and brought many distractions. I had, for instance, to deal with an angry Jew stockbroker who said that my men had absolutely cleared the stream of the trout with which he had carefully stocked it, and which was strictly preserved. My men did not improve the occasion. They conferred in my cabbage patch and sent the little trumpeter out to tell the stockbroker ⟨that⟩ {"begging} ⟨Mr⟩ Lichtenfeld to trouble himself no further as the gentlemen were not partial to fresh water fish!" Then I went, full of a romantic idea that all rivers were clean and cool, to Maidenhead which turned out to be a Yoshiwara[2] covered with geraniums. I moved from there to another riverside inn which would have been delightful had not the landlord and his daughter escaped out of a Conrad novel. The father was an apish man with a monosyllabic manner ⟨and ma⟩ who had come from South Africa, his daughter was beautiful and passionate—that is, she used to wander about the hotel caressing her opulent figure, which is what I have always suspected Conrad heroines of doing. And at night they used to have fierce sharp monosyllabic quarrels. One evening I was standing on the verandah when a voice suddenly came out of the dusk. I quote the remark with diffidence, but it does really seem to me to be one of the most marvellous remarks ever made. "If it were not for the great love of God in my heart I would strangle the damn bitch." I hope you will forgive me for quoting this foul language but it seemed such a Synge[3] like remark. After that my eyes went wrong and I have been rowing about in a sort of darkness. Now I've left the river and got my eyes right and am living in Suburbia, trying to work.

I'm so interested in your novel. For one thing it will be so interesting to read a novel which is not about how the author went to Oxford and left without, on the highest grounds, taking his degree. I am sure I shall like that novel because I remember your sketches so well. I forget nearly all fiction now, for your husband[4] has stunned my brains by those monstrous bludgeons of fiction he has given me. But I remember very well the insignificant woman who was rude to the fat young man.

I met a shorthaired lady called Anna Wickham (Mrs Hepburn)[5] the other day, who gave me a lively account of an evening you and she had spent at the home of Mr. W. L. George.[6] She gave me to understand that that evening had almost made her regret that she had taken up the literary life. It is a most singular thing that nearly all the men at Maidenhead looked just like George.

I hope that I may read that novel soon.

Yours sincerely,
Rebecca West

Rebecca West Collection   manuscript
University of Tulsa

[1] Horatio Herbert Kitchener (1850–1916), British field marshal who conquered the Sudan in 1898 and was chief of staff in the Boer War. He served as secretary of war (1914–1916).

[2] Area near Tokyo associated with brothels.

[3] John Millington Synge (1871–1909), Anglo-Irish playwright whose plays feature Hiberno-English.

[4] Robert Lynd (1879–1949), Belfast-born journalist and editor best known for weekly articles in the *Nation* and the *New Statesman*. As literary editor of the *Daily News,* Lynd often sent West several books at a time for review, starting in 1915.

[5] Anna Wickham (1884–1947), English poet reared in Australia. She presented challenging feminist ideas in relatively conventional verse forms.

[6] Walter Lionel George (1882–1926), Paris-born correspondent for various English newspapers and author of *The Making of an Englishman* (1914) and *The Intelligence of Women* (1917).

To: H. G. Wells   [1916]
Dearest Jaguar,

I ates being separated from my Jaguar. Do you realise you were away from me for a month and that I have only seen you twice since. I hate it. I am going up on Monday to see about that studio.[1] There is no life for us separately. Just a few nice hours over our books and articles and then when we can't write any longer an empty feeling.

Your loving Panther

Annetta is making the hell of a row about not being allowed to come. And oh *such* a joke. A long preciative[2] letter about Henry James from Arthur C. Benson.[3]

Rebecca West Papers   manuscript
Yale University

[1] The couple settled upon 51 Claverton Street in Pimlico as their London meeting place.

[2] Wells apparently returned this letter, as it bears his own response. "Preciative" for "appreciative" is circled and annotated "Jaguar cant read it prenative *Oh!* preciative of course!" He marks her first sentence in the margin and responds (like her, dropping the first letters of some words) "*me too.* Get your little home in order—make it a work place—very *fishient*—get not Wilma & all burrs—get your sisters & and your old circle there—& prepare for thorough lickings in the London studio. If you can get a place where we can sleep & have coffee and rolls in the morning without so much hardship so much the better. You *could* send a bed up. But you'll manage it best." He adorns the note with a sketch of a cat from rear view in the lower right corner.

[3] Benson was particularly noted for his public odes.

To: Sylvia Lynd

Alderton. Royston Park Road
Hatch End
[1916]

My dear Sylvia,

Here is everybody getting out nice fat books and I sit at home with a hacking cough and a kind of morbid infiltration of the brain with discontent that prevents me working. *I hate domesticity.* I don't want to stay here and I don't want to go to Westcliffe; I can't imagine any circumstances in which it would be really amusing to order 2 ounces of Lady Betty wool for socks for Anthony, or to try to get a fawn-coloured mail-cart. I want to live an unfettered and adventurous life like a [Bashibagonk?], and spend all my money on buying clothes in Bond Street. Anthony looks very nice in his blue lambs-wool coat, and I feel sure that in him I have laid up treasure for the hereafter (i.e. dinners at the Carlton in 1936) but what I want now is ROMANCE. Something with a white face and a slight natural wave in the dark hair and a large grey touring-car is what I really need. Are these a girl's natural aspirations when she is faced with last quarter's unpaid gas bill {—it isn't that I can't pay it but to pay for *gas!*}, or have I a wanton temperament?

I am so glad your domestic troubles have cleared up, but you don't say if you your precious self are better. Do get thoroughly well. As the mad baronet who lives near Violet Hueffer [Hunt] at Selsey used to whisper in one's ear when one was dancing with him—"Go on! go on! You're being such a help—just by being *you!*" I am glad the Zep story helped Sheila through the earache—I feel, ⟨as⟩ {in my} written-about domesticity, rather like Queen Mary.[1]

I had a most horrible afternoon last Wednesday going round Coubitt's shell {fuse} factory in the Grey's Inn Road with Tatcho. Tatcho has an oval paunch tightly encased in a fancy waistcoat and when one is taking an intelligent interest in the beautiful automatic machines (that cost £300 apiece) he arrests one's attention by placing a damp hand on one's bust and wheezing, "Yah see that hawspital over thah? Royal Free Hawspital? They carried Leopold Lewis in thah one night, they did, solicitah with red whiskers, wrote *The Bells*. Ever yuh see Irving in *The Bells?* . . ." He mixed very badly with Andrew Lang's[2] niece, an Oxford don, who was taking us round from the Ministry of Munitions. She didn't really like hearing how Bessie Bellwood, who had the neatest pair of legs Tatcho had ever seen, had disposed of the Duke's body. . . .[3]

I shall be in town on Thursday and Friday. Could we discuss your scheme for bringing light to countless brows on either of those days? Perhaps I might prepare myself for Shaw's Friday lecture on God by curling up on your hearthrug—although since Shaw has sent me half a dozen photographs which represent me as being exactly like Ethel Levey,[4] I refuse to believe him on any subject. I wish I was Ethel Levey, and had a Wedgwood blue door in Gloucester Place. Again I ask, are these a girl's natural aspirations or have I a wanton temperament?

Yours with love,
Rebecca

Did you see Harold Massingham[5] on me in the *Nation?*—with his discovery of an entirely new plot for *The Awkward Age?* It's good to be conceited—I don't mind a bit.

Robert and Sylvia Lynd Collection   manuscript
Boston University

[1] Queen Mary (1967–1953), wife of King George V (m. 1893).

[2] Andrew Lang (1844–1912), British poet, essayist, and translator best known for *The Blue Fairy Book* and others in the same series.

[3] West's ellipsis.

[4] Ethel Levey (1881–1955), an American actress and music hall singer associated with George M. Cohan (1901–1907), and a frequent performer in London.

[5] Harold John Massingham (1888–1952), English journalist who wrote for *Athenaeum* and the *Nation* before retiring to the country and writing on country subjects.

To: Sylvia Lynd   Southcliffe, Marine Parade
                                                 Leigh-on-sea
                                                 [10 October 1917]

Dear Sylvia,

Forgive me not answering your letter but I have been in a state of utter collapse. I got a sort of mild neurasthenia after I recovered from my dyspepsia which had just been dispelled by the news that the *Century* has taken my story and is going to publish it first as a serial and then as a book,[1] when these blasted air-raids began. The first three I did not mind at all, though they lasted three hours each and it is so unpleasing to sit down to dinner with a Gotha trying to nest on the roof and a noise filling the sky as though the Trinity were {(was?)} unskillfully moving a piano. But on Saturday it lasted from 8 o'clock till one and we were narrowly missed by an aerial torpedo, and on Sunday they dropped incendiary bombs in the bay, and I suddenly found that though I had never been consciously afraid I was simply gibbering and swept my young off to Watford without quite knowing what I was doing. I intended to sleep at Claverton Street but Miss Stern bore me off to a flock mill at West Wycombe—rather a blessing as four bombs fell round Claverton Street and one burst a watermain and flooded the street. I feel awfully ill and terrified about Anthony so I am sending him as a boarder to Anne Hillyard's Montessori School at Earls Court—intelligent teaching and six substantial storeys—and I will live on the doorstep. London is obviously going to be the safest place—we had twenty over us on nights when two got into London. They say the next treat for us here is going to be an aerial attack *and* a bombardment.

The flock mill was a great joy. The miller came in very drunk and insisted on shaking hands with me because Daily Newshthefineshtpaper intheworld and A.G.G.[2] the besht writer wegot andthatshthetruth. I hadn't thought that our austere Nonconformity could ever delight the drunken. I also discovered *Anna Lee, Maid, Wife, and Mother,* by T. S. Arthur, author of *Ten Nights in a Bar-room.* The villain was called William Archer, and he was always saying, "I'll lead you girl astray, or my name's not William Archer." And Anna said to her wayward friend, Florence, "What! Have you been to the theatre with William Archer?[3] But do you not understand that the purest woman is forever tainted by being seen in a public place with such a man?" Delightful also the way that babies suddenly appeared in the story, apparently to the intense surprise of their parents.

I liked G.H.'s epigram on that oh so different Passing of the Third Floor Back, the Malcolm case.[4] I hope that Douglas won't regard the verdict as a gun-license ⟨for⟩ in perpetuity. For the lady with the heavy jowl looks, as they say of carp and seagulls, a coarse feeder. I don't blame de Borch—I suppose he had to live up to his name. Talking of these nasty foreigners I can't agree with you ⟨that⟩ {about} Tolstoy. I wish I could. *Twice* have I read *War and Peace* and found nothing but stuffed Tolstoys, and such lots and lots of them. And plainly *Anna Karenina* was written simply to convince Tolstoy that there was nothing in this expensive and troublesome business of adultery and oh Gawd, oh Gawd, Kitty! And about *Resurrection* I cannot speak, but only yawn. And those short stories seem to me as fatuous as the fables of La Fontaine. But Dostoevsky—! The serenity of *The Brothers Karamazov,* the mental power of *The Possessed,* the art of *The Raw Youth!* Isn't it awful to think that nothing can ever decide this dispute?

I am so sorry you aren't radiantly well yet. But indeed there is nothing like the country. I am howling with rage at the thought of leaving (for a time) this jolly little house with its glorious view and its wonderful air. But except in bad weather I hardly feel at ease. If you're still in the West Country in Spring I may ask you to recommend rooms for me and the Great White Hope [Anthony West]. I hope you really will get strong soon. I believe there is something in the art of literature unsuited to women. Evidence:—

G. B. Stern	has	a	nervous	breakdown.
Sheila Kaye Smith[5]	"	"	"	" .
Clemence Dane[6]	"	"	"	" .
Olive Wadsley	"	"	"	" .

{ *The Flame* and other tigerskin romances}[7]

| *I* | have | " | " | " . |

F. Tennyson Jesse[8] is having an operation.
Such a lovely note about the last lady in "The Sketch" not long ago. "She is what the world will never believe in, a beautiful girl who is also clever." (Yes, Sylvia. They said that.) "She has a dear little house in Gordon Place, bought and furnished with her own money." Thank God, the reputation of one writing woman is cleared . . .[9]

I am going to remove Anthony from the danger zone tomorrow—and of course he is looking peculiarly adorable and babyish, and my heart is all cut [?] sore over it.

With love

Yours ever

Rebecca.

Tell Mr L. [Robert Lynd] (as they say in *Anna Lee*)[10] that Hirsey and the mixed grill he sent me are all being reviewed. He will have got Jean de Bosschère.[11] *Oh!* And I have lost your letter with the address of the man[12] who wrote *The Brook Kerith*. I'm *so* sorry. Could I have it again?

Rebecca West Collection   manuscript
University of Tulsa

[1] *The Return of the Soldier.*

[2] An inebriate's reference to H. G. Wells.

[3] West seems to be amused by the coincidence of this character's name with that of William Archer (1856–1924), Scottish drama critic, translator of Ibsen, and promoter of George Bernard Shaw. Her review of Archer's *India and the Future* appeared in the *Daily News* (17 December 1917).

[4] Lieutenant Douglas Malcolm was tried and found not guilty of the murder of Anton Baumberg, a foreigner posing as Count de Borch who seduced Malcolm's wife while Malcolm was off at war in France. Malcolm was told by Scotland Yard that Baumberg was suspected of being a German spy and of engaging in the white slave trade. The lieutenant went to Baumberg's residence prepared to horsewhip him and instead shot him numerous times—an action the jury found justified.

[5] Sheila Kaye-Smith (1887–1956), English novelist, poet, and autobiographer. She collaborated with G. B. Stern on *Talking of Jane Austen* (1943).

[6] Clemence Dane, pseudonym of Winifred Ashton (1888–1965), English novelist, feminist essayist, and playwright. She studied art in Germany and at the Slade School, was briefly an actress, and taught at an Irish girls' school. Her first novel, *The Regiment of Women* (1917), dealt with lesbian relationships at a girls' school. West expressed her distaste for her in a later letter to Lynd: "Have you ever seen anything more objectionable than Clemence Dane? I loathed her schoolgirlish book; I loathe her fatuous face; I loathe her round handwriting. She is going to be the Mrs Ward of our generation" (1918, Boston University).

[7] West's marginal note. Besides *The Flame* (1914), Wadsley's novels include *Instead* (1919), *Sand* (1922), and *Tournament* (1933), some of which were translated into Russian.

[8] Fryniwyd Tennyson Jesse (1888–1958), novelist, journalist, reviewer, playwright, and crime writer. Her work as a war correspondent in World War I resulted in an account of WACs, FANYs, and VADs in *Sword of Deborah* (1919). *A Pin to See the Peep Show* (1934) concerns a famous murder trial. West wrote an obituary praising her ideal beauty.

[9] Ellipsis in the original. West corresponded with Lynd about an article on "the younger

women novelists" that she was writing for the *Woman at Home* [Thursday 1917], requesting a picture from Lynd, who was to be included along with West, F. Tennyson Jesse, and Clemence Dane (1917, Boston University).

[10] *Anna Lee: The Maiden, the Wife, the Mother* (1892), novel by T. S. Arthur (1892).

[11] Jean De Bosschère (1878–1953), illustrator whose *Folk Tales of Flanders* appeared in 1918.

[12] George Augustus Moore (1852–1933), Anglo-Irish novelist influenced by study in France. *The Brook Kerith* (1916) was his most recent novel. His multivolume autobiography, *Hail and Farewell* (1911–1914), outlines his involvement in the Irish literary revival.

To: Sylvia Lynd   51 Claverton St.
                                                   London S.W. 1
                                                   Friday [late 1917]

My dear Sylvia,

I have at last sent off a column in on the Montessori book to the *News* and I feel I'm struggling back to normal life. "The patient['s] respiration has improved and she has done a review."[1] Sick times. After returning Anthony, very fat and lovely and reluctant to part with his nursemaid who never loses her temper having lived with a Scotch mother and an Irish father & subsequently with a genius, I returned to Leigh to sleep for a week or so. On Monday night saw the Gothas drop a bomb on a powder magazine at Sheerness—a tongue of flame about two miles high, then a ⟨x⟩ {red} incandescent cone. On Tuesday night two Gothas unloaded their bombs near us, seventeen in earth and some on the sea, and a Gotha came down within two miles of us. Came up to town to revel with Hugh Hart on leave. Was called on by a man called Britten Austen, who wrote a wonderful book called *In Action* and has written me beautiful letters once a fortnight for two years. I saw him as a splendid clear-eyed young man, the kind that wears a belt and no braces & looks very nice in flannels, very keen on his three kiddies, a wholesome Englishman that I could look at with reverent appreciation. O Sylvia. He was a stockbroker's clerk before he was a Captain, and he still has the snigger. His eyes are like grey glass marbles and he talks like this. "I kep' all your letters." (Encouragingly?) "I wouldn't 'ave kep' them if they'd been compromisin'. Naow. Never made a bloomer that way." Went back to Leigh discouraged. And then the trouble began—

You see, one evening at Brighton they brought Bertie in with the breakfast. He was visiting his mother who retired to Hove after giving birth to him. They say she is good to the poor and that you would never know. Bertie rapidly told me he was going to have a baby in a fortnight, asked who Anthony's father was, and said he loved *The Return of the Soldier,* and might he come & see me about it the first night I got back to town. I replied that that would be inconvenient, but he invited himself to dinner & duly appeared. Anthony was in bed, ⟨and⟩ {in} the next room, and wouldn't go to sleep, and sat up crying, between the hours of 7 and 11, "Panther! Panther! Open the door! I want to see the funny man!" and Bertie produced sheafs of opinions about *The Return.* He had sent it for opinions to William Archer, Alice Meynell, the publisher with the Elgin Marble head, and at least two other celebrities—probably Lord Morley and the Bishop of Oxford. He hadn't got to them when H. G. came in, so I never found out who the other two were. I had lent Bertie H. G.'s slippers as his feet were wet, and H. G. only found this out after he had been looking for them for some time, and Anthony began wailing "Tell the funny man to come & tell me a story!" And I was feeling confused because Bertie had looked in ⟨and⟩ {at} Anthony and said ecstatically, "Oh, he is like my Christopher!" and I couldn't get it right in my mind.

Well, Bertie said he'd publish *The Return,*[2] but I must give him my next two books. I hated this promise but said I would take his offer, & Pinker prepared the contract.[3] Meanwhile I got another offer {same terms but no future engagement} so I wired to Bertie that I must withdraw the manuscript unless he withdrew this clause. Bertie dashed round to Pinker—and Sylvia! he's a *cad!* He said the most awful things. That he had entertained me lavishly. So he has, of course, in a sense. Not the way he means. But fancy—! Also that he had taught me to write. — — — — — — — [sic] ! ! And that he had been on the most friendly terms with me and this was treachery! And he won't disgorge the manuscript, as he says he regards me as being already under a binding contract, and for all Pinker & I know he is probably printing it! Isn't it utterly fantastic and outrageous and beastly? I haven't, mind you, signed any contract! I withdrew the MS before I'd got the contract. But I'm horrified. I didn't think our little Robin Redbreast was such a bounder.

At this point Anthony got mumps. Mercifully the headmistress got it too so they are mumping together in an empty school, and now he's got over the bad bit of it it's no worry to me. It only means I have to look after him in the afternoons when the nurse is out. He's such an angel. But it all adds to the complexity of life. Miss Stern is a great standby in this life of struggle. To cheer me up she invited me to tea with Violet Hueffer & May Sinclair the other day but it was one of her failures. Violet was talking about C. F. Keary & his death, and said, exactly in the tone appropriate to—"It was so pretty— she's Irish, you know, so the bridesmaids wore emerald green sashes and there as a harp on the wedding-cake"—this different sentence—"You know, he'd died such an author's death—fell down by the table and dragged over the cloth, so that a bottle of ink fell all over his face!" It was the most macabre, insanely funny thing I have ever heard. Miss Stern & I went into peals of half hysterical laughter. May Sinclair stared at us, "You think *that* funny? Ought I to laugh? I'm sorry. It doesn't strike me as funny." And presently she left coldly. It was strange to see them exhibiting the essences of themselves—Violet saying something that was distraught and inappropriate but wholly memorable, and May being conscientious and genuinely enquiring but hopelessly missing the point of the situation.

I wish you'd come back so that I could sometimes see you. H. G. sends messages of respeckanaffection, as William Sutherland once said. He is being sculpted by Clare Sheridan[4] who is bringing out his attractive asymmetry rather well. If you are in town remember I'm here for another fortnight & not in the least infectious. I'm seriously thinking of abandoning Leigh; but do so love estuaries. It's awful to have a fancy for anything so large and rare. I hope you & all your fragile family ⟨x⟩ {are} well.

Love,

Rebecca

Will Bertie when he sues me charge more for the dinner I had with him alone than for the dinner I had with him & Yeats? It's a subtle point.

Robert and Sylvia Lynd Collection   manuscript
Boston University

[1] I have not found this review.

[2] "Bertie" worked as an agent for the Century Company, which published the novel first as a serial (February–March 1918) and then in its American first edition (March 1918). West reports on her vanquishing of Bertie in a later letter to Lynd: "Bertie has been brought down

in flames, with his crew burned to death, and the all clear has been sounded. I went to a delicious rugged person called Thring, solicitor to the Authors' Society, who at the mention of the words 'publisher' and 'agent' lifts up his head and looks like the Monarch of the Glen, and with his aid extracted a reasonable agreement from the screaming Bertie." She was relieved that "Never again, in the gilded splendour of the Berkeley . . . will Bertie stare at my ample bust, lavishly displayed by one of Violet's evening dresses, and say explosively, 'Never seen you without your hat on before' ([3 March 1918] University of Tulsa).

³ James Brand Pinker (1863–1922), well-known London literary agent. H. G. Wells referred James Joyce as well as Rebecca West to him. An ink blot masks her word for Pinker.

⁴ Clare Sheridan (1885–1970), English author whose works include *Russian Portraits* (1921) and *Across Europe with Satanella* (1925).

To: S. K. Ratcliffe   58 Lansdowne Place
                                                       Hove
                                                       [Christmas 1917]

Dear S. K. R.,

What a pig you are not to ⟨x⟩ have given some hints of your whereabouts on Monday in the letter I got on Sunday. For I had to fetch Anthony on Tuesday and conduct him here on Wednesday. So now I shall not see you till Heaven knows when—till, perhaps, I come over to America to avoid being verboten by our Prussian masters. Well, well.

Some business matters—*The Judge* will not be finished till the autumn, allowing for my slow rate. You see they have just got married, and her brother has to die, and his mother has to die, and he has to murder his brother and be hanged, and it's really only *then* that the exciting things begin to happen. I mean to try the *Century* soon—say Spring—with a shorter thing that I have a quarter written, and that I shall turn to when my story next comes to a halt. They are darlings. Their letters make me feel less than the dust beneath the Editor's chair. (Talking of Laurence Hope[1] did I tell you I got out *Stars of the Desert* {from the London library—for reference—} (and found among the leaves a sheet of notepaper inscribed in a fatigued female handwriting "Remember to order beeftea for baby"—potted tragedy). About the *Atlantic* I fear I am snuffed out. Sidgwick got irritated by my delay—and I admit I was to blame in not having {kept]} a copy of the 1st chapter which I had to rewrite—and plainly he didn't think that *The Return of the Soldier* was any great catch when he got it.[2] It may sound like the sour grapes touch but the *Atlantic Monthly* bears witness that his taste in fiction is orrible [*sic*]. Now for my confession—I can't send you any *New Republic* stuff by the 28th. I have the notes by me, notes chiefly of stuff I handed out to the Fabians two summers ago {& some stuff I wrote a fortnight ago} and it only needs what would be a couple of nights' work, {a} ⟨with⟩ few connecting paragraphs, compression, and a Beccas big bow wow peroration, and I cannot do it. I never now can sleep till 1, and Anthony wakes me up several times in the night and finally starts singing comic songs and doing conjuring tricks and otherwise hymning the dawn at 6.30. The consequence is that when I put him to bed at 6 I cannot do anything except sit and stare at my work. I am dog-tired. I may adapt myself to conditions but at any rate I won't have the stuff ironed out till the new year. Please don't be angry with me. Remember that since I was twenty I have had exactly seven weeks of the working conditions that people of my age & occupation usually have. In those seven weeks I've done no end of my novel and worked off my arrears for the *News* and written this stuff for the *New Republic*—I was glad to find I could still work! And on January 15 three more months of this blissful productivity begins. I wish you could imagine the ⟨exper⟩{conditions} under which I have worked for the last five years. Such that I cannot bear to be alone without some work to look at and think about in case I should start thinking about the million instances of cruelty & unkindness & meanness & treachery & imbecility & vamping that have happened to me with no intervals for refreshment since I was twenty. However it has opened my eyes to the ex-traordinary goodness of some of my friends. You have been the most won-derful person to me. Everybody else seems to deal with me for the purpose of getting something out of me but you have done nothing but give me things. You have been a dear. I don't wonder that President Wilson says like the man in the American ⟨x⟩ advertisement—"Yes, but it must be a Ratcliffe."[3]

I've run out of ink & am doing ⟨x⟩{what I} can with my landlady's ink-jelly. It's rather like being cut off on the telephone. I may leave Leigh {for a time}, as God now does us much more handsomely with the daily bomb than with the daily bread, & though I am more than usual calm my maid is talking of leaving. I am not sure either of Claverton St.[4] But for the mean-time it is a safe address & I'll notify you of any change. I am here till the 12th or so.

With such hopes as can be exchanged between two members of the Cold Feet Brigade.

Yours affectionately,
Cicily

Rebecca West Papers   manuscript
Yale University

Pinker is a [flop?]. I resorted to him to sell my serial rights—which he hasn't touched. Ach!

---

[1] Laurence Hope, pseudonym of Adela Florence Cory (1865–1904), a poet resident in Madras. Some of her poems were set to music. *Stars of the Desert* (1903) offers her typical exotic Eastern setting.
[2] See letter to Ratcliffe (4 February 1916).
[3] Cigarette advertisement.
[4] London rooms shared with Wells.

To: George Bernard Shaw   Southcliffe
                                                                         Marine Parade
                                                                         Leigh-on-Sea
                                                                         [1917–1918]

Dear G. B. S.

You have given me many hours of exquisite pleasure by sending me those two volumes. I admit that Frank is, in a certain sense, a very great man indeed.[1] Marvellous the way that without direct statement he gives one to understand that he is over eight feet in height and the authentic person referred to in the well-known saga—

There's a friend for little children
Above the bright blue sky.

But I still refuse to accept him as an artist. Perhaps I am prejudiced by my one encounter with him. Very shortly after I had come up to London I was taken by Austin Harrison[2] to a night club called the Cave of the Golden Calf.[3] It was kept by one of Strindberg's wives, a cornucopia of a woman who was apt to try and distract attention from the poorness of the liqueurs by telling how Strindberg (with a ready commonsense I would never have credited him for) kept a carving-knife under their pillow. There was a cabaret show, a Spanish dancer who, on being addressed in Spanish by Austin Harrison, enquired "Wot's that, dearie?" and a German hairdresser from Hull who recited poems which were considered richly exotic but which only suggested to me that he had been hanging round Hull docks too much and listening to rough men talking. To this entered Frank Harris, in a very new dress suit, which one felt was part of an outfit which he had procured from some trustful spinster by fraudulent representations, and delivered a lecture on Style. I admit it was plucky of him, for he was very drunk. His manner was foully offensive: a barking arrogance with oily declensions at the points where he was moved to speak of the necessity of the artist to feel pity and love—awful passages as though the Sermon on the Mount had kittened, and there were its progeny. But the thing that really horrified me was that his lecture consisted entirely of a criticism of an incident in *Madame Bovary* which that book does not contain. He had invented it. There is nothing in any of Flaubert's books remotely resembling it. I sat there with the intense solemnity of eighteen, horrified by this charlatan: and even more horrified by the way that not a soul in the room—and it was full of writers, Moore and Hueffer and Housman and Cunningham-Graham[4] and s[u]ch—had detected him. So this, I thought, was London. I picked up some consolation from the reflection that if London was such a mug I ought to be able to get some sort of income out of it. But I have never lost my horror of Harris as an impudent trafficker with sacred things, a conjurer who uses literature as his lowlier and more honest fellow-conjurers use white rabbits and bowls of goldfish. And I feel it here. Those lurching, brawling passages about beauty, and English Puritanism, and Christianity. And a certain indefinable quality about the prose. He has worked at it hard. But he had not the intention of making it a sharp instrument of truth. He polished it up with furniture-cream to make it nice and glossy.

I never can make out why there is all this fuss about Wilde. Of course it is impossible for people of my generation to give any just estimate of his position as an artist because you have so completely wiped him up in the theatre. And I have always been prejudiced against him because of the plea that his sentence should have been remitted because he was an artist, which seems to me unworthy of the aristocrat that an artist should be. But what an argument for Home Rule the book is. There are things in it which increase one's contempt for Ireland—notably the photograph of Sir William Wilde.[5] A country where a man who looked like an embittered mandril could have a family in every farmhouse must be in a deplorable state. But the book's exposure of what you call "Merrion Square Protestant pretentiousness," is a valuable contribution to the only important argument in favour of Home Rule. Those Protestant Irish of the governing class who were reared up with the understanding that they had been born kings and that it was their duty to hate the rest of the world, and so acquired a lifelong incapacity for love, are the most beastly of human beings. My father also was a "Dublin snob" and the circumstances of his upbringing {were exactly similar to those} of Wilde, even to the home in Merrion Square, and it has been most interesting to me to note how everything you say of Wilde was true of my father. My grandmother refused to go to Dublin Castle because the Viceroy had refused to pardon a Protestant servant of hers for what she considered the trifling offence of murdering a Catholic; and so you can imagine the kind of education in hate my father received. It bore fruit in the most horrible snobbery; he married my mother, who was a great pianist, and destroyed her musical genius and ruined her life with the most complete and well-mannered imperturbability, because she came of low people of peasant extraction. He had the maddening charlatan attitude to art that you complain of in Wilde; he always talked about any piece of art with condescension and an insolent refusal to take the slightest trouble to find out what it was up to, as if it had been a snuff-box his mother had bought for the silver-table in Merrion Square from some improvident Catholic. He had that appalling lovelessness of soul that was Wilde's real trouble. I suppose Wilde's abnormalities were really due to a desire to enjoy love without any responsibilities and without even any obligation of deference. (He probably felt kind to those children in prison because they were complete strangers and could not make any claim upon him). My father was a more imaginative and fastidious man and instead of indulging in abnormalities (so that we never had the satisfaction of seeing him go to prison) he used to go on exploring expeditions in Africa, where he behaved with most splendid courage and dash and performed one or two deeds of such daring that somebody afterwards made a bracing boys' book out of them, while my mother and sisters and I starved at home. He was quite a decent human being I believe, but it was this horrible Irish Protestant education in hatred and contempt which spiritually deformed him. You can imagine therefore that the figure of Wilde does not amuse me. He is no more a subject for art than a congenital cripple is for a picture.

Forgive this long letter. I will post back the exquisite Frank tomorrow. Many thanks for the loan—

Yours sincerely,

Rebecca

Shaw Papers   typescript with manuscript addition
British Library Ms. 50.522

[1] Frank Harris (1856–1931), iconoclastic Irish-born playwright, author of short stories and memoirs. As editor of the *Saturday Review* (1894–1898), he published Shaw, Wells, and Max Beerbohm. Shaw has probably presented West with a copy of Harris's *Oscar Wilde: His Life and Confessions* (1916), which contained Shaw's "Memories of Oscar Wilde."

[2] Austin Harrison (1873–1928), English literary and political journalist and editor of the *English Review* (1910–1923). His books on Germany include *Pan-Germanic Doctrine* (1904), *England and Germany* (1907), and *The Kaiser's War* (1914). *Frederic Harrison: Thoughts and Memories* (1925), concerning his father, is probably his best book.

[3] Run by Mme Strindberg, the club was decorated with contemporary paintings and became one of the favorite gathering places for the Vorticists and Wyndham Lewis.

[4] Robert Bontine Cunninghame Graham (1852–1936), rancher, traveler, M.P., and short-story writer, admired by both Shaw and Conrad.

[5] Irish surgeon, the father of Oscar Wilde.

To: Sylvia Lynd   [28 July 1918]
My dear Sylvia,

Life has been so full lately what with six teeth stopped by my blue-eyed dentist and my lunatic with erotic delusions about the entire staff of the Ministry of Reconstruction and the Billing case[1] (but why weren't Mrs Webb,[2] Hugh Walpole, and Maud Royden[3] mentioned) and trying to get some work done that I don't believe I answered your letter, which made me feel as though I had been most kindly stroked and given a full saucer of milk. I horribly envied your account of your real country environment for the gardener came when I was up in town and he's bin and gawn and put in scarlet geraniums and marguerites and a special kind of petunia made not by God but by a wallpaper designer and now the garden makes the intellectual 'eave. There is God knows no use. I am having a snap with that little ray of sunshine, Massingham. *He* says Orpen's *The Refugee*[4] is a German spy who was shot. He *likes* to think she was shot because it would be so brutal of the French to have shot her. *I* say she is a lady known as "The Mother of Rouen," who continues to mother Rouen. I intend to send her to the office of that full-of-smiles weekly the *Nation*—for she is said to be in England and I believe I have seen her—with the promise that there she will really see life. This arises out of an altercation at the Shaws—at which Barker[5] also was present. Oh Sylvia you have taken the words out of my mouth in a certain sketch in *The Thrush and the Jay*.[6] When we were waiting together before the Shaws came in there was an awful feeling that we were going to be "discovered on"; and all the time I felt as though I should be getting further down stage and be careful not to cover him. He is *nicht appetitlich*. I had a weekend with Violet [Hunt] and Ford {here} during which Ford explained to me elaborately the imperfection of *The Return of the Soldier* compared to any of his works—a statement with which I profoundly agree but which oughtn't to be made, because it rouses emulation. I desired to save my selfrespect by going off to stay with Hugh Walpole and explaining the imperfections of his work compared with mine—and then I suppose he would go off somewhere and stay with someone else & explain etc. etc. etc. and God knows where the chain would end and think of all the incidental scandal—and meanwhile dear old Violet dropped—*coram populo* on a Sunday morning—drawers trimmed with lace off the gown she had worn when courted by George Moore at the Earl's Court Exhibition—over my balcony on to the petunias— not now and again but again and again. Perfect dears they are, though. I have found out a way of brightening people's lives. I heard from Laurence Binyon's[7] secretary a yarn that May Sinclair was married to a Guardsman. I immediately wrote and ⟨told⟩ {asked} her if it was true. It was not, but she is immensely pleased, and wonders who it is she can have been seen about with. Now, when one can't think how to squeeze in one's daily good deed one knows what to do. *The Return* is doing rather nicely—1600 in the first fortnight—and I believe Bertie[8] is doing his best for it. You've all been pets to me over it. But oh God this new book. Do all new books lie on one's mental chest like an undercooked suet dumpling? And *when* is your masterpiece about the perils of stage life (throwing I hope some light on the 47000) coming out? H. G. and I may appear in your garden on bicycles some day in the next fortnight or three weeks, for we are going down to stay with the Neil Lyonses[9] and I believe it is a possible ride over. May we?—we will come separately if you like—I mean I will come alone. But H. G. has a new song —

My father suffered hell from his rheumatics
Till he mastered his pain by repeating mathematics
    Showing science is a benefit to all
    Shoowing science is a benefit to a-a-all.

Which helps me to forget the war. If you see Olive Heseltine[10] I wish you'd tell her how pleased and flattered I was by her review. And if you see [Bethany?] — !

Love,
Rebecca.

The *National News* is an amiable newspaper & I refuse to speak ill of it any more. After all we don't know its temptations and perhaps it had no mother—for it has reviewed *The Return twice*. Anthony is going to be President of a Railway Season-Ticket-Holders' Association when he grows up. He said, when I was bringing him back here the other day and the train stopped between stations, "When we get out at Leigh we must stop before we leave the station and beat the engine driver for being so slow."[11]

Rebecca West Collection   manuscript
University of Tulsa

[1] Case for obscene and criminal libel (29 May–4 June 1918) against M. P. Noel Pemberton Billing, editor of the *Vigilante,* for publishing a statement that connected the lesbian actress Maud Allen's forthcoming private performance of Oscar Wilde's *Salome* with "the Cult of the Clitoris." He suspected that the nation's purity and its defenses against the Germans were both threatened by the revival of this banned one-act play.
[2] Beatrice Webb (1858–1943), economist, essayist, diarist, and leading member of the Fabian Society.
[3] Agnes Maude Royden (1876–1956), preacher and feminist author who wrote on pacifist and theological issues.
[4] Sir William Orpen (1878–1931), Dublin-born British painter whose World War I sketches were exhibited in London (March–June 1918). His painting *The Refugee* portrays a beautiful young woman. Apparently, West and Massingham were arguing about the identity of this unknown refugee.

⁵ Harley Granville-Barker (1877–1946), director of the Royal Court Theatre. His role in establishing the reputation of George Bernard Shaw would account for his presence at the Shaws' party.

⁶ Lynd's *Thrush and the Jay* (1917) is a collection of prose and poetry.

⁷ Laurence Binyon (1869–1943), English poet and dramatist who published numerous works on English and oriental art.

⁸ See letter to Lynd, late 1917, for description of "Bertie."

⁹ A. (Arthur) Neil Lyons (1880–1940), English author of biography and fiction whose works include *Robert Blatchford, Sixpenny Pieces* (1914), and *Short Stories of To-day and Yesterday* (1929).

¹⁰ Heseltine wrote *Conversation* (1927).

¹¹ Written in left margin.

To: Sally Melville

Casa Solitaria
Isola di Capri
[late 1920]

Dearest S. M.

If you sent me the *Morning Post* with the Carthew case in it many thanks. But just in case you didn't and I sent the postcard to the wrong address I'm sending this letter to Winnie to forward. This is a heaven upon earth. (But man is very vile.) Faith Mackenzie's house is built halfway up a limestone cliff,¹ 300 ft. above the water, which usually looks (in this recent rough weather) like dark blue crystal, just above the three famous rocks I Faraglioni. The exact position was used by Turner in his picture of Ulysses and Polyphemus.² This place, by the way, completely explains Turner's pictures. The mountains are limestone, which is light in colour and very smooth, so that it reflects colour with extreme vividness—consequently under any strong light they simply cease to look as if they had any form at all and become masses of different tones of the same colour, losing all suggestion of solidity. Turner's wildest pictures are really strictly realistic. We are within ten minutes of the Grotto of Mithras and have the most glorious view from it of the Leap of Tiberius—serrated cliffs rising nearly 1000 ft. sheer from the water. It's not five square miles, this island, but it is inexhaustibly beautiful, and full of thrills. The days when the sirocco is blowing (the south wind, when the ⟨sky⟩{sun} passes across the sky looking silver as the moon) or the tramontana (the North, when all the Bay of Naples is brilliant blue flecked with brilliant white houses) we go down to a neck of rock that joins the nearest Faraglioni to the land. I discovered some brickwork there and some funny black stuff like mud gone solid—I found that the one was the remains of Tiberius' harbour—the other a sample of the lava that fell on the island 2000 years ago! I had a tremendous thrill at Anacapri, the village on the slope of Monte Solaro, 600 ft. above the sea, where the people are very pure in race (mostly Greek) and have kept their blood and their customs very pure. I heard a woman use "oras" for tomorrow! Society here has lost none of its sparkle since the days of Tiberius. My experience, which I had thought not to be narrow, has embraced much totally new material. There is a marvellous red haired Marchesa Casati, the wife of a very mild and oh so aristocratic Marchese that I met in London at Clare Sheridan's[3] in Spring. She used to come down to the Piazza in tartan pantalettes designed by Poiret,[4] followed by an enormous negro servant. This negro was very much afraid of being ill used, having had, poor soul, sad experiences; so if anybody met him alone he used to draw himself up and say defensively in ⟨English⟩ {Italie} and then in French: "I am attached to the person of the Marchese Casati." The delicate wit of the Italians took hold of this and he is known as "The Marchesa's flea." The Marchesa sat for her portrait to a woman called Romaine Brooks,[5] an American of real genius who has just been given the Legion of Honor for her work, which is amazing. We were all asked to tea to see its unveiling, at Miss Brooks' studio. I was prepared for something extraordinary from the conversation of two Russian princesses, who murmured to each other in dove like voices "People are so *unkind* about la Casati! Yes, are they not! They actually say she had to be put in an asylum for erotomania!—Yes is it not unkind!—Yes, indeed, you could never really have called it erotomania!—No, it was never quite as bad as that—no, not nearly!—Besides I know the truth. It is only this. La Casati had been dabbling in black magic, and she became overwrought and believed that she was to be the mother of the Anti-Christ and that the father was to be Cardinal Amcette, and she approached him—yes, and there was unpleasantness. Yes that was all. . . ."[6] When the picture was unveiled it showed the Casati standing without a stitch on, on a ledge of rock against a cliff. An Austrian doctor standing beside me was so overcome that he lifted up his voice: "What is it possible that in this country a hochgeborne frau [aristocratic woman] will present herself to be painted *stark* naked?" There are also some Russian aristocrats who completely explain the Bolshevik Revolution and its little faults of impatience—one a worthless old hussy of Tiberian vices who is *ruined* by the Bolshevists—but absolutely ruined, ma chère, as she says—and who still has 4,000,000 lire a year and keeps a fleet of eight yachts. {I don't know if they made her sign a separate peace.} There is a quite charming woman in this lot, however, who is engagingly helpless. The first time I met her her hair was the colour of a 2d stamp—the next it was the colour of a pillar box—she artlessly explained to me quite sans jêne that it was because she was now having to dye her hair herself, while her maid had always done it before, and "my hands have not yet a backbone." Oh, it's all very amusing, and the place is past all belief beautiful. H. G. says he is coming straight here from America in the middle of March, but men being what they are there may be some other lady in possession by then. I really do like him much more than most other men—besides loving him, as I do. We dined together with your friend Beaverbrook the night before I left. I found him one of the most fascinating talkers I've ever met, and full of the real vitality—the geniusy kind that exists mystically apart from all physical conditions, just as it does in H. G. I wish you and J. B. M. could get out here.[7] Just think yesterday I wrote all morning in the open air, my writing pad resting on the hot marble—baked by the sun! There is cold of course and three days gales, but the air is never poisoned. And my tummy blossoms like the rose. It may be simply the drugs I'm swallowing but I think not. I think it's really my resistance is improving because I'm not wasting my strength battling with bad weather and catching cold. So you see what you must do. Oh, Beaverbrook said lovely things about you—"a marvellous brain"—"and a wonderful character! If you knew all I do about that woman you'd go down on your knees to her." But I do that already, even on my knowledge! My salutation to Mary Patrice and I do hope you're well, and J B M too.

Yours ever
Rebecca

Rebecca West Collection   manuscript
Yale University

[1] Faith Compton Mackenzie (d. 1960), author of historical and autobiographical novels such as *The Cardinal's Niece* (1935) and *Napoleon at the Briars* (1935). Wife of Compton Mackenzie.

[2] J. M. W. Turner (1775–1851), the English Romantic painter best known for his study of

light in landscapes and seascapes, which influenced the late Impressionist painters. *Ulysses Deriding Polyphemus* (1829) is an outstanding work.

[3] Marchesa Luisa Casati (1875–1957), wealthy Bohemian who lived in Paris (1915–1930) and was the lover of D'Annunzio.

[4] Paul Poiret (1879–1944), French fashion designer popular in pre–World War II Paris. His creations included the hobble skirt, knee-length tunics, and flowing Greek costumes.

[5] Romaine Brooks (1874–1970), American expatriate portrait artist who arrived in Paris via Capri, after studying in Rome. Brooks was the lifetime partner of Natalie Barney and was associated with her Paris salon.

[6] West's ellipsis.

[7] James B. Melville, Sally Melville's husband and the legal counsel for Lord Beaverbrook's press.

To: Jane Wells

Casa Solitaria
Isola di Capri
6 December [1920]

Dear Mrs Wells,

I have just heard from H. G. how ill you have been and wanted to tell you how sorry I am to hear that you have had such a distressing time and how glad I am to hear that you are getting on well. I make this last remark with a terrified sense that it is of ill omen—letters containing such expressions usually arrive when one has had a relapse and is feeling particularly unhappy and are then likely to cause resentment against the letter writer! I hope my good wishes won't have any such ill-effect and that you will feel better soon.

Yours ever,
Rebecca

Rebecca West Papers
Yale University

manuscript

To: H. G. Wells

5 Chatham Close
N.W. 4
[August 1921][1]

Dear Jaguar,

When I got here Lettie said she was doubtful about Mother so wouldn't go away till Monday. Mother was like a skeleton, and I knew she was terribly ill but I thought she'd just sleep away out of sheer feebleness. In the meantime she was quite gay and we had a good evening together and she rejoiced to hear that Anthony wasn't in danger of drowning at Weyborne. But when night came on she began to have an attack partly heart and partly a mysterious pain. And she went on for thirty six hours. There were one or two bright times when she talked of Anthony—and when she made Winnie bring her baby in and almost played with it. But all the rest of the time she was in agony. She was climbing in and out of bed, she could get no ease in any attitude, she had an agonising pain in her stomach. She implored us to give her something deadening—and we were giving her chloral and bromide which was the only safe thing. We knew if we gave her morphia she would die. And in the end the doctor came on Monday morning and we decided that the time had come when she must have ⟨the prescription⟩ {morphia and} I went down and had the prescription made up—it was funny I felt quite happy and even flippant while I was doing it—and Lettie gave her a couple of doses and she said how comfortable she felt, and then slipped away. She looked the essence of herself at the moment when she died. Now I realise how terribly I loved her—what a queer passionate genius she was and how all through me I belong to her. I only quarreled with her more than most people do with their mothers because we loved each other so much more. I can't bear her to be dead. The only thing is that it is lovely how you don't feel any terror of the dead when you love them. I helped Nurse to bind up her jaw when she was getting her ready to lay out and it was just like doing a ⟨favour⟩ {service} to her when she was alive. The funeral's to be on Thursday. I will try to take Lettie down to Kelling on Saturday—I will try to get Peary to find you ⟨another⟩ {a room} out.[2] You do understand the necessity, don't you, pussy? She is in collapse—it was awful for her (after she'd been nursing Mother for weeks) to have this culminating thirty-six hours—with the decision to make about the morphia. I wish I had a Jaguar to rub up against, and tell how anxious I am about Mother. I don't feel easy in my mind about her! I am really quite calm and am being useful.

                                             Panther

[1] Someone, perhaps West, has supplied the erroneous date 1920.

[2] "Peary," Ada Pears, who took care of Anthony starting in 1919, when West moved into London.

To: Anthony West   [1922]

I have seen several people dancing like this.[1] They make a tremendous noise with castanets and stamping their heels on the floor. If I do it when I come home the people ⟨won't like it⟩ {underneath} won't like it at all.

Love,
Panther

Rebecca West Papers   manuscript
Yale University

[1] The picture side of this post-card, sent from Spain, features two women dancing flamenco style, in native costume.

To: Louis Golding[1]   36 Queen's Gate Terrace, S.W. 7
                                  [circa 1922]

My dear Louis.

Since you would certainly have received a copy of *The Judge* if you had stayed put among my coffee-cups your suggestion that I should send it to you is very sound. But I am broke, so I will wait till I get my American presentation copies. I do hope you'll like the second part better than the first, because all nice people do. Thomas Hardy[2] makes his wife read it to him over and over again, it being the only book ever written as gloomy as his own. His wife told me this in accents of incredible bitterness.

I did not come and see you because I myself was in a state of pitiful, infectious collapse. Do you know that I haven't got at any decent writing since *The Judge?* My family vampires me. There seems no way out ⟨for⟩ save the suicide's noose. As an alternative I have been learning to ride. This process is extremely perilous because my dramatic instinct makes me look and behave as if I could ride magnificently the minute I put on my riding kit. I force myself to tell the people at any new stables I go to that I can't ride but in spite of myself I do this in such accents that they don't believe me and put me on the bloodiest of all their blood hunters. The result of this ⟨was that⟩

{when I went} to Exmoor I was bolted with for three miles—but there again my damned dramatic instinct told—for I looked as if I was enjoying it so convincingly that some people who saw me insisted on me following the staghounds next day because it was over specially dangerous country that they knew I could tackle. {Black terror it was, black terror.} Some day I will stray into the foxhunting country and that will be the death of me. They'll make me the Master of the Pytchley on sight and I will break my neck over the first gate.

I haven't seen you since I was in Spain. I did so wish you were there, you would so greatly have loved Rinva with its incredible scenery of intersecting planes and its Esquimaux huts of bracken and sweet smelling herbs that stand in pinewoods—and oh endless Granada—endless in space and time—for there's a jolly modern town and the Alhambra and hills of wine purple earth with olives and tanks of Moorish palaces on them and then miles and miles and miles of buff rock with paths leading along razor-edges that go down to canyons where there are benevolent villages toggled up with almond blossom on their buttonholes—and above all snow mountains—and nobody ever goes to bed. Though talking of beauty I had a revelation the other day when overcoming my objection to dreaming spires, I went to Oxford. I had no idea it was so glorious. I had been staying at Garsington with Lady Ottoline Morrell—do you know her? People laugh at her but she is an innocent and generous creature—and I came in on Monday and was toted round—unfortunately for most part of the day among people who were obsessed by the theory of conflicts held by a gentleman named Mallik[3]—he is said to be an Indian but I believe he is an plain white bore who has been paid to go to Willy Clarkson and be painted black by some foe of Indian nationalism. ⟨If⟩ {In case} you are not acquainted with it I had better outline this theory. Mallik could not do it himself—he was looking highly deliquescent—as if he himself were engaged in a conflict as to whether he would stay an Indian or become dripping. It was explained to me that he was exhausted, having, on the previous day enunciated his theory. A disciple, therefore, took on the job. The theory rests on the assumption of the equality of all desires. If you and I were in a room with some flowers or cigarettes or books and we both wanted them a conflict would arise and we would both be right and both be wrong. It would not matter which of us had paid for them, and whether we desired to ⟨x⟩ {make} a reasonable use of them or to destroy them wantonly to annoy the others—our desires would be of equal sacredness. It would be our duty to find a compromise that would satisfy both of us . . . . [West's ellipsis] "Well? Well?" I asked. But to them it seemed very well. A lady has already produced a study of *Hamlet* based on this theory and Robert Graves[4] has revised his conception of poetry because of it. (I didn't like him and his wife—they're like very bad weather.) From this I crept away, feeling rather like a secret eater of caviare, to Anthony Asquith's[5] rooms. There I fell in love with a young man named David Cecil.[6] As he is one of the younger sons of Lord Salisbury I fear my passion is hopeless. Perhaps as his hair was very long and curly it is doubly hopeless.

I have had Francis Brett Young[7] and his wife staying with me—lovely people. He is harassed beyond measure by money miseries and the refusal of any more than three thousand inhabitants of the British Isles to read his books but bearing it really beautifully. They will be up at Anacapri till January so if you are in those parts go and see them. He is going to America to lecture in January—(as I am going to next September.) I tried to take him to a lecture by Agate at which I took the chair for the Tomorrow—or as Agate suggested, more properly speaking—The Yesterday Club, but he was too ill to meet one strange James.[8] The more I meet that being the less I understand him. He looks so virile, so hearty, and is so neurotic and meagre. He labours with his whole body to do what you or I do with our little finger. And who are these strange, heavy, unhouseled friends?

I do look forward to the light book. I am sitting about among my own mental ruins, trying to cut reviewing and concentrate on short stories—one that you will like when you have been in Italy. Really it is about the tortures of a passive sodomite who is beloved by an active lesbian but it has plenty of flesh on those sinister bones. And there you are, writing with the greatest of ease a light book. Grrrr!

Violet [Hunt] is ever so much better. Though she has had a bad internal chill which she insists on ascribing to shock at hearing that Ford is going abroad for the winter. The Pen Club grows and grows and redder than the cherry is Mrs Dawson Scott who, poor old thing, had an appalling blow.[9] Her husband, as I expect you know, was divorced and lived in sin with a lady in Wales. This Welsh lady suddenly sent telegrams to Mrs Dawson Scott to know where he had got to—which struck her as awfully funny. She giggled about it to me at the Pen Club ⟨dinner⟩ {committee} meeting and said to me how funny it was to feel that someone who had once been everything to me was now nothing—absolutely nothing—to me. An hour after I got back home the telephone bell rang. I went and could hear nothing but uncontrollable weeping—it was Mrs Dawson Scott—to tell me that she would not be at the dinner, because her husband had killed himself with prussic acid and she could hardly bear to go on living. V Sackville West has been elected to the committee—Russian toques, sables, perversions.[10] The innocent Club elected her instead of Amber Reeves,[11] thinking she would give us tone, little knowing that she had come to us because London society had held its breath till it fainted away and had recovered only to give orders that it was not at home. But, indeed, literary life is getting very respectable. D. H. Lawrence has suddenly sent back money to everybody he owed it to, from somewhere in Texas, which he has visited *via* Western Australia after having been driven out of a Buddhist monastery in Ceylon for lack of urbanity—or perhaps Nirvanity, it should be. Gilbert Frankau[12] has set up a stately home of England in Lancaster gate. ("I have been hunting in The Shires," he told Michael Arlen[13] and me when we met him. "Ah Ah!" said Michael Arlen. "But *I*'ve been paying a round of country house visits. So we're quits.") If you go to Florence please go see Reginald Turner—35 Viale Milton—a dear, *dear* friend of mine, one of the great "originals." There is a man on the [Loug'?] Arno who keeps a bookshop Oriole, who is a pet lamb and will tell you where everybody like Norman Douglas[14] and Leo Stein[15] (whom people will tell you is a bore but isn't) [is].

Yours ever,

Rebecca West

I have a letter from a Swedish lady offering to translate *The Judge*. Her exact words are "Would you have made the arrangements for the translation of the Judge? Else would I enjoy." The feeling behind it seems good.[16]

L. Golding Papers   manuscript
University of Texas at Austin

---

[1] Louis Golding (1895–1958), English novelist who wrote about Jewish life. His works include *Magnolia Street* (1931), *Five Silver Daughters* (1934), and a study of James Joyce (1933).

[2] On a trip to Dorset with Wells in early 1919, West had visited the novelist and poet Thomas Hardy (1840–1928) and his wife.

[3] Basanta Kumar Mallik (1879–1958), Indian philosopher and social commentator. Robert Graves included his actionless drama, *Interchange of Selves*, in his *Mock Beggar Hall* (1924). Mallik's other works include *The Individual and the Group: An Indian Study in Conflict* (1939), and *The Real and the Negative* (1940).

[4] Robert Graves (1895–1985), English writer of poetry, essays, and novels whose notable works include the novel *I Claudius* (1934), the mythical study *The White Goddess* (1948), and his autobiography, *Goodbye to All That* (1929). West probably refers here to his first wife, and not to author Laura Riding, his associate from 1926 to 1939.

[5] Anthony Asquith (1902–1968), English film director and script writer who specialized in adaptations of West End plays, including *Pygmalion* (1938), *The Importance of Being Earnest* (1951), and numerous works by Terence Rattigan. He was a founding member of the Film Society in London.

[6] David (Gascoyne-) Cecil (1902–), English critic and literary historian, the younger son of the Marquess of Salisbury and a regular at Garsington. He wrote biographies of William Cowper and Max Beerbohm.

[7] Francis Brett Young (1884–1954), physician, novelist, and poet who settled in Anacapri after service in East Africa during World War I. *The Black Diamond* (1921) and *Portrait of Clare* (1927) concern the West Midlands. His most ambitious work is *The Island* (1944). Like West, he reviewed for *Herald Tribune Books*.

[8] James Agate (1877–1947), drama critic for the *Sunday Times* and autobiographer.

[9] Catherine Amy Dawson Scott (1865–1934), "Sappho," English feminist, poet, and novelist who founded the international PEN Club. Her epic poem *Sappho* was published at her own expense in 1889.

[10] Vita Sackville-West (1892–1962), English poet, novelist, travel writer, and gardener, reared at Knole and commemorated in Virginia Woolf's *Orlando*. Both she and her husband Harold Nicolson became acquaintances of West. Sackville-West's works include poetry, *The Land* (1926), and the novels *Seducers in Ecuador* (1924), *The Edwardians* (1930), and *All Passion Spent* (1931).

[11] Amber Reeves (1887–1981), novelist, nonfiction writer, the daughter of prominent members of the Fabian Society. Her first child, born in 1909, was fathered by H. G. Wells. Her novels include *The Reward of Virtue* (1911) and *A Lady and Her Husband* (1914); *Worry in Women* (1941), drawing on Freudian psychology, studies women's new responsibilities.

[12] Gilbert Frankau (1884–1952), poet and novelist, best known for *Peter Jackson, Cigar Merchant* (1919).

[13] Michael Arlen (1895–1956), pseudonym for Dikran Kouyoumdjian, born of Armenian parents in Bulgaria. Writer of short stories, some collected in *The Romantic Lady* (1921), and novels, the best known being *The Green Hat* (1924).

[14] Norman Douglas (1868–1952), English novelist and travel writer who lived for many years on Capri, which is evoked in his best known work, *South Wind* (1917), and in southern Italy, treated in *Old Calabria* (1915). His cynicism and his interest in geology, biology, archaeology, and classics mingle in his work.

[15] Leo Stein (1872–1947), American author and art critic, an early collector of Cézanne, Matisse, and Picasso who lived in Paris with his sister, Gertrude Stein (1903–1912), before settling on his own near Florence (1921).

[16] This postscript is written along the left margin of the last page.

To: S. K. Ratcliffe   The Ship Inn
                                             Porlock,[1] North Somerset
                                             [summer 1922]

My dear S. K. R.,

Yes—I'd heard of Carruthers Gould's[2] proud tenure of the senior visitor-
ship at the Ship—and I feel I could punch his head every time I see him in
the High Street here for the false impression thus given of the Ship which is a
detestable inn run by Miss Murdstone.[3] Instead I simply score him as a Polar
Beaver. But all the same this is as good a place as one could spend these sun-
less days—it is not bad walking in a mist if Exmoor ponies run out of it and
rainbows stand about in it. Thank you very much for the corrections for *The
Judge* which alack are too late. I hold by achievement less however, but I am
amazed to find how right you are about June Cakebread—of four intelligent
well-read people here not one had ever heard of her. This is very amazing to
me. I have come to the conclusion that *The Judge* must be a very bad book as
no one sees its thesis—the way the pleasant vices of Harry pile up into this
tragedy which involves the innocent Ellen.[4] I could beat the heads of all the
people who talk about the Oedipus complex on a stone pavement—it is I
suppose a graceful compliment to me on the part of Providence that to prove
how right I am three men have committed suicide because of the death of
their mothers since the book was published. I feel dead beat and never want
to write another line—I hate *hate* HATE journalism. I want to write a light
book before I do my vast ghost story but there is no lightness in me. I am
trying to get some by furious riding and was getting some when I was sent
Dorothy Canfield's *The Bent Twig*. Oh God! Oh God the *Father!* as they say
in *This Freedom*.[5] My heart sinks when I see that that modern *Dairyman's
Daughter* went into 10 editions.[6] I can't write intelligently just now—partly
because I am troubled about {various matters} partly because I am shaken up
by violent exercise and new country (about which I shall write some day).
But I do want to see you—I shall be back about the 8th.

                                             Yours ever,
                                             Rebecca

I cannot believe [Tanhauson?] I wrote that review in the *Nation*. It's more—
surely—like Edward Garnett?[7] There hasn't been one sensible review; and
how all the people who have only a thimbleful of story and consequently

write novels the size and shape of a thimble—Frank Swinnerton[8] for instance
set the pace.

Rebecca West Papers   manuscript
Yale University

[1] West took this holiday apart from H. G. Wells and in the company of her sister Lettie
Fairfield, her novelist colleague G. B. Stern, and Hugh Hart, who seems to have aroused
Wells's jealousy.

[2] Francis Carruthers Gould (1844–1925), caricaturist who pioneered the spolitical cartoon in
the *Pall Mall Gazette* in 1888; later he took his talent to the newly founded *Westminster Gazette*.

[3] Miss Jane Murdstone, the villainess in Charles Dickens's novel *David Copperfield* (1849–
1850) who is largely responsible for the premature death of David's mother, who has taken
Murdstone's equally reprehensible brother as a second husband.

[4] In another letter written in 1922 to Ratcliffe from London, West explains that the subject
of *The Judge* is "the eternal swatting of that fly youth and beauty by the accumulations of evil
done by careless handling of beautiful things" (n.d., Yale University).

[5] A 1922 novel by A. M. S. Hutchinson.

[6] Dorothy Canfield Fisher (1879–1958) published *The Bent Twig* in 1915. West's objection
seems to be to fiction that serves pious purposes. The *Dairyman's Daughter* by Richmond
Legh is part of the *Annals of the Poor,* tales of conversion that began appearing in 1814,
published by various tract societies.

[7] Edward Garnett (1868–1936) was best known as a reader for Jonathan Cape (one of West's
publishers) who advised writers such as D. H. Lawrence, Joseph Conrad, Dorothy Richard-
son, and E. M. Forster. West commented in another letter to Ratcliffe, "Many reviewers seem
to have a Rebecca West complex. Violet Scott-James had it badly in 'The Yorkshire Post'"
(manuscript, West papers, Yale University).

[8] Frank Swinnerton (1884–1982), novelist and literary critic known for his reviews in the
Observer. He was a colleague of Arnold Bennett, one of the elder critics West savaged.

To: Letitia Fairfield   [Porlock]
                                                       20 August 192[2]

Dear Lettie,

Thank you for your letter—I am very grateful for your dear kind offers of
help. I've had two other letters from H. G. of the most amazing abusive
sort—the first concentrating on his pleasant idea about Hugh Hart and
including one allusion which I couldn't quite understand to my N.S. [*New
Statesman*] article. The second revealing that he objected to my N.S. article
because I praised Stacy Aumonier's past work[1] and this showed that I must
have liked his talking to me impertinently when he was tight at the Pen Club

dinner and containing terrible denunciations of my work which it appears is all worthless from start to finish—and I will never be able to write novels. It also appears that I am not doing my work. The time has come, it appears, when I "must work {hard} like a man." (Of course all this is a commonplace. I've felt his hatred of my work for a year or two—and of course the accusations of laziness are frequent—particularly when I'm ill or dead with overwork.) Then came a fourth letter in which he hoped I would mark the importance of these letters—if I would promise to try to reform he will come and take me away for a holiday. This is of course nothing new but the megalomania queerness of it is much more open than it was—though that I thought amounted almost to definite insanity at Algeciras and again at Madrid. In any case, I have told him definitely I won't live with him any more, and I mean to stick to it. H. G. ⟨will⟩ {might} take up this attitude to Anthony in time so I've no compunctions.

It is very dull down here ⟨after⟩ {now} that you have gone. I thought we had a heavenly day at Horner. My luck is not in riding. I went out with Beckett and a girl of about 16 {on a white horse} this afternoon—had a lovely ride for an hour—but then the girl's horse bolted and she was thrown in a valley—and conducted to me by an indignant tripper who said, "You ought to be ashamed of yourself maddam letting your daughter ride such a wild horse." I then had to walk my horse home with her (she wasn't hurt) while on distant hilltops we saw Beckett chasing the white horse—which got down into Minehead before he got it. Peary is much better and has really been quite nice during the last few days when the flood of abuse through the post has made me feel miserable! It is all the sadder because though I dare say you can't believe it we might be so perfectly happy if these fits of madness didn't come on him.

Love, Anne

Do look at the *New Age*. There is a marvelous slating of *The Judge* by Frances Low.[2]

West, R., MSS   manuscript
Indiana University, Bloomington

[1] West's "Notes on Novels" in the *New Statesman* 19 (19 August 1922) included a review of Aumonier's *Heartbeat*.
[2] Frances Low, English journalist, critic, and friend of H. G. Wells. Her works include *Press Work for Women: A Text Book for the Young Woman Journalist* (1904).

To: Ottoline Morrell   36 Queen's Gate Terrace, S.W. 7
                                         28 December 1922

Dear Lady Ottoline,

Thank you so much for the diary. Its blue watered silk is a special joy to me as I hate leather anywhere except on my feet. I hope you had a pleasant Christmas. I am feeling rather uninterested in New Years, as I feel so doubtful of having one of my own, as I am going over to Paris by air tomorrow. If I arrive there whole I am going to leave flowers for Katherine Mansfield, who is out at Fontainebleau and (I hear) very very much worse. I shall be back about the 10th—do let me know if you're in town. I lunched the other day with Mary Somerville who talked much of you. I think she's so picturesque—like the youth of a Raeburn[1] old lady. With best wishes for the New Year.

                        Yours very sincerely,
                        Rebecca West

O. Morrell papers   manuscript
University of Texas at Austin

[1] Sir Henry Raeburn (1756–1823), Scottish portrait painter known for his use of contrasting light.

To: S. K. Ratcliffe   36 Queen's Gate Terrace, S.W. 7
                                         21 March 1923

My dear S. K. R.—

What is this story that I hear from Lettie about a moral lady in Boston who is making hell about me? I heard something of it today from her but she seemed not very definite. I wish you would tell me exactly how bad it is. It is for various reasons an extraordinarily embittering piece of news. I may as well tell you exactly why—I have had an appalling life with H. G. during the last five years, due partly to the domestic difficulties arising out of our relationship, partly to an increasing nervous instability on his part, which leads to long periods which begin with fits of almost maniacal rage and then end in weeks on end of childish dependence. I had for instance two months of last year with him in Spain when for only ten days could he be described as normal. I have stuck to him partly for his own sake—mainly for Anthony's sake—but really quite a lot for his own sake as he has, to an extent nobody quite realises, not a soul on earth who looks after him. I have however increasingly felt that I cannot go on—for one thing I cannot spend most of my time sick nursing while I also have to keep an eye on Anthony *and* do my work—and I can assure you I am getting no adequate financial recompense. Also I am getting (as is natural from a person in such a neurotic state) no gratitude whatsoever. I feel that perhaps *if* I could go on it would be my duty to do so. But I can't. I'm sleepless and collapsing physically in strange ways—my feet and ankles swell and I feel sick half the time—and I can't do it. I have tried to leave H. G. innumerable times, but never without his following me and asking me to come back. I have as a matter of fact left him at the moment but I am dreading another attempt to get me to come back. It is also as I have a steady monogamous nature and would have been the most wifely wife on earth extremely difficult not to take on the job again. My one hope therefore of getting and keeping ⟨x⟩ clear is to get to America! Therefore this news does depress me. I would be glad if you would tell me all about it. I have a book (about 30,000 words) in my head, *Second Thoughts on Feminism* which I could write—if I keep free—in 2,000 word articles—which would make it plain where I stood and how unlikely it was that I should preach anything too revolutionary. But I suppose the ⟨suggestion⟩ {antagonistic} feeling is purely personal and can't be ⟨x⟩{overcome}. Well, I will come over to America in any case, just to look round and write a bit.

There really isn't much news from the writing world. The Lynds gave a party last Sunday night with the old gang—the Guedallas[1] and the Ervines (who would be nice if it weren't for her) and Naomi Royd Smith[2] and so on. Nobody thinks anything very much worth reading except David Garnett's *Lady into Fox* and Gerhardi's *Futility.*[3] Stella Benson's[4] book hasn't done as well as I think it might. But I'll write more when I feel more cheerful.

Yours ever,
Rebecca

Rebecca West Papers   manuscript
Yale University

[1] Philip Guedalla (1889–1944) and Nellie Maude. An Englishman whose father was of Spanish-Jewish ancestry, Guedalla was an essayist, historian, and biographer who worked

briefly as a barrister. He assisted H. G. Wells on his *Outline of History* and lived near Easton Glebe. His writings include *Ignes Fatui: A Book of Parodies* (1911), *Palmerston* (1926), *The Queen and Mr. Gladstone* (1933), and *Mr. Churchill* (1941).

[2] Naomi Gwladys Royde-Smith (1875–1964), English biographer, playwright, and novelist whose works include the novels *The Tortoiseshell Cat, A Delicate Situation,* and *Love and a Birdcage* and the play *A Balcony.* She was editor of the *Westminster Gazette* (1912–1922).

[3] William Alexander Gerhardie (1895–1977), eccentric Russian-born novelist best known for *The Polyglots* (1925) and for his writing on Russian subjects, including Chekhov and the Romanovs. His work was admired by Wells and Beaverbrook, and he became Beaverbrook's biographer (1964).

[4] Stella Benson (1892–1933), suffragette, novelist, poet, and travel writer. Born in Shropshire, she settled in China in 1921. Her works include the suffragette novel *I Pose* (1915), *The Poor Man* (1922), and *Tobit Transplanted* (1931).

To: John Middleton Murry   36 Queen's Gate Terrace, S.W. 7
                                  30 May [1923]

Dear Mr Murry,

Forgive me for not answering your letter before—my life has been greatly disorganised by the illness of a friend of mine. Thank you very much for the invitation to stand in with the *Adelphi*.[1] I haven't yet seen it (for my life really has been very much disorganised) but I admired the *Athenaeum* above all literary weeklies and I have the completest confidence in the *Adelphi*—and I'm very glad you think my work worthy of it.

I've got some sketches and things coming along that you might like. And the Contributors' Club ⟨which⟩ {appeals} to me strongly.

I would like to tell you how deeply I feel the loss of Katherine Mansfield. It has meant more to me (and many of our generation) than I would have thought any but a personal bereavement could mean. She gave one the pleasure of feeling absolutely unstinted admiration.

With many thanks for your letter.

Yours sincerely,
Rebecca West

J. M. Murry papers   manuscript
University of Texas at Austin

[1] The *Adelphi,* a monthly magazine edited by Murry (1923–1927). West reprinted a version of her *Elegy* to D. H. Lawrence in its successor, the *New Adelphi* 3 (June–August 1930).

To: Sally Melville   [summer 1923]
Dear Sally,

I am as miserable as Hell. I have gone back to H. G. I am going down to the country with him this evening. What else can I do? He says that if I go back to him he will leave Anthony as much money as his other boys—that will mean about £20,000. I daren't gamble on making that myself because I feel dead beat—and though I might marry I could never get any man to give Anthony £20,000. So there it all is. I could cry when I think of how I'd planned to go to Italy alone—I've never been alone in my life. I am sick of it all. I could have made H. G. get divorced and marry me—he wanted so much to get me back, but I thought it wiser not to. I don't want Lettie to know of this. I'll have to tell her later but not now.

                                    Yours,
                                        Rebecca

I had dinner with Beaverbrook and his wife last Thursday—it was so funny—I must tell you about it.

Rebecca West Collection   manuscript
Yale University

To: Sally Melville   [October 1923]
Dear Sally,

Alas! I couldn't see a soul. H. G. has been giving me an awful time lately, firstly by absolute dependence on me—Then a fortnight ago he began to realize I really was going—then he got horrid—tiresome and jealous and quarrelsome—and never left me alone an instant—Then this last week he got very affectionate—he really is very fond of me—but still was dreadfully jealous—and wouldn't let me see a *soul*—man or woman. It's rather trying— and I've had no time to do my lectures—no energy pray Heaven I'm not sick on the boat for I shall have to do them there—and I feel so *dog* tired.

I don't know when I shall be back. My dear, I've often thought of giving you the enclosed—it's what Violet Trefusis[1] gave me and is fairly good (very old, I believe) I've often thought it would suit your style. Take it, dear S. M, as a token of my very great affection for you.

My best wishes to both you and J. B. It's midnight and H. G. has just gone and I've still to go over my papers!

Yours wildly,

Rebecca

Rebecca West Collection   manuscript
Yale University

[1] Violet Trefusis (1894–1972), English novelist and autobiographer who settled in France and wrote mainly in French. West met her in Florence, just after the breakup of Trefusis's love affair with Vita Sackville-West. Trefusis's works include *Sortie de secours* (1929), *Tandem* (1933), and *Don't Look Round* (1952).

PART TWO *1923-1930*

Rebecca Goes West

REBECCA WENT WEST TO AMERICA LARGELY TO ESTABLISH HER PERSONAL AND professional independence from H. G. Wells. There she made lifelong friends, many of them eager to greet her on later visits. Her loathing and love of the United States proved a lasting topic, though she quickly decided against settling there permanently with Anthony. "Baedekering" (descriptions, sometimes of tremendous length of places encountered in her travels) becomes a staple of her letters, many of which are directed to her sisters. It was the era of grand and gracious cruise ships and ceremonial arrivals, complete with problematic greetings from the press, which was more interested in her past love than in her current writing.

In the case of the early writing from America, her impressions of people and landscape could be remade for journalism and fiction. West also found the South of France, which became a cherished retreat for Anthony's holidays, a place for gathering women together, and a vantage point for observing the international set. These experiences also could be tapped for serious writing. Once she had communicative literary agents, A. D. Peters and George Bye, situated on both sides of the Atlantic, West could establish independent finances. In her letters she often shares her delight at the rates offered by American periodicals—a sign that she is becoming a canny businesswoman.

With *The Strange Necessity* (1928), West established herself as a critic to be reckoned with by the older generation. She gives progress reports, self-assessments, and reactions to her critical fortunes with the novel *Harriet Hume* and various journalistic projects; she struggles with, then states her reasons for abandoning, *Sunflower.* She also reports on her rigorous lecture schedules, the strain of overwork, and harrowing episodes of sexual harassment.

Ill health, and its symptoms and treatments, feature regularly in her letters, as do modes of transportation and the summer heat in America. Her relationship with her sister Lettie becomes the subject of complaints to various confidantes. In a more spirited vein, West indulges in good-natured jesting with her correspondents—particularly with single males such as Vyvyan Holland. She is concerned with finding a "boof" (Fairfield language for a beautiful male) and has considerable misfortune in the endeavor, both in the failed liaison with Lord Beaverbrook and in her romance with an American lover who promptly dies. In the late 1920s West undergoes psychoanalysis to learn (among other things) why she has had such difficulty forming a stable relationship with a man. By the end of this section, she has met Henry Andrews, her partner in a long, if sometimes troubling, marriage.

There are numerous adjustments to be made with Anthony, now being educated in a series of private schools. He misses his mother when she is abroad. The letters show concern over Anthony's problems at school, his serious illness (originally diagnosed as tuberculosis), and his financial and personal relationship to Wells. He too is psychoanalyzed. Her letters to Wells during this period would later feed Anthony's resentment of his mother, particularly as he sought out financial details.

West's letters show contact with such fascinating and varied figures as Fannie Hurst (an important confidante at this stage), Irita Van Doren, John Gunther (both a lover and a supportive friend), Charlie Chaplin, Noël Coward, Bertrand Russell (whom she approached to serve as Anthony's guardian), and Emma Goldman.

To: Winifred Macleod   The Bellevue Stratford
                                         Philadelphia
                                         2 November 1923

Dear Podgers,

I haven't had a moment to write a line before. I had a fair voyage on the Mauretania—was only a little uncomfy the first day which was very rough, but then started an attack of colitis and had bad tummy pain till a day off New York. When the Immigration officer came aboard I went before him and got my passport visaed and so on. After I had done this a steward came up to me and said—"The Chief Immigration Officer wishes to see you." I nearly died—when I got down to him he said, "I have a letter from Mr Curran the Commissioner of Labor asking you to treat me with special courtesy and to give you this pass through the Customs." So that was all right. It turned out that Henry James Forman[1] had written to Curran who is a friend of his.

The view going up New York Harbour is gorgeous. Miles and miles of shore covered with low dock buildings—incredibly strange erections of a Robot civilisation—then this cluster of skyscrapers white and slim like lilies.

The Statue of Liberty is a washout—she gets her stays at the same place as Queen Mary.[2] I was met by Miss Laurent—& my publisher's publicity agent—& my London literary agent Andrew Dakers who happened to be in N. Y. (most unfortunately as you will hear), and my lecture agent's manager. I then had a hectic day. Two hours with reporters—five of them, during which one or two of them tried to make me say something unwise. One published an impertinent interview—"when asked if she were a literary protégé of Mr Wells she quickly changed the subject." The rest were all right. I was then taken off to a literary tea at Somerset Maugham's—he has a small flat here just now while a play is being produced—not so nice as mine—The rent unfurnished is $5000 a year. Then I wound up with a dinner of the business people—Sunday I spent in the same way. I woke up at 9 with a start and found a pale sad looking woman in my room. She said, "I am Miss Something of the Something or Other," and opened a notebook, and leaned over the end of my bed. "We would like to know, Miss West," she said in an unutterably tired and flat voice, "if you would like to marry an American." One way and another I wasn't alone till eleven that night. Among other people I saw a woman theatrical manager who wants to put on a dramatic version of *The Return of the Soldier* in January. She has paid various playwrights $3000 to prepare versions of it and hasn't got anything that gets the essence of the play. It was a fascinating couple of days—the air in New York is intoxicating—the architectural beauty sublime—but I simply cannot convey to you how unlike America is to what it says it is and gets other people to say it is. I have been in three places now—New York, Springfield (Mass.)—and here—everywhere the women are hideous and beyond all belief slovenly. A certain number are good looking between the ages of seventeen and twenty-five—they get even that good looks simply by force of slimness and careful management—There are very few good looking women of thirty—the middle aged women are repulsive wrecks—bad skins, and untidy though elaborately dressed hair—and at all ages the most terribly bad carriage. They wear very expensive and solid clothes which they huddle round them in such a way as to spoil all their lines—and they walk and dance with their feet wide apart. Almost every woman not theatrical who has spoken to me has worn an untidily adjusted hairnet dragging over her forehead and round the nape of her neck. Their utter and complete lack of sex attraction is simply terrifying. Not that it matters—for the men seem entirely lacking in virility. They wear spectacles almost as commonly as the Germans—and they are beyond belief slow. The mechanical side of life here whirls—telephones, taxis, trolleys— but a pale humanity patters along in the midst of it. (The only attractive and thoroughly male personality I met in New York was my publisher George Doran—an elderly man—between sixty and seventy—and he turned out to be a Canadian.) They are slow in speech, slow in movement, slow in thought. The irritation of ⟨listening⟩ {receiving} a telephone message from an American is almost past belief—the service is incredibly quick and good— one is connected at once—and then a slow, dry voice drawls interminably.

I went off to Springfield (Mass.) on Monday—travelled with Somerset Maugham and his theatrical manager Edgar Selwyn, who were taking the play to a New England town further out. It was a four hours run through first of all the most incredible suburbs. Luxurious bright bungalows in the midst of lovely scenery—the Autumn tints here are wonderful—they are past their brightest and the woods are burning with a curious dark remote flame—(as autumn tints depend on the chemistry of the air you can imagine what the difference in appearance from a European autumn means—how utterly different life is) ⟨But⟩ {Each} of these houses had a garage—round the neat clean factories there is a fleet of cars belonging to the workmen. But at the same time the most incredible unkemptness—no gardens at all—just grass plots—and here and there within sight of the houses the most horrible rubbish-heaps—twenty or thirty square yards covered with old tires and dirt of all sorts. As we got into New England the scenery became heartrendingly beautiful. The Connecticut river, broad and calm, fringed with these red woods, and the great bluffs—cliffs tipped with woods—were marvellous— but all so sad, so haunted by the ghosts of the Indians. The main crop raised there—or the most conspicuous—is the Indian corn. ⟨They⟩ {Just} now it is standing in stooks—grey they are and the height ⟨of⟩ {and} girth of a small man—and somehow the way they are tied gives the air of a tragic attitude. In Springfield I was received by the College Club secretary—and I was faced by the miracle of New England that faced us when as cubs we read Mary Wilkins.[3] Where when all the adult population of New England are bus-beasts[4] do they get their little pupils? There were hordes of women in Springfield—charming—good—with a peculiar wistful affectionateness— and hardly any of them married. It was dreadful to see how they made a fuss of the few cubs that existed. The secretary was typical of all I felt {and guessed} about New England—she was really a gentlewoman, delightful manners—a sweet pleasing face—soft voice—very well bred in everything she felt and said—interested in everything—but oh so plainly never get a boof[5] now—very dowdily dressed—very domesticated—she had a dear old Mamma with silver hair and the tiniest feet and hands—*and* she (the secretary) had the most terrible mouth I've ever seen—full of those Hutchinson incisors which came of congenital syphilis![6] They gave me a lovely time—took me to Mount Holyoke College—a college built with the most incredible luxury of panelling and parquet floors—standing in woodland beside beautiful lakes—inhabited by the most terrible slummocks of college girls, stamping about in sloppy {long thick} coats of dull colours, with inanimate and yet assertive faces: I was abducted for lunch by a very funny Mrs. Leo Hunter who asked me questions like this all through the meal. "Miss West, what do you think of the problem of surplus women?" The hotel I was in, by the way, had better service and far nummier staffing than the best hotel in London—and Springfield has only 120,000 inhabitants. The negro servants were delightful and helpful—and told me, with (I found afterwards, scrupulous honesty) what I ought to tip them. It is an awesome thing to speak a negro [*sic*] and be answered in measured and musical English—and to speak to a telephone girl (whose parents were both born in England, I discovered) and not be able to understand one word of the queer whining mumble she answers you in. This particular girl was a great joke. She took some cables {for me} and then chatted to me—"I guess it's nice for you to travel about but give me the United States all the time. I guess there's a finer feeling ⟨x⟩ {about} our lil old home that you don't get nowhere else. No, I ain't never been abroad . . ."[7]

I spoke in the evening to four or five hundred people—the College Club—and gave them a lecture on the novel—how more and more people are writing in fiction the kind of lyrical emotion they would have ⟨reserved for⟩ {expressed in} poetry before with special references to Conrad and Katherine Mansfield. ⟨They⟩ {It was} a fairly close wrought thesis, and they loved it—came crowding to me afterwards and saying quite interesting things and asking interesting questions. The thing that startled me and will give you an idea of how odd the atmosphere of New England is that several of them said things like—"I must tell you something—I hope you won't think it odd for me to say it. But you did look so beautiful against that rose-coloured curtain.

And how lovely your dress is." Can you imagine anything so queer—said with a curious earnestness? It is a *queer* country—the villages of ⟨board⟩ wooden houses (exactly like lots you see on the road out to Barnet) in their unfenced grass plots—built round the oblong village greens (the regular pioneer formation when they were practically besieged by Indians)—and no flowers anywhere. The orchards are lovely things—they don't send {all} their apples to town any longer—they stack them in lovely baskets by the road and sell them to the people in the automobiles. (Oh the automobiles! The {back} streets are lined with them {parking}—all set at an angle to the curb—all glistening black—it's very Robot-looking, this place.)

I went back from Springfield with two notabilities—a "Mayflower" woman—the trouble is Mayflower doesn't mean a thing except that your ancestors like to take their Bible reading seriously; it doesn't give you any breed at all. I don't suppose democratic pioneering does for an aristocratic type—you have to have the element of leadership. My other fellow traveller was Miss Skinner—the silk millionairess who has rebuilt a town in the devastated area in France—a cultured, travelled woman, with a wonderful Paris suit and marvellous jewellery—and ugly long cloth underclothing showing—and her dull lustreless hair pulled off her large ears—and a perfect dear all the same. She told me she had ⟨meant⟩ {been} living nearly all her time in France but she was coming back to live in America—"one finds out suddenly one's really a foreigner however much one has been at home there. They don't really think and feel as we do."

I got to New York at lunch time and then my bad day began. I had to lunch with George Doran and the editor of the Hearst magazines at the Ritz. The most gorgeous food, the most slovenly women sitting over their meals humped up in heavy and priceless clothes—I then went back to ⟨his⟩ {Doran's} office and met a few useful people—went back to my hotel and was interviewed steadily and slowly—oh *God* how slowly—by a few extra people who hadn't got me in at first. The ⟨x⟩ {day} then began to turn funny in my hands. My agent {Dakers} brought in his New York partner and his wife ⟨also⟩ {to} introduce them. They left soon, and Dakers who has always seemed a sensible sort of person flung himself down on the sofa and buried his head in the cushions and ⟨explained⟩ {made noises} like a sick cow. When (I had been up since 7 and this was 5 and I hadn't been alone all day) I rather wearily but in great alarm asked what the matter was he said that he had

been in love with me for five years and these last three days in New York I
had been so wonderful that he couldn't bear it any longer and he must tell
me about it. He writhed and panted and kept on kissing my hands—once
giving himself an awful jab with that Sicilian ring Gladys Holdsworth [G. B.
Stern] gave me—until an interviewer whom I couldn't avoid because he's
quite influential was announced, and Dakers had to go. By this time the fact
that I had to ⟨go to⟩ {pack} for a month some time before I caught the train
for Philadelphia the next morning at 10 was beginning to pulse through my
consciousness. This journalist Burton Rascoe[8] appeared with a lady friend,
whose appearance appalled me. She was radiantly beautifully [*sic*] and I
should say had not more than a week to live. Her eyes were brimful of light—
she had that half smile, that ⟨x⟩ {soft} acquiescent radiance that comes to
people who are nearly dead of phthisis[9]—she was shaken perpetually by the
most dreadful cough. I was too tired to go out to dinner—so I gave them
dinner in my room. She ate three clams and then said, "I feel terribly ill. I
must lie down." She then lay down on the sofa, disturbed already by Dakers'
passion, and proceeded to fall into a sort of coma, ⟨disturbed⟩ {occasionally}
shattering herself with this appalling cough. Rascoe, who was a loathsome
young cub of the kind that goes about here with a flask of Scotch drinking all
day and talking of James Joyce occasionally went up to her and smoothed her
hair and kissed her ⟨xxx⟩ ({at which she} looked up with the most heavenly
smile) in rather an absent-minded way and then turned to me and said "And
what do you think of T. S. Eliot's *The Waste Land?* or some similar question.
They remained giving this singular performance—he asking these damnfool
"post" questions, she noisily dying—until 9:30. Then I did a little packing
before I was fetched to a party which the Dudley Field Malones[10] were
giving for me—which I couldn't miss as some very influential people were
there—of the newspaper world. The men all danced divinely—the women
were incredibly uninteresting even in their evening clothes—everybody
drank far too much whisky—you can't imagine how strange it is to see how
quite young women drink whisky here! — and I left at 2.—packed for an
hour—and caught a Philadelphia train at 11, which went through the most
incredibly unkempt industrial districts fringing undrained marshes. We
passed various small towns of terrifying ugliness—one very characteristically
American thing was an inscription on a store. "Forty years of faithful service." This was the American business cant for "established forty years." I

arrived at Philadelphia at 1 and found my lecture was at 3 instead of 4—and the interval was entirely filled in with lunch with interviewers. One amazingly pretty little girl interviewer did an ⟨amazingly⟩ {astonishingly} skillful interview with me—disguising the fact that she hadn't the least idea whether I was an actress or a writer. I was so dog tired by my twenty-hour day in New York and the journey and the interviewing that my lecture didn't go nearly so well as it did in Springfield, though I did it practically word for word the same. The older people in the audience plainly thought me odd and crazy—⟨x⟩ {and I} really felt among them as exotic as a Chinese woman in full dress would if she walked down Oxford Street. A few of the younger women were very keen on me and enjoyed the lecture and took me about all the next day. I went to the Curtis Publishing Company—the largest magazine company in the world—an incredible palace of marble and mellow red brick—built in a conscious ecstasy of pretentiousness beside Independence Hall where the Liberty Bell is—but really a palace, of rare marbles and wonderful woods, full of grace and dignity. Mr Lorimer—the editor of the Curtis publications—has as his office a room which for beauty and spaciousness cannot have its equal in Europe—except in the Villa d'Este perhaps[11]—and he took me over the printing presses—where they print 2,000,000 copies of the *Saturday Evening Post*—the perfectly imitative and second rate publication which is the best thing that is produced by all this magnificence. Lorimer is a magnificent creature physically—middle height, broad shoulders, great grizzled head—but full of the terrible superficiality of the man who has never known anything but success. It was so characteristic of America—we went down in a lift that was worked by a half idiot negro porter—he ⟨exp⟩ {was} greatly irritated by this man and explained they had imported a lot of negroes from the South to try to break down the high wages here. Seeing that the negro was an idiot—and that the white labour looked very formidable—I said, "Oh yes, you've got a great many problems here." He said placidly, "Oh, no. Why do you say that? You've got plenty of problems over in Europe. ⟨you⟩ {we have} practically none. All we've got to do is to go on piling up the dollars."

In order to find out what the older people wanted from a literary lecture I went to hear William Lyon Phelps[12]—who is the most popular literary lecturer here—and Professor of English literature at Yale. It was amazing. There was a whole theatre full of people—I should say 2000. Phelps, a terribly underbred and unctuous person, came out and delivered very flat and trivial reviews of six or seven entirely unconnected books—with the most unbelievably cheap and common phrasing. He was an American equivalent of Cousin Tom.[13] He said things like this. "I read the Bible all through when I was five years old. (This in accents of Home-and-mother piety). I did it because my mother gave me five dollars for it. (Roars of laughter.) My price has risen since then. (Roars and roars of laughter.) But I reckon that was the best five dollars my mother ever invested." (Sympathetic hush.) They handed up questions at the end in the course of {answering} which he warmly recommended the works of Archibald Marshall[14] and A. S. M. Hutchinson[15]—and ⟨aft⟩ {when} he was asked about Ludwig Lewisohn,[16] who is quite a serious writer (though I don't think much of him) he answered, ⟨x⟩ "I'll tell you what's the matter with Ludwig Lewisohn. The matter is that he's a German Jew." (Roars of laughter). I can't convey to you the horrible vulgarity, the canting pietism and moralising, of this obscene being—who is a Professor at Yale! or the not less horrible receptivity of his audience. I was led into his room afterwards and forcibly introduced to him. I fancy he had denounced *The Judge*—if he didn't it was by accident—but he was loathsomely amiable in case I turned out a winner. There entered suddenly into this loathsome scene of fawning and hypocrisy the pale figure of Dakers who had come from New York to spend the night in Philadelphia so that he could say goodbye to me. I nearly went mad with rage when I saw him, for I saw bed receding to a still later hour. And indeed I had to sit till midnight in a Grill Room of my hotel while he explained how marvellous I was and how unhappy he was in competition with a jazz band to which three wrinkled and pallid young women danced flat-footedly with fattish and unmasculine young men with horn-rimmed spectacles. We had to pay rent by ordering temperance drink after temperance drink—loathsome things that leave one's mouth in a horrible blotting paper state. I felt an infinite melancholy for this unwanted young man's passion was very much like those temperance drinks. The same nervous instability was caused by ⟨hearing⟩ {listening} to it as by listening to the genuine article, but there was no intoxication.

The journey from Philadelphia here (I am finishing this letter in Chicago) took eighteen hours—The first six followed alongside the Susquehanna and Julietta Rivers. Nothing in the world could convey the wistful beauty of

American river scenery—the serenity of the wooded heights—wave-like in their skyline—the beauty of the wide shallow waters. I was adopted in the train by a charming old Texan, who called me "Ma'am," paid me old fashioned compliments ("If I may ask, Ma'am, how is it that such a charming lady as yourself have escaped matrimony?") insisted on treating me to all my meals, and escorted me to my hotel here. The amount of attention one gets from men here would turn one's head if one didn't look round at the sallow hags of American women and realise that the standard is very different from Europe! This hotel is an extraordinary palace in the Italian style built on the edge of Lake Michigan—today a grey waste of thundering breakers. I really must stop and put in some work on my next lecture. I won't make much money out of this but it is gorgeous fun—and if there is any trouble enough people in New York feel friendly to give me a graceful exit. Very much love.

Anne

West, R., MSS   manuscript
private collection
Indiana University, Bloomington

[1] Henry James Forman (1879–1966), American lecturer who taught creative writing at Temple University. He reviewed books for the *New York Times* and was managing editor of *Colliers* (1913–1919). His *Pony Express* was made into a film (1925).

[2] West seems to suggest that Queen Mary's well-endowed figure was kept under firm control.

[3] Mary E. Wilkins Freeman (1852–1930), American author known for her stories of New England. One collection is *A New England Nun and Other Tales* (1891).

[4] The overworked, undernourished horses used to pull buses before they became motorized.

[5] Fairfield language for "beautiful man."

[6] Teeth tapered on the sides and usually notched on the edge, due to the lack of a calcification center. This is usually associated with congenital syphilis, as West suggests.

[7] West's ellipsis.

[8] Burton Rascoe (1892–1957), American critic and editor who recognized contemporary American writers. His works include *A Bookman's Daybook* (1929) and a biography of Dreiser (1925).

[9] Tuberculosis.

[10] Dudley Field Malone (1882–1950), liberal American lawyer who supported women's suffrage, argued the defense in the Scopes evolution trial, and fought Prohibition. He was married at the time to Doris Stevens (1892–1963), an American suffragist who carried the message of the National Women's Party to Woodrow Wilson. West reviewed her *Jailed for Freedom* (1922) for *Time and Tide*. Stevens campaigned for an equal rights amendment (1923)

and headed the Inter-American Commission of Women (1928–1933). In the 1950s, she became a champion of Senator Joseph McCarthy.

[11] Villa d'Este, mansion constructed 1549 near Rome in Tivoli, from a design by Pirro Ligorio.

[12] William Lyon Phelps (1865–1943), Lampson Professor of English at Yale, where he introduced the first course on the novel. The author of *Essays on Russian Novelists* (1911) and articles in *Scribner's Magazine,* he reached a wide audience through public lectures and his syndicated newspaper column, "A Daily Thought."

[13] Probably Isabella Fairfield's second cousin.

[14] Archibald Marshall (1866–1934), journalist, comic novelist, and author of humor in *Punch: Simple Stories.*

[15] Arthur Stuart-Menteth Hutchinson (1879–1971), journalist, editor of the *Daily Graphic,* and author of the popular novel *If Winter Comes* (1920).

[16] Ludwig Lewisohn (1882–1955), German-born Jewish American novelist, translator, and drama editor for the *Nation* (1920–1924). A German professor and an ardent Zionist, he wrote numerous studies of American, German, and French literature and had an interest in works of the modern period.

To: Sinclair and Gracie Lewis

William Penn Hotel
Pittsburgh
9 December 1923

Dear Gracie and Red,

This is truly the first minute I've had when I could write. The minute I landed in New York America seemed to take a [pill?] and I was swept madly in. Whenever I've had a spare moment I've simply collapsed in the nearest bed. I had two and a half days in New York, then made a dash into New England then Philadelphia—then Chicago and a tour of the Babbitts. Minneapolis, Iowa City, Rockford (Ill.), Milwaukee, Indianapolis, Saint Louis. My God, you are a genius. And how you and Gracie have suffered. In Chicago I presented your letter to Tommy (you will understand why I couldn't thank you for those letters!) and I adore both him and Lida.[1] I had a great time in the Palazzo Drake (where there ought to be guides to say Ecco! veritable spurioso antico)[2] and I loved its view more than anything I've seen outside Spain. The lake got into my system. Oh, I *love* your water here—the Connecticut and the Susquehanna and the Mississippi—I got a great thrill out of that. I *hate* the talking though now I've got into a sort of state when I stand from under my own lecture and watch the thing spouting out among the old gals. I met a peach of an elderly clubwoman in Milwaukee who pleased me very much by telling me that it didn't really matter if the young

American girls got tight at dances and stripped to the skin—"because the American man is, beyond the comprehension of you Europeans—PURE." So there. The Clubwoman I've hated worst yet was one who penetrated to my room at the Drake and for one hour and a half read me the poems of her deceased daughter, aged twelve, {collected} under the title "Lovely Thoughts of an Angel Child." You can guess what lovely thoughts this angel child had. I love America and I loathe it. I can understand that people like you must be in an amazing state of conflict about it. I wish I could talk to you two now!

 I don't know how long I'm staying. I don't feel like ever going home, it's all so interesting!

Best love—

Rebecca

Dorothy Thompson papers   manuscript
Syracuse University

 [1] Tommy and Lida Thomas. West stayed in touch with the latter for years after the death of her businessman husband and helped her financially.
 [2] West's hotel in Chicago. ("Behold, genuine false antiquity.")

To: Fannie Hurst   36 Queen's Gate Terrace, S.W. 7
                                                              12 June 1924

My dear Fannie,

 I write to tell you the great news that I've seen Max [Beaverbrook]. The day after my second article in the *Sunday Times* he called me up and said he wanted to see me very much. We talked casually and politely and arranged a meeting at the end of the week. He called me up two days later when I was out: then left me alone till he suddenly appeared here yesterday and insisted on me coming out to lunch at his house in Fulham. We were alone. That was a queer thing, for nearly always he has had a crowd round him. We had lunch, and we walked round the garden for a time. He then talked quite lightly of our past infatuation as if it were a tremendous joke. He laughed about it. I suddenly realised that he was physically quite indifferent to me. Fannie, I'm not telling you the truth. I'm leaving out the point. He casually implied in a phrase that when he had made love to me in London first he had been drunk, and that it had been very awkward for him when he found I took it seriously. New York he didn't explain at all. Then we went back to town in the car, and he dropped me on his way. Later that afternoon {I heard} he ⟨was⟩ {is} making ardent love to Gwen Ffrangcon-Davies,[1] the young actress who is playing Juliet very successfully.

Fannie, this is the end. Is it true? I don't think he was drunk. And what about New York? Why did he set his secretaries to look for me—or was that only because he wanted to see me as a friend, and never told me he was making enquiries in case he revived the hopes he had raised in me—when he was drunk? I can't quite get over that phrase. I think I never will. Then why did he make love to me at the Ritz? Or is he just running away from me to another woman, away from me whom for some reason he hates as much as he loves? At any rate he's vile. He is vile if it is true. He is vile if it is not true and he has invented it. And I have loved him for seven years. I feel as if I were really going to die this time, but one doesn't. If it wasn't for Anthony I really would kill myself. Not talking for effect. I feel so dirty, so fouled, so infected. The rest of my life will never be clean or proud again. This happened yesterday and I haven't slept since—and it's nearly three on this morning and I know I'm not going to sleep this second night. It's over but I'm over too. Forgive me for bringing anything so sordid and squalid before you—but it isn't my fault it's that. I thought at Christmas I'd got something to give Max—that there was something worth while to be got out of it. But why was he so stricken when I told him that I couldn't have a child? I shall go mad wondering. But that's nothing. He says he feels the greatest friendliness for me. It may have been that. It must have been that. The New York business was I suppose a panic stricken response to what he realised was my clinging to the idea he loved me. In any case Fannie I don't want to go on living. And even that door's shut. It's come at the wrong time. I've had too much.

H. G. is irrelevantly round the house all the time proposing marriage to me. I've turned him down a little brutally yesterday because I wanted to be alone and today he sends me the ⟨proof⟩ {typescript} of an article in the Hearst papers attacking me pettishly for my articles in the *Sunday Times*. I'm afraid it'll make some scandal. Haven't I had rather hard luck with the men I'm in with?

[no signature]

F. Hurst Papers   manuscript
University of Texas at Austin

[1] Dame Gwen Ffrangcon-Davies (1891–1992), English actress who performed in leading roles from Shakespeare, Shaw, Wilde, Ibsen, and O'Neill. She taped her last television performance at the age of one hundred.

To: Walter White[1]   Grand Hotel
69, Fifth Avenue   St. Wolfgang
New York City   Saltzkammergut
                                                  Austria
                                                  23 August 1924

My Dear Mr. White,

Thank your very much for your kind letter. As a matter of fact I had only two days in New York before I sailed, as I lingered too long in Utah. I very much wanted to see you and Mrs. White again, but I have already told you that the aspects of American life which you showed me seemed to me certainly the most attractive.

I did not write any articles for the *London Times,* the *London Times* belongs to Major Astor[2] and you may imagine a frank description of American affairs are not likely to appear in its pages. I wrote three articles for the *Sunday Times* and these I will send you when I return to London.

I look forward very much to reading your novel, I am sure I shall not be disappointed, you know so *much* and feel so intensely about what you know that your book cannot be anything but interesting.

I don't know when I am going back to the United States but I am quite eager to do so, so never be surprised if I descend on you. Meanwhile, my kind regards to Mrs. White and Jane.[3]

                                        Yours sincerely,
                                        Rebecca West

NAACP Records   typescript with autograph signature
Library of Congress

[1] Walter Francis White (1893–1955), African-American civil rights leader who served as executive secretary of the NAACP (1931–1955). He had just completed the novel *Fire in the Flint* (1924). White arranged West's visit to Harlem churches in January 1924 and helped set up a luncheon given by the *Nation* in her honor.
[2] William Waldorf Astor (1879–1954).
[3] White's daughter.

To: H. G. Wells

36 Queen's Gate Terrace, S.W. 7
1925 (?) to check, dates of Emma
Goldman's arrival in England[1]
[1924]

Dear Cat,

A miserable Panther is sitting in murky London. I have given up the habit of sleeping except between the hours of half past eight and eleven in the morning, and this is playing old Harry with my work ⟨and⟩ {so} two infernal magazine commissions have been blocking my novel so that it still stands at 4000 words. To finish it all Alfred Sutro[2] decoyed the poor Panther to lunch at the Garrick Club, and it was really a Jewish plot, and the little creature was fed poisoned oysters, so that for the last twenty four hours she has either been afraid she was going to be sick or afraid that she wasn't. So life is not smoove. I hope Jaguar is finding it smoova.

There really isn't much to tell. The *Sunday Times* articles created a mild furor—which means that, people stroke your fur. I've been shepherding Emma Goldman who is a very sensible body. She has a lot of very interesting facts about the treatment of intellectuals. Shaw won't see her at all, and the D. H. [*Daily Herald*] and Labor Party people ⟨of⟩ {are} rude to her before she begins to speak. Clever, flexible Jaguar that has always kept himself out of these fossilising party influences.

There really isn't much to tell. I'm going back to America in January 1926, and till then I suppose I will be labouring on my book. Bryant[3] has written saying that Anthony has greatly improved this term, and suggesting he should stay on another term, but I think Anthony will decide otherwise. It will be a tight fit in the flat but I think Anthony really does need the reassurance that he is wanted at home.

I hope you're having a nice time, Pussy.

Love,

Panther

I broadcasted the other day—a horrible experience. You do it in an un-ventilated room lined with moth grey crepe—to cover pad to deafen the echoes—and they put me up against a hostile-looking microphone with one's interview typed on thin paper, and tell one not to rustle it.

Rebecca West Papers   manuscript
Yale University

¹This annotation (with its uncertainty about dates) was apparently made by West in 1950, when she recovered a few of her letters to Wells from Marjorie Wells.

²Alfred Sutro (1863–1937), playwright and translator of Maurice Maeterlinck whose works include *The Builder of Bridges* (1908) and *Five Little Plays* (1916).

³Anthony's headmaster at St. Piran's.

To: Lord Beaverbrook   36 Queen's Gate Terrace, S.W. 7
                                        [autumn 1924]

Heart of my heart, {without prejudice}¹

You have spilled some of my very best beans. The *Express* published today a story about Emma Goldman in which your (not inappropriately) rabbit-witted subordinates laid stress on her anarchist record, and mentioned casually that she had returned from Russia disillusioned with the Bolshevists. The effect of the article was distinctly unfavourable to Emma Goldman. Now, not only is Emma Goldman worth six of you (or three or me) but she is the most powerful Anti-Bolsh eyewitness I have yet encountered. Her effect as an Anti-Bolsh speaker ought to be tremendous. (Some of us are getting up a Queen's Hall meeting for her.) I know that your interest in politics is restricted to personal gossip, but you might try to understand and sympathise with people who are interested in deeper issues. If you attack her as an anarchist she (being as pigheaded as a mule) will probably get defiant and declare that she still is an anarchist and queer her own and the Anti-Bolsh pitch. Therefore it would be seemly and consistent with its own politics if the *Daily Express* and the *Evening Standard* refrained from attacking Emma.

This I have explained to Mr Baxter and one of your underlings. But I suppose they sometimes have to consult you.

I am sorry you are ill.

                                        Yours ever,
                                        Rebecca

A large number of American citizens must have decided that the *Express* cared nothing for accuracy when they saw the headline describing Emma as a Red Virgin. Emma was a bright girl once.²

Hist. Coll. 184, Beaverbrook Papers   manuscript
House of Lords Record Office

[1] West describes this letter to her sister, Winifred (17 November 1924, Indiana University, Bloomington), saying, "I wrote Max a letter of such unparalleled venom that he has not replied, but he shut down the campaign and gave her [Goldman's] dinner a good show."

[2] The following manuscript was preserved along with Beaverbrook's few surviving letters from West of the mid-1920s:

Cherkley, Leatherhead, Surrey   [1924–1925]

Mrs. Fenwick

Mrs. Fitz

Miss Parsons

Me

A wicked newspaper proprietor owner (Max) lives at Leatherhead with two familiars—one a negro (Angus Maidmato) one a brother with sidewhiskers (Evelyn Fitzgerald)—he receives four letters—warns his familiars that he is expecting four wives—also receives visit from pure young enemy—whom he laughs to scorn and dismisses. The four wives arrive— each with marriage lives—each with baby. The negro and the butler each ⟨pick up⟩ {take charge} of babies—parked in a row on the lawn. "Children are parked here." Each wife is poisoned with cocktail on terrace. Removed by negro and butler and dumped in flowerbed. Four pairs of feet sticking out. Clergyman also murdered. The pure enemy returns— watches horrible sight—runs for help. The newspaper proprietor orders babies buried first—little boards 336–337–338–339. The corpses of adults taken in wheelbarrow strewn regularly in drive—explains to policeman—accident—exceeded speed limit—ran them down. Then panic—for among the effects on the bodies the familiars find that all corpses are insured with the *Daily Express* and will draw the million pound benefit. He will be bankrupted—and have to face life. In desperation he commits suicide in the pond. The pure young enemy comes back—gives the corpses Yadil—they all revive. A little doubtful as to what to do—the enemy says he is a Mormon and will take them all to Salt Lake City. The clergyman says he has always wanted to be a Mormon. They all depart together down the drive.

So to the great open spaces where men are Mormons and

The End

To: Emma Goldman   36 Queen's Gate Terrace, S.W. 7

16 April 1925

Dearest Emma

I am so sorry that both the hours you have given me for meeting the Hapgoods[1] are quite impossible for me—I am so disappointed about this— do tell them how sorry I am. Secondly, I do not know anybody in Norwich, Manchester or Bristol but I do know a Town Councillor of great influence at Leeds.

You have not told me the date you are speaking at Leeds or the place? If you will tell me that I will write to Councillor Leigh who will be able to interest a great many of the women belonging to the Leeds Luncheon Club.

What I meant about getting lectures through *Time & Tide* is that this paper is very widely read by Women's Organisations & that your Articles would want to make them hear your lecture [*sic*].
There is nothing more direct.[2]

I am afraid the world is full of translators at present—I hope your friend has some luck.

Do please use my name if you wish to on the Pamphlet

Yours ever

Rebecca

Emma Goldman Papers   photocopy of manuscript
New York University

[1] Hutchins Hapgood (1869–1944) and Neith Boyce (1887–1951), both charter members of the Provincetown Players. He was a journalist, best known for *The Spirit of the Ghetto* (1902). She wrote novels and plays.

[2] West continued to advise Goldman about her possibilities in England. A letter written in the 1930s suggests: "About the lectures. I was lecturing for the Universities and for various English Societies so I had no manager or agent. I received no pay. I cannot suggest anything but the usual agents like Massie, who, I believe you have already tried, but I warn you as I have done before that the lecture is not an English institution. The English care really only for highly specialised lectures on concrete national problems and I am sure you would not get any audience to listen to lectures on the drama, unless it was some very elementary dramatic society, and they wouldn't want anything as advanced as yours. I am sorry to be so discouraging, but there it is!" (28 November [1931], New York University Library).

To: Vyvyan Holland   Dictated to 1st Under Secretary[1]
                                             36 Queens Gate Terrace, S.W. 7
                                             21 April 1925

Darling Vyvyan

Now that you have left Florence with words of complaint on your lips, I may as well admit to you that I loathe the place! It has the pictorial charm of Manchester with all that greystone, and its noise is infernal. I may say that I think things might go worse in Florence than they would in other places—it infects people for one thing, with a perverted passion for crowds and parties, in which, as we have noticed before, delicate charm, such as our own, does not show to the best advantage. You will look very beautiful at Marlowe before the Summer is out.

It is fun writing a novel, but I think one ought to put aside at least ten years for the purpose & I think it would be the perfect form for you to show off your neat spiritual ankle. When you come back to England, do ring me up—one of my regiment of secretaries, if at that moment at liberty, will probably answer the telephone.

I have many anecdotes to tell you—my life is a series of anecdotes, all of which seem to me in the worst possible taste!

Yours ever

Rebecca West

A lady once longed to be wild
But kept herself quite undefiled—
   By thinking of Jesus
   And venereal diseases—
And the danger of having a child.

Rebecca West

private collection   manuscript[2]

[1] West had taunted Holland at the end of her previous letter, "I dictated this to show I have a secretary. Have you a secretary? No, I thought not." (25 March 1925, private collection). A subsequent letter (14 April 1925, private collection) was "dictated to the 3rd Secretary."

[2] The handwriting for this letter is not West's, though she signs it. The enclosed poem is written and signed in her hand.

To: Emma Goldman,   36 Queens Gate Terrace, S.W. 7
From Rebecca West,   25 September 1925

Dear Emma,

Herewith the volume of the drama.[1] I have written H. G. about Berkman's Memoirs[2] and you will get an answer, I should think, at the weekend. I am awfully glad to hear that your lectures are going on well.

About dinner with the Robesons.[3] I am afraid I had better make no definite promise for I am very seedy indeed and I really cannot get about very easily. I am a lot worse since I saw you. {I don't mean this as unkindly as it sounds!}[4]

I am looking forward very much to the Russian book.

Yours sincerely,

Rebecca West

Emma Goldman Papers   photocopy of typescript with
New York University   manuscript signature

[1] The following blurb was saved among Goldman's letters:

Bray Court, Ltd.

Bray, Maidenhead

I read Miss Goldman's lectures on the Drama with great interest because I had during a visit to the United States come across many evidences of the effect they made on their time. It is largely due to the interest they aroused that the theatre of the United States ⟨can xxxxxx.⟩ {is in such a state of vitality and receptiveness: that Shaw and Tchekov}, for example, find vast audiences. Now that I have read her lectures I can well understand their effect. The lectures on Strindberg and Tchekov strike me as especially remarkable in their elucidation of complex and subtle literary personalities. I know that Miss Goldman knows much of the modern European drama (such as the German Expressionists) and I am confident that her explanations of them will be as admirable, particularly when I remember not only the literary content of her lectures but the ⟨x⟩ {impressive} method of her delivery.

Rebecca West

(Photocopy of manuscript, New York University)

[2] Alexander Berkman (1870–1936), Goldman's partner in anarchy. He too was deported for obstructing the draft in 1919.

[3] Paul Robeson and his wife Eslanda Goode Robeson (1896–1965). She was a lifelong activist, trained in chemistry, and author of a biography of her husband, and *African Journey* (1945). West described a meeting with them in a letter to S. K. Ratcliffe ([November 1925], Yale University): "I went over to Villefranche to see Paul Robeson and his wife—the *Emperor Jones* man. Many of the Woman's Club members would I think have rejoiced to see ⟨x⟩ {me} taking a 6 ft 4″ negro to lunch at the Hotel de Paris in Monte Carlo! It did take a bit of nerve, even with only Anglo-Indians to face!"

[4] West's manuscript note.

To: Vyvyan Holland   [Ventimiglia]

[9 April 1926]

I shall be at the Hotel Josse, Antibes, from about April 15th till the end of June. If you are wantoning in the neighbourhood let me know. I had a lovely time in America (score now 11, and would have gone higher but I went back to 5).[1] I saw Ruby[2] in Paris just before I sailed dominating the Ritz bar in a two year old Molyneux dress. Marvellous woman. Best love.

R. W.

private collection   manuscript, picture postcard[3]

[1] West may well be counting lovers.

[2] Ruby Melville, a love interest of Holland at the time.

[3] The card pictures a pensive young woman, chin in hands, gazing into the distance, beside a wrought-iron stand that supports a bowl of flaming oil and offers the caption "L'amor mio arderà sempre" (My love will always burn). She sent Holland two other cards in the same series in October, one captioned "T'offro le rose della mia purezza" (I offer you the roses of my purity) and the second, "Perchè non mi risponde?" (Why don't you answer me?).

To: Letitia Fairfield   Hotel Josse
                                                      Antibes A.M.
                                                      France
                                                      [1926]

Dear Lettie,

Thank you so much for going to Maidenhead. I am the more worried about Bryant,[1] because he is now censoring all the outgoing letters from the boys which puts me in a most difficult position, as it certainly is quite an indefensible proceeding, and I don't know what to do when Anthony attacks it, as you don't like to agree with a boy against school rules. I'm also very sorry that Bryant showed you my letter, in view of the reference to you, but I'm also glad because it raises a point that I thought when you were here I ought to talk over with you and yet I hadn't the courage. You're in so many ways the best and sweetest person in the world but you have a fault of manner that has grown on you. Because of Papa's shortcomings you were given a degree of authority over Winnie and myself that wasn't usual or wholesome, and I don't think you realise to what extent that has given you a tendency to behave with a kind of fussiness and bossiness that gives people who don't know you a totally false impression. I know that you are quite unconscious of it, but you very often don't behave as if you were a woman moving among your equals, but as if you had some sort of authority like a prefect, and people do not like this. I realise perfectly that you don't mean it in the least and I know the causes for it, but other people don't. That is the source of Anthony's naughtiness when you're about. I twice had difficulties with him during these holidays over this very thing, and you had better know exactly what he said. The first time he said to me after we had been at Cannes that day, "Why does Aunt Lettie talk as if she thought herself better than us? When you were long buying that hat she should {have} come in and asked you to hurry up, not spoken to you so rudely and told you to stop. And anyway you had a right to take as long as you like." Another time he said, "You see the difference between Aunt Lettie and you. When you are late for lunch she scolds you, when she is late you smooth it over and say it doesn't matter. I don't see why you stand her behaving like a teacher." Of course I told him it was nonsense and it is nonsense, but at the same time that is the impression you give. Understand that I perfectly realise it is only a question of manner and that you are a dear modest Frisk but you can't expect other people to realise it who don't know you. I know you'll be surprised to hear that when we were down in Cornwall last year I had trouble with both Louise and young Evans over remarks you made without the slightest idea that you were speaking with any undue authority. I hate writing in this way but do remember that none of us have had a fair chance in this matter as poor Mother was far too distracted to criticise us as we grew up. I don't even expect one but it really is the truth that you are inclined to irritate people not by being exactly rude {but} by being talking [*sic*] as if you had an authority that nobody in grown-up life ever has, which produces the same effect as rudeness. I also don't want to give you the impression that Anthony isn't fond of you, for he is devoted to you, but this resentment does spring up from time to time. I mentioned these things to Bryant because I thought it necessary to explain why Anthony was feeling such enthusiasm for male society. (Though in view of Bryant's later proceedings I think him merely an ass.)

I shall enquire about the mirror, which was consigned to you by some devious proceedings in connection with a Society of Antique Dealers. Your extra expenses amounted to about 240 francs—but I've lost the note. Let it be quits in view of the half holiday Maidenhead expenses. Charlotte[2] and Ian have bought a motor boat and we all were nearly blown to Kingdom

Come off the Cap on a rough sea owing to Ian attending to the engine with a cigarette in his mouth. It is still wet and cold.

Yours with much love,
Anne

West, R., MSS   manuscript
Indiana University, Bloomington

[1] St. Piran's suffered from this headmaster's alcoholism.
[2] Charlotte Boissevain, a friend with whom West sometimes stayed on the Riviera. Pamela Frankau imagines an unkind letter from West to Boissevain in her *Letter from R*b*cc* W*st* (1986).

To: John Gunther   Hotel Josse
                                                Antibes, A.M.
                                                France
                                                [summer 1926]

My dear John,

All your letters have arrived within four days of each other. I have been worrying about where you are and even now I am not clear. But I haven't worried as much as I would have, because I have been having a real old-fashioned nervous breakdown, and it hasn't seemed to me that it mattered where anybody was as all people on this globe seemed equally miserable anywhere. This nervous breakdown earned its keep, I think, because I am now so tough that I could keep my head up and see where I collapsed and why, and I have found out something useful. My breakdown was due to Lettie. And it was due to the fact that she hasn't a thought about me that goes more than two centimetres below the surface which isn't dislike and shame. She wishes I didn't exist. She thinks I look awful. She thinks my career is a despicable failure. (Do you know that when I gave her my little book on Henry James all she said was that she hoped his relatives wouldn't mind and be able to do me any harm; and when I gave her *The Return of the Soldier* all she said was that she hoped that the present occupants of the inn at Monkey Island wouldn't be offended; and when I gave her *The Judge* all she said was that she couldn't understand how I could invent anything so unpleasant as

Roger. And that's that.) She is constantly embarrassed by my conversation and my manner. She treats Anthony as if he were the most appalling freak because he is mine. She actually has delusions about him. She alleged to me quite solemnly just before she left that he was so dark that of course it would be a handicap to him all through his life because people would think he had coloured blood in him. She is nearly crazy with an elder sister desire to call little sister down. And that is a force that all my life has been depressing and annoying me. I [am] perfectly sure that it is that and nothing in the way of a morbid neurosis which makes me dread going back to England. It isn't, as my family has always conspired to make me believe and as H. G. in his sadism loved to tell me, that I am a neurotic who cannot stand up to life, but that I am healthy and I have been preyed on by neurotics till they have bled me nearly white. So there we are. I feel better, but accursedly lonely. I have felt during the last four weeks quite miserable because you were so far away and because there is so slender a hope that I shall for months to come have more than a nibble at your dear company.

But you had a good time. I have goggled with envy over those letters. What is it about Islam that makes it armour-clad in every way except unity? Did you ever read the History of Islam in Spain? {particularly a book by a Dutchman called [Dozy]}.[1] There is no reason under the sun why they should not be there now and doing very much better than their Catholic Majesties were it not for just such damfoolishness as seems to have informed your Congress. I have had a quiet time here. It has been the most iniquitous weather, wet for days at a time, and extremely cold. The chief guffaws I have had lately have been at the letters I have had from America, on the subject of the General Strike in England. As you will have guessed it was as calm a bean-feast as may be, but America would have it that it was a Revolution. I had one dolourous letter which contained the quite serious sentence "How dreadful you will all feel when Ramsay Macdonald[2] moves into Buckingham Palace." To an English mind that does seem so deliciously irrelevant. I have spent a good many evenings talking to rather a nice American who is staying here, Lloyd Morris,[3] who seems to have done quite a bit of reviewing as well as some books and gives lectures on Contemporary Literature at Columbia. He has been here dreadfully ill ever since March, and has had one operation. It is a dreadful modern tragedy. He is the son of a widow, and has, I think, been a very decent and sweet soul up till a year ago, contented with his social life and his books. Then he met a young man whom I met at Villefranche with Paul Robeson, I think I wrote you about him, called Glenway Wescott.[4] And Glenway has pretty well made hay of this gentle creature, has conveyed to him that it is the chic way to be a genius to be a homo and take dope. Glenway being an ox with as much nerves as belongs to the ox-like state can do it, but this Morris boy is just a quivering mass of nerves. I am desperately sorry for him.

I have written a bit, but not so much as I had hoped, for I have been struggling with this desperate depression. For about a fortnight I found it difficult to be alone without bursting into nervous tears. But the place has done me a lot of good. There have been two days fine weather, and I spent all yesterday writing on the beach in a bathing-dress. And I like the Casino, where one has food such as is not in the whole of New York for about a dollar. And oh, I do like the pinewoods when the broom is out. But I shall never live in these parts. I would fondly love to live someday on the Cote des Maures. Do you remember it? That quite lonely stretch of woodland tumbling to the seas before you get to Toulon. Hereabouts is being covered with villas while you look.

Oh, such a queer thing happened at the hotel at Marseilles. I came down in the morning and asked for the bill in a hurry. They said "What room?" I said, "Room 225." The two cashiers looked at each other and said, "There is no such room." I said, "Well, that's where I slept." They said, "Where's your Key?" I said, "Oh, I left [it] in the door." I then turned to the man who had brought down my bag, and said, "What room was it?" He said, "Room 225." The two cashiers got very excited, and the bag-bringer confided to me it was the first day he had worked in the hotel. Finally they alleged you had paid. I said, "But what about the mineral water I have [had] since Monsieur left, and so forth?" They shrugged their shoulders and did nothing about it. So there you are. Do you think the God-streak that is in both of us had been functioning and we had created a bedroom? It is odd. (Let's thank God that's all we did.)

I am crazy with joy at the thought of your coming up from Genoa. It is a grand idea. Stay a few days, and we'll have such a good time. I am also thrilled by the scarf. I think I know what it looks like—like a coat of mail that has gone in for the gay life. It was a good idea to buy it white. Oh, but what's the good of anyfink? I want to talk to you, to John Gunther himself.

Yours ever, with ever such love[5]
Rebecca

Papers of John Gunther, Addenda   typescript with partially autograph
University of Chicago   closing and signature

[1] West's note in left margin.
[2] James Ramsay Macdonald (1866–1937), the first Labour Party prime minister (1924, 1929–1931, 1931–1935), residing at No. 10 Downing Street, of course, and not the royal residence.
[3] Lloyd Morris (1893–1954), American critic and reviewer. His books include *The Celtic Dawn* (1917), *Curtain Time* (1953), and studies of Edwin Arlington Robinson, Nathaniel Hawthorne, and Henry James.
[4] Glenway Wescott (1901–1987), American writer of novels, short stories, and essays. His novels include *The Apple of the Eye* (1924) and *The Pilgrim Hawk* (1940).
[5] The second phrase of the closing is handwritten.

To: John Gunther   On board the Cunard
R. M. S. Berengaria
Between Cherborg and
Southampton
[December 1926]

My dear John,

I very much wanted to see you. For I wanted to tell you that I've fallen in love. Someone[1] whom I have known very slightly for the last three years suddenly turned up and assumed a significance I hadn't thought anybody would ever again, and he was my lover for the last three weeks I was in New York. It isn't what I felt for Max [Beaverbrook]—what, in an odd way this has made me realise, I still feel for Max; but it is love. I don't know if it will last, I don't want to marry him, but I definitely want to be with him for some time to come. I put this out as crudely as possible because I am so disconcerted by not being able to talk about it, and I'm terrified of being vague and dishonest about it. The queer thing is that I don't feel as if it affected the essentials of our relationship. I do want you to say you'll come back to me and be my nice sweet friend you've always been. I truly love you, John, and I'm enormously grateful to you for all the dearness you've shown me. You really did fill my flat with yellow flowers. Come and see me the very first moment you can.

I am practically commuting! The day before I sailed on the Berengaria I was told by the *Cosmopolitan* people that they wanted me back to edit my serial at the end of January. So I take some big boat about the 21st—as Anthony goes back to school on the 20th. I shall stay there probably till early April.

I sent you that cable about Frances[2] because I found she had created the impression in Chicago that you had played with her, that you had perpetually led her on and then dropped her, and led her on again. I also found that in New York she rather specialised in creating an impression that men whom she hardly knew were extremely interested in her—which after all is natural enough reaction to hurt pride and for which I don't blame her in the least—but which I thought showed a tendency to hysteria that might make her get you into trouble. I think that provided she doesn't get you into any trouble what you did was quite right. It will probably make her feel much better and ease off the situation.

I fancy I wrote you the last time I saw Jerry. Didn't I tell you that the deplorable Billie was married to her Yiddish boss and having her honeymoon at the Biltmore of chaste memory and had disconcerted the bridegroom by manifesting herself as a dyed-in-the-wool dope addict? It is morphine and I understand of years' standing. Jerry consoled himself by an affair with a woman called Catherine Brodie (Jerry doesn't know I know this) who is almost as offensive as Billie except that she has a good figure. She has a face like a skull and all her light chitchat is of her husband's strange sexual habits. I rather weary of Jerry's crescendo of undesirable females. I weary also of Zelma. Of all the stupid, grouching spectres. . . But Carl is a lamb.[3] It's a funny thing that I stumbled on the fact that a certain girl in New York— young, quite exquisitely lovely, with a really beautiful character and a first rate wife and mother (being a young widow) is madly in love with Carl and has been for years, and he just doesn't notice it out of the depths of his obsession with Zelma.

The *Herald Tribune* reviews took me two days apiece. The difficulty was to get books from the office. They really never thought I would need more than 48 hours for reading and writing. I didn't see Saxton but momentarily.[4] I didn't meet Darrow[5] or Sandburg but am crazy on Lincoln. Hansen is a flop just because his stuff is so hopelessly and dreadfully bald and bad.[6] It's like the worst book notes in the cheapest London daily. I wish the poor dear soul had spoken to me for I liked him awfully when we met.

I didn't write that short story or any more of *Sunflower,* for I've not had time. But the middle of February will see me with 10,000 dollars clear! I've also made 2,500 dollars profit on some Wall Street gambling I did last January! So I'm fairly well-off (but the 2,500 dollars I've reinvested.)

I grieve to hear your family responsibilities have increased. But I suppose your sister will soon be on her own. I fancy *The Red Pavilion* will be something of a wow. I don't agree at all with your estimate of *The Sun Also Rises.*[7] I think *The Red Pavilion* a lot better insofar as they compete. But I think *The Sun Also Rises* beats your book in its fault of not being about anything. If it's about the fact that Brett got drunk and went to bed with everyone she saw clearly enough to distinguish their sex you get that all in a couple of chapters.

I hope this won't interfere between us. After all we have shared the common experience of Gerhardie—that ought to weld us together.

I oddly don't want to tell you who my lover is. Not one soul knows of it. He is a Californian, and a banker, and a terrific gambler, and he is so illiterate that he reads poetry and remembers it and gets a kick out of words, and he is broke one day and a millionaire the next, and he has been in love with me for three years without knowing me. I don't know if it'll last. I am terrified till my heart stops that when I go back to New York at the end of January he will seem just a dull man with a drawl. And I am terrified to let him know that the thing that delivered me into his hands was that his voice, when he let it go, was like Max's. I am so sick with fear about the whole thing that you may guess how much I want it to be real and lasting. I haven't told him about you. I mean he knows there is someone, but I haven't told him your name, because I think you might like each other when you met.

I wish I could talk to you. I don't say anything about wishing you to be happy because that sounds as if we were at the end of something. We aren't, are we? And anyway you will be happy, you fortunate child.

Yours ever,

Rebecca

Papers of John Gunther, Addenda   manuscript
University of Chicago

[1] Steven Martin, American banker and speculator whom she met in 1923 and took as a lover in 1926. She reported his untimely death to both Gunther and Vyvyan Holland, spring 1927.

[2] Frances Fineman became Gunther's first wife.

[3] Carl and Zelma Brandt. Carl Brandt (1889–1957), a highly respected New York literary agent, who was credited with talent in editing. His agency still exists.

[4] Eugene Francis Saxton (1884–1943), American editor and publisher who revived Harper & Bros. after moving to New York City in 1926.

[5] Clarence Seward Darrow (1857–1938), American defense attorney best known for his defense during the Scopes trial (1925) of the teaching of evolution.

[6] Harry Hansen, American editor of the *Daily News* and author of *Midwest Portraits* (1923).

[7] Contrary to West's expectations, Ernest Hemingway's 1926 novel made his reputation. Gunther's *Red Pavilion* (1926), set in Chicago, dealt with a set of sophisticated friends.

To: Letitia Fairfield

Hotel Majestic
West Seventy-Second St.
at Central Park
New York
Thursday [3 April 1927]

My dear Lettie,

I am so agitated by these cables. I feel I'm giving an awful lot of trouble. But I don't see how it could be avoided. If you saw me you might be pacified for I'm having a terrible time. I've had the most ghastly experience of my life. I feared the last also. Just when I was up and well after this anti-typhoid fever {last Friday} I went out to dinner and met one of the presidents of a movie concern that's been making me offers. He was a very charming, very attractive young Jew of about twenty-eight—not a Kike, he belongs to a very old-established Jewish family—rather grave and neurotic. He ⟨xx⟩ {told} me he wanted me very much to do some work like the "Magician of Pell Street."[1] He finally came back to my hotel with a woman who was there and we talked ⟨till⟩ {in} my sitting room till midnight. Then they went and I went to bed. An hour later I heard a ring at my door. (I have a complete little suite, sitting-room, bedroom, and bathroom, in an angle of the building—it is just like a flat on its own, and is entered by quite a long corridor.) I went and opened it, as sometimes cables and telegrams are delivered quite late, and here was this man. He looked ghastly. I saw something was wrong, but he forced himself in. Then he told me that he had always wanted to meet me, that he had always been fascinated by the photograph of me in ⟨xx⟩ Dr Devol's office, then now I met him I had destroyed him, he knows I had made him impotent and that he had been walking about in Central Park ever since he'd left me, and that he'd come back to kill me. Then he went for me. I didn't know what to do. I was frightened to scream as I knew that if I got people to come one of the bellboys would be sure to sell the story to the papers. Finally after we had dashed round and round the room I got in a corner behind a sofa, but he dragged me out and started strangling me. I thought I was gone, but suddenly he fell on his knees and had a kind of fit. I rushed out of the room, but had to go out into the passage as he was between me and my bedroom door. I still didn't dare fetch anybody, so I locked myself into a public lavatory, and waited till it was light, thinking what on earth I would do if he had killed himself or died or was still unconscious. I thought I could possibly get the manager to do something to avoid a scandal—carrying him into another room. I was so sick I could hardly move. But when I went back he had gone. I've never been so torn to pieces by anything in my life. He wasn't drunk, he hadn't had anything but water at the party. It was sheer madness. I can't tell you the effect it had on me—partly obviously because of Max [Beaverbrook], partly because I had about a fortnight ago a painful scene with Charlie Chaplin.[2] I never told anybody but when I was out in Los Angeles in 1924 Charlie made violent love to me and asked me to marry him. Finally, the last weekend of my visit, he got so pressing that I went away to Santa Barbara[3] without telling him where I was going. ⟨x⟩ {I never heard from him} again but heard that he tried to find me very hard after I had left. The other day I had a long talk with him and he told me that he was pressing me so hard to live with him then because he had suddenly become terrified of impotence and wanted to see if it were so. Then when I went he experienced one of the regressive movements he has had at intervals all his life, and became interested in very young children—I mean little girls of thirteen or fourteen. It was then he took Lita Grey,[4] though knowing it would lead to trouble. But for six months afterwards he was impotent with mature women, and remained so till he took up with Marion Davies, who is the original of Lorelei in *Gentlemen Prefer Blondes*,[5] the very antithesis of myself.

I suppose you can imagine how perfectly ghastly all this is. Also when this man was strangling me I got an awful conviction that if he didn't get me some other one of those lunatics who are clustering round me will. The thing is getting so bad and fantastic that it can't go on much longer—there must be some frightful disaster. I wouldn't tell you all these horrors if it wasn't that I want you to understand why I'm going to Florence, and being analysed. This can't be just ill-luck unless the world is completely insane. There must be some mental cause for it in me. And so far as I can see if I don't discover it I run quite a risk of departing this life.

It's nearly a week ago. I can't finish my serial,[6] I'm so shattered. I shake all over for a couple of hours after I get up in the morning.

Do forgive me if getting off my fambly is a nuisance. I hope *we'll* have a good time when we foregather.

Yours ever,
Anne

West, R., MSS   manuscript
Indiana University, Bloomington

[1] Short story by West published in *Hearst's International Cosmopolitan* (February 1926); rpt. *The Only Poet*.

[2] West's first impressions of Chaplin are recorded in a letter to Reginald Turner (6 October 1921, Yale University), describing him as "a darling" and "a very serious little cockney" who told her anecdotes about the Queen's dollhouse. Of his recent marriage, he had said "You know, I dropped into it with a blonde," to which she reacted, "I don't think you can better that as a concise statement." Chaplin told William Saroyan that West was "a piece of cake" (quoted in Carl Rollyson, *Rebecca West: A Saga of the Century*, 75).

[3] City on southern California coast, fifty miles north of Los Angeles.

[4] Grey and Chaplin married later in 1924.

[5] Marion Davies (1897–1961), silent film actress in works such as *When Knighthood Was in Flower* and *The Fair Coed*. She was the lifetime consort of William Randolph Hearst, who spent millions on her career. West refers to Anita Loos's *Gentlemen Prefer Blondes* (1926). Marilyn Monroe played Lorelei in the 1953 film version.

[6] *War Nurse*, contracted for by the Hearst Corporation, was based on another woman's experiences.

To: Vyvyan Holland   Frifri Palace
                                                      Comp Long.
                                                      par Agay (Var)
                                                      [July 1927]

My dear Vyvyan,

The above is my address, though I hardly believe it myself. It is not as you might suppose a place for fri-fri love but a sedate old-fashioned villa in a little village near St Raphael of which the only other inhabitant is Polaire.[1] It is really rather a charming house with balconies up among mimosa branches and I have a marvellous cook, a form of consolation which I need, considering all things. I got back to my gunrunner to find him ill.[2] He got steadily worse and after an operation died at the end of March. I really do feel I have bad luck, because this was badly what I wanted. He was so sweet, and such fun. I thought of consoling myself with a very rich young man, but he drank too much, and suddenly I got too damn tired for anything and went away to Florence and was psychoanalysed. After three weeks my psychoanalyst turned pale and went to America. But she's reculéd and is mieux sautering down here soon,[3] I hope. It's done me a lot of good, as I felt absolutely finished.

Come and see me if you are anywhere near here. You can have a pleasant bedroom if you come in July—or a quite good sofa in the drawingroom in August.[4] Ruby [Melville] I hear is going to Nice for the summer. I just missed her in Florence. Gerald Huxton tells {me} she is looking radiant. Divorce suits that girl.

I knew about Jane [Wells].[5] H. G. wrote and told me about it in a cold what-do-you-know-about-the-mystery-of-death letter. ⟨xxxxxxxxx⟩. {So I left him to it. He's apparently being very} good to Jane, which must be the last tragedy of her poor life, for I'm sure she's been bored to death with him for years.

Write to me and tell me all about your lewd life in London. I'm going back there to live this autumn. I want to be near a decent library. I like your notes on idleness though they're pure boasting.[6]

Reggie [Turner] was very sweet in Florence. We spoke lovingly of you. Don't tell anybody about Steve, because I feel my bad luck is comic.

Yours ever,
Rebecca

So glad to hear from you.

private collection   manuscript

---

[1] Emile-Marie Polaire (1877–1939), Algerian-born French actress and singer, known for her tiny waist and bobbed hair. She played memorably in Colette's *Claudine in Paris* (1906).

[2] Steven Martin.

[3] From the French, "reculer pour mieux sauter," to retreat in order to jump better.

⁴When staying in Padstow in 1925, West had humorously denied Holland accommodation. "I am indeed pining for companionship, but as the house is now full and you would have to choose between sleeping with me or my son's tutor, which choice would inevitably be followed by ill-feeling in the evening by the one who was not chosen, and in the morning by the one who was, I cannot invite you, as I long to do" (17 August 1925, private collection, manuscript).

⁵Jane Wells was dying of cancer.

⁶*A Few Odd Reflections on Idleness* was a pamphlet compiled by Vyvyan Holland. He was a member of the male dining club, Ye Sette of Odde Volumes, where he presented the pamphlet on ladies' night (22 June 1927).

To: Letitia Fairfield

Frifri Palace
Comp Long.
par Agay (Var)
France
[August 1927]

My dear Lettie,

Herewith a cheque for £20 which leaves me still ten pounds in your debt. I have paid the full £50 into my account. This is the mortgage money I am reclaiming isn't it? I am all of a dither about this sum. The animal [Anthony West] and its keeper arrived this morning and I was struck dumb by the immense improvement in its mouth and its nose! Its nose is now quite human and wholly free from all Pekinese suggestion. Its report is poor except for a lyrical outburst about its drawing. ⟨But⟩ {However} the prevalent complaint is one of inattention in class, but his examination marks don't seem so bad. It is unfortunate that he seems to have a great resistance to psychoanalysis.

My analysis by the way has been conducted under circumstances that will make your hair stand on end. Mrs Wilshire¹ has been living in the house and we have been working anything from four to ten hours a day! I had however complete confidence in Mrs Wilshire. I knew she understood the engine—and you may judge of her conscientiousness from the fact that she came back from San Francisco for three months solely to do my analysis because she feared the effect a broken analysis would have on me. Mrs. Wilshire says that so far as she knows there is not the element {considered} vital to the conduct of an analysis that hasn't been broken—but that she thought it wisest to handle me this way. The length of the bouts of analysis she says were particularly necessary for me and could hardly have been done by any other patient she has ever had.

Now I feel immensely better. It was a terribly intricate and complex business, based on an inconceivably disguised and ⟨x⟩ {hidden} father fixation. I wish you would tell me one or two things—what was the family doing during the first twelve months of my life? How were we disposed of when Mother was away having her eyes treated? When did we have a servant called Kate? There seems to have been an incident in my first three or four years when I had a mustard plaster or something similar applied to my chest. There was one occasion when it was put on too hot—of course the recovery of this memory exaggerates the importance of this incident—it possibly only meant that there was a moment's pain. But what seems mysterious to me is that this seems to have ⟨x⟩ terminated or at least interrupted a series of visits to a doctor. Can you throw any light on this? And was there anyone in our young lives called Miss O'Rare? O'Reagh?[2]

The animal seems well pleased with the Frifri Palace, and it ate heartily of fresh sardines and peaches for its lunch. It seems a little tired but that is natural enough. I hope it likes this place for I would like to come here again and again. I will send it home on the 19th and it will bring you the blue dress. I will stay here till the 26th or 27th to clear up the house.

Best love,
Anne

West, R., MSS   manuscript
Indiana University, Bloomington

[1] Mary Wilshire, American lay analyst whom West met in California in 1923. She analyzed both Rebecca and Anthony.
[2] West offered the following explanation for her psychoanalysis to Wells:
I have had a difficult time lately, and I want to understand why nobody will let me get on with my work but always makes impossible demands on me. In my whole life nobody has come to me and offered me quiet companionship of the sort that would help me and Anthony and my work. You dear Pussy never gave me any sort of rest and peace—if we had a few days of quiet you always had to break them up by scenes—you're much nicer to me now we're separated. I found the same prospect stretching before me in New York these last few ⟨years⟩ {months}—with a handsome young millionaire who proposed to fight with his alcoholic family history all over my exhausted body while even as you did feeling great love and 'votion for me but giving me no sort of peace or quiet and not for one minute

recognising the slightest need for self-restraint in order to spare my nerves. I want to ⟨x⟩ {find} out why I'm a host for parasites, as you yourself have noticed, and there's nothing for it but psychoanalysis. (1926, Yale University)

To: John Gunther

1 Raymond Buildings
Grays Inn, W.C.
[fall 1927]

My dear John,

I am sorry too I saw so little of you. But what a wild gay time it was. It ended queerly for me with a ⟨night⟩ {scene} when the Prince[1] came in about midnight to say goodnight to me—and it appeared then and after that that Mrs. Brennan was ragingly, tearingly jealous about him! She hasn't written to me since though I have written to her and sent her some money she ought to have acknowledged. The queer thing is that she really hardly knows him. Attaprince! He had a wonderful goodbye scene staged for me the next morning—in bed, of course, with the famous black crepe-de-chine garment, and some marvellous lines, most of them bland anticipations of the future. However I don't expect I shall ever see him again. Over here life is boring. This flat has a lovely view, but a bathroom that only a virgin could tolerate, and the whole of London is *muggy*. H. G.'s wife [Jane Wells] has just died, poor soul, and I fear he may become tiresome in various ways. Bless you. I shall be glad when you come over for that week-end.

Yours ever,
Rebecca

Papers of John Gunther, Addenda
University of Chicago

manuscript

[1] Prince Antoine Bibesco, once Romanian ambassador to the United States and Spain. A close friend of Proust, he married Elizabeth Asquith, daughter of the prime minister (1919). West was still adding to the account in a letter to Gunther (June 1962):

I have had lately an odd experience of hearing a voice from a grave—the grave belonging to Antoine Bibesco. The son of a servant of his came to see me the other day, who remembered me because of a romantic passage in Belgrade not recorded in *Black Lamb and Grey Falcon,* and half a dozen times since then there have been reminders of him, my sister suddenly found an unopened letter from him to me at the back of her desk, and such odd things. Probably for that reason I had a dream last night in which you and I were again sitting in Antoine's house on the Isle St Louis. Antoine was there and Jerome Frank it was perfectly pleasant. When I woke up I cried and cried to think of the past being the past, and was so happy to think that your life had turned out so well.

However, she confided to Fanny Hurst ([fall 1927], University of Texas at Austin) that Bibesco

did something to me so perverse, so cruel, so queer, so fantastic, that you could not believe it. It was something entirely independent of me. I didn't bring it on myself in any way. When I came round, so to speak, I asked him why he had done it. This a day later. He was genuinely distressed, and told me that from the moment he had known I was in Paris he had had an impulse which it was not in his power to resist to do something eccentric and insulting to me. He was genuinely miserable because I would not see him any more or accept any apology. The whole thing was entirely in line—not in circumstances but in emotional feeling—with Max, with [Gelricks?], with [Wanger?], mixed desire and hate and death. I am entirely convinced now that there is an external force working against me. I have been down into myself in the analysis so deeply that this isn't a superficial point of view. This is rather frightening. I am going to live so far as possible utterly and absolutely alone from now on, because simply and straightly I believe that if I don't I am going to get killed.

To: Jonathan Cape   80 Onslow Gardens, S.W. 7
                                     [December 1927]

My dear Jonathan,

I have had the draft of a blurb by me for days but I am suspended between my old flat and my new flat and everything has broken down. So here goes in my own fist.

The title I suggest is:

THE STRANGE NECESSITY: ESSAYS AND REVIEWS

The essay "The Strange Necessity" (god dammit) has gone from 6,000 to 30,000 words. It begins with a discussion of James Joyce's *Ulysses* which is probably the first estimate to be done neither praying nor vomiting. In it I come to the conclusion that though it is ugly and incompetent it is ⟨an art⟩ {a work} of art. That is to say it is *necessary*. Then I go on to discuss what is this "strange necessity, art" which is so inclusive of opposites?—as for instance the paintings of Ingres and the books of James Joyce? This leads to an analysis of literature, and the discovery of a double and vital function it fulfills for men. Firstly it makes a collective external brain for man; secondly it presents certain formal relations to man which suggest a ⟨x⟩ universe more easy in certain respects than the one he knows.[1]

I cannot tell you how anxious I am to write the last 5000 words of this or how determined the painters, telephone authorities, and gas companies seem that I shall not get into my new flat and do so. I hope when I'm settled that you and Mrs. Cape will come to dinner some evening. A Merry Christmas to you both.

Yours ever,
Rebecca W.

Jonathan Cape archive   manuscript
Reading University

[1] In a note a few months later, West suggested the following about the marketing of the collection: "*The Strange Necessity*—can you see to it that it's treated as a *technical, highbrow* book? Reviewable really as a *book on psychology*" (1928, Reading University).

To: H. G. Wells   [late 1927]
Dear Pussy,

Thank you for your letter. I am glad about Gyp [Wells] and the meeting shall be arranged as soon as possible. But I've been able to do nothing about it before now as I've had a trying time owing to Anthony being stricken down with chickenpox. He was not bad with it but the type that afflicted the school was unusually virulent. I have had to go up every day, and as I am getting the new flat ready for the Christmas holidays (which is in Kensington) I have been spending about two hours a day on busses and taxis—and I am finishing my book of criticisms. I am so tired I could cry. But the minute it can be done I shall. I am bringing A. back here for a week to feed him up—he is getting dreadfully tall and thin. He's drawn all the time in bed, some beautiful things. He is a gifted creature, I think.

I am here for another three weeks. Then we move into the new flat—80 Onslow Gardens, S. W. It's exceptionally beautiful—part of an old fashioned house with big rooms and a roof-garden—the place a boy will adore, and runnable with one servant. £275 a year.

I'm afraid the poor cat got down to Grasse just in time for the rain—but anyway it's better than this terrible gloom.

Love,
P.

I hope you're giving me the life interest on this £5000? It is going to be difficult if after A. comes of age I am dependant on him for the rent of the house. It's not a good or normal relationship. You know well that you can trust me to hand it over properly. I've taken very good care of all his funds. Also it's not good for him to feel I haven't anything.[1]

Rebecca West Papers   manuscript
Yale University

[1] This note is probably one of the documents that caused Anthony West distress when this correspondence came into his hands in 1944.

To: Jonathan Cape   80 Onslow Gardens, S.W. 7
                                               7 March 1928
My dear Jonathan,

Alas that I was snatched away from your arms on Friday night by Lord Castlerosse's[1] necessity to confide to me the secrets of his heart—which were extensive and peculiar. I hear that you became more and more a social success as the evening went on.

Thank you very much for your kind offer about books. There are one or two books that I would be very glad to have. I should very much like Salvemini's *The Fascist Dictatorship*.[2] I should also like *The Pilgrimage of Henry James* by Van Wyck Brooks. I should also like, partly to see if I can do anything with them, everything you have got of Laura Riding.[3] I have just had out of the Times Book Club her *Contemporaries and Snobs*. I think she writes quite atrociously, almost as badly as anybody I have ever come across, with the obvious exception of Middleton Murry—another of your authors, dear Jonathan. (You are slightly promiscuous, aren't you?) But I think she may have something to say. It doesn't appear for certain in "Contemporaries and Snobs," but her attack on Elliot [*sic*]—which I think extremely well founded—suggests to me that she may know more than she says there.[4] If you will send me the whole lot along I will see if I can write about them, as I thought she got a very unfair notice from that old ass Arnold Bennett.

What has happened to *Lions and Lambs?*[5] I am getting the wind up about it because the Grim Reaper is so busy just now and I suppose I shall have to perjure my immortal soul and say sweet things about Masterman and Lord Oxford as the studies that I wrote do not come under the heading of nil nisi bonum.[6]

I like your nerve, the way you yap for my MS, considering that when I send you any MS you keep it in the cellar along with the winter bulbs for eight months or so! ⟨x⟩ May God have mercy on your soul.

Yours ever,

Rebecca West

Jonathan Cape archive   typescript
Reading University

[1] Viscount Valentine Castlerosse, Earl of Kenmare (1891–1943), Irish journalist for the *Evening Standard* and author of *Valentine's Day*.

[2] Gaetano Salvemini's *The Fascist Dictatorship in Italy* (1927).

[3] Laura Riding (1901–1991), American poet and critic, resident in Europe (1925–1939). *The Fugitive* and *Poetry* were published by the Woolfs' Hogarth Press. *A Survey of Modernistic Poetry* (1927), written with her long-term companion, Robert Graves, influenced New Criticism.

[4] Riding urged poets to write of their own experience in this 1928 book, prepared in association with Graves. West would launch her own attack on T. S. Eliot in her final article for the *Bookman* (August 1930), "What Is Mr. Eliot's Authority as a Critic?"

[5] *Lions and Lambs* included West's commentary on David Low's cartoons of prominent literary and political figures, including "the late C. F. G. Masterman" and "the late Lord Oxford." It was published by Cape (1928).

[6] Nothing unless good.

To: Fannie Hurst   80 Onslow Gardens, S.W. 7
[spring 1928]

My dear Fannie,

This is just to say I've read *The President has been Born* a second time and I love the prairie feeling—I mean the feeling of being in the middle of America, that I get in the Middle West. It's grand. Bless you. *Bless* you.

Cape is publishing "The Strange Necessity," an essay on art bound in with my *Herald Tribune* articles, on May 15th.[1] It is 45,000 words long, and I meant it to be 5,000. I think it's the best thing I have ever done. You shall have the first copy I lay hands on. I had to dedicate it to Irita van Doren, because she has been very decent collecting the stuff for me. I want to dedicate the next one I do to you.

I should finish *Sunflower* in three months time. And there has jumped up a bogey. Not from my indiscretion but from the indiscretion of several subsequent ladies, it is now generally known about M.'s [Beaverbrook's] troubles in life. Not from my indiscretion but from his (because he has talked of it perpetually) it's begun to be known that we were closely involved some years back. He is now, I hear, half mad, bitterly vindictive, and ⟨x⟩ unscrupulous. In other words, I am scared to death that people will identify the persons in *Sunflower* and that he will wreak some awful vengeance on me. So I am sitting down to finish *Sunflower* (which I don't mind saying is remarkably good) in the knowledge I may have to suppress it for years. It doesn't matter as much as it would at any other time, because I now write with such comparative speed that I will have another novel quite soon. I wrote *The Strange Necessity* in ⟨three⟩{four} months *and* moved into a new flat *and* minded G. B. [Stern] in her horrific breakdown.

I sail to your blessed shores at the end of September, & stay there for two months I should think. I *long* to see you.

Best love,

Rebecca

F. Hurst Papers   manuscript
University of Texas at Austin

[1] The first of the essays was "Uncle Bennett," commissioned by Irita Van Doren, editor of the *New York Herald Tribune Books* and published in October 1926.

To: Fannie Hurst   80 Onslow Gardens, S.W. 7
                                              [May 1928]

My dear Fannie,

I'm off again!—for the last few days Anthony has been looking white and has had a nasty cough. This morning I called in a doctor. I saw by his face at once that something was wrong. Another doctor came this afternoon—and they told me there was no doubt it was T. B. He is to be X-rayed on Monday—I am to get expert advice as to where to go in Switzerland—and ⟨x⟩ {in as} short a time as possible. I have to be out of England with him in anything as near a week as possible. This is obviously a bad story—but what makes it worse is that he has been more exultantly happy in this new flat than anything I've ever known, and we have never been so much to each other. Also he's done very well at school, is very happy there, and was {looking forward to} going to Stowe in the autumn. I know there's every chance for him—it's probably not been going more than a month—but over and above the physical peril there's the dreariness of sanatorium life for a kid of thirteen with a mind that's just fully awakening. I did think I had at last secured his happiness. What scares me moreover is that up till now I have always been most painfully affected by high altitudes (I think its my low blood pressure) and I must not fail him up there. I don't know whether he'll ever be able to winter in England—in which case my flat, in which we were both so heavenly happy, is no use whatsoever![1] This is not just a grouse. It is also to tell you that if you are coming to England my flat and my servant will be waiting for you until the beginning of ⟨July⟩ {August}. I've told the Thomases they can have it when they come—but {the date of} that visit I don't know. Ring em up and find out if there's any chance of your using the flat. Anthony's room will be fumigated.

I'll tell Cape to send you a copy of *The Strange Necessity*. I won't be here to inscribe it, alas! Not that I mind a fig leaving London—if there was a pleasant alternative for Anthony. But it will be the devil's own job to make it pleasant.

What grouses I always write you! I'm ashamed of myself. But this is harrowing. I haven't told Anthony yet {that} he has to go, and one of the things I dread most is to intimate that he'll have to be parted from his first dog, a disreputable Sealyham. He never had been able to keep a dog till now. Oh, every way this is damnable.

Letters sent here will be forwarded. I haven't a notion where I'll be here in Switzerland—if it's suitable Arosa, but I don't know if it will be.

RW

Don't tell this to anybody. If it gets about and A gets better quickly—he might have an awkward time getting into Stowe. I am telling Lida Thomas and nobody else.[2]

F. Hurst Papers   manuscript
University of Texas at Austin

¹ The story unfolded in additional letters. She told Hurst a few days later that a specialist had told her, "He will get through if the best that can be done for him is done—*but you have no margin*. Mercifully he does not approve of Switzerland in the summer—so we are trying to get Anthony into an English Sanatorium—on the East Coast—and I will take a house nearby. I will be living between London and there—mostly ⟨London⟩ {there}" (1928, University of Texas at Austin). On stationery of the Royal Links Hotel, Cromer, where she stayed off and on into August while Anthony was in a Norfolk sanatorium, West thanks John Gunther for a visit when she had been feeling particularly down: "When I got here at 7 I was done in and almost crying with fatigue. But inside I felt so refreshed and happy because you made that tiresome journey ⟨and⟩ {to} see me and were so kind and friendly and loving. There is something between us that is very real and will never be broken" (1928, University of Chicago). Anthony had a mild case and was able to enter Stowe on schedule, though not without additional alarms from the specialists.

² Postscript written along left side margin of first page.

To: Fannie Hurst   80 Onslow Gardens, S.W. 7
                                                         27 August 1928

My dear Fannie:

I am awfully disappointed not to see you but I quite understand. I sail on the 23rd September, so get your Middle Westing over before October.

I am sending you *The Strange Necessity,* so cancel that order at Brentano's.

I have been enmeshed in the most sickening business for the last few days. Arnold Bennett, whom I have always loathed, and who has always loathed me, wrote a very hostile review of *The Strange Necessity* in the *Evening Standard* (which is one of Max's [Beaverbrook] papers). This I never saw as I was in the country and was not getting my Press Cuttings. One day an *Evening Standard* reporter presented himself and I did not even know what he had come to see me about. He produced this cutting, about which I said a few things, just the things one would say. He went away. I came back to town and had a good old-fashioned attack of colitis, which kept me busy for three days. On the third day I arose, as they say in the Bible, and found that the *Evening Standard* interview had been a tissue of lies simply beyond belief, representing me as having covered Bennett with the lowest kind of insults. On several succeeding days they had published letters insulting and deriding me for this interview, and they finished up by starting a literary competition for the readers to supply the best imaginary conversation between Bennett and myself. I then went down to a lawyer and within two days writted them for libel, as they would not apologise—an almost unknown thing, of course, for a journalist to do to a newspaper, but everyone agreed I had to do it. I can get no apology out of them so I am afraid the unsavory business will have to come into Court in the autumn. All this tallies with the extraordinary behaviour that is reported concerning Max these days.

Tyler has entirely lost interest in *The Return of the Soldier* he does not even hold the Rights. I simply could not bear the Play, because of its material ugliness.

Well, my lamb, I hope that I shall see you round and about October,

Love,

Rebecca

F. Hurst Papers   typescript with autograph signature
University of Texas at Austin

To: Arnold Bennett   14 September 1928

When I went to France ten days ago for a rest I was too ill after this dreadful summer of domestic misfortune to write any personal letters: and as I had informed the Press Association that I have issued a writ for libel against the *Evening Standard* on account of the interview they published with me on August 14th on the subject of yourself, I had believed this would be published in the press and you would learn of it in that way. I am extremely sorry to find that for some reason the Press Association have not been able to give publicity to this fact, and I am concerned lest you should have no knowledge of it. It is awkward to speak of anything which is the subject of legal proceedings—but I do most earnestly wish to assure you that I have never in my life been so aghast as when I read that interview (which I did only some days after it had appeared): so aghast, and so humiliated, and so bewildered. The rest must wait till another time to be explained. But I could not rest until I had given you some intimation of my feelings.[1]

Yours sincerely,

REBECCA WEST

Rebecca West Papers   typescript copy
Yale University

[1] Bennett was unperturbed in his reply.

To: Letitia Fairfield

The Langdon
2 East 56th St.
New York
[autumn 1928]

Dear Lettie,

Forgive me for not writing but I have had a most trying time—unlucky in every possible way! I had a nice rest on the boat until Lady Astor found me out—and of all the silly, tactless, dithering females she is the worst. She announced me without my consent as a speaker at the Ship's Concert and herself made a speech that was so silly that everybody was in a state of revolt—a most nervewracking experience. When I got to New York Emanie Sachs[1] met me on the dock and took me for the weekend to their seaside place in Connecticut which was lovely—But after that everything went wrong. Two stories {were} turned back for tedious and unnecessary alterations which were a bother to do—and Ray Lang sent for me, coolly announced the time was past for straight war-stuff and demanded that I should turn the *War Nurse* into a novel! He is willing to pay me a lot more money but that doesn't relieve it from being a strangling job. However they gave me an indefinite time to do it.[2] Then also I had found the only thoroughly dirty and uncomfortable hotel in New York, from which I had presently to remove to this place, which is beautiful—I look down Fifth Avenue to Central Park, and the light and the traffic and the new skyscrapers are superb. My secretary failed me—and I found it terribly hard to work—and felt so miserable I didn't know what to do. It occurred to me to take my temperature and I found I was in another bout of ⟨temperature⟩ {fever}. I was too busy to do anything about it—nor does there seem anything to do. But about five days ago it died down to normal. I feel dreadfully tired however—This summer seems to have broken something in me. New York is more beautiful than ever—the newest buildings are glorious—but the whole atmosphere is ghastly. The gang warfare here (especially in Brooklyn) is becoming as bad as Chicago—and everybody is simply thrilled and amused by it. Nobody reads anything but murder stories—and all the plays are about crime. The other night some people took me to a nightclub and we got in just as the police were taking charge of it because Texas Guinian's[3] brother had struck a chorus-girl there the night before and during the day she had died. All these horrors simply amuse people, though the crime is just as sordid as {it is} anywhere else.

I have just had a letter from Mrs Hopkins and hope to see her next week. I wish I were staying longer though there is really no point in my being here except for work. It is depressing to live on the outskirts of an attractive world in which one has no real foothold. I am glad Anthony is all right—suggest he should write me a postcard. I went to spend the night with some terribly rich people on Long Island and met Lindbergh. He struck me as a most curious neurotic type, but beautiful to look at—Nobody has conveyed half his radiant good looks. The district where I stayed was thick with the beautiful homes of the unfortunate Guggenheims—this Mrs. Waldman whose children fell off the roof was Peggy Guggenheim.[4] Her mother was insane and she has been eccentric from childhood—she had separated from her husband and there were great disputes about the guardianship of these children. Her cousin was in seeing me yesterday and it was appalling to see how the whole family evidently hadn't a doubt as to what had happened.

Thanks ever so for the cable. I'll be back on the Mauretania sailing November 7th.

Yours with love,
Anne

West, R., MSS   manuscript
Indiana University, Bloomington

[1] Emanie Arling after divorce.
[2] The Cosmopolitan Book Corporation published *War Nurse* (1930).
[3] Owner of a speakeasy in New York.
[4] Peggy Guggenheim (1898–1979), American patron of the arts whose collection is housed at the Peggy Guggenheim Foundation in Venice, also a patron of Djuna Barnes. Her autobiography is *Out of This Century: Confessions of an Art Addict* (1980).

To: Noel Coward   15 November 1928
My dear Noel,

I was at your show on the first night but had to leave it at 10.30 to go on the Mauretania. I meant to send you a wireless to tell you how grand I thought it, but dearie, I don't love you so much tha[t] I can go on thinking of you when the Atlantic is making me stand on my head. Love has its limits.

Why I am writing to you is not to express my belated admiration but to tell you of a very nasty situation that has arisen. At various times a lad named Sewell Stokes[2] has blown into my house, has frequently been my guest, has borrowed books from me that he needed for his work. He published about six weeks ago a book called *Pilloried* which I only saw yesterday, which has a chapter called "Gossipary" which gives as malignant an account of me as human pen could put to paper. I am represented as {a} "blousy and actressy" (the word is used) person who perpetually talks about her celebrated friends in a malicious manner. Pages and pages of samples are given and one considerable passage relates to yourself. I am made to refer to you with weary loathing as having been a terrible bore on a trip we made together on the Olympic. The fact is that I told him that I was certain that people had thought that Syrie Maugham, Diana Cooper[3] and you and I and the rest of that group were all engaged in highly sophisticated practices probably of a distinctly vicious nature when we all went off together after dinner and that actually we played quite simple games. I did say that I thought Diana Cooper extremely socially gauche and tiresome but at no time did I express anything regarding you except the greatest admiration and liking. You can ask Mrs Holdsworth [G. B. Stern] if I am likely to have expressed any other emotion. I tell you this because I feel that if you opened the book you might get a distinct facer at finding that somebody to whom you have always been very amiable had spoken ill of you behind your back. Believe me that if I disliked you I should tell you so with all the well known punch and vigour. So that's that.

I thought you were great in *Lilac Time* and *Mazurka*. I did hate going off on the boat. That girl Madeline Gibson[4] struck me as being so really pretty and sweet that you didn't mind that odd flavour of virginity that even the kindliest nature could not help but notice.

I hope you have a grand time for the rest of your stay in New York.

Blessings,

Rebecca West Papers   carbon typescript
Yale University

[1] Sir Noël Pierce Coward (1899–1973), English playwright and composer whose most successful works included *Vortex* (1923), *Hay Fever* (1925), *Private Lives* (1930), and *Blithe Spirit* (1941). His comedies featured a smart, sophisticated set; amorous, amoral themes; and clipped dialogue.

[2] Sewall Stokes (1902–), author of *Pilloried!* (1928), as well as joint author of two plays, *Out of Sight: A Play About Prison* (1937), and *Oscar Wilde: A Play* (1938).

[3] Syrie Maugham, wife of Somerset Maugham. In their marital disputes, West typically took her part.

Lady Diana Olivia Winifred Maud Cooper (1892–1986), actress renowned for her beauty, autobiographer, and hostess in support of the political career of her husband, Duff Cooper. She made her fame and fortune playing the Madonna in *The Miracle* (1923).

[4] Madeline Gibson (1909–), English actress.

To: George Bye   80 Onslow Gardens, S.W. 7
                                         25 January 1929

My dear George,

Thank you for your letter. West Prose Corporation sounds to me like a company formed to build bungalows on some dull place on Long Island called West Prose. I can just see it with three filling stations and five road houses advertising chicken dinner with waffles at $1. I think it is just terrible, and just what we need for the purpose, so I am all for it.[1]

As for the salary that I would require, I want to live this year as much as possible on what I am making over here, so I think what I should like would be say $2500. I should like it to be paid quarterly. I still have, as a matter of fact, something over $3000 debt to the Bank on stocks which I bought, which I want badly to pay off.

I got Jonathan Cape and Harrison Smith's[2] letter about ten days after your wire. I have been dreadfully busy during the last few days and have not answered it but as I have got a contract for two more books with Doran it all looks pretty remote—though these two books will be delivered fairly soon now. Besides their letter is absolutely no concrete business proposal, it is just an announcement that the business is starting, and that is all.

Blessings on you. The business all seems perfectly smooth.

Yours
Rebecca West

P. S. By the way I hear that Louis Golding is telling extraordinary stories of what I said about America. What is all this?

J. O. Brown Collection   typescript with autograph signature
Columbia University

[1] West was in the process of incorporating to avoid income taxes, an idea she got from John Van Druten, Michael Arlen, and Noël Coward (letter to Bye, 5 December 1928, Columbia University). The corporation was dissolved in 1934 (letter to Bye, 1 September 1934, Columbia University).

[2] Harrison Smith (1888–1971), American critic and editor whose works include *Sinclair Lewis* (1925) and *From Main Street to Stockholm: Letters of Sinclair Lewis, 1919–1930* (1952).

To: Winifred Macleod   80 Onslow Gardens, S.W. 7

                                                     [January 1929]

Dear Podge,

Forgive me for not writing to thank you for the exquisite ivory napkin rings. Peggy (my little secretary) whose people have a lot of Eastern things thinks they are a sword and dagger scabbard cut up in slices. I have rarely seen an Eastern design I liked better. It is a most rich gift. I didn't write and thank you because I have been agonizing over the last five thousand words of *Harriet Hume*. This ghastly incubus has been my ruin. I began it on December 1st intending it to be a short story 5,000 words long—it has turned out to be just short of 70,000 words. I have sold no short stories and have been living from hand to mouth. However it has turned out rather good and pretty—I think as new in its ideas as *The Return of the Soldier*. This is fantasy, not a novel. I will come down some time during the next few days—but have now to finish the fair copy of *Harriet* and make the money for my holidays—in the course of the next fortnight. I am going down to see Anthony at Stowe on Sunday. Lettie looks ever so much better and said again and again how lovely it had been to have you with her.

                                      [letter ends sideways in left
                                      margin; no signature]

West, R., MSS   manuscript
Indiana University, Bloomington

To: Anthony West

Villa Mysto
Anthéor
Var, S. France
23 July 1929

Dear Anthony

Write to H. G.—THIS IS IMPORTANT—and say I have told you he wants you to go to Easton with a tutor in September but that you would like to have the tutor here because you don't want to miss the swimming. If you like tell him you would rather go in the Christmas or Easter holidays than now.

Be sure to do this—because the place will be at its best in September—Lady Rhondda[1] and the Melvilles are coming and the Bromfields[2] have asked us to go over to their place at Biarritz.

I will meet you at the pier at Calais Tuesday the 30th! Then we will leap southwards. Oh, the water is so good!

Love

Rebecca West Papers   carbon typescript
Yale University

[1] Margaret Haig Rhondda, Viscountess (1883–1958), suffragette, editor, essayist, and auto-biographer who founded the journal *Time and Tide* (1920), giving West a forum for her political ideas. Her *Leisured Women* (1928) sets the agenda for women following their acquisition of the vote.

[2] Louis Bromfield (1896–1956), American journalist and novelist whose works included *Early Autumn* (1926) and *The Strange Case of Miss Annie Spragg* (1928).

To: Sylvia Lynd

Mysto
Anthéor: Var [S. France]
[31 August 1929]

Dear Sylvia,

Walter Hutchinson has done the strangest things over *Harriet Hume*. It is to come out on September 13th and the proofs were flung at me only a few days ago. There was no chance whatsoever of sending you the proofs for your approval, so I have left the dedication simply "To Sylvia and Robert" and if *Harriet* displeases you you can say that you know naught of it! I hope you will like it in its unpretentious way—it's only an hour's crazy entertainment.

I wish you were converted to the idea of summer holidays in the South of France. This is such a heaven on earth, with rocks at the bottom of the garden from which one steps into fifteen feet of nicely warmed Mediterranean. I would give anything in the world to own this particular villa, which is just as I like it—the property of an old opera singer, entirely decorated with portraits of herself. It must be so funny to sit in a room with portraits of yourself for the last 40 years candidly showing the change from black to red that came about 1895 and the change from red to gold that came about 1902. I am staying here till the end of September. Anthony goes back in about a week's time, not to school but to Easton. I don't know if you know the hell I have been through lately with H. G. I put down £60 of my hard-earned money to adopt Anthony so that he could show an adoption instead of a birth certificate and need not pay strangers' death duties on my estate. H. G. opposed this—alleging that I was claiming the child only because I was jealous of his writing and wanted to wound him in his paternal love, that I never let him see Anthony! [(]He's never seen him in his life except at my suggestion) that I was bringing up Anthony in undesirable "third-rate literary society." I got the certificate in spite of him but as it turned out that all the settlements on Anthony H. G. had very cleverly made revocable I had to promise I would send him to Easton for part of the holidays. This {legal bother} and the fact that I now have to pay all the Stowe school fees is stripping me of every penny. I paid over three hundred pounds last summer for his illness. This of course is only a side lure—what he wants to take from me is Anthony. Now Anthony is no trouble, and a very desirable object he thinks it is an {excellent} ⟨good thing⟩ {idea just} to take him over—after he's never done one single thing for him. The horrible eerie thing is that I can't help feeling the spirit of Jane has entered into him. He isn't just cruel and petulant and greedy as he used to be—there's also that kind of inventive malice with which she used to think out ways of ⟨being⟩ {making} servants and secretaries' wives and people suffer. It is awful that after I thought I had got rid of these nightmare people they come back at me. I have always brought up Anthony to adore H. G. because I'd never thought he'd see anything of him—even last summer he behaved with the most utter callousness about Anthony's illness and only went to see him once during the whole six months he was in a sanitarium. I never thought he'd turn to this new way of tormenting me. It's been bitter learning what sort of stories H. G.'s been telling ⟨me about⟩ {about me} for years—I don't wonder that people like Arnold Bennett have regarded me with disapproval.

Anthony and I had such a lovely time coming down here—we stopped at Dijon. I must confess I love France more and more—though what an insane people! We have neighbours in the next villa who glower ⟨and⟩ {at} us and insult us in every way to such a ⟨way⟩ {degree} that in England would make one go to the nearest police station to report the presence of lunatics. The explanation is that they have a row with the opera singer who let us the villa. On the other hand the servants and the tradesmen are as amusing and kindly and considerate as if one had known them for forty years and had conferred endless benefits on them. The odd thing is that no one says a word about Snowden.[1] It seems distinctly the thing the French understand and (though they are likely to keep it a secret) admire.

I hope you'll like *Harriet*!

Till October,

Yours ever,
Rebecca

Rebecca West Collection   manuscript
University of Tulsa

[1] Philip Snowden, first viscount (1864–1937), chancellor of the Exchequer, ousted along with the Labour Party (1931).

To: A. D. Peters   Mysto
                                                              Anthéor
                                                              Var.
                                                              [1929]

Dear Peter,

I haven't been correspondentially inclined because I've been wrestling with the Gissing preface and I've been badly ragged about my private af-fairs.[1] But today I've been moved to amazement and gratitude by receiving a cheque for £224 on account of *Harriet* which came through Pinker but must be due to you. I can't tell you how grateful I am. As a matter of fact I've just been precipitated into desperate straits financially again by the fact that the

Ladies Home Journal has coolly turned down "Gossip"—American editors simply do not seem to understand what a commission means—chiefly on the grounds that they had really wanted an article about something else! This left me short of another £180, and this cheque of yours has just saved the situation.

Of course I love Whistler's cover—could I buy it, do you think? I don't think anything more perfect could have been done. I'll send you a note thanking him when I finish the Gissing stuff. There isn't another man in the world who could have done it.

I've only seen the *Morning Post* and the *Sunday Times*. ⟨x⟩ They amazed me with their amiability. I wish I could go on writing—but I seem to have every drop of blood drained out of my body by worry. I got a letter from H. G. praising *Harriet Hume* but expressing wonder that I should have been capable of writing it in my state of deplorable abandonment to sloth and bad habits—and I see there is picture of me (I recognize it from certain ⟨details⟩{phrases} he has used to me) as Pomander Poole in his new serial in *Nash's*[2] ⟨x⟩{which} is utterly insane. I can't tell you what it's like to have Anthony at Easton with this man who's turning out this stuff about me. Forgive this complaint—but don't think I'm lazy if I don't write!

Bless you for all you have done!

R.W.

Rebecca West Collection   manuscript
University of Tulsa

---

[1] George Robert Gissing (1857–1903), English novelist best known for his works concerning poverty and failure, including *New Grub Street* (1891), *Born in Exile* (1892), and *Odd Women* (1893). He was a friend of H. G. Wells. West wrote an introduction for an edition of Gissing's first novel, *Workers in the Dawn* (1880), but the work was apparently not published (1930).

[2] Pomander Poole was a character in Wells's novel *The Autocracy of Mr Parham* (1930).

To: Bertrand Russell   [Agay, France, September 1929]
Dear Mr. Russell,

I cut off from England in a state of such despair that I couldn't see anybody. Otherwise I had very much wanted to see you and tell you about a problem that has vexed me very much. Now other circumstances have turned up, and although I'm still too stupid to tell you about things I'm driven to write to you about it after all.

May I tell you the story of my life? I'm afraid it amounts almost to that.

I left H. G. in 1923 when Anthony was nine years old, for various good and sufficient reasons. He demanded from me rather more than a husband usually demands in the way of continual help and care, he would give me only the barest amount of money, he prevented me from doing much work and the money I earned, such as I could do, he insisted on my spending immediately on the household expenses, he was extremely bad-tempered and cruel in case of illness or any difficulty arising out of our illegal relationship, and, above all, he was jealous and hostile to my son. He grudged every penny he spent on him, and even objected to my spending my own earnings on him. He was furious if I devoted any time to the child, and he loved exposing the child to strangers by advertising that he was his illegitimate child. This is to give you only the bare outlines of the relationship. The details would persuade you that I was compelled to leave him out of consideration for Anthony.

I had several times tried to leave him before but I never succeeded till I went to America for six months. During my absence he caused ghastly trouble by going to Anthony's school and parading his parenthood before the other children so that some of them tormented the child about it. But when I came back things went along fairly indifferently until last year.

Last year H. G. took a violent loathing to me. I don't know why. He hadn't seen me for several months. Just about this time Anthony fell dangerously ill with a novel form of pneumonia which was at first mistaken for T. B. H. G. came to see him when he was most dangerously ill, but left for the Continent and sent no word of enquiry for five weeks. At the end of that time I wrote and told him that Anthony was better and got a curt letter of acknowledgment. During the six months Anthony was in the sanatorium he visited him once, for about an hour. He made no move to pay the expenses of the illness, which amounted to over £300, until I sent him a bill for £30 and told him that he had got to pay it because I had no more money. He paid that bill but offered no further assistance. (I had better explain that my sole private income derived from H. G. amounts to less that £300 a year).

During the autumn I was more and more conscious of an insane antagonism, which came to a head at Christmas. Gyp and Marjorie Wells asked

Anthony down to Easton, either for Christmas or a later weekend. As we had made our Christmas plans I accepted the alternative and received innumerable insane letters abusing me for keeping Anthony with me for Christmas. He also refused to pay Anthony's school fees for Stowe unless he was described at school as H. G. Wells' illegitimate son. I was pursued by letters so insulting and accusing me of such unheard of offences—such as having wasted enormous sums of money he had given me and having prevented him from seeing Anthony (he has never in his life seen Anthony except at my suggestion) that I went to Charles Russell[1] and said that he must carry on all communications for me.

It happened that Russell advised me to adopt Anthony legally to save death duties and save him various minor inconveniences. This I did. It should have cost me about £50. H. G. turned up and opposed it. And what alarms me is that he instructed his counsel to bring forward all these stories about me—which shows that he believes them. I was of course able to produce all his letters showing that he had never been denied access to Anthony, so it didn't matter. Also he assured the court that I was an unsuitable person to bring up Anthony, and exposed him to the society of persons who were not respectable.

This did not impress the court—but what did was that the £8,000 he has settled on Anthony (which is mostly tied up till he is 21) are all the subject of revocable settlements. Therefore I had to buy him off. I had to promise to let Anthony spend part of his holidays with H. G. and to consult with H. G. about his education, and to make him one of Anthony's guardians in my will.

Now this last is what strikes me as serious. His behaviour seems to me insane. I am aware from my knowledge of him that he has a violent anti-sex complex like Tolstoy's—You punish the female who evokes your lust. But it seems to me to be reaching ⟨x⟩ demented extremes. I hear from the lady with whom he lives at present (who is quite mad) that he frequently hits her and gives her black eyes, and so on, which is surely not done in our set. (This was not cited as evidence of cruelty, but as evidence that they were living a rich and satisfying life.) Also this month has shown him quite unbalanced. He went down to Stowe before the term ended and created more trouble, and has removed Anthony to Easton from this perfectly lovely villa for the last three weeks of his holidays. (The boy adores him—I've always brought him up to do so, which I rather regret now.) This has all been done with an extraordinary and insane air of a saint struggling with the personification of evil. He has shown in every way of late the most extraordinary unwillingness to let anybody have their own way. For example, he opposed his son Frank's marriage most virulently on the ground that the selected female was common, and then summarily forbade them to have children.

You may perceive that I do not feel the smallest confidence in leaving H. G. as guardian of my only child. I think that if I died he would get bored with the boy, and would get his fun by frustrating him at any crisis.

Therefore—

I wonder if you would be Anthony's testamentary guardian also? I haven't a soul I can turn to in this difficulty. The man who would have attended to it out of affection for me died two years ago. My sisters are silly and inexperienced. I have few friends who are sufficiently interested and enlightened to understand children. I am sure you would always want an adolescent to have just the freedom that I would. Obviously you would be the best person in the world. It plainly wouldn't be any adequate compensation but I would also provide in my will that so long as you were Anthony's guardian you could have so much a year paid into the funds of your school. We could settle the amount later.

Would you do this? I know it's a lot to ask—but I feel you are a really merciful human being—and Anthony ought not to be left in the ⟨x⟩ care of this lunati[c].

I'm here till the beginning of October.

Yours ever,

Rebecca West

I haven't explained this well—but the point about having you as guardian is that H. G. is afraid of you and wouldn't dare to oppose you or do anything in your sight that was manifestly reactionary.[2]

Rebecca West Papers   carbon typescript copy[3]
Yale University

[1] West's solicitor.
[2] Several fragmentary carbon typescripts of a letter to Gordon Ray (4–30 July 1972 University of Tulsa) and one actually sent (7 July 1972, Pierpont Morgan Library) relate to this letter:

I have dug out the Russell letter, and after not having seen it since 1967 I am shocked by it. I wish I had not written it. My excuse is that I then believed Bertrand Russell to be an angelic being, and a real friend. My only other excuse is that I was at the end of my tether. The trouble is that I cannot ignore it because after I refused to let Russell publish it in 1967 it went into the Russell archives, and will presumably emerge in the fulness of time.

I am sorry that I wrote this letter, but not because anything in it is untrue. But it is the only record of things I had suppressed and made light of, and I would have been pleased to go on doing just that. I wish I had not said that "he insisted on my spending immediately on the household expenses" the money I had earned, because he afterwards made up for this handsomely. I have no complaints against his generosity in the long run—I have asked you to take into consideration his really shakey financial sense. (⟨29⟩ {30} July, University of Tulsa)

[3] West denied Russell permission to publish and returned the copy of her 1929 letter that he had sent (16 June 1967, University of Tulsa). She must have retained another copy. Russell's immediate response was to postpone a decision, though ultimately he did not accept the role of guardian (letter to West, 10 September 1929, University of Tulsa). In this letter, Russell worried that Wells might regard his guardianship with hostility, and that there would be domestic friction with Mrs. Russell (who liked Wells), if Russell had to oppose him. Russell suggested that he should probably discuss the matter with a third party, such as West's lawyer. In his letter Russell also listed a series of experiences that had contributed to his dislike of Wells. This had begun with an unpleasant weekend visit in 1905, increased with the Amber Reeves affair, and grown further owing to the attacks Wells had made on Russell during World War I. Russell offered his own psychological analysis of Wells, which differed from West's. He attributed Wells's presumed antisex complex to ambition and vanity, rather than to a Tolstoyan wish to punish the person who evoked his lust. Russell also felt that much of Wells's recent hostility could have resulted from remorse once he learned about Jane Wells's cancer.

To: Irita Van Doren   80 Onslow Gardens, S.W. 7

                                                               [autumn 1929]

Dear Irita,

Cut this as you like and do not curse me. I *could* go on for another 4000 words—let that be my only excuse. Listen to what happened—your letters went to France and stayed there. I thought I just had to write reviews—and you could have knocked me down with a fevver [*sic*] when I found I had to write four general articles. I found I could write of nothing but my sick loathing for every blighter writing except James Joyce whom I think a pretentious nitwit but who has guts, guts of the moonlight, beautiful guts, as Lewis Carroll nearly wrote. I feel the interest in these articles is much too special and limited but I hadn't time to pull out of my mood. Give me another chance in a year's time and I will do better.

I have had three months down with advanced anaemia—millions of pi-qures and all the liver in the world. I am now supposed to be half well, but I feel marvellous, except that I hate all but about three books. I understand so well what these Faustian half-wits mean when they say they want to express and not to communicate. Who is there to communicate with or to? This is ungracious because everybody I care about has been handsome about *Harriet Hume*. My life has been complicated by the fact that since I finished *Harriet* I have been unable to write anything with pleasure except masses of *very* bad poetry of the sort I particularly despise.

As a result of the reflection of this on my material affairs I became engaged to a man named Cohen, but I couldn't go through with it. Since then however I have discovered that earth has few negative pleasures greater than not being engaged to a man named Cohen.

I'm writing at 4 o'clock in the morning, having just finished this article. I have really done this all against the grain dripping with dissatisfaction because I can't say what I mean. It's a great mistake ever starting to mean something different from everything else.

The [Leviathan?] *should* have got you that last article in time, but it winced so under the burden that it didn't put to sea for two days.

Do come over soon! I may come over next autumn for two months.

Bless you
RW

Irita Van Doren Papers   manuscript
Library of Congress

To: William Troy[1]   80 Onslow Gardens, S.W. 7
                                              [19 January 1930]

Dear Sir,

I was amused to come across the phrase—"Rebecca West discussed rather tamely on modern marriage"—in your paragraph on *Blast* in "The Story of the Little Magazines." It may interest you to know that that story was written in my teens to amuse some friends, as a pastiche of the stories Austin Harrison was then publishing in the *English Review*. It was published in *Blast*—a publication of which I knew nothing—by Wyndham Lewis[2]—

whom I never met till years after—for no other reason than that Wyndham Lewis found the manuscript in the chest of drawers in the spare room of Violet Hunt & Ford Madox Hueffer's home at Selsey, a week or so after I had left. But I was literary editor of the *Egoist* for some months at the beginning of its career, and set its tone before I left: a fact I would rather you had mentioned than my fictional appearance in *Blast*.

In case you are reprinting your essay—you have passed T. *H* Hulme instead of T. E. Hulme.[3] My own pages seem to breed misprints so I have a sympathetic feeling when I see one!

Yours sincerely,
Rebecca West

Léonie Adams papers   manuscript
Yale University

[1] William Troy (1903–1961), American literary critic for the *Nation* and the *Partisan Review* whose works include *T. S. Eliot, Grand Inquisitor* (1934) and *The Lawrence Myth* (1938).

[2] (Percy) Wyndham Lewis (1882–1957), Canadian-born British artist, critic, and novelist. He edited the journal *Blast* (1914–1915), which advanced the Vorticist movement. His novels include *Tarr* (1914) and *The Revenge for Love* (1937). Writing to West soon after the publication of *The Strange Necessity*, he agrees with much of what she says about Joyce, including his relation to tradition (21 July 1928, Yale University). Lewis's *Time and Western Man* (1927) attacked Joyce and Stein. Lewis was attracted to Fascism in the 1930s, and in critiquing civilization, he cast himself in the role of the "enemy."

[3] Thomas Ernest Hulme (1883–1917), poet, essayist, and philosopher whose doctrines influenced literary Imagism and Vorticism—the latter advocated by *Blast* editor Wyndham Lewis.

To: Henry Andrews   Raphael
                                                                             17 Avenue Kléber 17
                                                                             Paris
                                                                             [spring 1930]

Dear Henry,

I knew you were trying to get through this morning but they kept on calling me and then saying it was a mistake. The journey yesterday was exquisite only so long as we were in England. The crossing was as rough as I have ever known it—suitcases lunging all over the place—and when we got to France it was too hot. It was fun going the same journey to Amiens. They were very kind and civil when we got here—it is a friendly hotel. Then at night I went to dinner with Tom Beer[1] who had Tony de Sanchez and his wife (he's in Morgan's and most intelligent) and Chester Dales (they have the finest private collection of modern art in the world.)[2] After dinner to my great joy they suggested going round to Jean Lurçat's studio.[3] Don't on any account miss his show at the Lefevre Galleries—it starts on May 6th, I think. It's queer stuff but quite authentic. It was fascinating seeing his work in various stages and he had done these panels of tapestry which were more gorgeous than any tapestry I've ever seen since the XVth century. Miss West's grammar is here unfortunate. It was a lovely evening and I won't tell you about it now because I have people crowding round. I hope this is the last Spring I shall ever spend apart from you. I hate not sharing it with you. But everything even Lurçat's studio seems of less value because it isn't shared with you. I'm writing in such difficulties—but you know what I mean.

Love,

Rebecca Cicily

Rebecca West Papers   manuscript
Yale University

[1] Thomas Beer (1889–1940), American novelist, short-story writer, and biographer of Stephen Crane. He is best known for *The Mauve Decade* (1926), a witty ridicule of late nineteenth-century Americans.
[2] Dale gave his collection to the National Gallery, Washington, D.C., which named its Chester Dale Fellowships in Art History in his honor.
[3] Jean Lurçat (1892–1966), French painter who turned to the design and weaving of tapestry.

To: Henry Andrews   Mysto
                                                     Anthéor
                                                     Var: France
                                                     Sunday [spring 1930]

My Dearest Henry:

I'm back in bed with another attack of bronchitis—and how I hate it! But the doctor says that if I'm very careful I'll be able to travel on Friday, and I shall try my best. I had a fatiguing and annoying day at Nice on Thursday.

My agent was worrying me to get a contract sworn before the American consul and send it back to him as soon as possible. So I wired to the American consul at Nice asking when it was convenient for me to come to his office. I got back the amorous sounding wire—"Come tomorrow before three—Honey"—so I obeyed the summons. It is a two-and-a half hours journey and this I found tiring, although the usually dull flat road ⟨with⟩ {between} Cannes and Nice was glorious with poppies and mallows and purple thistles. But when we got there we found the American consulate shut up—with only the imbecile Mr Honey who was exactly like a fat and half-witted old baby waiting on the doorstep to confess he had sent off the telegram in momentary forgetfulness of the fact that the office was going to be shut up for the next two days (for Ascension Day and Memorial Day). He insisted on making me sign the contract (I think in all the wrong places) and retain it in order that the clerk who knew about these things (he knew nothing) could affix the seals in two days time. After we had reluctantly consented to this possibly illegal procedure we—Pamela [Frankau] and I—lunched at the Ruhl on blue trout and fraises du bois,[1] with a terrific sea pounding on the Promenade des Anglais, and turned homeward. I've stopped for a cup of tea at Joseph Négres in Cannes—a confiserie with a garden that I love—a slit of ground beneath tall houses with green shutters all palm-trees and bamboos—pure 1870 Cannes. There I enquired about a litter of kittens that had obviously been about to bless the shop cat the last time I was there, and was told ."On les a supprimés . . ."[2] It's a ruthless language. Well, I got home just in time to see poor G. B. [Stern] fall on the rocks and cut her knee, so badly that the doctor had to be called to stitch it, and he has forbidden her to walk for a week. There's a disaster! Since then I have felt very miserable and tired, and couldn't get on with an article I was trying to write, and this morning I woke up again with a temperature and a pain under the shoulderblades. I am being very good, though, and I ought to be well enough to travel on Friday.

I liked your last long letters so much. I was amused by the young man who took you out to dinner to talk about his love-affairs on the sound assumption you knew a great deal about love. He sounded so much less nice than you are that I can't help feeling a little sorry for the girl. But this involves me in being sorry for all girls—except myself. I am glad you are so nice about Harriet.[3] She has had such a strange story—of people getting near her and winning a place by her simply in order to gratify something jealous in themselves by refusing her the tenderness and honour she ought to have—that that self-assertion is pardonable. It is, I know quite well, as "shymaking"—to use Evelyn Waugh's[4] word—as anything I know, and you are a darling to get behind it.

I am looking forward to being with you, dearest! This month has been one of endless disappointment. I've done virtually no work save finish the *Bookman* book, and I had counted on getting on with my story. This bronchitis makes me feel tired and weak, and I loathe the South in bad weather. I want to come back and curl up close to you and have it all made up to me by the pleasure of being with you. I love you so very much. I shan't make any engagements at all for town before I get there. I feel as if the gods had wanted to say about me *on l'a supprimée* and only you could stop them. I can't tell you how safe and comforting the thought of you is.

I suppose you will get this on Tuesday. If all's well you will be talking to me on the telephone on Saturday morning at the Savoy. It will be lovely to hear your voice again

Yours ever—with all my love,
Rebecca Cicily

Rebecca West Papers   manuscript
Yale University

[1] Wild strawberries.
[2] They were suppressed (i.e., killed).
[3] Harriet Cohen, pianist and the model for the title character of *Harriet Hume*.
[4] Evelyn Waugh (1903–1966), English novelist, journalist, and travel writer whose works include *Decline and Fall* (1928), *Vile Bodies* (1930), and *Brideshead Revisited* (1945) and reflect his conversion to Catholicism. *Sword of Honour* (1965) records wartime experiences in Crete and Yugoslavia.

To: George Bye   80 Onslow Gardens, S.W. 7
                                                  [30 August 1930]

Dear George Bye,

My secretary left me in France to go to some friends in Germany. I posted her a long letter to Bellancy and an article on a book by Eve Lavallière[1] and told her to type them and post them off. I imagined it would go off by last

Saturday's mail. It is only today that I hear that though I registered them she never got them. Damn careless of me I know—but just at this moment I am damned careless because I'm almost dead with overwork, arising out of a certain situation. I blush to confess it but at my advanced age I am being led to the altar. I have been moved to this extreme step by the fact that a man named Henry Maxwell Andrews insists on it and anyway seems to be the nicest man I ever met, barring you, of course, sweetheart—So I've acceded to the suggestion. He says he's going to look after me and let me write, so it ought to be grand. This has rather come to a crisis since I got back—because it has become unsporting of me not to take charge of him at once, whereas it had seemed up till now that we could safely leave it till Spring without hurting ourselves. But he is in a banking house and he is working (like all bankers over here just now) about fourteen hours a day trying to pick up the pieces—and it's too much for him dashing between here and his place which is the other side of London. So I have to look for a house. I guess I've found one already, but until I get that settled I'll be a bit distrait. I'll get that done very soon however.

This is all a dead secret. If a reporter comes to see me before I'm married it'll be the halter for me and not the altar. I feel black death about publicity.

Good news about *The Return [of the Soldier]* {talkie} film-rights. Bless you for everything.

But do you think I will ever fit into the *Outlook*? It seems so damned earnest. But my first outside was, so perhaps It'll be all right. They aren't quite as literary as I'd like 'em either. But still we'll push on.

> Yours ever,
> R. W.

J. O. Brown Collection   manuscript
Columbia University

---

[1] West's "Penance of Eve Lavallière" concerning *Ma Conversion* (1930) appeared in *Outlook* (24 December 1930).

The young Rebecca in costume,
1909. Used by permission of
McFarlin Library, University of
Tulsa.

Winifred Fairfield as a young woman.
Used by permission of Alison Selford.

Letitia Fairfield in World War I uniform.
Used by permission of Alison Selford.

George Bernard Shaw, from a picture
postcard he sent to West. © Robert de
Smet. Used by permission of McFarlin
Library, University of Tulsa.

G. B. Stern, Rebecca West, and H. G. Wells, circa 1917. Used by permission of McFarlin Library, University of Tulsa.

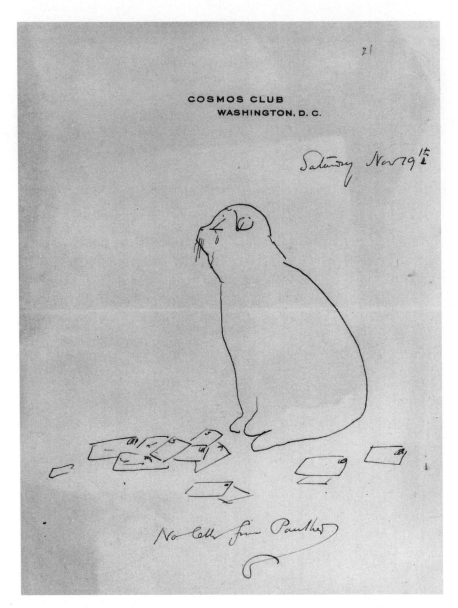

"No Letter from Panther," a "picshua" by H. G. Wells, Yale University. Used by permission of A. P. Watt Ltd. on behalf of the literary executors of the Wells estate.

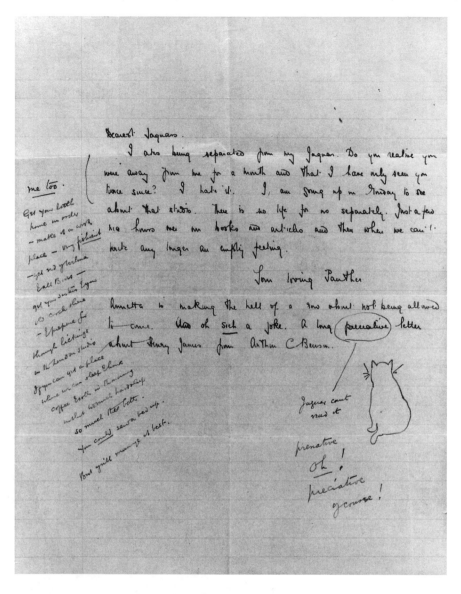

Letter from West to Wells, with his additions, including cat, 1916, Yale University. Used by permission of the Wells estate.

Rebecca West, circa 1923. Used
by permission of Kit Wright.

Max Beaverbrook. Used by permission of the House of Lords
Records Office.

PART THREE

1930-1945

Ric, Rac, and the Fight
Against Fascism

WEST MARRIED HENRY ANDREWS IN AN ANGLICAN CHURCH CEREMONY ON
1 November 1930. In a letter to her sister Lettie from Genoa, West reported
on the honeymoon. Not only were the older sections of the city glorious, but
"Boof is so sweet to travel you'd hardly believe! So altogether it's lovely." The
only sour note was in reaction to the "illiterate idiots" of the newspaper corps
who noted the absence of "obey" in her vows: "Had they never heard of the
Revised Version of the marriage service? I suppose they just had to look for
some aggressive aspect of the situation until they found it!" (November 1930,
Indiana University, Bloomington).

West's daily life expanded to encompass her new husband's business and
family concerns, and under his influence she took new interest in describing
art and architecture. His German background made him a good negotiator
for the banking firm Schroders, which gave him responsibility for reorganiz-
ing the Berlin Power and Light Company. Henry traveled frequently to Germany, sometimes in Rebecca's company, and thus she could gauge the rise of
fascism from their own experiences. On a visit to Berlin, Rebecca reported to
her sister Winnie (autumn 1931, Indiana University, Bloomington):

> I never loathed any place so much as Berlin. The people have all the bad
> characteristics of the Scotch without any of their virtues. They have that
> habit which used to madden you in Scotland—and which I think is
> found nowhere else in the world—of keeping you out in the street at the
> garden gate until they pull a lever indoors. They are perpetually in a state
> of inflamed exaltation ⟨because⟩ {over their} own commonsense and
> other people's lack of it. This, considering that they have got themselves
> into the worst scrape the world has ever known and are trying to get
> everybody who comes along to help them out, ⟨x⟩ {is} faintly irritating.

By late 1933, Henry was at odds with his employers. He resigned when they
replaced a Jewish employee of his choosing with a Nazi. Rebecca lamented
the death of her "great surgeon" in Berlin, a man of "a most angelic character" who was "tortured to suicide by the Nazis, being a Jew" (23 May 1934,
private collection). Both Ric (Henry) and Rac (Rebecca), as they called
themselves, were wary of the economic and military exploits of the Germans
and concerned themselves increasingly with the welfare of Jews and refugees
from various affected nations.

The couple lived briefly with Henry's mother and then moved to a modern flat near Regent's Park, in Portman Square, London. The location was chosen for its proximity to Henry's demanding uncle Ernest, who had funded Henry's education after his father's death. After Uncle Ernest's death in July 1936, Henry inherited his sizable estate, though as the letters testify, he brought few resources into the marriage. In 1939 the Andrews found the place where they settled for the remainder of their long marriage—Ibstone House, the surviving portion of a Regency-era manor located about an hour from London on the one side, half an hour from Oxford on the other, in the Chiltern Hills of Buckinghamshire. Its situation, dominating a great basin of fields and woods, was ideal for walking as well as farming. The farming operation and expansive grounds were to provide a mixture of delight and frustration. Henry's lavish expenditures and his inefficient management of personnel would become a topic in many of Rebecca's letters.

Anthony West did not qualify for Oxford, despite the years of careful tutoring and private schools. He did go on to other things—painting, writing, and managing a dairy farm. In 1936, he married the artist Katharine Church, thereby establishing a whole new arena of family negotiations for West. He did not join the armed forces during the war, though West kept writing to her friends that he was on the verge of enlisting in various forms of service.

Assisted by her agent George Bye, West kept up her lucrative commissions in America. Bye was sometimes treated to intimate disclosures as Rebecca aged:

> What I feel is (to be perfectly [honest] between you and me) that sitting here cold-sober in the autumn of my days (my 41st birthday is happening right *now*) I realise that sleeping with people is a whole lot of fun but it doesn't amount to a row of pins (after a period of a few hours— fill⟨ing⟩ in the time yourself, George) unless you sleep with someone who is capable of a grand attitude to life and is better than you. I've found it extremely hard to express this, because I really cannot bring myself to describe my early amatory exploits, and I've found the second part hard to express without priggishness and sentimentality. But hell maybe I am a prig and sentimental. (16 December 1933, Columbia University)

She kept a portion of her revenues in the United States and by late 1934 was eager to travel there again and be with old friends. The letters report on new writing projects, *A Letter to a Grandfather* (1933, commissioned by Virginia Woolf), *St Augustine* (1933), *The Harsh Voice* (1935), and *The Thinking Reed* (1936).

As the thirties progressed, West turned, in many of her letters as in her other writing, toward cultural and political analysis. She describes the differences among the factions in the Spanish Civil War, Ireland's position during the war, the Italianization of Albania, a long series of accommodations to Hitler, and wartime conditions in Britain. Henry's interests in art and architecture are indulged in her letters home. West launched into a new international phase with British Council lecture tours begun in 1935—the most notable of which took her to Yugoslavia. Her detailed travel letters from a total of three visits to Yugoslavia anticipate *Black Lamb and Grey Falcon* (1941)—the work considered by many her masterpiece. The accounts of her first visit, which vary tremendously according to their audience, hint at various intrigues, including the aggressive sexual advances made by Stanislav Vinaver, who was also her valued guide. Her long, fussy missive to the British Council (parts of which have been condensed here), suggested how its programs could be improved. To her editors at Viking Press, West defended her attacks on Germans for their attitudes toward Slavic culture. She worried that "the Germans have led out into Roumania very large numbers of Yugoslav soldiers and boys down to the age of ten. These are presumably to be treated as the young Poles have been treated" (letter to Marshall Best, 8 May 1941, Viking Press archive). West's concern over Yugoslavia continued, extending to its refugees, some of whom she and Henry housed after their flight from fascism. She expresses her indignation over Britain's acceptance of Tito.

Notables reported on or to in West's letters from this period include D. H. Lawrence, Virginia Woolf, Harold Nicolson, Naomi Mitchison, Alexander Woollcott, Dorothy Thompson (a new confidante), Sinclair Lewis, Somerset Maugham, and V. S. Pritchett. Her observation of Mrs. Simpson and the Prince of Wales betrays a fascination with aristocrats and nourishes her persistent theme of the winding down of the British empire.

To: Gerald Bullett[1]   80 Onslow Gardens, S.W.
                                               11 December 1930
Dear Mr Bullett,

   You once wrote me a charming little note thanking me for some very inconsiderable service I had done you—which I didn't answer because I was then in very great trouble of various sorts. Since then I've read more than one book and article by you which has made me regret that I should have laid myself open to the suspicion of rudeness in the eyes of the author. So I now very gladly take the opportunity you have given me by the review you have written of the little book on Lawrence in the *Fortnightly Review*.[2] I am so glad you quoted and approved the ⟨sentence⟩ passage about *Lady Chatterley's Lover*, because I think it was such a great and endearing effort of Lawrence's mind, and I am very conscious of how it wasn't honored by the world in the horrible reviews I am getting of this book—⟨x⟩ not that I attach any great importance to it as far as my own literary powers are concerned, because I wrote it as my monthly letter to the American *Bookman* and it was entirely Secker's idea to reprint it. ⟨x⟩ What I hate is the sniggering about Lawrence and the actual candid joy in his death which is expressed in review after review—particularly in the illustrated weeklies and the provincial papers. The tone is savage and indecent. There is a kind of lewd hysteria about it—which declares itself more unpleasantly still in the personal letters, most of them anonymous, that I am receiving. He was right—he was and is hated. And that he was hated by the ⟨wrong⟩ vile people makes one revere him more—but the frightful vitality of their vileness, and the amount of it, makes one despair—if it wasn't for such pleasant reviews as your own.[3]

   Thank you so much. I hope your work goes well in every way.

                                        Yours sincerely,
                                        Cicily Andrews
                                        (Rebecca West)

Rebecca West Collection   manuscript
Yale University

[1] Gerald William Bullett (1893–1958), English essayist and novelist who wrote *The Progress of Kay* while serving in the RAF (1916). His other works include *The History of Egg Pandervil* (1928), *The Jury* (1935), *Cricket in Heaven* (1949), and critical studies of the writings of G. K. Chesterton and Walt Whitman and of modern fiction as a genre.

[2] Martin Secker published West's *D. H. Lawrence* (1930).

[3] Through Norman Douglas, West met D. H. Lawrence at a hotel outside Florence in 1921, as described in her elegy. Another account occurs in a letter to the novelist Francis Brett Young (8 June 1921, University of Birmingham): "I *admire* D. H. Lawrence. His beard was very thin and waved about his head like a scarf and his clothes had *not* been washed with Lux (see Well Roman advertisement). He must have them sent home to an English laundry to get shrunk. His voice was all you reported it to be. I wish you'd heard the story of how he hated the Sicilians—culminating in (I indicate high and low notes. 'ᐱDo you know˅ I can go into ᐱany antique˅ shop in ᐱTarquinia˅ and buy ᐱanything I ˅like at my ᐱown price˅—at my ᐱown price˅ and howᐱ do I do˅ it? By taunting them with their ᐱlack of ˅virility˅ by taunting them with their lack of ᐱvirility.˅' Jessie, we must try and do a little shopping on this principle when you come to London. He was going to Baden-Baden to meet Freda. He only stayed in Florence a day and a half."

To: Virginia Woolf   15 Orchard Court
                                                      Portman Square, N.W. 1
                                                      26 November 1931

Dear Mrs Woolf,

Your letter went out to France, and just stayed there, enviably enough, in a comfortable hotel on Agay Bay, until I happened to write to the manager the other day. I cannot tell you how flattered I am by the invitation to write a letter for the series. There is something I would like to do for the series. It is a letter to a grandfather, from a woman whose family has the power of seeing visions and who has just seen what is this age's form of what would have in other ages been a vision of the Gadama or Christ.[1] I could have it done in January—it would be about 4000 words. Would that do?

Again I must thank you for the invitation and apologise for the delay. More than a dozen letters, including one useful cheque, were held up in France.

                                        Yours sincerely,
                                        Rebecca West

Hogarth Press archive   manuscript
Reading University

[1] *A Letter to a Grandfather*, published by Hogarth Press (1933).

To: H. G. Wells[1]   15 Orchard Court
                                            Portman Square, London, W. 1
                                            [1932]

Dear H. G.,

This is all very startling about Aunt Letty. She is indeed awful, poor thing, and lives in a state of shame about all living beings (not especially about me and Anthony, whom indeed she wistfully admires) except my repulsive little niece Alison [Selford] and a few crazy Catholic friends.[2] I find her a fearful trial—but she plays no part in Anthony's life whatsoever. For years he has never seen her more than an hour or two at a time at rare intervals, and I have quite frankly owned to ⟨them⟩ {him} that I find her a dreadful trial. He has never exchanged {two words} with her alone for years—it is five years since I refused to let her spend any part of the holidays with us—and, as Henry finds it difficult to be civil to her for more than ten minutes, she certainly doesn't create the atmosphere here. I can't help having her in for a meal on such festivities as Christmas Day as she is lonely and elderly, but I don't think that that need make Anthony feel he is "being thwarted, apologised for, and forced into an attitude of genteel atonement." I find her so maddening myself that for years I have ⟨refused to let her split my part of our⟩ {come between her and Anthony on every possible} occasion.

Nobody so far as I know regards Anthony as an Unfortunate Accident. Except to very stupid people, who feel a peculiarly bitter resentment against him, he is most attractive. Henry admires him greatly and thinks he is a budding genius, and most people he meets here seem to take a real liking to him. He certainly can't be under any delusion that he is not the principal thing in my life.

As for the educational business, I don't think I quite like your tone. "I've interfered very little in his education so far because I have trusted to your love for and pride in him." Gammon and spinach![3] You interfered very little because you couldn't be bothered. I have in my time received a large number of letters from you, and when I was going through them not long ago picking out the amusing ones with drawings, to leave to Anthony, I was struck by the very large number which referred to Anthony with indifference and hostility. A letter written when Anthony was six months old upbraiding me for not letting Anthony be adopted by someone, on the ground that you found it so boring to come and see me in a country house where there was no tennis court. Letters expressing rage because I had to look after Anthony because his school was closed ⟨with⟩ {for} mumps. Letters in answer to three of mine begging you to let me remove Anthony from St Piran's because I thought he was unhappy, expressing complete indifference and saying Anthony was not worth while taking any trouble over. A letter in answer to mine saying that I must stay in America because my contract had been interrupted by illness and I had to stay on an extra month, and asking you to go and see Anthony, refusing on the ground that you had been to see him once, and could not be bothered to go again. The financial letters, showing how you grudged every penny of yours or even mine that was spent on Anthony, are also interesting. There is no reason why Anthony should see these letters (I hope he never will) if it can possibly be avoided. But he certainly will if there is any trouble made by the suggestion that you have always been a loving father separated from your child by me.

So leave that out in future. As you know I've always wanted you to take an interest in Anthony, and I'm delighted that you do, and I'll welcome any useful suggestion about education. I think Stowe was thoroughly bad—the food poor, the staff (as their reports showed) thoroughly silly, the method of Latin teaching contemptible. On the other hand, the climate was mild, much milder than most schools. But this crammer is supposed to teach Latin remarkably well, it is a quiet place, only two other boys, and it was suggested by Roy Harrod of Christchurch, who is a brilliant person in touch with all the best Continental economists. I must ask you, for Anthony's sake, to make all suggestions through me. I know that it will irritate you to hear, but the fact is that both in regard to Anthony's public school and University education several people of acknowledged standing have refused to have anything to do with Anthony because it might involve them in correspondence with you. Doubtless this feeling is very unjust, but we cannot hold up Anthony's education till we remove it.

I know this letter will offend you, and I grieve, for though I know you are a great humbug I also know you're a great man. Nor do I see any real reason why we should wrangle over Anthony's education, as obviously he is going to follow his own line, and if he gets to Oxford he gets put in touch with the means of self-education. He is so near to finding his special means of expression through writing and painting that the more general subjects of education mean little to him. I am quite confident about his ultimate state, but he needs help through this period. You can go on sympathising with him over Aunt Letty—that would be best—but his feeling for her springs from some remoter rage. And certainly you needn't blame me for exposing him to her influence, for I don't think he ever sees her more than five times a year, {at most} and then casually.

Yours ever,
Rebecca

Rebecca West Papers   manuscript
Yale University

[1] A typescript copy with variants also exists (University of Tulsa).
[2] The typescript copy omits the words *repulsive* and *Catholic* from this sentence.
[3] The typescript substitutes "This is nonsense" for the "gammon and spinach."

To: Ruth Lowinsky   15 Orchard Court
                                               Portman Square, London W. 1
                                               [misdated] October 1930 [1932]
Dear Ruth,

I've just got back from my lecture tour and I feel as yet completely dead, in fact I have repaired to bed to-day.

I hear from Miss Shimmel that you are not as well as I hoped you would be by this time. Forgive my bothering you about this, but it is urgent. I have just been rung up and told about the fate of a {German} Jewish Analyst, Miss Edith Jacobsen.[1] She has continued at her work up till now although most analysts have fled the country. She went on with her work for the reason that she had no money at all and would have had to leave the country absolutely penniless. A short time ago one of her patients was arrested for being concerned in a Communist plot. Now she has been arrested and is being held for interrogation—in other words the Nazis think that, as she is his analyst he must have told her everything about his life, and you can guess how they will try to get it out of her. I am told by people who ought to know that the Nazis do not care a fig about exposure in the Press, and that the only way to do anything is to get hold of a "friend of Germany" and put it to them that the matter is causing a good deal of criticism in England. I dare not follow through this procedure with Enid Bagnold[2] because Henry is in Germany at this moment, and I do not believe she could keep her stupid trap shut as to where she got the information. I know that you know her, and that you do not go to Germany, so could you possibly write her a letter saying that you have heard these facts and that she would be in a position to find out the truth and add that you suppose that the usual routine will be gone through, and the Nazis will say that no such person ever existed, but that if you are pressed you can produce all sorts of people who have known Miss Jacobsen, and they would be quite satisfied if they could see her in her home in Berlin.

If you don't want to do this yourself can you think of any other friend of Lady Jones who would do it? Will you leave my name out all the time because of Henry? Pray God we {I meant Andrews, but we could extend the prayer to England—how can we have anything to do with these cannibals?}[3] soon sever all connection with this horrible country.

Henry will be back on Sunday, I hope, and if you and Tommy can come and dine on Wednesday we shall be so pleased.

Yours ever,

Rebecca

Rebecca West Collection   typescript with autograph signature
University of Tulsa

[1] I have not been able to establish definitely the fate of Miss Jacobson. The 1986 "Gedenk-buch" (memorial book) of victims from Germany lists an Edith Jacobsohn (the spelling is thus different), born 18 June 1900 and resident in Berlin before the war, who died in Lodz on 13 February 1943.

[2] Enid Algerine Bagnold, Lady Jones (1889–1981), English novelist and playwright. *A Diary Without Dates* (1917) describes her experience nursing in World War I. *National Velvet* (1935) is her best-loved work. Her husband, Sir Roderick Jones, head of the Reuters News Agency (m. 1920), may have provided her with access to the information West was seeking.

[3] West's handwritten note.

To: Winifred Holtby[1]   15 Orchard Court
                                          Portman Square, W. 1.
                                          [spring 1933]

Dear Winifred,

I have meant again and again to write and thank you for your review of what is known in this household as Gus.[2] This understanding and sympathy are just what I would have expected from you, but I always am surprised by what Yeats calls the peacock's feather in the cap,[3] the extra touch by which you make those things even more desirable than they always must be. I had wanted to review *Mandoa! Mandoa!* but I could not do so for a reason most flattering to you—that Raymond Mortimer[4] who of all human beings I would have thought least akin to you [in] every way, and prevented most effectually by his Bloomsbury prejudices from susceptibility to your merits, was so bowled over by your book that he insisted on doing it for the D. T. [*Daily Telegraph*] (and I believe he also did it somewhere else, though he hates doing a book twice.) Such a triumph over the resolute-not-to-be-defeated I have never seen. I have been working like mad lately, but I'm now freer, and I wish you'd come to lunch some day—you're coming on March 9th anyway, I hope, but would you also come alone or nearly so on March 6th? Monday?

Yours ever,
Rebecca

Winifred Holtby Collection   manuscript
Central Library, Hull, U.K.

[1] Winifred Holtby (1898–1935), English novelist, journalist, pacifist, and feminist who lived with and worked in close association with Vera Brittain. Like West, she wrote regularly for *Time and Tide.* Among her novels are *The Crowded Street* (1924) and *South Riding* (1936). She wrote an antifascist play, *Take Back Your Freedom* (1939), visited South Africa to unionize black workers there, and did an early study of Virginia Woolf.

[2] West's *St. Augustine,* published in 1933.

[3] This may refer to Yeats's poem "The Peacock," which asks, "What's riches to him / That has made a great peacock / With the pride of his eye? . . . His ghost will be gay / Adding feather to feather."

[4] Raymond Mortimer (1895–1980), British critic and editor of the *New Statesman.* Among his works, the collection *Channel Packet* (1942) is noteworthy. He wrote on the paintings of Bloomsbury's Duncan Grant and was one of Harold Nicolson's partners.

To: Alexander Woollcott   [November 1933]
Dear Alec,

I am down in this austere hostelry with Henry, who is convalescing after a minor operation. On Tuesday we went up to London for the night because I had to speak at a meeting defending the right of married women to engage in paid employment.[1] Lady Astor was also one of the speakers, and we dined with her before the meeting. There was present a distinguished company, including Dr Ethel Smythe,[2] the composer, whose memoirs you may have read, a typical eccentric *grande dame* such as only England produces; Mrs Charles Dana Gibson[3] and Mrs Brand (both Nancy's sisters): Brand, Lord Lothian,[4] Clarence Dillon, Professor Hoffer. Dr Smythe is {slightly} deaf, and presently Nancy said to her, "My sister is trying to tell you that you were at her wedding 38 years ago; and you won't take any notice. I don't think you realise who she is. {She's Mrs Charles Dana Gibson.} You know all about the Gibson girl, don't you?" To this Dr Smythe replied, with the most charming desire to be courteous that I've ever seen, "Yes, indeed, I've often heard of her. But, do you know, I'm afraid I can't remember what it was she did."

This struck us all flat with joy: and it still delights me, so I hand it on, though it may become deflated during its passage across the Atlantic.[5]

My blessings on you,
Rebecca

Woollcott Collection, bMS Am 1449 (484)   manuscript
Harvard University

[1] Virginia Woolf remarks respectfully on the presence of West and Smyth at this very meeting in her diary (14 November 1933).

[2] Dame Ethel Mary Smyth (1858–1944), English composer, suffragette, and memoirist. She composed the WSPU anthem "The March of the Women" and was imprisoned in Holloway Prison for suffragist activities. *The Wreckers* (1906 production) is the best known of her six operas. *A Final Burning of Boats* (1928) and *Female Pipings in Eden* (1933) make up her autobiography.

[3] Mrs. Charles Dana Gibson, née Irene Langhorn, a noted beauty immortalized as the 1890's American ideal, the Gibson girl, in illustrations by her husband.

[4] Philip Henry Kerr (1882–1940), English journalist and statesman who began his career in South Africa. He eventually became secretary to Prime Minister Lloyd George and ambassador to the United States during World War II.

[5] West, who regularly reported to Woollcott on her travels, sometimes reused the descriptions in her later writing. A notable example, written from Vienna, is this description of Mayerling (site of the suicide of the crown prince and his mistress), which was recycled in *Black Lamb and Grey Falcon:*
Yesterday afternoon we went to Mayerling, a place that has {been} holding a gloomy performance in my imagination since childhood. This lonely hunting-box set in a dark forest, a flat & dreary expanse of black pines, through which there was practically no traffic except an occasional Erl Konig, and where the sounds of an orgy or a murder were lost in eerie silence.
Mayerling is in fact a comfortable yellow house, indestructible homelike and jolly, that

sits on a hill with orchards all round it, and no trees in any direction for about half a mile. . . .

Inside there is one touch of horror. The place is in the hands of Carmelites, and the ⟨x⟩ room where the tragedy happened is a chapel in the most ghastly German taste. Off this is a {very small} chapel with the most indecent object I have ever seen—a priedieu which the Empress Elizabeth had made out of the end of the Crown Prince's bed, a baroque piece of bulging gilt cherubs and whatnottery. There is also a confessional box made out of the rest of the bed, ⟨x⟩ {and a} life-size statue, in fact a wormwork, of the Empress Elizabeth as a mater dolorosa, with a sword sticking in her breast. But this isn't eerie, it just has a jolly bloodcurdling suggestion of spiritual incest taking its fences as they come. (Woollcott Collection, Harvard University)

To: Henry Andrews   15 Orchard Court
                                                     Portman Square, W. 1
                                                     Sunday [1933–1934?]

Dear Ric,

Yesterday I went to dinner with Anna May Wong and Joe[1]—and we had a lovely dinner but Anna May Wong is too stupid to be a useful Rac.[2] Old Joe said, "Anna May, you look so lovely you've made me fall in love with you," and instead of taking this as tummy-rubbing she said gravely, "Oh, Mr Hergesheimer, I hope not, that would spoil our friendship. For I am very much in love with someone else." We went on to Lilly's party[3]—which was very pretty but not very good—the food was inaccessible and we couldn't go home at a reasonable hour—for why? There was a superb dialogue—Mrs Gilbert Miller (a horrid very snobbish daughter of Julius Bache) came in and rustled over to Lilly and said—"I am so sorry—will you forgive me—we had a guest and when he heard where we were going to he did so want to come—I do hope you won't mind me bringing him—I know it's so awkward having this sort of guest at a party because of all the curtseying—you see it's the King of Greece." Lilly lethargically replied, "I wouldn't mind a bit if he'd only get out of the doorway—he's standing right in the way of the Prince of Wales."[4]

The full horror of the situation broke on us all about half an hour after he got there—we couldn't leave till he did, and he didn't choose to do that till half past three. Lee Ashton,[5] the Lowinskys, Joe Hergesheimer, and I huddled in a sleepy heap! Dear Rac Lowinsky was going about in such a smart frock of black taffeta with bits cut out—through one of them one saw a pair of twill corsets (laces very wide apart, poor Rac) and the stout elastic running through a pair of Sensible Cambridge blue knickers. But everybody loved her. Joe Hergesheimer said she was "the most physically attractive woman in the room—she's got warrrmth." Lilly had a lovely sham Chinese dress on. I said to Joe "Hasn't Lilly a tiny behind?" He said, "it's so tiny that I'm all discouraged," which amused Paul very much. And indeed the Prince of Wales had come, with a party including his new artificial Rac who has displaced Lady Furness.[6] She is a Mrs Simpson—about 34—very smart but very common and trivial. She was a quite low-class American who married a bad lot who deserted her in Shanghai,[7] where she picked up a living anyhow until she married a business man called Ernest Simpson. Then she came to England and has resolutely climbed and climbed (on the slender basis of an introduction to Lady Sackville)[8] till she attained this objective. The Prince looked dreadfully common and ostlerish and the women he came with were very second-rate, but he was quite sober and seemed very pleasant and amiable.[9]

Longing to see my dear Ric,

Love
From Rac.

Rebecca West Collection   manuscript
Yale University

[1] Anna May Wong (1907–1961), European actress of silent film and, less successfully, in Hollywood, where she played oriental villainesses. She played opposite Douglas Fairbanks in *The Thief of Baghdad* (1924).

Joseph Hergesheimer (1880–1954), American novelist who was popular in Britain for *The Three Black Pennys* (1917), *Gold and Iron* (1918), and *Java Head* (1919). He stopped writing after the publication of *The Foolscap Rose* (1934).

[2] West uses their pet names, Ric and Rac, generically, to mean male and female, respectively, throughout this and other letters.

[3] Probably Lilly Bonner; West describes Lilly and Henry Bonner as friends of Mrs. Simpson in a letter to Stanislav Vinaver (14 December [1936], University of Tulsa). The Bonners are remembered as cultivated, well-off American friends of West.

[4] The Prince of Wales (1894–1972), later King Edward VIII (1936), who abdicated the throne to marry Wallis Warfield Simpson (1937).

[5] Leigh Ashton (1897–1983), English arts curator. Beginning in the Department of Ceramics, he rose to become secretary and then director of the Victoria and Albert Museum.

[6] Thelma Furness, daughter of an American consul and sister of Gloria Vanderbilt, married to the much older scion of a shipping family, Lord Furness, and the former love interest of the Prince of Wales.

[7] Wallis Warfield Simpson, later Duchess of Windsor (1896–1986). Several aspects of West's account are unreliable, though consistent with stories put out by Scotland Yard. The duchess came from prominent Maryland and Virginia stock (the Warfields and the Montagues). She divorced her first husband because he was an alcoholic. Though she and the prince met in January 1931, she became known to the public as his favorite only in 1934.

[8] Victoria Sackville (1862–1936), wealthy English hostess, the cousin and wife of Lionel Edward Sackville-West and the mother of Vita Sackville-West. She left her husband and the great family house at Knole to live at Brighton in 1919.

[9] This letter contained a second installment which is omitted. The letter to Stanislav Vinaver, written shortly after the abdication (14 December 1936), summarizes in great detail the developing relationship of the king and Mrs. Simpson. In it West blames Lady Cunard for a marriage that even Mrs. Simpson may not have wanted. West ends with observations on the Nazi sympathies of the former king: "I see with great regret that he's gone to Austria, and I have no doubt that the Nazis, though they must be disappointed in the failure of their coup to produce any disorganisation in England, will try to use him again. If they do it won't wash. He is, as this story may convey, such an incredible fool that it would be almost impossible to use him; and his folly has really betrayed itself to the people. But even I . . . suffered the deepest pain through this, I did not realise how much I am part of my country."

To: George Bye

Private

Dear George,

15 Orchard Court
Portman Square, W. 1
6 February 1934

I got my little love notes from Mr. Spock.[1] The $1500 arrived in good time to go straight to the Income Tax. I want to be a native with a very short lava-lava and no Income Tax.

Rutger Bleeker Jewett I adore for himself and for his name, which sounds like a series of strange abusive epithets. Rogue! Scoundrel! Blackmailer! Rutger! Bleeker! Jewett! But I think he's wrong about "Murderee" making a lovely short book. I would much rather it went into THAT book of short stories.[2]

The *New York Herald Tribune* is not so friendly to me as you think. I had a hell of a dust up with Mrs. Meloney[3] who is a damn fool, about a highly offensive personal article concerning me by a piece of mud called Patrick Thompson. She behaved like a fiend over it and I do not think she would buy the novel for $10,000 or anything else, but we had better leave the whole discussion until I send you the manuscript.

I think you are going to be turned loose to regularise a nice commission for *Cosmopolitan* on character sketches. With regard to other articles, I feel myself I would like to leave this over until I come to America myself. I am quite out of touch with New York and the magazine market in general. You may possibly see me in October. You can certainly go right ahead now that the novel is {nearly} finished, and would have been quite but for a series of maladies on the part of my husband and myself. The Knopfs seem to love me, and I love Alfred but I do not like Blanche's prehensile methods.[4] Stanley Rinehart says he loves me,[5] but that doesn't amount to very much, or doesn't it? Harpers I rather smile on, especially as the bald-headed lecher Tommy Wells has gone to live in Paris and I like the bald-headed non-lecher, Mr. Gene Saxton,[6] who has taken his place. Thayer Hobson has also made passes at me, but gosh how I hate Honore Willsie Morrow.[7] I feel she is one of those good women from whom all other women ought to draw aside the hems of their skirts. There is also a paralytic bloke called, I think, Horace Stokes.[8] All we can remember about him is that when I signed a book for him he leaned tenderly over my chair and said, "The name is Horace," but I think the rest was Stokes. That is all I can remember, so I'll leave you to pick and choose. If you show them all this letter it might be a help.

Did you know that Simon & Schuster cabled to the Dickens family that if they were entrusted with the publishing of Dickens' Life of Christ, they would issue it "con amore and in reverence." The phrase is pleasing ⟨to⟩ quite a lot of people over here.[9]

The $30 cheque was never sent, so that is why it has never been presented. A photograph will follow. I have had some new ones done. I don't want to send you any of the old ones, which represent me as a simple girl, and the new ones that seem really to do justice to the ruins of Rebecca West by moonlight aren't ready yet.

With love,
Rebecca West

J. O. Brown Collection
Columbia University

typescript with autograph signature

[1] Jasper Spock sent the accounts of Rebecca West's earnings for Bye's firm and forwarded her income checks.

[2] It did appear in *The Harsh Voice* (1935), retitled "The Salt of the Earth."

[3] Marie Mattingly Meloney, *Herald Tribune* editor of the *Sunday Magazine* and director of the Herald Tribune Forum, a speakers series at the Waldorf Astoria. She did have an easier relationship with Irita Van Doren at the *Herald Tribune*.

[4] Alfred A. Knopf (1892–1984), American publisher and chairman of the publishing house that bears his name. He and his partner and wife, Blanche Knopf (1894–1966), attracted cosmopolitan works of high quality and cultivated contributors on both sides of the Atlantic. He had sought a manuscript from West in 1917. She rarely had good things to say of Blanche.

[5] Stanley Marshall Rinehart, Jr. (1897–1969), American publisher, then president of Farrar and Rinehart. He made bookselling an aggressive, commercial venture.

[6] Eugene Francis Saxton (1884–1943), American editor and publisher who revived Harper & Bros. after moving there in 1926.

[7] Honoré Willsie Morrow (1880–1940), American novelist and biographer who moved to England in 1931. Notable among her works are *The Forbidden Trail* (1919), *We Must March* (1925), and a Lincoln trilogy.

[8] Horace Winston Stokes (1886–1950), American publisher associated with Crowell Publishing and Frederick A. Stokes Co. (1926–1941), of which he became president (1939–1941).

[9] Simon and Schuster published Dickens's *Life of our Lord* (written originally for Dickens's own children) in 1934.

To: H. G. Wells

The London Clinic & Nursing Home
20 Devonshire Place, London W. 1.
[October 1934]

Dear Jaguar,

Many thanks for the kind and calming visit the other afternoon, which I really needed, for these operations leave one a trembling reed.[1] But I am distraught again, on account of an article by Odette on you in *Time and Tide*.[2] Did you give them or her permission to print? I don't like any real person's "sexual vitality" being attacked in print (let alone that the thesis is silly and superficial, and the allegation of "dishonesty" based on an idiotic foundation.) I am on the board of directors and I don't like it. But if in some moment of handsomeness you passed it I would have nothing to say.

Yours ever,
Panther

Rebecca West Papers   manuscript
Yale University

[1] West had had her appendix out.

[2] Odette Keun, journalist who was Wells's lover (1923–1933). They shared a house part of the year in the South of France, near Grasse. She wrote negatively of the relationship, first in letters to Winifred Holtby, and then for *Time and Tide* ("H. G. Wells the Player," 27 October 1934). Keun's article coincided with the publication of his *Experiment in Autobiography*.

To: Virginia Woolf

15 Orchard Court
Portman Square, W. 1
[June 1935]

Dear Mrs. Woolf,

I just don't know about the Paris Conference. I feel I am not worthy, for reasons of which I am secretly proud, I fear.[1] Morgan [E. M.] Forster made a most enchanting speech at the Prize giving otherwise you missed nothing. Miss Elizabeth Jenkins[2] was worse than I feared, a disordered blonde, about whom I felt something that could only be expressed by the haughty words I heard a lady use to another at 1 in the morning at the corner of Dover St. "What are you doing here with us? You are the Strand cut, not Piccadilly." Do come in some evening, any evening, about 6 or 6.30? Just telephone me the day before or even that morning. Or wouldn't you dine on the 24th or 26th, here, at 8, don't dress if you don't want to?[3] I should love that.

Yours ever,
Rebecca West

University of Sussex   manuscript

[1] The Femina–Vie Heureuse prize for imaginative literature was awarded annually by the two named journals for imaginative work best suited to giving the French an understanding of the English. There was a corresponding Northcliffe prize for the French. The selection process is described by West in "Prizes and Handicaps," in *Ending in Earnest.* Also see letter to Gordon Ray, 11 February 1958. West served on the British selection committee and attended the awards ceremony regularly.

[2] Elizabeth Jenkins (1915–), English novelist and biographer. She received the Femina–Vie Heureuse prize for *Harriet* (1934). Woolf's reply indicated that she had not interpreted West's remarks about Jenkins as they were intended. In a subsequent letter (Sussex), confirming a visit on the 26th at 8, West clarifies: "I meant nothing about Miss Jenkins' virtue, it was her pile of battered blondeness, her brightly coloured but insubstantial garments, and that very thin coat I meant. I am sorry to have caused a misapprehension. I am sure she's quite a good girl."

West also advised Woolf that "Mrs Melony has all the money on earth to spend on her deplorable rag, if you succeed in writing anything she could use you will be able to buy Leonard (who is coming too I hope) diamond studs from Cartiers, but it is a difficult market for the literate to satisfy."

[3] Virginia did dine with West on 26 June 1935, an event recorded in Woolf's diary for Thursday, 27 June. Though Woolf critiqued the glitz of the flat, she ended with a positive note on West: "She has great vitality: is a broad browed very vigorous, undistinguished woman: but a buffeter & battler: has taken the waves, I suppose; & can talk in any language: why then this sense of her being a lit up modern block, floodlit by electricity?" (Woolf *Diary,* vol. 4, 326–27)

To: Henry Andrews   [22 April 1936]
Dearest Ric,

I have been [on] the most incredible journey. I went down on Saturday last in a packed train the 10 hour journey to Skoplje,[1] with this poet who is also Chief of the Press Bureau—half Polish Jew, half Serb, the son of a famous surgeon, the most extraordinary person [Stanislav Vinaver]. He did not get on with his family so at the age of 10 they gave him a house and an allowance—and from that age he travelled all over Europe alone. I've ⟨stayed at the⟩ {went that} night to the Easter ceremony—you know, candles and three processions round the church. I was very tired, but extremely interested—it was so like [St.] Augustine. The next day we went in the morning to an old monastery up in the hills [of] Naesi and saw the most glorious frescoes and met the angelic old priest from Lake Ladoga I told you about in the post card, {then saw a procession in the afternoon, next morning visited the mosques and} then spent the afternoon going from village to village seeing the Rics and Racs dancing in their lovely clothes—then in the evening went a round of cabarets.[2] I know you've been in these parts—I wish I could remember where—but isn't it fantastic the way that there's almost nothing except bread and cabarets. Poverty & entertainment—it's very odd. Then the next day we went a 7 hours ride to Lake Ochrida.[3] What a journey—what a place! Oh, Ric, we must go there together. We were very churchy there—went to a festival ⟨by⟩ {in} a church by the sea with such a racket of people selling cakes & smacking babies and singing hymns and climbing over the rocks round the church—all *so* Augustine—and we spent the night at the miracle-working monastery of St Ann—a very nice monk looked after us, a North Serbian doctor who had joined the church to work better as a Macedonian pioneer—he wants to start a nursing school & so on.—and I sat at the right hand of the Bishop of Ochrida at a curious ⟨feast⟩ lunch that took place in the porch of a church that the Bishop likes specially because he succeeded in ridding it of a poltergeist who used to snatch the marriage-crowns from the heads of people being married there. There were children underfoot & people begging & prophetic old women all over the show & we munched young garlic, and I was elected "honorary guest" for next Easter. So that's where we'll have to go for Easter. We also acquired a young poet somehow & we all went up to a monastery in the hills & he read us his verses while the priest (who said he had six or seven sons & whose mother was 100 and had been 50 when he was born) gave us some very good wine & it all was very rosey & mellow. Then we drove to Bitolj[4] that used to be Manastir, a lovely but villainous town, where we went to a café where the waiter palmed 10 dinars Vinaver had given him to pay the bill. "There isn't any coin here," he said, after it had run up into his sleeve. We came on a fair there, with people wearing the most heavenly clothes—I bought some from a gentleman who said, "When you come back here, you'll be able to find me quite easily, I've a very uncommon name—Abraham Cohen." Then the next day we went to Prilep—oh, God, what a city, how degraded, how it makes you hate the Turk—and through desolate Macedonia—to the remains of Stoki, which are most interesting—it's such a glorious situation. Then back to Skoplje, where I met some nice people—the Serbian wife of a Moslem who played a great part in '12 in turning out the Turk, and who {she?} sits in Skoplje writing about Plato.[5] Then the next day we came up by the filthy Athens train to Beograd [Belgrade]. All the time Vinaver had told me about his beautiful German wife & when the train came in there was a waddlinger! As I tell you waddlingers have their public.[6] But in this filthy train I caught a cold, and I woke up this morning with my ears as bad as in February & March. It makes me feel too awful, and I have stayed in bed today—I must stay here to fulfill my promise to the Press Bureau to broadcast, which I think will be on Thursday or Friday—then I will go straight to Vienna & the Kurhaus; for I really have seen enough to keep me going, and I am desperately tired. I am dining with the Jack Balfours[7] on Thursday night, they are very friendly. I shall wire you when my exact plans for Vienna are known. I am so sorry you are having such a bad time with the uncle [Ernest]. I am hungry to see you—I do miss you frightful even in the midst of excitements. I love my Ric fondly. I got the cuttings you sent to Athens on my arrival here, and I'm very pleased with them, especially the *Times Lit. Supp.* I hope the thing sells well.[8] I feel very detached about it. I am much more interested in life here than I am in England; and I feel so ashamed of our national policy. If only we were solid with the French we could have filled this part of the world with light. How frightened they are, poor dears! I wish I could have stayed in Macedonia much longer, but I must get home to you.

> My best love,
> Your devoted Rac.

I did tell Louisa to send the mattress from our bed to be remade, didn't I?

Would you enquire what are the best books on St Columba,[9] and the Scottish and Irish saints? Four really good ones would be handsome. Then send them to Dr Stanislaus Vinaver, Pressburo, Beograd, Yugoslave, with a note inside "For Bishop Nicolas of Ochrid."

I am staying on till Monday because my cold is so bad I am going to bed, and I am consenting to radio later and stop at a town on the way to the frontier to speak. The Macedonian trip was so good that I must be agreeable. But even so I won't stop at Budapest—I'm too tired to see any more.

Rebecca West Papers   manuscript
Yale University

[1] Capital city of Macedonia, or southern Serbia, a part of Yugoslavia as it existed in 1936.

[2] In the couple's intimate language, *Ric* can refer to males in general, *Rac* to females; canine terms also apply.

[3] The lake (which gives its name to a city) lies on the border with Albania in the south-ernmost part of (then) Yugoslavia.

[4] City east of Ochrid. Many of the locations mentioned in her letters to Henry appear on the map supplied in *Black Lamb and Grey Falcon*. Her spelling has been preserved.

[5] Anica Šević-Rebac, Yugoslavian teacher and poet. As the character Militsa, she is treated with great admiration in *Black Lamb and Grey Falcon*. "She talks with the brilliance of a firefly, but her flight is not wandering, it is a swift passage from one logically determined point to another" (*Black Lamb and Grey Falcon*, 808).

[6] I have been unable to find the meaning of this pet term shared by Henry and Rebecca.

[7] John Balfour, chargé d'affaires of the British legation in Belgrade, had known Paul, the prince regent of Yugoslavia, at Oxford.

[8] *The Thinking Reed*, published in March 1936.

[9] St. Columba, or Columcille (521–597), Irish priest who spread Christianity to Scotland and established a monastery there.

To: Henry Andrews   Kurhaus Semmering [Austria]
Dear Ric,   [May 1936]

I hope I didn't alarm you too much by my telephone conversation, but I felt I'd better tell you to explain what must have seemed my extraordinary uncommunicativeness. It happened like this. I was asked on my arrival at Belgrade from Athens if I would care to go down to Southern Serbia to see Easter—as the Government's guest, the same tour that Irene Ward the M. P. had done. I was introduced to an inoffensive young man who, I was told, would go with me. Then I met a man called Stanislaus Vinaver, who was the head of the Pressburo, who arranges all these tours for foreigners. He was a man of 45, short, fat, like a Jewish Mr Pickwick, with a head like a cone with the apex cut off thatched with coarse black curls. He is a quite reputed poet, was Bergson's favourite pupil before the war,[1] and had a very distinguished career in the war—and now holds a very important position. He is going now as the special Legate to Vienna. (Not, I'm glad to say, for some months). He seemed therefore a completely safe and vouched-for person, and as it was in the papers, and as Miss Ward had done it, no doubt ever crossed my mind, particularly as he was such a tubbinger.[2] (But of course Rics never feel they are really tubbingers.) {On Thursday before} we went out to see the King's tomb at Topala and spent the day there seeing the Karageorgeovic village and so on, and he was most agreeable and very brilliant. But all that day I had threats of tummy pain, so stayed in bed all Good Friday, not even going downstairs. On Saturday we started for Skoplje—and in the morning a gruesome woman came in to ask me to get her an appointment, under the British Council. Suddenly Vinaver telephoned saying he could not fetch me—would I meet him at the station and at once, as he had heard that the trains were jammed. I therefore shot out of the hotel without changing my money—I had £15 with me in your fivers, and my railway ticket, and about 100 dinars in loose change. (About[£]9/-.) The train was indeed jammed, though it didn't matter as much as it would anywhere else, the people were so pleasant. You never get a sour look from these people. But the journey took 10 hours and during this time Mr Vinaver never stopped talking—it was really abnormal. For 1 hour he left me, because I said I must sleep, all the rest of the time was brilliant conversation (really quite brilliant) accompanied by spouting. ⟨It⟩ {This whole incident} would be more to Rac's credit if she could say that Mr Vinaver was a booful and desirable Ric ⟨but·it⟩ {that it} was hard to resist, but she ⟨x⟩ {must own} he was orrible. Then we got to Skoplje, got rooms in a very clean little hotel, dined, and went to the Easter midnight ceremony, which I shall never forget. I think you will have gathered from my cards what we did at Skoplje—we were there two days, monasteries, mosques, peasants dancing, so on. Then on the third day we went to Ochrid. I tried to change my money before I went, but it was not possible, the banks were still Eastering. We then went a 150 km. drive, over a mountain pass, and through two wild valleys, right down to the Albanian border. At Ochrid we found a clean hotel by the lakeside with admirable food. We went out after dinner to a café and I found Mr Vinaver's manner ominous. Presently we went back to the hotel and there Mr Vinaver jumped up on poor Rac. I was polite at first, then I got violent, then I got frightened—because in these days I had learned that Mr Vinaver was a pretty hard case. He had been caught by the revolution in Russia, and had been condemned to death, & had saved himself by turning Bolshevik and he had been a Bolshevik Commissar from 1918–1921. I had a pretty clear idea as to what that had meant. But I came to the conclusion that on the whole I'd rather die, and I went on being violent. It came to a stand-up fight in my bedroom, we rolled over and over, I hammered him with my fists, and finally manoeuvered him out of my bedroom, in a scene that was funny at the end, I must describe it to you in detail when I see you. I then locked the door and reflected that I was in a fairly bad way. I had now about 65 dinars, and I was 150 km. from Skoplje, from which I had a railway ticket. I believed there was a station in Ochrid, but I knew it was 30 hours to Belgrade and that the fare would be big, and that there was nobody in Ochrid who could speak English except the Bishop, and I had no way of finding him. I made up my mind to walk out of the hotel and start on the 150 km. walk. There was a town called Struga not far away, and I imagined I could try there to send a telegram to the British Legation telling them to wire me money—if 65 dinars was not enough for that I knew there was some sort of biological station there where I could possibly find someone who spoke a little German or French, who might lend me money for a telegram, and I could stay at the inn till the money came. If there had been nobody there I was simply going to start on the 150 km. walk, because I calculated I could get yoghurt and bread enough for the journey and possibly get a bus for part of the way. This may sound farfetched but I was frozen with terror—because for one thing, not a soul in the hotel had taken the slightest notice of the frightful row we made. Remember this man was an important official & we were in the Governor's car. But then I realised I had no passport. I'd given it up to the hotel keeper. I knew I couldn't get out of the town on the highroad without being questioned, or into any other town. (Everywhere you are questioned by the military police if you are a stranger.) I just gave up at that, and went to bed, and fell asleep at once, deadly fatigued. {Some of the postcards I sent you from S. Serbia I wrote really not knowing if I would ever see you again.}[3] The next morning Vinaver was perfectly nice. He apologised, but would not take me back to Skoplje, and told me that if I went away he would have me stopped. He knew I had no money—the banks in Ochrid were closed because of a local saint's day—so I could only get away in some slow way, He said that he was doing this to protect me, because my bourgeois prudishness would otherwise prevent me seeing the beauties of South Serbia. But at night I had exactly the same experience. I fought and fought and fought for about two hours. Then I thought we would have to go back to Skoplje because the time he had invited {me} for was up, but no, he placidly told me he had arranged to stay for ten days! That night I accepted an invitation at the Monastery which the head monk gave us, and Vinaver could not get out of it. That was heaven. Then we went to Bitolj, and there fortunately we found ourselves in a very proper hotel, with a colleague of Vinaver's staying in the hotel with a Roumanian professor who spoke French. That again was heaven. But in the morning he told me that we were going to spend the night in the mountain hut on the mountain where the Serbians broke the Austro-German front. He was half activated by honest patriotism in wanting to show me this mountain, but I thought the hut business was likely to be appalling. There would only have been the Governor's chauffeur and a guide, and I would have found it extremely embarrassing to call to them if he had left his cubicle for mine. (It is a pilgrimage place, {there is a chapel,} so the hut is big, but we would have been the first people up that season.) I was plucking up courage to refuse to go, but mercifully news came that the road was covered with new snow, and we couldn't get up. So we had to return to Skoplje. He then {at Bitolj} let me cash a fiver, and I bought some beautiful costumes for very little money. In Skoplje he was all right—I was free, I could get money, I had my railway ticket from there, and also he had become really fond of me. (All day he had been delightful always, though rather a bore and too exuberant) we stayed there two nights, because we got in on a Saturday night, very late, and we did not find out till after the day train had gone that the night one was not running. But indeed it seemed not to matter as he seemed quite to have quieted down. I must explain to you there was some excuse for him in one way—apparently all French women journalists sleep with the officials of the Pressburo, and at first he was genuinely amazed to find I didn't intend to be agreeable. (This is a confirmation of what Rac has always said about foreign Racs). Also he was completely uncivilised. He just didn't see why he shouldn't if he could. But he was very tiresome in the train. He obviously could not hope for anything ultimate but he kissed me sentimentally which was horrible. {I was actuated in this by fear. I would not care to go back to Jugoslavia if this man was my enemy.}[4] But we were met on arrival by "ma femme qui est très belle," who was a German waddlinger. She asked me to a family lunch, I accepted, and I thought it was done with. The waddlinger is really dotty, by the way, she's put her head in a gas oven and wanted to kill the children because he is half-Jewish. She has been in an asylum several times since the Nazis came in. She is a sister of Karl Silex, who is editor of some big German newspaper. I had a quite nice lunch there, thought it was then over, & an extraordinary incident. The English Club people asked me to stay a little longer to speak at Navigad—and I consented. It would have meant going on Sunday, and speaking there on Monday, & so on. I had a bad cold which made me glad of the delay, particularly as my ears went again. Then I began to feel very ill. I had to broadcast about my visit to southern Serbia, as the understanding had been, & wrote it & spoke it in a dream. Then I just caved in. I telephoned to Jack Balfour and they sent me a doctor who said I had erysipelas[5] and bronchitis. He, as I now know, was right. I was in a panic. I asked him to get me into a clinic, he said none would take me, as it was such a dangerous infection. But he promised he would send me a nurse. I was in great perturbation as I knew erysipelas could be fatal. Meanwhile Vinaver rang up and asked me to see him. I told him I couldn't that I had erysipelas, and rang off. I had determined to avoid seeing him for the rest of my stay in Belgrade, so far as that could be done without offending him.

It was then that my life became utterly intolerable. Twenty minutes afterwards Vinaver burst into my room, protesting that because he love me he had no fear of infection. I had a temperature of 40°,[6] was wheezing and gasping, I wanted sleep more than I wanted anything in the world. I was in pyjamas. For *3 hours* he stamped and raved and blustered beside my bed. I should have changed the dressings every hour, I didn't dare get up, I should have had milk regularly. I {could} just ⟨x⟩ {lie} and groan. There was a hitch about the nurse, so she did not come till the next evening. Vinaver telephoned the next day—I said he could not see me—in twenty minutes he was there pounding on the door, but I had locked it and left the key in. What happened I shall never understand, but I went to the bathroom which was off the hallway about twenty minutes—I saw the key kick forward on to the floor and Vinaver came in. Again he stayed, ranting and raving, for hours, while I lay & wept with misery. Then two {other} doctors came—one of whom said he couldn't make out what was the matter. The other of them said I had dengo fever. This the Viennese professor says is most unlikely, that I presented all the classic symptoms of erysipelas. Then the nurse came, a nice girl, but she couldn't speak one word of {anything but} Serbian. I begged the doctor to tell the hotel people to keep out all visitors—they apparently did not dare to keep {him} out, as he is a Government official. Every day he appeared, bringing flowers, papers, fruit, nearly driving me mad, poor creature, by his love making, his hideous physical presence, his "But you don't understand, you treat my love as England treated Lord Byron," this roaring, bubbling, spluttering demand on me that went on always two or three hours a day—and I never knew exactly when, so that I screamed with apprehension whenever the door opened. The nurse did what she could, but I was helpless with agony. Then the doctor told me that I was sufficiently uninfectious to go to a clinic, {though still disfigured} and that I had better go, though it was obviously not as comfortable as the hotel, because I obviously could not stand the strain & we could keep him out of the clinic. But they couldn't. He walked right in, and as I was better & dressed I had such a frightful go of it that I felt at the end of everything. After he had gone I found myself going to the window and looking down at a beautiful pink chestnut and deciding that if he came into the room I would throw myself down on the branches and that it would be quite a pleasant death. I realised that I was slipping and just then Joel Balfour rung me up—I asked him to come round, and I threw myself on his mercy, & without a moment's hesitation he said I must go and stay with them (though I looked as if a hyena had clawed half my face) and that he would call for me the next day. Unluckily Vinaver rang up the next day & ⟨then was⟩ {was told} I was leaving. He had before suggested that I should go and stay with him & his wife—he now insisted on it. I had to fight him back for hours, and I was so tired. When I got to the Balfours it was heaven. I can't tell you how I felt. But I had to speak to Vinaver on the telephone, & he was at the station when I left and I didn't feel really free of this frightful incubus till I got to Vienna.

I look too frightful. The Professor thought I was fifty. I am too thin, and my face looks worn and scored. But he says there's nothing wrong with me but anaemia {and weakness following the erysipelas} and low blood pressure, & this last I don't attach any importance to, as I think I'm always too low by nature in that way. He has sent me here with several prescriptions including injections—but I've refused to have them in the meantime, I couldn't bear it. I didn't feel able to tell the Professor about this experience. This is a queer, shabby, untidy place in a beautiful situation, the food is very good, the nurses are nice, and the light treatment seems properly handled, and that of course I need more than anything else. But curiously I feel as if I were really injured by this. I have deep lines on my face and my hair is much greyer than it was, and also I can't get enthusiastic about getting better. I suppose it was the awfulness of struggling with an infection and knowing I ought to have rest and instead having this ghastly struggle every day. I shall never forget one day when I lay with my eyelids falling like lead and this maniac sat by my bed running his horrible hands over my hair and saying again and again and again, "Venez près de moi." When I say he used to come in for three and four hours at a time I'm not exaggerating. His office was shut from 1 till 4 and very often he stayed longer than that. ⟨x⟩ The bother is that he meant to be kind, but was just a stupid uncivilised brute; and one can do nothing what-soever about it, because if he was my enemy I would never dare go back into or through Serbia. And I do want to go back. I will tell you more about this when I see you—more about my apprehensions. I'm too tired now, and somehow it's fatiguing to write of melodrama. The only bright spot in the situation is that after all there can't be many Rics who have to worry about the dogstealers when their Racs are forty-three years old.

The bother is I do love Jugoslavia. This country seems so flavourless after it—and when an Austrian woman who brought some mended shoes in and got a big tip from me started to beg from me I really felt quite sick. For the last six weeks I haven't seen a soul capable of cringing, (I except the Greeks and the Turks!), who however poor wouldn't hold out their hand for me to shake as an equal, and would have asked for a sliver if they were starving. I miss the food too—the yoghurt here isn't like ⟨that⟩ {the} Serbian, and I did so like the lovely "plates" they give you, with all sorts of vegetables and a fick gravy. But if I'd stayed there another week I think I would have gone right over the edge—anything to get away from that poor brute.

I am quite comfortable here, but it's rather shabby and casual. I didn't ask the Vaorick because I must be alone. She was obviously worried about something, I found out she was in low water, I gave her a 100 marks. I have nearly spent £25! That 100 marks, 80 marks for the doctor, 50 marks to the hotel, a complete day outfit—for I sent everything to the cleaners when I got to Vienna, I was anxious to get rid of the infection, and I bought myself ⟨some⟩ {a} knitted coat and skirt, sweater, and hat, and two pairs of brown shoes. I had an idea I would be able to walk, but I walked about ¾ mile today, and was completely done. If I don't feel much better in a fortnight I would like to come home, perhaps we could go down to Crawley for a bit.[7] I think in any case I'd like to come home, as the Jugoslavian Government is anxious I should broadcast, and I could do that, and then we could go abroad when you are free.

I do hope Ralli doesn't let the company in for anything illegal. I have always had a feeling that that mine was "ju-ju" for us—don't let it do anything more to you, my dear love. Please believe me on this, I feel my hackles rise on good intuitive grounds over that mine, for some obscure reason.[8]

It's very grey dirty weather—that's my only complaint now. Don't worry about me—and don't fret about doing anything about Vinaver. *Don't write to Balfour about it*—all English letters are read, and anything to do with me or the people I was connected with will be read for some time to come. Isn't this William le [Quex!?]

My love, I'm too tired to write any more and I expect you're tired of reading.

Yours ever, with all my love,
Rebecca Rac

Rebecca West Papers   manuscript
Yale University

[1] Henri Bergson (1859–1941), French philosopher whose theory of time in relation to human intuition and perception influenced Marcel Proust, among others. Bergson's major works include *Creative Evolution* (trans. 1913), *Time and Free Will* (trans. 1910), and *The Laugh* (trans. 1914).

[2] Part of West's private language, as are *pussinger* and *waddlinger*. Vinaver was rotund.

[3] West's note in top margin.

[4] West's note in left margin.

[5] An infectious, diffusely spreading, deep red inflammation of skin and mucous membranes caused by a streptococcus.

[6] 40° Centigrade corresponds to 104° Fahrenheit.

[7] Village near Winchester, said to be the model for Queen's Cawley in *Vanity Fair*.

[8] In this paragraph West seems to be advising Henry against an investment in a mine that she superstitiously finds interdicted—"ju ju."

To: Colonel Charles Bridge   [marked received 27 May 1936][1]
Dear Colonel Bridge,

I am not at all happy about the tour in Austria, Jugoslavia, and Greece, from which I have just returned. It was in great part a waste of your money and my time; and as the failure was due to mistakes of organisation I will describe my tour in detail. I consented to what was obviously a hurried itinerary because I am anxious to start work on a new book; but I thought it was merely hurried, and not, as it proved to be, impossible to carry out with any regard for the purpose for which I had gone abroad. I had thought that the journeys would be undertaken in reasonably comfortable trains, and that as the towns I visited were all small I should get enough sleep, and that the lectures I had arranged to give would be suitable for the audiences, and I am sure the Council made the same assumptions. As you read my account you will see how far we were mistaken.

I started at Vienna; and while it was very pleasant for me to lecture there I do not think an isolated lecture given by a person of less than international standing does very much to help Anglo-Austrian relations. There is a plethora of lectures in Vienna, and it is very obviously a place where cultural propaganda should be handled through the Universities and learned Societies by the lending of distinguished lecturers to give series of lectures. My friend Dr. Morgenstein,[2] the well-known economist, who has great influence on the Viennese students, would be delighted to discuss this matter with the British Council.

I then went to Ljubljana;[3] and that was perhaps the only properly planned visit of my entire tour. I stayed there two nights and that was just as long as I needed. The Society here consists of very simple people whose enthusiasm for English is great, but whose knowledge of it is considerably less than one thinks at first. They speak English quickly and correctly, but they tire very soon, and they follow a lecture with effort. It struck me as significant that Miss Irene Ward had told me that I would find them a very intelligent audience; and that I found that while they all remembered her vividly, practically none of them had any idea of what she had talked about. For myself I found a few people in the audience, about half a dozen, followed my lecture with intense interest, but I am sure the rest found it a strain. It seemed to me that this was a town to be cultivated mainly on an entertainment basis, and that Mrs Lewis's folk songs and her great social charm were more useful to them than I could ever be. . . . The members of the Ljubljana club were most courteous people, and probably wrote appreciative letters after my visit; but the sober fact is that the only member who had any knowledge of her own or any other literature was the young woman who is secretary of the Club Library, but unfortunately she wished to converse with me only regarding the Legalisation of Abortion, a subject on which I had received no instructions from the British Council. . . .

I then went to Zagreb, arriving at noon and leaving early next morning. I cannot think what was in the mind of the person responsible for making that arrangement. I should have spent at least three days there, as it is quite as important as Belgrade, and there are several distinct groups who could have made use of me. . . .

It was necessary that I should lunch with Dr. Čučin [a Croat patriot]; but I met nobody at lunch there except Mr. and Mrs Sterling of the theatrical company which performs English plays all over Europe. It was in fact Dr. Čučin's hope that I should be so struck by their personalities that I should beg the British council to subsidise them. This I perceived while I was under the thought that they must have spread far and wide through Europe as standard English the most vicious form of telephone-girl accent imaginable. This plan of Dr. Čučin's wasted a lot of my time, as I had to see all the people I might have seen at his lunch, either at a long tea party given by a wealthy Jewish family (a gastronomical ordeal, since we had to eat relays of heavy food, consisting chiefly of different sorts of tipsycake, for two hours) and a gathering at a café, after my lecture, which lasted till one in the morning. Even then I never met the young intellectuals or any of the University people, though they were present at my lecture and, I am told, enjoyed it. The audience for the lecture was extraordinarily intelligent, as good as a good Scandinavian audience. They had a working knowledge of European literature, and had no difficulty in following any allusion, and asked intelligent questions and took down titles. Many of them belonged to influential

Croat families and were themselves distinguished. This is a field worth cultivating, and as Zagreb is the nursery of Croat intelligence (which is very considerable) it should be well worth while to send them lectures to give isolated lectures and (let me reiterate) series of lectures.

Repacking my mended suitcase, I got to bed at 2 a.m. At 7 a.m. I was at the railway station, and after twelve hours of travelling in a fairly comfortable train I reached Split.[4] I will record my experience there in detail, asking you to remember that I had spent two nights there, as against twenty-four hours in Zagreb. I stepped out of the train and was met by a young man from Zagreb, active rather than intelligent, Dr. Petrinchkey; a Croat patriot, Dr. Lupič-Vukič, and a young woman of charming manners but feeble intellect, called Miss Peričič, who could speak a little, but not much English. Through the darkness I perceived that Dr. Lupič-Vukič was one of nature's Hindus. He immediately began to address me on the subject of the sufferings he had undergone when he had languished in Austrian prisons, in a flow of language recalling by its substance the late Mr. Saklatvala, but made uniquely horrible because he had learned his English in Louisiana and spoke with a marked Southern drawl. His oratory made it very difficult for me to collect my luggage in the night, and as he was the local Gandhi, both Dr. ⟨x⟩ Petnitchkey and Miss Peričič listened to him respectfully instead of coming to my aid. Eventually I sat down to dinner at the hotel, but Dr. Lupič-Vukič and Miss Peričič sat down too, and he addressed me unceasingly on his achievements and merits. At a quarter past eleven I arose and said that I was so constituted that I could not sleep unless I had a short walk before I went to bed. I led them out into the street and at the first turning shook hands with them and said goodnight. But Miss Peričič ran after me, and offered to take me to her coiffeurs the following day at 5.0. I never discovered what provoked this offer, since my hair was as tidy as Vienna could make it, and a great deal tidier than hers, and I refused it. But it had its consequence later.

It had been arranged that the next morning Dr. Lupič-Vukič should call for me and take me ⟨out⟩ a tour of the sights of Split and tell me about the Club and my lecture. He appeared at 9.30 and we walked about in the heat till 12.30. When we had exhausted the palace of Diocletian he took me to several spots bearing on his own career, including a church, some distance from the town along a very dusty road, where he acted as best man at a friend's wedding. Never once during these hours did I get a chance even to ask him how big my audience would be. When I tried to interrupt his unceasing flow of words he merely held up his hand and continued. He fortunately left me alone for lunch, and as I was sitting drinking coffee outside the hotel a young man named Mr. Patrick Johnson introduced himself to me and explained that he had for some months been teaching English there. Presently he said, "I hope you realise that the people understand hardly any English." He told me that only Dr. Petnitchkey and Dr. Lupič-Vukič knew English well, and that the mass of Club members had been learning English only for a short time, and few knew it as well as Miss Peričič. He warned me that they would not be able to understand English spoken at a normal pace, and could not possibly listen for more than half an hour, had read no English books, and were not highly educated people. At this point Dr. Lupič-Vukič and Dr. Petnitchkey arrived to show me more of Split. Immediately Dr. Lupič-Vukič began to recount again the story of his Martyrdom, but after twenty minutes horror inspired me to point out a hill behind the town and to declare I intended to climb it. As I had hoped, Dr. Lupič-Vukič, who is an elderly man, felt unable to perform the feat, and I managed to get off alone with Dr. Petnitchkey. . . .

Split is far less literate than Ljubljana. The atmosphere was more friendly but just as uncultured as a small Italian town; and in spite of the raptures the term "Mediterranean culture" raises in the bosom of Mr. Belloc,[5] one can perhaps say little worse. There was nobody in the town, except some of the families of the doctors in the big hospital and a few Jews, who was aware of the existence of art or literature, or who had any interest in the outer world. The propaganda in such a town must be planned on an entertainment basis, and at that the entertainment must be fairly simple. It was certainly useless to have sent me there.

The next day I spent going by boat to Dubrovnik,[6] and had a most enjoyable trip, choosing at least two places at which, should anything happen to my husband and should some suitor with a taste for maturity present himself, I should spend my honeymoon. But that was not the purpose for which the British Council sent me to Dalmatia and I therefore cannot imagine why no arrangements were made for me to speak at Dubrovnik {(provided I found myself there.)} Dr. Torbarina, the secretary of the chief Club at Zagreb comes from Dubrovnik, and informed me that he could have put me in touch with a group there who would be much better than I should find in Split. If you are going to organise lectures in Jugoslavia, somebody has got to know such facts as Torbarina's tie with Dalmatia, as there is much ground you can only explore through using such connections.

I spent the night at ⟨x⟩ Dubrovnik and left there at 11.40 in the morning for a twelve hours journey on the dirtiest train I have ever seen. It was a narrow gauge line, and the train rocked and bumped perpetually. There are over a hundred evil-smelling and filthy tunnels, which made it necessary to keep the window of the compartment shut. . . . I arrived at Sarajevo at 11.30, cold, tired, and hungry and was met by three officials of the Club, all so eager to speak English that they sat with me at supper and did not leave until 12.45. They were so charming and enthusiastic that I was delighted that they should do so. But such a day is only possible if one has ample time to rest on the following day; and that was certainly not possible at Sarajevo. The whole of the day I spent there was crammed with appointments. I had to talk with several Serbian men who had been educated in England during the war; I had to talk with Mrs Rudoi, an Englishwoman who does much to organise the Club on the social side, and with some members of the Czech and the Jewish groups; and with some returned immigrants from America. I also had to spend some time with Mr. Sutton-Palmer, the Consul, who has since died (By the way he showed me the greatest kindness ⟨in going⟩ and {went} to a lot of trouble to advise me regarding my journey.) All this, with a prolonged teaparty and the lecture, kept me out of bed till midnight.

In Sofia[7] I had a busy day, because there are so many writers, and because one has to speak French; and I am happy to find that Sir Ronald Campbell bears me out in my opinion that listening to Balkan French and replying to it is a form of physical torture only to be compared with the bastinado.[8] That day, and the following morning were entirely filled up with engagements, and I found that there was a lot more work that I could usefully have done, had I had a little time, such as to read to the English class in the University, which is taught by a Professor especially interested in spoken English. I append a separate note on opportunities that I thought were open to us in Sofia. In the following afternoon I travelled back to Nish, which was not a long journey, but extremely fatiguing because first of all the British Legation believed my ⟨x⟩ passport to be out of order, which it was not, and insisted on my taking various steps, and because secondly my ticket was indeed out of order. I had no right to be on that particular train, either with my Bulgarian or Jugoslavian ticket and I had to pay a supplement in Bulgarian currency, of which I had been told to bring nothing whatsoever out of Sofia. This involved conversations with five different railway officials, only two of which spoke either French or German. I arrived at Nish exceedingly tired, and was greeted {on the platform} by a small and aged governess, Miss Grosser, two Generals and the Mayor.

The Club at Nish is one of the most extraordinary organisations imaginable. It depends on the genius of Miss Grosser, who arrived there during the war, with two shillings in her pocket, having escaped from Russia, where she had been a "Miss" for over twenty years. She dragged with her her employers, a Prince and his wife, who soon after died of privations. She was taken care of by some Scottish Ambulance Corps and has remained there ever since, teaching English at the Orphanage outside Nish, which still carries on, officered by Scotchwomen who try to leave Serbia, go home, hate it, and come back again. She also teaches English to many of the young doctors at the Military Hospital, and therein lies the charm of the situation. It happens that the General in charge of the Military Hospital is a bully and a lunatic, and he has insisted on being made President of the English Club so that he can see if there is any spying going on there. He and the tiny Miss Grosser have thundering rows and she defies him while the young doctors, who all hate him, sit round and worship her for it. I wish I could have done this Club a better turn. It is worth cultivating. Thanks to the remarkable little Miss Grosser and the Scottish sisters, there is a warm atmosphere about the Club, and the young doctors form a very influential body, drawn from all parts of Jugoslavia. But obviously my lecture could not be an important part of the proceedings, as all these were practical people, very overworked, who wanted entertainment rather than instruction, and many of the young men were only beginners. The important thing was to be a good talkative guest, particularly at the big dinner-party afterwards, at the inn, which lasted until long after midnight. But needless to say after this appalling ten days that had passed since I left Ljubljana I was not at my best.

The next morning I started on my twenty-four hour journey to Athens. . . . The audience was intelligent and easy to address; though I do not think it worth while sending speakers to give single lectures there because they get a great many lecturers deposited on their shores by Lunn from the Anglo-Hellenic Cruises. The lecture itself was no strain, but the atmosphere of the English Colony was, and I had to take to the countryside for my rest, to avoid a situation which I will describe in detail later.[10]

I returned to Belgrade, and spoke on successive nights at the Pen Club and to the English ⟨x⟩ Societies. I was not, I found, sufficiently recovered from the early days of the trip to speak as well as I had hoped at Belgrade. I think you will realise that to cope with the conditions at Split I had to draw on what reserves I had of good temper and self-possession; and I was faced by the same necessity in Belgrade. I have only once before in all my years of lecturing experience had a lecture so completely wrecked by a member of the committee in charge of the occasion. I found that the Legation people in Belgrade believed Dr. Popovic to be a competent person, but I most emphatically dissent. I could not rest the next day after I got back from Athens, because he had made a number of futile appointments without consulting me, and said "it would be awkward" to cancel them. On the morning of my lecture he ⟨again⟩ insisted on my making a tedious and quite unnecessary visit to the University which was empty of all students owing to Easter vacation. At the lecture itself which took place in the Popular University, he insisted on fetching me an hour before it began, which meant that I sat in a stuffy room and had to respond to the atrocious French of the men of letters of Belgrade, while Dr. Popovic fussed round me and broke it to me that my lecture had been announced in two separate newspapers as starting at 6. and 6.30. This broke my nerve, and it was indeed the cause of a deplorable situation. At 6.30 I stood up before an audience consisting of the readers of one newspaper, who were irritated by my unpunctuality, while readers of the other newspaper straggled in all the time up to 7 o'clock; certainly more than half of my audience came in between 6.30 and 6.50. At 7.10 Dr Popovic made signs to me to stop, though I had been asked to speak for an hour, and I had to bring my speech to an abrupt conclusion. He then told me that I should have calculated the hour as beginning at 6.0 because the lecture room might have been required for another class, though I had myself enquired if this was so and had been assured by the head of the Popular University that I could go on. There were other annoyances too trivial to relate, but distinctly trying to the nerves. If I had been fit I could have dealt with this half-wit in my stride; as it was I cannot conceal from myself the fact that I allowed these things to submerge me and did not give as good a lecture as I would have wished. Jugoslavia is distinctly a country where one has to be in a state to deal with the unexpected.

. . . .

The moral of this is, I think, that you cannot organise a Jugoslavian lecture-tour from London. I have already mentioned that I do not think accurate information about the railway journeys can be obtained outside the country. I am quite sure that in planning any future lecture-tour you must act on local advice. It is not simply my physical weediness that made me think the journeys you sent me intolerable. Everywhere the Jugoslavians expressed amazement at my itinerary; and I also heard it said again and again, "Poor Mrs Lewis, she was so tired when she got here. Why does the Council send you on such terrible trips?" I also saw some whitened bones by the trail, which I was told belonged to two musicians who had fallen by the wayside going to Bucharest, and I was not surprised. Whoever it is who advises you on these Balkan journeys must know nothing about either the Balkans, or journeys, or the physical limitations of those who make public appearances. There is in the Legation at Belgrade a Dr. Pepič, who is, I think, in charge of the publicity, whom the Legation people themselves would use for such a purpose, and he has certainly a thorough knowledge of the country, and can in any case get any information he wants from the Jugoslavia Pressburo. But he tells me that he was never consulted about my journey.

Only local information will be of any use in deciding what towns are to be visited, and it seems to me this had hardly been tapped, even from the obvious source of the Legation. Both Mr. Bentinck at Sofia and Sir Sidney Waterlow at Athens mentioned to me that the British Council had not asked them if there was any other work I could usefully perform as well as my lecture, and in each case there were schools and colleges which would have been glad of a visit. But in Jugoslavia, of course, there is another equally obvious source of information. When I mentioned to Dr. Popovič that I had been to Split he immediately said "But what a waste of your time, there is nobody there who speaks English well except Lupič-Vukič and Petnitchkey." I then found that Split was in fact a branch of the Belgrade Club, and that in any case (as the Belgrade Club is the chief recipient of the Government grant to English-speaking Clubs) he is well acquainted with the condition of the Clubs all over the country. But he told me that he too had never been consulted about this tour. I think that a great pity. {Though he is a muddler he could give you facts.} Of course the antagonism between the Serbs and Croats and Slovenes is so great that Dr. Popovič could not be trusted to give advice regarding the whole country. I noticed that he showed the greatest jealousy of the Zagreb club, and quite unfairly mocked at its cultural pretensions. It is significant that the Zagreb Club is so anti-Serb that it refuses the Government subsidy, and that the Belgrade Club bitterly resents this refusal. But Dr. Torbarina of the Zagreb branch is a far abler man than Dr. Popovic, and could certainly give you all information about the Croatian and Slovenian Clubs. The young man who holds the Scholarship for Slavonic students in Jugoslavia, Mr. Hubert Butler, with whom you are already in touch, is extremely intelligent and has lived in both Zagreb and Belgrade and could give you a great deal of information regarding these matters.

Needless to say that in spite of the flaws in my tour I enjoyed it enormously. I found everywhere that there was a substantial residue left of the pro-English feeling that began in the war; and since the French influence is so rapidly fading there is an appetite for culture and liberalism which will be unsatisfied unless we take steps to fill it. It is a field worth cultivating. But I would like to point out that much more work can be done in countries like Jugoslavia and Bulgaria by entertainers than by serious lecturers. I cannot tell you how much good has been done by Mrs Lewis's tour. Everybody speaks of her with the greatest admiration, and as I saw for myself at Zagreb she is not only a delightful singer but a complete charmer, who can interest and be interested in everybody she meets. I am sure you want people like her, lecturers who play or sing or use picturesque lantern slides. I wonder if one could send out half a dozen clever young people who had just gone through the Academy of Dramatic Art or the Embassy School of Acting to do scenes from famous plays? But the young women would have to be chaperoned. It is love that makes the Balkans go round.

I append my notes on Sofia and Athens separately, since they are of a grossly offensive nature, and if this letter seems longwinded and complaining please forgive me. I was very pleased to do this tour, and honoured that you asked me to do it, and all that troubles me is that the conditions seemed to prevent me from being as useful as I might have been.

Yours very sincerely,

Rebecca West

Literature Department   typescript with manuscript insertions
British Council

[1] Originally more than six thousand words in length, this letter has been abridged to just over four thousand; most of the passages that have been cut deal with personal inconveniences.

[2] Possibly Oskar Morgenstern (1902–1977), best known for his *Theory of Games and Economic Behavior* (1947). He was a friend of both Henry and Rebecca, mentioned as visiting frequently at Ibstone.

[3] Major city in Slovenia, near its western border with Italy.

[4] City on the Dalmatian coast, on the Adriatic Sea.

[5] Joseph Hilaire Pierre Belloc (1870–1953), French-born English essayist, poet, political analyst, historian, and travel writer. His most memorable travel book is *The Path to Rome* (1902).

[6] City on the southern end of the Dalmatian coast, on the Adriatic Sea.

[7] Capital of Bulgaria, located near its western border with the former Yugoslavia.

[8] Oriental form of punishment involving the striking of the soles of the feet or the buttocks with a stick.

[9] City in eastern Serbia. The usual spelling is Niš.

[10] Space does not permit publication of West's additional eight pages on Sofia and Athens. Much of the Greek account is given over to squabbles between Sir Sidney Waterlow, the ambassador, and Mr. and Mrs. Miller, participants in the Anglo-Hellenic League. The following portrait of Waterlow has been preserved:

He represents the type of eccentric English gentleman at its very best. I have never felt prouder than when I stood bathed in the Attic sunlight on the steps of the Parthenon beside the stately form of the British Minister, whose strong resemblance to Vercingetorix, as he is portrayed in the mural decorations of provincial French hotels de Ville, added to my sense of the richness of the classical world. The Greeks adore his superb floridity, his kingly bearing, his arrogance and courtliness. It is popularly believed in Athens that he has the rich and damp plum cake, which he consumes in such large quantities every afternoon, sent out to him in the bag. I discovered (to my deep regret) that this was not the case; but the myth is excellent for British prestige. He is kindly, generous, full of enthusiasm for what pleases his scholarly and aesthetic sense, and is obviously shrewd enough when it is borne on him that he has to be. But he has the defects of his qualities. He is a character whom only those with a certain amount of talent and breeding can appreciate, and the Millers and their following are ill-bred people. He is also impulsive, spoiled and given to flagrant breaches of good manners whenever he feels like it.

To: Nancy Cunard[1]   15 Orchard Court
                                                             Portman Square, W.1
                                                             28 July 1937

I am for the legal government of Republican Spain against Franco, since
Spain herself, at a properly conducted election, chose that Government and
rejected the party which now supports Franco.

I am also against Fascism; the reforms of Diocletian[2] were a work of genius
and made many people temporarily happy, and in the end added greatly to
human misery. I see no reason why this inferior modern copy of them should
succeed.

Rebecca West Papers   copy of typescript
Yale University

[1] Nancy Cunard (1896–1965), English poet, essayist, journalist, activist, avant-garde publisher, and memoirist. West's prorepublican statement was one of 126 collected for the pamphlet *Authors Take Sides on the Spanish War.* Five contributors were pro-Franco; sixteen
(including Eliot and Pound) were neutral. Like West, Cunard was outspokenly antifascist.
[2] Diocletian, Valerius (245–316), Illyrian soldier and emperor of Rome (284–305), who
instituted numerous administrative reforms yet failed to check the decline of the empire.

To: Henry Andrews   Patriarchate,
                                                             Peč
                                                             [Whitsunday, 15 May 1938][1]

Dear Ric,

    I have been here two days and found it a great refreshment after Skoplje,
partly because the diet though really ample seems deliciously abstinent. The
frescoes are less interesting than I had remembered, but the interest for me
has been the pious old Racs from the neighbouring villages who turn up for
every service, grizzled and wirey old things wearing close jackets, very gaudy
check & striped waistbelts, and full trousers of sober window-curtain material, all such decent old things. Today was Whit Sunday—I ⟨said⟩ asked them
if it would be anything out of the ordinary, they said no, just an ordinary
service. ⟨They had⟩ But when I went in at seven I found the church carpeted
with new mown hay and wild-rose petals, which seemed to me hardly
ordinary. They also had iron candelabra all round the church which were

blazing with candles in the sunshine. Then a lot of poopingers[2] arrived on a motor-lorry, rushed about the monastery garden hooting and cheering, posed round the fountain for their photographs, then rushed into the church and sang right through the service most beautifully, all in parts. Such tricks as there were in this service you never did see. At one point a lot of Racs from different villages turned up with their puppies—some in extraordinary costumes—pink trousers in purple ankle bands, white {striped} silk blouses (from Prizreu) fawn velvet boleros, modern court shoes with buckles and a rather smart ⟨large⟩ {leather handbag}, a headdress covered with filigree silver butterflies, make a strange mixture. There was one superb village wearing classic Montenegrin dress with mantillas, composed entirely of slight variations on our Amabel, mostly dark but still definitely Amabel. ⟨All the Racs⟩ Their puppies were all signed with the cross in oil on the left temple by the priest, I can't imagine why. Then after about 2 ½ hours, ⟨they all⟩ I went out & found the porch filled with old peasant women of the type that as I say always comes here all with armfuls of long grass. {So had some of the women in the church.} I stood at the door so that I could look in right down to the altar {through the inner door also}. Suddenly there was some ecstatic singing and they all crashed down on their knees and began to weave the grass into garlands. This I believe they put on the family graves after-wards. This happened three times. Then at the end the priest tossed good hefty branches of flowering lime from the altar and the congregation fought for them. There was then a most curious feast—not like the one at Ochrid—there was a table set in the porch with plates of that sweet wheaten porridge and bits of bread and glasses of wine & the whole congregation fed by it—first Racs then Rics, and took a spoonful of the porridge and a handful of bread dipped in the wine, then crossing themselves. No priest was there. It was an odd sort of semi-secular Communion. The effect of the whole thing was of a festival in honour of summer with placation to the dead (winter) but of a fervour that you cannot imagine. There were quite as many men as women in the church today.

I am going to Decani[3] today in the afternoon. I am glad ⟨you⟩ I did not plan to stay there for the priests are in the hands of the horrid little bearded blonde monk we noticed last year when we were there as suspicious in his manners. Do you remember we said it was the only time we had seen signs of

Ricking and Ricking[4] in a monastery? He turns out to be an Austrian and a violent pro-Nazi, and he can ill conceal his rage about Czechoslovakia,[5] though I am having to go over to Decani with him in the afternoon and he is trying to be polite. They say Göring and Hitler are coming here on a triumphal tour in the autumn.[6]

They are fetching me from Trepča tomorrow. I am going to see how the land lies there.[7] If there is an inn I will sit down and write for a week, for I am terribly behindhand. All time in Skoplje on this trip has been wasted, except for knowing the Rebacs who are darlings—but the life is not compatible with work. But not possibly—though with my books anything seems possible—can there be more than 25,000 words to the damn thing. And I have written 50,000 since I have been out here. Oh, how it will all have to be cut.

It was well worth coming this time. I had forgotten the atmosphere. And the sacrifice on the stone is now the clou of my book. Yow, as the natives say, what luck it was that I insisted on being at Skoplje for St George's Day. I cannot tell you how I am homesick, only the stern desire to get this book done keeps me out here. But I have a feeling that once I have done this book all my work & my life will be simpler. A better Rac.

I will write you from Trepča.

Best love

⟨x⟩ Rac.

Rebecca West Papers   manuscript
Yale University

[1] West, now on her third visit to Yugoslavia, refers to the second, taken with Henry. Peč is located just north of the Albanian border.

[2] One of West's private terms, presumably a negative set, as opposed to the positive *pussingers*. It is followed by a number of dog substitutions for humans.

[3] Town slightly southeast of Petch (Peč) on West's map.

[4] Possibly homosexuality.

[5] Throughout the 1930s Hitler had been agitating for the unification of the Sudetenland— an area on the northern border of Czechoslovakia, heavily populated by Germans. The Munich pact (29 September 1938) would accomplish this. By March 1939 Czechoslovakia had been dismembered by Germany, Poland, and Hungary.

[6] Hermann Wilhelm Göring (1893–1946), German military and political leader, the designated successor to Hitler. As prime minister and air minister he set up the Gestapo and the

concentration camps and mobilized the country for war. He was tried at Nuremberg and condemned to death, but he committed suicide before this could be carried out.

[7] Trepča mines, site of valuable zinc and lead mines designed by the British, near Kosovo.

To: Ben Huebsch[1]   15 Orchard Court
                                            Portman Square, W. 1
                                            22 December 1938

Dear Ben,

I haven't written before because I have just got the dithers about Landau.[2] I must explain how I got to know him—he is, as I think I told you, married to the sister of the Nazi journalist Karl Silex—whose other sister is married to my Serbian friend, Stanislaus Vinaver, a poet and eccentric, also a Jew. I was interested in him entirely because of Vinaver, who is a queer card but a genius. {Now I've seen him I think he's good and would have helped him for his own sake.} But Mrs Vinaver is mad. She has spent some time in various clinics, and there is no question of mere eccentricity. The Nazi business has made her madder, indeed she has tried to kill herself and her children because ⟨they⟩ {she} had polluted the sacred Nordic blood in them by marrying a Jew. ⟨Thus⟩ I know *her* madness quite well—just as you know ⟨x⟩{somebody's} touch on the piano. The day I got your last letter from ⟨Ne⟩ {you} about Landau I got a letter from Mrs Landau, queer and silly and exalted, with just the same note of madness that I am accustomed to in her sister. There was nothing mad {though a lot very silly} in the substance of the letter, but the tone was unmistakable. I just sat and looked at it and sagged. And, indeed, expected to hear more of her. But nothing has come, and in a letter to me Landau says how he longs for her company. So maybe it's all right.

Bless you for what you've done. You are an angel. I cannot sufficiently express my gratitude to you, the poor battered thing would have been hideously on my conscience. Here is another cheque for 250 dollars. When it is ⟨expe⟩ {spent} I'll send another. But could I pay say 1000 dollars a year to some institution to employ him, if that would help him to get into the country? Then some other people might put up ⟨another⟩ {some} more money and we might give him a tiny living.

Oh, Lordy. Oh, Lordy. I wish we could give a lot more money, and that this incubus of a book [*Black Lamb and Grey Falcon*] was done so that I could earn again.

Blessings on you again.

Yours ever,
Rebecca West

Ben Huebsch papers   manuscript
Library of Congress

[1] West's American editor at Viking Press.
[2] Walter Landau, a Jewish specialist on tuberculosis who was fleeing Nazi Germany. West wrote in October that she was willing to spend up to five hundred dollars to get him settled, and she requested Huebsch's help with immigration and introductions.

To: Irita Van Doren   [December 1940]

This is a beastly war—like the stage of seasickness when you are not sure you are seasick but realise that everything but seasickness has ceased to exist. Henry works like a dog at the Ministry of Economic Warfare—I have forgotten what he looks like by daylight (which recalls—inexactly!—the legend of Cupid and Psyche). We are all working like dogs, indeed, because in an odd way the ⟨fabric⟩{connective} tissue of life has gone. Everybody is living miles away from where they usually do and has shut up their house and if anybody gets ill the relevant doctors and surgeons aren't to be found, so if you have stayed in London life goes in endless odd jobs. If it weren't for the sailors being drowned one could stand it, and of course it's a disappointment about the Finns. It did seem that once we had declared war we wouldn't have this awful business of being comparatively safe and seeing the smaller peoples being butchered. Do please give our love to all your blessed crowd.

I have bought a derelict farm & put it on its legs, we are now parents of a small herd of cattle, and a lovely house goes with it, the sort of house you can imagine Alice in Wonderland living in, (I mean the very stodgy house she really lived in, there's nothing wonderlandish about it.) It's almost impossible to get there so we can't live there. I bump my behind into a most curious flattened shape in byroad motor buses ⟨and⟩{to} talk about oil-cake and pig food with my retainers, and come back at a snail's pace through the blackout. But really it will be a nice place for you to come and stay at when this thing is over.

Yours ever,

Rebecca.

Loving greetings
from Henry

Irita Van Doren Papers   manuscript on Christmas card
Library of Congress

To: Alexander Woollcott   Ibstone House
                                           Ibstone, near High Wycombe
                                           Bucks
                                           April 1941

Dear Alec,

I am grateful for the bouquets. The Yugoslavian book now seems to me a preternatural event in my life. Why should I be moved in 1936 to devote the following 5 years of my life, at great financial sacrifice and to the utter exhaustion of my mind and body, to take an inventory of a country down to its last vest-button, in a form insane from any ordinary artistic or commercial point of view—a country which ceases to exist? I find the hair raising on my scalp at the extraordinary usefulness of this apparently utterly futile act. By the way, I wish you'd hunt about in the latter part of the book—the last quarter—and find a section called "St George's Night." I think this one of the strangest experiences ⟨xxxxxx⟩ {a human being could have in} passing through different levels of being—and under the New Order probably not to be repeated by any of our race. I cannot bear to read the proofs. Probably every soul I write of has passed through such agony that, even though one may have to face it oneself later, is not bearable to contemplate. (This sounds illogical, but I mean that usually you can't be sorry for people who are ⟨x⟩ {only} going to endure what one is going to oneself, but there were such gems and wild flowers of people that their fate is apart and specially, infinitely regrettable).[1] Please note that the best part of the book is the last part. I often of late have in this connection recalled how old Sir Robertson Nicoll,[2] informed that his opinion of one of Sir John Buchan's[3] books was unjust as the final chapters were very fine, dourly replied, "Mebbe, but there's few but our John will ever know that."

I enclose a letter which is, I think, a supreme achievement. It just cannot conceivably be surpassed, {ever or anywhere.} The ghoul who wrote is the wife of the Bishop of Lincoln. She wrote a letter in the summer before Munich to the *Times,* complaining that the B. B. C. gave forth such alarming news bulletins, full of unpleasant stuff about the dictators, which might cause panic among the public and irritate these dictators, and prevented her from "going happily to bed—" which I should have thought was a matter to be attended to by the Bishop of Lincoln rather than the B.B.C. I wept with rage and a bruised feeling that the God who looks after these times is without pity and without shame—but actually it's Dickens {and ?}. I still ache to think Leonard Woolf must have read it. It is not a good dream to ⟨x⟩ {imagine} Virginia walking out of that exquisite garden he had made for her—he was a "green finger" and everything flowers more brightly and lavishly than for anybody else—and going down into the ⟨x⟩ {landscape} they'd looked on together—the garden was a high terrace, which looked over the ⟨marshes⟩ {water-meadows} along the valley to Lewes, which lies round its castle, it was a very definite place, a real relevant image of them.[4]

 . . . . From this confusion of discomforts I arise to the miraculous beauty of this place in Spring. It is unlike any⟨thing⟩ {where} else—shabby, austere, & right to the last branch, perfect in composition. We have a 50 acre field that falls down the slope of a hill into the trough of a valley which is exquisite in shape. The new crops are pale green transparencies painted over chalky fields and the beechwoods are a soft rose brown with unopened buds. I arise also to the unbearable war news. In which connection—everything I write or say, whether admired or not admired, flows past people without ⟨x⟩ {leaving} the faintest impression on them. I wonder if you remember what I said at the meeting of the Town Hall when you were chairman? I bet you don't. I bet nobody who was in the audience does. I said that a reorganisation of society was imperative, because the conditions of the mechanised world gave no satisfaction to the primitive instincts, & that these would burst out in violent action and in a search for a new basis for the exercise of power if the old system couldn't find a legitimate channel for these instincts. The townspeople, factory and office workers, I informed uninterested New York, would act up. I don't think the audience got their money's value in political or social prescription, and probably not even in oratory, but I think they got fair value in prophecy.

Yes, the deathbed scene is straight out of a work on Macmillan's list by the author of Elizabeth.[5] (I am so glad, by the way, that Pat is in America, she seems to me one of the human species most deserving of survival.) I do not remember if I've ever told you the *close* of our conversation in ⟨x⟩ {her} garden at Monguis (or wherever on The Alpes Maritimes) in 1935. The first time we had ever met, so long and so bitterly did she resent ⟨my⟩ {the} loss of H. G. We had a long and pungent conversation, I don't think I ever ate a better curry. It occurs to me, illustrative of the impossibility of biography, that I am probably the only living person to know what determined Elizabeth's life for a period of some years and affected it slightly for ever after—not only factually but with a full realisation of its quality—and she was the only person I ever knew who had the corresponding knowledge about myself. But as it is in the realm of possibility that to the third generation from now we shall be as incomprehensible as Esquimaux I don't suppose it matters.

I have written only to Emanie [Arling] and you as yet, and probably both of you will believe without reserve when I say that my mind is working like a very old Victrola. Emanie, by the way, has been angelic beyond belief in standing by with every offer of help and promise of welcome, if I ship Kitty who is expecting a baby in September, to America. But Kitty says she won't leave Anthony. It is odd to sit and wonder if ⟨you⟩ {I} have everything ⟨you⟩ {I} want (as the poverty we are all doomed to even in case of victory doesn't matter) or if the horsefaced type of Englishwoman I have always hated has done me out of the lot. In the meantime I am knitting a white pullover for Henry (can't read much, eyes and head tire) and sowing flowers for naturalisation in our woodlands. It is maddening not to know what has really happened in Greece (the Prime Minister's death seems ominous)[6] but there is nothing to do [but] to continue with these light distractions, although I ache to write—but I don't know what & certainly couldn't.

Much love,
Rebecca West

Woollcott Collection, bMS Am 1449 (494)   manuscript
Harvard University

[1] In another letter to Woollcott concerning *Black Lamb and Grey Falcon* (27 December 1940, Harvard University), West records another wartime loss:

I picked up a book which is one of the London Library ones I am firmly housing here. (I got out every book I thought indispensable on my pet Balkan subjects and brought them down here—if the London Library has not sense to evacuate themselves I must do it for them.) I picked up this one which was called *Byzance après Byzance*—about the perpetuation of Byzantine culture by the aristocrats driven out of Constantinople by the Turks and scattered through Roumania and Italy—such a lovely appreciation of the survival of a few pleasant human activities in a general headachy chaos. Such pride in the men who did it—the book was by Iorgo, the old Professor who had been butchered in Roumania a few days before by the Nazis—and this was the copy he himself had presented to the London Library. Ai, ai.

She reported to him on 22 May 1940 (Harvard University): "We are all going about our business, with one eye on the map and a certain amount of curious feeling about the bowels. I have never felt so coldly ferocious in my life, and optimistically carry a couple of linoleum knives wherever I go."

[2] Sir William Robertson Nicoll (1851–1923), Scottish-born minister and editor of the nonconformist London journal the *British Weekly,* who contributed weekly book reviews. He also wrote biographies.

[3] John Buchan (1875–1940), Australian-born statesman, novelist, and biographer of Sir Walter Scott and Oliver Cromwell. His adventure stories include *The Thirty-Nine Steps* (1915), *Greenmantle* (1916), and *Three Hostages* (1924).

[4] This allusion to Woolf's suicide, which followed her "walking out of that exquisite garden" resembles the final walk of Marion in West's novel *The Judge.*

Much of the remainder of the letter (which has been cut) concerns West's operation for fibroids, conducted in a maternity hospital, and her slow recovery. She felt oppressed by a nurse who seemed to dislike her, by her surgeon who told her she would soon need her gall bladder removed (an operation more painful than the one just completed), and by her sister Letitia, about whom she had the following revelation:

The member of my family, whom I have recorded, perhaps too favourably, as Alice in "Salt of the Earth" and Eva in the S. E. P. *[Saturday Evening Post]* piece you approved, came in for a visit. ⟨xxxx⟩. I breathed out that I felt rather alarmed by what the surgeon had said—she leaned over me with that absent look I wrote about and confirmed ⟨what⟩ the surgeon's remarks with a gentle convincing flatness, refusing, in spite of all Henry's efforts, to leave or change the subject. I lay and gasped, not caring so much about the gall bladder as realising how my life had been unnecessarily darkened from its beginning, by this little dear, who has always been at my side when life was at its darkest, to make it as bloody black as she could possibly help, with the most ⟨x⟩ {firm} persuasion, & the drive that such persuasion gives, that she belongs to the forces of light.

[5] Mary Annette "Elizabeth" von Arnim (1866–1941), New Zealand-born novelist, first married to a Prussian count. She was involved with H. G. Wells when West first met him. Her unhappy second marriage to the brother of Bertrand Russell is reflected in *Vera* (1921), which West admired; *Enchanted April* (1923) is her best-known work.

[6] John (Yanni) Metaxas (1871–1941), with the consent of the Greek king, had assumed dictatorial powers in 1936 to prevent a communist coup. His forces successfully repulsed an attempted Italian invasion through Albania (1939–1940). He died on 29 January 1941. The Germans invaded Greece through Bulgaria and Yugoslavia (April 1941).

To: John Gunther   15 Orchard Court
                                              Portman Square, W. 1
                                              [late April–10 May 1941]

Dear John,

I am staggered by your kindness in giving an affidavit for Anthony and Kitty [West]! I must explain how it happened. I suddenly got a cable from Emanie Arling saying {that} with great nobility she had signed an affidavit committing her self to support Henry & myself for the rest of our lives and asking us to suggest sponsors for Anthony and Kitty.[1] I was struck dumb because I didn't like to send any such cable, because it might have looked as if Anthony (who is waiting for his call-up) was trying to get out of the country, an idea which drives us all frantic!—and also I think that such affidavits are of academic value. If the Germans win (which I don't think they're going to) Henry & I will be dead or in prison, and the same applies to Anthony, who ⟨will⟩ {might} cop it ⟨all ways⟩ {in still another} way and be conscripted in a Germany army. If we win we'll have to face a difficult period of resettlement when nobody worth their salt must leave. But I can't say this to affectionate little Emanie, who will mourn us as dead and think we're having a hell of a time, whereas sitting on a firework has a curious wild charm. So I didn't cable, & she ran around among my friends. But anyway it was magnificent of you to sign, and you are all I ever thought you and a good deal more.

I would have given something to be in France in the crash. You couldn't understand why I wrote *The Thinking Reed*—everybody in it except Marc and Isabelle were the Fifth Column, & I always thought of it as having a sequel in which Marc and Isabelle would die violent deaths in a revolution.[2] The funny thing is the French here are like drugged people. They look at you with blank eyes & say that the important thing is for de Gaulle to have no politics! I am told by an old lady who was a lady-in-waiting at Court that the ⟨two people⟩ {only person} who prophesied this day was—you'll faint!— Queen Alexandra.[3] Everybody thought her a fool because she was deaf, but apparently she was a wizard about international politics and always foresaw this.

London is fascinating now. The queer thing is the burden of coping the war brings. Henry spends his life seeing to odd things for the interned anti-Nazi refugees in such hours as are left him from the Ministry of Economic

Warfare, and I having done a 350,000 words [*sic*] on Yugoslavia (!)[4] and acquired a farm find that every ⟨thing is⟩ {moment is} filled with relatives who've had to leave their houses and so on, while there's a lot of occasions for a sudden spring back into journalism. Harold Nicolson is a great success, easing the tension of the inevitable spy-scare,[5] and being civilised in war-time. Sibyl Colefax[6] does a good job by having dinner-parties where people in the ministries whose wives are evacuated & haven't any homes can meet each other—but her letters to America are often sent back, as possibly [damaging?] of aircraft. I wish I could write you a really candid letter about the extraordinary liveliness of England, but I couldn't do it without indiscretion. Chamberlain[7] and constipation have more in common than that they both begin with C and we all feel as if the Tascol had worked and everything was grand. I was talking of you the other day to a nice Canadian called Holton, who was with you at Leipzig and had pleasant recollections of you. Blessings on you, and all my good wishes to Frances.

Yours ever,

Rebecca

Papers of John Gunther, Addenda   manuscript
University of Chicago

[1] In an earlier letter (17 April 1941), West had mentioned the possibility of Kitty's coming to the United States on Gunther's affidavit, as she was expecting a baby. West told Lady Rhondda that Anthony had tried to get assigned to a minesweeper, but in the meantime he was "running a 68 acre farm, & gets up at 4.30 every morning, and sends 40 gallons of milk into the nearest town, and is ploughing up derelict land in his spare time" (28 July 1940, University of Texas at Austin).

[2] The wealthy American widow Isabelle marries the millionaire Marc Sallafranque in the course of *The Thinking Reed* (1936), a novel set in France around 1928. "Fifth Column" refers to subversives who work from within to undermine a nation.

[3] Queen Alexandra (1844–1925), former Danish princess and consort to King Edward VII (m. 1863).

[4] Gunther responded to *Black Lamb and Grey Falcon* in a letter dated 6 October 1944 (University of Chicago): "Just let me say that I thought *Black Lamb and Grey Falcon* belongs with Velasquez, the third act of *King Lear,* and all nine symphonies of Beethoven. I read it when it came out with slow and loving care. Then this spring I went through most of it again, comma by comma. You should see my marked copy. I haven't read a book so carefully since *War and Peace*. I was revolted by most of the reviews I saw because they missed the two things I thought most admirably notable: 1) the application of the book's theme—that is the conflict

between love of life and love of death—to every kind of human problem; 2) the fact that it surely contains some of the finest descriptions of *nature* in the English language. And it somehow pleased me too that it was not so much a book about Jugoslavia as about Rebecca West."

⁵ There was a universal fear that Nazi spies might be abroad in Britain.

⁶ Sibyl Colefax (d. 1950), celebrated hostess (wife of Sir Arthur Colefax) who entertained political and cultural figures at their home in Chelsea, Argyll House. Henry Andrews commented to Wendell Wilkie that she was "full of knowledge, discretion, and judgment" (Wilkie folder, West papers, Yale University).

⁷ Neville Chamberlain (1869–1940), British prime minister (1937–1940), forced to resign in May 1940, after the British failed to keep the Germans out of Norway (April 1940). At Munich (1938) he had favored appeasing Hitler.

To: V. S. Pritchett¹   Ibstone House
                                                             Ibstone
                                                             High Wycombe
                                                             Bucks
                                                             11 July 1941

Dear Mr. Pritchett,

I sent you the Letters the other day, which I think you may find interesting. I have long wanted to write something about Madame de Staël,² whom I think a much misjudged character. I think that it is very remarkable how all the people who were closely associated with her liked her very much, and I also think her book on the French Revolution really superbly written. I think the chapter on Mirabeau a masterly evocation of a personality. One gathers from the writing that she was not insensitive to the gentleman's charm, though I do not think charm is quite the right word. Obviously something stronger would meet the case better. I also think that Madame de Staël obviously had perfect hell over the complicated financial life of her husband. I believe in one of Lonôtre's books there is a very curious essay on de Staël's financial relations with a French actress, I think Mademoiselle Clarion.

By the way, much that has been written about Madame de Staël in English shows our curious national habit of writing monographs on one subject without looking into its context. Again and again one reads abuses of Madame de Staël for not subordinating herself to her husband's career as a Swedish diplomat, and her insistance on making him live in France. But, of course, she was acting exactly like an American woman who was married to an anti-Nazi German who was in the German Diplomatic [Corps], and trying to get him a safe job in the U. S.

I suppose that you know that the descendants of Madame de Staël, the de Panges, have loads of private papers concerning Madame de Staël, which they release every now and then most annoyingly.[3] All these releases, I must say, do seem to redound to the credit of the old girl.

I wonder if you know David Glass Larg's unfinished work on the life of Madame de Staël? He got T. B. and ran a teashop to keep himself on the Isle of Wight, and took to writing worse and worse books, which did his reputation a lot of harm. But the two volumes on Madame de Staël,[4] which he wrote in French, were extremely fine.

I shall look forward to your writing some day an exciting work about Madame de Staël. I think that the Benjamin Constant[5] set were the ancestors of all the people who have plagued our day by renouncing normal love, not for the sake of direct asceticism with a religious motive, but just in order to increase the amount of disagreeableness in life for purely secular motives. As such I think they are very important. I believe, of course, that this attitude has been carried on throughout the ages, but I think that in this group it first got definitely associated with intellectuals.

With all good wishes,
Yours sincerely,

Rebecca West Papers   carbon typescript
Yale University

---

[1] Sir V. S. [Victor Sawdon] Pritchett (1901–1997), English novelist, critic, short-story writer, and autobiographer. He started his career as a journalist in Ireland and Spain; his first collection of stories was *The Spanish Virgin and Other Stories* (1930). His other works include studies of Balzac and Turgenev and *The Living Novel* (1946).

[2] Anne-Louise-Germaine Necker, Baroness de Staël-Holstein (1766–1817), French-Swiss author of novels, plays, and political writings, noted for her salon. She developed a theory of Romanticism and was immersed in the culture of her period. For her opposition to Napoleon, she was exiled from Paris. Her friends included Wilhelm von Schlegel and Lord Byron.

[3] Mme la Comtesse de Pange, a descendant of de Staël, related by marriage to Count François de Pange (of whom de Staël was enamored), published *Madame de Staël et la découverte de l'Allemagne* (1929), based on family papers.

[4] *Madame de Staël: La vie dans l'oeuvre (1766–1800)* (1924). His work on Dante Gabriel Rossetti (1933) remained unfinished.

[5] Benjamin Constant de Rebecque (1767–1830), Franco-Swiss novelist and political writer whose *Adolphe* (1816) anticipates the modern psychological novel. He divorced his wife in order to pursue a relationship with the decidedly older Madame de Staël (1794–1806).

To: Alexander Woollcott   11 October 1941

Dear Alec,

I have been rolling in ecstasy on the floor all round my parcel of food and my dear Secretary (she is typing this letter!) and my dear Nancy (the parlour-maid), say they would like some razor blades for their loved ones.

I am just appending a list of what we really are short of over here:

1. Lemon juice and orange juice.
2. Sugar
3. (for town dwellers) Butter
4. Also for town dwellers, De-hydrated onions.
5. For all of us, town dwellers as well as country dwellers, as this year's crop is a failure, dehydrated apples.
6. Silk Stockings.

If you ever saw anybody who was coming over with luggage to spare, who is a friend of mine, you might tell them that what I ache for is a good raincoat. I could wear a small man's raincoat. These are becoming more and more difficult to obtain, and if one is in the country, they are very necessary.

As I told you when I saw you, the trouble is that the shortages are intermittent, and cover the whole of life. I am not suggesting that anyone should send this from America, but [it] is an extraordinary fact that you cannot buy a dustbin for love or money at present, or any saucepans for a high combustion stove.

I cannot tell you how lovely it was to see you.[1] We are waiting here wagging our tails in the hope of the master's voice. By the way, if you have to see the Lowinskys about their children, they live just about fifteen miles away.

Blessings on you.

Rebecca West Collection   carbon typescript
University of Tulsa

[1] West's sketch "The Man Who Came to Dinner" is based on Woollcott's wartime visit.

To: Harold Nicolson   16 January 1942
Dear Harold,

As doubtless many a woman has said before, "God may forgive you Harold Nicolson, I never shall." I really nearly fell dead while I was reading that first paragraph of your letter.[1] I then handed it to my secretary and she almost fell to the ground. Lindbergh too was very fond of practical jokes.

I enclose a letter that I have just found in the debris of the Christmas post. I think from the heading and general tone of the communication that it must really be meant for Vita [Sackville-West].

There, I have done all I can in the way of revenge.[2]

Thank you very much for the kind words that you said. I am afraid that you may be repelled by my remarks about Prince Paul,[3] but I must say I got rather a grim view of him when I was in Yugoslavia. He really did do his job, it seems to me, very badly. Old Moslem gentlemen of great dignity and learning, graduates of the Sorbonne, who had devoted their lives to the making and the service of Yugoslavia, and who had always been received as honoured guests at the palace by King Alexander, were treated by Prince Paul when they went to the palace on public business as if they were tedious country bumpkins. Not only were they not country bumpkins, but one must not be as choosy as that if one has taken on a royal job. So my remarks about Prince Paul are not written out of a snap judgment of his behaviour in the crisis.

I wish you would lunch with us some day in Town. It is terrible the way the war is closing in on us, and one sees so little of one's friends.

Rebecca West Papers   carbon typescript
Yale University

---

[1] In his letter of 13 January 1942 (Rebecca West Papers, Yale), Nicolson pretends to have an acquaintance recently arrived from Yugoslavia whom he wants her to meet, "the wife of a dear little Jew in the Jugoslave Ministry of Information whom I met when I was out there on the British Council. She is actually a German by origin but a most patriotic Jugoslav." This describes West's source for Greta, the arch-villainess of *Black Lamb and Grey Falcon*. Nicolson's closes with the jibe, "She seemed so lost that I have lent her your two volumes to cheer her up."

[2] In his reply Nicolson said nothing about the letter to Vita enclosed by Rebecca West, but he didn't like the comparison to Lindbergh, who had rented Long Barn from the Nicolson family in 1930. He later regretted in the *Spectator* that Lindbergh had turned so anti-British.

[3] West's epilogue to *Black Lamb and Grey Falcon* implicates Prince Paul in a deal made by his ministers in Vienna that allowed German troops passage through Yugoslavia to attack Greece. She also acknowledges that Paul had supporters in the British diplomatic corps who analyzed some of his moves as pro-British. In his response (20 January 1942, Yale University), Nicolson expresses sympathy for her view of Prince Paul and explains, "The only reason why I defended him in any way was that I always rush about looking for lost causes."

To: Edward Sackville-West[1]　　　　　　25 February 1942

Dear Eddy,

I do not think Elizabeth Montagu means anything to anybody except myself.[2] I rashly consented to write an essay on her six or seven years ago, and found that the existing essays about her had been written by people who had simply copied and re-copied a very empty essay written in the [90's?]. There are four huge volumes of selections from her letters done by a rather silly man, but full of amusing stuff. I think there is quite a lot of dramatic stuff in her life. She had quite a dramatic row with Voltaire, Laurence Stern was her cousin and she had a life long bickering with him and his wife which is really quite funny—she felt he was not respectable and she knew that he had something she hadn't got. She also had trouble with Dr. Johnson, and she gave a grand tea-party to chimney sweeps in the garden of her house in Portman Square, and her last years have a great deal of charm in them, because of the contrast between enormous prestige and enormous wealth and her inner dissatisfaction, which showed itself in a very pathetic and sometimes beautifully expressed pre-occupation with her child who had died many years before.

Of course, I quite realise you can turn it down, but don't feel that it is something quite without a basis.

I was so sorry to hear from the Jebbs the other day that you were ill. We have all been ill here, and I can sympathise with the havoc that can be worked on the soul by a bug cooperating with the war news.

Rebecca West Papers　　　　　　　　　　　　carbon typescript
Yale University

[1] Edward Charles Sackville-West, fifth Baron Sackville of Knole (1901–1965), music and book critic for the *New Statesman,* essayist, and novelist. His novels include *Piano Quintet* (1925), and *The Sun in Capricorn* (1934). Vita Sackville-West was his cousin.

[2] Elizabeth Montagu (1720–1800), leading English bluestocking (1750–1800) and author of *Essay on the Writings and Genius of Shakespeare* (1769). West's essay appeared in the collection *Elizabeth Montague*, ed. Bonamy Dobrée (London: Cassell, 1937), 164–87.

To: Hermon Ould: Ibstone House
                                                         Ibstone
                                                         Nr. High Wycombe
                                                         Bucks
                                                         23 April 1942

Dear Hermon Ould,

Herewith the corrected copy of my few words at the P. E. N. Club Lunch. I told you that they would give your secretary fits, and I don't wonder he was worsted.

I could not agree with you more about the way that the Press treated that Lunch. There seems to be any amount of room for Austro-Hungarian propaganda and not a line for these poor blighters,[1] and I thought the attitude of the papers was so uncivil. I am taking the whole thing up with the *Evening Standard* and the *Daily Telegraph,* both papers that I know, because I really think it is a scandal. It is the effect of that extraordinary principle of British education that all British children should be taught to be cold and rude to strangers, and I think it may have disastrous effects after the war.

I may say that everybody I have seen who was at the Lunch thought that it was so awfully well arranged, and compared it most favourably to various other lunches, which I shall not name, but which I am sure you can think of. Cheer up, you will get your reward in heaven—I cannot honestly hold out any promise before then. We should have been born not only in a different world but in a different universe.

                                         Yours sincerely,
                                         Rebecca West

Rebecca West Collection   typescript with autograph signature
University of Tulsa

[1] The guests of honor on this occasion were a group of Slavic notables: King Peter of Yugoslavia, M. Rackiewicz, president of the Polish Republic, M. Beneš, president of the Czechoslovak Republic, M. Krek, vice-premier of Yugoslavia, M. Zinchenko, of the Soviet

embassy, Dr. Milan Grol, president of the Belgrade PEN, and members of the Yugoslavian PEN. West honored them because "all of them might to-day be sitting safe and comfortable in their own homes had they but yielded to the Germans. But when Hitler offered them peace and good treatment on condition that their peoples collaborated with Germany and Italy in the establishment of a reign of evil on earth, all these men said, 'No.'"

To: Ben Huebsch

Ibstone House
Ibstone
Nr. High Wycombe
Bucks
22 July 1943

My dear Ben,

Having put on cherries to simmer with the red-currants and the raspberries, which they have to do for fifteen minutes before I add the sugar, which is warming in the cool oven, {I have not gone mad, but this is how I spend my life these days; and cows come in quite a lot too.} I now sit down to consider your interesting proposition about a book on the British Empire. It is a thing I would like to do, and I am thinking of it all the time. But on the other hand, Lady Rhondda has written a series of papers in *Time and Tide* on the subject, which is really about as good as it could be. Except for the fancy bits on religion and metaphysics that I would throw in in my demented way, she really gives all that I could give and I would like you to have a look at her stuff and either accept it or turn it down before I started writing such a pamphlet for wartime. I mean to treat the subject in a book that I plan for after the war, but I am rather reluctant to do it now, unless I have to.

It was lovely to get the news of my friends. I do hope Dorothy's [Dorothy Thompson's] marriage is going to be a success. It cannot anyway be worse than the others![1]

Yours ever,
Rebecca

Ben Huebsch Papers   typescript with manuscript closing,
Library of Congress   signature, and note

[1] Thompson's most recent marriage had been to Sinclair Lewis.

To: Ruth Lowinsky

Ibstone House
Ibstone
Nr. High Wycombe
Bucks
4 March 1944

Dear Ruth,

Henry and I send Tommy and you our deepest love. It must be torment to lose any son, and I can't imagine what it's like to lose such a good and dear son.[1] Still you did give him a glorious life. I remember how once at lunch Martin did something with a bottle that made it burst and flow all over the place—and he cried out, "Oh, Mummy!" quite reproachfully though you had nothing to do with it. He wondered afterwards why he had said it—but I remember thinking, "How wonderful, his mother is such a defence from all ills in his eyes that when something inconvenient happens it is as if it must be her defence that has broken down." It impressed me tremendously. I hoped Anthony might think of me in the same way. You and Tommy gave him such firm ground under his feet, he never seemed uncertain. He must have known much more happiness in his short life than most people who live a long time, and it was your doing. ⟨But⟩ I know nothing can count with you just now except the sin and crime of his being taken away, but do try to remember what a lovely job you made of his life. I have had convincing evidence of a life after this, though oddly enough it's a subject that has never interested me very much, but I don't know that anybody else's experience is much use. I can only tell you I did have evidence that a boy of twenty-two killed in a plane accident was still an active mind twenty-four hours after his body had been smashed to pieces. It is a story difficult to put on paper. I will tell you some day if you want to hear it. I therefore think it certain that Martin is somewhere just as much as ever, and I hope it seems the same to you, though of course the separation is in itself a torture. But even if it weren't, so the happiness you and Tommy gave him would give you a right to feel you had, so to speak, outwitted destiny and made things right in spite of their end.

Do forgive me if I seem to be writing too intimately. We are so very fond of you both. Let me know if there's anything I can do. If you would like to get away there's always a bed here. I am so glad you have got Clare and Justin back from America.[2] Don't bother to answer this unless there is something we can do.

Yours ever,
Rebecca

Rebecca West Collection   manuscript
University of Tulsa

[1] Martin Lowinsky was killed in the war.
[2] The Lowinskys' other two children.

To: Anthony West   Ibstone House
                                                        Ibstone
                                                        Nr. High Wycombe
                                                        Bucks
                                                        3 June 1944

Dear Anthony,

I ask you to read this letter carefully, to take it seriously, to destroy it and not to answer it. Last week I was urged to see a person unknown to me, on important business. On Friday I went up to town and did so. This person told me that as I knew too much about certain affairs, which is quite true, and as I have refused to make certain false statements which were put to me—and that again is quite true—certain steps were to be taken about me. These concerned you. You, I was told, had been "got hold of" by a group of people who had won your confidence.[1] It was the job of some among this group to see that you ultimately got into trouble. This would probably take the form of maneuvering you into a position where you would seem guilty of some offence and either having you put away under Regulation 18B or as an ordinary offender—or blackmailing me by the threat of doing so. The intention is to discredit me by discrediting you. My informant seemed to know something about you—he certainly knew a lot about my business and what clinches the matter for me, knew a lot about the curious circumstances in which the daughter of a friend of mine left home recently. (I don't know the identity of my informant.) I remembered too that H. G. had said you had spoken to him of some new friends you had made. I realise this may have some shocking implications for you—I cannot throw any light on them, because my informant was interested in me and not in you, and had not troubled, or probably could not trouble if he had wanted to do so, to fill in the details so far as you were concerned. Please, please, <u>please</u> take this seriously. Don't tell anybody about this—and when I say anybody I mean *anybody*. I have a fancy that it might be more disagreeable for me, and possibly you, if the matter were known to be known by us. I ask you urgently for both {our} sakes to behave with the utmost caution. Do not try to find out what has happened or who is responsible, simply sit quiet and hold your tongue. I went to H. G.'s on Friday to try to find you, but was told you had gone till Tuesday. I meant to write all sorts of things to you but I am afraid this rather preoccupies me.

> Much love,
> Rac.

I shall be up in town one day next week. I will send a card to H. G.'s

private collection   manuscript

[1] West was concerned about the friends Anthony was making as a pacifist. Her failure to go along with Britain's acceptance of Tito is probably behind her reference to a refusal to make false statements. Anthony felt that West's suspicions had damaged H. G. Wells's opinion of him at this time. She told Gordon Ray that H. G. had heard that Anthony was involved in a Nazi conspiracy. This remark suggests that Wells knew this story before West did, and that Anthony's suspicions were misplaced.

To: Kit Freund[1]   24 October 1944
Dear Mrs Freund,

If I haven't written to you long ago to tell you of my pleasure in meeting your husband and to thank you for having restored my skin's self respect—it really came to that—it isn't because I'm uncivil, it's because I'm unlucky. In May my son had a complete breakdown after years of overwork as a farmer, and not long after my daughter-in-law became ill. When they were on their feet the doodlebugs were at their worst and my house was filled with refugees, some of whom I knew, some of whom I didn't. When we had got that straight I had a minor, a minimus of an operation; and by some strange misfortune I got blood poisoning. I was for three weeks under M.&B.[2] and for six weeks in bed. I then got up and went to stay with a friend to convalesce. In three days I was returned home with bronchitis. This brought me to the middle of September, since when I have been quietly wheezing, not violently, but monotonously. I came here a week ago—here being a hotel at Bournemouth—to convalesce and I go back to Ibstone tomorrow. This is literally the first day I haven't felt too stupid to write a letter of any importance for about five months. So that is why you haven't heard from me.

I expect you have heard of your husband's visit to us—how everything had gone wrong, and I received him with a patch of flour on my nose and a frying-pan in one hand. Margaret Hodges, my secretary, and I forgot our shame in delight at what your husband is—which I needn't explain to you. When he told us you were about to have another baby she and I burst out in what may have seemed excessive pleasure, but really both of us were so glad the strain was being perpetuated at such a brisk rate. I don't want to be impertinent and intrusive, but there is something very wonderful in that Prince out of a Persian miniature with his enormous capacity for delight and appreciation who yet is not afraid of tragedy, who is curious about suffering also. I was very proud to think my book had bought me an entrance into the world of you two.

I was sorry we couldn't give him a better show in Oxford—Roy Harrod, who showed him over Christchurch, was too tired to be as revealing a guide to Oxford as he usually is. But Stanley Carson's memorial service was something for him to see—my husband's old uncle, Professor Myres, preaching the memorial sermon for one of his most gifted pupils was {a} touching old stoic, very noble. Still, it would all have been better if it hadn't been for this war which has gone on so much too long for us civilians, who haven't *la gloire* to smarten us up. All the same, as my husband said, your husband's personability made that day one he would put among his pleasantest Oxford memories, and he loves Oxford very much.

I thought of your marvellous stockings and vests and panties today [as] I was walking through the garden of one of the villas here—I must explain this hotel is in a suburb of Bournemouth, a fantastic place. I knew it first when I was a child of nine and it was a vast ⟨tangle⟩ {forest} of ⟨pinewoods⟩ {pines and cedars} standing in a tangle of bracken and rhododendron and bramble, with only one great grey house standing on a cliff looking out to sea, which had been built by a M. P. of great gifts and his beautiful wife, who had so loved the wilderness that they directed that their bodies should be buried in a chapel ⟨among⟩ {in} the loneliest part of the woods. They died in about 1870—in the rich years of Edward VII the place was sold and it was cut up into huge plots where villas with twelve to twenty bedrooms stand on huge stone terraces, and in the twenties and thirties smaller houses were built. The tomb of the original owners is now squeezed in between the back gardens of two of the houses in the meanest of these terraces—the wooden fences bulge round it. The dead can now, I observed this afternoon, when I found the tomb, listen to the radio very comfortably. Well—today I went ⟨through⟩ {to} one of the vast villas whose owner I knew—I found it for sale, the top of its tower cut off {so as not} to be a landmark out at sea, and a heartbroken gardener wandering about a garden gone to rack and ruin. The war has made this place inaccessible, there is no transport, there are no servants—and peace won't bring recovery, nobody will ever be able to live there again—it will be too dear. As the gardener moaned to me a cat wandered by. I bent down and patted it, and it was *fat*. No English cats are fat now—my cat has enough to eat, but only because he hunts rabbits, and the hunting makes him thin. But this cat was round and buttery. I remarked on it, and the gardener said, very peevishly and almost enviously, "Of course she's fat, she's a stray that's been picked up by those American soldiers ⟨living⟩ {billeted} across the road." I thought of the stockings and vests and paints I was wearing and loved to feel that the cat and I, in a plunging and catastrophic world, enjoyed such well-being as the result of Christopher Columbus. I really can't tell you what a godsend your present was. I was hideously short of clothes because I had been ill with a tumor which I wouldn't have operated on till I had finished my book, and in that period it wasn't worth while buying any clothes. Then after my operation I lived between town and country and had to restock practically a double set of garments—I had to have a mackintosh, for example, and country boots, which ate up coupons. But thanks to you I am absolutely straight, I need nothing more—and, oh the—in an odd way—spiritual peace of matching all over!

Forgive this long and rambling letter—I don't know why I·should inflict a description of Bournemouth on you, but I have been profoundly impressed by it and it's pervading my mind. It really was odd to go and see the boarding-school I went to as a child of nine, which was even for forty years ago exceptionally prunes and prism, and find it occupied by Negro troops. It is all like a more romantic Proust.

I hope you and your children are well, and I hope very much that you have good news of your husband. We think of him very often, and Margaret Hodges' husband, who is in the Tanks, has an absurd commission to look out for him. But indeed they might meet over there.

My regards, ⟨x⟩ and regards from all of us—my husband and Margaret Hodges—and all good wishes.

Yours ever,
Rebecca West

private collection   manuscript

¹ Katherine Freund, then married to Richard Freund, an American soldier, and who later became an employee at the State Department. He had gone to West to have a copy of *Black Lamb and Grey Falcon* autographed for Kit, and West invited him to tea at Ibstone. After the war, West visited the Freunds in Washington, D.C., and in the 1960s she stayed with Kit and her second husband, Thew Wright, in Mexico.

² *M. & B.* probably refers to a pioneer antibiotic introduced by the May & Baker pharmaceutical company. As in this case, *blood poisoning* is often used as a vague term to indicate the presence of bacteria in the circulating blood. West had had a cyst removed.

To: Miss G. Rotherham¹   11 December 1944
Dear Madam,

When your letter arrived I looked at it with great distress, because I did not know whether I could safely answer your enquiry without fear of legal consequences, but the author I warned my readers about vaguely died just about that time. This was M. E. Durham,² who had lived in the Balkans a great part of her life, and who should have had a unique knowledge of them. I found her books fantastically unreliable. In one of them she has an account of two Montanegrin Prince Bishops, one of whom was a drunken barbarian, the other a great law giver and saint. Something about the dates worried me, and I discovered she had made two people out of one person, and had been misled by a trifling divergence between two travellers. This was a mistake of quite serious import as it happens. Her anthropology was completely wild, and her account of some of the native customs, when you check them by the younger authors who have worked in the same field, are quite wildly incorrect. She was also a person of wild political likes and dislikes, and her accounts of historical events were often distorted. This I feel very strongly, and I was justified when my book came out, because as it was more or less pro-Serb, and she was violently anti-Serb, she attempted to stop the publication of the book by launching an absurd libel action, which involved her withdrawing from a statement of an event, which she had made before several witnesses. I do not charge this latter event against her, because she was very old, over eighty and it was quite apparent that she was not what she used to be but her books gave me so much trouble when I was working on my book that I do hold that against her still.

Sarajevo, by Seton Watson[3] is indeed an excellent book, and though a certain number of documents have turned up since, they have not been put into book form. There is a French reprint of the trial of Sarajevo which is extremely interesting.

Living Space by Stoyan Pribitchevitch is an extremely interesting book, but its knowledge is only partial, it is written very much from the point of view of the people from the north, and Pribitchevitch is an incredibly silly person. He sent me a telegram once to ask me to use my influence to stop civil war in Yugoslavia; but I may be speaking of the dead—a consideration which does not seem to be worrying me much while writing this letter— because he was certainly captured by the Germans when they made that raid on Tito's H. Q. in Bosnia and he had to fly to Vis.

Thank you very much for your kind words about my book. It is indeed heartbreaking for me to know about my friends.

Yours sincerely,

Rebecca West Papers   carbon typescript
Yale University

---

[1] The letter is addressed to Queen Mary's Library, St. Leonards School, St. Andrews, Fife.

[2] M. E. (Mary Edith) Durham (1863–1944), English travel writer and anthropologist whose works interpreted the collapse of the Ottoman Empire and championed the Albanian mountaineers. Among her works are *Through the Lands of the Serb* (1904), *High Albania* (1909), and *Some Tribal Origins, Laws, and Customs of the Balkans* (1928).

[3] Hugh Seton-Watson (1916–1984), English historian and political scientist whose major works concern East European and Russian history. He served in the British legation in Belgrade until the German invasion of 1941 and spent most of his academic career at the University of London.

To: Stoyan Pribicevic[1]   Ibstone House
                                                   Ibstone
                                                   Near High Wycombe
                                                   Bucks
                                                   5 June 1945

Dear Mr Pribicevic,

The trouble about you, my lad, is that you are beautiful but dumb. Your review shows that you did not understand a page of my book. I don't use the lamb and the falcon in the symbolic sense you imagine, my portrait of Bishop Nikolai is not "biting" but an admiring tribute to someone who was doing his job superbly and who had a proper attitude to Stoyadinovitch,[2] and I write page after page celebrating the courage and worth of the peasant—who was the figure in the Yugoslav landscape which made me write that book. It was not honest of you to mention that Vinaver censored *Inside Europe*[3] without saying that you derived that knowledge from a passage in my book describing how I had attacked him for that act. Go and sit in the corner and think over the family tradition and come out a better boy, I will be delighted to welcome you.

About the political aspects of your review: please cut out that stuff about the Belgrade Press Bureau, which is an obsession among you émigrés. It had no influence on my views of Yugoslav politics. My connection with that body was formed after I had decided to write a book on Yugoslavia on roughly the same lines as I wrote it, and it was a straightforward and unimportant connection. To make a long story as short as I can, I went to Finland in 1935 and saw a lot of people there including the Communist leader, Vuoluoki, who seemed to me a superb woman, and I wanted to write a book on small nation[s] torn between the conflicts of greater powers. I meant to go back to Finland from time to time for a matter of years, but I went to Yugoslavia some months later on a lecture-tour for the British Council, and realised that this was a far more exciting and noble subject. I went with some experience of Nazi Germany and Fascist Italy and a supreme loathing of both, and a great distaste for Austria, which I thought the nastiest of the old European powers and in her present phase very willing to hold the bag for Nazi Germany. I had also thirty years of experience as a journalist behind me, and this had given me something quite other than the naiveté that you have so naively ascribed to me. I very soon after my arrival in Yugoslavia had some illuminating conversations in the clubs and universities I addressed, I met some English friends in Belgrade and thought they had got it not quite right, I had a very revealing evening with some Croat, Serb and Slovene students at the Army Medical College at Nish, I went off to Greece and Bulgaria resolved to go home, get together a good foundation of reading, and then come out and see the place again, and do a book. It was then that the Belgrade Press Bureau approached me with the request that as a repre- sentative of the British Council I should go to Macedonia for ten days and broadcast in English for the Belgrade radio when I returned, and the British Council asked me to accept. That was my first contact with that body. The Press Bureau sent Vinaver with me, and in this I was very lucky.[4] He was criminally voluble, I have never known any human being talk so much, but he was a kind creature with great enthusiasm and affection for works of art and human beings, he loved meeting the people we came across on the road and drew them out, he had a lot of information, and his situation was of course a godsend to the writer—as a defeated liberal, as the Jewish husband of a Nazi wife, as an assimilated Jew, as a gifted human being who had not realised his promise and was conscious of it and was therefore a symbol of humanity everywhere. He spoke rarely of the dictature and if you think it over you will realise that this was natural enough. He never spoke one word that I can remember of serious criticism of any Left Wing leader, and the only person I can remember him seriously attempting to blacken in my eyes (and very properly too) was Koroshets.

I went back to London and worked on Yugoslavia, and found out a great deal about the country and the part it played in the dream of other countries. I may tell you that while your friends were chattering about the Belgrade Press Bureau there were forces at work against them which were much more deserving of their attention. I came back and told everybody I could who had any influence that Stoyadinovitch was purely venal and that if he were persuaded that England would take an interest in him he would abandon his near-Fascist tactics at the drop of a hat and there would then be a Liberal Yugoslavia which would be friendly to England and a bulwark against Fas- cism, and that the next stage would be the exit of Stoyadinovitch. In conse- quence of this I learned quite a number of things. There were in Belgrade a number of people who posed as ⟨xxx⟩ sympathisers with the enemies of the regime and spread over Europe stories against the regime—but not because they were friends of liberty. Their aim was to discredit Yugoslavia and make it seem an uncivilised country, which deserved to be partitioned between Italy, Hungary, and Nazified Austria. It was partly to defend your country against this ⟨x⟩ {propaganda} that I wrote my book.

The second time I went to Yugoslavia the Press Bureau lent me Vinaver for some weeks, which was most helpful, and the Ban of the Vardar Provinces lent me his car and chauffeur for a fortnight, I was careful to wip[e] off any financial obligation by certain gifts of money and books to various institutions. Again Vinaver concentrated in his talk on other subjects than modern politics, though of course he did mention them when our situation—as in Zagreb—thrust the subject on him.

The third time I went to Yugoslavia I saw Vinaver only twice as I stayed only three days in Belgrade, and I spent the rest of the time entirely with various friends of mine who were all anti-Stoyadinovitch. (I wonder that you think the Belgrade Press Bureau would have inspired me to write a book in which I make such remarks about Stoyadinovitch as that I had in the whole of the country only found two people who would say a good word for him and that his hand had fallen with merciless cruelty on the working class, I saw no other person connected with the Press Bureau during any of my visits to Yugoslavia except Lukevitch, whom I saw for perhaps ten minutes, and three local representatives with whom I had the most superficial encounters. With none of them except Vinaver did I have any conversation at all about the political situation in Yugoslavia. I have had some correspondence with the Press Bureau of a totally uninteresting nature—for example concerning permission to stay in monasteries where I wanted to study the frescoes and wished to stay longer than the usual three days. Once I discovered that Lukevitch imagined I had written some grossly offensive articles about Yugoslavia which had appeared in a foreign newspaper (describing the Yugoslav peasant as an animal and Yugoslav towns, especially those in the Vanat and the Vojvodina as contrasts to their neighbours' towns in their bestial filth) and wrote him a letter disclaiming them, and received a civil answer. Once, out of curiosity I wrote to them for particulars concerning incidents of which I happened to have eyewitnesses' accounts—one [w]as the Senj riots—and got back statements that suppressed a bit but were on the whole more accurate than I had expected.

As a routine precaution I wrote about no place (except, for quite good reasons, Jajce and Travnik) I had visited with Vinaver unless I had visited it also with a non-official Yugoslav.

In view of these facts I would be glad if you would kindly refrain from making the allegation that I got my views from the Press Bureau. . . .[5]

As for the second part of your letter, I have not advocated "foreign rule over a part of the Yugoslav people." I do not wish the Italians to rule over a single acre, or for that matter, square inch, of Slovene territory. But the Yugoslavs should not break the common understanding of the United Nations by attempting to occupy territory before the Peace Conference. ⟨where the problem can be discussed with full knowledge of the issue, including the degree to which Tito's government implies Russian absorption of Yugoslavia. For⟩ {I must point out that} it is your friends, not mine, who approve of "foreign rule over a part"—indeed, the whole—"of the Yugoslav people."

I require no reminder that it is necessary to differentiate between a country and its regime and have often done so in the case of my own. And when you say "it is facile to be a friend of Yugoslavia when your personal friends are in power" you show that misunderstanding which makes your review of my book so deplorable, I am really not such a barbarian or such a simpleton as to confuse friendship with government. To take an example, I am very fond indeed of Father Kuhar, but as I disapprove of the political influence of the Roman Catholic Church I should be sorry if at a free election the Slovenes should vote his Party into power. I do not feel any feeling of warm liking for Mr Krnjevitch, but I should think it right and natural if he were in a Yugoslav Government. I like Yugoslavia very much indeed when Stoyadinovitch, who is the kind of person I despise, was near-dictator. I could give you examples from my own country which would add to this proof that I require no such lesson as you are attempting to give me. But when you tell me to "be a friend of Yugoslavia when your personal enemies are in power" you are talking nonsense. Marshal Tito is not my personal friend or my personal enemy. He is not even my enemy because he is a Communist, for I can imagine that a free and spontaneously Communist Yugoslavia might be an inspiring spectacle. But Marshal Tito seems to me the tyrannical instrument of a foreign domination, and when you appeal for support of him for the sake of your country you are speaking {in} the same accents as those who urged people to be loyal Frenchmen and worked for the good of France under Petain or to be loyal Norwegians and work for the good of Norway under Quisling.[6]

As for you[r] last sentiment, "A nation, Miss West, has the supreme right to disown its sons without giving any reason, but no man on earth has the right to disown his country, native or adopted, for any reason whatsoever." I can only beg you to believe that I am not in the Seton-Watson or Kingsley Martin[7] or Dorothy Woodman class,[8] but am much too much like yourself for it to be worth your while to make that sort of remark to me. A nation cannot disown its sons by any theory of international law if it recognises law at all; and, my lad, you went pretty near disowning your country when you refused to do your military service, and what you did then you could have done again, and should have done, when it was a case of aiding a foreign domination. And that reminds me, you have a heck of a nerve for talking contemptuously about the Yugoslavs who "consider themselves as martyrs for not getting pensions from Tito or for being called up for military service in wartime." Possibly there is some medical reason why you did not fight the Germans and Italians and are not fighting the Japanese, but even so it ill becomes you to say ill words about people who have never refused to fight, but only to fight under Tito. And as for pensions, you move out of Dorchester House[9] before you start reproaching people who are left on their uppers because they have been deprived of allowances which they were guaranteed by the State when it hired them, and which they have lawfully earned.

I regret that you continue to commit yourself to this propaganda. You will in all probability work yourself right out of America, where you can get on terms with life, into a community where you will not last a couple of years. This is none of my business, so it is good of me to mention it. I shall be up in town next Monday and will stay over to Tuesday. I expect my husband will be up there too, and we will be most pleased to meet you. You will be far better off with us than with these influential ⟨visitors⟩{Britishers}, who either can't read or are of imperfect honesty.

With all good wishes,
I am,
yours sincerely,
Rebecca West

Rebecca West Papers
Yale University

typescript with autograph signature and
insertions, probably a draft

[1] On 13 August 1943, Pribicevitch sent a telegram headed "Yugoslavia" to West in reaction to her letter. It was published in *Time and Tide* (24 July 1943). He urged her to throw her influence behind a compromise between Mihailovitch and the Partisans, rather than perpetuate a civil war. He reviewed *Black Lamb and Grey Falcon* in the *Nation* (1941) and sent her a typed copy in a letter (31 May 1945, Rebecca West Papers, Yale University). This letter responds to his criticisms.

[2] Milan Stoyadinovitch (1888–1961), Serbian politician who served as Yugoslavia's minister of finance (1922–1926) and premier and foreign minister (1935–1939). In managing foreign affairs, he abandoned traditional allies, Czechoslovakia and France, in favor of Nazi Germany. Prince Paul accepted his resignation.

[3] John Gunther's study focusing on Hitler, Mussolini, and Stalin (1936) was also banned in Germany.

[4] Of course, this description may seem somewhat at odds with West's letter to Henry Andrews, April 1936, in which she complains about Vinaver's behavior on her first visit to Yugoslavia.

[5] West discusses several very specific points involving the historical accounts of Yugoslavia made by Pribicevitch's father, which have been cut.

[6] Vidkun Quisling (1887–1945), the Fascist puppet prime minister of Norway (1940–1945) during the German occupation, was executed after the war.

[7] Kingsley Martin (1897–1969), English historian and biographer who edited the *New Statesman* (1931–1960). Notable works include his biography of prominent British Labour Party Member turned Marxist Harold Laski (1953) and *French Liberal Thought in the Eighteenth Century* (1929).

[8] Dorothy Woodman (1902–1970), English journalist for the *New Statesman,* the companion and co-worker of Kingsley Martin. An anti-imperialist and anti-fascist, she reported on World War II resistance movements and refugees and, unlike West, garnered support for Tito. Her books include *Europe Rises: The Story of Resistance in Occupied Europe* (1943) and *The Republic of Indonesia* (1955). She supported the independence movements in Burma and India.

[9] Probably what is now the Dorchester Hotel, which provides fine accommodations near the U.S. embassy in London.

To: Leonard Woolf   ⟨The Lansdowne Club
                                      Berkeley Square. W. 1⟩
                                      Ibstone House
                                      Ibstone, near High Wycombe
                                      [August 1945]

Dear Mr Woolf,

Long ago you wrote me such a delightful letter about *Black Lamb and Grey Falcon,* but I didn't answer it, I couldn't. I have a house packed with people with discordant minds and perpetually ailing bodies, and I myself am torn between two or more kinds of work. (The fact is one wants to be God.)

In the end I fell ill with a tired heart, and I have just come back to more or less real life. My heart, the specialists say, is "irritable and ineffective," which is just how I feel. Hence my silence.

I am so glad you liked my book. It is at any rate a faithful mirror, because what has happened since isn't incongruous with what I wrote. I don't know if you remember what I wrote about the body of King Lazar in {one of} the Monasteries of the Frushka Gora—The Germans stripped the tomb of its jewel-work and threw the body into the river, from which it was rescued and taken to Belgrade, where it was reburied before the Cathedral, and is now the object of a cult, but, of course, more fervent than in the first days after Kossovo. What is the use of thinking about human beings as if such things were not done, and are not of value?

I don't see any possible re-education of Central Europe and Italy save by renewal of poetry, that is to say, of religion, a transformation of Judaism and Christianity. {Not of unreason⟨able⟩. I mean the symbolic representation of what is real, behind which a reasonable pattern is always to be assumed and sought. This sounds pontifical, like Mrs Eddy, but I want to make myself clear.}[1]

I was so horrified by the article on Yugoslavia in this week's *New Statesman*.[2] The facts don't exist—*nobody* is in a position to give such a clear picture of life in Yugoslavia—it is guesswork. The attack on the Yugoslav Government was sheer dyspepsia—it has many Left Wing men of undoubted integrity in it, & Right Wing men, too, if it comes to that. And to attack Draza Mihailovitch on the assumption he is really pro-Axis is so grotesque—worse than grotesque—4,100 men and women were killed in Belgrade on Christmas Eve, Christmas Day, & Boxing Day, on the charge they were pro-Mihailovitch. But the most recent refugee from Yugoslavia, who escaped at the end of October, and could best bear testimony to the days of Draza (who is pro-British) was on arrival shut up for *three weeks* in the Patriotic School and only released on the understanding that he did not write a speech about the situation in Yugoslavia! He is a perfectly respectable member of the ⟨Yugoslav⟩ {Serb} Peasant Party, pro-British since childhood. So the Right and the Left join to make confusion, and the poor Yugs don't know where they are.

Thank you *so* much for your letter. I am now trying to write a novel about treachery,[3] which seems to me more and more the root of all our human misery—the desire to frustrate ourselves, not to be what we are.

I do hope we meet again some time.

Yours very sincerely,

Rebecca West

Leonard Woolf Papers   manuscript
University of Sussex

[1] West's note at bottom and in left margin.

[2] Hal Lehrman's "Report from Yugoslavia," the *New Statesman* 30 (15 August 1945): 120. Lehrman claimed "Mihailovitch was not the victim of his subordinates—as his apologists always maintained—but was himself the prime mover in the policy of intimate cooperation with the invaders."

[3] *The Birds Fall Down* (1966) was started this early.

PART FOUR

1944–1955

Confronting Communism

REBECCA WEST'S LETTERS, RARELY BRIEF, BECAME EVEN LONGER IN THE DE-
cade from the mid-1940s to the mid-1950s, as she labored over her own
versions of personal and political issues. A higher proportion of letters from
those years than from earlier decades has survived, some of them in carbon
copies kept by the secretaries who were by then regularly in her employ. The
carbons introduce new problems of transcription—fading impressions and
uncertainty whether some letters were actually sent.

West remained attentive to Yugoslavia and to the postwar challenges of
Europe. Many letters express her outrage over Britain's acceptance of Tito as
the ruler of Yugoslavia or register her concern for displaced persons. West,
who traveled repeatedly to Germany, reported on the final stages of the
Nuremberg war tribunal and in 1949 made an official visit in the company of
Henry Andrews and the American journalist Dorothy Thompson. Charles
Curran, her editor at the *Evening Standard,* became a valuable sounding
board for her investigative reporting, and she valued his assessment of communist activities in Britain.

This was also the period of West's greatest transatlantic journalism, much
of it aimed at interpreting American culture for a British audience. In 1948,
benefiting from Thompson's knowledge of the U.S. political system, West
reported on three presidential conventions. Her letters discuss problems
with syndication and differing deadlines for British and American publications. They also describe the ways of the Amish in the Pennsylvania Dutch
area she visited. In 1945, West became affiliated with the *New Yorker* and,
with the encouragement of its editor Harold Ross, explored her interest in
criminal trials. Her letters concerning Ross betray occasional weariness with
his editing regimen but also amusement and a high degree of respect. He
often marked the best passages of letters from her. By the time of his death
she had "come to love him dearly" (letter to John and Jane Gunther, 14 December 1951, University of Chicago). West, taking time as always to share her
literary and aesthetic opinions, praised and encouraged good work but
scorned Henry Miller and Roberto Rossellini.

A more problematic endeavor on the American front was her study of the
investigative committees of the U.S. Congress, a series of articles written for
the London *Sunday Times* and syndicated in *U.S. News and World Report.*
This was part of West's assault on international communism, and on those

who failed to see it as she did. When such eminent men as Arthur D. Schlesinger, Jr., and J. B. Priestley suggested that she was perceived as a supporter of Senator McCarthy, and hence as a lost liberal, they received hard-nosed responses.

We also learn about day-to-day operation of Ibstone, with its market garden, pedigreed cattle, and staff of seven—many of whom are the subject of extended anecdotes. The mid-1940s inaugurated another era of difficulties with West's son, Anthony West. He left his first wife, Katharine Church, temporarily in 1944 and finally in 1950, when he emigrated to the United States. Rebecca West was concerned about Kitty's financial welfare and the emotional shock to the couple's two children. Speaking with me in 1996, Kitty said that she had never really liked her mother-in-law. Kitty was far more accepting of Anthony's decision than West was, as is shown in Rebecca's bewildered letters to confidantes such as Emanie Arling.

Issues of biography also came to the fore during this period. One incident, indicative of West's desire for control, occurred in 1947 when she prevailed on *Time* magazine to remove from a cover story about her a paragraph discussing Wells's paternity of Anthony. After H. G. Wells died in 1946, Anthony was given permission to borrow papers from the estate in order to work on his father's biography. It was, however, not acceptable that he removed the uncatalogued and unduplicated papers when he left for the United States, or that he destroyed some of his mother's letters included in the archive. It did not help matters that it was West who revealed Anthony's imminent departure to Marjorie Wells. West wrote ahead to friends such as Harold Ross in the United States to prepare them for Anthony's character, as she saw it, but by early 1951, she was expressing pleasure that Anthony had made the grade at the *New Yorker.* He availed himself of her contacts and the hospitality of her friends. Anthony's own story discredited her as a mother by emphasizing the ways he had felt poorly provided for since infancy. West found even old friends such as John Gunther beginning to take his part.

Her correspondence at this time involved an amazing variety of fascinating people, including Anaïs Nin, Henry Miller, Colette, Lionel Trilling, Eleanor Roosevelt, T. E. Lawrence, Harold Macmillan, Kay Boyle, and Ingrid Bergman. There are brief references to Francis Biddle, her lover during the Nuremberg trials, though the actual nature of the affair has to be surmised from his letters, for hers to him have not been recovered. Henry remained supportive, but West's letters express increasing concern for his health, annoyance at his quirks, and the occasional need to get away. She reveals her complicated sense of loss over the death of Wells. West varies her opinions of her former lover Lord Beaverbrook according to the interlocutor and continues to bait Max about his publishing practices and his political role in Churchill's wartime government. Margaret and Evelyn Hutchinson, the latter a zoology professor at Yale, emerge as supportive American friends, and the recipients of West's longest and most comprehensive letters. In 1949, by giving some of these letters to the Beinecke, the Hutchinsons started the Rebecca West Collection at Yale. When West's offer to donate letters she had received from Wells to the British Library met with complications, she began efforts to build the archive at Yale—a decision that has made matters more convenient for the American editor of this volume.

To: H. G. Wells

Ibstone House
Ibstone
Nr. High Wycombe
Bucks
28 May 1944

Dearest Jaguar,

I enclose a letter from Kitty, which I think you ought to see because it is so greatly to her credit. I think it would be as well if you didn't mention it to Anthony.[1]

I have written to her saying that both you and I thought Anthony in a queer state. I felt it was as well to mention this, as the set-up {she describes} seems to me a good deal worse than she suspects.

This is the most shattering blow to me, for while I had had many worries about Anthony when he was 16–19, he had seemed to me completely sta-bilised, and he certainly had shown signs of remarkable practical ability. I had thought him sure of a happy life. He also had shown great kindness and sympathy, I really could not have wished for more loving support in any difficulty. I feel numb.

My dear Jaguar, I hate your having these worries when you are ill. But may I point out that as one who has known the furry carcass for over thirty years it strikes me the doctors have all been wrong, and you need not worry at the moment about removal to

another sphere of $\left\{ \begin{array}{l} \text{usefulness?} \\ \text{controversy?} \\ \text{whatever.} \end{array} \right.$

> Much love,
> Panther

Rebecca West Collection   manuscript
University of Tulsa

[1] The letter relates to Anthony's plan to divorce Kitty.

{must have been written in 1944.}[1]
To: Anthony West

> Ibstone House
> Ibstone
> Nr. High Wycombe
> Bucks
> [1944]

My dear Anthony,

I got your message from Joyce Seligman.[2] Why do you think I think you damnable? My feelings are largely conditioned by my knowledge that if you do anything wrong you will never forgive yourself. You aren't truthful, but you are scrupulous. You are also living through a situation that your father and my father lived through, and the way they took it resulted in their lasting unhappiness. I am anxious that however you take it, it shouldn't be that way. But there are several alternatives. If you can settle this matter by yourself do so. If you find it difficult to do that ask me what I think about it—I've collected a certain amount of relevant material during the last thirty years. But in any case I wish you'd remember that the excitement and support you seek will probably—for you—never be found except in your own work. (It's no use expecting personal relations to do your work for you— they won't.) But I am so very much afraid that as well as everybody else in this business, you are very unhappy, even though you may in a way be very happy.

Much love,

Rac

{I have found this letter in a book left here by Kitty—I have an odd feeling it is a copy made by me, however.}[3]

Rebecca West Papers   manuscript
Yale University

[1] West's note at top, apparently made long after 1944. Letters concerning Anthony's marital difficulties are deliberately gathered together in Part 4 of this volume for the sake of coherence, even though this arrangement violates strict chronology.

[2] A neighbor who befriended Anthony.

[3] West's note at bottom, added later.

To: Harold Ross   18 July 1945
Dear Mr. Ross,

I was so glad to get your letter. I think there has been a long misunderstanding on this subject. I would in any case not have been a frequent contributor to your pages during the war, as I have had a lot of ill health and worry, but about two months ago I received a cable from George Bye asking if I would do a series for you. I wired back that I would be delighted and waited for news of what series was to be, and I never received any information. Then I had a letter saying that you would be glad to have short stories and articles, and when I was trying after some lapse of time to cope with this, I received a cable from George Bye saying that you wanted a London Letter. I knew that Molly Panter Downes[1] had been doing this for several years and had no intention of busting in on her preserves. I would much rather write short stories or articles, as now that I live in the country a London Letter would be difficult to do.

I will send you along a piece on William Joyce.[2] I presume you want this by airmail. It should be rather an astonishing experience, because I have listened so much to Joyce that he is a very familiar personality, and it will be extraordinary to see him for the first time in these circumstances. I am also trying, as I cabled today, to get a card of admission to Amery's [trial] which will be even more poignant, as all of us know [his] father so well.[3]

About the books: it is very kind of you to offer to send me one of them. I think I would rather have the book about Alice Miller. I do not find it [word cut off margin] to read what other people write about Alec [Woollcott]. There [are] all sorts of things too subtle and contradictory for journalistic handl[ing]. For example, that play of his which you have had so much experience of perpetually quarreling with people he really liked and respected this I find so distorted by superficial presentation th[at] it pains me a lot, and I got a good deal of that pain from Mr. Samuel Hopkins Adams' book.[4] So I would rather have the book about Alice Miller.[5] It is very kind of y[ou] to send me an American book, because it is so hard to get hold of them here. May I say in a deprecating way that some very kind friend has been sending me the *New Yorker* for years, and on this matter I wish to make two comments: (a) that if it was you, I cannot tell you what pleasure I, my family and my village have had from them, and (b) that the stream now appears to have stopped. If you like to relate these circumstances in any way it is of course not my doing.

I hope you will like what I send you about Joyce. You have not given me any indication of length. I should imagine that for that kind of thing about 2500 words would be right. Does that suit you?

Rebecca West Papers   carbon typescript
Yale University

[1] Mollie Panter Downes (1906–97), London-born novelist and journalist. Her "Letter from London" ran in the *New Yorker* (1939–1984). She is known for *One Fine Day* (1947), a novel. She supplied the introduction to the Virago edition of *A Train of Powder* (1984).

[2] William Joyce, "Lord Haw-Haw" (1906–1946), Irish traitor to Britain convicted of treason for his radio broadcasts from Nazi Germany during World War II. West followed through with a series titled "A Reporter at Large," which included "The Crown Versus William Joyce," the *New Yorker* (29 September 1945), and "William Joyce: Conclusion" (26 January 1946). She felt empathy for Joyce, even as she defended the British system of justice. Joyce became the subject of the lead essay of *The Meaning of Treason* (1947).

[3] John Amery (1912–1945), convicted and hung as a British traitor, having recruited British prisoners of war to fight alongside Germans and broadcast messages to Britain urging defection to Nazi Germany. West's "The Crown Versus John Amery" appeared in her *New Yorker* series "A Reporter at Large" (15 December 1945). Though West did not name Amery's father, Leopold Charles Maurice Stennett Amery (1873–1955), she described him as "a gifted English-

man who had rendered service to his country" (*The New Meaning of Treason*, 91). He was a staunch conservative M.P. (1911–1945) and a journalist for the *Manchester Guardian* and the *Times*.

[4] *A. Woollcott: His Life and World* (1945). Adams (1871–1958), American journalist who exposed scandals of the Harding administration and the patent medicine industry. He wrote on his native New York State for the *New Yorker* and in his novel *Canal Town* (1944). He was a lifelong friend of Woollcott, who had died recently.

[5] Alice Dure Miller (1874–1942), American writer who was briefly celebrated for her poetry on the war effort, *The White Cliffs of Dover* (1940). Her novels include *Come Out of the Kitchen* (1916) and *The Charm School* (1919).

To: Letitia Fairfield

Ibstone House
Ibstone
Nr. High Wycombe
Bucks
25 September [1945]

Dear Lettie,

The honey had arrived during my absence at the Joyce trial—I will send it off to you as soon as the carrier can take it which will be next Friday. {No—Henry has dispatched it by rail.} The Joyce trial was very fascinating—it was entirely an Irish set-up, Michael Joyce[1] had been a Dublin Castle man, I thought from the Royal Irish Constabulary's letter about him to the Lancashire Police in the last war, which said in effect, "Yes, we know this man is breaking the Aliens Regulations but he isn't *really* an alien," and added, "he is one of the loyalest ⟨x⟩ men in the county." The family came over here after Home Rule and were genuinely passionately loyal to England, and anti-Liberal. I am sure they thought Hitler would kindly restore England to its Victorian state. The 1813 internees in Court were nearly all Irish and a much better crowd than the Mosleyites.[2] It is a bore—the *New Yorker* now reaches London so quickly they have had to delay printing my stuff, as it would get here before the Appeal if it were printed now. There were many things I longed to know—why Michael Joyce had lied about his citizenship since 1908, instead of getting renaturalised as his friend Holland had done, and what Joyce had felt like when he got over to Germany and found {after a few days} that the Germans had signed a Pact with Stalin. It was a great mistake of Slade's not to put Joyce in the box, as Joyce's personality (though he is remarkably plain) is much less repellent than Slade's.[3] I understand Slade rarely appears in Court, and I've never seen a counsel so irritate a Judge, and he bored the jury. The solicitors' work on both sides seemed to me very badly done. The Crown could have got Joyce on the ground that he had left his effects in England (an admitted proof of the intention to continue enjoyment of the King's protection from a 1707 ruling), a policeman in the court told me his friend had searched Joyce's lodgings and he had had everything moved to his father's house. But nobody had thought of that. Perhaps the Crown wanted to get a ruling as to the possession of a passport. I was very much surprised that nobody read the Jury the wording of the passport which specifically alludes to the protection of the King.[4]

It was rather distressing to sit as I did among the American correspondents. The younger ones had never heard of Casement.[5] None of them could follow the legal argument—and could not understand why people born in Lancashire should have strong Irish accents—and they were inclined to think Joyce was "framed" and a good thing too! I am bound to say he showed superb courage. He is a poor little runt—and hideously disfigured with a scar from mouth to ear—his voice was incredible for that physique—when he said "Not guilty" you looked round to see who had really said it.

I am having to engage a cook whom I know will be no real good—and ⟨x⟩ who has a child of six—we are so bored with having children about the house, they always hate their mothers working or are (like Robin Plunket) reared to regard us as exploitable. Mrs Hodges will have to go at Christmas, and I shall be heartbroken. We are both so fond of her. I loathe starting out with all new faces around me. I expect you feel the same.

Much love,
Anne

I do not know if I had got that batch of American cuttings before you left—I do not think so. The situation in America with which we are having to ⟨x⟩ {deal} is a very painful one—since July there have been coming into light a series of appalling "crookeries" by Elliott Roosevelt—he raised $800,000 at least for a {radio} network he started which collapsed almost at once, borrowed from people to whom Roosevelt afterwards gave appointments at some such advantages and who were afterwards asked to settle for small amounts, loan and settlement being negotiated by relatives of the Roosevelts or business associates.[6] A Committee of the House of Representatives has pronounced that President Roosevelt ⟨x⟩ {must have} been privy to these proceedings. This on top of his will, which was very long and grandiose, and left half of all he could to his secretary, who had died six months before—the feeling being it was extraordinary he had not used the time to cancel such a compromising bequest, has caused an anti-Roosevelt feeling which must be anti-British. I think the British press is being too secretive about this.

West, R., MSS   manuscript
Indiana University, Bloomington

[1] Father of William Joyce.

[2] Followers of Sir Oswald Ernald Mosley (1896–1980), head of the British League of Fascists, which he founded in 1932. As a result of his anti-Jewish campaign and support of the Nazis, he was imprisoned (1940–1943).

[3] Gerald Slade, counsel for William Joyce and John Amery.

[4] Because William Joyce was born in the United States to a father who was then a naturalized citizen, one argument was that he did not owe allegiance to Britain. West suggests that he was living under British protection and thus was liable for treason.

[5] Sir Roger (David) Casement (1864–1916), Irish-born British consular agent, knighted for his investigative work into trade in the Congo and the Amazon. He was executed as a traitor for attempting to smuggle German armaments into Ireland to support the Easter Rising (1916).

[6] Elliott Roosevelt (1910–), second son of FDR and Eleanor. With his second wife, Ruth Googins, he purchased Texas radio stations. His father did indeed get Jesse Jones, chairman of the RFC, to make arrangements with Elliott's creditors on the five-hundred-thousand-dollar deal. Among his creditors was John A. Hartford, president of A&P, who was being sued by the Federal Trade Commission on monopoly charges and thus gladly obliged.

To: George Orwell   Ibstone House
                                                                Ibstone
                                                    .   Nr. High Wycombe
                                                                Bucks
                                                                22 February 1946

Dear Mr Orwell,

I feel you don't understand Henry Miller[1] as I do, an extremely offensive assumption, and I shall forgive you if you resent it. I can only offer as an excuse that possibly you haven't seen as much of him as I have for you say Henry Miller "for forty years or more. . . had led an insecure, disreputable kind of life."² Now I have been in touch with Henry Miller since 1933, and it is my firm belief that however disreputable he may have been he has never known a day of insecurity—not at least till the beginning of the war. Miller is a German-American—his German origin accounts for his prose—who after a good Spießburger [petty bourgeois] upbringing, took a job with the Western Union Cable Corporation, of which he eventually became a Vice-President. He then married a lurid trollop of curiously mixed atmosphere³— she was Baudelaire + Jean Lorraine⁴ + early Hemingway—and she upset him and led him astray into all sorts of trouble that didn't go too well with the Western Union. It then occurred to him that there was a way of getting out of all this trouble with the Western Union, ⟨xxxxxx⟩ {and} getting ⟨xxx⟩ into a new and amazing world; and that was to write obscure literature as an expatriate in Paris. He thought this out quite coolly. As part of this Lucien de Rubempré⁵ de nos jours stunt he froze on to a guileless pair—a young American bank representative named Guiler who was married to a beautiful woman called Anais Nin, whom I think the only real genius I have ever known in my life, though her work has abated as the result of the influence of Henry Miller and his wife. I don't think that from the minute ⟨x⟩ {he} got in touch with these people and their friends he had a moment's anxiety about food, clothing, or shelter. He had a particularly delightful flat in Paris which I greatly envied.

He wrote a completely silly book about Lawrence (D. H.)⁶ which Anais Nin asked me to sell in England, but this, to the credit of English publishers, I couldn't do. He was under the delusion that Lawrence had been neglected in England and had been read and rewarded in America, which is not the case, as his sales were five times greater in England. He is very anti-English, and I think this is probably due to his strongly German character. But I feel very doubtful about the "via Newhaven-Dieppe" adventure, as I think it odd that he didn't apply to me for aid, or to T. S. Eliot, to name only two English people with whom he was in contact in 1935.⁷ I must record my whole-hearted conviction that if he had an unpleasant experience with a police-man, or anybody else, it was probably because he had been very unpleasant to the policeman.

The commonplaceness of his opinions and the emptiness of his language, of which you so rightly complain are, I think, due to the fact that he is, beyond all possible doubt, a humbug. But I do not find him personally an unpleasant humbug, and I feel—as you suggest in your remarks about his sojourn in California—that if he stopped being a humbug he might, with the aid of the fluency he has acquired while writing as a humbug, become quite a valuable writer.

Today some[body] said to me that if only Disney would do *Animal Farm* we would have a really contemporary work of art on the cinema. I thought it a grand idea. I very much admired the completeness of that story—every sentence was at the highest level of satire.

Yours sincerely,
Rebecca West

{I must explain that my childhood was spent in extreme poverty and that this has left me with an eye for the real thing and the counterfeit.}[8]

George Orwell Archive   manuscript
University College London

[1] Henry Valentine Miller (1891–1980), American novelist and essayist raised in Brooklyn. He settled in Paris after knocking around the world. Miller is best known for his autobiographical *Tropic of Cancer* (1936), long banned as pornographic in the United States and Britain, as was *Tropic of Capricorn* (1939). Orwell's appreciative essay on Miller "Inside the Whale" (1940) suggests that Miller might institute a new "school" of literature announcing the impending ruin of civilization.

[2] West is quoting from Orwell's review, "*The Cosmological Eye* by Henry Miller" in the *Tribune* (22 February 1946).

[3] June Smith, Miller's second wife, a dance-hall hostess when they met. She told exotic stories about her origins.

[4] Jean de Lorraine (1498–1550), French cardinal, a patron of scholars, artists, and writers, known for his dissolute, extravagant entertainments.

[5] Lucien de Rubempré, a young man from the provinces who was on the make in Balzac's *Les illusions perdues*.

[6] *The World of D. H. Lawrence: A Passionate Appreciation* (1980).

[7] In order to escape his wife June, then in Paris, Miller took a boat from Dieppe to Newhaven, where immigration authorities jailed him overnight as a suspected vagrant. When he did not come up with a guarantor in England, he was shipped back to Dieppe. His story "Via Dieppe-Newhaven" is based on the incident.

[8] Written along left margin of last page.

To: Lady Grigg[1]   29 April 1946
Dear Lady Grigg,

I am writing to you in what I fear may seem to you a rather foolhardy spirit. I am interested in Yugoslavia, and have ties with that country which go back for the last ten years. I was never at all satisfied with the anti-Mihailovitch propaganda which was made during a certain period of the war, partly because I got indirect news throughout of friends of mine of the most perfect loyalty to the cause of the Allies and life-long hostility to the Nazis, who joined Mihailovitch; partly because the case against Mihailovitch as put to me by various persons in the Foreign Office and the War Office do[es] not stand up to investigation when you scrutinise it with the most elementary care (e.g. a gentleman has given evidence that Mihailovitch was collaborating with the Germans when he himself had been in his grave for some years) and partly because the people who gave evidence against Mihailovitch were, even to my certain knowledge both English and Yugoslav, the most shocking villains.

I now find that large numbers of Yugoslavs are in a S.E.P. camp and likely to be abandoned to the charge of U. N. [R]. R. A.[2] when the British Army gets out. In that case they will be quietly kidnapped from U. N. [R]. R. A. and taken back to Yugoslavia. I am quite certain that a very large proportion, if not all of these people, had not the slightest sympathy with the Nazis or Fascists, and did everything they could to fight Germany and Italy. They could be saved if the British Army took them with them when they went and dumped them somewhere in North Africa.

Can you tell me of any person in the War Office who would be approachable on this subject? I have had a long talk with the Bishop of Gibraltar who has been out to see the camps, and has been assured by people who have been watching them day in and day out that they are completely inoffensive people, whom it is ridiculous to suspect of Nazi or Fascist leanings because if they had had them they would not have been there, they would have got away. I may say that most of the people that I knew who were pro-Nazi and pro-Fascist have joined Tito.

Forgive me writing to you when I have not seen you for so long and our acquaintance is so limited, but I feel that you are one of the most practical people I have ever met and decidedly on the side of the angels, and as I am really most anxious about these people I have ventured to write to you.

Yours sincerely,

Rebecca West Papers   carbon typescript
Yale University

[1] Wife of Sir James Grigg, secretary for war during World War II.
[2] United Nations Relief and Rehabilitation Administration, formed in 1943 to distribute food and supplies and assist persons displaced by war.

To: Kitty West   Ibstone House
                                                      Ibstone
                                                      Nr. High Wycombe
                                                      Bucks
                                                      20 May 1946

Dear Kitty,

I gather from various sources that nothing decisive is being done at once, and I hear from my family we will probably have you near us after Whitsun.[1] I can't express how horrified I was by your letter, and how anxious I am, for everybody's sake, that there should be no divorce. I hope it's unnecessary to tell you that I love you and admire you greatly. We will have to talk about the situation, but in the meantime I would like to put some things before you that might be useful.

Since you were both in your twenties when you married, one or other of you, and indeed both, were ⟨likely⟩ {bound} to fall in love again at some future date. I hoped there would be some way for you to smoothe this over, but I think it had to come, inevitably. It may have come for you temporarily and maybe you did smoothe it over. I don't think, whatever the situation, that you ought to think of this as an abnormal catastrophe—it is the necessary price you pay for early happiness. The only thing is that everyone should behave well, and that the later attack shouldn't prejudice what you've made of your marriage—I am deeply sorry that Anthony should have failed to realise this.

I would like to say that I think the present conditions of life make it specially difficult for both of you to cope with the situation. I don't suppose you realise—it took me till the forties to realise it—how immensely less staying-power men have than women. They cannot stand up to any sort of difficulty unless they are the kind of suet puddings, in which case they are really not likely to be in one's life. It has not been easy for you to live a life of hardship on that farm, cooped up with two small children, and isolated by the war. But you naturally stood up to it, and did not ever find any great effort in doing so. But this is not a strain a man would be likely to stand well. I am sure you both want a holiday (we all do) but it is unlikely that you would signal your need of a holiday by behaving stupidly and cruelly—many men, however would. It is of course infernal nonsense—they are Anthony's children as well as yours, but it is ⟨x⟩ {a characteristically} male piece of nonsense. I think you have to accept it and its like if you want to have anything to do with the male.

It's also true that Anthony has special difficulties. He had an appalling childhood. This was, I can say honestly, not my fault. It was due to H. G.'s weakness and the appalling fantastic wickedness of his wife Jane. (By the way, I did not break that marriage up. H. G. and Jane had not lived together for many years before I appeared.) I had to send him to school at three—for the reason that H. G. suddenly wrote to me and said he never wanted to see me again. (This is apparently a family habit.) I had no money, no friends, and was in wretched health. I had to send Anthony to school ⟨x⟩ {in} order to get on with my work, and in a way this was the wisest decision I ever took (though H. G. reappeared in ten day's time) but Anthony felt it terribly—and at school he heard two teachers saying that I had obviously sent him there because I did not love him. My life was full of horrors, and he felt, quite wrongly, that I could not be bothered with him, when actually I was aching to make a settled home for him, and was prevented by one infernal misery after another. Then when I left H. G. finally I could only do it by going to America, and it was not easy for Anthony—and he was pushed about ⟨x⟩ {to an} awful school ⟨x⟩ {which H. G. chose} for him. Then H. G. was so angry {at me for leaving him} that he did everything to make my relations with Anthony difficult, in his eleven–thirteen period. Then he had this six months in a sanatorium, which was not easy for him, and spoiled his career at Stowe—and as you know he had health difficulties after that. I have always done what I could for him; but I know I've been able to do little for him. For years I did not dare to discipline him, because H. G. was always at hand to say I was wrong. And it is the worse story, because H. G. and I really loved one another, and in a sense still do. But it was not a good training for Anthony, and you must reckon him as shell-shocked. If his shell shock should ever take the form of his going out of the happiness you can give him, you must forgive him. But I really don't think it will take that form. I am deeply sorry my failure should have given you such a thorny problem to solve. But I know that Anthony—whom I often misjudge, because he looks ⟨is⟩ physically so like me that I often assume he is like me mentally, though I think we have very few qualities in common—has a deep desire for love,—which has led him to appreciate the love you gave him—together with a tendency to snarl at it, worry it, and chase it in a corner, which is a torment to himself and ⟨every⟩ {the} persons he loves. I cannot believe many people would have coped with this condition {as you have done}, and I think Anthony will realise this again (as he has realised it in the past).

H. G. tells me he has talked to Anthony about it, and dissuaded him from doing anything decisive, and found him not at all difficult to dissuade. I think H. G., who is very good and sweet just now, will help Anthony to keep his sense of values. I think he is also trying to help him about his work—if only Anthony could get on satisfactory terms with his writing I think he would be more balanced. H. G. spoke with the greatest admiration and affection of you. By the way, I agree with you—as I asked my family to tell you—that H. G.'s illness is affecting Anthony most severely.

When you come over here we must talk about how you can get back to painting. Possibly you can't do it for some little time, but it must be planned for.

I know nothing about Joan.[2] Anthony has not written or spoken a word about the business to me.

Please, *please* hang on. There will certainly be moments when you will not want to, when you will want to walk out. But possibly all things will come right—for all of you. I can't write what I feel about you, and Caroline and Edmund, but Henry and I are heartbroken over this.

Our best love—

Rac

Rebecca West Collection   manuscript
University of Tulsa

¹ Whitsun, the seventh Sunday after Easter, or Pentecost, the descending of the Holy Spirit to earth.

² Presumably the fellow worker at the BBC whom Anthony wanted to marry.

To: Emanie Arling

Ibstone House
Ibstone
Nr. High Wycombe
Bucks
13 August 1946

My dear Emanie,

This is the queerest thing. Today I woke up feeling sick and ill and apprehensive, and got worse and worse till I was in a state of hysteria. At three I got Henry to drive me to the head of a valley three miles away, and I walked home. After a time I suddenly got ⟨home⟩ {calm}. When I reached home Henry told me that Marjorie Wells had rung up to say H. G. had died suddenly at ⟨3⟩ {4}.45—he was dressing to go downstairs for tea when he fell back dead. I feel very sad because I had ⟨x⟩ {arranged} to go and see him on Friday and show him the photographs of Nuremberg I brought back. Dear H. G., he was a devil, he ruined my life, he starved me, he was an inexhaustible source of love and friendship to me for thirty-four years, we should never have met, I was the one person he cared to see to the end, I feel desolate because he has gone.

And it is all so strange, because in Nuremberg I had what will certainly be my last lover.¹ He is a man I have met at intervals during the last twenty years, and when he came into the room at Lord Lawrence's he said to me, "Why have you let yourself go? You could be as wonderful as ever." He guessed the tragedy of my marriage, and for a week set himself to correct it. I realised why my life as a woman has been a failure. We were gloriously happy together. We could always have been so, and he had felt it for twenty years. I don't think I would have had a chance if his wife had been there. He adored her and prattled of her . . . [West's ellipsis]. She objected to child bearing and after the birth of her second child wouldn't sleep with him for eighteen months, just to punish him—it wasn't to avoid {having} more children, she knew all about that. This was the mildest of her tricks. He mentioned them with indulgence as pretty little feminine ⟨x⟩ oddities. What chance have you and I when men have such alligators? What chance had I against Jane?

But I was gloriously happy there in Nuremberg for a week, and now I don't think I'll ever see him again, and I hardly want to, for I'm fifty-three, and I might as well put the shutters up. I had, but he made me take them down.

I've a new fantastic tragedy in my family. My sister Lettie has always managed the family estate, and has always resisted my efforts to look into it. And I thought she could not—with her legal training—be doing very wrong. It turns out that she has parted with house after house to a dishonest solicitor who has been buying them from her at a fraction of their real value, and we have lost somewhere between £15,000 and £20,000. This is confidential, for the solicitor might finish up by suing us for libel and she has lost every relevant paper. All my love—I hope you had a lovely holiday and oh! How awful I am! The parcels are lovely, I am in heaven—and oh! the Rose Land box, I nearly died with joy. The present I should love and would give up one monthly box for would be a really lavish pot of lemon cleansing cream. Can you still get it? Cleansing cream is very difficult here. It's sticky and harsh. And there is something else—could you for my daughter-in-law, Mrs West, 52 Carlton Hill, London, N.W., buy two or three really nice sketching blocks? Sketch books that artists use? There are none here. I will repay you all this when I see you. My book is taking ages. I have had such an awful spring. I have had such a contretemps over my new secretary, who is a failure and worse than a failure, a damn nuisance. She ended up by having an {(perfectly postponable)} operation on her shoulder without saying she was insured, while I was away, which has cost her $200, which I shall have to pay—and she has had to have a fortnight's holiday, just as I return from Nuremberg. I am trying to write a piece for the *New Yorker* about it but my head is boiling. I can't write anything about it that doesn't give me away. I want to write nothing. I want to live and I have left it too long. Nothing H. G. did against me compares with what Henry has done against me, and Henry's love and care for me never fails. Oh, God, what a world. My best love—

Rebecca

This envelope is transparent.

Rebecca West Collection   manuscript
Yale University

[1] Francis B. Biddle (1886–1968), attorney general for FDR and American chief prosecutor at the Nuremberg war tribunal. He married Katherine Garrison Chapin (1918). His letters to West contain plans for a rendezvous in Paris in August 1946 (Yale University). The two also visited Prague together, using a military plane. West's letters to Biddle seem not to have survived. A letter to Monica Sterling gives some details of the Paris weekend, which included a visit to the French author Colette: "I was foolish when I went in to see Colette, I tried to tell her too much, she got scared. And I was so tired, and I made such a stupid mistake in French. But she tried to like me, she was generous, and she did love Francis. I am writing Colette a long letter which she needn't read if she doesn't want. It was angelic of you to take us, it is one of the greatest things in my life. And the Palais Royal was so right for Francis, he was so enchanting there and at the Café de la Régence where we sat and looked at the lit fountains. I hope that when I said I preferred Henry I didn't suggest that Francis wasn't perfect in any way, he really is" ([1946], University of Tulsa).

To: Dorothy Thompson

Ibstone House
Ibstone
Nr. High Wycombe
Bucks
31 August 1946

My dear Dorothy,

I am going to cast myself on your mercy. I have had an emotional upset, which has left me horribly aware of the fact that in some ways my life has been a failure. The death of H. G., who devoured my youth and nagged and bullied me and was so much made for me that to the last he glowed when I came to see him, helped to rub that in. The worst of the life I live here is that it drives me back on the fundamentals, which are gaunt. I would do anything to have a month or two in America—say from about the 15th of October. I haven't got the guts to say to Henry that I just want to go. If you aren't coming to Europe just at that time (which would be my luck) could you possibly cable to me and suggest I should come over for some vague reason—or if there is a political ⟨do⟩ {event} I could attend—or just an invitation would, I suppose, do. I don't want Henry to feel my terrific discontent. I would give anything to see new people and be in new places, and it is the American thing I want. I wish to Heaven I could have settled down in America, the dreariness of English life is something I cannot master. If you ever go up to the farm in ⟨x⟩ {the fall} I should love to go with you ⟨x⟩ {if} that was ever convenient. I long for American countryside. In New York I will probably stay with Emanie Arling.

I hope you won't mind me asking you to do this. My love to Maxi,[1] and of course to you!

Yours ever,

Rebecca

Dorothy Thompson Papers   manuscript
Syracuse University

[1] Maxim Knopf, a Czech artist, was Thompson's third husband (m. 1943).

To: Anne Charles (McBurney)   Ibstone House
                                                     Ibstone
                                                     Nr. High Wycombe
                                                     Bucks
                                                     18 October 1946

Dear Miss Charles,

The conditions of the post we have to offer are these. My husband farms the land we own and rent near the house, running a pedigree Jersey herd and supplying all the milk to Wycombe Abbey school, is interested in various economic and international questions, and is a Rural District Councillor. I write books and am interested in various activities of one kind and another. We live here with what should be a staff of three, butler, cook, and house-maid, and four gardeners. (The garden is run as a market-garden.) The house is about ten miles from High Wycombe and eight from Henley. There are several buses a day to High Wycombe, and we have two cars.

I want someone who will run the house, type my manuscripts, take down my husband's correspondence, and do the odd jobs that come up in connec-tion with the farm and the garden. We have a good farm-bailiff and a good head gardener, so these jobs are not so very numerous, I simply mention them to show there are odd jobs to be done and this is in no sense an office job. It sounds rather heavy, but I don't think it is, except at moments when I have to get an article off in a hurry. This Spring we lost a secretary who had been first my husband's secretary, the[n] mine, then ours, over a period of twelve years. She left us because her husband was starting a school. After that we replaced her with someone who has proved a failure, owing to lack of detachment with the staff and a number of other faults springing from lack of education.

If you would care to look at the job, I shall be in town on the 23rd., but think it would be really better if you came and looked at the place. If you tell us what day you could come we could meet you at High Wycombe station. There is a good train from Marylebone at 12.15.

If you can take correspondence in longhand your lack of shorthand would not matter very much. But if you cannot handle correspondence at all that would be a pity.

> Yours truly,
> Rebecca West
> (Mrs Henry Andrews)

private collection   typescript with autograph signature

To: Lord Beaverbrook   Ibstone House
                                        Ibstone
                                        Nr. High Wycombe
                                        Bucks
                                        4 December 1947

My dear Max,

How I wish you were in England! I am in a difficulty about the Amery's. I understood that they did not care what was published about John {That they had made up their mind to take it.} and that Mrs Amery had liked what I had written about the trial. But I have had a strange mad letter from her, full of ecstasy about John, and I hear old Amery asked the *Standard* not to reprint my article about his trial. (Which I had hoped from the first they would not use.) Now, for the English edition I am taking everything out about John Amery except the facts that will convict the Germans of black wickedness in using him and will prove the lack of integrity of the totalitarian governments; and I am coming down hard on the mother's side (which is probably the father's side also) that she knew something about John Amery which the rest of the world did not know.[1] But—you can trust me—there will be no violation of family intimacies. Only—I cannot leave

Amery out. This material about treason will go down the drain if I do not record it; and it is valuable not only to the historian but to everybody who wants humanity to survive. There isn't only the fact that treason in modern condition [sic] works out as cruelty to prisoners of war—that is the real fruit of my book, from an *immediate* point of view. There is the fact that treason is an attempt to live without love of country, which humanity can't do—any more than love of family. I don't know how to write to the Amery's. I am going to see her at her request, but how far I will make all this plain I don't know. So I wish you were here. {I'm not asking you to ⟨xx⟩ do anything about this! I must settle it myself.}

How disgraceful—not to have begun my letter with thanks to you ⟨xxx⟩ {for your intervention} in the *Time* business.[2] But, whatever you are, you are at least one of those—rewarded with a special halo in heaven—whom people always forget to thank. This struck me as the oddest business. I do not think the fat oaf John Osborne[3] has the slightest idea that I was not distressed at the exposure of my private life but that I was angry because a person whom I had treated as a guest and a colleague should coolly disregard my wishes. I know nothing about Luce, but he seems to have acted well and promptly in this business.[4] But I regard Osborne's part in this business as disgraceful, and I think Matthews—the New York editor—has been an incredible ass also. I gather that your enchanting Herbert Gunn sent you my letter and the copy of Osborne's letter. My God, what a letter! [Sheer?] dynamite. A friend of mine who is a lawyer had a look at it and tells me that if *Time* libelled anyone and I chose to give evidence and put in this letter the Judge and jury would gather together to take a running kick at John Osborne's ⟨ugly⟩ {most} characteristic aperture. This is the *oddest* thing that has ever happened to me in thirty-seven years of journalism. John Osborne was inspired to write me a letter in which he ascribed the removal of the paragraph to ⟨my⟩ {his} pity for my *distress*. For distress read disgust. But anyway I knew the matter was settled by Dorothy Thompson before John Osborne ever heard of my distress {disgust}. This oaf hasn't learned what *we* knew before we were born—don't lie except about matters concerning which you can't be found out.

You have a pleasant crowd working for you at the *Evening Standard.* Gunn is of course a wonder. But I like Charles Curran, who, God knows why, adores you, to the extent of maintaining that you are really quite a tall man, who stoops.

On this note I close. Bless you.[5]

Yours ever,
Rebecca West

Hist. Coll. 184 Beaverbrook Papers   manuscript
House of Lords Record Office

[1] West seems to have been touched, despite John Amery's treason, by the affectionate relationship he had with his mother.

[2] For a cover story in *Time* magazine, West had invited reporters and photographers to Ibstone. She was distressed by a paragraph alluding to her relationship with Wells, to Anthony West's birth, and to his first novel. She had requested help from Beaverbrook as well as Dorothy Thompson in suppressing the passage.

[3] John Osborne was editor of *Time*.

[4] Dorothy Thompson had spoken with Henry Luce, owner of *Time*, and prevailed. West's letter to her explained her objection as follows:

The trouble about this business is that it is manifold. I object to any discussion of my relations with H. G. for many reasons. First of all, it gives me a spurious glamour on which I have no desire to cash in. Second, it isn't possible to tell the whole story until the Wells family is dead, and till it is told by me nobody knows what happened. Thirdly, it is too interesting, how can I go about my business as a reporter with this albatross round my neck? And fourthly, which bulks far the largest in my mind, the immediate repercussions are too troublesome. Apart from the fact that my sister would make my life unendurable for weeks if she had read the original article, I don't see why she, a hardworking woman who is doing magnificent work when she is old and tired, should be excited and worried just because two young men think it would be amusing to print a news item—and why the hell should I, who have been a good and loyal and, if I may say so, tactful friend to the Wells family for thirty-five years, be converted against my will into a trouble-maker? (26 November 1947, Dorothy Thompson papers, Syracuse University)

[5] Writing to Henry Andrews from New York (April 1947, Yale University), where Beaverbrook made an unexpected call, West expressed a very different attitude, questioning Beaverbrook's disavowal of support for Tito, and his demeanor:

He behaved to me as if he were a tender and loving friend. Nobody could have deduced that he had ever done me a mortal injury and inflicted on me a supreme humiliation. And he behaved so exactly as I had thought he had behaved, as a kind, loving, dignified person, that I looked at him with astonishment, I could not fit it in with the drunken, lying, cheating little vagabond I had learned to see him as during the last months when I saw him and as he has been reported to me ever since. I looked at him and could not realise what all the disaster had been about. . . . It was extraordinarily disturbing. His charm, his sweetness, his convincing assumption of affection for me, which was so callous in its overlooking of what he had done to me, his assumption that he could wipe out a deep injury by coming in to see me for an hour, this crazy and cowardly lying.

To: G. B. Stern

Ibstone House
Ibstone
Nr. High Wycombe
Bucks
5 May 1948

Dearest Tynx,

I had just sat down to thank you for your book when an incident which I regard as characteristic of my life happened. I had four long beds planted on my lawn with parrot tulips—some pink and green Fantasies, some yellow flecked with red, some mauve and silver Lady Derby's, some lilac and green, and there was a long bed planted with wallflowers which runs the length of the lawn, in which there were some amber and bronze and maroon tulips. They were working up to perfection and I was going to suggest you came over to see them if that were possible. There were three hundred of them. I have looked after them myself and put bone meal on the beds and so on. Then I had to go down to the gardener and tell him that someone wanted to buy some tomato-plants. When I came back in ten minutes time there was not one single tulip left. Not one. I found a married couple and their two children living in horrible circumstances in a caravan in a wood, and I brought them here, to fill in when my Lithuanians left and before my new people came. The wife then had a nervous breakdown and we have had a great deal of trouble looking after her. We have now moved them into one of our cottages. The little boy, who is three and a half, had gone into the garden with a stick and had chopped off the head of every tulip.

Hell.

My dear, forgive me if my first reaction to your book is purely personal. Did you go to Swanston? That country is so much a part of my early life that I cannot go back, but the reference to Caerkerton made me dissolve with longing. I can't bear to go to Edinburgh partly because of my mother and partly because of my friend Flora Duncan who died a few years ago. We used to walk over all that country. In those days Swanston wasn't open to the public as I think it is now, but it lay to the right of a road we often followed, and I can see it now. The part of the book that moved me most was the chapter about Barrie, which I thought wonderful, and a perfect illustration of what evil is—of how one shouldn't dare treat one's fellow beings, of how the devil treats human creatures.[1] Really worse than Marcus. The whole book struck me as subtle and penetrating in its study of relationships. How good your use of the Grenadier is. Bless you.

I shall be up in town on May 12, and 13, and could come in for tea on the twelfth. If not could I dine with you on the night of the twentieth. I am going to America again on June 2 till July 25. I would love to see you and tell you of the odd time I had at Washington. Henry is in Germany at the moment. If you care to come and stay the night here or day here, it would be grand. I am in terror about Henry going to Germany, as I am afraid that the sight of the desolation may have an unfortunate effect on him. He is getting wilder and wilder, in odd sorts of ways. One of them has resulted in my having in my garden now enough cabbage plants to carpet the whole of Buckinghamshire. It's an awfully prosaic form of wealth.[2]

I saw Charlotte[3] in New York, perfectly beautiful in an elderly way, very distinguished, and awfully tiresome. She's a bore as usually old men only are. She is very anti-Willie now, but no more than I am after our last meeting. I met ⟨x⟩ Marshall Dill's[4] aunt, who said that Mrs Dill, senior, really loves Pamela [Frankau], and had the greatest regard for her as a person—not just American gush. Which is good news.

Love,

Panther

Rebecca West Collection   typescript with autograph signature
University of Tulsa

[1] In chap. 10 of Stern's 1948 novel *No Son of Mine,* the hero visits a famous author (modeled on J. M. Barrie), whom he adores. He leaves severely disappointed over his treatment by the great man.

[2] West described Henry's growing eccentricity to a number of correspondents, one of them her publisher at Viking Press, Ben Huebsch ([March 1947], Library of Congress): "My life has been a nightmare. He has engaged people of an unsuitable type without fixing their wages so that they have stuck us up for enormous sums. He has committed every possible folly—I could not get him interested in the fact that the central heating had broken down, I had to get out of bed as the two Irish servants had walked out because the house was so cold, and in this icy temperature cook for two cornmen who laughed at my husband as an idiot. While I was cooking for these two men and other workmen my husband had sent down a vanload of his mother's china and glass, which the vanmen insisted on unpacking and leaving on the floor— 16 cases of it. Not a day but he does something completely imbecile which causes me a great deal of trouble, and often humiliation."

³ Charlotte Boissevain, an old friend from her days on the French Riviera. Copies of letters to her are at the University of Tulsa.

⁴ Marshall Dill (1916–), American history professor.

To: Henry Andrews

Hickory Hill: Gap: PA
[25 June 1948]

Dearest Ric,

I hope you didn't feel aggrieved because I have not written or cabled ⟨because⟩ but I could not. Life completely broke down. I had to wait ten minutes to get an elevator up to my room at any time except in the early morning. I could not get a reply from my telephone. Breakfast took an hour and a half to get to one's room and downstairs there were queues. You had to wait ten minutes to get your mail at the desk and as long at another desk to get a stamp. The first day I had a terrible time getting back from the Convention¹ because though there were press busses they were put in an out of the way place and nobody told the press. You cannot pick up a taxi on the street except in the central area because they are directed by radio from the head office and only go where they are telephoned for—but nobody could get near the telephone in the Convention Hall. Hence the first morning I ⟨xx⟩ walked home thirty-five minutes in the broiling heat. But my colleagues either waited for hours or waited in the Hall till the evening session, sleeping in the basement. I had at once to face a most tiresome situation concerning the syndication. The syndicate ⟨xxx⟩ had sold my articles—but there was not one chance that they ⟨x⟩ could use them. The deadline for the American press was eight at night—for the English press it was half past two. To get peace to do my English article and not be worried about it I have had to write TWO articles a day. The American I made very light but it meant that I did not have one second's rest a day, and while the others were having showers I had just to sit at my typewriter. To add to the horror of the occasion my typewriter went wrong owing to the humidity. The various parts stuck and swelled. Fortunately there was a charming man in the night office of the Western Union in the hotel and he used to let me come down and write my piece on one of his typewriters when it got too bad. Meanwhile I had a horrible time being pestered by radio and television people to appear on their programmes (for nothing) and when I had my telephone shut off so that I could sleep they still got through. I am told that they bribe the switchboard girls. As I was selling my stuff to the *Philadelphia Bulletin* I was unable to avoid appearing on television for their radio station. This meant an hour and a half wasted. This is a shameful racket. It means that a lot of second-rate people get highly paid jobs on these stations and fill their programmes by badgering celebrities. The man for whom I broadcast was a lazy lout who had got no programme ready and was quite indignant that the four people whom he had badgered into coming would not get together and invent a really thrilling script. I then had a curious adventure which I tell you because it had the oddest consequence. I shut off my telephone and was enraged to be called at seven-thirty—having gone to bed at three. This was a woman called Anne Schapiro who told me that she ⟨x⟩ wanted to interview me and was doing so for the *Philadelphia Bulletin,* that Walter Lister, the managing director, had told her to do so. I got a little sleep then rang up the *Bulletin* and told them in strong terms what I thought of them for ⟨x⟩ allowing somebody to ring me up at that hour. I was told they had ⟨sent⟩ {asked} nobody to do this and were sending somebody called Frances Blackwood to interview me as had arranged before at half past nine. I had told Anne Schapiro to wait in the lobby at nine. But she came up to my room at ten to. I opened the door and asked me what she meant by saying that she was sent by the *Bulletin* when she was not. She disarmed me by a most peculiar appearance, very ugly, very eager, and very strained on this one particular. She admitted the *Bulletin* had not sent her and then said that she was doing this for her agent Brandt & Brandt and had not cared to say so as this meant that she was freelancing and many people will not see a free lance. She was so anxious to write the article that I wondered if poverty was at the back of this, although Frances Blackwood appeared and thought it insanity. Certainly she was odd. In case it was poverty I telegraphed Carl Brandt to know if he had commissioned the article in which case I would have seen her before I left the Convention, awkward as that was. That afternoon I came back to write my article and was deeply distressed to find that CARL BRANDT HAD IMMEDIATELY TOLD HER I HAD TELEGRAPHED ENQUIRING ABOUT HER although I had begun my telegram with the word Confidentially. She had left an aggrieved and really unhappy letter, evidently very upset because I had so naturally felt doubt about her. By this time I realised from the whole tone of the incident that she was an eccentric, and so felt committed to seeing her again. Now we will leave her—but be assured she comes back. You will know from my articles the main outlines of what happened to me. You cannot know the discomfort of it—the dripping heat and the noise and the glare and the determination of everybody to interrupt one. Dorothy [Thompson] was of ⟨x⟩ great use to me and did everything she could to help me, but she was slow in moving and cannot get round nearly as fast as I can, and she is getting appallingly deaf. Had I not been with her she would have missed a great deal as she misheard a great many of the instructions, and I was very happy about that. She was the most delightful and sweet-tempered companion. We lunched with Alice Roosevelt I mean Longworth[2] once, who is getting more and more beautiful. She is now so lovely that you cannot take your eyes off her, and she looked perfectly cool, the only woman in Philadelphia who was not deliquescent. Her young daughter was with her and is the image of Senator Borah. Bill Bullitt[3] turned up at this lunch and was a bore, but I saw him at another dinner and he was very entertaining. These lunches and dinners were in the Ritz, to which we could only get admission by these illustrious friends as they would have nothing to do with the Convention. I had lunch there three times and dinner there twice and one dinner at a marvellous restaurant called Bookbinder's where they cook steaks three inches thick—and these six meals were the only meals I had during the five days I was there, and all except the Bookbinder's meal were rushed and skimpy. The rest of the time I lived on hot coffee or iced coffee or cartons of ice-cream. The Bookbinder's meal was horrible because I'd gone out with ⟨x⟩ Dorothy to eat there at half past nine, meaning to write most of my article for the *Standard* after I returned. Dorothy took with her her piece which had to be in the next day and *lost* it—and it was hours before we found it. The day of the nominations we got to bed at six having had breakfast after we got back from the Convention Hall—but it was so hot I could do nothing except down a glass of pasteurized milk. (But having seen American cow-sheds believe me I would not drink milk that was not pasteurized.) I slept till nearly one the next morning which left me short on time but I needed it. While I was dressing I had a telephone call from a man who wanted to take me out to dinner who said he was the brother of Gordon Richards the jockey and had horses over here and he offered to help me make all the money I wanted over here by tipping me winners—this is something I would not have anticipated. When I was back during the recess I was called up by a man who said that I would not remember him but his name was Parry, and said he had been introduced to me rather over twenty years ago by the editor of *Nash's Magazine*. But I remembered him at once—I don't know why. Nor did I remember anything about him except his appearance and a vague feeling that I had later heard something disagreeable about him. He said he must see me. I rather angrily told him I was here to write and would not be free till I had filed my story at half past two. He said that he would be in the lobby ⟨x⟩ by the desk at that hour. He was, and he put to me an extraordinary proposition which was that if I wrote an article attacking Randolph Churchill for an organization the identity of which would not be revealed till I had written he would pay me five thousand dollars. When I expressed some indignation he offered to pay me more. I explained that it wasn't quite that, and he enlarged on the ease with which it could be done, saying that they had a lot of material about Randolph on which I could work. ⟨x⟩ He asked me what reason I could have for tenderness towards Randolph considering that "Winston Churchill opposed you over Tito." This wa[y] of putting it enchanted me. I left him and went up to my room and felt very upset. I assumed it was some personal vendetta, which shows how tired and stupid I was. I went down and cabled Curran asking him to tell the *Evening News* for which Randolph is, I think, over here, of this curious offer, and saying that I did not want to make any personal contact with Randolph myself. I went down in the elevator with a party of fairly drunk young people obviously rich including a fat blonde man. When I went up again it was in the same elevator which was now empty and the elevator man told me that the fat ⟨x⟩ blonde was Randolph Churchill. The hair stood up on my head, it was so odd. The next day I told Ed, the Damon Runyon character[4] who looks after me for the Syndicate, and he immediately said it was Zionist work. So I think it must have been, and that same day Parry rang up again and offered me double the money to do the article and if I made it a good one it could be published anonymously. This is beyond reason and means that Parry has any amount of money to spend and can waste it as he likes. Also once I had done that I would have to do anything. Better not talk of this. On Friday I wrote my last article and packed and prepared to come out here but could not get the Ogilvies[5] on the telephone nor could I find out the times of the trains. The telephone was still disrupted, I could not get hold of the porter to find out the times of the trains, and there is no way of getting a railway timetable in America except by going to the station, and the station was wholly disrupted by people going up to the Joe Louis[6] fight. Anne Schapiro rang up and asked me what I was doing. I told her my plight, thinking she would have no suggestions, and she said that she knew of a way I could get out. Later I was rung up by the Yellow Cab company which said they were sending a conveyance and I couldn't quite understand what they said about this but I did realise that it was coming, for me at eight and that it was bringing me out here for sixteen dollars—which was dirt cheap for a journey of ⟨x⟩ fifty miles (and back—) late at night. When I went down with my luggage there was an AMBULANCE. With Anne Schapiro in it. She could not explain why she had engaged it—there is a Yellow Cab limousine service—but there was no time to argue as I wanted to get down here—but as the bed was slipping about the place as there was nobody in it I insisted on the driver calling in at the garage and taking out the bed. He also removed blankets, a macintosh sheet, and a bedpan. I think this is the craziest thing that ever happened. Anne Schapiro then proceeded to sit in the ambulance with me and confide her plan—which was this. "West is covering the Convention, I am going to cover West. I won't be a bother, I'm not going to question you, I'll just go wherever you go, just tag right along, and see what sort of person you are." How I am going to cope with this I don't know. But she is not unpleasant, just mad. She is useful to me as she has a fund of local knowledge, her husband being a Philadelphia newspaper man, it isn't a case of impertinence and empty chatter. But it is going to be difficult on my return to Philadelphia. We then started off on a three hours drive, the last two hours of which were in total darkness. We stopped and had cocktails and frozen steak sandwiches (these are wonderful) at a roadhouse where they were televising the Louis fight, which drew us together with our taxidriver who was utterly amazed by the whole expedition. ("Ain't you sick, lady? Not at all?") Then we got into the area of villages which are inhabited by the Amish Brethren and got into the line of four in which David and Melinda live. Their names are Bird in Hand, Paradise, Intercourse, and Fertility. The little hamlet where they live is alongside Intercourse and Fertility—that is Gap. Nobody in Gap could tell us where Hickory Hill was and we telephoned to David who came out to guide us with an old Ford and was flummoxed when he saw the ambulance. To my horror they began asking Anne Schapiro to stay the night but I indicated that this was a mistake. It was wonderful to come in out of the night into a very eighteenth century room and see the picture of my grandfather Major Charles George Fairfield which I had always seen hanging in my loathsome aunt's house—and see how like it is to Anthony and young Norman [Macleod]. We all sat down, it now being after midnight, taxidriver included and drank American Rhine wine and seltzer which is a wonderful drink, and David explained the family portraits to the taxi-driver, who was enchanted. At one we went to bed and I slept till eleven. The little boy was not there, he was away staying with his best friend, who is the son of an Amish farmer. ⟨xxx⟩ The farm is charming and Melinda has cut down the work to the minimum and has no servants at all. Always the people who strike me as supremely able in practical matters are Southerners. This is not what one is led to believe. The heat is terrible. I have a bath in the morning and a shower about every two hours after that. They have Holstein cows, which are usual here for a peculiar reason. This is diversified farming, very mixed indeed, and they work it at all with horses—it is funny, they theoretically have no machinery—the Amishes, I mean,—but they use milking machines run on gas and not electricity. Such diversified farming means that sometimes the hours of milking are irregular and Holsteins stand it better than any other dairy breed. We went to a steel town near by (where there had just happened an extraordinary tragedy—the middle aged son of a very Puritanical old millowner and his wife had married a disreputable but worthy lady who had been married three times ⟨xx⟩ before—he kept the marriage secret but it was revealed lately—they went to a party and it was suddenly discovered she had passed out—the family picked her up and took her home in their automobile in frozen disapproval—and when they got her out they found that she was not drunk but dead) to pick up a man called Paul Scott-Rankine who is Reuter's correspondent in Washington—an ex-Civil Servant whom I thought very poorly of, but ⟨x⟩ was an amiable soul. The next morning we rose at seven and at nine were at the ⟨x⟩ local Amish church service. We had on our way ⟨x⟩ from the steel town called in to fetch Fairfield from the Amish household where he had been staying, and the farmer had invited us to come to this meeting, which was a tribute to the Ogilvies position in the district. This service went on for three and a half hours in terrible heat and I did not understand more than a word here and there—it was not even in German it was in Palatinate German—modified by two hundred years over here—and I have never had a more wonderful experience since I was in the Balkans. The ⟨x⟩ spectacle was unbelievably beautiful. I sat among the women who are plain but very dignified with very strong, calm faces. They wear white lawn caps such as Palatinate farmers wives' would have worn in the early eighteenth century, and very plain dresses of black or rich dark colors with a fichu effect on the bodice and full skirts. They all have good though stout figures, with well defined waists, though the married ones have nearly all over seven children and some have as many as seventeen. The little girls stood beside them, in the loveliest dresses I have ever seen for children outside the Balkans. They were dressed in long dresses almost to their ankles of ⟨x⟩ clear but not pastel colors—a fairly strong green in the light register, but not washy, or lilac, or blue, or crimson, over which they wore muslin aprons and fichus which almost entirely covered their dresses and were transparent. Their faces were entrancing in the little muslin caps. Then, on benches facing the same way as the women's, sat the boys. All this, I should have explained, happened in a barn, with the bags of fertilizer pushed to one end and a pile of logs at the other. The men of the community are much handsomer than the women, and the boys were beautiful. They wore black trousers and waistcoats with touches of black satin and ⟨x⟩ white shirts with little black bow-ties—all home-made but very well made and of beautiful material. Then facing them sat the grown men, with the preachers and the Bishop in the front row, all with beards, some of a strange Semitic handsomeness. The little girls, under about five, sat in their mother's arms, and the little boys in their father's arms. As the service went on the children cried from boredom and they were made to stick it out, but nobody was cross with them or seemed irritated with their cries. They sang hymns in unison, very strange old Gregorian plainsong, I believe. This is never written down. The birds sat on the rafters and sang madly all throughout the sermons. Once a cat came in and walked about. After three and a half hours we went out with the young people because there was a church council and we were asked ⟨x⟩ to stay to the church meal. It was in the farmer's house, everybody rushed in with trestle tables and in a very short time all the old Racs were sitting down—in another room the old Rics sat down. I was with the old Racs though I was about fifteen years junior to all of that lot. (There were in all about three hundred and fifty to four hundred people present.) We had coffee and bits of cheese which I had to eat on the point of my knife and apricot jam and masses of very spongey bread and superb butter and dill pickles and beet and thick cream—the only thick cream I have ever yet seen in America. There is a long silent grace before and after and one does not talk during the meal. Then they popped up and the youngsters took their place and would all be fed by relays—and we went out on the garden and some of the farmers talked to us about the Convention and about England. They were so cut off from the world that one man said, when we had explained how a Prime Minister was elected and the differences from the office of President, "And how do you get your King? Do you vote him in too?" But the same man gave us a most brilliant analysis of the system of subsidised prices and how the Amish's rejection of the system had in the long run paid them. We went home and on the way paused at an Amish farm where there was a grandmother, mother, and daughter, all called Rebecca, who were very friendly. Then we slept, and had a dinner-party of local lawyers and newspaper men and their wives, and had a long good fight about Palestine.[7] At ⟨x⟩ each evening meal till now there has been Henry Bonner, Lilly's second son, it is the oddest coincidence he should have got into David's orbit—we are not far from Lancaster where Lilly's family mill's is. He is married and has one child, and his wife has gone home to her parents to have another. He is oddly unattractive, he looks quite coloured and though amiable is not intelligent. It seems Paul got into great trouble in Rome through distributing funds before the election, but I don't know how far he or his superiors were to blame, and as he has not been recalled I suppose it was all right. I am going up to New York tomorrow because the *Herald-Tribune* is giving a lunch for me. I think I shall stay there two days and then go to Doris Stevens for two days and then come down here again till I go to Bruce and Beatrice Gould[8] for the weekend of the ⟨x⟩ 9th, after which I shall go down to the Democratic Convention. This will not be so hard partly because of my circumstances and partly because of the Democratic Party's circumstances. Unless Eleanor Roosevelt nominates Eisenhower (who might have consented to become the Democratic nominee straight away if an isolationist had been nominated as Republican candidate) and he dislikes Dewey enough to consent to stand there will be very little going on.[9] And I am writing to Curran and telling him how impossible the syndication has proved to be. I shall then have a margin of rest and less necessity to work late. It will also probably be a day shorter. David and Melinda are delightful and intelligent and kind and the child is charming. It is like a more delicate Edmund [West]. I have not yet written to you about your news because I have felt that I had better get all this off my chest. I am grieved about your teeth, I realise that you have actually had some out. I am so sorry about this—and still more that you should now have the bother of getting false tusks in such weather as this—but I am now supposing that your summer is like the one here. The accident sounds horrible. I am dropping a note to Margaret to say that I will probably be in New York about the 15th or 16th—on my way up to Dorothy's. I will write you later from New York. I have not had time to send a single parcel—but Ross will be sending you some wonderful detergent.

Love RAC

Please send my *Standard* articles to Mrs F. Lyman ⟨Randolph⟩ Weir 1041 Woods Ave, Lancaster, Pa. She is a darling I have just met with a ravishing husband and we have had a stand to fight about Palestine.[10]

Rebecca West Papers   typescript
Yale University

[1] The Republican National Convention. West wrote a series of articles in the *Herald Tribune* for U.S. audiences and one for the British in the *Evening Standard*. On the same visit she reported on the Democratic and the Progressive Parties' presidential conventions.

[2] Alice Roosevelt Longworth (1884–1980), American socialite, the only child of president Theodore Roosevelt and his first wife Alice Hathaway Lee, famous for her political jibes. She was courted for her political opinions by numerous presidents. Her only child, Paulina (b. 1925), was rumored to be the child of Senator William E. Borah.

[3] William C. Bullitt (1891–1967), American diplomat who tried as part of Wilson's peace delegation to negotiate a settlement of the Civil War in the Soviet Union (1918). In serving as the first ambassador to the USSR (1934–1936), he developed a strongly anticommunist line. He was ambassador to France (1936–1940) until it fell to Germany. Louise Bryant was his second wife.

[4] Damon Runyon (1884–1946), American short-story writer and journalist best known for the character types in *Guys and Dolls* (1931)—racy Broadway types, including gamblers, bookies, and fight promoters, who speak in slang.

[5] David Ogilvy (1911–1999), English-born advertising executive and West's cousin (see family tree) and his wife Melinda. His autobiography, *Blood, Brains, and Beer* (1978) describes various occupations including chef's apprentice, wartime work in the Secret Service, work with pollster George Gallup, and retirement to Touffou Castle in France.

[6] The American heavyweight champion scored a knockout against Jersey Joe Walcott in the eleventh round, 25 June 1948.

[7] Britain had a mandate over Palestine (1922–1948), during which time various schemes for partition into Jewish, Arab, and British sectors were proposed, and Jewish immigration and

land tenure were limited. Revelation of the Holocaust (1945) increased international sympathy for a Jewish state. The British occupation force withdrew in May 1948, on the establishment of the State of Israel.

⁸ Beatrice (1898–1989) and Bruce Gould (1898–1989), the American couple who as editors
of the *Ladies' Home Journal* (1935–1962) made it the largest-circulation magazine of its day and
brought quality articles and fiction to its pages. They also wrote plays together and she
published short stories in the *Saturday Evening Post* and *Cosmopolitan.*

⁹ The move, favored by the Roosevelt sons, to dump Harry Truman as the Democratic
nominee did not prevail. Thomas Dewey, the Republican nominee, was narrowly defeated by
Truman.

¹⁰ West's postscript is written upside down at the top of the first page.

To: Margaret Hodges

Ibstone House
Ibstone
Nr. High Wycombe
Bucks
9 January 1949

My dear Margaret,

This afternoon the memorial tablets to the Ibstone boys who fell in the
war and to Geoffrey Tilley¹ were unveiled and dedicated by the Bishop of
Buckingham. And I do not think that anything will ever happen again in
Ibstone, because it reached its climax today. The service ended with an
incident which can never be surpassed, or even equalled.

Mr Wheen had the Bishop to lunch, with the Golds, because Norman
Gold is going to be the churchwarden at Fingest in place of Mrs Montefiore.
So the Wheens and the Golds came late with the Bishop, and they went up
into the gallery, where they were joined by the Parkers. At the close of the
service Mrs Wheen descended the staircase, with Clare [Parker] just behind
her. As Mrs Wheen reached the bottom she found the Bishop standing
beside the font, and she made some remark to him about the beauty of the
service. He is a little deaf, and he inclined his head down to her. Mrs Wheen
said nothing, and he inclined his head lower still. A puzzled look came over
Mrs Wheen's face, and then, with an air of doing her duty, *she kissed the
Bishop.*

Nobody saw the incident except Clare and, I think, the Golds. Either
⟨everybody⟩ the people had left the church, or they were standing with their
backs to the gallery. Mrs Wheen quietly went out and left the Bishop
standing petrified, his mitre slightly on one side. Clare rushed out into the

churchyard ⟨with Jimmie⟩ and surprised us all by going into strange chokes and gurgles. We all went up to meet the Bishop at tea at the school, and there Clare told us, one by one. Marjorie was completely cheered up. When the Bishop came he was still looking perplexed. It was wonderful to think that he couldn't possibly have asked anybody about it, he was bound to nourish this curious secret in his bosom. When he left us he told us several times that he thought this a most remarkable village.

Blessings on you, and all our love.

S[2]

private collection   typescript with manuscript initial

[1] The simple stone plaque set in the side wall of tiny St. Nicolas church, down the hill from Ibstone, reads, "In loving memory of Geoffrey Tilley, Died June 14th 1947, Aged 52 years." Marjorie Tilley was a good friend of West's.

[2] S stands for Simpkin, one of the pet names West used with Hodges.

To: Charles Curran   The Lansdowne
                                                       Club
                                                       Berkeley Square, W. 1
                                                       26 January 1949

My dear Charles,

I feel so wretched that I must tell you the cause of it.

I am very fond of you and have from the first felt an untroubled affection for you. I can have such an affection for men quite easily for reasons apart from my age. Since you know so much you might as well know more. I have lived a completely celibate life for eighteen years.[1] I don't mind so doing, I prefer it. If at any time in that period men have made advances to me of an insistent kind I have not even become hysterical. I have remained completely wooden, in a way that has often been regarded as most insulting. I am perfectly happy as I am, and in the last few years I have liked some men, like Paul Gallico[2] and Bill Gaines,[3] better than I have ever liked men before. I have felt like that before. I assumed you either had a happy relationship with someone or like me had chosen to forget about sex.

I hated you last night when you talked about sex, when you talked again and again about lust. You were repudiating it, but you were so much aware of it that you practically felt it. It was worse for having no object, it seemed an abstraction that possessed you. I sleepily went on trying to talk you back to the person I knew. I couldn't do it, and I can't take the you I saw. I am frightened of you. It sounds insulting and a revocation of what was good, but I don't want to see you. In the night I lay and thought of you as a part of the darkness.[4] You aren't that but that's how you have made me see you. You aren't evil but at this moment I feel you in league with evil.

I don't know why I am telling you anything so rude and crude as this, except that if I had to speak to you on the telephone I should probably say something extraordinary and susceptible ⟨of⟩ {to} misinterpretation. Also affection has a {probably unfounded} belief in honesty.

Yours,
Rebecca

Rebecca West Collection   manuscript
University of Tulsa

[1] West is overlooking her fling with Francis Biddle in describing the span of her marriage.

[2] Paul Gallico (1897–1976), English author of fiction whose works include *The Snow Goose* (1945), *A Small Miracle* (1953), *Trial by Terror* (1954), and *Thief Is an Ugly Word* (1951); his *Poseidon Adventure* was adapted for film (1996).

[3] William Maxwell Gaines (1922–), publisher who took over his family business in 1947 and eventually launched *Mad* magazine.

[4] In a follow-up letter (1 February 1949, Rebecca West Collection University of Tulsa), West expressed this in the Manichaean terms she favors in much of her writing: "It seemed to me that as you spoke you showed that Catholic teaching—and surely {British, non-Continental} Catholic teaching has been wholly conquered from within by Manichaeism—has won such a victory over you that threw overboard the non-Manichaean elements in Christianity and hugged the rest to you. You scrapped an interpretation of the universe which is probably true—oh, certainly so unless you want to insist that the Holy Ghost has got to be as tangible as Mrs Braddock or you won't have anything to do with it—and you retained the rationalisation of the hatred of life which is the primal sin."

To: Anne Charles (McBurney)   Baden-Baden
                                                               [28–29 May 1949]
Dear Anne,

Forgive me for not writing—but we have literally not had a moment till we got here. We arrived at Frankfurt and had to circle over the airport for half an hour before we could land—which I found very sickmaking. Then

Mrs Hughes took us to her house, and indeed Daddy[1] was right—she is an angel. She was a dancer and is slightly common, and has a view of Doris & Elsie Waters combined with an ethereally lively appearance. We had a quiet dinner and the next morning got our papers all morning and shopped for presents at the PX—the American Army shop—which is fantastic. Quite a lot of things they don't have—for 3 months there wasn't a toothbrush—but there are quantities of the finest Swedish cut glass (I wish I could bring some vases home) and of the *vilest* French perfume which the G. I.'s frauleins won't accept—so they are being sold off at bargain prices. If I were an American taxpayer I should be awfully curious about the buyers for this institution. We got back to lunch & ⟨had⟩ {the} *Daily Mail* correspondent & Hughes assistant told us various things including that the Fine Mind was quite a danger.[2] We then went on to [Mespelbrun?] to ⟨talk⟩ {stay} with the Ingelheims—a glorious drive took us to a heavenly medieval castle standing in a moat with forest around. The Countess was sweet and was having an awful time because her husband is going dottier and dottier. She told me that Brunson Halter whom I had known when as a boy he worked in Heinemann's lived nearby and had asked us to lunch on the way to Nuremberg. {Before we left we went to early service in the (R. C.) chapel, an octagon hanging over the moat.} We found him & his very nice wife and four children as beautiful as angels living in the stables of their bombed baroque country house. ⟨They⟩ He took us on to dinner with the Countess Schinborce at Pennersfelden, a baroque roccoco palace *as big as Buckingham Palace,* with a vast collection of good 2nd class paintings and priceless Japanese and Chinese porcelain. The Countess and her sister Princess Wittgenstein (who was there) were elderly Italian aristocrats—they were not touched by American authorities but were specifically honoured because the Countess and her husband (who oddly enough ⟨ws⟩ practised as a doctor though they were fantastically rich from vineyards) had protected all Jews on their properties, defying Hitler, and many Jews they had got over to America had testified for them. All these people thought Hitler was not only a bad man but "dreadfully vulgar"! At the Countess's we met a Nuremberg judge who wouldn't hear of us going to ⟨his⟩ {a} hotel but took us to spend the night at his villa in Nuremberg— furnished with Hitler's things from his Nuremberg flat.

That was our first day—none has been less full. The next day we went to the Courts of Justice and saw the prosecution for the Weizsacker[3] trial (the old diplomat who got 7 years for working with Hitler—which distresses the fine mind). We got much of the documents from them (we are now travelling with about a stone of papers) and had to ring them up in between whiles. We pushed off to Munich in the afternoon—and dined with some old friends—and the next morning Dorothy turned up. From then on we worked incessantly—seeing Ministers and officials about the state of the country, looking into the Weizsacker case, and into the Resistance Movement, visiting D.P. [displaced persons] camps (of which the most interesting was a White Russian camp.) We included a long drive to the country to see the German General who had negotiated with Vlassov, the Russian general who brought over 100,000 ⟨xxx⟩ {men to fight with} the Germans against Stalin. This was up in the mountains and was superb. We had an appalling day on Friday—beginning with an interview with a Minister who had to handle refugees (not Displaced Persons, German {speaking persons} turned out of Eastern countries, where they had been for 2 or 3 centuries, to please Stalin) at *8.30* in the morning—and ending with a dinner where we put Weizsacker's defense counsel through it till 2.30 in the morning! Your employer is giving at the seams. The next day we had a glorious drive to Stuttgart, where we met a couple of as rank Nazis as I ever saw or smelled, and for the first time got out of the Press Camp and official houses on to "the German economy," as it's called {paying in German marks}. We went to a German restaurant and {five of us} had a large and fussy but not good ice and a slice of inferior iced cake. The bill was £3"10|—the chauffeurs (two, as we had a baggage car lent us, our car is tiny) had an ice and a coffee apiece which cost a pound! The rank Nazis explained to us how awful Hitler had been, and all they meant was that he was such a damned fool they couldn't get on with the job of Nazifying the country. This was our first very hot day—or even hot day. We then went through the most glorious wooded mountainous country, and landed in the French zone, which is extraordinary. The French are living in the country which the English and the Americans fall over backwards doing [*sic*], and it seems to be working beautifully. We are in a hotel, in which only Germans are staying, which the French have allowed to refit—it is an old and magnificent hotel. It has been ENTIRELY REFURNISHED, there is particularly good linen and wonderful towels. I don't think such an enterprise has been carried out in England. *Everywhere* the Germans look well, are well dressed, the shops are full of goods, if they didn't have to keep the refugees (12,000,000) the Marshall Aid[4] would have put them in a far better position than us. But it may not last, and the rich are not particularly kind to the poor.

The Fine Mind turned up last night—she *is* rather like me—but looks incredibly young for 38. She might be 23, and is quite nice and has very good manners, but is dreadfully German in the sense of hidden dark forces, and wouldn't be repelled by violence. If a sane Hitler turned up all these people would follow him. From all accounts Hitler was so raving that whether there was a Resistance movement or not there certainly should have been a Certification Movement. All the recollections of these people, by the way, describe fearful quarrels amongst themselves—how they ever got a war going, I can't think.

They are a set of wets.[5]

I am determined to stop this pace. Had to cross the river at Kehl and buy a [futringer?] of foie gras for a picnic—I now have to go to lunch. *Ever* so much love, dear Anne. (and love from Ric)

> Blessings,
> Rac

Daddy is good—but sometimes AWFUL. Whenever I need the car it turns out he has told the driver he can have a few hours off. And the *names* he introduces people under!

Tell Glen[6] that after living nearly a fortnight in a society of dachshunds we long for the dignity and seriousness of a Labrador. Tell Pounce[7] that there are no cats here and we long for a marmalade form to glide before us. (But tell him we think it possible that the Germans got rid of the cats because they ⟨x⟩ {found} their disagreeableness a trial in the war and the post-war period."

private collection   manuscript

[1] West regularly refers to Henry Andrews as Daddy in letters to Anne Charles.

[2] In writing to Anne, West is using Henry Andrews's phrase, "but she has a very fine Mind," to describe a charming German socialite who entranced him, but whom West suspected of Nazi sympathies.

[3] Ernst Freiherr von Weizsäcker (1882–1951), German diplomat, state secretary for the Third Reich, later ambassador to the Vatican (1943–1945). He served eighteen months of a five-year sentence before being released under a general amnesty. Though he claimed to be anti-Nazi, he initialed documents that brought about the murder of innocents.

[4] Funds from the Marshall Plan (named for U.S. secretary of state General George Marshall, who originated it), for European recovery after World War II (1948–1952). More than twelve billion dollars in economic aid was provided.

[5] British slang for "spineless individuals," "wimps."

[6] Anne Charles's labrador retriever. Glen remained at Ibstone when she left her job to be married.

[7] West's cat, memorialized in a letter to Emanie Arling (6 November 1952, Yale University): "I am suffering to a degree that I wouldn't have thought possible from grief over my poor old marmalade cat, Ginger Pounce. He was thirteen years old, and we had had him from a kitten. He thought I was neurotic and apt to be intrusive, and was always very careful not to make a fuss of me, but in a cagey way let me know that he knew I was doing pretty well for him and there were no hard feelings. He had a very reserved, reluctant way of licking my hand in a way that suggested he was saying to himself, 'I hope to God the woman won't start to think I want to marry her.' It really is a close tie—for every day of the thirteen years that I have been at home I've fussed about his meals and opened doors for him and taken him round the garden, and I miss him so much that the house seems dreary."

To: John Gunther

Ibstone House
Ibstone
Nr. High Wycombe
Bucks
1 August 1949

Dear John,

I have not written to you for a long time, and I feel ashamed of myself. I went to Germany for five weeks with Dorothy Thompson and Henry, and when I came back I worked through the first few days of what I took to be a sore throat but which was some deep infection, so I made myself horribly ill. The first time I got up was when I went to Buckingham Palace to get my C. B. E. [Companion of the British Empire], and it wasn't a bad idea. I was so ill that the King and the Beefeaters and the tapestries and the throne with the scarlet canopy and the Guards and in the musicians' gallery (playing the Valse des Fleurs of course) all swam together, and it was lovely.

You have asked me and Hamish[1] has asked me if I got *Death Be not Proud*. I did, and I loved your account of the boy. I also loved the book because it reminded me of the superb steadfastness, the courageous unyielding love, I saw you show towards the boy during those last months of his life. Staying at that mad hotel while you were doing that great work was one of the experiences for which I have been most grateful.[2] Yet I had a strange feeling about the book. I tell you this frankly for the (perhaps cowardly) reason that if you ever spoke to me about it I couldn't dissemble it; it would come out. I thought you gave an odd, disingenuous picture of Frances.[3] I do not doubt that she behaved as well as the Frances in the book. But she isn't the Frances in the book. And that seemed mysterious to me, and not fair to you.

But of course it was a wonderful job. And bless you for having written it, and bless you for having sent it to me.

Yours ever,
Rebecca

Papers of John Gunther, Addenda   typescript with manuscript signature
University of Chicago

[1] Hamish Hamilton (1900–1988), English publisher of Gunther's *Death Be Not Proud.* He founded the firm that bears his name (1931).

[2] Soon after the boy's death, West had written, saying, "The horror of illness is that you get bored and that you feel you are a bother to people, and all through his illness your son can never have felt that for an instant. . . . In your dealings with your son you showed in a grand way that your good humour and good temper are the outward and visible signs of a profound goodness and sweetness; which you showed in a little way, or I should say a less way, in your kindness to me when I was ill. Bless you for ever" (4 November 1947, University of Chicago).

[3] Gunther's first wife and the mother of the child.

To: Anthony West   16 September 1949[1]
My dear Anthony,

You really must stop tormenting yourself over these things.

You have wholly misunderstood this passage in my letter of 1927.[2] I was not trying to prevent H. G. making a settlement on you. I am suggesting to him that if you and I had shared a common home—and I had no reason to expect that you would marry so very early—it would be an absurd and unnatural position that I had to come to you to ask you for money to pay the rent, supposing that I had a run of ill luck or ill health. I explicitly say that he could trust me to hand over the income to you. I don't think that the financial relations between you and me can have led [you] to suppose that I would have failed in this undertaking.

I made this suggestion under the advice of Theo Mathew,[3] who pointed out to me that young people were often thoughtless about money, and that this arrangement would perhaps be better for the relationship of a mother and son living together. So far from making this suggestion because I saw in the settlement "a possible source of humiliation and embarrassment" to myself at some future date, I made it because an adviser who always was careful of your interests thought it would remove a possible source of friction between us.

I wish you would show this letter of 1927 to a solicitor and tell him what I'm telling you and what you think. I am sure he would tell you that there is nothing wrong or discreditable in my request, but that it was a sensible and natural attempt to deal with a difficult situation. Surely you understand that if Kitty were left to bring up Em [Edmund West], and she had no income and he had, there might be trouble in his adolescence and youth. I am the more surprised that you do not see this, because I thought you were of the opinion that having the uncontrolled disposal of your income from such an early age had been unsettling and had prevented you from getting down to work.

I think it would be a good thing if you sat down and thought about the financial side of your life, and asked yourself if you have any grounds for suspecting that I or anybody else close to you has ever dealt with you unfairly or greedily over money.

I find it difficult to deal with the other matters which are troubling because I really do not know what picture is in your mind. I gather that you think that I came between you and your father. There is not one word of truth in that. It is true that I left him, but that was in part because it was clearly impossible to go on living with him and provide you with a stable and orderly home. But I did everything I could to strengthen the tie between you, partly because you were both at your most charming and your happiest when you were together. Surely you realise that it must have been delightful for me too, when he used to do those little drawings for you. I would have thought it a dreadful thing, considering the intense affection you felt for H. G. if I had ever prevented you from seeing him when he said he wanted to see you; and I can safely say that not on one single occasion did I do so. As for material matters, I always told H. G.—and the last time I told him this was, I think, just before the war—that I thought it not just or kind or courteous to you or to me that you should not inherit on exactly the same terms as Gip and Frank [Wells]. But his strange complex forbade him to do this though I am sure he was as fond of you as he was of Gip and Frank, and possibly more.

It is very hard for us to come to an understanding on this. You see, you were only ten years old when H. G. and I separated; after that you saw him briefly during the holidays, and then occasionally till the end of his life. Obviously I couldn't describe to you when you were a child or adolescent what was an intense and subtle and tragic relationship—I doubt if I could ever describe it to you in any fullness, obviously that too is an impossibility, at any age. But when you were twenty you went down to the country an lived away from me and from all the people from whom you could have gathered anything about H. G. and myself. So far as I can make out you have spent much of the fifteen years which have passed since then telling yourself a story about your parents and their relationship to you and each other. It unfortunately happens that part of this story is the representation of myself as a crazed old lady. This began, so far as I can remember, when I was about forty-two, and is unaffected by the fact that I carry on a fairly successful and active professional life. It means that you do not believe one word that I say; and when I tell you anything about H. G. you don't believe it. I can't enlighten you. I can't even convey to you that you are living in a dreamland. But surely it might occur to you that if Kitty and you parted in three years' time, Kitty and you might know more about the relationship between you than Caro [Caroline West] ever would, however hard she might work on the subject later. It might occur to you that Caro would, almost certainly, be influenced by her fantasies.

Forgive me if I say that I don't like what you have done with the story of us three. So far as I can make out you have painted a picture of H. G. as a great man and a healthy, normal character, with whom you might have had a happy life had it not been for my aberrant self. This disregards the real and suffering self of H. G. It really was a source of misery to him that he had to take a hammer and smash up life whenever it formed the pattern that he most liked. If you saw him as a happy man it was because he seeing you and was temporarily happy. He was a witty and a humorous man, which is quite different from a happy man. I had indeed an aberrant self, and my aberration was to burden with my demands for a common happiness a man who was committed to unhappiness. I wish that instead of ignoring his tragedy you were sorry for him. You ⟨x⟩ are letting yourself forget what he was actually like and what you felt about him, I wish you could think and get back to a sense of his private life.

All sorts of things are worrying me in case they have fostered your feeling that I came between you and H. G. After the cremation it struck me as a pity that you had not gone up with Gip and Frank and Marjorie [Wells] and myself to see the last stage of the ceremony. But I had so hated the whole service and knew you were hating it, and so dreaded the last stage we had to see, that I did not think of it as an experience to be shared, but as something that it was a pity for any of us to see, something H. G. himself would not have approved of. I should perhaps have spoken of this, but I thought you felt as I did. There is also a trivial matter about his carpet. I mentioned that I might give it to you; and twenty times I have started to tell you and been interrupted that I thought it would be better for me to keep it, it is very long, has a very short pile, in any of your rooms would have to be put under furniture, and would be ruined in no time, according to the man who comes and cleans our carpets in situ. I am taking it out of the hall, as it is wearing out even there, and putting it in the library. I ⟨x⟩ feel that all sorts of things that mean nothing to me because I didn't feel this desire to separate you and take from him what should be yours for that very reason may seem to you evidence of that nightmare.

I think it is better that we do not see each other or write to each other for some time. You know quite well that H. G. would prefer you to get on with your life and not worry about the life that he and I lived. I realise fully that what I say has [no] reality to you just now, so don't trouble to set down my wishes for the book[4] and your future.

Yours ever,
Rac

Rebecca West Papers   typescript with autograph signature
Yale University

[1] Another typescript version of this letter, dated 15 September 1949, exists in the Yale Rebecca West Papers. The version given here is probably the final form of the letter.

[2] See the postscript of the letter to H. G. Wells, [late 1927].

[3] Theobald Mathew (1889–1964), solicitor with Charles Russell & Co. when he advised West. He became head of the criminal division of the Home Office and was appointed director of public prosecutions (1944).

[4] Anthony's biography of Wells.

To: Harold Ross

Ibstone House, Ibstone
Near High Wycombe, Bucks
18 December 1949

My dear Ross,

If you don't like this I shall come over to New York and cut you up like Mr Setty.[1] The contrast between this poor empty racketeer and the damned fool who murdered him (he killed him single-handed, in circumstances of the greatest brutality) for the sake of the notes he carried on him, not realizing that every racketeer files the numbers of the notes he carries on him) and this good and kind and gentle and wise creature Mr Tiffen. But I doubt if I've got down on paper half of what Tiffen was. . . .[2]

I should expect you to cut this piece hugely between pages 16 and 25. But of course you may not like it. If you do send me proofs if you can. I will send you cuttings as soon as I know you want it. If you take it I wish you would send two hundred and fifty dollars to Charles Curran, c/o *Evening Standard*, 47 Shoe Lane, London, E. C., for he took me to Burnham and did all the pub stuff with me, which I could not have done myself. My secretary Anne Charles was also with me and tried hard to find the head. She has never got over the thrill of falling over the container in which Mr Haigh[3] dissolved Mrs Durand when we went down to Lewes.

As for Haigh, the forger business has gone into reverse. There is an extraordinary development over that. At the last moment they discovered that Haigh had been the forger of all time, and that the Guildford mistake was made when he worked *with* a forger. And where is that forger now? I think the restitution cases may yet come on. But curiously enough it was a dull case, so far as it came into court. All that was interesting was the surrounding facts, and some day I will do a piece on them.

Henry and I, my sister Letitia, my nephew Norman [Macleod], and Anne Charles [McBurney] are all going to Amiens for five days at Christmas on what remains of the expense money you sent to France in the summer. We will all be calling your name blessed.

All love and Christmas wishes to Ariane,[4] and please God that 1950 will see [you b] me back among your contributors. By the way, surely that is a magnificent story about the woman and her coloured servants by Peter Taylor.[5] That struck me as one of the truest pictures of female life that I had ever read.

That is a horrible thing about Hokinson.[6] So utterly inappropriate. But she loved her life, she gently burbled about how it was the most astonishing luck that she had got into the *New Yorker,* and what a time you all gave her, and so on.

Yours ever,
Rebecca

New Yorker Collection
New York Public Library

signed typescript

[1] The *New Yorker* ran a three-part serial, "Annals of Crime London Masque" (December 1950), reprinted as "Mr. Setty and Mr. Hume" in *A Train of Powder.* With social and psychological deftness, West tells the story of the murder of Stanley Setty, a secondhand auto dealer and curbside banker. A farmworker, Sidney Tiffen, found his body, minus head and legs, bundled up in a package floating off the Essex coast. Brian Donald Hume was accused of the murder.

[2] In an omitted paragraph West describes a second part that did not appear.

[3] John George Haigh, who shot Mrs. Olive Durand-Deacon and dumped her in a barrel of sulphuric acid, was hanged in 1949. After previous murders he had written letters to his victims' families pretending that they were still alive and well, which may explain his identification as a forger.

[4] Ariane Allen Ross, aspiring young actress who became Ross's third wife in 1940.

[5] Peter Hillsman Taylor (1917–1994), American author of short stories and plays. He won a Pulitzer Prize for *A Summons to Memphis* (1967). West was praising "A Wife of Nashville" (3 December 1949).

[6] Helen Elna Hokinson (1893–1949), cartoonist for the *New Yorker* whose drawings of plump suburban clubwomen were often paired with captions and situations supplied by James Reid Parker. She died in an airplane crash in Washington, D.C.

To: Marjorie Wells[1]

Ibstone House
Ibstone
Nr. High Wycombe
Bucks
14 February 1950

My dear Marjorie,

This is a nightmare. It is no good telling you again how ashamed I am. Apart from anything else, those letters were your property. The copyright was mine but the letters themselves were your property. Anthony has no right to think you and your husband and Frank anything but generous and high-minded people, and even if he did not want to consult me (though why he shouldn't I can't imagine) it was his plain duty to write to you and say, "I would like to destroy some letters written by my mother, may I do so?" and abide by the answer.

As you know, all this business about letters full of melodramatic revelations is sheer delirium. But I really do not think Anthony is in his right mind just now. I noticed a most peculiar thing concerning this correspondence the other day. I think you may remember that he wrote Henry a furious letter ⟨xxx⟩ about a letter of mine which put forward a suggestion my solicitor had made about a settlement H. G. made on him. He gave a date to this, some day in July, 1927. When I looked up the letter in the file you sent me I found that not only was the letter completely innocuous but it was undated. I concluded that he had found it in an envelope and had taken the date from the postmark and then destroyed the envelope. But since then I have checked up the date from other correspondence, and I found it must have been written in February or March 1928.[2] Why on earth would anybody do that? what point is there in it?

I feel so ashamed of the tone of Kitty's letter to you and her unmannerly lack of response to your suggestion that she and you should meet. (I hope you won't bear a suspicion against Caro [Caroline West (Duer)] and Em [Edmund West], they really are very sweet). I [sic] The phrase "his only motives were to save his mother from any unpleasant repercussions" is indeed amusing, but I must say that I feel a chill run over me at the naive remark—"He refused to show them to me although my curiosity was much aroused." I need hardly tell you that if I had come across any correspondence between Anthony and Kitty [West] I would not have thought of reading it.

I think Kitty has had a very hard life with Anthony, I know she is an excellent mother and a very good painter, I am much afraid Anthony will leave her, but my God she makes it difficult for one to feel friendly towards her.

I was a little afraid that you thought that I was making a fuss over the letter which I thought had unbalanced Anthony by making him realize that H. G. had in his childhood been indifferent or hostile to him. But I realise perfectly that the letter would have done no harm if Anthony had been well-balanced—in the first place he would not have read the letter, and, if he had, he would not have interpreted it in the sense that he did. I am sure that he did interpret it in that sense because several phrases he had used lately—to

Henry and to some of our friends—were echoes from that letter. I can't tell you, ⟨x⟩ although like you I find it hard to believe, how convinced he is that he was enormously important to H. G., and that he and H. G. might have had a close and happy relationship had it not been for me.

Incidentally, Anthony never mentioned my letters to *me*, only to Henry, which was perhaps worse. But really this is not the sane Anthony at all.

> Yours ever,
> Rebecca

H. G. Wells Archive   Typescript with autograph signature
University of Illinois

[1] An earlier, briefer version of this letter survives (University of Tulsa), but this one was apparently sent. The earlier version disclosed more about West's disposition of her letters: "By the way, I am giving all my letters from H. G. to Yale. The librarian is very keen to have them, will keep the gift a secret until whatever term of years I name. What term seems suitable to you? I have weeded out these letters carefully and there are none which are not charming and delightful and the best of H. G., except for some irritable ones which are also amusing. And those I am annotating so that they will do nobody any harm."

[2] See letter to Wells which I have dated late 1927 because it mentions her plan to move to Kensington by the time of Anthony's Christmas holidays.

To: Harold Ross   Ibstone House
                                       Ibstone
                                       Nr. High Wycombe
                                       Bucks
                                       3 May 1951

My dear Ross,

I imagine you are feeling fairly sick about O'Dwyer.[1] I rage about it. I can imagine that he got into a job where he couldn't rebuild the premises into a morally satisfactory edifice for the simple reason that he didn't happen to be God. But as for this damned silly story about his standing on the steps of Gracie Mansion and taking an envelope full of money, it makes my blood boil that an entire nation should swallow it on the evidence of a crook. It is so odd that many people were indignant that Hiss[2] had to answer the charge against him when there was a strong prima facie case against him, but don't seem to feel any indignation at the assassination of a man against whom nothing has been proved except participation in a corruption which the people of the United States enforce on anybody who takes any of a large number of jobs *which have to be filled by someone*. If the United States did not want O'Dwyer to have faintly dirty hands they should have tidied up their politics many years ago. In any case there is no excuse for accepting a story that he has not merely faintly dirty hands but is filthy throughout, on the unsupported evidence of a witness who was almost everything you don't want a witness to be if you have to accept his evidence unsupported.[3]

I went to Chartres for Easter and it was damned cold. Did I tell you about the procession on Easter Sunday, that wound round the Cathedral, preceded by two lines of nuns in the floppy linen head dresses of the order of St Vincent de Paul—the mother house of that order being in Chartres and specialising in sending nurses out to the Far East—and God knows how many of the little dears being sunk without trace in China and Korea—and many of the little dears who were there being Chinese and Korean, as one sometimes saw with a shock of surprise when the wind blew back a fold of linen. After my return I went down with influenza which turned into a hell of sinusitis and a revival of that arthritis which appeared in my spine after that fall I had, and I then went stone deaf, with an exaggeration of the sound of my pulse so colossal that hardly any dose of barbitone would get me sleep. That is over, but I have lost about a month of work.

Before I was {again} in possession of my normal hearing I did a television with Eleanor Roosevelt, in company with Hartley Shawcross.[4] It was a difficult position for him, as Eleanor Roosevelt is deaf anyway, and I was still deaf, and we both looked at him hungrily for directions with an expression which I feel may easily be mistaken by the televisors for lust. I was very much interested to see Eleanor on the job. I love her voice and her eyes and her manners and the occasional revelation of a nice woman baffled by marriage to what must have been the largest known extrovert which you get in her books. But it was curious to meet her not socially, but on a job. The first thing Shawcross and I noticed was that everybody in the studio kept on telling us how wonderful she was for her age. But actually she is incredibly old for her age. She is something like sixty-six, and she looks nearly as old as our Queen Mary, who is in [her] eighties, and who still does a considerable job of work.[5] It was also odd that she was physically on her toes, she arrived at the studio at an ungodly hour on time, and she was always dashing about the studio, but it was impossible to get her to take any interest ⟨about⟩ in the subjects we were discussing. She had a list of questions typed out. We tried to warm her up by talking about them beforehand, but she wouldn't have it. She read her piece from cards behind the camera, and neither of us could get a flash out of her till we had nearly broken our backs. But I'm sure the show will look as if we were frightful and she was grand. I think this lack of interest is due to worry. She was accompanied by Elliott, who is surely an unmanageable great hunk of Roosevelt, and his fourth wife,[6] who was extraordinary. She is a pleasant woman with excellent manners, well-made, with good jewels and a marvellous platinum mink coat, and a make-up which reduced both Henry and Hartley to speechless gaping, though ⟨it was⟩ both are wellmannered lads. Her face was plastered with mud. It was brown, as if she had stopped her automobile by a ploughed field, and smeared the earth thick on her skin. But you knew she hadn't done anything of the sort, that really it had cost an awful lot of money. I don't believe Eleanor wanted {her} life to hold that sort of thing.

You had a very good story about a hospital by Winifred Williams.[7] By the way, I have suddenly had a letter from a lady called Mrs Louise Biles Hill making me an honorary member of the Mary Mildred Sullivan Chapter of the United Daughters of the Confederacy in consequence of the services my father rendered to the Confederate Army as a stretcher-bearer when as a very young man he was on furlough from the Rifle Brigade, which was stationed in Canada. This is literally the only thing I could possibly regard as an inheritance left me by my father.

An American landed here the other day with a story that Ariane had gone West to get a divorce.[8] I mention this because I may thereby save you the trouble of telling me, should the story be true. Do not trouble to allude to it, unless it happens not to be true. If it is true, let me say how sorry I am that you should both have had to go through this particular form of pain, and how much I hope that both of you will find other happiness.

Over here we are of course in fear that the Russians go into Persia any moment now. I lunched with my publisher two days ago, Harold Macmillan, who is a Conservative leader, and he tells me that some people think that the Russians may go into Yugoslavia instead. But I doubt that, for it is further afield and there is no food there, the collective farming has broken

down entirely, and the Russians would have difficulty in supporting themselves though I am quite sure Tito would put up no real resistance.

Blessings on you.

Rebecca

A note that was never sent as I was ill is appended.[9]

New Yorker Collection   typescript with autograph signature
New York Public Library   and postscript

[1] William O'Dwyer (1890–1964), Irish-born American lawyer and Democratic Party politician. He began as a policeman and rose to become mayor of New York City (1945–1950). The
Senate Crime Committee, headed by Estes Kefauver, found in March 1951 that O'Dwyer had
had dealings with racketeers such as Frank Costello. O'Dwyer was a close friend of Ross.

[2] Alger Hiss (1904–1996), U.S. State Department official accused of spying for the Russians.
He was convicted of perjury for concealing his membership in the Communist Party (1950),
in a sensational trial that brought Richard Nixon to prominence and fueled the investigations
of Senator Joseph McCarthy.

[3] Ross frequently marked his letters from West. In this case he has bracketed this first
paragraph and added quotation marks, as if for the purpose of quotation. There is a circled *A*
in the left margin.

[4] Hartley Shawcross, attorney-general and chief prosecutor for the British at the Nuremberg war trials. He was also prosecuting counsel in the Amery case and is referred to frequently
in *The Meaning of Treason*.

[5] West reported on Mrs. Roosevelt's personal appearance in a letter to Winifred Macleod:
"Eleanor Roosevelt is the most hideous being imaginable and was dressed fantastically badly
and radiated charm and vitality, partly the result of her lovely voice" (n.d., Indiana University,
Bloomington).

[6] Minnewa Bell, an oil heiress (m. 1951). He went on to marry a fifth wife, Patricia White-
head Peabody (m. 1960).

[7] Winifred Williams's "Visiting Day" (14 April 1951). She also wrote *The Beehive* (1941).

[8] Ross left Ariane on 29 September 1951. She filed for a formal separation on 21 November
1951, shortly before his death.

[9] In a letter to John and Jane Gunther (14 December 1951, University of Chicago) West
expressed her shock at Ross's death within the year: "He not only gave me the most wonderful
time in 1948 and 1949, but since then he had written to me regularly, and I had come to love
him dearly. Indeed, as to 1948 and 1949, I had some of the happiest days of my life in that
house of his at Stamford, doing nothing in particular. His letters stopped this Spring, but I
thought that was due to his matrimonial troubles more than to pleurisy. Then my daughter-
in-law brought back the news that he was very ill, and in late October I wrote and asked
Hawley Truax if he would like to see me if I hopped a boat. I got back a letter from Ross
himself absolutely cockahoop about his return to health."

To: Anne McBurney   Ibstone
                                                17 February 1952

My dear Anne,

I have just one thing to say about your account of Gerard:[1] Anthony had his pneumonia on this level for three months and one week. It just went on and on. And in three months' time he was better than he had ever been in his life. But I know very well what you and Gerard are feeling. . . .[2]

I had an exhausting time over the King's funeral.[3] I can't remember when last I wrote to you. There was the wild day when I stood in the snow and watched the coffin arrive at Westminster Hall. It was sleeting and icy cold, and the Queen Mother[4] suddenly told all the officials to go to blazes and decided that the family would receive the coffin at the door. And there they stood, all of them, the old Queen Mary looking marvellous, and remembering to thank people when they handed her things though she was plainly transported with grief. Then I rushed off to Pentonville and combined a lecture on the United States with an account of the cortege, which interested them all tremendously. There was a very nice Governor who had been Governor of Parkhurst when several of my traitors had been there, and said that I had been right about their characters, which pleased me. Then I rushed down again to Westminster Hall and went through the Hall before the public were admitted. You will have seen the pictures, but nothing can convey the solemnity and beauty, particularly of the changing of the guard which was like the ballet and high mass mixed. Then I went home and wrote part of a piece and went to bed at half past eleven and was down in the queue outside Westminster Hall at five in the morning. At half past eight I had been through the Hall with the first comers, and was back at the Club and had breakfast then went off to the *Evening Standard* office and wrote the end of my piece—all round a man who was a caretaker from Birkenhead and was a comic character, just like somebody out of Itma—I invented a catch phrase for him, "Have you ever been to Uttoxeter?"[5] and disguised him for fear of libel, and then wound up with a final paragraph saying how appropriate it was that the King who loved Itma would have had this man as one of the first people in the queue. I finished it with pleasure, feeling that I had done a good job, and as I was on the last page found that Charles [Curran] had throughout it cut the man from Uttoxeter, as he thought it had really happened like that, so we were left with an article which had absolutely no point and was rubbish. I nearly wept—he should have come and asked me, of course. I then realised that there was a spate of photographs and I would have to reckon with huge cuts, which nobody would be calm enough to do intelligently, and so I said I would do no more. . . .⁶ I retired from the *Evening Standard*, but then the syndicate who had been handling my stuff, which had gone to the *N. Y. Herald Tribune* and a mass of Canadian papers, came after me, and said that people had liked my stuff because it was more personal than anybody else's and wouldn't I do the funeral from inside St. George's Chapel. I said I would, and we arrived at Windsor at half past nine. Nobody could tell when the Chapel was open to the press, which was a nuisance as there was then a great sensation over the flowers, and I had to describe them straight away as the beginning of my article. You can't think what they were like. They covered every bit of flat ground anywhere near St George's chapel, and stacked up the cloisters as well. Lots of little bunches from France, from people who had been connected with the R. A. F., lots of interesting things, like a cushion of daffodils from a group of streets in Fulham, and a bunch of polyanthuses with a note, "To a good King, from one decorated by him, and proud of it, Royal Marines." My headquarters were a pub down by the bridge to Eton. I went back there and sent off a thousand words to the early editions on this subject, then went back to Windsor Castle, and was standing by the North Porch of the Chapel when it opened, by chance, so went in, and found Johnny⁷ gorgeous in an embroidered jacket and his wonderful breeks. But neither he nor anyone else could find the press box, I had to hang about for a quarter of an hour. At last I found where I had to go. The agencies went up to a curious chapel that is up under the roof and saw everything, but we correspondents had had our noses rubbed in the dirt. It was a scandalous business. We were shown into the ambulatory of the choir, which, although they had been preparing the Chapel for a week, had been turned into a lumber-room. It was really a most shocking sight, considering that it was within a few yards of the place where the King was to be laid to rest. They had piled up bits of wood from the stands, pots of paints and paste, doormats and cushions, all anyhow—though there cannot be lack of storage room in Windsor Castle. There was even a sewing-machine on a table. Not in the most sluttish French or Italian church have I ever seen such a disgraceful scene. Picking our way through this mess, we arrived at our seats. These were behind the grille which protects the tomb of Henry VI, and showed us almost nothing except the doorway opposite, through which the guests who had seats in the [Order of the] Garter stalls entered, and a sideways squint to the left, which we hoped would show us the head of the coffin, and a sideways squint to the right, which showed us part of the altar. This filled us all with consternation, but we did think we would see the Archbishops conducting the service. But now we had some interesting sights of the entering guests—Eisenhower and Churchill, who very nearly broke his neck, he tripped on the chancel step, and seemed likely to fall very heavily indeed, but just recovered himself in time. I thought he was going to kill himself. And it is a most extraordinary thing that there spread just at this time, outside the church, a rumour that he had died. It started long before anybody could have heard of this incident. But that was the end of our sights. When the processions arrived a ⟨x⟩ number of representatives of the Army and Navy and Air Force and diplomatic service arrived and fanned out across the chancel, just below the altar steps, interposing a solid block between us and the ceremony. So far as the newspaper correspondents' eyes could tell, it might have been a marriage service. Most people stood on their chairs, I got hold of some pew cushions and put them on the step that ran round the outer wall of the ambulatory, and so did Gilbert Harding,[8] and we stood on them. It was all appallingly irreverent, and many people among the correspondents were furious at the religious aspect of it. Two men said to me, "I don't like behaving like this in a church." But even so we saw nothing except the magnificent head of Lord Clarendon,[9] which was not enough for a story. . . .[10]

When I got out of the Chapel I saw Helen Dashwood,[11] who needless to say had had a wonderful seat, but who looked like death. She looks very thin and terribly old. (So too, by the way, did Mrs Churchill, she looked a hundred.) I don't think she can be well. Then I rushed down the hill and typed steadily for four hours, and then had a most interesting time in the bar, while they were getting my stuff off over the cables. (They had a cable room installed.) The bar was full of the journalists, who were staying over to do a last story on the flowers the next day. They were all dead tired, but they were all talking with such absolutely romantic passion for Queen Elizabeth. Ronald Camp of the *Daily Mail*, who is as hard-boiled as can be, said, "Well, I take it as part of my duty from now on to back her up every way we can." And old Nichols of the *Evening News* said, "Of course, we must look forward. She's bound to make mistakes some time. We must do the best we can for her then." It was enough to make one cry. There were discussions as to how to make the proprietors lay off Princess Margaret—it is apparently much resented by the reporters that they have to do all the Dalkeith business.[12] I felt proud of my profession. We got home at half past nine, and I don't think I have ever worked a harder ⟨thirt⟩ fourteen hours in my life. It must have been all right, for I have already been booked by the syndicate for the Coronation.[13]

Oh, one funny story I couldn't use. The {Negro} racing tipster, Prince Monolulu, was there standing in the crowd. How, God knows, he recognized me, and called out to me and held my hand fervently. He was in mourning—usually he wears red and green and blue feathers round his woolly head, they were black and white. A French photographer came up and Monolulu spoke to him in the most beautiful old-fashioned French, he must have learned it in Martinique or somewhere, and in French he explained that he had known the King personally, and then broke into English and said, "I am not a good man, but the King was a good man, here, I give you something, not for money, ⟨but⟩ just because I'm so sorry," and thrust something into my hand. I put it into my pocket and slunk away from a scene which I had been anxious to leave from the first moment, all things considered. The next day I took the paper out of my pocket and it was a slip tipping Pearly King for the Grand National, and two other horses for two other races. I think this a most curious way of showing grief, the free distribution of tips by a tipster. . . .[14]

By the way, where are the safe-keys?

Much love from us both, Daddy [Henry Andrews] has gone to fetch the French widow from Andover.

Rac

private collection   typescript with autograph signature

---

[1] Anne Charles had gone to the Gold Coast to be with her ailing brother Gerard, who died there.

[2] A comic paragraph on the comings and goings of servants is omitted.

[3] George VI died 6 February 1952.

[4] Elizabeth, mother of the new queen, Elizabeth II, and widow of the king.

[5] *Itma* was a radio program, "It's That Man Again," featuring Thomas Handley. Uttoxeter is a town west of Derby in Derbyshire (northwest England).

[6] A description of the new cameras used has been cut.

[7] Sir John Dashwood, premier baronet of England.

[8] Gilbert Charles Harding (1907–1960), broadcasting and television star on programs such as the *Brains Trust* and *Twenty Questions,* where he consistently displayed anti-establishment attitudes.

[9] George Herbert Hyde Villiers (1877–1955), public servant who pursued Conservative politics in the House of Lords and served as chairman of the BBC (1927–1930) and governor general of South Africa (1931–1937) before becoming Lord Chamberlain to the household of George VI. His last official act was to break his wand of office over the coffin of the king he had served; he retired thereafter.

[10] A description of rudeness of Windsor authorities to foreign correspondents has been cut.

[11] Wife of Sir John Dashwood.

[12] Reporters had to inquire into rumors (January 1952) that Princess Margaret was engaged to the Earl of Dalkeith.

[13] West also gave McBurney a memorable description of the toilet facilities at the coronation: "Thank you kindly, there were masses of lavatories, Elsans, in the Abbey. They stood in pairs in odd angles of what, by force of association, I find myself constrained to term the noble pile, though it is not a phrase I use in ordinary circumstances. I particularly like the pairs marked 'Peeresses' and 'Ladies,' and 'Bishops' and 'Judges.' All the toilet paper was marked on each separate leaf 'Government Property,' and as there is a penalty for destroying Government Property, one hardly knew what to do."

[14] A description of Ibstone neighbors has been cut.

To: Lionel Trilling[1]

Ibstone House
Ibstone
Nr. High Wycombe
Bucks
15 March 1952

Dear Mr Trilling,

First let me say that I am one of your greatest admirers.

The other night I was delighted to hear a speaker on the Third Programme of our radio, a Mr John Raymond, delivering a panegyric on your works; and when he singled out for special admiration your essay on *The Princess Casamassima*[2] I remembered that this was the one essay in *The Liberal Imagination* which I had never read. I turned to it and was startled to find that the essay contained a reference to myself which was bewildering for several reasons. You allude grimly to my "exuberant little study" of Henry James and you convey that I showed gross ignorance by casting doubt on the probability of the conspiratorial events described in *The Princess Casamassima.*[3]

Now, I attach little importance to that book, for it would have been strange indeed if a girl of twenty-two could have written well on one of the greatest of writers. But I knew at once that I had not expressed the opinion that you ascribed to me for the reason that it was historically impossible that I or any of my generation could have held such an opinion. I had not read it for twenty years, but when I hunted it out I found that in fact I had not expressed the faintest shade of doubt regarding the probability of the conspiratorial events described in *The Princess Casamassima.*

What may have misled you is that I begin my account of *The Princess Casamassima,* with the words: "Politics play a great part, and in the same sense, in *The Princess Casamassima."* But if you had turned back the page you would have seen that the reference is {to} the feeling of dread regarding Left Wing or reformist politics which Henry James had shown in *The Bostonians.* He certainly also expressed this in *The Princess Casamassima* and retained it to the end of his life. But I expressed no doubt as to the existence of his revolutionaries and the nature of their plans—and indeed mention the Poupins as faithful and vigorous portraits—for the reason that no contemporary of mine would not [have] been aware of the situation he described. Least of all could I have been unaware of it.[4]

You quote, I observe, from James' own declaration of his reliance on his general knowledge, for his description of the revolutionary activities, and you lay stress on his refusal to make any special study of the matter, and appear to regard it as a unique proof of his genius. But in fact any educated person of the time knew as much about Continental terrorism as is manifested in *The Princess Casamassima.*

This was partly due to the space and order of writing which was devoted to such subjects by the press. Any reader of the *Daily Telegraph* or the *Illustrated London News* would have quite a fair idea of the state of anarchist and terrorist movements on the Continent. George Augustus Sala,[5] for example, was a mine of information on the subject. Furthermore, if you belonged to the sort of family which travelled abroad, you were almost bound to have some experience which brought you within the sphere of revolutionary activity. Very few educated persons were not fully aware of all the circumstances that surrounded the assassination of the Empress Elizabeth of Austria;[6] and if you will look at the files of the English press for the period you will find that a wide knowledge of the Russian revolutionary movement was shown by the English public when the Tsar proposed to visit England some years before the First World War.

It would indeed never have occurred to anybody of my generation to doubt the existence of the Sun and Moon Club and the sinister activities of Muniment, any more than it would have occurred to a young American in the twenties to doubt the existence of bootleggers. But it is peculiarly absurd to imagine that I could have been in this situation. I do not know if you have ever heard of the Reclus brothers,[7] but any book on the French anarchist movement or on the Commune will tell you who they were. It happened that after they had left France to avoid the consequences of the Coup d'Etat they met my grandmother, Mrs Charles George Fairfield, who engaged first one and then (briefly) the other as tutors for her sons, and they became intimates of her family in County Kerry. My father regarded both Elie and Elysée with the greatest affection and respect, and though he like the rest of his family was strongly Conservative he retained his liking for them throughout his life. I therefore grew up into a family where the various varieties of anarchism, and the conflict between pacifist and terrorist anarchism, were frequently the subject of conversation. When I became interested in the Labour Movement at the age of fourteen I went into it with a certain amount of knowledge which made me extremely interested in the foreign groups associated with it, and before I left Edinburgh at the age of seventeen I had already quite a number of acquaintances which would have preserved me from the remarkable degree of ignorance you ascribe to me.

I may also mention that I feel puzzled at your implication that in some way I am or was a defender of the naturalistic novel to the exclusion of other kinds. As I disliked Gissing and detested Galsworthy[8] and Arnold Bennett this seems a singular judgment. I am also at a loss to understand why you describe me as "a loyal Fabian," or should ascribe to those who were loyal Fabians any kind of incredulity at the statement that "a lower-class character" might become Prime Minister of England.[9] It was anticipated by a great many people outside and inside the Fabian Society that this would happen a long time before it did. I also could wish that you had not framed a sentence in such a way that it appears as if I had used the words "able" and "meticulous" as if they were both adjectives expressive of approval. I learned my Latin in Scotland and I am incapable of using the word "meticulous" as other than a term of abuse.[10]

I must own that had I extended space to deal with *The Princess Casamassima* my conclusions would not coincide with your own. I think you lay a stress on the relationship between Christina and Muniment which is hardly warranted in view of the popularity of such relationships as the subject of novels at that time, and I think also that it needs to be discussed how far James' treatment of the story was determined by his decision to transpose the real events on which he was drawing for his plot to another age than that in which they actually happened. This, from the ideological point of view, is quite important. But I see in your essay many of the brilliant qualities which have delighted me in your work before, and I wish I had not to write this querulous letter. But it is irritating to find oneself alluded to in a tone of undisguised contempt on the ground that one has held an opinion which it is impossible that one could have held and which one did not hold.

Yours sincerely,
Rebecca West

Lionel Trilling papers   typescript
Columbia University Library

[1] Lionel Trilling (1905–1975), noted American professor of English at Columbia University. Author of *The Liberal Imagination* (1950), *The Opposing Self* (1955), and *Sincerity and Authenticity* (1972). He reviewed *The Meaning of Treason* in the *Nation* (10 January 1948).

[2] Novel by Henry James (1886).

[3] In West's first book, *Henry James* (1916). Trilling's response to West's letter includes the following: "I really haven't wronged you as much as you think, but I have wronged you a little, for which you have repaid me with a very charming letter. . . .
You quite mistake the intention of what I say of your brook. When I alluded to your 'exuberant little study' of James I didn't in the least make the allusion to 'grimly'—couldn't have done so because it is a book toward which I have always had the happiest feelings. When I was young it seemed to me the enviable model of the way a young writer should be able and dare to write." (17 June 1952, Trilling papers, Columbia University).

[4] Trilling stands by his interpretation of p. 73 of West's book but then on the evidence of her letter sees that this was mistaken.

[5] George Augustus Sala (1828–1895), legendary English journalist who began writing for Dickens's *Household Words* (1851–1857). He ran a gossip column for the *Illustrated London News*. But it was in the *Daily Telegraph* that he began covering world events such as the American Civil War, in a humanistic but florid style.

[6] Empress Elizabeth of Austria, wife of Emperor Franz Joseph. West gave an account of her assassination by an anarchist (1898) in the prologue to *Black Lamb and Grey Falcon*.

[7] [Jean-Jacques-] Elysée Reclus (1830–1905), geographer and anarchist and his less famous brother Michel-Elie (1827–1904); both were active in the Commune (1871). West recalls Elie as her father's tutor in *Family Memories* (175).

[8] John Galsworthy (1867–1933), British novelist best known for *The Forsyte Saga* (1922). In her 1922 essay "Mr Bennett," published in *The Strange Necessity* (1928), West compares

Galsworthy to a "phagocyte" in the blood system, "rushing to eat up the invading hosts." She declares his work "minor" in *Ending in Earnest*.

[9] In his response, Trilling explains that "loyal Fabian" was not meant to refer to her.

[10] Trilling identified his Latin as "the dimmish New York Schools variety," but claimed American usage: "We say "meticulous workmanship" and mean it as praise."

To: Kingsley Martin   Ibstone House
                                                        Ibstone
                                                        Nr. High Wycombe
                                                        Bucks
                                                        23 April 1952

Dear Kingsley,

I haven't acknowledged your letter before because of a complex of domestic disasters, including one death. (My secretary's [Anne Charles McBurney's] brother, aged thirty-eight, the best type of colonial administrator, who loved Africa and the Africans—I wonder if you find like me that you feel a sense of guilt when gifted people younger than oneself disappear into the void.) At first I was puzzled by your letter and thought that you were pulling my leg, but I realised from your reference to my book that you weren't, and I am grateful for your kind words. What is odd about the reception of that book[1] is that what moved me to write it—the pitifulness of Joyce's ambition and his unfitness for any sort of eminence, and the pitifulness of the poor fools who were dragged before those horrible courts martial—has excited the interest of only a few ⟨x⟩ {readers}, I think I have had fifteen letters in all {concerning the courts martial}, mainly from well-to-do people not in Who's Who, and only one reviewer. (He did get quite agitated, a middle-aged Liberal.) Though this book has been used a lot by people in the thick of the struggle over the reform by courts martial, it has not interested the general public from this point of view at all. Gilbert Murray once said to me that what struck him most about the first world war is the decay of pity, and I think I agree.

                                        Yours ever,
                                        Rebecca W.

University of Sussex Library   manuscript

[1] *The Meaning of Treason*, with its treatment of William Joyce.

To: Lionel Trilling

Ibstone House
Ibstone
Nr. High Wycombe
Bucks
22 June 1952

Dear Mr Trilling,

Thank you for a most charming letter. I had been a little worried at not hearing from you, because I am dogged through life by the personal hatred of people whom I have never met. (I do not mean that people whom I have met never hate me, but I think I have been unusually subject to fierce resentments on imaginary scores; I once was most savagely attacked by an Italian critic, who on being informed by a friend that what he said seemed to apply to nothing I had ever written, said that that might be so, but he himself could never forgive me for having so grossly offended Benedetto Croce[1] that afternoon at Ravenna—which you will admit, to one who never met Croce and has never been to Ravenna was very eerie). I quite see the points you raise. But I do not know what large matters you think are subjects for dispute between us. I have an idea that in a review of *The Meaning of Treason* you alleged that the idea of nationality on which I lay so much stress is an outmoded superstition laid aside by all reasonable people. But, if I may say so, the only faults that I ever find in your work are due to the fact that you do not know post-war Europe. For the last nineteen years I have been coming more and more in contact with exiles and refugees as they presented themselves before me in increasing destitution and hopelessness, and I know very well what ideas they have cast off, and what have survived in their minds as true. In none of them has the idea of internationalism and univer-sality had any strength, it was nationalism, the pride of a people in their own country and in their own culture, which kept them in a state to have an international use and universal value. But I do not remember coming across anything in your writing which gives me a clue to any fundamental differ-ence between us, and I hope there are few.

By the way, regarding your excellent paper on Orwell; I wish that you would some time write, or impose the task on your most beloved disciple, a history of the part the Spanish Civil War played in the lives of literary men and women.[2] A study of that overpopulated Missolonghi[3] could be a beauti-ful exploration of the relations between myth and experience.

Please do not trouble to acknowledge this note. I hope I may meet you some time when I am in America.

Yours very sincerely,
Rebecca West

Lionel Trilling papers   typescript
Columbia University Library

[1] Benedetto Croce (1866–1952), Italian philosopher, literary critic, and historian. His aesthetics emphasizes the intuitive nature of art and reflects German idealism. He was a liberal throughout the Fascist era and was a delegate to the Italian parliament (1945–1947) when its new constitution was made.
[2] See letter to George Orwell, 22 February 1946, for note.
[3] Greek town on the Gulf of Petras, where Byron died.

To: Charles Curran   Grand Hotel, Rome
                                                                        1 January 195[3]

My dear Charles,

Happy New Year to you. May every day of 1953 make you a contented man by bringing the conviction of a Labour member for drunkenness, if not for some more disgraceful crime—and may you be able to explain to me why your party[1] is asking Tito to come to England. But let us pass on to less contentious matters, and let me thank you for those glorious poinsettias, which were brought into my room at the villa at Settignano, where we were staying, when I was in bed with an attack of colitis. This I owed to the fierce winter climate of Florence, and my habit of going to museums, and my acute disgust at the Rossellinis.[2] The poinsettias which came as a result of your superb command of remote control were deep crimson things about a foot across.

I am coming home with Henry in a few days, for the Rossellini business is incredible. We got here on the 14th, and my understanding was that I was to confer with Rossellini for a week to see if I would consent to write the dialogue for his film of Colette's *Duo*.[3] For the week I was to get the equivalent of five hundred dollars, plus ten thousand lire a day for my expenses, and my return fare. If I took up the contract I was to be paid a thousand dollars a week but pay my own expenses, for a term not less than four and not more than ten weeks. ⟨When⟩ I was primarily moved by the idea of getting to Italy—but also by Rossellini's great reputation as a film director.

But when we got here I recognised an old pattern. Rossellini wasn't here—he was producing an opera in Naples. Then during the two days that passed before he came back we saw his last film, and I was startled. *Europe 1951* is its name, and it is the purest punk—except for a good performance by Ingrid Bergman it is childish, the plot, dialogue, and production is amateurish and out of date. We then went to dinner with the Rossellinis, and were still further disconcerted. Ingrid Bergman is a nice soul, but (when one sees her out of her American background, where she was following the stream) common and mannerless, with a flatness of which Henry discovered the secret when he found that she was half-German—her mother came from Hamburg, and she might well be a housemaid in a big Hamburg hotel. The big blow was Rossellini. He is surprising from a physical point of view—the great lover is forty, flabby, lolloping, with a fish mouth, fish eyes, no chin, a paunch, and a peculiarly revolting habit of waving about fat hands; and his conversation very soon shows that the man knows nothing about anything and has no talent of any sort. I thought I could not be right, and gave him every chance of setting down something which would show that he had ideas and a technique. But nothing has come out of this, though the man through which we deal (for I have only seen Rossellini twice) is able and anxious to get on with things. It turned out Colette's *Duo* had been scrapped, for very dubious reasons. I was told that there was a story—which turned out not to be a story; it became obvious that though I had been hired to write dialogue, I was to be persuaded to write a story which would afterwards be presented as Rossellini's. When I put this to him I was presented with a rubbishy improvised synopsis, of a rather dirty-postcard tone, and I found that his ambition was to represent Miss Bergman in the light of passion, which would certainly sink her ship. This all seemed rather mysterious. The complete absence of talent was explained eventually by the fact that Rossellini hasn't in fact ever himself made a successful picture. In his documentaries, he was helped, he was then the lover (I can't explain the mystery of his attraction) {Have just realised that Anne Magnani must be queer this way, her first husband has only one eye, which makes R's appeal to her more plausible.} of Anna Magnani, who saw him through the *Open City* with the aid of a very good writer, and who got him another good writer to do *Paesano* with him.

The film, *Miracle,* was Anna Magnani's too. He is in fact a camera man who has worked his way up on a ladder of sheets and blankets. Since he left Anna Magnani he has made a very few films which are all failures. *But* his career has been assured by the close link between the state and the film industry in Italy. The subsidy system is generous and intricate—it leads to such things as there existing a volume of sequences amounting to about 150 pages which are supposed to be the sequences of the production for which I have not written the story yet (so that not a dozen ⟨xx⟩ sequences could honestly be set down). This volume of sequences is a dummy, whipped up to be sent to the Ministry so that the department can be sure that a new production is going forward— and as a producer receives back part of the money received at the cinema theatres from his old pictures in order to finance his new pictures, if he is going on producing. What a cancer the film industry is in the body of civilisation.[4]

I have told him I won't take up the contract, and we are just waiting till the situation is confirmed by Rossellini, and we have eaten a little more veal, and seen some more churches, before we come home. Our stay with Bernard Berenson[5] at Settignano was interesting, but to me a little painful. Here is this wonderful little creature, eighty-seven now, with a little voice like the tune of a musical box, everything exquisite about him, so full of learning that it is not to be believed, right about everything, but nevertheless a Jew born in Wilna, and carrying to his grave the infatuation with Germany, the hatred of all Slav peoples, which is inborn in the Jew. He was quite angry with me when I told how Reuter, the mayor of Berlin, on hearing what Henry had done in the way of coming into Germany to protect the anti-Nazi and Jew employees of the Berlin Light and Power Company (of which Henry was a director) and various persecuted friends of his, had said ⟨after⟩ "Aber warum?"—meaning he wasn't German, why did he bother and run the risk? The old man assured me that a German Professor of Greek could not have said that.

While we were there Katherine Dunham, the Negro dancer,[6] came in, in great distress. A nice, silly, honest creature, she has been persuaded by some- one to create a ballet about lynching, and run a season of it in Paris for six weeks. Thornton Wilder had seen it and begged her not to do it, because of its effect on Communist propaganda; Bernard Berenson told her she must withdraw it; she came up to talk to me in bed about it. She had had no idea that it would lead to any trouble. In the course of conversation it turned out that she had never been in the South, did not know the lynching figures, and had no idea what lynching was about. She said she was not a Communist, but from her account of a difficulty she had had about appearing on a television programme it was apparent that she was surrounded by them, and that her lawyer, a Jew, had given her very bad advice, likely to make her appear as a persecuted Communist when the authorities were not persecuting her at all. There also came in a couple of Communists called Louis Untermeyer and his wife Jean Starr Untermeyer[7] (he a nephew of the famous Sam Untermeyer) who called to deliver a Christmas present from Berenson's publishers in New York, Simon & Schuster, with whom Joe Barnes now works. Barenson tells me he is constantly sought after by Communists, that Louis Adamic[8] worked on him for a long time. How they cover the ground. The Untermeyers worked hard to sell Arthur Miller,[9] of the *Death of a Salesman,* to Berenson. I thought that success had not happened quite by accident. I had myself a feeling that the Untermeyers might have come abroad {for a trip} because they might find it difficult to get passports under the new regime.

How it rains!

Yours ever,

R

Rebecca West Collection   typescript with manuscript insertions
University of Tulsa

[1] The Conservative Party.

[2] Roberto Rossellini (1906–1977), Italian film director and producer who developed Italian neorealist cinema in the film *Open City* (1945). The actress Anna Magnani appeared in a pair of films titled *L'Amore*. His then wife Ingrid Bergman starred in *Stromboli* (1949), *Europe '51* (1952), and *Viaggio in Italia* (1953). They divorced in 1958.

[3] Colette (1873–1954), novelist, dramatist, and journalist best known for her *Claudine* series of novels. West described her first meeting with Colette (when they collided in the St.-Raphael train station) in the *Bookman* (November 1929), reprinted as "Formidable" in *Ending in Earnest.*

[4] West wrote a comparable assessment of the Rossellinis to Margaret Hodges on the same date.

[5] Bernard Berenson (1865–1959), American art critic, connoisseur, and diarist who was born in Lithuania and was long resident in the villa I Tatti near Florence. He specialized in Italian art and wrote several books on Renaissance painters, starting with *Venetian Painters of the Renaissance* (1894). Other works include *Sketch for a Self-Portrait* (1945), and *Rumor and Reflection* (1952). West sought his help in motivating Henry to write.

[6] Katherine Dunham (1910–), American dancer and choreographer whose anthropological

research into "primitive" dance influenced her *Tropics* (1937) and *Le jazz hot* (1938). She organized an African-American dance group (1940) that toured the world. Her autobiography is *A Touch of Innocence* (1959).

[7] Louis Untermeyer (1885–1977), American critic of modern poetry. He recalls the visit, at which West served the tea, in *Bygones* (1965). He says Berenson wanted to hear about new Jewish-American writers and recent science fiction (pp. 183–184), but makes no mention of Miller. Jean Starr Untermeyer (1886–1970), poet and anthologist whose works include *Wingèd Child* (1936).

[8] Louis Adamic (1899–1951), Slovenian-American journalist and novelist who wrote of the experience of immigrants in *Laughing in the Jungle* (1932) and of a return to Yugoslavia in *The Native's Return* (1934). He was a supporter of Tito.

[9] Arthur Miller (1915–), American playwright who established himself with *Death of a Salesman* (1949). The Salem witch trials in his play *The Crucible* (1952) are often seen as a parallel to McCarthyism.

To: Leonard Russell[1]

Ibstone House
Ibstone
Nr. High Wycombe
Bucks
16 February 1953

My dear Leonard,

The date will suit me perfectly. But I want to do something rather more novel and interesting than concentrate on Whittaker Chambers.[2] I want to start with an affirmation that it is quite unjust to the United States to believe that the Investigating Committees are simply "witch-hunting." I go on to describe how first Elizabeth Bentley[3] and then Whittaker Chambers went into the Committee room on successive sittings and named a number of civil servants as Communist bottlewashers. I then give a brief description of the Hiss case, turning aside to point out that the arrest of Fuchs[4] turned up a lot of evidence which started a trial which ended in establishing the veracity of Elizabeth Bentley. I go on to describe the book that Chambers published after the case, which shows himself as a dispossessed member of the middle-classes, who turned to Communism to give him a foothold in society when his family had proved unable to face the terrific competition which the middle-classes have to face today if they are to keep their privileges. I then point out that in this he is a typical Communist. The backbone of the Communist Party in America was composed of people who (like Hiss and Chambers) wanted to keep their middle-class privileges or people who were trying to establish themself in the privileged middle-class (like Rosenberg and his wife)[5] and found that the Communist Party gave them an edge over people ⟨who⟩ of their own sort who had no backing. In the meantime I have indicated the character of Harry Dexter White, who was a Russian Jew of superb intellectual gifts who could not help joining up with *any* party—was just as busy in linking up with Keynes as he was with the Communists, and therefore could not be counted as an idealist or a ⟨x⟩ Marxist or any of the things Communists are supposed to be. I indicate from quotations from the Government reports just what sort the professional Communists were by describing Nathan Silvermaster[6] (whose wife is the daughter of the Czarist statesman Count Witte.) I then point out that the Hiss trial was a matter of slight importance to the American people, and that a much more important issue is before them. This is the infiltration of their Civil Service. The Committees have pursued this issue through sittings and sittings and sittings and it is now difficult for any lay reader to grasp the situation—impossible for most Europeans ever to get hold of the material. But the case of Irving Kaplan[7] shows that a man—to whom attention was drawn because he got Whittaker Chambers a job in the Civil Service at $6000 a year at the drop of a hat because he was a fellow-Communist.—can rise rapidly through the civil service with no qualifications, or few qualifications, referring for recommendations to other civil servants, who in this case for the most part, when they are traced, turned out to be people who had refused to answer the question "Are you a member of the Communist Party?" on the ground of their constitutional right to refuse to give an answer that might lead to self-incrimination. Irving Kaplan himself refused to answer this question. A number of civil servants have refused to say who they gave as their references. This would seem a slight matter, as surely their references can be traced in the files. But this is not the case, since the election of Eisenhower it has been shown that the files of the State Department, to give only one Government agency, have been accessible to almost anyone and that they have been robbed in many case[s] of essential information regarding personnel. (This evidence has just been given and I am having cuttings air-mailed to me for the next fortnight.) Quite obviously it was a tremendous advantage to an ambitious young man or woman to be a Communist if they wanted quick advancement in the American civil service. This was hard on the ambitious young man or woman who was not a Communist. It was also hard on the

American people, for this preference does not stop at a certain level. Hiss was at Yalta.[8] But the matter is not bounded by whether treachery is at work. The system may cut across the basis necessary for a satisfactory civil service. Lauchlin Currie, the President's personal adviser, let Owen Lattimore open his mail in his absence, this is objectionable ⟨x⟩ {even if} Lattimore is as innocent as the lamb.[9] (This last reference has to be tactfully handled, but I will make the point.) It goes still further, because it is now doubtful whether Communist influence did not affect the China policy of the State Department. The investigation of the Institute of Pacific Relations (the American branch) shows that it had many Communist[s] on the staff, and that it had close relations with many Government agencies. This is leading to a desire to investigate whether the policy-deciding Civil Servants were Communists or under Communist influence—but this is a most dangerous line of investigation, because it might mean that no Civil Servant would ever dare to take a line of any decision for fear he might later be investigated. In fact, the infiltration of the American Civil Service has accomplished a notable triumph along a certain line of Communist endeavour—it has thrown a spanner into the workings of the capitalist state. But this arises out of the struggle of a group for supremacy which has nothing to do with Communism. Both Elizabeth Bentley and Whittaker Chambers were members of the middle classes who fell into Communism because it gave them membership of a class within a class—a privileged class within the underprivileged middle class. Elizabeth Bentley's book [*Out of Bondage* (1951)] was not well written and didn't illuminate the case. Whittaker Chambers' book [*Witness* (1952)] did, and ⟨that it s⟩ that is why he is so much hated.

You will be saying, this is all too damned complicated. But I will sort it {out}. I have *some* experience as a journalist. By God, forty-three years of it. And never being believed for most of the time. All this mess springs out of the administrative inefficiency of Roosevelt, which I described in a series of articles on the New Deal in Washington in 1935 which the *Daily Telegraph* turned down with a large sweeping gesture.[10]

The post-trial material regarding Hiss himself is not so much. I am able to link together the evidence of Whittaker Chambers and Gouzenko[11] and Bill Bullitt that they had reason to believe that Hiss was a Communist; and that if he is the victim of a conspiracy then there is some individual or organisation in command of funds and influence enough to enable him {or it} to suborn an editor of *Time,* an attache in the Soviet Embassy at Ottawa, and the United States Ambassador in France to tell the same story, though they never met. But the really new material is the tracing of the associates of Hiss and Harry Dexter White through the American Civil Service and into the administration of the United Nations. That I don't think anybody else will have in detail, and it is fairly sensational. But I won't forget that above all you want me to be clear and readable.

I hope I can handle this, the material is there. Blessings on you.[12]

Yours ever,

Rebecca

I'd like you to keep this confidential till you get my typescript, if you could keep it out of the office.

Rebecca West Collection
Yale University

typescript with autograph note, corrections, signature, and postscript

[1] Leonard Russell was editor of the *Sunday Times.*

[2] Whittaker Chambers (1901–1961), former Communist Party member and courier for a spy ring in Washington, D.C. Also a journalist and editor of *New Masses,* the *National Review,* and *Time* magazine. He named Alger Hiss as a conspirator in the Russian spy ring (1948).

[3] Elizabeth Bentley, courier for the Communist Party who testified before the House Un-American Activities Committee. Doris Stevens interviewed her for West.

[4] Klaus Emil Fuchs (1911–1988), German-born British physicist who worked on the atomic bomb at Los Alamos in the United States (1943–1946). Having passed secrets to the Soviets since 1943, he was exposed as a spy in 1950.

[5] Julius (1918–1953) and Ethel (1916–1953) Rosenberg, U.S. civilians convicted and put to death for allegedly transmitting to the Soviets in 1944–1945 information about the atom bomb obtained from Ethel's brother, David Greenglass, who worked at the Los Alamos project. Efforts to obtain clemency failed.

[6] Nathan Gregory Silvermaster, Russian-born economist who while employed by the Farm Security Administration helped organize a communist espionage ring within the government and later implicated White and Irving Kaplan.

[7] Irving Kaplan, American official in the War Production Board and a member of Silvermaster's group.

[8] At the Yalta Conference (4–11 February 1945), the Allies (with Joseph Stalin representing Russia) planned for the postwar occupation of Germany and the reorganization of Europe.

[9] Owen Lattimore (1900–1989), American writer and Orientalist who served as U.S. political adviser to Chiang Kai-shek. In 1955 he was cleared of accusations by Senator Joseph McCarthy that he was a major communist spy.

[10] Her series of four articles on the New Deal ran in *Time and Tide* (August–September 1935).

[11] Igor Gouzenko, Soviet cypher clerk who, on defecting in 1945, revealed extensive Soviet spying operations in Canada and the United States, described in *The Meaning of Treason.*

[12] Russell was cautious, and with reason, as reactions to West's articles were to prove. He advised her to make clear her love for the United States and cautioned that people would think she had ceased to be a liberal.

To: Ingrid Bergman

Ibstone House
Ibstone
Nr. High Wycombe
Bucks
10 March 1953

Dear Miss Bergman,

Thank you very much for your letter, which I am going to answer honestly. My feelings were not in the least hurt by the abandonment of what was for both of us a trial trip. But I was distressed by the whole incident, from your point of view. I had been asked to write the dialogue of a film which was being founded on an important novel, *Duo,* by an important writer, Colette. Instead I was faced with a ridiculous idea, incapable of development in any way not likely to be prejudicial to your reputation.

You may love your husband very much, but you should face the fact that he has no talent. You have great talent and a great personality, and it is absurd that for the sake of your private emotions you should allow these gifts to be wasted in a film like *Europe 1951,* which is so inept that even your performance, which excites admiration by itself, cannot save it.

You will not believe this when you read it, and you will think me an odious woman. But when your husband has made two more films for you, you remember this letter, and think about putting yourself in the hands of a competent director.

I never wrote such an extraordinary letter as this in my life. But I have also never seen such an extraordinary situation as the wreck of your artistic life.

With all good wishes,
I am, Yours sincerely,
REBECCA WEST

Rebecca West Papers   typescript copy
Yale University

To: Arthur Schlesinger, Jr.[1]   [4 June 1953]

UNABLE UNDERSTAND MOTIVE BEHIND GROSSLY OFFENSIVE LETTER YOU HAVE
HAD IMPERTINENCE TO SEND ME STOP MY ARTICLE CONTAINS NO DEFENCE
MACARTHY WHATSOEVER STOP ARTICLE ADDRESSED BRITISH PUBLIC [DIS-
COUNT] HARM DONE BY MALICIOUS ANTI AMERICAN IDENTIFICATION ALL
AMERICAN COUNTER COMMUNIST ACTIVITIES WITH MACARTHYISM STOP THIS
IS CLEAR ANY HONEST AND INTELLIGENT READER STOP ALSO THAT ARTICLES
REFERED PRE MACARTHY INVESTIGATIONS HAVE NO OFFICIAL REPORTS THESE
HAVE REACHED BRITAIN AND BOHLEN WECHSLER[2] INCIDENT INCOMPLETE
STOP MY RECORD ENTITLES ME REGARD YOUR REMARKS REGARDING PRETTY-
FICATION AND EXCUSE OF MACARTHY AND IMPLYING DEFENCE OF SCATTER-
GUN DENUNCIATIONS AS SMEARS WORTHY GOEBBELS STOP IT HAS COST ME
CONSIDERABLE EFFORT FRAME THIS CABLE IN THESE RESTRAINED TERMS

REBECCA WEST

private collection   telegram

[1] Schlesinger's letter to West (29 May 1953, private collection) opens, "As an old admirer of your work, I am taking the liberty of writing you about your *Sunday Times* articles on 'McCarthyism,' which, as you know, have just been reprinted here by *U.S. News and World Report.* These articles have caused considerable surprise and dismay in the United States. As one who vigorously shares your conviction of the danger of Communist conspiracy and your alarm over democratic complacency in the face of this danger, I want to explain why I share too this surprise and dismay over your article." He then goes on to provide two single spaced pages of background concerning early anticommunist movements, proceeding to a discussion of McCarthy's recent "scatter-gun denunciation" of various figures, and the dangers he sees in them. He ends "I hope you will reconsider your evident belief that this fight can be helped by excusing and prettifying all those who seize the banner of anti-Communism to sanctify their own passion for destruction and their own lust for power."

[2] Schlesinger's letter identifies Bohlen and Wechsler as men he consulted for information on communist movements. Charles E. Bohlen (1904–1974), State Department official who served in the U.S. Embassy in Moscow in the 1930s and became U.S. ambassador to the USSR (1953–1957). He was aware of the communist threat. James Wechsler (1915–), briefly a member of the Young Communist League, became an anticommunist newspaper man, editor of the *New York Post,* and the author of *Labor Baron: A Portrait of John Lewis* (1944), and *The Age of Suspicion* (1953), concerning the McCarthy era.

To: Arthur Schlesinger, Jr.

Ibstone House
Ibstone
Nr. High Wycombe
Bucks
7 June 1953

Sir,

I wish for reasons which I will make clear later, to put before you certain matters relating to the articles which I wrote for the *Sunday Times*, which were reprinted in the *U. S. News and World Report*, and which form the subject of the letter you have addressed to me.[1]

These articles were written because I have been extremely disturbed of late years by the virulence of the anti-American campaign in Great Britain which has been inspired by the Communists and carried on by various grades of the Left and of the Right. During the last year or so a change has come over the form of this campaign. Up till now great use has been made of lynching, to such purpose that I have often heard it said by British people that "of course there is a lynching every day in the United States." This has been replaced recently by propaganda based on the investigation committees which are described as "witch-hunts."

Stories are spread which lead countless British people to believe that there is a complete suspension of civil rights in the United States; that all over America people are dragged in front of investigation committees, and if they are found guilty of having a communist or liberal affiliations are sent to prison and deprived of the right to earn their living, which last punishment is inflicted on the [innocent] also. For according to these stories the mere fact of appearing before an investigation committee is sufficient to put the most innocent person under a social ban, inflicted by a cowed community. Strangely enough, long before the expiry of the Truman administration, Senator McCarthy was named as the sole controller of all these committees, and he is represented as condemning and sentencing the accused persons. It is asserted that there is no evidence whatsoever that Communists have ever engaged in any mischievous activity whatsoever in the United States, and that, indeed, it would be fair enough to say that there are no American Communists, only innocent people who have been labelled Communists by Senator McCarthy.

On the basis of this nonsense there has been built up, in certain parts of

Great Britain, an attitude towards the United States which is revolting. Out of these lies is engendered hatred. The vast mass of the British resist this indoctrination, but the poison is there, and it is of a recognisable type. ⟨But⟩ A friend of mine, who knows well a certain factory district where the dominant Trade Union is Communist-infiltrated, put it well when he wrote: These people are being taught by the Communists to hate the Americans just as the Germans were taught by the Nazis to hate the Jews." And the poison has filtered into the middle-classes, largely through one Left-Wing and one Right-Wing journalistic sources.

I have a long record as an anti-Fascist and an anti-Communist writer, and I have some power to get space to lay my work before the public. I thought it my duty to expose this situation. So I read 105 volumes of the official reports of the proceedings of the investigation committees, and wrote these articles, with the sound liberal ambition of substituting the calming truth for inflammatory lies. There was no question of dealing with Senator McCarthy's investigations, because at the time I wrote no official record of them had, so far as I know, reached any private person in Great Britain. Nor did I feel called upon to pronounce upon Senator McCarthy's merits or demerits; since he has been voted into office by American electors, such a task is for American writers to perform rather than British. I dealt with Senator McCarthy solely insofar as he enters into the British situation which I was discussing.

I undertook this enterprise knowing that it would take all the courage I possessed. For I knew that ⟨they⟩ it would make me the target of the poisoned arrows of every fool who has got hold of the word "liberalism" without knowing what it means, and of every knave who [knows] how that word can be misused to serve totalitarian interests.

These expectations did not, however, prepare me for the surprising experience of opening a letter and finding myself called to account for these articles in a manner recalling that of a schoolmaster reproving a backward pupil, by a person named Arthur Schlesinger Jr. My surprise is not due to the fact that I do not know who you are. It is due to the fact that I know who you are. My knowledge of you makes me quite certain that you are not experienced enough, or clever enough, or wise enough, to adopt the attitude towards me of a schoolmaster instructing a backward pupil, or indeed, any pupil at all. This is not my individual opinion. If I could put the matter to arbitration, quite a number of people would be on my side. Wounding as it may be to our egos, there are very many people whom neither you nor myself can venture to treat as our inferiors.

Not only is your letter highly offensive by reason of its insolent tone, it is packed from start to finish with mendacious misrepresentations of my article. You ignore the fact that I was writing them for the British public to deal with a British situation, though this is evident in the text and is explicitly stated in the banner headline on p. 61 of the *U. S. News*. You have written me pages in which you rebuke me for writing an article which has no relation to that which I actually wrote, or to any which I could conceivably produce.

Let us examine this impudent nonsense piece by piece.

You have the effrontery to write:

> The greatest fraud perpetrated on the American people in recent [years] is McCarthy's success in persuading some of them that nothing was done about Communism until he came along. *This illusion I think you avoid.*

Since you have written this letter to me you must be able to read, and you must know that in my article I not merely "avoid" this illusion, I denounce it as an illusion, on pp 77–78. You become more brazen still in the sentence:

> But you do fall victim, it seems to me, to the next greatest fraud— that is the theory that McCarthy is genuinely interested in exposing Communists.

There is not a line in my article which give you grounds for this assumption. I never discussed the question of McCarthy's sincerity, because it was not relevant to my thesis.

You then "beg" me to look at "the names of the people on whom [he] has launched his main attack" and give a string of names of people with whom I have never concerned myself and could not concern myself for two reasons: either they had never come before an investigation committee, or they had come before one after my articles were written. You then ask me:

> Do you really regard this scattergun denunciation as useful in the fight against Communism? Or can you really excuse it as merely amiable

ignorance on McCarthy's part of how he is to use (as you perhaps over-delicately put it) "his gifts in harmony with the established practice of civilisation?" If so Goebbels and Zhdanov[2] had the same disarming failing.

By these sentences you show yourself a blood brother of Goebbels and Zhdanov. There is not a single phrase in my article to justify your pretence that I regard this "scattergun denunciation" as useful for any purpose whatsoever, or to account for it by Senator McCarthy's ignorance or by any other of his qualities.

Your impudence takes a comic form when you write:

It is necessary to criticise equally those on the right who would attempt to be anti-Communist without being anti-totalitarian.

Nobody is in a position to address this admonition to me or to any other of the persons who were on the Gestapo[3] list of persons marked for immediate arrest if the Nazis invaded Britain.

The rest of your letter consists of turgid restatements of principles familiar to me since I was fourteen, which you have couched in hackneyed phrases that might have been swept off the floor of a Convention Hall after the speeches nominating an unsuccessful candidate. But you make a further revelation of your essential affinity with Goebbels when you suggest that I "minimise the problem of McCarthy and seek to discredit those who attack McCarthy." There is not a phrase in my article which supports this charge, and I would direct your attention to this sentence in my article.

It is time we admitted that, while Cleon[4] the demagogue was an unpleasant fellow, so was Charles Peace; and if a community spends all its energy in hostility to Cleon it may find itself with none to spare for the pursuit of Charles Peace.

There is nothing here to suggest that Cleon does not still present a problem, and the validity of the point I raise [you] yourself prove. For obviously you are devoting all your energy, such as it is, to attacking McCarthy. You are incapable of reading my articles intelligently, and following the argument or recognising the liberal aim inspiring them, because you can think of nothing but Senator McCarthy. You cannot understand that, if British people are led to accept a lying story about the United States which involves Senator McCarthy discreditably, it would be better for them not to believe that story, even if they then cease to think of the Senator in that particular derogatory sense, *because that story is not true.* You have indeed gone very far indeed in the direction of Goebbelisation, and it is a matter of distress to me that a person in such a state of mind should be associated with ADA,[5] an organisation which I know to contain many respectable members.

I am not writing to you in the hope that I may persuade you to approve of me. Should the writer of such a letter as you have sent me express approval of me, I should feel gravely tainted. I have other purposes in writing to you. First: I think you must have known that you are slandering me when you ascribed to me an "evident belief that this fight can be helped by excusing and prettifying all those who seize the banner of anti-Communism to sanctify their own passion for destruction and their own lust for power." (As I repeat this sentence I am filled with wonder. Are you in the habit of bombarding people with the grossest possible accusations of blackguardism which their records make it most unlikely that they have ever committed? Do you do it to Americans too? And do you not have a number of stern-faced people calling on you to teach you manners and morals and to demand apologies? If you do not, then you are a very, very lucky man.) I want therefore to put down your misstatements in black and white, together with the proofs that they are misstatements, in order to secure that should you repeat them, there will be absolutely no doubt that you know [what] you are doing.

Second: Since you have played the schoolmaster, I will play the schoolmistress. I therefore append for your consideration the opening sentences from a review of Alistair Cooke's book, *A Generation on Trial*,[6] which I wrote for the *University of Chicago Law Review* ⟨last⟩ {two} years {ago}.

It is never possible to serve the interests of liberalism by believing that which is false to be true. The liberal must have as exact a view of the universe on the common sense plane as it is possible for his perception and his intellect to give him, because it is the aim of liberalism to grant each individual the fullest degree of liberty which can be enjoyed without damage to the claims of liberty justly presented by other individuals.

This is the creed by which I, as a writer and as a private individual, live. Let me recommend it to you.

Rebecca West

private collection   typescript

[1] The four *Sunday Times* articles were: "Hiss Case Hid Graver Issue" (22 March 1953), "The Surprising Mr. Kaplan" (22 March 1953), "The Terrified Teacher" (5 April 1953), and "Behind the Witch-Hunts: McCarthy the Demagogue" (12 April 1953). These were reprinted as the cover story on "McCarthyism" *U.S. News and World Report* (22 May 1953). West attempted to clarify her position in regard to McCarthy in "Miss West Files an Answer," the *Herald Tribune* (22 June 1953): 12, and "Memo from Rebecca West: More About McCarthyism," *U.S. News and World Report* (3 July 1953): 34–35.

[2] Andrei Aleksandrov Zhdanov (1896–1948), Russian communist general and a hard-line supporter of Stalin. He organized the Cominform, the Communist Information Bureau. As propaganda minister for Hitler, Goebbels provided a comparable service to the Germans.

[3] Nazi German secret service police, founded in 1933.

[4] Cleon (d. 422 BC), Athenian politician with a reputation as a demagogue. He opposed Pericles early in his career and was killed fighting in the Peloponnesian Wars.

[5] Americans for Democratic Action, an anticommunist organization founded in 1947. Schlesinger mentions it as evidence of growing U.S. awareness of the communist threat.

[6] Subtitled *U.S.A. vs. Alger Hiss* (1950).

To: Nancy A. Potter[1]   2 November 1953
Dear Miss Potter,

So far as I know I have no letters from Elinor Wylie.[2] We had a steady friendship, which was renewed every time we met at exactly the point where it had been when we had last met, and we rarely wrote except to confirm a date or give a friend's address. My files are in great disorder, owing to the war and to post-war irregularities, and I can't be sure. But I really don't think I can have anything that would interest you.

During her last trip to England she made no comment to me that indicated that she was specially annoyed with anything but the fact that she had fallen downstairs, or that she was frustrated with anything but the fact that she could not get about as much as usual. You are on very sound ground when you say that "she often appeared to be playing frantically with life to make each year count." I don't really believe, however, that people are right when they lay stress on this as an indication of a neurosis. I am sure that her conduct was largely dictated by her appallingly high blood-pressure. She must, for years and years, have been feeling quite dreadfully ill, and was racing to get away from her own discomfort.

I know she was an egotist. But so are most people who achieve a great deal, or rather who push their achievement ⟨xx⟩ above a certain level. It often seemed to me that when other people called her egotistical when she was being honest—she *was* exceptionally beautiful, she *was* exceptionally gifted, and it would have been stupid of her not to have known this. Her self-knowledge was expressed often in febrile terms, but really she had enough blood-pressure to make this understandable. It seems to me that it would be dangerous to consider Elinor Wylie without taking into account the extraordinary spitefulness of the age in which she lived. Looking back at it, the world seems to me to have been overfull of people who spent their lives saying, "We went to the Smith's party last night—it was just *terrible,*" or "Have you met Freda Jones, we met her last night—she is just *terrible,*" with a screech on the *terrible* that I recognized during the war in the wail of the air-raid sirens. The gentler and more civilised the Smiths or Freda Brown might be the more the screech. Elinor Wylie was the chosen victim of the screechers. I daresay she often behaved tiresomely. But twice it happened to me that I was at a party with Elinor where she was gay and funny and brilliant, and that a few nights later I went to a cocktail party where people who had not been at that party described the ludicrous remarks Elinor had made at it and what a nuisance she had been.

She had an enormous sense of duty. It hurt her tremendously that she had failed in her duties as a step-mother; and of course she had failed, she was as unsuited to be a stepmother as any romantic character could be. She seemed to me to be often arrogant in her judgment of other people, but arrogant only in the sense that she dismissed people for lacking certain qualities before she had looked round to see if they had any other qualities; when those other qualities hit her in the eye she was just and humble. Once she met a friend of mine at my room in the old Majestic and spoke of her afterwards with candid contempt, wondering why I cared for this woman. I arranged for them to meet again, under better circumstances, as the woman adored Elinor's work and wanted to ask her permission to do something with one of her poems; and she got on to her character this time, and rang me up and admitted her error very handsomely (Not because she knew the woman wanted to do something with one of her poems—the woman hadn't then mentioned it). And though she was arrogant I don't remember her ever being spiteful. I should have been very much surprised indeed if she had ever repeated me a story about anybody which was even slanted, and I could not have believed it if anybody had ever accused Elinor of inventing a story against anybody, though that was the vice of the time. As you know, she had a very uneasy relationship (this is an example of British understatement) with Kathleen Norris.[3] She always spoke of her, even in her most confidential moments, with reserve, with a well-bred blankness.

You know, of course, the incident that touched off the explosion in her early life, when she left her first husband and her child. I haven't any reason to disbelieve it, but I have no authority but Elinor's own statement, which however she repeated to me several times. She always repeated it in the same form, though many other items in the context in which this story was embedded varied considerably. Apparently, after her father died, it was discovered that he had been in love with a woman who was not his wife, over a period of many years. Elinor described the scene of this discovery with deep feeling, and always expected me to take it for granted that when you found out that your father had been in love with someone not your mother, why, *of course*, you left your own husband, you just had to, you were so upset. The thing came up as strong and clear as a Racine play. Quite beyond argument. It was something she could no more help than her blood-pressure.

The wonderful thing about Elinor, which none of you who did not know her will ever realise, was her astonishing beauty; which was as significant, as much of a bridge beyond the real and the imaginary world, as the beauty of Rosamund Lehmann.[4] I don't suppose she had anything to give that had a higher value than that, it was sublime; and to me it appeared not at all a sexual beauty, it made not a heterosexual or homosexual appeal, it made an imaginative appeal. About her relationships—I don't know enough about them. But I fancy you would find that the people who knew her best liked her best, that her apparent victims would always speak of her with tenderness and affection.

I hear people speaking and writing of her in a patronising spirit. I must own that I found it delightful to know her, and thought and think that she did me considerable honour by wanting to know me.

I hope you have a happy time with your study, and I wish you could have received a letter from me saying, "Yes, indeed, I have a correspondence with Elinor Wylie rather larger in bulk than the Holmes-Laski letters."[5] But, alas, I have always had too many family ties to get on with my writing or my letter-writing as I would have wished.

Yours sincerely,

Rebecca West Papers   carbon typescript
Yale University

[1] Potter wrote (15 October 1953) seeking information for *Elinor Wylie: A Biographical and Critical Study* (1954). She cited West's description of Wylie's last days in her column "A Commentary" in the *Bookman* (March 1929). West's recollections of their meeting at the Lynds' house in Hampstead were republished as "Manibus Date Lilia Plenis" in *Ending in Earnest.*
[2] Elinor Wylie (1885–1928), American poet and novelist who first achieved notice in *Poetry* magazine. Collections include *Nets to Catch the Wind* (1921) and *Black Armour* (1923). Her historical novels include *Jennifer Lorn* (1923) and *The Venetian Glass Nephew* (1925). West later helped Stanley Olson with his biography of Wylie.
[3] Kathleen Norris (1880–1966), American novelist, journalist and short-story writer, whose novels include *Mother* (1911), *The Rich Mrs. Burgoyne* (1913), and *Noon* (1925). A member of the Women's International League for Peace and Freedom, she also wrote *What Price Peace? A Handbook of Peace for American Women* (1928).
[4] Rosamund Lehmann (1901–1990), English novelist, translator, and memoirist best known for *Dusty Answer* (1927), which like many of her works deals with a woman's inner life.
[5] Letters between Justice Oliver Wendell Holmes and Harold Laski, *Holmes-Laski Letters* (1953), edited by Mark De Wolf Howe. Their correspondence amounted to two volumes and nearly fifteen hundred pages.

To: Emily Hahn[1]   Ibstone House
                                                         Ibstone
                                                         Nr. High Wycombe
                                                         Bucks
                                                         28 July 1954

My Dear Emily,
    Kitty [West] rang me up suddenly and told me that it had just occurred to her that I might like to come to the school show, so I leapt at it. And we thoroughly enjoyed it. I don't know what to make of Kitty, it does seem too odd that when I repeatedly ask her to bring the children here she shouldn't realise, over years, that I would like to see them on such occasions. But on

the other hand it is obvious that she is handling those children well, both the girl and the boy are getting on with life in spite of the shock over Anthony and what seems to me the unsettling business of these visits to the new household in America—and therefore I owe her a debt of gratitude, and she must have something much more than oddity in her.

I came home and found the *New Yorker* with your account of your terrifying experience with Carola at Hamley's.[2] Believe me, this sort of thing, this gluing together of girls in groups and this loss of individual initiative, is something entirely new. If you were very wealthy in the past, you went about with a governess; but at that you and your governess might go lonely rides and walks and journeys. But if you weren't, young girls were quite astonishingly independent compared to the girls of today. My recollections go back a long way, because I was the child of old parents—my mother was forty when I was born. She was one of the five children of a woman of quite aristocratic birth who had run away with a successful musician, and when their father died they were brought up in Edinburgh, according to the customs of the bourgeois families of the time. My mother was sent to Germany alone, at the age of fourteen, in the sixties of the last century. She had her tickets given her and written instructions as to what to do in all imaginable circumstances, and off she went, to Dusseldorff, which was then not on the main track. From the age of twelve my elder sister, Winifred, travelled alone from Edinburgh to Cheltenham College every term—this in the first decade of the century. I travelled from Edinburgh to stay with people in Yorkshire alone when I was twelve years old. Your family spoke to the guard of the train and that was all. We thoroughly enjoyed our solitary journeys.

But I got curious intimation that things were changing. I arranged for Anthony to travel out alone to me when he was thirteen and I was in Italy one Easter. I got a travel agency to speak to the people on the trains about him. The other day I discovered that he remembered this with great resentment, though nothing had happened to him, and that Kitty had thought it eccentric of me to send him out alone. I don't think that Caro [Caroline Duah] or Em [Edmund West] would at all enjoy making any journey alone. And I think it is very odd.

It amused me to see how your child and my grandchild ruled the roost in the Art Exhibition at the school. And there I thought I saw another change, but one for the better. When I got scholarships at my school in Edinburgh and acted the best part in the play and all that sort of thing I got hell from my fellow-pupils. It didn't seem to me that my Caro or your Carola were having at all a bad time in that way.

It's all much cosier and gentle. But I also relate it to a queer feeling of the middle and upper classes that somehow God has got to look after them, they can't stand on their own feet and it isn't fair to ask them, and so the question can't possibly arise. I daren't say to Kitty, if she gets a cheque from the Wells estate for the sale of the Wells papers, "You had better treat that as capital," because she would not think it decent to put it to her that there is a difference between capital and income and it might be frightfully important to keep that difference in mind. I don't believe she ever faces for a minute the thought that she won't have a steady income if the world gets any tougher, and that the children may be entirely dependent on their own activities. So you get this clinging together in a nice, kind, helpless mass.

On my way home I went I to see Raymond Mortimer at what is humorously known as Haworth Parsonage.[3] And I had a dose of anti-anti-Communism. Quite sweetly he reproved me for not being a champion of Dr Cort, on the ground that if we kept Cort out then there was a precedent for sending people back behind the Iron Curtain, and that it was not liberal to throw people out. I felt it slightly exasperating, considering that people like Kitty Atholl and Miss Blackett and myself have been tearing down the Home Office with our fingernails trying to protect people who were being unfairly turned out by the Home Office, and we never got a bit of sympathy from people like Mortimer—who rally round Cort, who seems to me as suspicious as hell. And I notice the *Observer* has suddenly dropped his case. I mentioned to the three of them that Iverchapel[4] had been a Communist—and they looked at me as if I were mad. But I haven't the slightest doubt that the Security people who looked into the state of the American Embassy after the disappearance of MacLean and Burgess[5] were shocked to the marrow by what they found out about Iverchapel—and you know the Chinese story.[6]

At Berkhamstead you will be under an hour from us, which delights us very much. It was lovely seeing you and your very nice young.

Yours ever,
Rebecca

Since I began this letter the issue of the *New Yorker* that followed the one in which you told your grisly tale has arrived, and I am just appalled. It couldn't, couldn't be duller.[7]

Hahn MSS   typescript with autograph signature
Indiana University, Bloomington

[1] Emily "Mickey" Hahn (1902–1997), American roving reporter for the *New Yorker* and author of fifty-two books, including tales of her travels, biographies of D. H. Lawrence and Aphra Behn, and novels for children. Her early career took her to the Congo and China. Hahn helped West keep in touch with her grandchildren, who knew Hahn's daughter, Carola.

[2] "A Question of Deportment," the *New Yorker* (10 July 1954): 61–64, which describes Hahn's reactions when her twelve-year-old daughter became separated from her in a crowd in front of the Regent Street, London, toy store Hamley's.

[3] The somber Haworth Parsonage, set among gravestones in a Yorkshire village, was the home of the Brontë sisters.

[4] Lord Iverchapel, British ambassador to Moscow, Peking, and Washington. West describes his inflicting bagpipes on guests at embassy dinners, and although she does not charge him with treachery, she regrets the courtesies he extended to those who shared his enthusiasm for the Soviets (*New Meaning of Treason*, 245).

[5] Guy Burgess and Donald Maclean, British officers in the Foreign Office who fled Britain for Moscow in May 1951, when Maclean learned that he was suspected of espionage. Burgess (1911–1963) had been recalled from Washington for exhibiting a disorderly lifestyle. He had been a BBC correspondent and a member of the MI-6 intelligence agency (1939–1941), then a second secretary in the Foreign Service. Maclean (1913–1983), held a more senior position as counsellor in the Foreign Service, head of the American Department in the Foreign Office, and secretary of the Combined Policy Committee on Atomic Development. West's articles on the case first appeared in the *New Yorker.*

[6] According to West, Iverchapel had given a British passport to a German involved in a Soviet spy ring in the Pacific (*The New Meaning of Treason*, 245).

[7] Perhaps it is a twenty-four-page article on the evils of DDT that did her in.

To: Charles Curran   Ibstone House
                                            Ibstone
                                            Nr. High Wycombe
                                            Bucks
                                            6 August 1954

My dear Charles,

It seems to me damned hard luck on Farouk[1] that he should have imperfect enjoyment on a number of occasions which must have promised well, and had to square the disappointed ladies with gifts and then should have the whole business clawed over years later by a number of total strangers who make a fuss about something that hurt him more than it hurt them and tell you all about it. No more privacy than a goldfish in circumstances more humiliating than a goldfish ever knows. The use of the palaces shows how cheap and nasty life is becoming—the sideshow of Blackpool and the Tottenham Court Road invading the land of the Pharaohs.

I have the Oppenheimer transcripts[2] given me by this American diplomat Chipman.[3] It is very hard reading. I do not think anybody, however experienced, could read it in less than a week, so you may imagine what the American press got out of it. It clearly reveals that there *was* a conspiracy to stop the H-bomb. Oppenheimer and four men, all, I think, Jews. The Tribunal must have been profoundly impressed by the evidence of one of these men, a pro-Oppenheimer witness named Hans Bethe,[4] a German refugee, which fairly sizzles on the page, such is his venom against the Hungarian, Teller,[5] and his supporters, who insisted, with incredible courage, in going on with the researches into the H-bomb. Oppenheimer lied about everything; but another very important physicist, not in the conspiracy, Vannevar Bush,[6] lied preposterously on one matter of fact, plainly for fear of offending the scientific climate, and Lilienthal[7] gave very shifty evidence which I haven't yet sorted out, but it's obvious he was caught out in something. The septuagenarian chemist, Evans,[8] who put in a minority report in favour of Oppenheimer was senile, and was interested in nothing but General Groves'[9] statement that he found scientists difficult and untrustworthy. He kept on asking witnesses with a snort if *they* had found scientists crazy, also enquiring whether old Fred who used to be at their university fifty years ago. An odd thing—Oppenheimer's alcoholic Communist wife is a cousin of the Nazi General Keitel.[10] Sefton Delmer[11] has long been said to be a Communist—he is supposed, and I think I told you that it was said in *Die Zeit,* to have been in the Red Chapel. He is a rootless creature, his father was in Ruleben with Henry during the First World War, and was a Lector in English in Berlin University. Delmer was brought up there from childhood. I met him at Nuremberg and didn't like him. But the curious thing is that more and more do I feel that the Old Man [Beaverbrook] is under the influence of someone who presses the Communist line on him, and that this has been going on for years. I never think you realise quite how stupid the Old Man is about anything and everything except making money. I saw Max [Beaverbrook] again the other day and he said of his father, "The only thing he can read is a company prospectus and he can read that like a flash of lightning." But the Old Man is running this anti-German thing, Max Aitken told me (twice over) that he had been wildly pro-Hiss and had wanted to load the paper down with it, and he has this mania about Burgess and Maclean. (I simply am astounded at the rage that seems to have filled him because I declined to write that book.) It looks to me very much as if Burgess and MacLean had been withdrawn—as I think Dr John has been withdrawn—simply to weaken public confidence and make mischief between America and England—and the Old Man's passionate desire to go on hounding the F. O. [Foreign Office] about them fits in with that campaign.

I spoke at Wormwood Scrubs[12] on Wednesday, Mrs Field not there—but what a nice man Holland is. In Mrs Field's place was a silly woman lawyer, rather sweet—who gave me an odd sidelight. The poor silly had been in UNRRA[13] and had gone with the team that wrote the history of UNRRA (never published, I think) to America, where she had met Harry Dexter White,[14] and had both worked with him on the book (he had a lot to do with UNRRA) and had known him socially through friends—and she and the friends felt that he was "radiantly sincere and could not have been a Communist, he was incapable of deception." I asked who the friends were—the Woodbridges. Mrs Woodbridge was Katherine Skinner, one of the five Skinner males and females, who are all physicists, and all suspect. Herbert Skinner was the running mate of Fuchs, and was wafted out of Harwell when Fuchs was arrested and made Professor at Liverpool, and Mrs Skinner was supposed to have had a love-affair with Fuchs—but the authorities thought she hadn't, that it was a device to cover some correspondence. I thought this was an odd bit of information to pick up at Wormwood Scrubs.

This may be true about Craig and the evacuee business, I am sure the process worked that way in innumerable cases. (But in the reverse way often enough—we had a boy down here who was the son of a prostitute in East London who stayed down in the country and had made himself a very good life as a herdsman, and I am sure there are many cases like that). But

Scotland Yard thought very badly of the Craig parents, I forget why. By the way, strictly under your hat, I hear Ronny Howe's[15] health is very bad.

See you some time I hope.

R

Rebecca West Collection   typescript with manuscript initial
University of Tulsa

[1] Farouk I (1920–1965), king of Egypt (1936–1952) whose unpopular policies, together with Egypt's 1948 defeat by Israel, led to his overthrow by Gamal Abdel Nasser and Muhammad Naguib (1952).

[2] J. Robert Oppenheimer (1904–1967), American physicist, in charge of the development of the atomic bomb, and, after World War II, chairman of the General Advisory Committee to the Atomic Energy Commission (AEC). In a 1953 report on military security, Oppenheimer was accused of having communist associates, delaying the naming of Soviet agents, and opposing development of the hydrogen bomb. Although not found guilty of treason, he was denied access to military secrets and service on the AEC, to the outrage of the scientific community.

[3] Norris B. Chipman, a member of the foreign service.

[4] Hans A. Bethe, along with Edward Teller, had been a part of Oppenheimer's study group at Berkeley in 1942. A professor at Cornell and a consultant at Los Alamos, he testified that he had "absolute faith in Dr. Oppenheimer's loyalty."

[5] Edward Teller (1908–), Hungarian-born American physicist who worked on the atomic bomb and supported the development of the hydrogen bomb.

[6] Vannevar Bush, chairman of the New Weapons Committee of the Joint Chiefs of Staff in World War II, later president of the Carnegie Institution. He opposed testing of the hydrogen bomb, and gave a strong endorsement of Oppenheimer's performance, loyalty, and right to express strong opinions.

[7] David E. Lilienthal, former chairman of the AEC responsible for Oppenheimer's security clearance in 1947, when he consulted the FBI record. West may be calling lapses of memory lies in this case, as Lilienthal was not permitted to review the records. He too supported Oppenheimer.

[8] Ward Evans, a professor of chemistry at Northwestern and Loyola Universities, was the dissenting member of the Personnel Security Board. He stated that Oppenheimer deserved the same clearance he had received in 1947.

[9] General Leslie R. Groves, in charge of the Manhattan Engineer District, who agreed to the establishment of a civilian laboratory at Los Alamos and made Oppenheimer its director. Part of the hearing hinged on the way Oppenheimer belatedly reported attempts at espionage to Groves, who affirmed at the hearing that he would be "amazed" if Oppenheimer committed a disloyal act.

[10] Katherine Oppenheimer had been twice married before she wed Robert Oppenheimer (1940), and had been briefly a member of the Communist Party while married to Joe Dallet, an organizer in Youngstown, Ohio, who was killed in the Spanish Civil War.

Wilhelm Keitel (1882–1946), general field marshal and chief of staff of the high command of the armed forces in the Third Reich (1938–1945), Hitler's submissive military adviser. He condoned mass murder, and he was executed following trial at Nuremberg.

[11] Sefton Delmer (1904–1979), German-born journalist whose Australian parents settled in England in 1917. He headed the Berlin bureau of the *Daily Express* and during the 1930s met and moved about with Hitler, thereby arousing the suspicion of the Foreign Office. During World War II he produced black propaganda broadcasts aimed at Germany. After the war he was chief foreign affairs reporter for the *Daily Express*.

[12] Prison on the western side of London. West describes it as a Victorian "work of great vigour, which recalls at one and the same time Ravenna and Pisa and a giant model of a lodging house cruet" (116). William Joyce awaited the outcome of his appeals there.

[13] United Nations Relief and Rehabilitation Administration, a social relief program to repair the ravages of World War II (1943–1947).

[14] Harry Dexter White, American Treasury Department official suspected of harboring communist sympathies, who was accused of espionage in 1953.

[15] Sir Ronald Howe (1896–1977), English Criminal Investigation Department official and author of *The Pursuit of Crime* (1961) and *The Story of Scotland Yard* (1965).

To: Vyvyan Holland

Ibstone House
Ibstone
Nr. High Wycombe
Bucks
22 October 1954

My dear Vyvyan,

Forgive me for not answering you before, but I had an acute attack of nervous dyspepsia which put me to bed for four days with the feeling that I had swallowed a toasting-fork. I returned these shocking records of brigandage with the utmost sympathy. For one thing, I realise that you and your wife cannot have believed that such a thing could really happen, and you must have been sure that there would be a happy issue.[1]

About the boy, Henry and I will gladly pay his school-fees till the end of this school year, in the simplest manner, by paying a cheque. But after that there will have to be a plan which I am even now devising, which will dodge income tax as far as possible, and take into account the fact that Henry and I might die before the boy was fully educated. I intend to work out something pretty, put it to my solicitor, and then ask you and your wife to a meal where we can discuss it. This should be a week or so ahead, possibly a fortnight. But I think I can say definitely that you need not worry about the boy's education, unless of course the earth blows up.[2]

It is a great pleasure to be able to do this, for I have always had a great affection for you, and I hate to think of you being worried, and worried over such an important matter as that delightful little boy, and worried as the result of such a hell's brew as your documents disclose.

Much love—may I say to you both. I do admire you both for putting such a good face on it at that lunch,[3] when you must have been shattered.

Blessings,
Rebecca

Please send me the estimated total of school fees at Summer Fields[4]—and the name of the public school you favour.

private collection   typescript with autograph signature and postscript

[1] Vyvyan Holland had been benefiting from the royalties of his father's plays, but when copyright ran out in 1950, he had not saved sufficient funds to cover the backlog in income tax, let alone his son's education.

[2] West arranged for Margaret Rawlings and John Van Druten to be contributors to a fund that allowed the claiming of tax rebates.

[3] The lunch at the Savoy Hotel, London, 16 October 1954, commemorated the centenary of Wilde's birth, following the unveiling of a plaque on Wilde's Tite Street house by Sir Compton Mackenzie. Messages of support had come from Laurence Housman and Sir Max Beerbohm, who were too elderly to attend.

[4] Merlin Holland attended another preparatory school, the Old Malthouse, in Dorset.

To: Charles Curran

Ibstone House
Ibstone
Nr. High Wycombe
Bucks
6 February 1955

My dear Charles,

The Bacchanalia to which you took me knocked me all out, not for me participation in these wild dances of nymphs and satyrs, not for me the grape-clusters and the leopard-skins and the cymbals. I succumbed to influenza on my return and have had a relapse. I spent my time in bed the first time reading the Lawrence book, and what a pity that Aldington has spoiled a great historical study by writing like a disgruntled Grub Street hack.[1] This is a pity because he is much more in a position to criticise Lawrence as a scholar than might be supposed. (Though perhaps the fact that he is London University and Lawrence was Oxford weighs a good deal in this balance.) Many years ago, when he was twenty-one, he married the imagist poet, Hilda Doolittle (H. D.) the daughter of the great American classicist,[2] a horse-faced but brilliant girl, and herself a great classical scholar, and they worked together for years. By the way, I don't believe that anybody will ever describe Lawrence as well as he is described in Flaubert's *La Tentation de St Antoine*—in the description of Appolonius and Damis. (The early version of the book, I've never read the later, and don't know if they survived the rewriting.) The great heretic and his disciple visit the hermit—and in the picture of the two men you get a wonderful sense of Lawrence, who was a schizophrenic and might well be represented by two men. You feel that Apollonius might be a great man, but his disciple is a shoddy fair-barker who adores him and lies about him and is his "manager," and it does not seem possible that Apollonius would have such an uninviting companion if he were not unappetising himself, and the suspicion grows. That was always the feeling that Lawrence gave me—two men in one skin, and why had the one given the hospitality of his body to the other little horror.

I don't believe a word about [T. E.] Lawrence[3] suffering horror and shame at the thought of his birth. There is after all no reason why an illegitimate child should have a greater sense of the grossness of lust than a legitimate child, if its parents behave themselves, and I can't see that Mrs Lawrence who so remarkably solved the problem of what to do with five illegitimate sons by making {most of} them missionaries, could possibly have anything to do with the very specific obsessions of Lawrence. I fancy he put up that line to suit Mrs Bernard Shaw[4] who was cracked on this very subject. Mrs Shaw was filled with an extraordinary horror of the normal processes of reproduction. She once told me that her one hope for the world was that science might invent a new and pleasureless method of reproduction. Both she and Shaw, believe it or not, were profoundly impressed by a lady called, I think, Mary Everest Boole, who claimed that she had found a way of enabling women to become parthenogenetic. (This movement seems to have perished from lack of support, I wonder why.) Mrs Shaw was a big healthy woman, a great meat-eater, and she married Shaw on the understanding that the marriage was never consummated, and I am sure he always observed this condition. He was a eunuch perpetually inflamed by flirtation, and I imagine that no house hold in the Yoshiwara was more continually occupied with the thought of sex than the Shaw family was. Anybody who wanted to dominate the Shaws through Mrs Shaw would have followed just the line that Lawrence did. The passage in his letters about children inflaming their parents' desires might have been cut to Charlotte's measure, for she went in for Indian wafflings about Reincarnation and The Way and The Return.

Of such was the kingdom of the intellect, in the twentieth century.

My guess was that Lawrence was a fairly earthy homosexual of the type that Walpole was, no use for women, and no use for men either, unless they were of an inferior social rank—and no doubt another race would help. He had a habit of attaching himself to women but I don't believe that this was due to a psychic drive, as Aldington suggests. I didn't see him in the relationship with older women of whom Aldington talks, for he was four years older than I was. But he did attach himself to us when he was at Wool, and we were at Swanage for the summer, and he had very much the English male attitude, natural enough in a closed society, that it was pleasant to go in and enjoy the amenities of someone else's home ⟨—which, let me say, is⟩ when you are away from your own. Let me also point out that this attitude has developed in the older universities to something that is simply a tough form of scrounging. Occasionally we have people from Oxford over to see us, and we have in recent years (owing to Anne) had a good many contacts with Cambridge. I don't myself feel that Lawrence felt anything very deeply except the drive of egotism and his particular sexual obsessions. By the way, I have looked up the account of the sexual violation in *The Seven Pillars of Wisdom*[5]—and it is even more implausible than Aldington thinks it. The Bey took up a bayonet and ran it through a fold of flesh over Lawrence's ribs so that the blood ran down to his thighs, and then had him beaten by three soldiers . . .[6]

Rebecca West Collection   incomplete typescript
University of Tulsa

[1] Richard Aldington (1892–1962), English poet, essayist, and biographer, married to H. D. *Images, 1910–1915* was his first volume of poetry. West would have been reading *Lawrence of Arabia: A Biographical Inquiry* (1955), concerning T. E. Lawrence.

[2] "H. D.," Hilda Doolittle (1886–1961), American poet, novelist, and autobiographer, dubbed an *imagiste* by Ezra Pound. *Bid Me to Live* (1960) describes the breakup of her

marriage to Aldington. Her other works include *End to Torment* (1979), *Tribute to Freud* (1954), *Trilogy* (1944–1946), *Helen in Egypt* (1961), *The Gift* (1969), *Her* (1981), and *Asphodel* (1992). Her father was an astronomer at the University of Pennsylvania, not a classicist.

[3] T. E. (Thomas Edward) Lawrence, "Lawrence of Arabia" (1888–1935), English archeological scholar, author and military leader, who headed the Arab guerrilla forces against the Turks in World War I. His mother, Sara Maden, and his father, Sir Thomas Chapman, posed as a married couple; she had been governess to his children.

[4] Charlotte Shaw, of whom West spoke positively to me in 1981, preferring her to G. B. Shaw.

[5] Narrative of Lawrence's desert adventures. He was apparently brutalized homosexually when captured by the Turks in 1917.

[6] The rest of this letter is missing.

To: Bernard Kalb[1]   26 February 1955

Dear Mr Kalb,

Thank you very much for your letter, and the news that the *Saturday Review* is going to give me such a conspicuous position—though I don't know yet whether I go up all those steps before all those people in order to be crowned or to be executed. But thank you very much for saying that you have liked what I have already written.

As for the questions you ask, let me first condole with whoever has to write the sketch—I always find such things so difficult to do.

I write because all my family do, it is in the blood. My father was an Army officer (for long resident in America, by the way) who became a follower of Herbert Spencer and thus drifted into political journalism and the writing of books. Both my elder sisters write—my eldest sister, Letitia Fairfield is a doctor of medicine and a lawyer, who after a long life in the public service is starting life afresh [as] an author to beguile the tedium of retirement, and is making her mark as a writer on crime. My other sister is a poet of great distinction who hardly ever bothers to publish anything. I started writing in my teens in Feminist publications, and have gone on and on.

This new book represents the second phase of a process which started when Hitler came into power, and I was quite sure (having long suspected it) that the world as we knew it was going to be rubbed out. I had been greatly attracted by the Balkans, and I went back to Yugoslavia and took an inventory of the country, because I knew that there would be a war and it would be transformed into something entirely different. That book took me five years to write and was called BLACK LAMB AND GREY FALCON. Then after the war I realised that I had been right and the world was changed—and Ross of the *New Yorker* asked me to report for him, and so did some English papers. *A Train of Powder* is an attempt to convey what I saw. I cannot believe the world changed so much in such a short time in any previous era. We are all in a disconcerting position. All human beings are in the same position to their environment that a man is if he gets his wife home after a road accident with amnesia and a transformation of personality. But he can at least give up and leave her, and humanity cannot leave its environment. I have tried to do what I can to chart the change.

I must make the reservation that I do not believe the world has changed so much that certain principles have lost their validity. The liberal faith still seems to me to hold its truth.

I live forty miles out of London on the Chiltern hills, in an extremely isolated house, which I regret because it means that something is always going on. Either one of the farm worker's children falls into a pond or an animal needs the vet or there is some other crisis. I remember Willa Cather[2] telling me that she left her country home to come to New York when she wanted to write a book, for the sake of the quiet. I sympathise.

I hope to get to America this year, but I am struggling with the second major tragedy of my career. Five years ago I sat down to write what I thought was going to be a long short story. It is now 400,000 words long, and it takes a family from the cradle to what I sometimes fear will be my grave.[3] I am within sight of the end, and after that I will come to America, for which I am horribly homesick.

Yours sincerely

Rebecca West Papers   carbon typescript
Yale University

---

[1] This was in answer to Kalb's request for an author's sketch for the *Saturday Review of Literature,* which published his interview with West on 19 March 1955.

[2] Willa Cather (1873–1947), American novelist and editor of *McClure's* magazine, whose Nebraska childhood inspired her to write *O Pioneers!* (1913) and *My Antonia* (1918). West praised her *Death Comes to the Archbishop* (1927) for its "mountain-pony sturdiness" in *Ending in Earnest.*

[3] West's final trilogy of novels did indeed take her to her grave. *The Fountain Overflows* was published in 1956, but *Cousin Rosamund* (1985) and *This Real Night* (1984) appeared posthumously.

To: Charles Curran

Ibstone House
Ibstone
Nr. High Wycombe
Bucks
22 March 1955

My dear Charles,

The Yalta papers haven't arrived, and will tomorrow, I expect, come to rejoice me. In the meantime I have been looking at the Bohlen reports as reprinted by the *U. S. News,* and I think you are misled because you were unaware of what had gone on in London before the Yalta Conference. Churchill's defence of the Poles was for the record and to impress the Americans and stop talk; but it cannot have been sincere, for he would not have treated the Poles as he had done from the moment they arrived in London, had he had any of the desire to safeguard their interests which he professed at Yalta.

Make a comparison. The references at Yalta to the arrangement between [Subasic][1] and Tito *look* all right; sensible and prudent, a clear case of bowing to the inevitable. Actually Churchill had savaged the Yugoslavs from the moment they came into the war. When Yugoslavia came into the war and the King and General Simovic and his staff arrived in London they were not welcomed. They saw nobody for some days except Foreign Office clerks, who treated them with no special politeness. The King, our King, sent for King Alexander. I think he arranged for a meeting with Churchill, but it was a perfunctory one. When the exiled Government was formed the Prime Minister was a scholar well-known all over Europe, an old liberal named Professor Jovanovic.[2] Neither he nor any member of his Cabinet ever met Churchill, or had any civil message from him then, or ever after. Their first Prime Minister of Yugoslavia ever to have a meeting with Churchill was Puric[3] (a career diplomat) who was in Cairo in the summer of 1943 (I think) and was suddenly, one morning, fetched by British soldiers from his hotel to go and see Churchill. He was lying in bed, unshaved and unwashed, and abused Puric like a pick-pocket, because he was still communicating by radio with his Commander-in-Chief, Mihailovitch. He brawled with him and ordered him to join Tito or pack up. Puric told me of this himself in most convincing terms. Later Churchill, without seeing Puric, without consulting any Yugoslav, sent for Subasic, who was an ex-Nazi-supporter, in America and brought him back and made him Prime Minister and got him to sign this deal with Tito. Meanwhile the whole Yugoslav administration was exposed to extreme humiliations and annoyance. As liaison officer between the F.O. {Foreign Office] and the Yug Government a drunken Communist named Alec Brown was employed, who blackmailed the functionaries by getting them to cash rubber cheques. In spite of repeated requests that this man should be removed, from the Yugoslavs, the F.O. kept him there. There was obviously a feeling that the Yugs had to be treated rough. The King's last interview with Churchill was a nightmare. (Not that I would say a word for the King, but I object to a Prime Minister of ours behaving like that—and he was not objecting to the King for sound but for unsound reasons.)

Throughout this nightmare I used to check up with people concerned with other exiles to see how Churchill treated them. The Poles also were continuously insulted. (We used to put up a parachutist here between his trips. It was quite obvious that the service was not being petted.) The Czechs also were insulted. The only people who had tolerable treatment among the exiles were the Greeks. I am not relying on the perhaps partisan statements of people like myself, who might have been sentimental. Tony Biddle,[4] who was Ambassador at Large for the exiled Governments, was outraged by the way they were treated; so was his wife, Margaret Biddle, who now runs Realites in Paris. So, too, were Ann Bridges and her husband.

If you ask me why Churchill did this, I can't answer. I think he is, though a great man, a peculiarly base and nasty person who would like to torment people who are out of luck. It still seems to me idiotic to insult one's allies in a Great War, however small {they may be}. And remember he gave the Yugoslavs this appalling time *before* Russia came into the war. But that he did behave in this way is known to everybody who had any contact with the exiled governments, and you are quite off the beam if you believe either what Churchill said at Yalta or the smoke-screen he puts up in those very dishonest books of reminiscence.

It amuses me, by the way, that there is this outcry about the Yalta papers, when all it means is that Bohlen did not use his notes as Churchill and Byrnes have used theirs, but [has] given them to the State for use—as I think all such papers should be used. The Hiss notes, you know, mysteriously disappeared from the files. I have a note of that somewhere. I like the very funny bit of backchat between Bohlen and Vishynsky.[5] What a good man Bohlen seems to be, and how he must have suffered. I hope you noted in the

U. S. News that among the censored bits is a proposal that Joseph Lash[6] should be alternate U. S. delegate to the U.N. meeting at San Francisco in 1945. Mr Lash was the boy friend of Mrs R., though I am sure that went a very small way, and what is more significant [is] that he was a young man who had begun life as a gym instructor (not many years before) and had been up to the neck in the Communist Party, being an active hand in the infiltration of the Youth Movements in America. I think he now admits he was a Communist.

But I am quite sure that in our judgment of all this mess a very considerable part of the blame lies on Churchill. He is irrational, ungracious, with no real liking for good; and he is a shocking judge of people. I have no doubt that the whole explanation of this odd business about the Yugs and the Poles was that some queer protégé had sold him some nonsensical plan of campaign. The only thing about the horrid old man is that he refuses to die, or let his people be killed. But it is the *only* thing. You said once that he was an aristocrat. But I think the trouble with him is that he isn't. It is the queer and crazy Jerome blood that has spoiled him. Not that the Marlborough strain is without its disadvantages.[7]

Yours ever,
Rebecca

Do not forget about *Time and Tide.* I am very anxious that Lady Rhondda should get some clear idea of who might take it over—though of course she would prefer it to be non-Party. The existing arrangement, of which you first warned me, is most undesirable. She is, as I think I told you, 72, and wants to get it straight before she dies, not parting with the control till she dies.

The Kay Boyle[8] (is most) story is most curious; the American Government says they have nothing against her (she was investigated only as the wife of an official in Germany, for indiscretion) and are quite clear that they think her no Communist (the investigation was never finished as her husband's term of service terminated) and the *Saturday Evening Post* have been most loyal to her, resented the investigation on her behalf, and though they turned down a serial of hers, it was only because it wasn't good, and they have since published one two-part serial and mean to publish another soon. But there is running round Paris, and now here, the most pathetic stories of how she was witch-hunted and the *Saturday Evening Post* basely deserted her, so that she lives in poverty.[9] Obviously she doesn't spread the story, it is just the Party, and the strange [damn fools] who like to think of persecutions. I wish you could remember who told you the story.

Yours ever,

R

Rebecca West Collection   typescript with manuscript initial
University of Tulsa

[1] Ivan Subasitch, head of the Yugoslavian government in exile when Tito was recognized as administrative foreign minister.

[2] Slobodan Jovanovitch, historian and supporter of Mihailovitch, opposed to Tito's Partisans. He became the first prime minister of the government in exile in January 1942.

[3] Bozidar Puritch, prime minister of Yugoslavian government in exile beginning in August 1943, also opposed to the Partisans.

[4] Anthony Joseph Biddle, Jr. (1896–1961), American diplomat who was serving as ambassador to Poland when Hitler invaded. Ambassador extraordinary to the refugee governments of Poland, Belgium, the Netherlands, Norway, Greece, Yugoslavia, and Czechoslovakia (1941–1944), he returned to the Army at the end of the war. Margaret Thompson Schulze, a copper heiress, became the second of his three wives (m. 1931).

[5] Andrei Vishinsky, Soviet diplomat who served as foreign minister and U.N. representative. He had presided at purge trials in the 1930s.

[6] Joseph Lash (1909–), American historian who met Mrs. Roosevelt in the 1930s when he was a young liberal involved in the Youth Congress. He is author of numerous books on the Roosevelts, including *Eleanor and Franklin* (1971), *Eleanor: The Years Alone* (1972), and *Love, Eleanor* (1982).

[7] The Jerome strain comes through Churchill's American-born mother, Jennie Jerome, daughter of a financier devoted to horse racing, Leonard W. Jerome. On his father's side Churchill was a direct descendent of John Churchill, first duke of Marlborough, a key figure in early eighteenth-century wars against Louis XIV.

[8] Kay Boyle (1902–1992), American author of short stories, poetry, and children's books. She was part of the expatriate generation in Paris, where she remained for thirty years as a foreign correspondent for the *New Yorker*. Her third husband, Joseph Franckenstein, who fled Nazi Austria, lost his job in 1953 under suspicion of having communist affiliations.

[9] In a letter to Evelyn and Margaret Hutchinson (2 April 1955, Yale University), West gave a more detailed explanation, provided by a diplomat in the American Embassy: "My friend told me that Kay Boyle and her husband had not been suspected of Communist activity, for their position was perfectly understood, they were simply liberals that had patted strange dogs in their time, and the Government had nothing against him. . . . Some Germans, I gathered, had complained that they were victims of indiscreet gossip, for which they thought Kay might have been guilty, and it had been necessary to investigate the matter, if only to clear her."
West's friends in Paris (among them Monica Stirling and Janet Flanner) believed that Kay was teaching in Darien "for a pittance" and connected the case with the *Saturday Evening Post*'s rejection of a serial by her. West made further inquiries, and Bruce Gould reported that

the serial was deemed "below her usual standard." She attributed Boyle's problems with the *New Yorker* to personality issues, not suspicion of communism. But West's efforts to suppress the story were failing, as were her relations with the friends in Paris, whom she considered subject to "mythomania." She also reported that Blanche Knopf "has bought the rejected serial for book publication and is selling the English rights over here. (Blanche is a maniac with strong Left Wing associations.)"

To: J. B. Priestley[1]

⟨Elysée Park Hotel
2 Rond Point, Paris⟩
Ibstone House, Ibstone: Bucks
22 juin 1955[2]

My dear Jack,

Your letter was a disagreeable surprise to me. I had thought that your unfavourable opinion of me, of which I have lately been assured, was due to the fact that you took a poor view of my refusal to blame Kilmuir[3] for the prosecution of the obscene books; and that I would have regarded as quite comprehensible on your part, since I had to do a lot of research before I realised that Goddard[4] was solely to blame, and luck played as much part in the discovery as research.

But you say, "I do disagree with your defence of McCarthy."

I have never written or spoken a single word in defence of McCarthy. I had from the beginning regarded him as a stupid and violent demagogue. The only time I have mentioned the name of McCarthy is in four articles in the *Sunday Times* which were published early in 1953;[5] and my references to him were contemptuous. I could not denounce him as I would denounce him today, for a reason that can be deduced from the date. McCarthy had then just become the Chairman of the Senate Committee, and the committee had sat on only a few occasions (not dealing with any very interesting material) and not a single official report of these had reached the country. I should certainly have denounced him for his attack on M. I. T. for its part in the foundation of the Baker East and Baker West radio stations,[6] but I am not a clairvoyant, and the sessions in which he made this attack did not take place until some weeks, even I think months, after the writing and publication of my articles, and the full facts were not unearthed for some time after that. I would have been only too delighted to write the attack on McCarthy which was afterwards written by Frederick Woltman,[7] but as he, an American living in America, was not able to write it for months (even, I think, more than a year) afterwards I hardly need to feel apologetic.

At the time McCarthy had conducted few investigations and no official reports were available. But he had been himself investigated, by the Tydings Committee, but there was no copy available in England, and my friends in America could not find a copy for me.[8] (As you probably know, it is increasingly difficult to get copies of these official reports.) I spent a small fortune and endless time on getting back press clippings and tracking those in other people's possessions, and formed an unfavourable view of McCarthy, which I expressed in these *Sunday Times* articles.

Not only have I never written a word in defence of McCarthy, I had spent a great deal of time in attacking him. Not in the press, for which I would have got paid, but in private letters. I have throughout the past two years written long letters to two members of the Republican Party who ⟨have⟩ found them so useful that they asked me to furnish them with ammunition. When I was in Paris during the visit of Cohn and Schine I spent two days translating press comments on the occasion from the French newspapers, and supplying my own fervent opinion of the situation, and the letter got to the White House.[9] I really do not think that I could have done more to fight McCarthy, and I shall be delighted to hear that you have done as many tedious and unrewarded chores as I have in this field.

It is no use trying to get round the fact that you have made an unfounded accusation against me by claiming that my articles, though they did not defend McCarthy, defended McCarthyism, since the proceedings of the committees whose investigations I defended were tainted with the faults of frivolity and brutality which are the main charges against McCarthy. But this would be a wholly unjustified smear against me.

I wrote those articles in the vain attempt to prevent the sabotaging of Anglo-American relations by the constant presentation of the United States as insane with anti-Communist hysteria and the Investigation committees as tribunals comparable to the Inquisition. My precise reason for writing these articles was [a] painful incident which occurred when our car broke down in West London and I sat down outside a cafe, and saw the little girl of the proprietress run out and spit on the pavement behind two American airmen. She explained to me that she encouraged her little girl to do this because the Americans were barbarians and that Senator McCarthy was worse than

Hitler. (This was some months before McCarthy held any office at all, and she was basing her opinion on the counsels her husband had received from that impartial body, the Electrical Trades Union.) I therefore thought somebody had better point out that the Communist Party had created so many new criminal problems in the United States that the Administration had to investigate them, just as we in this country would have to investigate them under the Tribunal of Enquiry Act if they emerged here in quite that form. I am afraid that I am the last liberal left, and I must confess that my obstinate liberalism cannot approve of Communist civil servants packing the civil service with Communist Party members and getting them employment and promotion over the heads of non-Communists, nor in Communist trade unions that extend their power by thuggery, or in Communist schoolteachers who employ the sort of tactics (such as sending telegrams announcing falsely the death of a relative and making all night successions of telephone calls) which the teachers and students at Brooklyn College employed against that great liberal, Harry Gideonse.[10] I do not know why you should want these peculiar activities protected by press silence. I was careful not to use any fact which I could not draw from the evidence of persons accused of these activities, or which were supposed to have occurred by organizations such as the C. I. O. or A. F. L. I had every fact vetted by ⟨organisations⟩ a paid researcher and by an independent American {not American born} lawyer, and usually consulted more than one person of authority in the relevant field. This does not strike me as the defence of McCarthy or of McCarthyism.

I might have attacked abuses of the process, but at that time very few had appeared; for example, only slowly could I determine that the committees took a contribution to the legal defence of an accused person as evidence of sympathy for the accused person's crime. I wish you would tell me of one case in which injustice had been done at the time when I wrote those articles. I have found in my reading and research since a very large number of cases in which it appeared or was alleged that injustice had been done, but in a very large number of cases there was no foundation for the allegations of injustice, or the injustice had been committed by individuals—and the question was one of legal redress, not of corrupt administrative practice. But in any case this refers to a period of time after my articles were written. "Red Channels" of course existed before my articles were written, but that is entirely a matter of individual action, not of action by the State or Federal Government, and it has no more ⟨x⟩ {governmental} support than the monkey-tricks of East End Fascists or Communists have here.

It does seem to me, however, that your quite unfounded allegation that I defended McCarthy is McCarthyism; and perhaps you will understand better what I feel when I tell you of a perplexing incident which occurred just after the *Sunday Times* articles appeared. An American with whom I have some business relations asked Henry and me to go to the theatre with him and took us on [to] the Caprice for supper. There then appeared, with rather a trapdoor effect, Ben Levvy and Constance Cummings.[11] I had not seen Ben Levvy for twenty years, and Constance Cummings I had never met. They regarded me in a peculiar manner and so did the American. Then apropos of absolutely nothing, Ben Levvy said to me, "You are a supporter of McCarthy." I said, "No, I've never said or written a word in his favour." To which Ben Levvy said, with a curious smile, "I know that, but all the same if we say so you're going to find it very hard to convince people that you are not." You can make what you like of this incident. At the time I felt slightly alarmed, but thought, "Well, it does not matter, people who know me and have read me will see through this skulduggery." I have since learned that I was wrong. But I hardly thought that you would be one of the people who would be taken in. Have you ever known me [to] write or say anything that would lead you to suppose that I could be a supporter of McCarthy? Can you suggest why, after sacrifices we made at that time, I should suddenly fall for a half-baked gorilla from the Middle West? Didn't it occur to you that I had published in the *Sunday Times* and in the *Evening Standard* and *The Meaning of Treason* some stuff that is faintly disadvantageous to the Communist Party and that they might possibly find it convenient to spread lies about me? And aren't you behaving to me like the asses who during the war, when you made your completely anti-totalitarian broadcasts, said that you were a Communist?

I am slightly startled by your remark, "Your book, like the last, is a brilliant piece of writing, but I am puzzled to understand why you should devote your superb talent to this particular theme." I don't know what you mean by "this particular theme," but it does seem to me odd that you should rebuke me for reprinting pieces which deal chiefly with the Nuremberg attempt to punish war by international law.[12] Of the other two pieces I have bound up with it, I can remember a time when you would have thought it worth while to write an account of a lynching trial and the attempt of a Southern town to rid itself of race hatred or of a trial in which a family's happiness was destroyed by the heartlessness of ideological fanatics. Have you really forgotten the faith you used to live by? Have you really gone over to the side of the people who think that one might just as well tell all the fashionable lies and deal with trivialities which offend nobody? I find it very hard to believe of you.

Yours ever,
Rebecca.

But do let us meet![13] How ungracious of me to overlook that suggestion—particularly as I wouldn't much care to meet anybody I thought a pro-McCarthyite.

J. B. Priestley papers	typescript with autograph heading,
University of Texas at Austin	signature, and postscript

[1] J. B. (John Boynton) Priestley (1894–1984), prolific, wide-ranging British author, journalist, critic, novelist, dramatist, and wartime broadcaster for the BBC. He wrote on travel, psychology, and—in *The English* (1970)—his countrymen.

[2] Though she crossed out the French letterhead, West used the French word for June.

[3] Maxwell Fyfe, Earl of Kilmuir (1900–1967), Scottish conservative M.P. (1935–1945), deputy chief prosecutor at Nuremberg, and lord chancellor (1954–1962).

[4] Raynor Goddard (1877–1971), English judge, a staunch conservative whose reputation had been made in criminal cases, where he favored corporal and capital punishment. He was lord chief justice (1946–1958).

[5] See letter to Arthur Schlesinger, 7 June 1953, for note on these articles.

[6] In the articles mentioned, West tells of the suicide of an MIT employee, Raymond Kaplan, who was involved in the selection of these apparently ill-suited sites for Voice of America stations. She takes interest in a peculiarly illiterate suicide note which suggests that he feared prosecution by McCarthy. See *U.S. News and World Report* (22 May 1953).

[7] Frederick Woltman (1905–1970), American reporter for Scripps-Howard, best known for his exposés of anticommunist activities; he discredited McCarthy's evidence in the Amerasia Case.

[8] McCarthy presented evidence of 110 supposed cases against communist sympathizers to the Tydings Commission, headed by veteran Democrat Millard Evelyn Tydings. The Tydings report of 14 July 1950 failed to find conclusive evidence in McCarthy's files and accused him of perpetrating a "fraud and a hoax." West requested information on this and other investigative committees from American friends such as Dorothy Thompson and Evelyn Hutchinson.

[9] Roy M. Cohn was appointed chief counsel to McCarthy's Rules Committee in 1953. G. David Schine was a hotel heir and friend of Cohn. They toured Europe in April 1953 to

uncover communist influence in the U.S. information services. Cohn tried to shield Schine from the draft (this was the Korean War era), and when he failed, he threatened Army investigations that would later backfire on McCarthy in the McCarthy Army hearings that led to his downfall.

[10] Controversial second president of Brooklyn College (1939–1966), credited with eliminating communists from the College. A case involving Harry Slochower, who took the Fifth Amendment when asked whether he had been a member of the Communist Party, was much publicized and reached the Supreme Court (1957). Gideonse publicly denounced McCarthy's tactics, and in less known cases resisted the efforts of the Joint Committee Against Communism in New York, when they took action based on insufficient evidence against numerous members of his faculty.

[11] Benn Levy (1900–1973), English playwright, director, writer, Fabian, and M.P. (1945–1950). He wrote politically conscious books favoring nuclear disarmament in his later years. Levy extended his hospitality to Hollywood victims of blacklisting in the McCarthy era.

Constance Cummings (1910–), celebrated English actress who married Levy in 1933 and starred in many of his plays and in films, including *Night After Night*.

[12] West refers here to *A Train of Powder* (1955), which included a three-part essay on the Nuremberg war tribunal, "Greenhouse with Cyclamens," as well as "Opera in Greenville," on a lynching trial in South Carolina, "Mr Setty and Mr Hume," and "The Better Mousetrap," a Soviet spy story incorporating a domestic tragedy.

[13] Their meetings were not always a success. Michael Denison and Dulcie Gray recall entertaining the two at a party. West and Priestley sought opposite ends of a large sofa (interview, July 1996).

Anthony West. Used by permission of Katharine Church.

Katharine Church with baby Caro West, circa 1942. Used by permission of Katharine Church.

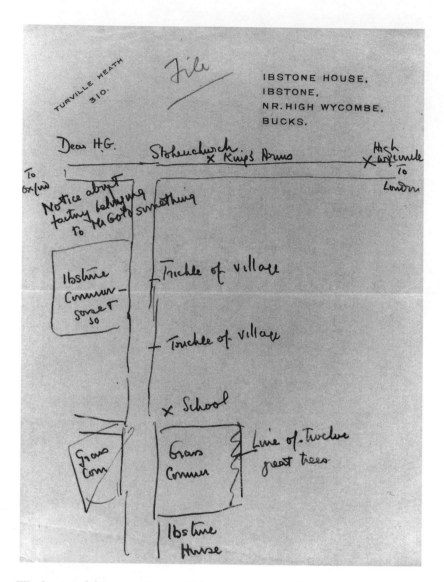

West's map of the way to Ibstone House, 1941, prepared for H. G. Wells. Used by permission of Yale University.

Aerial photo of Ibstone House
and farm. Used by permission of
Anne McBurney.

Rebecca West reviewing papers
with Henry Andrews, circa 1950.
Mark Gerson Photographers.
Used by permission of McFarlin
Library, University of Tulsa.

Dorothy Thompson. Used by permission of Syracuse University.

Rebecca West at Chartres Cathedral in France, 1951. Used by permission of Anne McBurney.

Rebecca West, Henry Andrews, and their yellow labrador, Albert, between her prized sphinxes at Ibstone, 1957. Used by permission of McFarlin Library, University of Tulsa.

Rebecca, Caro, and Edmund West, with Katharine Church in the background, at Caro's graduation from Oxford, circa 1962. Used by permission of Katharine Church.

Henry in formal dress, at Ibstone. Used by permission of McFarlin Library, University of Tulsa.

Rebecca West at her great circular desk, 1970. © Fay Godwin. Used by permission. McFarlin Library, University of Tulsa.

PART FIVE

1955-1969

Dame Commander of Letters

THIS ERA OF WEST'S LIFE BROUGHT NOT ONLY UNWELCOME NOTORIETY, WITH the publication of her son's autobiographical novel *Heritage* (1955), but also deserved recognition in the form of national and international awards, culminating in her designation as Dame Commander of the British Empire (1959). West responded to her son's autobiographical challenge by making papers pertaining to her relationship with Wells available to Gordon N. Ray. She assisted her niece, Alison, in finding publication outlets for her writing, developed a warm relationship with her nephew, Norman Macleod, and took an interest in Vyvyan Holland's son Merlin, whose education she was helping to finance.

West took on the new role of assisting scholars interested in such figures as Marcel Proust, James Joyce, H. G. Wells, May Sinclair, Ford Madox Ford, Violet Hunt, Bryher, Zelda Fitzgerald, and Harriet Shaw Weaver. She gave a series of lectures of Yale, later published by Yale University Press as *The Court and the Castle*. And she watched critically over adaptations of her fiction for the BBC. Andrew Brown, who worked on an adaptation of her story "The Abiding Vision," was told at length why his "presentation would do me severe professional damage, as it is a complete travesty of my story in content and style" (9 June 1968, University of Tulsa).

Once she entered her sixties, West's journalism slowed only slightly. Most notably, she traveled to South Africa. While there, she attended the Treason Trial—a proceeding that stretched over three and a half years and involved 156 individuals accused of secretly intending revolutionary action and violence. West suspected that the accused were guilty merely of affiliation with the African National Congress. She saw the Progressive Party as South Africa's greatest hope for the future. Her visit coincided with the Sharpeville shootings, which added a dimension of personal uncertainty and danger. Her insightful five-part series on apartheid, "In the Cauldron of South Africa," was published in the *Sunday Times*. West's letters are more replete with communist intrigues than were the published articles. On her return to London, West felt like a celebrity: "I found that my articles were being featured as very few articles have in recent times—the *Sunday Times* advertised them in huge electric lights in Piccadilly Circus. I did an Ed Murrow 'Small World' on Apartheid, and they showed it to a Labour Group in the House of Commons (a wonderful old room off Westminster Hall) the day before I spoke to the Commonwealth Council, . . . and I also addressed a large Sword of the Spirit meeting at the Overseas League" (Letter to Glen Wolfe, 9 June 1960, Yale University). A less fortunate outcome was that she was successfully sued for libel by Judge Alexander Angus Kennedy, whom she had misidentified in her report on the trial. Her letters offer an array of explanations and show disappointment over the role of the *Sunday Times* in defending her. In a letter detailing various intrigues and written to U.S. embassy official Glen Wolfe (9 June 1960, Yale University), West also reported her suspicions that the Communist Party had "well and truly laid hold of the South African situation in order to exploit it." Her accounts involve such prominent individuals as high commissioner and future ambassador to South Africa John Maud, the author Nadine Gordimer, the canon of St. Paul's Cathedral John Collins, a champion of the detainees in the Treason Trial, and the photojournalist Tom Hopkinson. Lulu Friedman, one of her hostesses during the South African stay, became a valued confidante and the recipient of lengthy letters for years afterwards.

West's interest in espionage culminated in her writing *The Meaning of Treason,* which caused Evelyn Waugh to threaten her with another lawsuit. West brought out a highly profitable best-selling novel, *The Fountain Overflows,* but she complained that domestic interruptions prevented the completion of two additional volumes in the series.

This was an era of personal losses for her, including the death of Winifred, the "Big Sister who protected me from the Bigger Sister." She puts Winnie to rest in the mystical manner that characterizes many of her accounts of death, in this case detecting "a curious 'mirror' happening":

> Her funeral was intensely moving, because she was buried in the most beautiful cemetery on the outskirts of London, with tall trees, and they had found a grave for her under a graceful tree of some kind I wasn't in a state to identify, but it was not very tall and it bent protectively over her—and it was romantic in an eighteenth century, no later, early nineteenth century way, absolutely in accord with what she was as a young girl. It was as if life, never having given her anything that was in accord with her physical or mental nature, suddenly pulled itself together and fitted the setting to the jewel. (Letter to Lulu Friedman, 6 June 1960, private collection.)

West's correspondence continued, on Ibstone House stationery. The farm had become a necessary occupation for Henry, whose problems with deafness, cerebral arteriosclerosis, and erratic driving are frequently reported. He died in late 1968. Henry had proved in some ways a delightful companion but in others a distracting husband for a writer, and his death brought with it disillusionment and the need for West to compose a satisfactory version of their life together. She prepared to leave Ibstone House and all that she had loved about it, from oversized bookcases to walks with her labrador retriever in the beautiful landscape around the house. She sought a more manageable lifestyle in the city of her birth, London.

To: Kitty West

Ibstone House
Ibstone
Nr. High Wycombe
Bucks
[fall 1955]

My dear Kitty,

Thank you for warning me. I got another copy this morning,[1] and I started the book, but could not face its monstrous, clotted spite. I have only fluttered the pages. But the curious thing is that on every page I had a queer sense as if the book wasn't just by Anthony—as if there was a second person concerned in it. Somebody with a much more vulgar, direct personality, with much less imaginative power, and with no knowledge of the real circumstances—who every now and then said, "Here, let's put this in, it is good and damaging." I thought the vulgarity of the book astounding.

I had one smile out of the book—the idea of there being County Court summonses on *my* breakfast tray. That my solicitor will particularly enjoy. But what I could not endure was the report of my saying to Anthony that I had had an affair with his father because "it was a short cut to the top of the tree." That *is* Anthony—at his worst—and after that I decided I wouldn't read any more.

It is—selfishly—an immense relief to me that he hadn't any real grievances to write about. You know how one worries about whether one didn't say or do something that may have hurt their feelings. But in the pages I read there was nothing leading back to anything real.

This is as strange as any nightmare.

Yours ever,

Rac

Rebecca West Collection   manuscript
University of Tulsa

[1] A copy of *Heritage,* Anthony's autobiographical novel which has characters very like his family members, including himself, Rebecca, H. G. Wells, and Henry Andrews. Rebecca is cast as a self-centered actress who neglects her son. Concerning *Heritage,* Anthony wrote to his mother as follows:

Dearest Poss,

Bless you for writing such a temperate letter about your feelings. The only thing I would argue with in it was your use of the word malicious. You can call me selfish if you like. The truth is that I care more about writing than anything else. I found that I wanted to write that book not to pay off old scores or anything of that kind—but simply to describe areas of feeling that I know about. If I'd been thinking of good manners I'd have kept off them—but I was thinking of Lawrence and Dickens and Balzac and the imprint of truth that their work bears and how it came to bear it. They didn't, they couldn't, deny themselves the right to use the central experiences in their lives in their writing. I can't either. Don't think for a moment, because of the names I've just mentioned, that its a matter of wanting to be "famous" or anything like that. It's just that I want people who read what I write to feel as they read it that this is the truth as I know it. I felt that as long as I had to withhold the major part of my experience from my writing I would go on producing flawed books which were in the end evasive about the realities I know, and which would seem false. I didn't want to go on writing inferior stuff—that's all there is to it and whatever it is it isn't malice. I'm sad that you should have used the word but not a bit cross.

Unimpressed, West noted at this point: "I particularly enjoy this sentence" (typescript letter of Anthony West to Rebecca West with her annotation, Yale University).

To: Lord Beaverbrook   Ibstone House
                                                        Ibstone
                                                        Nr. High Wycombe
                                                        Bucks
                                                        4 November 1955

My dear Max,

Don't think that in my old age I am developing a mania for writing to you. But I want to thank you for your very kind (though I fear too optimistic) note about *Heritage,* and to comment on a passage in your letter which certainly surprised me.

You write:

Anthony West told me in England that he would not write H. G.'s biography because it would give you pain.

I have no idea what he can have meant. The literary executors of the Wells estate, H. G.'s two elder sons, G. P. and Frank, and Mrs. G. P. Wells, gave Anthony the task of writing a political and literary biography of his father. There could be no other sort of biography. There could not be a personal biography. I had nothing to do with this decision, but it is an entirely reasonable recognition of the fact that there is no material for a personal biography. H. G. did not wish one to be written, and to that end destroyed all his personal letters a short time before his last illness, except for a few letters from me and from Amber Reeves.[1] It is impossible to fill the gap, for there are very few people alive who knew Wells prior to a comparatively recent date. Were he alive today he would be ninety, and most of his close friends, such as Maurice Low[2] and George Whale,[3] predeceased him by many years. Even Philip Guedalla, who was much his junior, died before he did.

I was delighted that Anthony should write this political and literary biography, and never opposed the idea in any way. I remember that the day he went to see you he came here first, and I had asked him how he was getting on with the biography, and we had a general talk about it. Indeed, I understood that the purpose of his visit to you was to ask for your personal reminiscences of H. G.

The only reason that the project was abandoned was that the literary executors found out that Anthony was sailing for America, and was taking with him such part of the Wells papers (nearly three-quarters) as he had been working on, and forbade him to take them with him. Anthony preferred to go to America and of his own free will dropped the biography, though the executors very kindly kept the door open for him to start work again for quite a long time. I had nothing to do with the decision of the executors in refusing to let the papers go out of the country, but I think it was inevitable. The papers were uncatalogued, uninsured, and of great value, and the executors were responsible for them to the estate.

You will see that the statement you repeat is quite wide of the mark. Forgive me for explaining the facts at length, but I would not like you to think I had stood in Anthony's way.

I object to *Heritage* very much indeed. As you say, the picture is not clear, and obviously I am not feckless or given to debt or a snob. But there is enough in the parallel, which seemed to be exploited by the publisher and enjoyed by various reviewers, to compel some identification; and I most strongly object to having it thought that I neglected Anthony. I never came to America till he was in prep school, and except for one Christmas, when for reasons quite beyond my control I was kept in New York to finish some lectures, I never missed the school holidays; and I visited America only once a year. If I had not come to America and built up my very profitable connections here, Anthony would certainly not have had the comfort and opportunities he had as a child and young man. You know this, for at the time I told you about the extremely strange financial conditions of my life, and you gave me very good advice. But the book grieves me also because it gives an ungracious account of the Wells family, who have always been most friendly and generous towards Anthony. Had he written the biography, he was to be given the right to draw all the proceeds, giving nothing back to the estate, which is the ordinary custom; and all they asked was that he should submit what he wrote for their approval, and they would not have withheld the approval unreasonably. But the real trouble of the book is the storm which will arise if it gets into the hands of Odette Keun. You may remember her. You may, I repeat, remember her. For this reason there has had to be a certain amount of consideration.

I agree with you that Anthony will go far. He has a magic power over words and a good mind behind it. But he will not get a step further by gratifying this odd desire he has shown of late years to get publicity by advertising the facts of his private life. It is a matter of sheer advertisement. I have seen correspondence with his former publisher in which it was discussed simply as a matter of selling his earlier novel. That strikes me as vulgar; and it creates prejudice against him. It is also not necessary, as he can get ahead on his work.[4]

Do not trouble to answer this.

Again many thanks for your letter,

Yours ever,
Rebecca

Hist. Coll. 184, Beaverbrook Papers   typescript
House of Lords Record Office

[1] Before meeting West, Wells had an affair with Amber Reeves, a woman twenty years his junior and the daughter of prominent Fabians. She bore his daughter (1909), after a hasty marriage to Rivers Blanco White. Wells had a severe falling-out with the Fabians over the ensuing scandal.

[2] A. Maurice Low (1860–1929), journalist for the *Morning Post*. His books include *The American People* (1909), *The Law of Blockade* (1916), and *Woodrow Wilson* (1918).

[3] George Whale (1849–1925), English solicitor, mayor of Woolwich, and literary clubman active in the Rationalist Press Association. The benevolent solicitor in Wells's *Joan and Peter* is based on him. Whale advised West to leave Wells if he wouldn't marry her.

[4] Concerning *Heritage*, West told G. B. Stern:

My fundamental objection is that Anthony apparently brings up against me all the objections to what H. G. made me do, and which I fought against—as if I had gladly inflicted them on him. When my life with H. G. was such unspeakable hell. I cannot bear it that Anthony, instead of looking on his childhood as something we had to go through together, should write a clownish account of H. G. and a glossy magazine story about an actress and a little lord Fauntleroy idyll about himself—out of that hell. It is so irreverent and disgusting, and so ungrateful for all the things I have done for him since, that I cannot be grateful for the testimonials to my personal appearance and a view of my theatrical gifts which I would have liked the A. D. A. [Academy of Dramatic Arts] to share but which is no use to me in this connection. (25 October 1955, G. B. Stern Collection, Boston University)

Dorothy Thompson was given some additional information:

You know I got Ross to give Anthony a job. Henry and I together put his affairs in order, which he had left in a mess, and we have paid out thousands for the support of Kitty and his two children. To meet that situation (though Anthony left his small private income at their disposal, he does give them something) I have had to settle half my available capital on the grandchildren. If anything happened to Henry's money I would now not have enough to live on. Meanwhile I have started an affectionate correspondence with Anthony, and in August he brought his second wife to this house, and we welcomed them warmly, and Anthony was given two hundred pounds by Henry as our delayed wedding present. We visited them in Dorset, and we all dined together at the Ritz the night before they left England. We were wondering why we had not heard from them, and then this book came out. Anthony made the most desperate attempts to get the book published over here, and when he failed Donald Klopfer came over and took a hand. Finally I received ⟨an offer⟩ {a request} through an agent that I would write a preface to it—he knew that it would be my instinct to refuse, he said, but if I wrote a preface some passages might be left out that would otherwise be left in. It must be the lot of few mothers to be blackmailed by their sons. I sent a message that if the publisher published I would sue, and I have heard no more, and I hear that the agent who was handling the book is not sending it out any more. (1955, Syracuse University)

A letter to Maboth Mosley and Vera Watson summarizing Anthony's history up through *Heritage* (5 February 1956) was published in the *New Yorker* (24 and 31 August 1998): 99.

To: Letitia Fairfield   La Posada
                                                         Santa Fe, New Mexico
                                                         [6 May 1956]

My dear Lettie—

   I have been very lazy in not writing to you—but there are really many
excuses for me! When I got to New York my friends the Goulds[1] asked me to
let [them] see the first part of the book, which is going to be published as a
separate novel. I told them it was quite useless for them, but they asked if
they might have it to read over the week-end, and I gave it to them on
Saturday morning—on Monday morning they called up and bought it for
35,000 dollars! I fell on the floor, so did Henry, then we realised that if they
paid [??] (as they offered to do) at once, Henry was ruined! So we had hastily
to devise a method by which we were paid in installments over the next few
years. This took quite a lot of time and also I had to see various people, such
as John Gunther & his wife, we had a dinner party ⟨almost⟩ {every} night
and other social engagements—and incidentally got involved with Greta
Garbo, who is a darling. Then in fear and trembling I went to Yale. I felt I
would not be able to lecture at all, I was so tired. But the lectures went well
and for the third one they moved me into a larger hall! We had some
delightful parties there, and met Wallace Notestein,[2] who sent the most
loving greetings to you. The scenery is glorious, and the Indian life entrancing, but it's very odd. The people living here are all arty people who take a
pride in living in the "old Spanish houses"—which are made of mud—and
they are actually hideous, like the worst emergency pre-fabs put up after the
blitz, and if anything are rather smaller, and they are dumped down among
[scrubley?] trees and shrubs beside miserable rivulets meandering through
mud. It is quite fantastic. But the surrounding country is marvellous, like the
best of Spain, with an added beauty of light due to the high altitude. The
second day we were here—that is yesterday—we went to an Indian village to
see a [?] dance—which is an astonishing sight indeed—a small village of
mud-houses on the banks of the Rio Grande produced two troupes of 150
people each, young and old, in magnificent costumes, performing without
fault elaborate dances of a semi-drill type. The young men and women were
many of them skilled technicians in the outer world. What surprises me are
the Indian children—the only well brought up children, who know how to
speak and move, on this side of the Atlantic. Today we went to Taos and we

called on D. H. Lawrence's widow [Frieda], whom I was delighted to see us [*sic*] after all [these] years, and was full of fire and vitality. Such a wonderful drive, through desert and through a mountain pine forest, of pines we don't have, that grow as beautifully as beeches, in glades. We ended up in a wonderful (really wonderful) Spanish farm, where a cracked old Bostonian lady lived who had written a book on Navaho religion ⟨x⟩ making them out as cracked as she was. (This is what nearly everybody is doing out here—I don't know how the Indians stand it!). Tomorrow I have been given a special permit to visit Los Alamos, I hope they won't blow me up. The woman who gave me the permit at the Atomic {Energy} Commission offices here told me with tears in her eyes that she hoped I would write about Oppenheimer, who was, she said, exactly like Jesus Christ. ⟨x⟩

When I got here I found that Warburg of Secher & Warburg was trying to buy Anthony's book for publication in London, and Anthony & his publishers were eager to sell. But Warburg's only doubt was whether I might not sue for libel—which I have always said I would. It turned out from what he said to publishers over here and others that Robert Senhouse and David Farrar (two pansy partners in Secher & Warburg, whom I have known for some time) have been expressing great concern over the book to Barbara Bach, who has transmitted their remarks to me in all good faith and even asked questions through her about the book—it now appears (from what Warburg says {in N. Y.}—and Warburg is a very old friend of Henry's!) that they were sounding B. B. to find if I really would sue and weren't sure! Fortunately I got a letter from first Marjorie and then Frank Wells saying that they were deeply sorry {for me} over the whole business and were so disgusted that if Secher & Warburg ⟨sued⟩ {published} the book *they* would sue {and I need worry no longer}. My publisher transmitted this to Warburg, who seemed taken aback, and there—as I had conveyed through B. B. and another friend of Senhouse we may *hope* the business may stop. The whole business becomes more and more repulsive—Anthony came over here (as you know with the intention of leaving Kitty and marrying a Mrs Prescott) and immediately started an elaborate impersonation of a poor boy who had never had a chance and had lived in garrets and had at last come to the New World to try to make a life for himself. I had to explain to Jane Gunther that he had had a large house, beautiful and comfortable, and a large number of friends and a successful career at the B.B.C. and as a writer! Dorothy

Thompson, with whom he stayed, is convinced he was sent over here by some people (presumably the C P [Communist Party]) who paid him to ruin me. At the same time he is now making desperate attempts to see me and get me to be on friendly terms, ⟨though he is to⟩ {on the grounds} he never intended to hurt or injure me by the book—though he is still trying to get it published in England. He was terribly upset when I appeared here and evidently hoped that he had made it impossible for me to come to America. This is so strange and horrible a sting I feel it has nothing to do with me.

Much love. I hope all goes well.

YourseverAnne.

West, R., MSS   manuscript
Indiana University, Bloomington

[1] Beatrice and Bruce Gould, editors at the *Ladies' Home Journal*, were interested in the first installment of *The Fountain Overflows*. Beatrice recalled, "We read it over a weekend, and I'd been reading in one room and Bruce had been reading in another, and when I was coming near the end, I came in to where he was and said, 'I have to sit with you while I read the end of this,' because I was so moved by it" (*Beatrice and Bruce Gould*, microfilmed typescript, Oral History Research Office, Columbia University).

[2] Wallace Notestein (1878–1969), historian and author best known for *The English People on the Eve of Colonization* (1954), though his *History of Witchcraft in England from 1558 to 1718* (1911) would have been of greatest interest to Lettie, who was fascinated by witches. Details of West's travel to Albuquerque, N.M. are omitted.

To: Mrs Tyson   30 August 1956
Dear Mrs Tyson,

Thank you very much for your very kind letter. I am very glad that the book on Yugoslavia was of help to you, and I hope you had a pleasant trip. I haven't published anything on Yugoslavia since the end of the war. Constantine is dead of heart disease after a painful struggle with authority; Dragutin has been chauffeur to some friends of mine; I do not know what has happened to the Bulbul and Selim; Mehmed died about two years ago, at the time of his death his wife attempted to commit suicide but was brought back to life, only to make the attempt again six months later, and succeed.[1] I feel that much of myself has died with these people, but that did not help them.

Thank you very much for your kind words about your expectations regarding my novel, I hope you will like it.

Yours very sincerely,

Rebecca West Papers   carbon typescript
Yale University

[1] These are all characters in *Black Lamb and Grey Falcon*. Constantine represented Stanislav Vinaver, her guide. The Bulbul and Selim were a Jewish couple she had encountered in Sarajevo. Mehmed's wife in life was Anica Šević-Rebac, for whom West had great affection. See letters to Henry Andrews of April–May 1936.

To: Norman Holmes Pearson[1]   30 August 1956
My dear Mr Pearson,

I found your letter on my return from Switzerland, where I have been laying out large amounts of horribly hard Swiss currency in return for uninterrupted thunderstorms and rain; and I was very much pleased to see that you had remembered me and had asked me to do something in the service of someone I admire as much as Bryher.[2] But Pantheon has till now sent me only H. D.'s *Tribute to Freud*; this may be a mistake, but if so Pantheon will realise it when they get my letter of thanks. I look forward to *Beowulf* with the greatest interest.

I do not think that Bryher is ignored because the British do not care for naturalism (they cared for Aldous Huxley a great deal till he went pharmaceutically silly) or for novels that deal with the middle and lower classes (Kingsley Amis and John Wain[3] deal with as common and drab a set of characters as can be found in what are justly termed prefabs). I think rather that Bryher was ignored because the influence of T. S. Eliot has been to make people distrust writers who have any substance to their work—who have anything to say. If a critic is as unsure of himself as Eliot he dislikes work that is different from other recognised work and cannot therefore be judged by reference to some handy precedent; and his dislike is as nothing to the dislike that his less gifted followers feel. I think this accounts for the silence that hangs around the name of Edwin Muir.[4] I think it accounts for the silence that hangs about the name of Bryher. I don't myself think that it is tragic, for she has gone on working, and so has Muir. But there must have been people of lesser character who were silenced.

Thank you for your kind words about my visit to Yale, which indeed made me very happy—I never met more charming people.

Yours sincerely,

Rebecca West Papers   carbon typescript
Yale University

[1] Norman Holmes Pearson (1909–1975), American professor at Yale, an editor and critic specializing in American literature. He was responsible for bringing out numerous works of H. D. as well as editions of Hawthorne.

[2] Bryher (1894–1983) pseudonym of Annie Winifred Ellerman, British poet, novelist, and editor. Her first marriage of convenience, to Robert McAlmon, provided freedom from her wealthy family. He invested in authors by founding Contact Press. She is noted for her support of the career of H. D. and for founding the pioneering film journal *Close-Up*.

[3] Aldous Huxley (1894–1963), whose works include the satires *Chrome Yellow, Antic Hay, Point Counterpoint,* and most famously, *Brave New World* (1932), with its caution about developments in reproductive science. By the 1950s he was interested in mysticism, parapsychology, and the effects of LSD.

Kingsley Amis (1922–1995), English novelist and poet, author of *Lucky Jim* (1954). He exemplified the angry young man.

John Wain (1925–1994), English poet, critic, and novelist who also wrote in the tradition of the angry young man. *Hurry on Down* (1953) was his first novel in the genre.

[4] Edwin Muir (1877–1959), Scottish poet, novelist, and critic. He was a socialist, contributed to Orage's *New Age,* and showed an interest in psychoanalysis. His poetry tends toward dream journeys and a mythic return to a threatened Eden. He collaborated on translations with his wife Willa.

To: Harold Guinzberg[1]   Ibstone House
                                                             Ibstone
                                                             Nr. High Wycombe
                                                             Bucks
                                                             [November 1956]

My dear Harold,

First things first. Leaving the international situation on one side, let me thank you for the copies of *The Fountain Overflows,* a prettier book than I could have wished. I like the wrapper, I like the binding, I like the print, I like the paper and I like Alice and you, so that makes the whole business perfect from my point of view. I am all too conscious that people may be a little too busy in the coming months to give my masterpiece the attention it deserves. So I apologise in advance for any disappointment you may suffer, and wish I had been a more negotiable author.

It is not easy over here. The situation is sheerly crazy, with a craziness that has been boiling up for a long time. I am, as you know, half-Scottish and half-Irish, and though my Irish half originally came from England that was some centuries ago, the time of Edward VI, to be exact, and I have never got used to the place, and have thought people madder and madder. Let me tell you how that madness has boiled up. J.B.S. Haldane[2] was at Oxford, with Henry, and I have known him and his sister Naomi Mitchison[3] all my life. J.B.S. is a hard-shelled Communist and director of the *Daily Worker,* and he married a good Jewish Communist, a very fine type, Charlotte,[4] who left the Party during the war and was consequently left by him. He then married a biologist, presumably of the right political complexion, called Helen Spurway. She has caused some sensation lately by writing a paper in favour of the theory that virgin births are possible and may be quite common. (Some argument about skin-grafting came in here.) This caused obscene merriment among their friends. It was unkindly said that after some years of marriage with J.B.S. the poor girl looked round on the landscape and seen the teeming populations [*sic*] and said to herself, "Well, there simply must be virgin births, that's all." She got herself into the tabloids with these views. When the Suez Canal landings came up the Haldanes got very excited; and two days ago she and her laboratory assistant, a young American, were arrested outside the University for being drunk and disorderly and assaulting a police-officer. I don't mean in the course of a demonstration, they were just drunk.[5]

It's all mad like that. I don't understand what made Eden[6] act. I can conceive that he is a fool or even a lunatic, but his Cabinet is neither of these things. Butler[7] and Macmillan (both of whom I used to know personally when I was younger—I still occasionally see Macmillan) are as sane as any men living. The Chiefs of Staff are sane and sensible. I can't think they would have consented to this business if there had not been some sense to it. And indeed Henry and I have had some uneasy feelings for the past month. We watched a family which we know to be CP go behind the Iron Curtain on what was supposed to be a business trip, but which seemed to be attended by such a degree of painful emotion that it was pretty obvious that they were being sent by the Party, called in from Moscow to do a job. I had imagined there was going to be some new peripheral war in which their advice would be useful as to propaganda in English-speaking countries. I would have said that there was going to be some trouble in the way of Arab aggression. But here we have Israeli aggression—and a precipitate action afterwards. There must be some whacking great suppression of news—or everybody has gone mad. It has been ironically beautiful weather and every morning I wake up to the most heavenly landscape—a white mist in the valley and the red woods below our garden glowing against it on [*sic*], and on the lawn the sun shining down through the yellow branches of our big chestnut on a pool of leaves on the lawn—and such a feeling of utter bewilderment and uncertainty.

And oh, the opposition has been so much worse than Eden. It has been contemptible. Anthony Nutting[8] behaved badly in resigning, because he was already on the skids. As you probably know, he was (as Eden's whiteheaded boy) sent over to New York to the UN, and fell in love with some Catholic girl in New York, the wife of a rich Catholic husband, and came home and had a very public quarrel with his wife, ending in the breaking up of the household—he is a spoiled, sulky young brute, very rich, and does everything in bad taste. He is serving out his time and it wasn't for him to pretend to resign on a matter of principle. Then a number of Oxford heads of colleges and dons signed a protest against the policy of the Government—one at least a CP member—which was practically an appeal to the public to panic, before they could possibly know what the issues were. On the other hand, the Communists are delighted because there is a distraction from watching what ⟨x⟩ is happening in Hungary, and the Labour people are exploiting their chances to get back into power at the next election. The opposition is so base that the best people are not taking part in it—see the enclosed letter from Gilbert Murray, with some of the best men in England as co-signatories.

Just in case I should get carried away with cheerfulness, I have caught up in a libel action by Evelyn Waugh. That filthy little creature has got my new cheap edition of *The Meaning of Treason* suppressed, and is suing me, my publisher, and the printer—for no other reason than that I mention him in a sentence in a new chapter dealing with Burgess and Maclean and the Korean prisoners of war. I pointed out that the people who have upset admiration for the classic virtues are not all on the left but that Graham Greene and Mauriac[9] and Evelyn Waugh have done their share. With fury I find that (a) the publisher of the edition never had it read for libel, and though I had had some queries they had been provided by a creature in the office (b) my solicitor, who fervently advised me to apologise, is also Evelyn Waugh's solicitor, and they wanted me to apologise and admit it was a libel because (d) Evelyn Waugh is engaged in a very silly libel action against the *Daily Express* over a trifling matter and (e) the *Daily Express,* though it had this libel action with Waugh on its hand had without having the article read quoted my remark about Waugh and headlined it and (f) Evelyn Waugh and his solicitor now [say] that if I would ⟨x⟩ admit that it was a libel, then they would go into court on their original suit against the *Daily Express* and a new one consisting of an action based on the quotation from my book, and the new one couldn't be defended if I had admitted it was a libel, and that would strengthen the first weak case. Because of this idiocy I have had endless tiresome interviews and telephone conversations and have much expense. But the slackness—! Neither the PAN publishers or the *Daily Express* having the stuff read for libel is what infuriates me. Oh, dear, how like France in 1940 England is in 1956.

I feel no affinity with anybody here, there is nobody here in this crisis who seems to me to be thinking straight or acting unselfishly. I am finishing my Yale lectures, but slowly, because I have not yet quite recovered. My fatigue has gone, to a certain extent, but I have got again a tiresome and obscure malady I had during the war, which gives me fits of giddiness if I get tired, and I have to go carefully.[10] But I shall get the next book to you before very long.

Yours ever,
Rebecca

I tuned in as I was writing this letter to get some music and heard the news of the riots in Paris—and a few sentences of Adlai's speech conceding the victory to Eisenhower.[11] What a charming, delightful, civilised personality it is. I hope that if the crisis continues and the matters thereto remain negotiable that Eisenhower will use him as Roosevelt used Wendell Willkie.[12]

Viking Press Archive   typescript

[1] West's publisher at Viking Press.

[2] J.B.S. Haldane (1892–1964), English geneticist, scientific popularizer, and chairman of the editorial board of the communist *Daily Worker.* His thinking about the future resembles that of the Huxleys. He left the Communist Party around 1950 in protest over Stalin's attitude toward science.

[3] Naomi Haldane Mitchison (1897–), Edinburgh-born historical novelist, poet, children's writer, and political advocate who was particularly concerned with women's issues. The censored *We Have Been Warned* (1935) concerned women's reproductive rights. Notable among her novels are *Cloud Cuckoo Land* (1925) and *The Corn King and the Spring Queen* (1931). *Small Talk* (1973) is her autobiography.

[4] Charlotte Haldane (1894–1969), English novelist and biographer who, like her husband, popularized biology. Her works include *Motherhood and Its Enemies* (1927) and *I Bring Not Peace* (1932). She was editor of *Woman Today.*

[5] In this bizarre incident, Spurway (1915–) stepped on a police dog's tail while returning from a pub, and when challenged by police, told them off. She was imprisoned in Holloway. Later she and Haldane resigned from their jobs at University College, London, and emigrated to India.

[6] Anthony Eden (1897–1977), British statesman, foreign minister under Neville Chamberlain and Winston Churchill, and prime minister (1955–1957). He was forced to resign over the Suez Canal crisis.

[7] R. A. "Rab" Butler (1902–1982), British Conservative Party statesman who held numerous ministerial posts and headed his party in the House of Commons (1955–1961). His vigorous support of Eden during the Suez crisis meant that Macmillan, rather than he, was tapped for prime minister in 1957.

[8] Sir Anthony Nutting (1920–), Conservative cabinet minister who resigned during the Suez crisis. He wrote numerous books on the Middle East, including a study of Lawrence of Arabia.

[9] Graham Greene (1904–1991), English novelist and playwright whose works are set in a variety of seedy places. His interest in moral dilemmas draws on a Catholic tradition. His works include *The Power and the Glory* (1940), *The Heart of the Matter* (1948), and *The Third Man* (1950).

François Mauriac (1885–1970), French novelist, dramatist, and essayist, awarded the Nobel Prize in 1952. Like Greene, his Catholicism contributed to intense concern with matters of sin and redemption. His works include *The Desert of Love* (1929), *Vipers' Tangle* (1932), *The Life of Jesus* (1936), and *A Woman of the Pharisees* (1941).

[10] West suffered from vascular problems and would experience vascular spasms and a mild heart attack in late 1958.

[11] West wrote to Emanie Arling, 6 November 1952, concerning the Eisenhower election.

[12] Wendell Lewis Willkie (1892–1944), American industrialist and Republican candidate for the presidency who ran against Roosevelt in 1940. He was a leading critic of the New Deal, yet he supported Roosevelt's war policies.

To: Kitty West

Ibstone House
Ibstone
Nr. High Wycombe
Bucks
[December 1956]

My dear Kitty,

Thank you so much for the lovely scarf—which indeed I don't deserve after my shocking performance. I am sending you two scarves which I meant to give you at that lunch—so I am posting them. If mouse [Caroline West Duah] thinks her black and pink one too sombre she can give it away. We rejoice over the prospect of the Ibstone plates, which we enjoy using very much indeed. We will come over when we can.

There is something I wish you would explain to Mouse—there is a horrid bother in my mind about something, for reasons with which I won't darken Christmas. Would you tell Mouse that the story of the book is not true,[1] except in the portrait of my mother, and very vaguely in the portrait of the father, which is really a portrait of all gamblers. He didn't sell my mother's furniture, he didn't desert his wife and children. At the time that I was as old as Rose is at the beginning of the book my father had been dead for some time—the last time I was together with my father and mother was when we went to church together when he was going on a wild-goose-chase to West Africa, after which, not unnaturally, at his age, he died. I must have been eight or nine at the time. My mother had a terrible time after he died, not because of anything like what happened in the book, but because of some incredibly melodramatic events connected with two embezzlements, and because first of all my sister Winifred and then I myself had slight T. B. I never lived with my two sisters on the terms described in the book because they were much too old—Lettie is eight years older than I am and as she started a five year course when she was sixteen (times have changed) she took her degree when I was thirteen, and we were never under the same roof again except for a fortnight or so a year for five years. Winnie was first at Cheltenham College all term time and then she went to various places after she got ill, and spent a year in France. I never had a brother, and we weren't musicians, and Cordelia is a very close portrait of a little girl who did want to be a violinist, so you may see that the story is not true. My mother was as good as I paint her, in far more difficult circumstances, but that is all the literal truth in the book.

We have had such a dose of London. Yesterday we went up and shopped, intending to lunch with Viva and Willie King, who have both been very ill, and ⟨come⟩ {start} home about four. We noted some fog before we started {quite early}, and telephoned the A. A., which told us that it would be all right if we went to London by Slough instead of Denham . . . [West's ellipsis] It was fog all the way, visibility about twenty yards, we got there just in time for lunch, and couldn't get back. Ruth Lowinsky very kindly put us up as everything was full of Christmas shoppers, and we came back this afternoon, crawling through slightly worse fog, and almost as soon as we got in we had a failure of electric light which lasted an hour.

I hope you have a lovely Christmas, and I am sorry to worry you about the book, but I don't want Mouse to feel that she comes of a family which behaves too oddly.

> Blessings on you all,
> Rac

Rebecca West Collection   typescript with autograph insertions and
University of Tulsa   signature

¹ *The Fountain Overflows.*

To: Gordon N. Ray¹   11 February 1958
Dear Professor Ray,

I have been uneasily aware that you must be thinking me very rude for my failure to thank you for the volume of H. G.'s juvenile work—and now you send me a second book to make it clear how long I have delayed. My excuse is that I have been ill since I saw you, almost continuously, with an obscure vascular ailment which makes it hard for me to keep abreast of my work and my correspondence.

The James-Wells book is most interesting,² and I admire the selection almost as much as the introduction. But there are one or two comments I would like to make. Has not the dispute between Wells and James some relevance to Trotsky's *Literature and Revolution*?³ It seems to me that the key to many things in Wells's life is that there was being played out in England a curious muted version of the great Continental drama which was to have its most spectacular performance in Russia. The dispute between Wells and the Webbs was in little a dispute between Menshevism and Bolshevism;[4] and I think the dispute between Wells and James was in little the dispute between the Right and the Left view of literature. I cannot see Wells' view of James as entirely due to his temperament when I think how, when I sat on the Femina–Vie Heureuse Committee (which was a Franco-British affair, the French committee giving an annual prize to an English novel which then got translated, the English committee doing the same thing for a French novel) the debate between the members usually resulting in a split into two parties—one holding the Jamesian view, the other the Wellsian view. But by this time the people who held the Wellsian view were anti-Wells, for they were Communists or fellow-travellers, and therefore hostile to him as a Social Democrat; so his influence could not account for their views.

There is a reference to me on page 39 which I wish you had asked me about. I have already discussed this letter with Mr Rupert Hart-Davies,[5] who showed it to me when he was writing his life of Walpole,[6] and I made it plain to him that I knew nothing of this letter nor of the circumstances which are described in it. I was the object of attack at that time which had nothing to do with my literary merits or demerits, from several quarters; and there were two attacks made on the book (to which I don't attach too much importance, though I think it a fair work for a writer of twenty-two) which I resented, because the writers made clear to me by private intimation that they were written in order to register the writers' disapproval of me. Neither of these was Mr Percy Lubbock,[7] and neither of their reviews appeared in the *Times Literary Supplement*. As it happens, I can be quite sure that I had no grievance against that journal, for I remember Bertram Christian who published the book, telling me that it was very probable that the *Times Lit Supp* did not review the book, as it was one of a low-priced series and might well not be sent out for that reason. Even if I had had such a grievance, I would have been most unlikely to express it in these terms, for I am fairly sure that I never heard Percy Lubbock's name for years after. I was one of the *Daily News* group, who had very little to do with the *Times Lit Sup;* we were led by the Lynds, and considered ourselves much more advanced and interesting. I may say that my blood froze in my veins when I read the letter at the time that Rupert Hart-Davies gave it to me, for it was bound to do me harm; and this sentence must, I think, have accounted for some difficulties I had later.

I hope you will not think me tiresome and demanding, if I tell you that I would think it most kind if you would, when you find a reference to me in the Wells papers, ask ⟨x⟩ me about it. H. G. had all manner of wonderful characteristics, which I realise more and more. But he was completely irresponsible. He was always involving me in fantastic imbroglio of which I knew nothing—once, in 1923, he managed to get me into a most disagreeable situation with, of all things, a member of the Nobel Prize Committee, because I told him something that this man had said to me at a dinner-party, and he gave a garbled account of it to John Middleton Murry for publication in his magazine!

While I am deeply grateful to H. G. for the affection he gave me (and the concern he shows in this letter) it is also the fact that he made my life a burden to me with the irresponsible stories he told about me, before and after I left him. I have not the least desire to point this out; it seems to me a matter on which it would be unpleasant to expatiate. But I would have welcomed it if the letter had been quoted with the explanation that I had not known of it when it was written and would not support any allegation that Percy Lubbock and the *Times Lit Sup* had treated me in this way.

My life is something of a nightmare, with these nonsensical stories lingering on after H. G. has gone, and others—worse than nonsensical, alas—now coming from my unhappy son.

I hope your work is going on in a way that satisfies you, and that we may have the pleasure of seeing you down here again.

Yours sincerely,

Rebecca West Collection   carbon typescript
University of Tulsa

[1] There are several overlapping and fragmentary carbon copies of letters to Ray, in which West reacts to a draft of the book. In one fragment, she attempts to correct his impression that she and Wells were "two quarrelsome people holding together by sexual attraction," by asserting instead that they were "much more compatible than incompatible." She claims that Wells had an "extraordinary habit of relieving tension by writing a frantic letter of abuse to someone, either to me or a publisher," such that a collection of only his letters gives a misleading impression.

[2] *Henry James and H. G. Wells: A Record of Their Friendship, and Their Debate on the Art of Fiction and Their Quarrel*, ed. and intro. Leon Edel and Gordon N. Ray (1958).

[3] Leon Trotsky (1879–1940), Russian communist leader who played a role as a theorist in the 1905 and 1917 revolutions. He lost in a power struggle with Stalin and was expelled from

Russia in 1929. Stalin sanctioned his assassination in Mexico City. Trotsky wrote an account of Wells's 1924 meeting with Lenin.

⁴Sidney James Webb (1858–1947) and Beatrice Webb (1858–1943), British socialists influential in the Labour Party. The Mensheviks sought to establish a party of the masses (which corresponds to Wells); they were defeated by Lenin's Bolsheviks, who favored a revolutionary elite (which corresponds to the Webbs).

⁵Rupert Hart-Davis (1907–), English publisher, editor, and biographer. His editions include the correspondence between Wilde and Max Beerbohm and the letters of Siegfried Sassoon.

⁶Edel and Ray quote from a 1916 letter from Wells to Hugh Walpole. In defending his parody of James in the novel *Boon,* Wells says: "Anyhow nothing I've ever written or said or anyone has ever written or said about James can balance the extravagant dirtiness of [Percy] Lubbock and his friends in boycotting Rebecca West's book on him in the *Times Literary Supplement.* My blood still boils at the thought of those pretentious academic greasers conspiring to down a friendless girl (who can write any of them out of sight) in the name of loyalty to literature" (39).

⁷Percy Lubbock (1879–1965), American critic, biographer, and editor of the letters of Henry James, best known for *The Craft of Fiction* (1921), an early example of New Criticism.

To: Raymond Mortimer   16 July 1958

My dear Raymond,

Thank you so much for your letter, which is the first intimation that I have received that the book is anywhere near publication.¹ But you done me wrong. I didn't mean ["] to take firmly if not explicitly a Calvinist position," I simply describe the Calvinism of others.² There is nothing about myself in the book, and if I ever wrote a sentence suggesting that I adhered to the beliefs of any of the writers I described it was through sheer inadvertence and incompetence. If I had chosen a spiritual teacher from among those writers it would have been Fielding, whom I so much prefer!

I hope you take into account the sub-title of the book, and the quotation from Blake on the last page, which I hoped made it clear that I am simply tracing in the works of the great the influence of the religious and political ideas of their time, and that I do not think that this influence ever completely accounts for their works, if it did they would not be works of art. (What a quotation that is from Blake, by the way!)³

I feel full of contrition when you tell me that I do not make enough allowance for the slowness of other people's wits, for your wits are as swift as a jet-plane, and if you find any difficulty with the book it must be because I am incoherent. But naturally I can't see where I am that.

Original sin seems to me a useful conception, to warn one that neither oneself nor other people have been brought into our place in the universe by a process which promotes kindness, unselfishness, or good sense, and that we therefore should always watch ourselves like detectives. But I wouldn't let it put on airs, and I have known one or two people who seemed to me to need no such detectives. The sombreness of the doctrine I think comes from a period when observers of the human character (and I suppose the Christian Fathers were that above all) put on the same portentous manner that scientists assume today.

The oddest confusion led to the statement that Conrad had gone with his parents to France. He once said to me something about being with his parents in France, and when I wrote that sentence I remembered this and thought, surely not, but checked in a reputable encyclopaedia, which said that he had gone to France with his parents. But of course he had been translating *parents* as parents, and the encyclopaedia was just plain wrong. About, Madame Ranevsky,[4] oh, shame. . . .

What horrible reviews this book will get.

Rebecca West Papers   carbon typescript
Yale University

---

[1] *The Court and the Castle.*

[2] In a second letter West elaborated: "I have a feeling that you think I am doing propaganda for something. In that you are behaving like a Victorian Bishop denouncing Darwin and Huxley for their evolutionary theories. I am simply describing how the political and religious ideas of various periods managed to engage the great writers of those periods, as the Victorian scientists tried to describe the phases in the evolution of various species. I am not myself 'engaged' in the medieval conception of monarchy, or in Calvinism, or in Pelagianism, or in the Proustian complex, or in the horrid Kafkan predicament, I am describing the engagement of others—and you really cannot deny that they were engaged."

[3] "If Homer's merit was only in these Historical combinations and rival sentiment he would be no better than Clarissa."

[4] Madame Ranevsky, also known as Alla Nazimova (1879–1945), Russian-born actress. Acclaimed on the New York stage for her performances of Ibsen, she went on to Hollywood (1915–1925) to star in numerous films. She assumed the name Madame Ranevsky when she returned to the stage in 1928.

To: Alison Selford   18 August 1958

My dear Alison,

I have heard from the *New Yorker,* and my particular editor (they have them in droves) says that while he likes a number of details in your stories they do not fit into the *New Yorker,* and he feels sure that you naturally belong to the big circulation magazines. This is not passing the buck, and there is nothing derogatory in the opinion. The *New Yorker* has certain special requirements which you evidently don't fulfill—and I am sure I only fulfill some of them and don't fulfill others—so as I have not read your stories I am rather in the dark as to how you stand. But from the way he writes the fault is not that you can't write, only that you can't write what the editorial policy demands. The big circulation magazines publish practically anything which can hold a reader's attention comfortably and has no violent shock in it—and I mean violent. Isak Dinesen[1] gets all her stories published in the *Ladies Home Journal,* and for serials they use Rumer Godden[2] and J. P. Marquand[3] and me. You come into the world padded with a few pages on fashion and one or two love-stories, otherwise there is a fair way for one's genius.

I am writing to the *Ladies Home Journal,* saying that Marion Saunders may be sending them something, and writing also to M. S.[4] I don't know if I said anything to you about our friendship with Pamela Sherek, who reads plays for her husband Henry Sherek.[5] We have known her casually for some time, but during the last few months we have seen more of her, as she was a great friend of my best friend, Ruth Lowinsky, who died in January. If you have anything you want to have produced and you think would be any good for the commercial theatre I would like very much to show it to [her], but I would like to see it first, as I know her taste, and the less you waste people's time with unsuitable material the more they are apt to snap up what is suitable. Also if you have anything that might make a film script, we have a friend here (Lenore Coffee) who is highly ⟨experienced⟩ {successful} in Hollywood and will be here for a few more weeks—she is a very fine technician and could really be trusted.

What a summer. I hope you had some decent weather.

Yours ever,

Rebecca West Collection   carbon typescript
University of Tulsa

[1] Isak Dinesen (pseudonym of Karen Blixen, 1885–1962), Danish author of stories, memoirs, and plays, she was manager of a coffee plantation in present-day Kenya (1914–1931), an experience that contributed to her best-known work, *Out of Africa* (1937). *Last Tales* (1957) contained the notable feminist allegory "The Blank Page."

[2] Rumer Godden (1907–1998), English novelist and biographer. She was reared in India, which provides the setting of many of her works, and wrote for and about children. Her works include *Black Narcissus* (1939), *Breakfast with the Nikolides* (1942), and *The Greengage Summer* (1958).

[3] J. P. (John Phillips) Marquand (1893–1960), American novelist best known for satirical works on New Englanders, including *The Late George Apley* (1937) and *Wickford Point* (1939). He also wrote a series of stories featuring the Japanese detective Mr. Moto.

[4] Marion Saunders, Alison Selford's agent in the United States.

[5] Henry Sherek (1900–), English theatrical producer and director, the author of *Not in Front of the Children* (1959).

To: Richard Ellmann[1]

Ibstone House
Ibstone
Nr. High Wycombe
Bucks
7 November 1958

Dear Mr Ellman,

I was literary editor of the *Egoist* for a very short time, and I resigned because of a disagreement with Dora Marsden, into which there is no point ⟨to go⟩ {in explaining} now. It is sufficient to say that I thought she showed a lack of prudence rather hard on our other writers, by the encouragement she had given to someone of whom I felt considerable doubts. Dora Marsden was, as you must know, a science graduate and a follower of Mrs Pankhurst in the Suffrage Movement. She was beautiful and charming in a fragile way, and it is a great horror to me that later she became insane, and spent many years in a lunatic asylum. She for many years failed to respond to any visitor and spent in time in doing exquisite needlework. I think I heard that she had died in the asylum; and indeed this is probable, for she would now be in her late seventies. Please check up on all this if you wish to publish it, for I have no written evidence to substantiate what I am telling you.

I certainly recommended Joyce's *Portrait of the Artist as a Young Man* to H. G. Wells—someone else had sent it to him, but he had not read it till I drew his attention to it. But I must own that this does not seem to me of the greatest importance—he probably would have read it anyway.

I had no association with Joyce at all. I had left the *Egoist* just as he was coming into that journal, and I remember only one conversation with Dora Marsden on the subject. I have an idea that the major part of the spadework regarding his publication in the *Egoist* was done by a man who is now in Ireland—I am seeing a friend of his and will ask him about it, next week. Some time afterwards—indeed in the early twenties I wrote an essay on Joyce in a book called *The Strange Necessity* in which I copied the form, killed stone dead since by T. S. Eliot, of criticism in a personal and almost fictional framework, such as Remy de Gourmont² and several other French writers had used. I tried to show the power of James Joyce breaking into a mind unprepared for it. This was taken *au pied de la lettre,* and brought many attacks on me {from the *aficionados*—many others were drawn by the essay to read Joyce.}—the more so because of a most unfortunate incident. A friend of mine who taught at Columbia sent me a letter from a student raising certain points regarding my essay on Joyce, and I answered it in an article [in] the *Herald-Tribune.* Unfortunately these points were all taken from an article by Carlos Williams³ in a volume of *Transition* devoted to Joyce, which I had not then seen and did not see for some time. Carlos Williams was very angry indeed because I had not mentioned him. In the early thirties he wrote about this very bitterly, and I answered him, explaining the situation, in Orage's *New Age.* But I don't think he ever believed that I had not meant to be offensive, though as I had not the slightest reason for wishing to offend him I was completely innocent.

Joyce's resentment of the essay was extreme, and as you know he made a long attack on me in *Finnegan's Wake* [*sic*]. The literary aspects of this business were complicated by the extraordinary story which I related to Mrs Hutchins, concerning a meeting between him and myself and the publisher George Doran, which certainly never took place.⁴ The result of this fantastic myth was that when I heard that Joyce was offended by my essay I did not dare to do anything that would have made him understand what I felt about him. This was certainly reverence (so far as his prose works were concerned) although I neither think that *Ulysses* is the only book in the world or believe that the hope for literature lies in the adoption of its form. (He is perhaps the one genius who invented a form and exhausted its possibilities at the same time). It is simply a work of genius, and that surely is enough. But I am writing too quickly to give you what I feel about James Joyce, and indeed that is not what you have asked me.

I would be obliged if you would let me see anything that you write concerning me before you publish it. You would not be surprised by this request if you saw some of the fantastic statements. Recently I had an extremely pleasant visit from a young man who appeared to be thoroughly aware of what he wanted from me but who afterwards sent me proofs that showed that he had confused me biographically with Vita Sackville-West and had been betrayed by a mistake in a foreign review into a belief that I was an enthusiastic admirer of the writer whom I consider the most objectionable of philistines. I do not take myself very seriously, and I really do not mind emotionally very much what is said about me, but I like to get the record straight.

Yours sincerely,
Rebecca West

Rebecca West Collection   typescript
University of Tulsa

[1] Richard Ellmann (1918–1987), American critic and scholar who became Goldsmiths Professor of English at Oxford (1970). He is best known for his biography, *James Joyce* (1959), which uses West's information. He also wrote studies of W. B. Yeats and a biography of Oscar Wilde.

[2] Rémy de Gourmont (1858–1915), French poet and journalist associated with the *Mercure de France*. He helped establish the Symbolist movement and was championed by Ezra Pound.

[3] William Carlos Williams (1883–1963), American poet and physician best known for his five-volume epic *Paterson* (1946–1958). Though influenced by Imagism, he broke with both Pound and Eliot to write more about ordinary experience. "A Point for American Criticism," his humorless rebuttal to West's *Strange Necessity,* was originally published in *transition.*

[4] Patricia Hutchins, author of *James Joyce's World* (1967). For West's description of Doran, see her letter to Winifred Macleod, 2 November 1923.

To: Norman Macleod   Ibstone House
                                                      Ibstone
                                                      Nr. High Wycombe
                                                      Bucks
                                                      25 November 1958

My dear Norman,

We are having the rum-punch party on Sunday the 28th, and will be very pleased to give you a bed. Kitty and the grandchildren will be here, and I will be interested to hear what you think of the boy, who seems to me to have come on a lot.

I haven't been to see your mother [Winifred Macleod] for some time, deliberately, because my doctor suggested that I should not do so. On his observation of her some years ago he thought that if I did not put myself out for her she would improve. I am very much of the opinion that her symptoms of senility are feigned, and the real disease is the feigning and some other ⟨x⟩ symptoms not so apparent. I don't know what she is eating, so I don't know what that has to do with her recent emaciation.[1]

There is another point I would like to write to you about, which is very difficult to tackle. I don't think that you, or anybody else in your family, quite understands the relationship between Lettie and myself. It is a very difficult relationship. Lettie was an extraordinary child, and it would be odd if I had a normal affection to her for she was so extremely unkind to your mother and myself when we were children. She cultivated a fantasy by which she was the good and beautiful little girl with two ugly and wicked sisters (Winnie was actually a most beautiful child, I think the most beautiful child I have ever seen). My blood curdled once when I was about six, when some visitors who had come to see my mother and had been received by her came out into the garden and stumbled on me—Lettie's face was as stricken as if she had had to own a repulsive idiot as her sister. When she was thirteen or fourteen she led Winnie and myself a most miserable life because she was always telling our mother of our misbehaviour at school, and our teachers of our misbehaviour at home. Your mother was an extremely good little girl and so far as she was concerned the stories were sheer imagination. The trouble about Lettie was that she hated my father and was afraid of him and had a sense of degradation about him {and her family}[2] which was largely fostered by a horrible woman named Aunt Sophie,[3] whom she adored; who was a drug-addict and a terrible liar.

When Lettie elected to become a doctor, which meant five years training in those days, it naturally involved great financial sacrifices for your mother and me, which we made quite placidly, because your grandmother was a woman of generous spirit and made us feel it quite natural that ⟨x⟩ we should do this. The situation became very hard to take when Lettie qualified, for she emerged with a fantasy that she had become a doctor in order to lift us from poverty, and a fear that neither your mother nor I would earn our living and that she would have to keep us. This was very disagreeable. My sister Winnie and I had a terrible experience when a woman called Christine Murrell, a middle-aged doctor, came down to our house in Hampstead Garden suburb and bullied us for being dependent on our eldest sister and told us we must learn to fend for ourselves. In point of fact my mother was by then better-off, neither Winnie nor myself derived any financial benefit from Lettie's being a doctor, both of us earned money from an early age—by nineteen I was making quite a good little income—and we were contributing to the upkeep of the home quite as generously as Lettie.

Your mother completely repressed her feelings over this and turned her resentment into hysterical manifestations of illness. I did not repress them, but I was utterly miserable. The situation became impossible when my mother got worse as a result of her Graves' Disease,[4] and became ill-tempered and irritable, which was exploited by Lettie. I cannot tell you what a hell my life was at home or how dreadful it was to go out to a party with Lettie—I simply had to leave home or I would have gone mad.

I am quite sure Lettie is quite unconscious of the part she has played. I know that she is extremely generous—she has, I understand, been very generous to your family, and she was very generous to Kitty and Anthony, giving them a hundred pounds at ⟨x⟩ the birth of each of the babies. But to me she has always been a heavy burden which I have had to carry through life. She is, and I wish you would try to believe me, to me someone who has constantly indulged in inconsiderate and irresponsible behaviour which I have had to cope with. I don't think there has been a year of my life when she has not provoked some crisis. Her present financial crisis worries me more than any other before—but she has always been in a mess about money. My mother died in 1920, and she was terribly worried about Lettie's inability to make ends meet on what was a very respectable income for a young girl. In 1922 Lettie borrowed a substantial sum from me, and I cannot for the life of me imagine why that was necessary. She has always talked indiscreetly, intervened in my private affairs without consulting me, gone to see my lawyer and my doctors and my friends and my employees without telling me to talk about my affairs behind my back, and has never, never done anything to help me in any difficulty. She was nice to me when Anthony was born, and that was the only occasion. Otherwise it has always been I who have had to cope with extraordinary situations, which she has provoked, and which have never caused her the smallest compunction. Lettie has never said to me, "I am sorry I did that," in her life.

Let me just tell you what I mean. She has always insisted on managing the Irish property. When I married in 1930 I had great reason to want all the money I could lay my hands on, and I with great difficulty extracted a list of our holdings in Dublin real estate from Lettie and sent them to Charles Russell. His opinion was that the list made no sense and that a surveyor ought to be sent over to vet the property and see why the properties were let at such fantastic rentals. (Thirty pounds a year for a large warehouse in a commercial part of the town). Lettie went into hysterics at the proposal. Your mother was apathetic, your father said that Lettie must know best. I was extremely disturbed over it—particularly as Lettie told me that she had spent two hundred and fifty pounds ⟨x⟩ on paying off a mortgage. This was the maddest {also extremely generous} thing to do, so long as there was a mortgage, the rate of interest of which was quite reasonable, the solicitors had to deal honestly with the property. I knew Lettie did not understand the situation at all. But I could hardly insist in the face of your parents' attitude. Then Lettie sold the solicitors the property piece-meal, then some years later your mother went to Dublin, and saw that the property had in fact been valuable. (I should think we sold it for a third to a quarter of the value.) When I spoke to Lettie about this, she then owned to me she had been anxious to get rid of it because the property was on her conscience. She believed that our grandfather, Major Charles George Fairfield, had embezzled the houses, so to speak, while he was acting as land agent for Lord Pembroke after he left the Coldstream Guards. Now (a) our grandfather was a perfectly respectable person, there is nothing known against him, and (b) the property, as I ascertained, never belonged to Lord Pembroke and (c) we owned the property legally, as the Statute of Limitations applies to land, and (d) to allow the solicitors to buy it at a fraction of the value did nothing to set the moral problem right, had there been one, as the rightful owners would hardly have benefited. But it had apparently tortured her that we had this land. Five minutes looking at the title-deeds would have ⟨comforted⟩ {revised} her scruples.

I cannot tell you how much trouble she has been to me, and how often she has done things of which I cannot approve. It is not only I who have complained of this. For example, she insisted during the war that she had left some clothes here; she insisted on my turning the house upside down twice over, she wrote and telephoned abusively, she paid a dreadful visit here when she raved at us. It turned out that she had left them at your mother's house at Hampstead Garden Suburb when your parents went to Bath. I then met Mrs Strachey and found she had done the same thing to her. She never apologised to Mrs Strachey or to myself. I find it embarrassing and humiliating that, after she had made that tremendous fuss about not having been left Maimie Mackenzie's money, she met Ian Barclay's mother Jessie here,[5] and in front of Ian's wife, said that she wished to be given Maimie's most valuable piece of jewellery, which she described. Jessie with great good humour said that she could have it if she liked but Maimie had given it to her as a Christmas present years before and it was in the North of England. Lettie said, "That will be all right then, please send it to me."

I know she is a different person to you. But that is the person she is to me. I don't take it well. I know that. I can't reconcile myself to being treated as an inferior scatterbrain by someone with whose crazy behaviour I have been coping all my life, without a word of thanks, or of regret. I wish you would realise that I have to act with that picture of Lettie in mind. I think you thought it very unnecessary of me once to take you to see Charles Russell (Richard Butler really) about an unfortunate incident in the family. I did it because I knew that if Lettie came to hear of this incident there would have been hell to pay, she would have rushed off and done something, and I wanted to be able to tell her that Charles Russell knew all about it and would be able to ⟨xx⟩ talk to her about it. But it is a little hard for me to be ⟨x⟩ aware that people think of me as having a wild prejudice against a kind and sensible person when actually I have at least not abandoned someone whom I think many people would not have remained on friendly terms with at all.

Tear this letter up as there is no use keeping this dismal record. But it is a little difficult for me to carry on with life when there are so many misunderstandings about of one kind or another—I mean this in general terms, I don't mean that you misunderstand, I mean that I have had rather a great deal to do with my life which has not appeared on the surface. Please believe that I understand that you may have the strongest possible reasons for feeling affection for Lettie and that she may have proved herself kindly and sensible towards you. But to me it has always been a relationship which has ⟨not⟩ been painful, although I see that the reason is pathetic enough, it springs from our unhappy childhood; and I think that possibly Lettie took it worse than your mother or myself because she was older and understood more, and had this very unpleasant woman Aunt Sophie ready to exploit her sensitiveness.

Blessings on you

R.-C.

private collection   manuscript

[1] Norman Macleod feels that West had "found it uncomfortable and unsettling over a period of many years either to visit . . . or to entertain" her sister Winnie, who "cared not at all for—and was indeed profoundly scornful of—the trappings of high life" (letter to Bonnie Scott, 30 July 1996). Winnie did not have a disabling disease at the time but encouraged her imagination to soar through enforced immobility, according to her son.

[2] Norman Macleod finds this hatred of the father hard to believe, noting that only Lettie "maintained some kind of continuous touch with that unfortunate after his return from the disaster of Sierra Leone" (letter to the editor, 30 July 1996).

[3] Sophia Blew Jones, who married West's uncle Arthur Fairfield. She was remembered more positively by her grandson, David Ogilvy. See family tree.

[4] A hyperthyroid condition that proved fatal to West's mother.

[5] See Isabella Fairfield's generation on the family tree. Mamie, who died in 1955, was the daughter of Isabella's brother Alexander Mackenzie. Jessie that West speaks of here was the daughter of Isabella's sister (also called Jessie).

To: Mark van Doren[1]   30 December 1958

Dear Professor van Doren,

I am wondering if you will think me an intrusive person if I take advantage of your nice letter to ask you for some help.

I have a friend in Washington called Milan Gavrilovic[2] who was a pre-war Socialist in Yugoslavia. He was leader of the Serb Peasant Party but he was not a communist and would not go along with Tito. This is not that he was narrow-minded in any way. He had worked hard for a rapprochement with Russia and fought all the old reactionary gang.

He is now 76 and has two married daughters in Washington. There remain of his family over here his wife, who is devoted to him, and her daughter, whose marriage was broken up, and her daughter's little child. The wife very much wants to spend her last years with her husband and the situation is getting urgent in view of the father's age. But Mrs. Gavrilovic does not want to leave her little granddaughter here and the granddaughter cannot be separated from her mother. This is a standard refugee tragedy and it is always poignant.

I was wondering if you could tell me how I could get the daughter [Kosa] a job in America. She is a graduate of Newnham who got good second class Honours in French and Russian. She has been teaching for seven years in a Government College which instructed members of the Armed Forces in Russian but this College has now been closed down. Since then she has been teaching in a very good girls' boarding-school, Cranbourne Chase, Crichel, which is quite famous over here and is the place where all the intellectuals who can afford it send their girls. She is an attractive and well-read woman of 35 and all her references are extremely good; but she does not know how to get a job in America of the right sort and as Milan Gavrilovic is so old her need to get such a job quickly is urgent.

Could you possibly advise me how best she could get into touch with people who would be likely to want such a teacher? Her general education is extremely good and she is very energetic.

I would be most grateful if you could just scribble me a card either with some names and addresses of schools and colleges on it or with any other suggestions you may have, if so be as this is not an impossible request.[3]

With all good wishes for 1959,

Yours sincerely,

Rebecca West Collection   carbon typescript
University of Tulsa

[1] Mark Van Doren (1894–1972), American poet, critic, biographer, and novelist who taught at Columbia University (1911–1930). He wrote on Dryden, Shakespeare, Thoreau, Hawthorne, and Lincoln and was influenced as a poet by Wordsworth. Carl Van Doren was his brother and Irita his sister-in-law.

[2] West wrote many letters to and on behalf of this family. A letter to Norris B. Chipman of the U.S. Foreign Service (3 October 1954, Yale University) attempting to get Milan Gavrilovitch a visa for Ireland, gives more details of the family members' separate flight from Yugoslavia following the German invasion in World War II. Gavrilovitch had been an ambassador in Moscow and was the minister of justice for the exiled Yugoslav government in London.

[3] Both Mark Van Doren and his wife responded with suggestions for Kosa's employment. Milan Gavrilovitch died in 1976, and at the family's request, West supplied the following epitaph for his gravestone: "Milan Gavrilovitch was one of the wise men of modern Europe,

and his wisdom was rejected; and what that rejection has cost us can be seen in our present miseries. But he himself kept all the virtues the rest of the world has cast away, and in possession of that treasure he was rich in exile. All those with whom he shared his spiritual and intellectual riches will never cease to feel love and gratitude. He was the very image of the day we threw away when we decided to stay in the night" (Rebecca West Collection, University of Tulsa).

To: Victor Wolfson[1]

Ibstone House
Ibstone
Nr. High Wycombe
Bucks
9 January 1959

My dear Victor,

Thank you so much for your letter! I am pained by letters from America which seem to think this is a medieval title.[2] It ain't. It is true that I am now entitled to be addressed as "My Lady" but as nobody knows this—I didn't—and I am unlikely to tell me [*sic*] this will be a sweet secret between me and the College of Heralds. But Dameship or Damehood or Damewhatever is a post-Pankhurst order, a mark of the response of the State to the feminist movement—it was invented as the first means of enabling a woman to get a title for her own achievements instead of getting a title that her husband had got for his achievements! And for me it is a dizzy Trade Union affair since I am as *Time* truly said a novelist-newshen, and this is [the] first top honour that a newshen has got.

Thank[s] again for your letter, and get Emanie [Arling] to take not a sip but a snootful of that champagne. Teach her to capitulate to the appetites of the flesh in every way she can!

Yours ever,
Rebecca

Wolfson Collection
Boston University

typescript with autograph signature

[1] Victor Wolfson (1910–1990), American dramatist, novelist, and biographer who wrote for the *New Yorker*. His works include *Excursion* (1937), *Bitter Stream* (1944), *My Prince! My King!* (1962), *The Mayerling Murder* (1969), and a biography of Truman.

[2] West was named Dame Commander of the Order of the British Empire in November 1958.

To: Arthur Schlesinger, Jr.

Private and Confidential

Ibstone House
Ibstone
Nr. High Wycombe
Bucks
20 January 1959

Dear Professor Schlesinger,

It was a great pleasure to have you both at our house, and we have been talking about you most of the time since.[1] I am selfishly glad we had nobody else here, because we were able to have you to ourselves.

I am wondering whether you will think me tiresome if I tell you why I felt some anxiety when I heard that you were mentioning my impression of Huey Long in your third volume.[2] I think I had better tell you the circumstances which make me feel anxious.

My contact with Huey Long was more interesting than must have appeared from my article on him (which appeared in *Time and Tide,* I think). A friend who wanted to see Huey Long took me to have an interview with him, and he graciously spared us a few moments from his legislative duties— and we were more impressed than we had thought we would be. We were both surprised by his vitality and his liveliness, which was combined with— though I did not care to say this in print—extreme physical repulsiveness. I don't think I have ever seen anybody who seemed to consist of sheer pulp under his clothes except this one man. In his vitality and his repulsiveness he was very like Laval.

Some days afterwards a Washington journalist, now dead, indeed he died shortly afterwards, whose name I cannot remember, came to see me and told me that Huey Long wanted to see me, and that he advised me to keep the appointment he offered me, as he himself thought it would be interesting. He told me not to tell anybody I was going to see Huey Long, and I have often wondered why, as the whole interview turned out to be very odd—or rather both the interviews.

I came down specially from New York to keep this appointment and went to an apartment house where Huey Long was staying, quite late at night, in company with the Washington journalist (whom I knew quite well). Huey Long was looking horrible in a sort of loose suit that might have been pyjamas except that he was wearing a sort of sweatshirt underneath which projected round his gross neck in a very unpleasing way. I had a strong feeling that he was not physically clean, and yet that he was healthy.

The substance of our conversation was really astonishing. He said to me, in effect: "I have been making enquiries about you. I learn that you recently had an operation for an unusual malady which has not been performed until comparatively recently, and that you went to a doctor who has often performed this operation since it was developed. The wife of a secretary of mine is in need of this operation. I would like to make arrangements for her to undergo the same operation, and I would also like you to arrange for this doctor to come and teach at the Medical school at Baton Rouge."

Now, the first odd thing was that I have no idea how he knew I had had this operation, which was not one I had talked about. It was a breast operation, which I had had performed because I was suffering from a condition which caused intolerable pain, and some doctors thought that this condition was so ⟨generally⟩ {often} found in patients suffering from cancer of the breast that the removal of the affected tissue was desirable. This was not the sort of thing one converses about lightly at Washington dinner-tables, and I don't think I had spoken of it to anybody except my two most intimate friends. It does seem possible that an American surgeon visiting England might in the course of his professional activities have heard of the operation and somebody may have told him confidentially that I had undergone it. If it got back to Huey Long, this shows how much attention he was giving to medical matters; and that {attention} astonished me quite apart from this.

I don't know whether he was starting a Medical School at Baton Rouge or reforming one. Anyway he wanted to have a first-rate one going there, and he had done a considerable amount of work on the idea. I have been told that after he died it was found that his work for the University had been bogus, but if that were so it must have been the result of administrative inefficiency, for the idea of reform was certainly in his mind. I do not mean that this was necessarily the result of idealism. To give you an idea of his mental climate, when I said to him "It's very nice of you to take such trouble over your secretary's ⟨x⟩ wife and to see that she has this operation," he replied quite clownishly that that wasn't what he really cared about, he didn't much like the woman, but he wanted to know about the operation and see if he could get the surgeon to come out to Baton Rouge.

I told him that I was sure the surgeon would not give [up] his position in London, which he found hard to believe, because he thought everybody in London and in England generally was poor and underpaid. In discussing the matter I told him that I knew something of the hospital system in London, as my sister [Letitia Fairfield] was one of the senior health officers under the L. C. C. [London County Council] and was a doctor and a lawyer. He then questioned me exhaustively about what I knew and I found that he had looked into the hospital system in London, and had grasped, for example, how the teaching hospitals fitted into the then system. I do not say that his grasp was very firm. He was handicapped by this native clownishness and a lack of general understanding, but he made lively enquiries—and it was manifest that somebody of a sort who usually would have had no interest in the idea of an efficient medical school or of efficient hospitals had great interest in these ideas. The thing was at once on a higher scale than one would suppose and on a lower. It was rather as if a pig suddenly looked at you out of its sty and asked if it could help in the Spastics Drive, and made some remark which showed that to some extent it *could* help in the Spastics Drive.

He was extremely anxious to be accepted. So anxious that I could not possibly have told him that the English surgeon would not be seen dead working for him—on humanitarian grounds I wouldn't have told him that, not because I was afraid of him. Though certainly I would have been afraid of him. His desire to be accepted and his humiliation at being rejected was shown, oddly enough, in a conversation we had about Jerome Frank.[3] He had either a book by Jerome or a printed judgment in his room and I told him that Jerome was a friend of mine. He said bitterly that though he admired Jerome he would never try to get in touch with him because Jerome would have nothing to do with him. It appeared to me possible that he would sooner or later accept the discipline of his Party, so intense was his ambition.

It sounds an impertinent thing to say about the South but I thought that for where he came from he was better than might have been expected. But what I mean, I suppose, is that he was better than might have been expected, considering what sort of a Southerner he was. I did not feel justified in being offhand with him, so I wrote to my surgeon a letter relaying the offer telling him that of course I knew he would not and could not accept it, and when I got the answer it contained a ⟨cover⟩ note which I was able to show Huey Long, whom I visited again, {who was extremely hurt and angry} in the company of my friend the Washington journalist. (I wish I could remember the name of this man, he was a close friend of Fleta Campbell Springer.) {This is a temporary amnesia. I could find out the name.} I don't know why he had this link with Huey Long, for he was very far Left.

I then wrote (I think briefly) about Huey Long, under the handicap that I could tell nothing of this curious interchange with him. I was also handicapped by the fact that I felt quite sure he would never get through any Convention and could not possibly have been made President, as many people, I think quite foolishly, imagined. I have not read what I ⟨have written, for⟩ {wrote} since ⟨much⟩ {many} of my records got lost in a hurried move in the war, for many years. It is possible that, as I took my own anti-Fascism for granted, that I may not have underlined the fact that dictators were never my cup of tea. But the whole business was revived for me in a very puzzling way three years ago.

My son then wrote a brook, *Heritage,* attacking us, for reasons which are obscure to my husband and myself, and indeed to most other people. John Gunther will, if it interests you in this connection—I can't think it would in any other—will tell you how bewildering the whole business has been. But the immediate point is that the actress, Naomi, who is supposed to be me, goes to America in the book and sees Huey Long and thought he was very handsome, or words to that effect. Now, I am sure my son never read anything I wrote about Huey Long, he was then quite uninterested in anything of that sort, and I am sure that he never heard me speak about Huey Long because I spoke of him very little to anybody when I returned from the States; nor, had I spoken about Huey Long, would I have described myself as feeling admiration for him, though I had felt interest—and certainly nobody could have described him as handsome.

Ever since I read that reference in my son's book I have felt extremely worried about my contact with Huey Long. I have wondered if someone had not put {by} the record of the facts that I met him three times and wrote of him, in order to injure me. I felt at the time an uneasy feeling that this might happen and it was for that reason I took a witness. But unfortunately my witness is dead.

You will now understand why I felt some alarm at hearing that you had mentioned my contact with Huey Long in your third volume. I did not want you to think I was repudiating anything that I had ever felt or done, and I was alarmed lest you had been guided to my *Time and Tide* article by the allusion in *Heritage*. So I felt I would like to make an explanation, and I regret that it is so long.

Do come and see us again some time.

> With all good wishes from us both,
>
> Rebecca West

private collection   typescript with autograph signature and insertions

[1] The tone of this letter is in stark contrast to her earliest correspondence with Schlesinger—see letter of 4 June 1953. West and the Schlesingers had become friends in the interval, and the couple had visited her for a long weekend at Ibstone in 1959.

[2] Huey Pierce Long (1893–1935), as governor of Louisiana (1928–1931), was head of a corrupt political machine and a presidential aspirant who proposed a "Share-the-Wealth" plan. His career was cut short by assassination. Schlesinger wrote of him in *The Politics of Upheaval* (1960), third in the series *The Age of Roosevelt;* in the book Schlesinger quoted from West's article "The Kaleidoscope that Is Washington," *New Republic* (12 May 1935).

[3] Jerome Frank (1889–1957) American judge, legal philosopher, and author of numerous legal studies, the most influential of them being *Law and the Modern Mind* (1930). He was special counsel to the Reconstruction Finance Corporation under Franklin Roosevelt.

To: Margaret Hutchinson

Ibstone House
Ibstone
Nr. High Wycombe
Bucks
14 February 1959

My dear Margaret,

I wish, I wish I could hear you sing. How wonderful that lesson sounds, with the right murderous ending. I was so enchanted by the version of yourself as "a middle-aged woman of uncertain health." That doesn't, dear one, quite cover the ground.

I will tell you about my two Buckingham Palace experiences. Did I tell you the funny Lady Bracknell thing I did?[1] The telephone rang about three weeks ago, and a voice said, "This is Buckingham Palace. Her Majesty the

Queen is giving a small luncheon-party on February 11, and would be glad if you could attend." At which the Dame said in a most Lady Bracknell voice, "Are you sure you mean February 11? THAT IS ASH WEDNESDAY." There was a slight stir at the end of the telephone and I was assured it was all right. But I received an amended invitation for the fifth, and when I got it I wrote and apologised and said I did not intend to keep up such a Bracknellike attitude. When I arrived there for the luncheon the Master of the household and the Lady in Waiting burst in happy laughter at the sight of me; and it appeared that the Master of the Household, having asked the other eight guests, then rang up a Bishop and said, "I've asked eight people to lunch with the Queen on Ash Wednesday, and I suppose it will be all right if the Queen goes to Church and then gives this luncheon party, but there's a new Dame, Dame Rebecca West who seems to think it won't do." The bishop said acidly, "Well, I do not know the lady, but you have cause to be grateful to her," which I think a glorious episcopal answer. We then went into the centre drawing-room of the Palace, which has four china cupboards with the most wonderful Sevres set of birds, now never used because they are getting scared of breakages, the cost of repairs in the Palace being so great. As the Master of the household said, "So far as rents in the upholstery are concerned, and moth, we can boast of being truly representative—we're keeping up with the Joneses." Actually it looks marvellously clean, particularly as there is no central heating in most of it (very difficult to put in) and they have open coal fires. I found to my horror that I was one of the YOUNGEST people present. There was Sir Harold Hartley, the president of the Society of the Advancement of Science, on crutches, telling everybody he had fallen off a horse, how he had ever got on seemed mysterious, Sir Edward Muir, head of the Ministry of Works, Sir Arthur Morse, head of the Holiday Association, and so on—the only persons younger than myself or out of the same age group being Terence Rattigan,[2] who is a pansy, and a most boring Australian journalist. Presently the Princess Margaret came in, very much prettier than she looks in evening dress; tiny; with uninteresting hair, but with a wonderful pale skin and violet eyes; beautifully dressed in a charcoal grey velveteen 〈dress〉 coat and skirt. Then the Queen came in; lovely, beyond belief, in this incredible way—because there is really not much reason why she should be, it's hard to pin down; tiny too, with tiny little feet and ankles; a skin beyond compare; an anthropologist who met her in Australia described her to me as "the most flawless person he had ever seen" and so she is; this clean, clean, fine-grained skin, a beautiful hair-line; a perfect neck, neither too long nor too short; a lovely light quick voice; and oh, so badly dressed. In something that is called, I think, saxe blue, [b]lack, with two inserts of pleated georgette, sort of plastrons on the bodice, and a panel of pleated georgette by the skirt, something one could buy in a dress-shop in the high street in High Wycombe—the work of a miscreant named Hartnell, probably, who can make evening dresses and nothing else. She spoke to the Australian journalist, after apologising for being late ("they didn't go," she said vaguely) and to me, and we spoke of her husband's tour,[3] it was apparent that she is deeply in love with him, her face glowed as she spoke of his success. It was obvious she finds it a little difficult to make conversation. ⟨Thus we went to⟩ I realised a terrible thing about her life. She asked the Australian journalist, who was being recalled from London to Australia after three years here, how he was going home. He told her, oh, he told her. He was going by air, his wife was going on a boat with the children, he would arrive on such and such a date, his wife would arrive on such a date, the boat she was going on was such and such a boat. The poor child spends her life asking questions *which people answer!* Then we went and had lunch. I sat between Sir Edward Muir and ⟨xx⟩ Lord Plunket, who is a bosom friend of my dear Ruth Lowinsky's daughter Clare and her husband—he is an A.D.C. [aide-de-camp]. Sitting round the table I realised the appalling amount of time that these two young girls must spend with much older people. We had an egg in a pastry case, roast beef (very good) and an Alaska, only white wine, not terribly good, a Moselle. There was no general conversation. After luncheon we went and stood in the drawing-room again, one stands all the time. The Queen spoke to me and the Australian journalist, it was heavy going I found myself breaking the law that she must choose the subject, "and now," I said, "there are two things I want to tell you." The first was how wonderful was the impression she had left in Paris, how they felt that they had arranged something wonderful and that she had come and made it more wonderful, and that an old Frenchman had said, "It was beautiful as a ballet and solemn as High Mass." I also told her how pleased people were with her for lending some of her best diamonds to the Diamond Exhibition at Christie's, that they did not like to stare at them when they met her, and it was lovely to look at them. (This Exhibition has been phenomenally successful, the queue was always a hundred yards long). She then told me that she had written a thoroughly nasty letter to the *Times* which had printed the photograph of a brooch ⟨x⟩ among her loans upside down, suggesting that they should take more care in future—and explained that she had a special feeling about diamonds because she went to Amsterdam and wore the brooch made out of {two} odd bits left over when the main gem was cut from the Cullinan Diamond, and had asked if anybody at Aschers, which she visited, remembered the cutting of them, and old Lucien Asher, 78 years old, came forward and burst into tears, because he said that he had been so frightened over the cutting of that gem when he had done it years before, and it was wonderful to see it again. I don't really remember what else we said, we chattered—oh, there was general conversation about the building of some new offices which overlook the Gardens of Buckingham Palace, they felt it a hardship, they see the line of white faces in the distance looking at them and the flash of opera-glasses, they daren't take a scamper with the dogs. Then Princess Margaret took me over to look at the family pictures on the other side of the room, there was an entrancing baby in a frilled gown, and she pointed out a part of the palace and told me that it was still not repaired from bomb damage. It was bombed several times in the war, and an entrance was destroyed. That has been replaced, but they have not yet got on to these repairs which are not visible from the outside and are in a part of the Palace not essential. She then said to me that she felt much more akin to people of any age who had been through the Blitz ⟨x⟩ than she did to people of her own age who had not been through the Blitz. I asked her how it had happened that she and her sister went through the ⟨x⟩ Blitz as so many people must have wished them to go to Canada, and she said that she had asked her Mamma that just the other day, and her Mamma had told her that it was a strange thing, she and the King had never thought of sending them away, people had suggested they should send their children away, but it had really never registered, they thought it so unsuitable—⟨it was⟩ she (the Queen Mother) now realised from written record that it had been put to them but had forgotten every occasion when it had. Princess Margaret said that she was deeply grateful for this. Then she suddenly said, "You don't think everything's awful now, do you? You don't think all the young people are going to pot, do you?" I said that I didn't, and told her about the young girl my nephew Bobtail is marrying, a working man's daughter, a virologist, pretty and gay and a gifted and hardworking girl, and she said, "Oh, that does sound splendid."[4] Then the Queen was summoned and had to go, and she went too.

On the day of St Scolastica [February 10] life seemed very strenuous indeed. Henry drove me to the Palace, after I had had my hair combed out at the hairdresser's, and he went to the Relatives' section, where he was joined by my grandson [Edmund West], who was allowed twenty-four hours off from school, while I went down to the cloakroom and left my coat—a cloakroom the size of Ibstone House, with perfect old-fashioned parlour-maids. Then I went up and found myself in a round room, with all the Knights and the only other Dame, a very plain and charming woman named Ruth Buckley, who is a Local Government expert—a beautiful carpet, some nice pictures—the Knights all followed a pattern, there was a strong resemblance between them. One was Roy Harrod, the economist, who is one of Henry's oldest friends, one of the Forbes-Robertston family, who was a standby, we stood by each other, for one's knees knock. I had been through it when I got the C.B.E., but still it makes one nervous. Then we trailed through galleries and up a staircase (I forgot to say that Alec Guinness[5] sought me out very sweetly though I don't know him) and entered the room that runs parallel to the ball-room where the awards are made. At the entrance of the room is the celebrated Winterhalter[6] picture of Queen Victoria and the Prince Consort with a haze of children and dogs floating about them. We queued down the room, in front of us were a few people with terrific G.C.B.s[7] and things, we came before the Knights. The Grenadier guards in the music gallery of the ball-room were playing the Valse des Fees and *Carousel* and *My Fair Lady*. We were told to wait till we heard the name of the person in front of us called (that was for me Ruth Buckley) and then go forward {into the Ball Room} and halt beside a certain Admiral. This Admiral had obviously been chosen because you couldn't miss him. He was about 5′2″ and must have been 46 round the chest, and had a vast projecting jaw, once seen he couldn't be forgotten. When I got into the ballroom there was the Queen on the dais, so lovely, but oh, such a dress! It was bright emerald-green and cut without any sort of distinction, and far too short. I had to walk forward and face her, curtsey, take two steps forward, and then she leaned over and pinned my two pretties on me—a cross and a steel star, one of those queer dazzle things. As she did so she said in her pretty voice, very low, "We did so much enjoy seeing you the other day, and it's a great pleasure to give you this, you have done so much work." Bless her heart, so I have, but I doubt if she will ever know what it was. But it couldn't have been more prettily said. Then she shook hands. She has a curious beautiful very bright blue line of veins on the inside of her wrist. Then, horrors, as of course I was wearing high heels, I had to back and curtsey again. The rapidity of the thing was extraordinary. She puts out her hand for the orders and an underling with a cushion moves it so that the required order is under her fingers. She puts the orders into little steel holders that are pinned on one's coat before one goes in. It is so quickly done that (Henry calculated) she did three people in one minute, with no apparent air of haste. Then I walked out into an antechamber, and as quickly an underling took out my orders and put them in a box, and took out the holders—like a flash—and I was free to watch the others, from a seat in the ball-room. It was not as interesting as it had been when I got my C. B. E., because then old Lord Clarendon was Lord Chamberlain and he read all the orders in a voice like Henry Ainley's[8] and one heard every word, and the citations, particularly of the George Medal, were entrancingly interesting. This present man could not be heard at all. At the end of it all the Queen went out, having been doing it at top speed for one hour and ten minutes, and Henry and my grandson and I got together. I showed him the curious line of American pictures on the staircase (there are a number of Benjamin Wests[9] and Copleys[10] just there) and downstairs I showed him what I think one of the best of the nineteenth century pictures (very French in appearance, I mean French impressionist) Winterhalter's not too kind picture of Queen Victoria's mother.

Then we went and had lunch at the Caprice, with Charles Curran and my sister Letitia. Then my grandson who had been asked where he wanted to go chose to go to the Corbusier[11] exhibition. He was there profoundly disconcerted because they had a great many of Corbusier's pictures, and he knew they were bad, though he liked the Indian buildings. Then we came back and had tea and in the evening went to the triple bill at Sadler's Well—a terrible bit of hamming by Vaughan Williams *The Riders of the Sea*,[12] a bit of froth by Menotti[13] (but good froth) and then, oh glory, glory, glory, Bartok's[14] *Bluebeard's Castle*. Very well sung, well staged, and the orchestra was just a little too loud, which is saying a good deal for a Bartok composition, where the temptation is to bang. But what beauty of argument, if you know what I mean, did ever music keep so close to intellect, to the actual expression of intellect. . . .[15]

All my love to you both,

Rebecca

My nephew [Norman Macleod] (you know him and were kind to him) is engaged to this pretty girl (a plump *mousse* Renoir) who also had a Commonwealth Scholarship.

Rebecca West Collection Yale University

typescript with autograph signature, postscript, and note

[1] Comic, outspoken character in Oscar Wilde's *The Importance of Being Ernest*.

[2] Terence Rattigan (1911–1977), English playwright whose work includes *Separate Tables* (1954) and *Ross* (1960), which is based on the life of T. E. Lawrence.

[3] Prince Philip was on a world tour which took him to India, Pakistan, Hong Kong, and various Pacific territories.

[4] Marion Macleod, who married her nephew Norman.

[5] Alec Guinness (1914–), British actor of stage and screen whose varied roles include renditions of Shakespeare and Dickens. He received the Academy Award for Best Actor in *The Bridge on the River Kwai* (1957), and he was knighted in 1960.

[6] Franz Xaver Winterhalter (1805–1873), German painter and lithographer who specialized in portraits of royalty. Queen Victoria invited him to the British court in 1841.

[7] The highest order of knighthood, the Most Honourable Order of the Bath.

[8] Henry Ainley (1879–1945), English actor known for his roles in Shakespearean plays and for diction so fine that it was preserved by the BBC. .

[9] Benjamin West (1738–1820), American-born painter known for his influence on perception of historical subjects. He was an associate of Sir Joshua Reynolds and became influential in Britain, where he served in the court of George III (1772–1801). He was a founder of the Royal Academy (1768).

[10] John Singleton Copley (1758–1813), colonial American painter known for portraits of people surrounded by objects from their daily lives and for depictions of historical subjects. He left Boston during the American Revolution and settled in London in 1776.

[11] Charles Edouard Le Corbusier (1887–1965), Swiss-born French architect associated with functionalism. He designed the major buildings of the Punjabi city of Chandigarh.

[12] Ralph Vaughan Williams (1872–1958), English composer of symphonies, choral music, and state performances who looked to folk music for inspiration. *Riders to the Sea* (1937) is his setting of John Millington Synge's play.

[13] Gian Carlo Menotti (1911–), Italian composer of operas and vocal music, including *The Saint of Bleeker Street* (1955), and *Amahl and the Night Visitors* (1951).

[14] Béla Bartók (1881–1945), Hungarian composer, pianist, ethnomusicologist, and teacher at the Royal Hungarian Academy of Music, whose compositions have a Hungarian flavor. The impressionistic *Duke Bluebeard's Castle* (1911) is his only opera.

[15] Further remarks on music, books, and her John Cavanagh outfit have been omitted.

To: Henry Andrews   [January 1960][1]

My dear Ric,

The journey from Nairobi to South Africa was veiled with clouds, through which I dropped to a first-class row. The plane was held on the runway till the M. O. [medical officer] came and saw our vaccination papers and there was then handed to me a letter from Sarah Gertrude Millin[2] saying that she and an Afrikanders friend were there to meet me and save me from the abominable Mr. Wilson,[3] who was a fool and an ass and a villain, who had practiced nameless abominations to her. With knocking knees I went through the Immigration and Customs, and emerged on the other side to find the inoffensive Mr. Wilson and a colleague cowering before the furious eyes of Mrs. Millin, while an elegant woman (the leader of Afrikaans society, the wife of a German, a gold man) was looking as if she had nothing to do with any of us. Mrs. Millin had no need to snatch me from Wilson and his friend, they fled, we went off in the Afrikaaner's car, and drove through the charming country—Johannesburg consists of suburbs scattered on a delight-ful plain, with open parks every here, and there, and the mine dumps, which are some of them like white shale-heaps, some like Egyptian temples, all gleaming white. The flowers should be magnificent—but are beaten down by the perpetual thunderstorms—during the three days I have been here we have had four. Presently Mrs. Millin quite suddenly began grossly insulting me, implying I was a fool to have come here and why did I come for the Anglo-American[4]—I said I hadn't and she said I shouldn't talk such non-sense. Then she went on to tell me of threatening telephone calls she had, from someone called Johnny and Johnny's friends. We arrived at the hotel where the local *Sunday Times* man had taken me quite a nice room (though shabby and old-fashioned) and she raised cain about the aspect, it looked west, that is apparently a bad thing. By this time I was nearly weeping with despair, as things seemed to have got into a rut; but the Afrikaner woman finally withdrew her. There were some lovely flowers, notably from Arthur Aiken. I went to bed, but had to get up, there was a rush of telephone calls from newspapers. I had dinner downstairs—there is absolutely no question of leaving my hotel. Never after dark, except in a known taxi or a friend's car. When the telephone calls had made me realise I would have no rest I went out and shopped for some typewriting paper and a book or two, and the woman said to me, "You are from abroad, you mustn't carry your bag like that"—I was carrying it by the strap—"carry it under your arm. I really mean it. Twice I have carried my bag as you are doing, and twice I have come to because I felt it was so light and a passer-by had deftly opened it and emptied it." She told me not to go out at night. And when after dinner I lean out of the window and look down on the streets, there is never a white person man or woman walking—only natives. The Bantu is a most odd-looking cuss, quite unlike the American Negro and it appears none of the American Negroes were taken from these parts.

The next day I had a Press Conference with a big heavy amusing man called Peter O'Malley—who turned out to be the son of Ann Bridge—and some other people, including a radio woman who took a tape-record[ing] of a conversation with me and made the most extravagant success because she leaned over me and said, "Now tell me, Dame Sybil,[5] why have you come to South Africa?" This caused general joy, and I went into quite a good imitation of Dame Sybil, *I* thought, and the tape was lovingly preserved. This has put me on a most pleasant footing with the newspaper people. There is also a most charming Public Relations woman at the hotel, who could not be more helpful—and coped with the situation that arose when I took my case off my Olivetti. The Comet trip had not been without deleterious effect, my coat and skirt is covered with a curious oil spray in patches, I can't think how this happened, it is all down one side and shoulder-blade—*and* the projecting handle of the Olivetti which switches from line to line, I don't know its name, was broken clean through. The P. R. O. [public relations office] woman sent it out to the Olivetti business and they sent it back repaired within two hours. It is fantastic how quickly everything gets done here—your dress is pressed in half an hour. On the other hand everybody, everybody, everybody is full of bitterness about the political situation.

I had lunch on the Friday with Mr. Wilson who discussed his offence against Mrs. Millin—I haven't told you what it was, he had cut and altered a radio script she had written about Smuts in the year 1941—with suitable levity, and two Anglo-American men, Lloyd Williams and a charming man called Francis Gerrard, who was a great friend of Marie Belloc Lowndes.[6] They spoke of things they could show me in the mines, and they also talked most sweetly and sensibly of the situation created by Mrs. Millin telling everybody that I had been hired by them to come out and write about them! Then in the afternoon I saw Nadine Gordimer,[7] who was delightful, had heard the rumor, looked at my *Sunday Times* card, and said she would tell everybody she had seen it, and told me that when she returned from England Sarah Millin had rung her up and abused her for her presumption in going to lunch with us! I then had a quiet dinner and went to bed, and this morning Wilson rang up and told me that he was giving a party for me tomorrow—Sunday. I am going out to lunch with de Guingand,[8] who rang me up earlier, and the Wilsons are fetching me, and taking me to their house where I am to sort out my notes of what happened with de Guingand, and to rest, and then there is to be a cocktail party, at which I am to meet Harry Oppenhiemer[9] and Hugh Vyvyan-Smith, and some people in charge of Native Affairs. It is very funny how things work out here. De Guingand is starting this South African Foundation and had Montgomery here; and he stands for Tube Investments. It is quite obvious that the Anglo-Americans ⟨x⟩ think him a silly tactless fellow and their feelings about Montgomery are undisguised. But Nadine Gordimer and the journalists think of de Guingand and the Anglo-Americans as buddies. Nadine Gordimer was, by the way, extremely funny about her experiences in London. She had met all the people who set themselves up as patrons of the South African Anti-Apartheid and couldn't abide them—her pet abomination being Canon Collins,[10] which as her publisher is Victor was not too easy.

I am dining with Arthur Aiken on Monday night, lunching with the editor of the *Rand Mail* on Tuesday, having a party with Nadine Gordimer on Friday, dining with Robert Barlow's chief, John Baxter, on Saturday. The interstices will be filled with going to see things. I doubt if I will get through with all I have to do before the end of January. But everybody tells me the Cape is so marvellous that I won't prolong my stay unless I have to.

I cannot tell you how unlike anywhere else this place is. Nobody of any importance lives in the centre of the town. This hotel is surrounded by blocks of flats (some remarkably strange in architecture and apt to break into corrugated iron at any moment) but nobody of any importance lives in them—they are the homes of office-workers and white-collared workers on a fairly high grade—the rich people all live in the suburbs. And suburby suburbs. Like the Tiarks house at Chislehurst,[11] as non-puss, and with garden suburb touches about them. The curious thing is this business of not going out at night. It is of course terribly limiting, by this time I would have been into several small restaurants, were this any other town. There are [?] of foreign restaurants about, I couldn't get to them if I wanted to, and I don't know if it would be proper to use them. I went into a Bantu shop to buy fruit (which was of excellent quality) and the assistants greeted me with consternation, and when I told one of the journalists he was amazed that I should have done this, he said. "But when you saw what it was didn't you know you ought to walk straight out?"

All very odd. I must now go and have tea with Sarah Millin, which will, I hope, be the end of my acquaintance with her here, as she is going to tend the sickbed of a brother who has had a coronary thrombosis in Swaziland, which I must own sounds rather funny.

Confidence of Viennese waiter in hotel—the Afrikaanders keep on pushing Germans at him, they don't understand it isn't the British he hates, but the Germans.

Much love to everybody, and much love to Ric.[12]
I meant to send picture postcards to the household, but everything is shut, I had forgotten it was Saturday in my disturbed life.

Rac

Rebecca West Papers   typescript
Yale University

[1] West departed for her three-month tour of South Africa on 6 January 1960. She wrote the series "In the Cauldron of South Africa" (10, 17, and 24 April and 1 May 1960) for the *Sunday Times.*

[2] Sarah Gertrude Millin (1889–1968), South African author of biographies, including *Cecil Rhodes* (1933) and *General Smuts* (1936), and novels, such as *The Dark River* (1920), *Mary Glenn* (1925), and *The Wizard Bird* (1962). She was the wife of a South African Supreme Court judge.

[3] Possibly Francis Wilson, an academic at the University of Cape Town, later head of the South African Labour Research and Development Unit.

[4] The Anglo-American Corporation, a wealthy conglomerate in diamonds and gold which provided vital financial support to the Progressive Party.

[5] She had probably confused West with Dame Sibyl Thorndyke (1882–1976), the noted British actress.

[6] Marie Belloc Lowndes (1868–1947), author of murder mysteries, novels, and autobiography.

[7] Nadine Gordimer (1923–), South African essayist, novelist, and short-story writer who addresses the conditions of apartheid. Like West's, her work was published in the *New Yorker.* She received the Nobel Prize for Literature (1991).

[8] Francis Wilfred de Guingand (1900–1979), South African general and author of *From Brass to Bowler Hat* (1979) and *Generals at War* (1964).

[9] Harry Oppenheimer (1908–), chairman of the Anglo-American Corporation of South Africa (1934–1982) and chancellor of the University of Cape Town (1967–1996).

[10] John Collins (1905–1982), English minister and social reformer who became canon of St. Paul's Cathedral (1948) and inspired the Christian Action movement. After his 1956 visit to South Africa, the sum of twenty thousand pounds was raised for the anti-apartheid detainees in Johannesburg. By 1958 he was director of the International Defence and Aid Fund and chair of the Campaign for Nuclear Disarmament. The Jewish liberal publisher Victor Gollancz, his close friend, repeatedly spoke on Collins's behalf, even appearing on Christian Action platforms.

[11] Chislehurst is a South London suburb, generally praised for its churches and the eighteenth- through twentieth-century homes scattered around its central common.

[12] West's loving attitude was soon to be shattered by a letter from Henry concerning his secretary, Lorna, who had been sent to a psychiatric hospital; unlike Henry, West had opposed her return. His letter had expressed some concern for West's failure to complete her current novel, to which she responded, in closing:

> I do not understand all this fuss and flurry about my work. My distress about Anthony's book and my illness made it difficult for me to get back to *This Real Night,* and I had a series of technical difficulties ⟨about⟩ to face as the book had to be taken ⟨out⟩ up and begun again after the breaking off of *The Fountain Overflows.* I had to write five new chapters of one sort for the beginning, thirty-five thousand words, which I did to the satisfaction of Harold Guinzberg. I then had to write three new ⟨books⟩ chapters of another sort, and I could not have these typed because I had constantly to modify the beginning to fit in with the middle and the end. I was astonished, when after Lorna had come back to us you came to me and said, "The kindest thing you could do to Lorna is to give her some of your book to type, she is so terribly worried about it." I looked at you in amazement. The idea of using my book as a medicine for a highly undesirable lunatic still makes me tingle with rage, and I think most people would take it as a sign that you had wholly lost your sense of the fitness of things. You then said in horror, "But there must be something to show after all these months," and looked at me and spoke with the suggestion that I had suffered a breakdown and was completely finished, an impression Lorna had worked hard to convey to me month after month. You and Lorna then turned the house into a bear-garden in which no writer alive could have got on with the job. . . .
>
> I really do not know what to do. I am devoted to you. Ibstone House is run entirely to suit you, and I seem to myself to have a good deal to do with its running. We live the life you want to live, and I have never grudged any sacrifice which seemed likely to make you happy. I have not done enough for you but I have done what ⟨you⟩ I can. Nothing seems worth while any more. Your letter is free from any sense that you may have your defects which make life with you difficult, and it is singularly free from any trace of gratitude. What is apparent is that anybody who comes into the house is put above me, is considered capable of passing judgment on me, and if the judgment is adverse I am supposed to accept it. (30 January 1960, Yale University)

After writing her sister Lettie about her problems with Henry, West reproached Lettie for trying to intervene (7 March 1960, Indiana University, Bloomington).

To: Emanie Arling

Ibstone House
Ibstone
Nr. High Wycombe
Bucks
25 April 1960

My dearest Emanie,

This is just a brief line to say how much I like *A Pot with Feeling,* it is like having a part of you in the house. I like all the autobiography, I like most of the pictures, and when I don't say I like all I only mean that some have too personal a meaning for me to allow me to consider them as pictures. Your Delphinium one, by the way, is very little different from a very good Lurcat,[1] which amuses me because I don't believe you have seen any Lurcats, nobody does nowadays (he's too much of an "agreeable painter," as an art dealer said of that excellent artist Winifred Nicholson). The paintings I like best are the ones on the marble and mosaic tables and the petunias at night, but probably you will tell me you were wrong. The autobiography of course puzzles me as so much about you does—flight from an inadequacy you allege but I don't perceive. By the way, what a good photograph of you on the blurb. An ironical Bambi.

This is so brief, there is much else I would like to say, simply because I am dead tired. I enjoyed every minute of South Africa, though it was full of unpredictable irks! I spent a month in Johannesburg studying the economy based on the mines which since then has become one of the least interesting subjects in the world—and was tormented by an excellent novelist called Sarah Gertrude Millin, who has turned into a fiend with old age. She would ring me up at 6.55—I mean it—and if I had told the switchboard not to put anybody thorough till I called she would bully them till they rang me—and for anything ⟨abo⟩ up to an hour and a quarter she would harangue me on South African politics and the absurdity of my hoping that I could write about South Africa. I have given her a home here whenever she wanted it, and she betrayed such jealousy and such a desire to crush my ego that I could hardly endure it. She insisted on calling for me and driving me to various places she declared I must see and drove like a maniac—once stopping her automobile in the middle of a busy street, in order to tell me an anecdote about General Smuts,[2] so that we were driven into—and another time she drove me very fast the wrong way down a one way street. I then went to Cape

Town and the Anglo-American Corporation said they would find me rooms
through an agent they had down there. He dumped me down in a most
terrible seaside place ten miles out of Cape Town with an unreliable bus
service, being as I afterwards found out given to a political way of thought
that is not mine. {I was put down among his pals who at once moved in on
me.} Then I ⟨went to a⟩ found myself rooms in a ghastly hotel in Cape Town
where I got a local {endemic germ} ⟨kind⟩ of gastro-enteritis, and the telephone switchboard developed an extraordinary fault so that every call to the
hotel went straight to my room—and did so for twenty-four hours! They
couldn't give me another room, so I was on a spot—from this I was rescued
by two marvellous old ladies, millionaires, whom I really loved—and it was
sad, I must write the whole story some day.[3] They were full of ability and
would have had happy lives if their mother had not attracted the love of a
millionaire, who got her to divorce her worthless husband and took on all
her children—so that they were brought up in luxury and in the most
aristocratic society in England—for everybody liked them. But they were
Jews and the millionaire was narrow-minded so that they were not allowed
to marry Gentiles, and both had loved Gentiles. They had thus been cheated
of their married lives and of the opportunity to earn their livings which they
could have done superbly. They were really *beautiful* people, the pair of
them. They wiped out the misery with which I had left England, and which
all the interest of a new country and situation hadn't been able to annul in
Johannesburg because of the accursed Sarah Gertrude. Then I went to the
Transkei, flew over wonderful coast scenery to the real African wilds—I took
a taxi one hundred and fifty miles and landed in the most enchanting little
African town called Umtata where I could happily have lived all my days.[4] I
wish I had come out to Africa in my youth, I could really have been very
happy there, I like the idyllic quality, there is still a lot of air that has never
been breathed; and the small towns are delightful, they have that angular
quality that Western towns used to have. There I found that the State
Information Officer in Cape Town had played a trick on me, he had hoped
to strand me there with nothing to do and no tie-ups so that I would have to
move on—he being an Apartheid fiend. I never had a better time, all the civil
servants were anti-Apartheid too, so I wandered about for five days seeing
everything, even sitting in on a [beer?]-drink in a kraal, which few white
visitors do. I sampled the injustice of life, the people in these kraals were

so beautiful that you could not believe it, there was a perfection of face and body such as I have never seen outside the ⟨most beautiful⟩ parts of Yugoslavia where the most beautiful people come from, the unmarried girls were naked to the waist and the set of their breasts and the grace of the way their heads were poised on their necks was something you couldn't believe. They were hard, knowing, and trivial, thoroughly hick, there was nothing inside to correspond with the outside.

I got linked with a B. B. C. man who was sheer lunatic, and we drove northwards through the mountains to Natal, after a very funny interview with a Paramount chief, and I had some days in Durban, which is like a Turkish bath, and there I [met] some enchanting Indians. Oddly enough they were much nicer than any Indians I have ever met from India. There was a doctor of philosophy who was one of the most brilliant and delightful people I have ever met: the great-grandson of an Indian who went to Natal as an indentured labourer. There were two women there who were far better than any Indian women I had ever met before except Mrs Pandit, one as beautiful as a most expensive doll. Both were graduates of Natal University— to which no non-white can now go. All these people are now in prison. The Indians had terrible grievances—there was a large block of shops and offices in the centre of the town, all occupied by Indian shopkeepers and business firms. The whole block is to be taken over by the whites and the wretched Indians have to move out four miles from the town—into something like the Jersey flats.

Then I went on via Johannesburg to Basutoland, which is like Scotland— and British territory—and oh, the relief of being in country where the Africans can come into the room and be treated like human beings. There is some degree of segregation, but nothing like apartheid, which is just loony. There I saw the installation of the new Paramount Chief which was rather a pathetic business. He was such a nice young man, and he loved his school in England which I happened to know—the Catholic school of Ampleforth. But he is in the midst of a witches' coven—only they are wizards—you don't know what witchcraft is like in Africa, it is like having an invisible flood of sewage running over the place, you step in it when you don't suspect it's there, you smell something but you don't know where it is coming from. A professor in Cape Town told me of a Basuto whom he thought most intel-ligent. I found him charming and most peenable [*sic*], {he} looked really

well in Western clothes (they do in South Africa, the men look nicer in Western clothes than most white men) and was intelligent and obviously well
grounded in a technical subject of great importance. Only he was strongly
suspected of being concerned in some revolting magic practices known as
medicine murders, people who are young and healthy and distinguished are
kidnapped and have their vital organs cut out of them while they are alive
and these are eaten by their fellow-Basutos in order to get power, vitality. If
he wasn't guilty he consorted with people who were.

Incidentally I nearly got crushed to death in a crowd—at the installation
of the Chief, the arrangements went wrong—a wave of brown humanity
suddenly rolled towards us. The situation was saved entirely by the self-
control and intelligence of the Basutos, when they grasped what had happened they acted I think more quickly than most white crowds would have
done. I went back to Johannesburg and lived, hiding from Sarah Gertrude,
with a Dr Friedman and his wife. He is a former ear nose and throat
specialist, quite first-rate, who had given up ⟨xxx⟩ medicine for politics, ⟨she
a difficult woman⟩ and was out on his ear because he had fought Apartheid
too hard, and she a difficult woman, crabbed, a pianist who would not play
but would try to translate Baudelaire, which I didn't think the most necessary of jobs. They had a beautiful very Germanic house, with the only tragic
garden I saw in South Africa—their gardens are glorious but suburban, this
could have been used as a set for a Shakespearean tragedy.[5] As I lived with
them, and they treated me with such kindness you cannot believe—such
kindness as you showed me long ago when I first went to America. . . .[6]

In Johannesburg we had a period from the Sharpeville[7] shootings till I
left—from March 22 till April 11—when we were, the whole household, the
Friedmans and myself, simultaneously afraid of an outbreak of the Africans
in the townships and of arrest by the Government. White people just disap-
peared; very silly white people most of them, but innocent of all offence. It
was illegal even to say they had gone. My chief worry was that I knew that if
they arrested me, as I thought they might, as my articles were going over the
cables and they did pick up that Canadian journalist, I would be put into
prison in close company with a number of Communist women who would
give me hell. It is odd that the worst didn't frighten me, I calculated quite
coldly on how I could dodge the various things that might happen, but my
capacity for horror was really exhausted by having that lunatic Lorna Yendoll

thrust on me here.[8] I cannot tell you what last autumn was like; and to my distress I find that though things appear to be all right here I do not like being at Ibstone. I have no feeling of security whatsoever, less than I had in Johannesburg!

A brief line indeed, but I couldn't stop.   Love,

Rebecca[9]

Rebecca West Collection   typescript with autograph signature and
Yale University   insertions

[1] See letter to Henry Andrews, spring 1930, for note on Lurçat.

[2] Jan Smuts (1870–1950), Cambridge-educated South African statesman and soldier of Dutch stock. An aloof leader who favored a united South Africa, he served twice as prime minister (1919–1924 and 1939–1948).

[3] They are identified as the Holt sisters in West's letter to Norman Macleod.

[4] West offers an expanded description of Umtata to her nephew, Norman Macleod: "I took a taxi to Umtata, a hundred and fifty miles, driven by an old gold-miner from the Rand, through marvellous country, and we got into mountainy country with rounded hills by the roadside covered with beehive huts, and people walking about barefoot with enormous grace, wearing various shades of red blankets, according to the district, anything from sharp light red to orange and deep crimson. The beehive huts are there set wide apart on the hills, and towards dusk you see all the little fires where they put their cooking-pots. Umtata was a charming little place, the African towns have a cosey domesticity of bungalows and suburban gardens plus all the angularity and cast-iron-ornamented verandahs and balconies of Western American towns (25 April 1960, private collection).

[5] West's description of South African politics to Lulu Friedman shares the same imagery: "But both in Johannesburg and in Cape Town one feels the situation of usurpation so much— it is as if we were living in a Shakespearean play where the King's brother had stolen the throne and the people were living in a state of indignation, not only against what he did but against an unjustifiable transfer of power." (21–22 February 1960, University of Tulsa).

[6] West's observations on the Friedmans' son, including comparisons to Anthony, have been omitted here.

[7] Black township where racial violence arose on 21 March 1960, when the Pan-Africanist Congress organized a nonviolent demonstration calling for the abolition of South Africa's pass laws. After some demonstrators stoned police, about sixty-nine demonstrators were killed when the police opened fire. The incident focused worldwide attention on apartheid.

[8] Henry's secretary. See n. 12 to previous letter for some of West's complaints; West sought her dismissal.

[9] West's postscript has been omitted.

To: Vyvyan Holland

Ibstone House
Ibstone
Nr. High Wycombe
Bucks
25 June 1960

Dearest Vyvyan,

Thank you so much for your letter—which I value highly, for you have not only an intellect, you have horse sense. About the young men of today, I find it significant that Colin Wilson has just published a novel in which, after immense effort, he discovers that there is something wrong about murder, and that Jack the Ripper was not an ideal character.[1]

As for the letters,[2] I feel for Thelma over this. It is a hateful thing to have to face, and I also feel for your unfortunate father, who cannot have written those letters with any idea that one day all could ⟨vie[w]⟩ read them. But I feel strongly that it is far better that your father's letters should be published by a reputable publisher, who would give you some control over the editing, rather than nameless wolves and jackals should get hold of them in the future. I am writing in the dark, as I don't know what the letters are like. But I feel that Thelma cannot hope that Merlin can fail to learn that his grandfather was homosexual, and I wonder if he will not be wearied of the subject by the very excess of attention which is given it. (Your poor father. He *also* wrote, didn't he? Sometimes one would never guess it.) But I can enter into Thelma's anxiety and distaste, and {her} tenderness for her delectable ewe lamb.

One things [*sic*] strikes me as odd. How on earth did your father's letters to Reggie Turner get into an American Public Library? Ross might have distributed the letters he had from your father to his horrid friends—I did not like Ross.[3] But I would not have believed that Reggie would have given O.W.'s letters to any body but you, and I cannot imagine him selling them. I mention this because there is a prodigious number of forged letters changing hands in America.

Thelma wrote me a charming letter which I didn't answer, for reasons which I know she will forgive. Not only did my sister Winifred die at the end of May, my favourite cousin [Jessie Barclay] died a week before I g[o]t back from Africa. Both these events had their bitter taste. These were two of the most beautiful and gifted women I have ever known, and they had, for no fault of their own, joyless and troubled lives. Some of the troubles of my cousin have taken up a lot of my time and Henry's, and it has come into my mind again and again that though the lives of such as you and me have tragedy and anxiety and fear in them, we have had a hell of a lot of fun; and some people—and it is rather extraordinary to realise this—really have almost none at all.

It is always lovely to see you both. And how lovely Thelma looked. I hope my life will quiet down after this, and we will see more of each other. I've had no time to send Merlin anything in the way of stores, so he must forgive me. I got a nice letter.

Yours ever,
Rebecca

private collection   typescript with autograph signature

[1] Colin Wilson (1931–), prolific English novelist whose works often deal with the psychology of crime and with the occult. West is probably referring to his first novel, *Ritual in the Dark* (1960). He later wrote *Jack the Ripper: Summing Up and Verdict* (1988).

[2] Holland consulted West (letter of 22 June 1960) about Rupert Hart-Davis's edition of Oscar Wilde's letters, including numerous ones to Wilde's homosexual friends Robert Ross and Reginald Turner. Holland favored publication: "Better that they should be published now, with explanatory notes by ourselves, than in bare fashion by unsympathetic editors." Vyvyan's second wife, Thelma (m. 1943) preferred censorship. In a later letter, he sent West samples of the homosexual texts, and she advised that he should leave in passages he had contemplated omitting: "They are very period—so period that they really are not shocking any more. And I have a dread of the letters being hawked about by people like Frank Harris as an 'unexpurgated version of what the cowardly son suppressed,' but, oh dear, I do feel so much for Thelma. It is such a pity that people don't exercise some sense about the letters that they keep." West also opined, "What your father did to little boys is not so criminal as what little boys did to your father's prose. Isn't the writing frightful when he lets himself go in that way?" (30 June 1960, private collection).

[3] Robert Baldwin Ross (1869–1918), Canadian-born literary journalist and art critic. He met Wilde in 1886 and became executor of his estate.

To: Janet Flanner

Ibstone House
Ibstone
Nr. High Wycombe
Bucks
13 July 1960

Dearest Janet,

Thank you so much for your letter. My first article was possibly emotional because you can hardly disguise a certain excitement which springs up when you are conscious that you may be arrested by white Africans at two in the morning or massacred by justly irritated black Africans at any hour of the day. It was really something the week after Sharpeville. The whole enterprise has become very difficult because people like things in black and white. I cannot say that the position of the black African is intolerable owing to apartheid without having a lot of people screaming at me that I am unjust, because the Africans are well-housed and very well looked after from the point of view of medical care; but if I say they are, then other people scream at me that I am overlooking the hideous sufferings that black Africans suffer under apartheid. Telling the truth is really a very difficult job indeed.

I was moved by the loss of Bevan,[1] but I had long felt very unhappy about him. I do not really think that there was any hope, even if he had lived, that he would manifest the power that was originally in him. He had been too long in opposition. He had gone very soft and self-indulgent, and Jennie Lee[2] is a poisonous influence. I don't think he altogether accepted what she said, but she is a upas tree. Moreover, to get support against the old guard in the Labour Party he had had to compromise with the lunatic fringe and other sordid elements. I cannot tell you what I think of Silverman or Mikardo.[3] But I thought that the test of his greatness was his performance at the time of Suez, when he behaved so well.

Henry said it was lovely to see you. I hope I shall be able to see you soon. I'd love to get over for that Poussin[4] exhibition.

Can nobody tell Shawn[5] that his stuff is too long? I cannot think that it serves a magazine when it publishes articles so long that you have to cut off the telephone, leave the milk bottles outside the front door to fool the neighbours, if you are to get a chance to read them. It is a most curious thing, by the way, that wherever I went in South Africa a peculiarly obnoxious type of Greenwich Villager said, "That is a perfectly wonderful book of Thurber on

Ross." It is as if the book had been scattered from the air with little notices saying, "Please give this book to the first objectionable person you meet."[6]

Yours ever,

Rebecca

Janet Flanner-Solita Solano Papers   typescript with autograph signature
Library of Congress

[1] Aneurin (Nye) Bevan (1897–1960), British orator, leader of the left wing of the Labour Party. As minister of health under Clement Attlee's Labour government he became the architect of the National Health Service.

[2] Janet Lee (1904–1988), British politician and Labour Party M.P., married to Bevan (1934). As minister for the arts (1964–1970), she doubled funding for the arts. She was made a peer in 1970.

[3] Abraham Silverman, English economist, chief economic adviser to the Analysis and Plans Section of the Air Force (1942–1945). He was accused of belonging to the Communist Party.

Ian Mikardo (1908–1993), British politician, an outspoken Labour Party M.P. (1945–1959 and 1964–1987). He introduced the resolution that led to the nationalization of British industry and was a leader of the Socialist International.

[4] Nicolas Poussin (1594–1665), French painter of the classical school.

[5] William Shawn (1907–1992), journalist and editor who joined the *New Yorker* as a reporter in 1932 and became managing editor in 1936 and editor in 1952, after the death of Ross on 6 December 1951. He is generally given credit for achieving an emphasis on serious political and social issues.

[6] West had written to Flanner about James Thurber's biography of Ross, and her debt to him: "The Ross book still shocks me and revolts me, particularly as I once saw Ross, in the very nadir of his desolation about poor Ariane, check himself in flight to stay back and do something to ease Thurber's life. I had no idea that there had been this business of unburying Ross's unhappy corpse and desecrating it. . . . He revived and partly created a vein of talent I wasn't using, he opened doors to me and gave me a share in the thing he had made which brought me friends and adventure . . ." (8 July 1959, Flanner papers, Library of Congress).

To: G. B. Stern   29 September 1960
My dear Tynx,

Oh, dear, if I have any vanity left, it must be bleeding. The letters arrive[d] this morning, and I was very glad of them, but I am full of a certain wonder. I have written a great number of letters in my life, and some are now being read by people (such as Sam Behrman)[1] who says that as letters they are good, and obviously they contain a great deal of material which will be and already is of some interest to literary historians—even and indeed especially when they deal with what seemed at the time purely personal matters. But obviously you attached no value to them, or you would not have destroyed so many; and several other people with whom I have corresponded have shown the same disregard for them. I have been writing to Emanie Arling regularly since 1923 and she has kept only a number running from 1944 to the present day—and she handed over these to Yale with the utmost reluctance. But ⟨they⟩ {the ones she had destroyed} would have been of overwhelming interest as records of political events before 1939 insofar as they affected our family—there really was no other record of all that Henry did to get people and money out of Germany under the Nazis from 1933 on. But Emanie was itching to burn ⟨them⟩{the rest}. The curious will to annihilate me and every trace of me which I don't understand. It is unfortunate that all my early letters to you have gone, for there is now no record of my years with H. G. He resolutely destroyed every scrap of my letters, except a few which escaped him through being in the wrong folder. He was moved by emotions which rather dumbfounded me when he told them, and apart from that I grieve because there was a great deal of stuff there of really serious interest. For instance we had an angry correspondence about the departure of Prince Mirsky to the Soviet Union. Moura[2] acted as an agent of Gorky[3] to persuade Mirsky[4] to go back to the Soviet Union, promising that he would be treated there as H. G. was treated in London, and the little snob loved the idea—H. G. had added his persuasion. I told H. G. he ought to be ashamed for himself, because Mirsky would be killed; and he did die in a concentration camp. I don't think the facts are anywhere else.

I have put in a note asking that my remarks on Humbert Wolfe's death be blacked out when the letters are opened, but I think you misjudge the situation.[5] I don't think Pamela would mind at all; and I am concerned about her on other grounds more realistic. How terribly ill she looks. She drifted into a party I was at two months ago, rather oddly for she did not know the people, and she sat and looked like a skeleton.[6] I am amused that you have forgotten who Odell was—he was a repulsive old creature who was supposed to be the oldest member of the Savage Club and was brutally and nastily rude—a Swaffer[7] cubed—and was the object of our combined detestation. Helen was a sandy-haired American who took photographs in partnership with a man called Maurice Beck from China, in Marylebone mews, and she and her very beautiful and tiresome octogenarian mother came here as evacuees after their Marylebone flat was bombed, and she proved very difficult—she posed as an expert cook and carried her pose into the kitchen and consequently cook after cook left, and we had in the end to employ *her* as a cook—upon which she never went into the kitchen. Cooking was her neurosis; she was fascinated by it and repelled by it—she hated to see Margaret Hodges and me cooking, though we had to or we would have got nothing to eat—but we had to do most of it in the middle of the night, to avoid scenes. Then somebody in California left her and her mother a substantial annuity, and Helen was much touched by our unselfish joy at her good fortune . . . [West's ellipsis] That joy was unfeigned. Poor thing, she was going dotty, it turned out, and after enjoying her annuity for a year or two went very dotty and died.

Did I tell you a queer thing about the letters which were sent back to me by the Lowinsky family [after] Ruth died? I reread them and found a reference to a rare malady suffered by a girl who had been our housemaid—and then left the village. Since then she had returned, and was at that moment in a situation when it was vital her doctor should know she had this disease, which hadn't been recorded. It was a most curious coincidence.

Do come over and see us when you can.

Much love,

Rebecca West Collection   carbon typescript
University of Tulsa

¹ S. N. (Samuel Nathaniel) Behrman (1893–1973), American dramatist and biographer. His plays include *The Second Man* (1927), *Rain from Heaven* (1934), *No Time for Comedy* (1939), and the musical *Fanny* (1954). His memoir of Max Beerbohm appeared in 1960.

² Moura Budberg (1892?–1974), formerly Zakrevskaya, Countess Benckendorff, whom Wells met in 1914. She afterwards became the secretary and mistress of Maxim Gorky, having been planted as a police spy. Wells met her again in Moscow in 1920 in the company of Gorky. Their liaison was renewed in the early 1930s, marred by his suspicion that she was spying on him as well. Budberg did a number of translations and coedited Gorky's short stories.

³ Maxim Gorky (1868–1936), Russian novelist, playwright, autobiographer, and short-story writer, known for his naturalistic depiction of social outcasts and laborers. An independent Marxist, often in exile, Gorky supported the Russian Revolution but criticized the postwar Bolsheviks. During the Stalinist era he advanced the socialist realism that became enforced as state art. Wells visited him in Moscow in 1920.

⁴ Dimitry S. Mirsky (1890–1939), Russian author of *Modern Russian Literature* (1925), *Pushkin* (1926), *Lenin* (1931), and *The Intelligentsia of Great Britain* (1935).

[5] West's story "The Addict" (1934) was based on the relationship of Humbert Wolfe and Pamela Frankau, who had bankrupted herself giving him money. Because of the incident, the friendship between Frankau and West was interrupted until after Wolfe's death (1940).

[6] West wrote to Pamela Frankau describing Stern's destruction of her letters and asking Frankau to preserve hers for the Yale collection, and to try to get more letters from Stern (1 October 1960, University of Tulsa).

[7] Hannen Swaffer (1879–1962), English journalist for the *Daily Mail* (1902–1912), drama critic for the *Daily Express* (1926), and gossip columnist for the *Daily Sketch* and *Daily Graphic*. He was called the Pope of Fleet Street, owing to his habit of pontification.

To: Norman Macleod

Ibstone House
Ibstone
Nr. High Wycombe
Bucks
10 November 1960

Dearest Bobtail,

I thought the picture of Graham[1] was good, but what I particularly preened myself on were the pictures of Marion! Which, I may say, have evoked wolf whistles from several people I have shown them to. I was only at the *Lady Chatterley's Lover* trial for one day and did not return because I found it really very painful.[2] The reasons for the jury's decision were manifest in the Judge's vile temper,[3] he scowled and wriggled on his seat, being a black Catholic, he really looked like a soul in hell. The prosecuting counsel, Mr Griffiths-Jones, was the most AWFUL cad, and what was funny, very sexy—a sort of male Jayne Mansfield,[4] a handsome overblown being who wears his striped trousers far too tight over his plump buttocks. He was very rude to the witnesses—I believe that his assault on Anne Scott-James[5] was quite fantastic, and this did not pay off, as she is a beautiful and well-mannered woman. I was in an embarrassing position, as I had to go into the box and persuade the jury that people did mean something specific when they talked about a work of art, which explains Ken Tynan's[6] venomous remark about me in the *Observer* (what a blight [he] is—you don't, when you are being subjected to examination in chief, say what comes into your head, you and the counsel and the solicitor cook it up together, and the solicitor sends you the result in what is known as "a proof," and to that you have to stick. You only can speak your mind when you are cross-examined, and that didn't happen to me. I don't know why Richard Hoggart's[7] evidence impressed people so much, I heard the first part of it, and I thought him very ordinary red-brick, and found his career rather puzzling, I don't know why he is put on all these commissions. The thing that strikes me as odd is that the evidence of the Churchmen was not understood or appreciated.[8] What they said was that the secret was out, and young people knew there was such a thing as sex and were discussing it in the broadest terms, and *Lady C.* was a high-minded contribution to the discussion. They said this, I thought, sensibly and moderately. I believe Graham Hough's[9] evidence was good, but I didn't hear it, because he was before me, but I found him the most unpleasant and ungenial person. Pinto of Nottingham[10] was mad as a coot, Helen Gardener of Oxford was rather a pet and very attractive,[11] and Elizabeth Bennet[12] of Girton turned out to be Pamela Frankau's aunt. . . .[13]

I am indeed still being pursued by the South African judge, and it is likely to work out as the final disaster of my life! I have the clearest recollection of this judge asking a number of questions, and so had Lulu Friedman[14] and her friends, with whom I discussed the matter at luncheon the same day. I actually wrote down the conclusions regarding these questions which were given to me by a lawyer. The Judge denies having ⟨x⟩ {asked these} questions, and has sent a court record transcribed from a tape recording which certainly does not show them! I can call no witnesses. I wouldn't dare put any of them in such danger. It is true that another Judge asked questions along the same lines of argument—but this the Judge is denying, and there might be some interminable legal argument over it. He calls for an apology and damages. The *Sunday Times* may give him this, but I can't, and it may cost me a fortune to fight it, probably singlehanded.[15] My problem is complicated by the fact that the defence, the people who would naturally be against the Judge and for me, are mostly Communist and won't lift a finger for me. It worries me a lot. It's so hard to work with this hanging over me.

Lettie seems much happier than she was, now she has Virginia (one of the O'Reilly clan) living with her. Your father was here and was in a very silent phase, but seemed contented enough—he left after a couple of days to fulfil some engagement, but we would willingly have had him longer.

Polanyi[16] has asked me to a mysterious conspiratorial dinner at Oxford, I always love seeing him.

Yours ever with love to all three
Auntie C.

A very rich woman who has had something to do with the Court Theatre tells me that Devien[17] gets a grant from somebody on condition that he encourages young dramatists and trains them, and that any young dramatist is useful to him as a name on a list that ⟨xxx⟩ {is produced to meet} these terms—but that she does not herself see how he could fit many of them into his schedule when it comes to production. I have not told Alison [Selford] this, as it seems discouraging, but if you ever are sent by her a play that seems hopeful try to persuade her to send it to an ordinary commercial manager.

private collection   typescript

[1] Son of Norman and Marion Macleod.

[2] Penguin Books was prosecuted under the Obscene Publications Act for its 1960 publication of Lawrence's 1928 novel. The trial was held at Old Bailey (20, 27, 28, 31 October and 1– 2 November 1960). West testified on the second day.

[3] Justice Byrne presided.

[4] Jayne Mansfield (1933–1967), American actress famed for dumb blonde roles, and for having the largest bust and smallest waist in Hollywood.

[5] Ann Scott-James (1913–), English journalist and horticulturalist. She worked for *Vogue* (1934), was women's editor of the *Picture Post* (1941), editor of *Harper's Bazaar* (1945–1951), women's editor of the *Sunday Express,* and a columnist for the *Daily Mail* (1960–1968).

[6] Kenneth Peacock Tynan (1927–1980), English theater critic for the *Evening Standard* (1952–1953), the *Daily Sketch,* the *Observer,* and the *New Yorker.* He was literary manager of the National Theatre (1963–1969) and devised and produced *Oh! Calcutta!* (1969).

[7] Richard Hoggart (1918–), English cultural studies specialist at the University of Leicester, best known for his work on Auden and for *The Uses of Literacy* (1957). Red bricks are British universities founded in the nineteenth century. He was a member of the Albemarle Committee Concerning Youth Services and the Pilkington Committee, which inquired into broadcasting practices.

[8] John Arthur Thomas Robinson, the Bishop of Woolwich, and Alfred Stephan Hopkinson, who testified on the second day of the trial.

[9] Graham Hough (1908–), English literary scholar on the faculty of Cambridge University and author of *The Dark Sun: A Study of D. H. Lawrence* (1956).

[10] Vivian de Sola Pinto (1895–1969), scholar at Nottingham University who testified at the trial. He is the author of *D. H. Lawrence: A Prophet of the Midlands* (1951) and, with Warren Roberts, edited the *Complete Poems of D. H. Lawrence* (1964).

[11] Dame Helen Louise Gardner (1908–), English literary scholar at Oxford University whose books on modern writers include several on T. S. Eliot.

[12] Joan Bennett (1896–1986), English literary scholar associated with Cambridge University. She wrote the groundbreaking *Virginia Woolf: Her Art as a Novelist* (2d ed. 1964).

[13] A brief comment on West's grandchildren has been omitted.

[14] The Friedmans are described in West's letter to Emanie Arling, 25 April 1960.

[15] Victoria Glendinning reports that the case was settled out of court for £3,500. In a letter to Lady Maud (29 August 1961, Yale University), West says parenthetically, "I must explain

that if Judge Kennedy's letter to me had been printed, the Treason Trial could have been annulled, for he had identified himself with the prosecution. A letter to A. D. Peters (15 November 1960) casts doubt on the efficacy of her solicitor.

[16] Michael Polanyi (1891–1976), Hungarian-born British physical chemist specializing in reaction kinetics, but also known for work in social philosophy. He is author of *Personal Knowledge* (1958), which supports his belief in the unhampered search for scientific truth.

[17] George Devine (1910–1966), English actor and theater director. He revolutionized theater training at the Old Vic Centre (1947–1952). His English Stage Company at the Royal Court Theatre (begun in 1956) favored new writers.

To: The Editor, *Daily Express*   1 February 1961
Dear Sir,

Will you forgive me if I write a note on the obituary you published on Dorothy Thompson. It might give her many friends living in this country an unhappy impression, though I am sure that the writer of the obituary had no such intention in mind.

She is described as frail and forgotten, and the headline runs "Dorothy Thompson dies, her fame over." Dorothy Thompson's last years were tragic, but not because she was forgotten. Her professional life was quite satisfying. Though her column was not syndicated as it had been, this was for political reasons of which she was proud. She had always other and well-paid work to do.

In 1958 her career was interrupted by the death of her husband, to whom she was devoted; and after that she underwent a serious operation and had two heart attacks which a frailer woman would not have survived. On her recovery she was offered a large sum of money for her memoirs, and during the last year or so, with characteristic resilience, she had been busy putting her mountainous collection of papers in order.

There was no pathos in her end. If fame had left her, it was because she had put it out in the ash-can.

Yours sincerely,

Rebecca West Papers   carbon of typescript
Yale University

To: A. L. Rowse[1]   27 February 1961
My dear Leslie,

Thank you so much for your heartening note, which I received on my return from Spain.

I am very glad that you approve of my opening line of attack. As a woman I have a great grievance on the physical plane because I was born at a time which meant that the periods when I was young, and not so young that I was miserably shy, and when I had money to spend on clothes, coincided with the period when the best clothes were made by Chanel.[2] The dresses that she made, or that other makers copied, were unbelievably hideous. I had to wear a hat bashed down on my head, and skinny and shapeless sacks that looked bad if one was made like a choirboy, and worse if one was not! Exactly the same thing seems to me to have happened in my time in literature, with T. S. Eliot preaching that you must not have three-quarters of an idea to every ten pages, and Leavis[3] using fastidiousness like a nouveau riche who buys asparagus tongs for eating asparagus. All this dreary nonsense has made the world more grave than the Galilean [Jesus Christ] succeeded in doing.

I am looking forward enormously to your book,[4] and I am wondering very much if you have detected a certain factor in the appeasement movement of which I have been conscious in recent years?

I shall be ringing you up soon to ask you to come over to lunch as soon as the weather is better. I have a couple of sphinxes on the terrace that I did not have when you were last here, and I think you might like them.

                                        Yours ever,

Rebecca West Collection   carbon typescript
University of Tulsa

[1] A. L. Rowse (1903–1997), English historian, biographer of Shakespeare, and poet who also wrote of his childhood in Cornwall. Rowse is best known for his historical trilogy *The Elizabethan Age* (1950–1972).

[2] Gabrielle "Coco" Chanel (1883–1971), French designer of haute couture dresses who set the style for nearly six decades. She liberated women from corseted styles with the comfortable jersey dress.

[3] F. R. Leavis (1895–1978), English literary critic, editor, and teacher at Cambridge, where he dominated the journal *Scrutiny* (1932–1953). He rose from humble origins and eschewed the supposed snobbery of Bloomsbury. Leavis turned criticism toward close analysis of texts

and sought to safeguard tradition by creating an intellectual elite in universities. His major works include *New Bearings in English Poetry* (1932) and *The Great Tradition* (1948).

⁴Possibly the third volume of his trilogy *The Elizabethan Renaissance* (1971–1972).

To: Jane and John Gunther

Ibstone House
Ibstone
Nr. High Wycombe
Bucks
28 February 1961

My dear Jane and John,

I should have written to you long ago, as I knew you would be as wretched as I was over the death of poor Dorothy [Thompson]. It came on us very grimly. I have been preoccupied over my own worries during the last six months, as a result of the wretched libel action which arose out of my South African articles. As an old reporter, what do you think of this? (Question should include Jane, but she can't be called old). In court, at a session of the Treason Trial, I said to a court official, "Who is that judge on the right of Mr Justice Rumpof?" and pointed at the man I meant. As a good subtle Afrikaner joke, he told me it was Mr Kennedy, whereas Mr Kennedy was sitting on the other side, and this was Bekker. Of course I checked, and for a reason as odd my check went wrong. From then things blew up—but never need have, had it not been for the filthy little snake, Harry Hodson, who edits the *Sunday Times*. The little creature panicked, I suppose because he has a new owner, Roy Thompson, and after he had insulted Kennedy (who is, in fact, not a bad man though an eccentric) with the inevitable result that he filed a case ⟨which⟩ {that} he originally had no intention of doing so, ⟨he⟩ {Hodson} turned to and worked off his feelings savaging me. And throughout this autumn and winter I have had a grisly time dealing with hostility that was also dam foolishness, and {a case} that never need have happened, and was happening at enormous expense.

In the midst of this I sat down and wrote a long letter to Dorothy; and I got no answer. I worried about this, and said to Henry that maybe I ought to see about taking a quick trip to America. But anyway I could not do this, as the libel action dragged on and on (settled in court with a lot of legal idiocy of a humiliating nature on February 8). Then one evening I was rung up by Henry who had heard the news in London, and later I heard it on the radio. I

wondered what in the world she was doing in Lisbon, and felt it was probably the result of some last rally when she had overestimated her strength and
had set off on a last tour. Needless to say I was very sad indeed, for Dorothy
has always been one of the great loves of my life. Even if I hadn't liked her, I
would have liked her, if you know what I mean. And I had known her for
forty one years, and at the time of our meeting she had been so handsome
and so fresh and so innocent and so ignorant and seemed so immune from all
disturbance that it breaks me to remember it. Later her resilience compelled
my respect, and I came to count it as heroism. Her marriage with Red
[Sinclair Lewis] I regard with such horror now. I never liked him, thinking
him a vain and heartless person from the first. Maybe I was less objective
than I might be, because of an astonishing moment when at the time I was
leaving H. G. Red asked me kindly if I was doing this because I was in love
with him! I have never forgotten my rage. Well, after I saw Red in action as a
parent, when [their son] Mike got into trouble here and went out to Red for
Christmas, and Red was a monster of coldness and cruelty, and finally turned
⟨out⟩ Mike out of doors, I realised what Dorothy's marriage must have been
like. I realise that what I am writing sounds as if I were hanging medals on
Dorothy, I am not doing anything so patronising, and anyway the thing that
was most remarkable was her unfailing generosity to me. She often found me
very irritating, but in spite of that I was always her welcome guest, she always
wanted to see me, I could always come to her home, she liked coming here.

It was a blow anyway, then something happened which may have happened to you! Did you get a letter from her after her death? I did, two days
afterwards, and it was a dreadful letter. Full of courage and affection, but the
chronicle of a martyrdom. Her love was really a great thing. It seems that before she started for Portugal she had had to go to Washington and there was
some slip-up at the station, no porters, and Mike, who was seeing her off,
was not allowed to take her bags down to the platform. He finally jumped on
to the escalator that was coming up and got down on to the platform that
way. He found Dorothy sitting on her bags and crying. I am sure from the
way that she wrote that according to the queer accountancy of love this
wiped out every debt he owed her and left a substantial surplus in his favour.
Dorothy also spoke with the warmest gratitude of the concern Bernadette[1]
had shown her when she got off the plane with pneumonia. But for the rest it
was an anguished story. It boiled down to the fact that she knew she ought to

rest and could not because of her financial responsibilities. She had received a letter from the Goulds[2] telling her they wanted less frequent contributions, and she was not resentful, for I think she knew very well that she could not have kept up her rate of work, but she did wearily note that this would make a hole in her income. She asked us to go out to Lisbon, and that we would cheerfully have done. She suggested a date some weeks ahead, to get into the spring weather—but actually if I had got this letter we would have got into a plane then and there, libel action or not. But we didn't, and there it is.

I can't really wish that Dorothy had lived a day longer. And yet how I wish she was still here. But obviously she was really winded, she could not have pushed on except in agony of soul and body. I cannot help thinking that if Red had left his son a greater share of his estate this all need not have happened.

I long to see you both. I hope all is going well with you. This business of the libel action has slowed up my work, and I have indeed done almost nothing for six months, since I had to buckle to in order to save myself from becoming involved to the degree of paying enormous expenses—as it is I have some sizable bills for legal costs coming in. But when I get something solid done, I will get back to America, for which I am very homesick.

All my love, to you and the super-brat.

Yours ever,
Rebecca

I see a good deal of Fleur,[3] whom I like enormously. She was exceedingly kind to me when my beloved sister Winifred died at the end of May. . . .[4]

Papers of John Gunther, Addenda   typescript
University of Chicago

[1] Bernadette Nansé Lewis, Thompson's daughter-in-law, then staying with her sister in Lisbon, while her husband Michael Lewis sought a divorce. Thompson had visited with her two grandsons there and died in a hotel on 30 January 1961.

[2] Editors of *Good Housekeeping*.

[3] Fleur Cowles (1910–), American author, editor, painter, art patron, and hostess. She edited *Look* and *Flair* magazines. Her memoirs, *She Made Friends and Kept Them* (1996), include quotations from West's letters to her. Cowles remained one of West's close friends to the end of her life and entertained her frequently in her London home.

[4] A tangential part of the postscript on Cowles is omitted.

To: A. D. Peters   29 March 1961
Dear Peter,

Not on your life would I give *The Meaning of Treason* to a film producer to do what he likes with it!

He might put out the most reactionary stuff without intending to do so, or the most Communist stuff for that matter, and then where would I be? There has been so much political skulduggery connected with this book that I simply cannot consent to such an arrangement.

You can assure him that I will not be unreasonable, and I shall be very glad to have you arbitrate between us, but I cannot possibly hand over a book with a title that is so well remembered to have Mr. Capra,[1] or anybody else, work their will on it.

Yours ever,

Rebecca West Collection   carbon typescript
University of Tulsa

[1] Frank Capra (1897–1991), American film director, best known for mildly satirical situation comedies such as *It Happened One Night* (1934), for which he received one of several Academy Awards, *Mr. Smith Goes to Washington* (1939), and *It's a Wonderful Life* (1946).

To: Anthony West   Ibstone House, Ibstone
                                               27 November 1961

My dear Anthony,

I shall be coming to America some time after the New Year. I shall stop just a couple of days in New York, to see various business people in New York, then we will go on to Barbados, and I shall be back in New York, possibly for a couple of weeks, on my way home. I hope {on} this second ⟨time⟩ {visit} to see you.

There is something I want very much to tell you. What worried me about *Heritage,* of course, was the feeling behind the book. A great deal of the book read to me as if you had not written it, but I did recognise that even if you had not only a deep resentment would account for the publication. The idea of this feeling not only distressed me but puzzled me—and continued to do so until Kitty told me various things which made it clearer. Because of recollections of your childhood which I spoke of to her, she told me that she thought you must have got a quite wrong memory of what had happened, for you had often told her (and someone else has told me this too) that I had sent you to school when you were two years old, because your presence was an embarrassment to me, and that you had hardly seen H. G. till you were 11, and then saw him often, the idea being that I had kept you from him till then.

I had no idea that you had this curious belief about the reason you were sent to school, and there is so little foundation for it that I could hardly have been expected to guess it. You were sent to school when you were three not two (not that that makes a great deal of difference, I know). We moved from a gloomy place called Hatch End to a very nice house in Leigh-on-Sea, when you were two and a half or more—I know that it was early spring and I remember also that H. G. came down when I was moving in and was staying in a cheap little boarding-house in Westcliff and after dinner he whispered in my ear that I must tell nobody but there had been a Russian Revolution. But unfortunately very shortly after we got into the house we were on the balcony one day and a plane went past so low that we could see the pilot, and it was the first German plane to fly over England. Subsequently we had (I think) about six plane raids, during one of which our cat was killed (a cat called Lieutenant Robinson, because it had been given me by the brother of the V. C.[1] who brought down the first Zeppelin). I [think] these happened during the early summer months. I was very anxious about your safety, but the raids tapered off, by daylight. As we got into the autumn of 1917 the raiders came by night, and there was a naval gun put onto the cliff in front of our house. It was quite impossible to shrug it off any longer (for one thing, though I could fool you about a daylight raid I could not pretend that all was pleasant when the night was full of shrapnel, you woke up howling) and for the first time I began to get apprehensive about our safety. I therefore sent you to Miss Hillyard's school at Earl's Court, because the racket was nothing like so great there, and the school had solid cellars. There was really nothing else to do. Travelling was more difficult in the First than in the Second World War, and I could not go househunting. Everybody agreed you must leave, and in fact along the long Parade there were only two families whose children were still there when you went off to Miss Hillyard's. I then looked out for a flat, but for some reason which I now forget it was entirely impossible to get one until the war came to an end. I went on living at Southend, for several weeks all alone at night because no servant would sleep in there. As soon as I could I got a flat in London and you came to live with me and went to school as a day-boy {and you remained so except for three months when I was in Italy getting well after double pneumonia and a brief period at Wohughan.} I can assure you that from first to last your illegitimacy had nothing to do with your being sent to school, nor had I the slightest desire to disembarrass myself of you. I now realise—and indeed realised very early in your life—that this was the worst thing that could have happened to you, and that any child who is reft from a comfortable home and suddenly plunged into an alien and coldish common establishment is going to have such a shock that it is not possible to ask him for a detached view of what has happened. *All the same,* I ask myself what I could have done instead, and I have to answer myself that I couldn't do anything else. But the queer thing is that I have told you all this again and again when you were small, surely you remember hearing about poor Lieutenant Robinson?—and I had no idea that you had misinterpreted your situation at school as being due to carelessness of your wellbeing—it was the very reverse.

About the idea that you had hardly seen H. G. till you were 11, then saw him often, the very reverse is true. You saw ⟨him⟩ {H. G.} constantly until I left ⟨H. G.⟩ {him} in 1923, because he was always with me, for at least two days a week and sometimes spent a week or a fortnight with us. After that you saw him not nearly so frequently and it is safe to say nearly always at my request. You may have got a contrary notion, partly, I rather fear, because H. G., who was not the most truthful man in the world, may have told you otherwise, and partly, I think, because you had come in H. G.'s papers on references to the adoption case. Now, this was a business which with your knowledge of H. G.'s character, you should have understood, or at least doubted whatever account he gave. I took steps to adopt you for one reason and no other—that it saved you the embarrassment of showing your birth certificate, you could show your adoption certificate instead. I told H. G. one half-term holiday when we were taking you to the cinema that I was doing this, and he warmly approved. The case then came on and to my utter amazement and the fury of my lawyers H. G. opposed the application, on two odd grounds. One was that he wished to have some control over your education, which as you know I had always left in his hands, with results so unfortunate that we have often talked of them as if they were comic. The other was that he wished to have you with him for some portion of the holidays, which I had always insisted on him doing, often in the face of his indignant protests. Because I thought it was in your interest to have the adoption certificate, I continued with the adoption proceedings, though I doubt if I would have done so had I known the use you were going to make of it thirty years later. The case was conducted by H. G.'s lawyers in the most disagreeable manner. A week after the case was finished H. G., perfectly at ease, bubbling with good humour, rang me up and asked me to lunch, and when I refused came round to my flat and explained that of course he hadn't meant anything unkind.

You have one grievance against me, and one only: that I did not have an abortion and kill you. This seems to me a most peculiar grievance for a man who has, I imagine, had a good deal of happiness out of his life, especially in recent years. But that you have any other seems to me a grotesque idea. You can't be so hopelessly stupid that you think that I, given my particular make-up, would have chosen to have an illegitimate child. I had a love-affair with H. G., and I loved him then as I was always to love him, on the understanding that he would not give me a child, a promise he wantonly broke simply because he wanted the panache of having a child by the infant prodigy of the day. I was appalled by the situation when it arose, the more so by the way that H. G. handled it, and I mean the situation in relation to you. I felt I had to make every sacrifice to compensate to you for the suffering you might undergo. It was no difficulty to make these sacrifices because I loved you very much. Hence—out of both a sense of duty and out of a love which I cannot understand you not recognising—I saw to it that you were never left about, you were never thrown into the background, anyone who wanted to be my friend had to accept the fact of your existence. If I failed you it was out of lack of understanding, and for no other reason; and for that I cannot now reproach myself, as it cannot have surpassed the lack of understanding which you have shown towards me. I did not guess at the degree of that understanding. I do not blame you for being more conscious of your own sufferings; but as a factual view of the situation surely you need not have interpreted as neglect on my part what were the hardships of our common victimisation by a raging egotist who loved us both and at the same time did not even faintly care what happened to either of us.

Because I loved H. G. and thought that life had turned out so that I would never have any need to remember the side of him which had better be forgotten, I feel some resentment because you have made it inevitable that I should remember it again. Realising that, perhaps you will understand why I did not explain many things to you which happened to us at the time they happened or later, and why this is the last explanation you will ever get from me. I wanted to get this point about the reason why you were sent to boarding-school so early quite clear, because that is the point where things began to go wrong in your mind, and I would like you to know that you were quite mistaken if you allowed that wrong slant to give you the feeling that this had been due to my neglect or indifference. But I am not on the defensive. I do not need to be that. But here is my love for you, you can have it again if you want.

At any rate it will be wonderful to see you, and I shall be in New York the second time some time between the end of March and the end of April. With much love,

Rac

private collection   manuscript

[1] Recipient of the Victoria Cross, the highest decoration for valor in the British armed forces.

To: Letitia Fairfield

Our address in Barbados
is Sandy Lane,
St. James.
S.S. United States
10 January 1962

My dear Lettie,

I have been most interested in Lizzie Borden[1] because it seems to me this was probably a true witch hunt, Lizzie was obviously a suffragette, and as such the town would be against her. The damming evidence against the maid is of course her own behaviour, which (though the author doesn't seem to see it) was oddly lacking in any human sympathy for the two daughters, by whom she might have offered to stay.

This is a most beautiful ship, very austere in design, and quiet in colour, and the last word in comfort. But getting on her was awful. The Pullman was unheated, and when we got to Southampton we were made to stay in the train because there was a strike and the gangways were not put up. Finally an old press photographer who had, it appeared, known me all my life from the first *Daily News* reviews, though I had never spoken to her broke it to me that there was a heated Immigration Hall just off the platform—which we then insisted on invading. But we had three hours in a freezing train and I had watched Henry's cold getting worse and worse—when we got on board he was really ill, all night his cough was like bad whooping-cough. The next day we got the doctor who gave him antihistamine pills and Henry and I were so utterly exhausted it never struck us that there might be any aspirin in it—but there was and Henry's allergy to aspirin presently declared itself in violent sickness and faintness. ⟨When⟩ All this kept us in the depths of misery for the first sixty hours, then things brightened and we have had a very pleasant three days. My publisher, Lovat Dickson[2] ⟨was⟩ is on board, which is pleasant—also a crime writer called John Creasey[3] who appears to write a lot for television, but is such an ass I can't believe he can write at all— *but* is enormously successful—also Sam Guinness (H. R. S. Guinness) the banker (of the brewer's family) who like his dead brother {Sir Arthur} insists we are relatives (you and I have been held up to the young of the family [as] examples of what the elect can do) and is certainly joined to us by a real link—apparently his father lent a lot of money to Henry Denny! We evidently represented the bottom of the barrel!

We should spend two days in New York—which I dread, so many of my friends are dead. Dorothy Thompson and my dear publisher Harold Guinzberg, are the last two losses.[4] Then we should fly down to Barbados, but there seems to be a weather explosion—the temperature in New York has dropped from 52° to 29° in two days and there has been a huge snow storm over the Southern States—8″ snow in Alabama—so whether we shall get off I don't know. The obstacles which have arisen between us and Barbados are just incredible! I can't tell you how I am longing to get there, the chance to see the sun and have a week or two without flu or a cold. I only wish you could have shown us the way through the Caribbean.

I am more and more despairing about Henry's hearing—while he was ill he could hear nothing. It seems so odd when the operation was successful— the stirrup-bone is still quite free—the deafness obviously comes from some other source.

Blessings on you—and thank you for Lizzie Borden, which is much better than any of the detective stories in the library here. I am sorry that even Ed McBain[5] whose earlier stories I thought excellent, has yielded to the convention that all American women cannot wait to embrace a police officer or a private eye—it's like the universal charm males are supposed to exercise on well brought up young women in the Victorian era.

Much love—and see you again in March.

Yours ever,
Anne

private collection   manuscript

[1] Lizzie Borden (1860–1927), American woman tried and acquitted for the axe murder of her father and stepmother, now a staple of popular culture. Edward Radin defended her in *Lizzie Borden: The Untold Story* (1961), which may have been the book Lettie gave to Rebecca.

[2] Lovat Dickson, Australian-born editor of the *Fortnightly Review*. He was an editor at Macmillan when West's *Black Lamb and Grey Falcon* was published.

[3] John Creasey (1908–1973), English writer of spy and crime fiction who wrote 562 books under numerous pseudonyms.

[4] Guinzberg was at Viking Press. See letter to him of November 1956.

[5] Ed McBain, pseudonym for Evan Hunter (1926–), American novelist best known for *The Blackboard Jungle* (1954), an exposé of the American high school. *Cop Hater* (1956) initiated a series of thrillers set in the eighty-seventh precinct of a nameless city and signed Ed McBain.

To: Vyvyan Holland   Ibstone House
                                                      Ibstone
                                                      Nr. High Wycombe
                                                      Bucks
                                                      5 June 1962

My dear Vyvyan and Thelma,

I haven't written to you before to thank you for your MUNIFICENT present, for the reason that poor Henry has been in the wars. He has not been well and has been dropping off to sleep at odd moments, and unfortunately one of these was when he was driving home from London one afternoon. He woke up to find himself charging a truck, which mercifully swerved, and though nobody was hurt our car was totally wrecked. He is badly shaken and is being charged with driving without due care etc., and there has been an endless running round of doctors and lawyers. Don't speak of this—even to him—but I am of course considerably worried, and indeed still am.

May I say that the impression left on me by the letters [is] that it was really not just advisable that they were published,[1] it was necessary. All the plays have gone except *The Importance of Being Earnest*, the poetry is unfashionable, the essays have been rendered unappreciable (if I may use the word in that sense) because of the Eliot pedantry—but the letters do show him as (a) a most charming creature, (b) an AFFECTIONATE creature, (c) a really gifted creature, and (d) a victim, brother of Phedre.[2] I don't think anybody could read the volume without liking your father more than before. I would think that from Merlin's point of view it was admirable that this clear view of his grandfather should be put before us. He no longer, for one thing, appears as primarily a homosexual. Which anybody could be, and there was no bravery involved, since people have been that throughout the ages (and I understand from a zoologist that the giraffes are always at it, which I would give anything to see). He was a sweet and delightful person and the letters show it. Oh, how touching those letters about his early love affair.

Indeed, the letters surprised me—(not really surprised me, for I had been told it long ago, but after reading these letters I realised it with the whole of me not just my mind, for he had never before touched my heart) by their revelation how little he was of a homosexual. It was really a question still of early influences and of that weakness for petits jeux which seems to get hold of people and which always seems to involve putting one's life in the hands of those who can't help betraying one. Oh, God, it is a volume which throws a light on the precariousness of the human condition—it is a great book.

I didn't expect to feel so intensely about it.

Much love,

Rebecca

If I may I'll be writing to you about a week-end here as soon as I get things sorted out.

Rebecca

private collection   typescript

[1] Vyvyan Holland sent West an advance copy of *The Letters of Oscar Wilde*.
[2] In Greek myth, Phaedra, the wife of Theseus and sister of Ariadne (whom he has deserted) commits suicide when her stepson Hippolytus scorns her love.

To: Jocelyn Brooke

Ibstone House: Ibstone
Near High Wycombe, Bucks
2 August 1962

Dear Mr Brooke,

Mr Grindea has just sent me *ADAM* with your very interesting article on Proust and Joyce.[1] Your inability to swallow Albertine interested me, as I treated of the same matter in a book I published about five years ago called *The Court and the Castle*. You probably do not admire my writing but you might be interested in the factual side of my treatment of Proust, and I will send you the book if you would care to have it.

I would like to explain to you why my own information convinces me. Just after the war I knew an Englishwoman, then in her twenties, who lived with her family outside London, but came up to London on various pretexts and spent much of her time with a foreign diplomat *en poste* here. He was a friend of Proust's and described his relationship with this girl to Proust in letters and when he went over to Paris. Later the foreign diplomat went to live in Paris, and there I came to know him well. He described to me his relationship with the girl in exactly the same terms that the "moi" of Proust describes Albertine. There was the same disapproval of her as middle-class and inelegant, and the same pedagogic attitude towards her mind. Later a friend of the diplomat told me that he had seen a letter to Proust in which the diplomat quoted a passage from a letter from the girl (this is very complicated) which ⟨was⟩ closely resembled the passage concerning ice-cream in one of the Albertine volumes, and made the same comment that "moi" did about[2] the intellectual advance shown by this "flight from fancy." My conversations with the diplomat preceded the publication of the Albertine volumes, not by a long time, but they certainly preceded it.

In fact, Proust just took a love-affair out of life and shoved it into the book, without troubling to join the flats; as you say, "he simply couldn't be bothered to exert himself." But I don't think he was doing anything but accurately mirror the life of his times when he represented "moi" as having a great horror of Lesbians, or perhaps it would be better to say that he mirrored national prejudice. If you think of Baudelaire's poem about Lesbianism, and Courbet's[3] pictures of embracing ladies, you will see that it was considered obligatory even by the rebels to carry on like mad over female homosexuality. I would remind you of that delightful story by Balzac, "La

Filles aux Yeux d'Or," in which a young man felt obliged to attempt murder on a young woman against whom he had nothing except that she had uttered a feminine name in a moment of ecstasy. This attitude survived into Proust's age. All the group of people I knew who had known Proust professed just the same horror of it, and it even survives today. People who invite male homosexuals to all their parties will not ask female homosexuals; and only a year or two ago the American wife of a French industrialist told me with considerable pleasure that her husband's partner had confided in her husband, with a heavy air of morality, that he had forbidden both his wife and his mistress to go to the funeral of the Duchesse d'Harcourt.

Proust's allusion to "Huxley's nephew" is certainly intended to be an allusion to Aldous Huxley, who was a friend of the foreign diplomat, who constantly sent him English books, and was closely in touch with the Bloomsbury school. I find the phrase "une de ses malades" even more puzzling, and I think it means that the anecdote came to him by way of his doctor brother and that he thought of Huxley as an English Charcot.[4]

You may be interested to hear that because of my lack of enthusiasm for "Chamber Music" I became victim of Joyce's paranoia.[5] Some time in the twenties he was visited by a woman with a strong Dublin accent wearing an emerald green cloak and a man whom Joyce believed to be an American (though apparently on no better basis than that he offered Joyce a cigar) and who appeared to be the lover of the lady with the accent and the cloak; and these two in some way excited his disfavour. It was an easy matter for him to identify this couple as myself (though I have no Dublin accent and no emerald cloak in my past) and my publisher, George Doran, {He was not my lover, and had no such intimate relation with any of his authors so far as I know.} and to incorporate a long attack on me in *Finnegan's Wake*.[6] I was told of this by the late Rene Crevel,[7] who had been told of this by Joyce (long before *Finnegan's Wake* was published or even completed, Joyce had just laid by some phrases in pickle) but nobody recognised them for something like a quarter of a century, when Padraic Colum[8] (who had been told about these phrases by Joyce) wrote of them. The fact that nobody had till then been aware of them seemed to indicate a defect in Joyce's method. But in the meantime I had suffered many irritations, such as rudeness from Joyce worshippers whom I encountered socially and mysterious denunciations in obscure reviews, as a consequence of this false identification.

I hope this essay of yours is reprinted in book form, but I would urge you to reconsider the passages regarding the attitude of "moi" to Lesbians, which may have been illogical but was the standard attitude of Proust's world, at least so far as amorous males were concerned.

With much gratitude for the pleasure you have given me by this essay and other of your writings,

I am yours sincerely,
Rebecca West

Rebecca West Papers   typescript copy with manuscript
Yale University   signature and note

[1] "Proust and Joyce: The Case for the Prosecution," *ADAM International Review* 297–98 (1961): 5–66. Brooke targets uncritical admiration of both authors. He considered *Albertine disparue* the least satisfactory volume of *A la recherche du temps perdu*. See letter to Kit Freund, 24 October 1944, for note on Proust.

[2] West inserts "how" here, perhaps by mistake.

[3] Gustave Courbet (1819–1877), French painter who offered realistic scenes of everyday life.

[4] Jean-Martin Charcot (1828–1893), French physician and teacher. His neurological clinic at the Salpêtrière Hospital, Paris, was key to the development of modern neurology. His use of hypnosis to study hysterics interested his student Sigmund Freud.

[5] In the essay "The Strange Necessity" West's persona probably purchases a copy of *Pomes Penyeach,* not the earlier *Chamber Music,* which she accuses of sentimentality.

[6] Joyce works "West" and "Rebecca" into *Finnegans Wake* numerous times, sometimes in association with hats, as she mixed her own discussion of his work with shopping for hats in "The Strange Necessity." See *Finnegans Wake* (203, 204, 453, 628). I discuss this procedure in *Joyce and Feminism* (118–21).

[7] René Crevel (1900–1935), poet and novelist.

[8] Padraic Colum (1881–1972), Irish-born poet and playwright active in the Irish Literary Revival before emigrating to the United States in 1914. He and his wife, the critic Mary Colum, relate their experiences with Joyce in *Our Friend James Joyce* (1959).

To: Emanie Arling   Ibstone House
                                       Ibstone
                                       Nr. High Wycombe
                                       Bucks
                                       14 September [1962][1]

My dear Emanie,

Would that you had given Anthony a black eye. I have just had a letter from him which infuriated me. It is written in a sort of "What Katy Did" infantile style—telling me that Lily has spent most of her time recently sitting in the shade of a grape-arbour, reading *Black Lamb and Grey Falcon,* and assuring me that my wise counsels have prevailed and he is not going to leave America except for the summers and that he and Lily hope to present me with my new grandchild next March in an air free from the alarming reek of burning or burnt boats. Where the hell did he learn to write like that? But what has got my goat is that he ends with a patronising passage about Em [Edmund West], saying that he is doing this and that, and really it isn't so bad, "I hope you are not disappointed in him. I know he is not an exciting boy, but I have hopes that something better will make an appearance. . . ."[2] and "he will break the shell of his diffidence." I'm not in the least disappointed in Em. He has good looks, good manners, he is kind to Kitty, he works like a dog, and he has given almost no trouble except that he is a bad correspondent, and is beautifully self-reliant and economical. When I think of the hell Anthony made of our lives when he was that age, with continual tale-bearing, extravagance, hysteria, and lying, I can't think how he has the nerve to speak like that of his admirable son. Well, that's that!

I should have gone with Henry to Belgium for an economists' congress, but the night before we should have started I had an attack of internal pain, which I think meant nothing, it wasn't gall bladder, and the doctor all the same said stay at home, just in case. And glad I was, it has been wonderful to do a little work, and live in peace. On Saturday (tomorrow) he returns and on Monday we have to winkle him in to Middlesex Hospital, for investigation by Kremer. I'm terribly afraid this means the slow descent into nullity of cerebral arteriosclerosis. His sight and hearing are both worse, his handwriting is notably deteriorating, his speech slightly slurred, and his performance so odd that people notice it—he has been writing endless business letters to the head of Schweppes, who said to a friend of mine, "That man's going off his head." Oh, dear, oh, dear, life isn't kind.

I don't know if you saw anything about the Writers' Conference at Edinburgh Festival. I wish you'd been there. It was the end. It was got up by a very rich young man who is going in for publishing named John Calder, and he's plainly one of the new diabolists. He just means to milk the beatnik craze. I have never in my life seen such degraded cantrips. The day devoted to Scottish writers was the most shameful thing I have ever seen, five of them sat in quiz formation and passed a gin bottle to and fro and visibly got drunk

before the audience—a Scottish poet was called to the microphone, not one
of the ones at the table, proved too drunk to speak, too drunk to be taken off
the platform, they just folded him up at the back of the platform—I have to
hand it to him, he presently after sleeping it off for an hour arose and went
back to the microphone and made a pretty fair speech—but the illuminating
thing was that the pride of place went to a dreadful man like a ferret, dressed
in a football jersey, Alexander Trocchi[3] from Glasgow (his name means that
his father probably sold ice-cream) who kept on announcing that he took
heroin and had been taught to be a junkie in the United States. He'd only
written one book and that was to announce the same fact in print. People
kept on going to the microphone and making extraordinary announce-
ments—there was a Dutch poet who kept on telling the audience he was
homosexual (he was wearing the oddest trousers I've ever seen, of white
sailcloth with brown silk scallops round the turn-ups) and got terrific cheers
from the homosexuals on the platform, who afterwards found he was the
wrong homosexual, he was also a religious maniac and I found him asking
three of his kind in agonised tones, "What are you not for Chesus, who was
the greatest of all homosexuals?" and getting the coldest looks. He ended up
by making a speech to express his other interest, which was of all things
disapproval of nudism—he made an interminable speech praising some laws
in Holland which allowed people to strip on the beach but prosecuted them
if they crossed the esplanade and went improperly dressed into a shop or a
cafe, and "right it is that we should haf these laws for public nekkedness is
{fery} ⟨most⟩ annoying." But don't think it was objectless, the thing was
a racket. There was a day on censorship and there on the platform was
Maurice Girodias,[4] who publishes dirty books in Paris, and he made a most
high-minded address on the subject. I had not been told he was to be there,
and bitterly regretted meeting him without the information that would have
enabled me to question him about the huge prices he charges for his filth and
the prices he buys it from the poor wretches who turn it out. I then looked
about me, and realised that we were beset with Gerodias' authors. There was
that old fraud Henry Miller, Laurence Durrell,[5] an unutterably disgusting
creature called William Burroughs,[6] an heir to the wealth of I. B. M. and the
author of a filthy book called *The Naked Lunch,* who was much publicised as
another drug addict, and that stupid lout Norman Mailer. Added to which
Miss Mary McCarthy,[7] whom I liked when we crossed the Atlantic together

but whom I learned to loathe, seemed curiously dedicated to the cause of Gerodias, among other things advertising Mr Nabokov, whom she named as the most important contemporary writer, and who seemed to be there to do a job. I then learned that though I and many other people were there without being paid—I would not have accepted anything had it been offered—and although Angus Wilson[8] had asked for a fee and been refused, some of us *were* paid. Laurence Durrell was, for one—a Gerodias author. And Miss McCarthy had very much the air of one doing a paid job. I can't tell you how badly she behaved, how foolishly—a man sent up ⟨his name⟩ a note to the platform to say he was an ex-professional writer of pornography, and might he speak—she beamed, and said she would of course be glad to call him, and would do so after some other people had spoken—and did so presently. There appeared a beatnik who announced that he was proud of having written and hawked pornography of no literary merit at all, because people had right to titillate their sexual sensations by pornography, and he was thus striking a blow for the rights of the people. I was in terror lest (a) He should be an undergraduate hoaxing us all or (b) he was a pornographer who dealt in such branches of sadism as flagellation which I has having nothing to do with. So when he had finished I went to the microphone and pointed out that pornography was tied up with sadism, and that Julius Streicher[9] who was hanged at Nuremberg had used pornography-cum-sadism to rouse anti-Semitic feeling in his filthy paper *Der Sturmer*, and therefore I was not going to issue an indiscriminate welcome to ⟨sadism⟩ pornography. Mr Norman Mailer then explained that we had to go through with all "this filth" to liberate ourselves—as if there wasn't enough pornography to have liberated us all, if that were the way liberation comes. I went home and reflected and wrote a letter to Calder saying I didn't think that the writers at the conference were being true to their intellectual standards or their integrity, and I was withdrawing. I was the only person who did this.

I can't tell you what nonsense Mary McCarthy talked. I was astonished. Also, who said she was beautiful? She has long greasy hair which she can't manage, and a behind built on the lines of a canal barge. And she can't speak. She grunts. . . .[10]

I forgot to mention that the party conversation at Edinburgh was unbelievably filthy. Laurence Durrell, at Lord Harewood's[11] party, asked me if I had ever been sodomised, and told me it was most enjoyable—Henry Miller bored a group stiff by describing the graffiti in public lavatories. Such old stuff.

Also an Edinburgh woman said to me about the poet who got drunk, "Oh, Sidney Goodsir Smith's[12] a streenge fellow. He has a daughter, you know, just a wee tot, and nobody has the faintest idea who the mother is." That I enjoyed.

Much love, and thanks for being so understanding—I would have died of rage if I hadn't been able to write to you about "I know he is not an exciting boy."

Love!

Rebecca

Rebecca West Collection   typescript with autograph signature
Yale University

[1] Misdated 1952.

[2] West's ellipsis.

[3] Alexander Trocchi (1923–1984), one of a group called the underground poets (circa 1950–1970), writer-performers who proposed an alternative society.

[4] Maurice Girodias, proprietor of Olympia Press, which published now-famous, sexually explicit books.

[5] Lawrence Durrell (1912–1990), English poet, novelist, and travel writer, born in India. He is best known for his lyrical love intrigue *The Alexandria Quartet* (1957–1960). His collections include *A Private Country* (1943) and *The Tree of Idleness* (1955).

[6] William S. Burroughs (1914–1997), American novelist and member of the Beat Generation whose works describe his life as a drug addict, the underworld, homosexual fantasies, and the evils of technology. His acidly satirical novels include *Junkie* (1953), *Naked Lunch* (1959), *The Wild Boys* (1971), and *Exterminator* (1973).

[7] Mary McCarthy (1912–), American novelist, drama critic, essayist, and short-story writer, best known for *Memories of a Catholic Girlhood* (1957) and *The Group* (1963). Her strong liberal politics ran counter to West's at the time. Her *Groves of Academe* (1952) concerns the persecutions of the McCarthy era, and *Vietnam* (1967) expresses opposition to the war there.

[8] Sir Angus Wilson (1913–1991), English novelist, critic, and short-story writer. His capacity for acute social observation, humor, and compassion are evident in *Anglo-Saxon Attitudes* (1956), *The Middle Age of Mrs Eliot* (1958), and *No Laughing Matter* (1967). He also wrote studies of Dickens and Kipling.

[9] Julius Streicher (1885–1946), German Nazi who spread hatred of Jews in his newspaper *Der Stürmer.*

[10] A paragraph is omitted concerning the family misfortunes of an old school friend whom she met again in Edinburgh.

[11] George, Earl of Harewood, director of the ENO (English National Opera). His mother was Princess Mary, the Princess Royal, sister of Edward VIII and George VI.

[12] Sidney Goodsir Smith (1915–1975), New Zealand-born poet, critic, and journalist who immigrated to Scotland. He participated in the revival of the Scots language. *Skail Wind* (1941) is one of his collections.

To: Theophilius E. M. Boll[1]   Ibstone House: Ibstone
                                                 Near High Wycombe, Bucks
                                                 England
                                                 3 November 1962

Dear Mr Boll,

Thank you for the kind words about my handwriting and my letter. I hope you won't be disappointed by the inferior quality of my typing, but that is due to the distaste for foreign travel felt by my typewriter.

I enclose a letter from G. B. Stern which may amuse you. The poetess was Charlotte Mew[2] (who was a very fine poetess). The amusing thing about it is that May could have leaped the bed. She was uncommonly athletic for her age and compact build.

Regarding your queries: May Sinclair helped G. B. Stern and Sheila[3] and myself by sympathetic interest in our work and our doings. Which was what we needed. Richard Aldington was in much less satisfactory a financial situation than we were. I was not well off, but certainly I could have paid for my own Library subscription and so could G. B. S[tern], while Sheila was very well-off, she made a lot of money, came of wealthy parents, and was to marry a man with a considerable income.

I would not say that May liked "admiring" people, she did not handle the relationship in that way. We—she and her younger friends—were dedicated to literature, and she was, so to speak, one of the senior priestesses. She took herself very seriously, but not egotistically. If there was something naive about her, she was less naive than those who thought themselves and think themselves not naive at all.

Neither Ford nor Violet [Hunt] mentioned her in their memoirs because they were consumed with their own troubles, which were indeed catastrophic. Remember that they were considerably older than she was, and both were better writers. (Ford was a great romantic writer, Violet was usually off her game but when she was on it she was superb.) Their literary relations with her were not seriously significant. They did not write much of their personal lives, in which she indeed played a part. Ford probably did not recognize it, for gratitude was not his strong suit. Violet was deeply grateful to ⟨him⟩ {her}; but darkness and disorder closed on that poor soul [Hunt] completely.

I am puzzled by your sentence about Richard Aldington.[4] May Sinclair was certainly in love with a man when she was young, and was prevented from marrying him by some barrier. She told me so in veiled terms. I cannot really believe that she loved Richard Aldington in that sense, and that the existence of H. D. was any barrier. Richard Aldington was almost exactly the same age as myself, and unless he assured you that he and May had been in love I would find it impossible to believe. I liked Aldington very much, and I am sure that whatever relationship there was would be full on his part of a generous recognition of what a delightful human being May was, but I can't think that he would have greatly desired to be her lover, nor can I have thought she would have wished for that tie.

With all good wishes,
I am, Yours sincerely,

Rebecca West Papers   carbon typescript
Yale University

[1] Theophilius Boll (1902–), American literary scholar at the University of Pennsylvania. He first wrote to West on 14 October, asking for recollections and letters for *Miss May Sinclair: Novelist: A Biographical and Critical Introduction* (1973). I have not located West's first letter, apparently in her neat hand.

[2] Charlotte Mew (1869–1928), English poet whose regular verses sometimes contained erotic, lesbian content. Among her poems are "The Farmer's Bride," "Madeline in Church," and "The Cenotaph," which questions the suitability of war memorials. May Sinclair supported her career. In an incident witnessed by Stern and West, she was supposedly chased around a bed by the admiring Mew.

[3] Sheila Kaye-Smith, who was married to the Reverend T. Penrose Fry (1924).

[4] Boll had a theory that Aldington was the only man Sinclair ever cared for, but that H. D. (who married Aldington in 1913) posed an obstacle.

To: Norman Macleod

Ibstone House
Ibstone
Nr. High Wycombe
Bucks
4 April 1963

My dear Bobtail,

I settle for *Cosi fan tutte,* which I love and hear is splendid on this occasion. I gather from the tone of your letter that you feel that *Fidelio* is a bind, and the prison was the proper place for all the characters and the composer—and Strauss's *Capriccio* is a perfect case of the than which.[1]

Congratulations on the elevation,[2] what a pity we are not in Germany and that automatically there would be a slight and gratifying change in the way in which Marion had to be addressed. This letter being of course as much addressed to her, I will add that I understand very well why any woman does not like living in the country. The damn place makes demands all the time. I am so constituted that I must have empty places round me to walk about in—the dog and I regret the ending of the snow, mile after mile we went over empty hillsides—but it does eat up time.

The Vassall Tribunal[3] hangs on, and it gets more complicated every day, even though the report is being prepared, because it vaguely links on with the Christine Keeler business, which is beyond belief, so Eric Ambler is it.[4] If you can imagine a brothel-keeper getting introduced into the highest society, and getting a number of people rash enough to go along to his brothel, people with something to lose, while the Russian Embassy kept tabs on the attendance! What is remarkable to those of us who had begun to doubt the virtue of our species is that apparently the yield politically was almost nil, our corrupt governors were too busy corruptly governing to do anything else corruptly, and unless they turn up with more revelations we must conclude that they really could not land anything more sinister than Mr Profumo's apparently quite remote admiration of Miss Keeler.[5]

I am not having an easy time. Henry's physical condition is far better than was expected. He had a fall not long before Christmas, of a sort which I knew from Dr Kremer he might have, which Kremer had thought might be followed by a physical collapse—but there is not the slightest sign of this. But he is much over-excited, and quite unreasonable in many ways, and curiously sour—he always used to be rather over-impressed by new people, he has taken a quite bitter dislike to my new secretary, who is invaluable and doesn't mind what she does. Our local doctor, who doesn't like patients who require any treatment, (not an N. H. [National Health] boy) simply will not come near us, and I have to communicate with Kremer quite outside the frame of etiquette ⟨wit⟩ through my osteopath (not the same as Miss Keeler's).

Much love,

Auntie C.

{It is dreadful the way one's friends die when one is old. *Two* of my friends have died within the last month.}[6]

[typed] P. S. My *Sunday Telegraph* boss, Michael Berry, asked me to lunch the other day. I was fascinated to find that he lived in the most marvellous small eighteenth century house in a dreary village called Oving, just outside Whitchurch, 6 miles out of Aylesbury. It is a riot of plaster work inside, the most glorious heynonny nonny and a hot cha-cha. What wonderful country that is, those drab fields (except for a sumptuous view over the Vale of Aylesbury) and those houses and churches bursting with ornament and general calloo-callay.

At lunch there was Adlai Stevenson whom I have seen turn from a bright hopeful rather wicked black-eyed little politician to a figure of grief. All done or most of it done by the heartbreak of U. N. and in particular misery over the Congo and Cruise O'Brien.[7] And by the leak Kennedy contrived over his part in the Cuban business. Something very nice about him, he was no end perked up by Pamela Berry taking him off to Waddesdon,[8] and he responds to little jokes.

I cannot tell you how sorry I am for Macmillan. He has {always} had the hell of a tragic family life, continual worries. Now he has had the Galbraith business,[9] followed by Mr Fletcher-Cook's[10] curious relations with a delinquent boy, and this Profumo mess. (Which has a further mess behind it, too awkward, though not discreditable to a politician). He looks ghastly.

Heavens I have forgotten to write to you about the thing that was most in my mind when I fell on the Olivetti. I have been asked to find some material for Audrey Hepburn, they cannot find films for her. I have [an] idea that she appeals to the public as a sort of Diana figure, and that therefore there is a tie up with the moon, and wouldn't she make a heavenly young astronomer?

Can you think of a scientific issue in the field in which an astronomer would have to make a stand against some ⟨xxx⟩body else's theories, and it would be important she stick to her guns? Give me a hint and I'll do the rest. The issue between the people who believe in a whoops creation and a gradual one is I imagine not of tremendous scientific interest is it? I would think there was so little ⟨x⟩ evidence that it couldn't matter. Forgive me if this sounds naive, but if you could have an idea on the subject, you in plural, I can see Marion milling round in the spirit to some profit, and the illiterates were sufficiently impressed, then we would share.[11]

> Much love,
> Auntie C.[12]

I have inscribed Fiona's[13] name on my copy of *John Buncle*—ask for it if I die—it is an amusing book and not easy to get.[14] If you have a piano I will send you a musical joke—a composition so bad it makes you laugh aloud as you play it—of some historical interest—if you haven't a piano I'll wait till you get back to Edinburgh.

> My love to you all,
> Yours,
> Auntie C.

private collection   typescript with autograph signature and
                                      two autograph continuations, each
                                      with autograph valediction and
                                      signature

[1] West is accepting to attend Mozart's 1790 opera, rather than *Fidelio* (1805), Beethoven's only opera. Strauss's late opera, *Capriccio,* has been described as an ideal fusion of the German Romantic and Neoclassical traditions.

[2] Norman Macleod had been promoted to the rank of senior lecturer.

[3] William John Christopher Vassall (1924–), British Admiralty clerk assigned to the embassy in Moscow, where he had a homosexual liaison with a Russian agent and handed over sensitive documents to the Russians. While at the Naval Intelligence Division and the Military Branch, he took photographs of sensitive materials for the Russians. He was arrested in 1962 and sentenced to eighteen years in prison. In *The New Meaning of Treason* West expresses exasperation because the prosecution too readily believed Vassall's story of entrapment.

[4] Eric Ambler (1909–1998), English author of spy and crime stories and novels, including *The Mask of Dimitrios* (1939), *The Night-Comers* (1956), and the two-novel series *The Light of Day* (1962) and *Dirty Story* (1967). In relating the Vassall case in *The New Meaning of Treason,* West compared life to an Eric Ambler plot (328).

[5] John Dennis Profumo, secretary of state for war, was seduced by a call girl, Christine Keeler, who also regularly served a Soviet embassy official. The affair gave rise to a major scandal (1960–1963), which contributed to the demise of the Conservative government of Harold Macmillan.

[6] Handwritten in top margin of second page. The P.S. that follows is typed.

[7] A 1963 uprising brought the Congo, which had achieved independence in 1960, under a Communist system. Conor Cruise O'Brien (1917–), Irish historian whose analysis of the Congo can be read in *To Katanga and Back, a UN Case History* (1962).

[8] Pamela Berry (1914–1989), political hostess and wife of *Daily Telegraph* proprietor Michael Berry. Waddesdon Manor, a French Renaissance-style château built in 1874–1889 for Baron Ferdinand de Rothschild near Aylesbury in Buckinghamshire, was the site for lavish entertainment of notables.

[9] T. G. D. Galbraith, M.P. for the Hillhead Division of Glasgow and Civil Lord of the Admiralty. Publication of his innocent letters to Vassall by Macmillan resulted in Galbraith's resignation. Members of the Labour Party accused Macmillan of unkindness to Galbraith, and Michael Foot compared the prime minister to McCarthy (*The New Meaning of Treason*, 333).

[10] Sir John Fletcher-Cook (1911–1989), British Colonial Office official and diplomat who served the Macmillan government as undersecretary of the Foreign Office. Andrew Roth reported in *Westminster Confidential* (the same organ that ran call girls' accounts of the Profumo affair) that Fletcher-Cook was in contact with a good-looking boy on remand from a borstal.

[11] Norman Macleod did make a suggestion concerning a revised view of interstellar distances, but he heard no more of her project of making an astronomer of Hepburn.

[12] The second continuation is handwritten in the left and top margins of the first page.

[13] Daughter of Norman and Marion Macleod.

[14] *The Life of John Buncle* by Thomas Amory, originally published in two volumes (1756 and 1766), a racy "autobiography" in which the main character marries a succession of seven wives, each representing a different feminine ideal.

To: Nancy Milford[1]

Ibstone House: Ibstone
Near High Wycombe: Bucks
10 August 1963

Dear Mrs Milford,

I am sorry not to have answered your letter before, but I have been much occupied, one hand dealing with Vassall and Ward, the other with an outbreak of illness in my household. My correspondence is standing round in drifts.

My relations with Mrs Fitzgerald were few and fragmentary. I don't know if you'll find anybody to confirm my impression that she was very plain. I had been told that she was very beautiful, but when I went to a party and saw her I had quite a shock. She was standing with her back to me, and her hair was quite lovely, it glistened like a child's. I am sure this was natural. Then she turned round and she startled me, I would almost go so far as to say that her face had a certain craggy homeliness. There was a curious unevenness about it, such as one sees in Gericault's pictures of the insane.[2] Her profile seemed on two different planes. Everybody told me how lovely she was, but that is and always has been my impression.

We got on quite well, though our relationship was interrupted by Scott Fitzgerald's anger at me because I did not come to a party, as related by Turnbull—the trouble was that nobody had told me where the party was.[3] Recently someone reminded me (and I can't remember who it was) that we had both been at a party where she had talked to us about her dancing. And there came back to me a very unpleasant memory. She had flapped her arms and looked very uncouth as she talked about her ballet ambitions. The odd thing to me always was that Scott Fitzgerald, who might have been expected from his writings to like someone sleek like Mrs Vernon Castle,[4] should have liked someone who was so inelegant. But she was not at all unlikeable. There was something very appealing about her. But frightening. Not that one was frightened from one's own point of hers, only from hers.

This is really all I can remember about her. When you ask me if I liked her as well as I liked Mr Fitzgerald, I think I did, but you must remember that I had my own preoccupations, which at that time were difficult and painful, and neither of them mattered to me very much.

Yours sincerely,

Rebecca West

Rebecca West Papers   carbon typescript
Yale University

---

[1] Milford had written with inquiries for *Zelda* (1970), her biography of Zelda Sayre Fitzgerald (1900–1948), the American fiction writer and artist who married the author F. Scott Fitzgerald in 1920. In December 1969, Milford wrote again, requesting permission to quote portions of this letter. In giving permission, West observed, "Doubtless it will bring down recriminations on me from believers in the legend" (21 January 1970, Yale University). West met the Fitzgeralds in New York during her first visit to the United States in 1923–1924 and again on the Riviera in 1926. By 1930, Zelda Fitzgerald was in and out of mental institutions. For additional samples of letters that West wrote helping scholars, see her letters to Stanley Weintraub (16 April 1966, Yale University) and Arthur Mizener (16 April 1968, Yale University).

[2] Théodore Géricault (1791–1824), French painter whose life-size, oil-on-canvas portraits of

the insane (1822–1823), depict the patients of a psychiatrist friend. His individualized subjects, gazing obliquely, in an uneasy state of meditation, are posed against dark backgrounds.

[3] According to Glendinning's account, West was invited to a dinner in her honor but was never called for at her hotel. In her absence, F. Scott Fitzgerald reportedly seated a pillow effigy in her place and mocked it for the benefit of his other guests. She refers to Andrew Turnbull's *Scott Fitzgerald* (1962).

[4] Irene (1893–1969) and Vernon (1887–1918) Castle, a famous husband-and-wife dancing team (m. 1911). They popularized such dances as the turkey trot, the tango, and the glide.

To: Emanie Arling

Ibstone House
Ibstone
Nr. High Wycombe
Bucks
[23 November 1963]

My dear Emanie,

We are all as wretched as you are. It is an odd thing that we take the death of your President as hard as we do the death of our King or Queen. When George died we grieved, and we grieved just the same over Roosevelt's death and we are grieving just the same over Kennedy's death, which came to me in an infuriating form in the end. The first intimation was amazing. I was sitting writing after tea, getting my last pages of the new version of *The Meaning of Treason* done, and at 7 Timmie came in and told me that Kennedy had been shot, she had heard it on the radio *thirty-five* minutes after it had happened. Then we sat by TV and when the news-caster was giving out news he heard the telephone ring beside him, he stretched out his hand, listened, and you saw him choking back the tears, and he announced that Kennedy was dead. We all cried, Henry and Timmie and I and the Spanish couple in the kitchen—and the dailies arrived this morning in tears. But what infuriated me was that the TV people put on a long line of Americans who nearly all kindly informed the world that *of course* it was a segregationist Southerner who had murdered Kennedy and one programme put on pictures of race riots to make the matter quite clear. I knew from the first it was no such thing, I was sure it would be a lunatic of some sort—though the funny thing was the Spanish couple said from the first it was a Communist who had done it. Hardly any of the Americans who came on TV didn't put forward this {anti-Southern} view. Most of them also kindly said that they didn't think Lyndon Johnson was much good. I could have beaned them all.

The best and most reverent part of the TV show consisted of interviews with the Americans who at once ⟨started⟩ {formed} a file (which went on all night) of people wanting to leave messages at the Embassy. They just picked people out of the crowd, but each and every one was restrained and good, and there was one woman who was superb—she said that she felt the world had come to an end, but she had felt that when Roosevelt died, but America had gone on, and she knew America would go on now, and she did it quite simply and quite superbly. We have spent some time before the TV here {today} an saw that silly, smooth loony face. It was ⟨rather⟩ significant I thought that lots of saints have been painted looking rather like Oswald,[1] people who went along a dead end and left things no better. I can't help feeling that now Madame Nhu[2] will feel that she had something. How I hate violence, how I hate murder, how I hate revolution and espionage and the lot. This is a horrible murder because though he had this back injury he was somehow the embodiment of good carnal health.

> All my blessings on you, and all
> my sympathy,
> R.

Rebecca West Collection   Typescript with autograph signature
Yale University   and inserions

[1] Lee Harvey Oswald (1939–1963), Kennedy's assassin, was a loner who had resided for a time in Russia. Though the finding remains controversial, he was determined by the Warren Commission to have acted alone.

[2] Madame Nhu, wife of Ngo Dinh Nhu, who directed spy operations to keep his brother Ngo Dinh Diem in power as dictatorial, narrowly Catholic president of South Vietnam. Both were killed in a military coup (1963).

To: Allen Dulles[1]   Ibstone House: Ibstone
                                   Near High Wycombe, Bucks
                                   22 February 1964

My dear Allen,

My review has now gone to the *Sunday Telegraph* and I hope it won't displease you. I enjoyed the book very much, though I was puzzled by the way that you don't seem to have been posted on English cases with perfect accuracy. Houghton[2] did not attract the attention of any security organisation by his extravagance and his investments in real estate or anything else. He is said to have been detected in the course of a dragnet investigation into the possible writers of an anti-Semitic anonymous letter; an alternative version being that a defector drew attention to the presence of a spy in his area on his level. Vassall's extravagance was not noticed, and a good part of the Tribunal was taken up by frenzied attempts of our Attorney-General (a moron of the first water)[3] to prove that our security organisations should not and did not notice it.

I have a strong suspicion that you have read the Vassall Report and not the volume of evidence etc published by His Majesty's Stationery Office. The two don't jibe too well. Radcliffe[4] is an over-rated talent and he fell down over this, and the Law Officers of the Crown were pitiable. I think someone had a hope that if they slapped down the press over the Vassall affair it would be muzzled over the Profumo case. It wasn't, and the whole thing just goes to show that one can't be too clever.

I have the oddest recollection, and an unpleasant one, of Mildred Harnack Fish.[5] She turned up with an introduction from an English writer now dead, at my flat in Orchard Court, and gravely told me that Hitler adored my books. She was empowered to tell me so, and bore the message gladly, because she and her husband were trying to civilise the Nazi state by working for it in the cultural sphere. She went on to say that every book I had written would be published in a beautiful German translation if I would only sign a declaration that I had no Jewish blood in me. At which I asked her to go. She went on, telling me the advantages I would secure if I did this little, little thing, even telling me that if I didn't people might think I had Jewish blood. I explained that I certainly hadn't, but that I would rather die than do such a thing as sign a declaration to curry favour with Hitler, and I threw her out of the front door, and as I did so, I made the uncharitable remark, "I hope Hitler does to you the worst thing he ever did to a Jew."

In 1949 I was in Hamburg with Henry and Dorothy Thompson and someone brought a book of anti-Nazi martyrs to the hotel, and I opened it at a page where there was the blond and vague face of Mildred Harnack Fish beside text which showed that Hitler had done that very thing. I felt considerable remorse, until an ex-Communist said to me, "Let me suggest to you, dear Rebecca, that she was not merely disguising her real convictions when she came to England on this mission. She was also engaged in a typical Communist attempt to tie bricks round the necks of all conspicuous anti-Communists."

Not a nice story, but this is not a nice age.

> All good wishes, and may we
> meet some time soon,
> Yours ever,

Rebecca West Collection   carbon typescript
Yale University

[1] Allen W. Dulles (1893–1969), American diplomat and author of books on foreign affairs. He was an early head of the Central Intelligence Agency (1953–1961). West's mixed review of his "bland" book *The Craft of Intelligence* (1963) appeared on March 15.

[2] Harry Houghton, clerk at the British embassy in Warsaw, and later at the Underwater Weapons Establishment in Portland, where he became a member of the Portland spy ring described in *The New Meaning of Treason*.

[3] Sir John Hobson.

[4] Lord Radcliffe, chair of the Vassall tribunal.

[5] Fish was hanged by the Nazis.

To: Anaïs Nin   Ibstone House: Ibstone
                                                Near High Wycombe, Bucks
My dear Anais,   8 November 1965

You will by now have got my cable accepting your kind offer to excise the parts of your diaries which refer to me. I found your diaries most interesting, but I am obliged to accept your offer for a number of reasons. One is that I loathe having the details of my private life published to the world, and I would never speak frankly to anybody about my personal affairs if it were not on the understanding that what I said was confidential. Another reason is that of necessity you have compressed your statements about my private life to such a degree that in some cases they are quite inaccurate, and in one instance you are unhappily mistaken. I am quite sure that there was no question of Anthony hating me, and I cannot have told you that he did. He was staying with us instead of in the country because he had had a long and dangerous illness, and we were on the best of terms. But what is most unfortunate is that your picture of my life is due to a curious misapprehension. I can't say I ever thought of my flat as very luxurious, and when the porter threw a red rug under your feet your were receiving a unique tribute, he certainly never did it for anybody else. It was perhaps an impersonal place, but it was not my fault that I was living there. Henry and I had had to give up a charming house in Kensington to find a flat near an uncle of his who lived in Cavendish Square and was slowly dying, and wished to see Henry every day on his way back from the office. If I was tired and uneasy, it was partly because of the amount of illness we had at that moment in our family. Anthony had been very ill, and Henry's uncle and a favourite relative of mine were both dying. But the real reason why the picture of my husband and myself would amuse people who knew us at that time is that the age was hardly propitious for such a vulgar and superficial life as you represent. Like you, I was a banker's wife, and my husband was concerned with Germany. He loathed the Nazis and was watching Hitler rise and burst into full infamy, and at the moment when you came he and I were deeply concerned with the fate of a Jewish director of a German company on whose board he himself represented the English investors, and this was only one of the disagreeable episodes of the time. Maugham's daughter and her husband had come to discuss with Henry how she could make arrangements for a former employee of her family, who had married a German Jew and was living in Germany as a widow with three adolescent children, to leave Germany and come to England. In view of this it is really rather funny that you represent me as unable to appreciate Miller's work because it didn't match with the pink ices. Miller's work struck me as empty and violent, and I don't remember that his reactions to that crisis in history were profound. I also had a case against his book on Lawrence which, if you will throw back your mind, was sternly factual. I don't think your account of your meeting with me does me justice, for it represents me as an unwelcoming and uninterested hostess, but it also does not do you justice. Kitty (Maugham) Bruce and her husband and John van Druten were charmed by you and we all found you a most grateful and refreshing guest. I don't think either of us will suffer if you omit these references to me. I hope the book will be a great success.

Yours ever,

Rebecca

Rebecca West Collection   carbon typescript
University of Tulsa

To: The Under-Secretary of State for Air   17 January 1966
Dear Sir,

With some reluctance I report to you an incident which occurred to me last week, on Friday, the 7th January, at about 2.45 in the afternoon, on my property here. I went for a walk, and followed a path from the foot of my garden across one of my fields, and joined a public path which runs down past some disused farm buildings. I append a rough map to show the position. As I was going down the steep hill to the farm buildings I noticed a man walking on my property along a track which leads to a ridge going down to the valley, at some distance to the right of the path I was following. He was trespassing, and it was an odd route for a trespasser to follow, as the access to it from the public road is difficult, and there is no point in taking it as the public path is easier. We have a permanent poacher, with whom we are on good terms, but I rather doubted if this were the man, and I have since established he was somewhere else. Nor was he the keeper employed by the neighbour who shoots over our land. He was walking very slowly, as if he had a purpose in mind, and I wondered if he had anything to do with any survey of the land, such as is going on in one or another part of the district. Presently he reached a point when the wood stopped and there is a hedge which runs down to the valley along a sharp ridge. The hedge is profiled against the skyline at the beginning of the ridge.

There is a gap in the hedge and the man stopped just past this and turned round, facing in the reverse direction, and stood still. This happened just long enough for me to come to a halt, just above the farm buildings, and wonder what he was going to do. Almost immediately I [saw] in the air above him, but to the right, an aerial construction. One moment it was not there, the next it was. It seemed to come down quite rapidly, on the other side of the hedge from the man, the further side, but very close to it. It did not come down very quickly but I had difficulty in seeing what it was, not because of the distance, for I have very long sight, but because it was so strangely shaped. I cannot pretend to describe it, but it consisted of something like a metal band, grey-blue in colour, flattened at one-point so as to seem almost leaflike, crossed with a sort of herring-bone system of metal strips, and the metal band was in itself odd, twisted, like a Moebius band. I could not be sure that there were not two of these curious bands, that there was not one behind the one I was looking at. There was also somehow attached to these an odd object like a bag with an opening that had points, made of a yellowish material. As I looked the whole thing collapsed towards the ground. I saw it crumpling downwards, but crumpling is not quite the word. The metal band seemed to curl backwards and disappear while the curious bag looked as if someone were squeezing the air out of the lower portion of it, so that all the points stood up, and then fell back. Comparing the height of the object with the height of the man, I should put it as something between fifteen and twenty feet.

The man's behaviour was very odd. He seemed to be watching the thing come down, and the minute it was down, without looking over the hedge to make a closer examination, he turned round and followed the hedge track down to the valley. Once or twice he looked to his left as if he were scrutinising the valley, and he did not seem to see me. But at the bottom of the track he stopped again and looked all round the slope on which I was standing, and this time he seemed to see me. We stood and looked at each other for quite a long time, and I had an uncomfortable feeling. I felt uneasy and went home. I thought that the object I had seen falling was possibly some gadget sent out by the meteorological office, though it seemed large for that. I then was told by a farm-labourer who had been burning the stubble in that field (but who had been at the other end of it when I was looking at the object) that a helicopter passed over the field while he was there. This seemed to make the problem easy, because earlier in that day a small plane had been flying in the district, perhaps three miles from this field, and had lost its propeller, part of which had not been recovered, and while I have made no enquiries, I think it possible that the Booker authorities might have sent out a helicopter to find it. But I have since looked at photographs of helicopters, and indeed I have seen many in my time, and I can't imagine how I could have seen a helicopter from any angle which would have made it present such an appearance. I have also wondered if some criminals had not arranged for a helicopter to drop some loot to be picked up later, and if the man walking by the hedge were not an accomplice who was to give the signal for someone to fetch it once he had seen it was dropped. But I have inspected the whole field and there is no sign of anything having landed or being dropped. The stubble is undisturbed. Nor can I see how a helicopter could have come into my angle of vision in that particular way at that particular spot, and if it had how it could have looked that way.

I feel most apologetic for burdening you with such an improbable story. But I did not like to report it to the local police, as I think you will agree that an elderly woman who went to the local police with a story of having seen the equivalent of a flying saucer would be adding considerably to the difficulties of her life. But it is possible that you may at least find my experience useful if only to be investigated as a case of an extremely convincing optical delusion.[1]

Yours faithfully,
Dame Rebecca West,
D. B. E.

Rebecca West Papers   carbon typescript
Yale University

[1] West received a reply on 31 January suggesting that the poor visibility reported in her area for that day probably masked the appearance of a helicopter, perhaps of the Bell 47G series, with its large transparent perspex "bubble" and latticelike fuselage, adaptable for spraying crops. Her response on 2 February raised several objections to this theory.

To: Jane Lidderdale[1]   Ibstone House: Ibstone
                                                 Near High Wycombe, Bucks
                                                 29 January 1967

Dear Mrs Lidderdale,

Thank you very much for sending me the typescript, and I give you full permission to quote from my letters according to the list you have furnished me, with the exceptions noted later.

But I would ask you to make certain alterations, which would removed from my mind a sense of injustice which I don't think altogether frivolous. Ezra Pound[2] was, so far as I am concerned, the cuckoo in the nest, and he has one way and another conveyed a wholly inaccurate picture of what happened in regard to the position which first I and then he occupied on Dora Marsden's paper—which I shall call the *Freewoman*[3] throughout to save time.

No "heroine of the Suffragette movement" visited him at Church Walk, Kensington, in order to tell him about the paper. He was about twenty-nine or thirty, and totally unknown {in this country} except to a small group of literary people, and the first time he ever heard about the paper was from me in the drawing-room of Violet Hunt's house in Campden Hill. If I ever wrote to him to ask him for contributions, it was not the first time we had discussed the matter and I can only think the letter was written for formal reasons or to jog his memory. But nobody ever sought him out in his home, you can imagine how unlikely {it was} ⟨that group as to h⟩ that any of that {*Freewoman*} group had ever heard of him.

At that time Ezra Pound struck me as highly intelligent and well-informed about French literature, but he was not very well-versed about contemporary English literature, about which he was learning at a rapid rate from Ford Madox Hueffer, H.D., Richard Aldington, Bridget Patmore,[4] and, if I may say so, myself. I knew he would be an asset to the paper, and I was anxious that Dora Marsden should accept him. But I saw grave objections and said so frequently, particularly to Miss Robinson, to this business of an unknown patron. I repeatedly urged Miss Marsden and I think Miss Robinson, that a meeting with Ezra Pound should take place, long before it did.

On 5.14. there are quoted some sentences {of an} ⟨regarding⟩ introduction to an article on Imagism, which are described as "new" and ascribed to Pound himself. These sentences are by me. My letter "I've got {no} copy to send. Sign that introductory column to Ezra Pound's stuff with my name," was the result of a discussion I had had with Pound who had inserted the reprint from *Poetry* and thereby disturbed me, because, so far as I can remember, we had not cleared it with the editor of *Poetry* in Chicago. I had talked of sending in a new article, but could not, and that is what I mean by "I've {got no} copy to send.

During the period you describe I felt a growing sense of unease. For one thing, I thought Miss Marsden increasingly peculiar, and half of the remarks she made to me seemed grotesque, also I became very unhappy about Ezra Pound. I felt that he was building up a paper which, if it became what he wanted, would probably swing right out of Miss Marsden's ken. I had no doubt that he would make a most interesting paper if he were given a free hand, but it would not be Miss Marsden's, and it seemed to me not fair to be aiding and abetting him in this enterprise, and I was careful not to do it, while also careful to give him his chance to do what he could. Then a difficulty arose. I was constantly suggesting the names of contributors to him, as it was his job to communicate with them, as I spent little time in the centre of London and did not go out much to literary parties. I was conscious that this arrangement was working in a way that was not good for my authority, which after all was a matter of responsibility to Miss Marsden. Finally I found that I asked Ezra Pound to sound out a writer, I cannot remember who it was, to contribute to the paper, and he did. Later, when I resigned the editorship, I met the author and found that my name had never been mentioned in the transaction. If you turn up the letters of this period in Pound's correspondence you will find letter after letter in which he writes to other authors asking them to contribute to the paper, in which my name is never mentioned, yet I can assure you that both before and after I had given up my post, I had suggested many of these writers as possible contributors. I remember, for instance, suggesting to Pound that he should send a copy of the paper as bait to Amy Lowell. You quote [a] letter he wrote. When I took up the {above-mentioned} matter of the poet (before I had made the discovery that my name had never been mentioned in the transaction) Pound said to me, "Oh, yes, I've got him all right, but did you suggest him? I thought I did," to which I replied, and I remember it vividly, "But you had never heard of him till I spoke of him."

I was giving up my job in any case, but if [I] hadn't been in that case, I think Ezra Pound would have done me out of my job. Probably he had persuaded himself that I was quite unworthy of the job, but it was still not a pretty proceeding. What I think the story you tell in these chapters represents is an early attempt at a take-over bid.[5] I think the Sanctus Patronus was almost certainly not W. B. Yeats, whom I don't think Pound knew very well at that time, if at all, though he married Yeats' cousin in 1914.[6] I think it is much more likely that Pound put up the money himself, for he was quite generously supported by his father, who was a business man, though a supplement may have come—or perhaps the whole—from John Gould Fletcher,[7] who was also quite well-off. What I think Pound was hoping for was that he would keep up his connection with the paper till it fell into such low water that Miss Marsden would be obliged to get out, and then he could induce some patron of the letters like the late Lady Rothermere[8] to finance it as a literary weekly. In fact, what I was watching was an early attempt at a take-over bid. It all worked out very well for literature in the long run, but what was going on was pure murder to the group who had started the paper. And if Ezra Pound had been more orthodox in his tactics the paper could have easily become the best in Europe, a super *New Statesman,* Harriet Shaw Weaver could have had her fun and much, much more.

Finally, I had a most disconcerting experience. Ezra Pound had told me and someone else in the office of some plans he had to get the paper into Oxford, and had told me of a professor he knew well {whose name I can't remember}, who had held out the prospect that he might give us a contribution regarding some controversy that was raging at the time. It happened that in the next few days I came into contact with this professor, spoke to him about it, and was told with some indignation that he did not know what I was talking about, he had never even heard of anybody called Pound, and never contributed to any journals but learned publications, and would not dream of writing about the controversy. I realised that the professor might have forgotten Pound, but all the same I made up my mind that this was not a person with ⟨xxx⟩ whom I could comfortably share responsibility; ⟨When⟩ {and when} at the same time Miss Marsden published an article about Lesbianism which I had been warned by a Fleet Street friend was a hoax, and refused to listen to my remonstrances, my position was obviously untenable.

All this is not for publication, I give it to you as background. I do not think well of Ezra Pound, and after this date he always spoke of me to other people with the greatest unkindness. I also found that there was a rift between Richard Aldington and myself, which lasted for years, and distressed me very much, for though I did not know him very well we had been on pleasant terms. I gathered this was through Ezra Pound's influence.

I would be glad if you would allay my feelings by altering the sentence at the end of 5.28. to read; "Within a very few weeks Ezra Pound had justified Rebecca West's choice of him as a literary mentor to the paper: he had introduced to the *New Freewoman* readers not only himself, but Ford Madox Hueffer, who had already been interested in the venture by Miss West, as well as Richard Aldington . . ." [West's ellipsis] I would also be glad if on 5.32, you could ⟨add to the epigraph⟩ {follow the letter} with a sentence reading: "This letter is hardly fair in its reference to Miss West. It was, after all, due to her that Ezra Pound had come to the paper, and though she had many literary contacts, being on the reviewing staff of the *Daily News,* she was under the disadvantage of not being able to offer {any substantial} payment to contributors." Moreover, I may say, I was constantly distracted by the other services I was rendering Miss Marsden. I cannot tell you how many publishers I visited in order to ask them to finance us {even after the advent of Miss Weaver}. It is an indication of how lush affairs were then that a number said they would think of it, if I would build the {paper} round myself and Ezra Pound {and even myself, without Ezra}, leaving poor Dora out. I am bound to say that the handsomest offer came from a publisher who went bankrupt in a very big way!

I am slightly shocked by the letter on 5.31, for the representations regarding Richard Aldington are quite shocking. It was the best luck for the paper that he worked for it, but the picture is odd. He was exactly my age {(born in 1892)}, and had published nothing, and had not even the journalistic experience I had had. I note from an old *Who's Who* that he puts down London University, as among the places where he was educated, but I can't think what this means. He had actually come up from Dover College and very shortly afterwards became dogs'body secretary to Ford Madox Hueffer, a job he left because he was insulted because he was asked by Ford in too seigniorial a way to call a cab for Joseph Conrad. You say that as Assistant-Editor I was "responsible for preparing copy for the printer," and that "Richard Aldington rallied round and dealt with the issue of November 1." I am puzzled by this. I never dealt with the copy, I know nothing to this day of technical journalism, and I doubt if Richard Aldington did, beyond handling a little proof-correcting for the last issues of the *English Review*, if he got there in time before its demise. I fancy Ezra Pound wanted him by him because he was a marvellous natural scholar, I have never known any man with a greater knowledge of French and English literature and that not superficial. My admiration for him is unbounded, and I am delighted he got to the paper, but it seems to me that Ezra's recommendation of him is very peculiar.[9]

I would also ask you to add to paragraph 1, 5.31., some sentence such as this: "She had also had a dispute with Dora Marsden regarding the credibility of a contributor, {of whom} ⟨regarding⟩ she felt doubts which were probably well-founded;[10] and, though she had not told Miss Marsden of it, she had been subjected to a most disagreeable experience owing to the anomalous position in the office so far as editorial responsibility was concerned. What influenced her most, however, was her conviction that Miss Marsden could not long go on exercising control over the paper, and it was not right that she should. But Miss Marsden had brought her into the paper, and she could not take part in any movement to oust Miss Marsden."

Confidentially, my diagnosis of Dora's state was a nightmare. She developed this extraordinary fusion of religion and William Morris[11] socialism and solipsism {and anarchism}, and there was something else beside. It was years before I heard that she had been at last relegated to an asylum, I had simply turned my mind away from the inevitable outcome of what she was, and it was a shock.

I would like to make it clear that I do not want to have it made ⟨x⟩ {obvious} that Ezra Pound's behaviour to me was unpleasant, though that it certainly was. There is no use dwelling on such things. But I would like it to be quite obvious that I performed a useful function in relation to the paper and that I behaved properly in a situation which offered, among other things, serious ethical problems. I must own that I have felt rather sad reading these chapters. I felt such affection and loyalty to Dora Marsden and I did everything I could for her, but I can't see that she was very conscious of what I was doing. The only thing that cheers me is that Harriet Shaw Weaver, whom I am sure I would have liked very much, has such a biographer as you, because the beautiful form of these chapters is something that delights the professional in me. You have done a most admirable piece of work

I am keeping these typescripts for a few days longer, in case I find other things that provoke a comment, but I send these notes in case you want to work on them at once.

Yours sincerely,
Rebecca West

I may say I protested against the appalling translation of Remy de Gourmont,[12] which did me no good with E. P.

Rebecca West Collection   typescript with autograph signature,
University of Tulsa   insertions, and postscript

---

[1] Jane Hester Lidderdale (1909–1996), English administrator and philanthropist instrumental in the successes of the Festival of Britain and the Bynam Shaw School of Art and founder of the Kensington Day Centre for the elderly. She was in the process of writing *Dear Miss Weaver* (1970), the biography of her godmother, Harriet Shaw Weaver, the longtime patron of James Joyce and Dora Marsden.

[2] Ezra Pound (1885–1972), American poet, essayist, and editor exiled to London, Paris, and Rapallo, Italy. He promoted Imagism and Vorticism, influenced journal selections on both sides of the Atlantic, and edited Yeats and Eliot. *The Cantos* (1917–1970) are Pound's major

poetic work. He supported Mussolini in radio broadcasts during World War II. Considered unfit to stand trial for treason, Pound was confined to a mental institution (1945–1958).

[3] It was revived after a brief hiatus as the *New Freewoman* and was renamed the *Egoist* shortly after West's departure. West had written of Pound and treason to the novelist James Cain (14 January 1945, Library of Congress): "I am heartily glad poor old Ezra went into the loony-bin, where the poor old dear, who had the kindest heart in the world, had long belonged. We all have a fantastic collection of postcards that he has sent us during the last twenty years. I have known him ever since he haunted the circle of Ford Madox Ford and Violet Hunt, and I hoped he would come through this safely. We used to listen to his broadcasts regularly and though we were anxious about him could not help laughing, they were usually one long sentence with about a thousand wholly unexpected relative clauses."

[4] Brigit Patmore (1882–1965), Irish-born fiction writer, translator, and memoirist. Her stories *This Impassioned Onlooker* (1926), are dedicated to H. D. Aldington was her lover.

[5] See my *Refiguring Modernism* (Bloomington: Indiana University Press, 1995), vol. 1, 47, for a summary of this complex history.

[6] West does not consider Yeats a likely patron. Pound's principal patron was the New York lawyer John Quinn. In 1914, Pound married Dorothy Shakespear, the daughter of Olivia Shakespear. Olivia introduced Pound to Years, and she also introduced Yeats to her brother's stepdaughter, Bertha Georgie Hyde-Lees, whom Yeats married in 1917. Though Dorothy is not Yeats's cousin, she might thus be called the stepcousin of Yeats's wife.

[7] John Gould Fletcher (1886–1950), American poet associated with Imagism in London (1909–1914). He also wrote on the painter Gauguin.

[8] Mary Lilian, Lady Rothermore (d. 1937), founder with T. S. Eliot of the *Criterion,* which she financed. She was married to the newspaper magnate Harold Sydney Harmsworth, first Viscount Rothermere.

[9] Three paragraphs concerning West and the defaulting *Freewoman* treasurer Selwyn Watson are omitted.

[10] West mistrusted contributions by Edith Ellis, wife of Havelock Ellis.

[11] See letter to Letitia Fairfield (20 March 1910) for note on Morris.

[12] De Gourmont's "The Horses of Diomedes" appeared in the journal. See letter to Ellmann, 7 November 1958, for note.

To: Merlin Holland

Ibstone House
Ibstone
Nr. High Wycombe
Bucks
11 November 1968

Dearest Merlin,

Thank you for your flowers and your letter. Don't worry about your being too young to support me—you did that splendidly by what you did for Henry—which was to give him something worth doing when his deafness and his age and his ill health made him feel he was out of the race. I mean this very seriously. Once at least you have been the right person in the right place, as it must have seemed if God were looking down on the world. I think it will happen to you again, and has happened to you before, in your family life.

I know you'll remember his sweetness. It's also worth remembering that he had a piling up of disappointments in his life which would have embittered anyone else. He had an arid childhood (his father was struck down with a fatal and lengthy illness and his mother gave all her attention to him) and it seemed to me very grim that when he was delirious in hospital he never spoke of his father or mother or any episode in his childhood. Later his deafness cut off his career. But it all resulted in the gentleness you saw. A gentleness that co-existed with extreme bravery.

Yes, his driving did excite me to cries of despairing love! As Justin Lowinsky,[1] who was very fond of him said when he went to see him in hospital, "How did he get onto the Surgical Floor? The Casualty Ward was where I'd expected him for years!" But it really was because it exhausted him that he wasn't allowed to drive—it has been a fight to keep him alive for quite a time, and I have to be grateful that we had quite a long period of victory.

All my love,
Rebecca

private collection   manuscript

[1] The economist son of Ruth Lowinsky.

To: Anthony West   Ibstone House: Ibstone
                                          Near High Wycombe, Bucks
                                          28 December 1968

My dearest Anthony,

I came back from spending Christmas with Kitty and Caro and found your letter, which partly made me very happy and partly appalled me. I felt like sending a cable to Sophie[1] saying I had heard she had been marvellously brave, then thought that you were probably trying to play it down in her mind. But I can't think of anything more awful for her or for you both. The five hours' wait must have been a crucifixion. The whole thing *is* worse because she is so pretty. It was, I remember, agony to have my nose hit violently by a revolving door when I was a child (my nose has been sideways ever since) but hers was a work of art and mine was not. I feel for her, and I feel for both of you, and wish, wish, wish it hadn't happened, and send you both my love. My sense of the demoniac nature of this event was increased because I left Dorset under blue and sunshine that was turning the winter woods bronze and even gold, and found this hill deep in snow under a grey sky, and sat down to read your letter with a drink, and had just got to the part about Sophie when the electric fire turned into a catherine wheel, sizzling and sending out from one of the bars a star with arms a foot long, I had to skirt round it to get to the wall switch. Tell Sophie to lay off the Julius Caesar in signs and portents, it is too much for the old. But oh, I do think this unfair to one who dispenses non–good-night kisses.

As for the rest of your letter, the question of citizenship is not quite relevant. I will get my lawyer to write you a scholard's [*sic*] letter about two points—one the impossibility of exporting a gift, (a bequest is quite easy but I can't go to all that trouble deliberately) and the difficulty of conferring benefit on an alien minor—when the time comes, I'll get him to write. For to my horror I have just learned that Henry is in the insurance business for three years after his death, or rather I am, and the Israeli may have walloped me hard.[2] I will be able to buy my flat and live in it, but there may not be, for a long time and perhaps ever, the surplus I hoped for. This is really one of the most extraordinary blows one could ever take—for really the attack seems to serve no other purpose, than to injure Lloyds. It's pure madness.[3]

About the other sadness I am so sorry. This sort of misery seems incidental to living. I have had a heart-rending time lately tearing up ⟨letters and sending to Yale⟩ old letters and papers. I am very unhappy about the end of my marriage. It seems, as I may or may not have told you in my last letter, that Henry had an undetected stroke a year or two after our marriage (I remember the occasion quite well but no doctor then attached any significance to it, I think it followed on a blow he had had when a civilian prisoner of war) and this set up a chain of cerebral misadventures, during which cerebral arterio-sclerosis became the controlling factor of disintegration. He was very far from the final stages but he was so trying that I was utterly exhausted most of the time. He was very deaf, and was always making muddles and would do thing he really should not have done, the chief being driving a car; I had to exercise self-control without ceasing, and the muddles I kept him out of could be judged from the ones he got into when I was by chance not around. I did a beautiful job, I'm told. But I had often to pretend to lose my self-control, and often Henry anyway thought that my opposition to him was because I was a bullying nuisance. The sort of thing I had to stop—he would hire a gardener who had in fact a criminal record and had a wife who was a nasty little tart, she was just manageable if [she] was living in the gardener's cottage on the far side of our garden, but Henry wanted her to go and live in one of the group of three cottages we have in the village, side by side to two quite pleasant and civilised families. (They were the sort of couple who were always pinching things.) I sometimes did lose my self-control: as when Henry would insist on meeting me with the car at Euston after I had come a long journey from the North, with the result that half an hour later we were still driving in circles, often through red lights, in driving rain, through Islington. I had every excuse for being impatient on many occasions, and I very often resisted the temptation—but all I know now is that I would give anything on earth to have the chance to live again and not be impatient at all. These old letters I have been reading show me that up to about eight years ago we were leading a life which was in some ways difficult, but bearably so, often relaxed and happy, full of a controlled quality which went out of sight, and through nobody's fault. It sounds terrible that I should have wished and still wish that Henry had died in that happy period—I couldn't wish that it had been I who died, for he couldn't have got on without me. It seems ghastly that an association which was so very, very pleasant should have ended in something not actually miserable, except at the moments when things suddenly went overboard and I faced a crisis, but which was testing and exhausting, so exhausting that I feel I was near the end of my strength. I also feel cheated, because I had at last got him to consent to sell the house and let me find a flat in London, with the sense (which I couldn't impart to him) that he ought to be near first-rate and familiar medical care—and I left it too long. He had to be bundled into a hospital, where the care was in many (but not all respects first-rate) but was certainly unfamiliar and rather frightening, at a moment's notice. I can't help blaming myself and feeling I should have got it all done earlier, though I know quite well that I had to do the thing at a snail's pace to prevent him getting obstinate. I was put in the position of having to be wrong, one way or another, and I find it hard. So I know exactly what you are feeling. You have learned, as they say, "the true value of happiness" and you wish the hell you hadn't had to learn it in this unfortunate way.

My dear pussinger, I wish you hadn't had all this sadness, ending in this shock. Anyway it was wonderful to hear from you again and have the opportunity to send you all my love.

Your affectionate Rac

private collection   typescript with autograph signature

¹ Anthony's second daughter and third child, born to Lily; Sophie had been seriously injured in a sledding accident.

² Claims about war damage from the three-day Israeli war of 1967.

³ Henry was a "name" at Lloyds, and hence his insurance investment stood to lose from the Arab-Israeli war.

To: Charles Curran   Ibstone House
                                                      Ibstone
                                                      Nr. High Wycombe
                                                      Bucks
                                                      6 March 1969

My dear Charles,

This is a terribly good book. The truth of it is so great that I found myself wondering whether it wasn't quite a good portrait of Max [Beaverbrook] in his middle age. Someone once said to me that Max's great gift was that he could pretend to understand any remark that was made to him, and I think it was the secret of his success. I believe he was always an empty man.

I find I mind leaving this house more than I thought I would. I have the most unwidowly attitude—the furniture is being removed in three lots, and the first lot has gone. The pictures are off the walls and I keep thinking that I would like to start life here all over again, with another labrador and another marmalade cat and absolutely no husband, it's really such a nice house, and I think I could make the farm a success. I have a different picture of Henry now I have read all his papers. He was a miracle, he had survived such ill-treatment in his youth as would have sent most of us into the mud. His father committed suicide when he was a small boy as a result of having the torturing disease of exophthalmic goitre, hyperthyroidism, you never see it now, they yank out the thyroid gland, my mother died of it, is a ghastly torment. Henry and his older brother and his mother were then left in charge of an uncle who was a moster. Immensely rich, he kept his brother's family in penury because he believed that the widow had driven her husband to suicide by her extravagance, which was pure nonsense, and held this over the family. When Henry wrote to him from prison camp during the First World War, and asked him to send him some books of poetry and the novels of Turgeniev and Dostoevsky,[1] the uncle replied that he did not know why he was bothering his head with fiction and poetry, when he came out he would have to follow a useful occupation. When he did come out, he was ill, and the uncle treated him with fantastic brutality. When I married Henry, the uncle was slowly dying, and Henry treated him with the utmost kindness and sweetness, though he did not know then that the uncle was going to leave him any money. (The uncle, like Henry, suffered in his last years the delusion that he had lost all his money.) What is tragic is the way that the individuality slowly drained out of Henry through the years, so that at the end he was a curious wooden creature. He never seems to have been conscious of any of the efforts I made to make his life tolerable and to get him a better time than he would otherwise have had—he just had no response, he really might have been made of wood. Roughly speaking, I get the impression from the letters that I married an odd but very nice man who to all intents and purposes died about 7 years after we were married, and I have been living with a zombie ever since. And hell it was.[2]

Many thanks for the book. I am here, in purdah, in packing-cases, rather, till the end of March—then at a hotel in London, when I intend to go to the theatre with you, the Kingston House North. It is a funny thing, I feel anguish, real anguish because I cannot take my drawing-room bookcase to my new flat. (Too high.) I have actually shed tears.

Yours ever,

Rebecca

[1] Ivan Sergeyevich Turgenev (1818–1883), Russian author of novels, stories, and plays. He achieved an international reputation for works such as *A Sportsman's Sketches* (1952), *A Nest of Gentlefolk* (1858), and *Fathers and Sons* (1862).

[2] West gave her most troubled assessment of Henry to Emanie Arling (1 January 196⟨8⟩{9}, Yale University):

> About Henry. The trouble is I'm so tired that I don't know how far I have brought you up to date. I think I told you that to my horror I found that Henry, who had told me that he was so poor that I had to pay the servants' wages and pay for the house-decoration, held £220,000 of free securities, on which the death duties will amount to 60%, so that, when the bequests to his cousins and the ballet-mistress are paid, there will be little for me. He never gave me anything except the house, ⟨for⟩ {and} that was the repayment of a loan, which I had some trouble to get him to make, although glad he had been of the loan (and indeed I would hardly have troubled to get him to repay it had I not been determined to live in a house which was not mortgaged or tied up in some way—and I knew that would happen to it if I didn't lay hold of it.) He also gave me £1600 worth of jewellery, plainly as an investment, for two of the most valuable items are ear-rings I can't wear. But what I cringe over is that there is something so queer that raises its head every now and then. Henry posed as a benefactor of young Merlin Holland, Oscar Wilde's grand-son, and he did take a great deal of trouble about him, that he really did, more than most men would. But as for money: Lady Barlow, who is Margaret Rawlings the actress, and Henry and I were supposed to put up the money. I find that in the last seven years, during which we have put Merlin through Eton and Oxford and various German courses at universities, Henry put up exactly £300. Margaret and I did all the rest; and he asked us an excess. The object of the enterprise is now accomplished, there is a balance of £960 in the account. Nothing but psychoanalytic theory accounts for this. If he was odd about money, he was odder about sex. I have been tearing up his old letters, I found a suit-case in which he had evidently put all his most secret correspondence. It defied belief by its futility and its activity. He chased every woman he met: there were countless letters acknowledging gifts of chocolate and cigarettes which were obviously the first steps toward courtship. The women he approached included—and this is just a rough list, just he names that come into my head—a perfectly awful Cockney secretary of ours, Rosamund Lehmann, her married sister, a German countess (who was a propagandist German journalist and not a person with whom anyone of my family should have been associated), a B. B. C. girl broadcaster, an actress who is a notorious and rather unsuccessful tart, Jane Canfield, Marcia Daven-port, the mad daughter of some neighbours of ours, Miss ⟨xx⟩ Yendol, my mad secretary with whom I had so much trouble, ⟨x⟩ and the ballet-mistress, and, [hold?] it, after her, in recent months, a horrible female Mr Sludge—the Medium bogus psychologist, with whom things seem to have gone to considerable lengths (She is the woman who created a scene at the funeral by appearing and to the bewilderment of everybody demanding a seat with the family.) There isn't a moment of charm in all this. The German Countess was down to business the whole time, doing propaganda, but for the rest it is just one long silly leer. What I passionately object to is the disregard for my dignity. I complained to Henry, that the Countess was habitually rude to me in my own house, and he told me I was imagining it and insisted on inviting her again and again. I had no idea that there was anything serious between them.
>
> I can't avoid thinking Henry repudiated me as his wife for fun, for the sadistic pleasure, and liked to kick me in the teeth by his succession of women—but, do you know, I was so

simple that it really never occurred to me that he was *sleeping* with all these women, and I still don't think he was doing so *much*. But oddly enough there is no doubt at all from one letter of the Mrs Sludge the Medium that they had been sleeping together. . . . I have a sort of feeling that Henry's dottiness consisted largely of his thinking quite seriously that no husbands slept with their wives but only with other women, and that meant as nearly all other women as could be managed. Which isn't really the social understanding. Do you know I found in his cupboards about £300-worth of shirts? If not much more. He had some made by the man who makes bullfighters' blouses in Madrid, which cost a fortune. And his drawers are, with symbolism I don't care much for, crammed and unshuttable and unclearable with disused spectacles and hearing aids.

You say "this has been a bad experience." But it's been more than that. It's been a bad life; and the only one I have.

Henry didn't really have a bad life. Hell, how many men of seventy-four have a mistress demanding to sit with the family at the funeral, whom he hadn't known for more than eighteen months? In a way it's a victory.

PART SIX

1969-1983

Auntie C. and Personal History

RETURNING TO HER FAVORITE PART OF LONDON IN THE FINAL PHASE OF HER life, West settled in a magnificent, spacious flat at Kingston House, North, facing Hyde Park. Re-entrance to London life allowed her to enjoy the theater, which was now more accessible, and fine restaurants. She collected a long list of friends for her gala birthday parties at the Empress Hotel.

West was still a traveler, venturing again to Mexico, which she had toured with Henry Andrews shortly before his death, visiting Merlin Holland in Lebanon, exploring family turf in Ireland with her long-lived elder sister Lettie, and making a trip to France for the 1978 filming of *The Birds Fall Down*. Her letters show what her never-completed book on Mexico might have been like. And her lifelong penchant for research continues, as, for example, in this rambling thumbnail sketch of Hester Stanhope (1776–1839), whose tomb she visited in Lebanon:

> I agree with you that the tomb of Lady Hester Stanhope is quite a discovery. I have been reading about her since I got back and she is rather maligned by legend. She was the daughter of Pitt's sister, who was an angel and died young, and a lunatic, a Red maniac, who would not let his children be educated, his sons were destined to be carpenters, shoemakers, and the like—and she rescued all her brothers from him, and then had a brief period of happiness and usefulness with her uncle, Pitt, which ended when he died. Meanwhile her elder brother, Lord Mahon, whom she had rescued from her father with great courage and resource, turned against her and she was very unhappy—and coming out to the Middle East was as sensible a thing [as] she could do. Her letters don't suggest to me that she was mad at all—but they read strangely to us because of her financial irresponsibility, which was, however, a class thing at that time. I must write a piece about this some time. . . . Her interest in sorcery is not so dotty either, for apparently the Arabian magicians, mediums, whatevers, were very advanced and put on superb shows. I have found a description of them by an American professor writing in the eighties, who gives an extraordinary description of high-power seances, they had some way of making shapes pass through well lit rooms, which looked like transparent people, fully operating ghosts, in fact. (Letter to Merlin Holland, 5 May 1971, private collection)

West was concerned over her own biography. She scrutinized the versions of her life that scholars had begun to produce, savaging them for their inaccuracies, though her own account of such events as her father's departure from the family were inconsistent at best. As she had for Wells, West questioned how much of the personal needed to be made public. She chose Victoria Glendinning and Stanley Olsen as her biographers and provided Glendinning with long self-explanatory narratives. To Jill Craigie and Jane Marcus she responded at first cautiously, but then affirmatively, to the feminist recuperation of her early activist journalism, published in *The Young Rebecca,* but she suggested that Marcus reduce the biographical content of her introduction.

In turning to her own family history, West reconsidered the lives of her parents in particular and presented in many letters material that eventually saw the light as *Family Memories.* Auntie Cissie indulged in the Fairfield passion for genealogy; in going over "pedigrees" with her niece, Alison Selford, West disputed both Alison's and Lettie's findings. She was remote from her son Anthony West, even when he resettled briefly in England with his second wife, Lily, and their two children, Sophie and Adam. She was particularly uncomfortable as he turned to biographical projects. Much of her correspondence seeks information from such friends as Emily Hahn about tragic events that beset her son and grandchildren.

West continued to vehemently defend her pro-Mihailovitch, anti-Tito stand on postwar Yugoslavia. Still positioning herself politically, she explained to Jane Marcus that "the Left-Wing has always hated me, although nobody could have been sounder against Fascism and Naziism than my husband and myself, because of *The Meaning of Treason*" (circa 1978, private collection). She worked through 1981 on the last new book published in her lifetime, *1900,* and, never tiring in her critique of such figures as Arnold Bennett, T. S. Eliot, Leo Tolstoy, and G. B. Shaw, wrote reviews until the end. When Bill Moyers interviewed her for television, she admitted to Jill Craigie to being "appalled by the *cost* of the thing—the crew numbered 22—and I found that the running cost was 12,000 dollars a day—for two shorts of me—goodness knows that I'm not worth that (though you would be)" (3 June 1980, University of Tulsa). West wrote frequently to a younger set of friends discussing travel, art, and Thatcherite politics. Even her final outings with supportive family and friends gave play to her considerable descriptive powers.

To: Lovat Dickson[1]

Ibstone House: Ibstone
Near High Wycombe, Bucks
26 January 1969

My dear Rache,

Forgive me for not having dealt with your typescript before. But I have been absurdly ill, really tormented by paroxysms of pain every day and much of the night, because of the ridiculous catastrophe that I caught whooping-cough from the cook's baby. Also, after the terrible month of suffering that Henry had before he died, I have been plunged into all sorts of fatiguing activity. Poor Henry left his affairs in the wildest confusion, and though he had for years been telling me he was poor and I had been paying for nearly everything, he left £220,000 in securities, nearly all of which {sum} goes in death duties and bequests but which has caused me to have endless conversations with solicitors and inland revenue officials, and has obliged me to spend a lot of time buying an annuity. I have also had for obscure tax reasons (to do with the farm) to sell my house and find a flat in London. I have only myself to take the responsibility for all this, and I have a grave personal irritant in my household—Henry's secretary, whom I have to keep on, as she alone knows the full finances of the farm and household, and who is the most exasperating woman.

I have simply been unable to go over your pages, and I did not want to send them back without comment. I have rewritten the passage about my youth. The trouble is that most of what you have written about me is—forgive me for my candour—the wildest nonsense. I don't only mean about fact, though almost every fact you give is wrong, even to the spelling of my Christian name, which I spell Cicily, after a collateral ancestress (Cicily Champernown).[2] But you have no idea of the story of my relationship with H. G., and what you say is completely misleading. I cannot correct your errors, because the only reason I have not ⟨x⟩{established the truth} long ago is that the corrections would be painful to people still living. I have told in the note on page 229 ⟨x⟩ {one} of the reasons which accounted for my state of mind when I ran away with H. G. There were other more powerful reasons which I cannot possibly make public, now, at any rate. I am also putting in a note about the passage on page 392. But again I cannot tell the whole truth. The real reason I separated from H. G. was that he nearly ruined himself and me by involvement with a lunatic woman, and I got him out of the mess, and received little thanks, and realised that I might run into even uglier situations, to the prejudice of Anthony. Your whole version of H. G.'s life is based on what he wrote about it, which was not true. The woman he loved most of all was his cousin, who in no way resembled the conformist lay figure which he draws—he wrote of her that way because he had left her and regretted it.[3] The character of Jane was not at all like H. G.'s description of it, she was more like Rosamund Lydgate in *Middlemarch*. The atmosphere of the Wells household was one of feckless extravagance. Your views of Odette and Moura do not come within miles of the reality, and I do not mean that they do not agree with my opinion of the two women, I mean that you have not detected the actual facts of their lies. I again say that I wish you had not written this book.

I would like you—it is only a small matter—to expunge the passage at the top of page 304 which links up my sojourn in a nursing-home with the birth of the baby Anthony. It had nothing to do with it. I had T. B. when I was about fifteen, and this left me with a curious disposition to hemorrhage from the mouth at long intervals, quite alarmingly. The event always terrifies everybody, but it seems to have no significance. I had had a particularly violent hemorrhage walking across Hampstead Heath, and was borne to a hospital. I also object (for reasons I can't quite explain except that the {statements} simply are not true) to the note written in on the margin of page 309. H. G. didn't make any such arrangements. It wasn't like that.

I don't expect you can understand the intense revulsion I feel to accounts of my life which are not true. It is like being dissolved into mist. I felt the same thing about Antonia Vallejtin's book. It is unlucky for both of us. And I apologise very much for keeping you waiting.

Yours ever,
Rebecca

Rebecca West Collection   carbon typescript with autograph signature
Yale University

[1] Dickson was writing the biography *H. G. Wells: His Turbulent Life and Times* (1969).
[2] I have not been able to locate this ancestress, but she would be on the paternal side of West's family tree, for Joan Champernown married Anthony Denny.
[3] Wells left his first wife, Isabel in December 1893.

To: Anthony West

48 Kingston House North
Prince's Gate, S.W. 7
31 May 1969

My dear Anthony,

Oh, woe and lamentation. That empty envelope. There could be no more impressive evidence that the demons who persecuted Strindberg[1] have moved in on me. I am in the most dreary mess, the worse because I foresaw it and did everything I could to prevent it but it's won, it's here. But to deal with what was in the letter:

An announcement made rather diffidently that I have signed an agreement with a film company which is taking out an option for the film rights of *The Birds [Fall Down]*, a small thing, meaning not more than a handful of dollars for each of the participants among whom are Sophy and Adam. More will come to them if the option is exercised, which probably it won't. I have never had luck with Films. I am acting as the beneficiaries' agent.

I have a lot of first editions of works by such guys as T. S. Eliot and Gertrude Stein and Wyndham Lewis and a first edition of *Ulysses,* and a rather nice portfolio of reproductions of drawings by Wyndham Lewis, one of them being a version of me. If you would like them, I will give them to Em [Edmund West] or post them to you; but if you are indifferent to such things, as I am, I will sell them as your property at Sotheby's, if you send me an authorisation, and you will get a hundred pounds or two, and it can wait here for a holiday. (Which my mad friend Dachine[2] says may be this year.) Hurry up over telling me what you want done. I have packed these {books} in a suit-case and twice helpful little hands have unpacked it and merged the books with the rest.

Not in the letter, but coming up since: I have a pleasant faded piece of eighteenth century embroidery which used to hang over the mantlepiece in the drawing-room, also an Aubusson rug which I made out of a runner cut in two and joined tother way round, considered rather beautiful, hung on the stairs at Ibstone. Shall I send these over to you? Or would you like them sold as your property here? I think the embroidery had better be kept. It is very pretty and Sophy [her granddaughter] might like it. The Aubusson you might get something for if you sold it over there—I sold an old Aubusson inherited from Henry's uncle for £350 at Sotheby's. The Labrador slept on it for years, having that sort of taste.

⟨But not in your letter⟩ Also, I have a number of Piranesi prints,[3] some of which came from H. G. Do you want them? Let me know. My flat is littered and I am almost singlehanded in coping.

But I am terribly worried by your letter, because of your sentence—"I was left out of my father's will altogether on the ground that I was 'amply provided elsewhere,' that being his reference to his understanding that I was to inherit something substantial from Henry." This throws me. Henry had no money when I married him, he had a good salary from Schroder's, but was deeply in debt. I know Pamela [Frankau] had an idea, but not from me, that he was very rich, which I couldn't counter, because of the embarrassing circumstances of the financial disaster which had struck him. He had expectations of about £70,000 or £80,000 from his uncle, who was a most curious character, and he had got into an appalling financial mess because he had engaged in a financial operation which was founded on his belief that he could use part of his family trust to back it. But this it turned out he could not do, owing to a blunder on the part of his uncle, which his uncle refused to admit. The uncle's £70,000 well and truly belonged to Henry, as the family finances had all worked out to the uncle's advantage, but he was alarmed lest the old man, who was very ill, would turn against him and leave the money away from him if he pointed out that he had been at fault. The only thing was to go on as if nothing had happened, and we had great difficulties, during which I backed Henry with my income. We had really quite a hard time. It was then his intention to leave me all his money, and his first will was in that sense, and he was prepared to leave you everything {if I died} which at one time would have been a lot, for the uncle left him not £70,000 nor yet £80,000 but £140,000.

But. I don't remember telling any of this to ⟨Henr⟩ H. G. There was no reason why I should have done so, and much emotional cause for my not doing so. I strongly objected to H. G. not treating you on an absolute equality with Gip and Frank, and resented the fact that for a long time he made no provision for you beyond leaving ⟨you⟩ me £2,000 in a codicil to his will, which was even then a small sum. Nor would he carry out a scheme worked out for me by Theo Mathew, which would have made the years of your minority easier for me, have given you a nest-egg and preserved some capital for the Wells estate. He simply could not bear to do anything for you, first because he had this superstitious fear of Jane, and he had a curious feeling that she alone had the right to spend this money—and spend she did. It was incredible what she spent. Both H. G. and Arnold Bennett lived as if they had masses of *capital* behind them, and in H. G.'s case it was Jane who called the tune. Then H. G.'s attitude got financially harder, for the curious reason that he resented my leaving him, the more because I said it was difficult giving you a childhood in our circumstances—and it was his case that there were NO difficulties. He never would have made a settlement on you had he not been screeched into it by Odette [Keun], with her legal sense of justice. But this was all, as you know, only pretty Fanny's way.

Let us continue. Henry certainly meant to make you his ultimate heir for some years, and may have told you so. But as you must realise things changed. He got less companionship out of you than he had hoped, and there was one thing and another. Towards the end of the war he was considerably encumbered by other responsibilities. H. G. made his will at the end of the war. By that time Henry's mother's brother and his wife, a lawyer from Esthonia, and a quite old woman, had come to England, and Henry had heard that his cousin Lewis, an agricultural scientist who had been caught when working in Hungary because his wife was dying of cancer and could not be moved, had survived, was in a concentration camp in Poland with a wife and two children, and he knew well that he would have to help them if they got out, which they did. I spoke to H. G. several times about this, because it interested him (how we had got the news and so on). Neither then or at any other time that I can remember did he say anything about having heard you had expectations from Henry. Had he done so, I would have expressed myself strongly. He should have treated you on an equality with Gip and Frank—and in any case it would have been absurd for a man in his late seventies to withhold his inheritance from his son, on the off chance his son might inherit money from another man, not related to him, who was just fifty and likely to live another quarter of a century—as Henry in fact did! For one thing, had I died, Henry would have married again and had children as like as not. I never heard the phrase "amply provided elsewhere" as occurring in the will till now. (I have never seen the will.) I would think that H. G. might have meant by his phrase the settlement he had made on you, which you later gave Kitty in lieu of alimony. I really don't think he had in his mind that you were going to inherit vast sums from Henry, for surely he would have mentioned it to me? . . . .[4]

As to Henry's estate, the estate duties were 60%, and the lawyers are on the level, though harried into inefficiency beyond their natural endowment of the same by the complications of the war. The accountants have been the real pests, they have been paid vast sums to do our accounts every year, and knew nothing about them. I have had to hire extra secretarial help to get some idea of what the books the accountants audited had really contained for they could not tell me. The fantastic figures are due partly to the huge death duties, and partly to the fact that Henry was deep in insurance, and has been shelling out capital since Hurricane Betsy, like everybody else in the trade. It is a dead duck. The figures are further complicated to the laity by the fact that the insurance business cannot be shed, you can't get out of it, I have to face three years of losses after Henry's death, for it's hardly possible the process can reverse, and that is all allowed for in the figures. Henry has properly left some money to needy cousins and an old friend of ours, and this has left nearly nothing for me, probably less than nothing. Against this, there is here and now in my hands what ought to mean a little for you, though not more than a little. Henry repaid me my loans during the early years of our marriage ⟨which⟩ by giving me Ibstone, which cost £4,000 for the house and gardens and paddock, £3,000 for extra land—and I sold it for £50,000, and have exchanged it virtually for this apartment, which should keep pace with inflation. It is one of the nicest apartments in London and requires little domestic help, and has a restaurant in the house, and has a number of porters. I have bought an annuity which goes on for five years after my death, and have kept some securities, and some pictures, and as I say there should be a little for you—but really the estate duties are sheer spoliation—and if my financial position is worse than I represent it here, I shall not be surprised. We can talk of this if I go over to America or you come over here.

Regarding the other matters, Vanessa[5] was awful, I thought, Isadora ĭght have been a bloat and she was certainly a bore (a beauty-lover if ever there was one) but she moved beautifully, while Vanessa is made so awkwardly, she is the shape of an unskilled undertaker's apprentice's first attempt at making a coffin. After all Isadora swam most beautifully and in rough seas too, if you remember. But we must get Vanessa to play the lead in our joint tragedy,

"Dysentery." Ruskin's[6] trouble was that he thought there were fewer orifices than Philip Roth[7] believes. He sodomised poor Effie when at last he decided to consummate the marriage, and she did not realise in her simple Victorian way that she was rehearsing what could have meant a first-rate contract on Broadway. Cheer up about Alexandra's marriage.[8] Nobody now in these broad-minded days will insist on you all carrying little bells and saying "Unclean, unclean." The bridegroom's utterances in print have always struck ⟨x⟩ me as eternally wrong, just as shrdlu etain can never be right.[9] Or, meaningful, would be his word. I am rather surprised by Tom Wolfe's book on Kesey,[10] in which he seems to get the quiet authority of the bogus seer to perfection.

Please let me know about the (a) first editions[11] (b) Aubusson and embroidery and (c) the Piranesis, and that quickly.

Much love,

Rac

What I foresaw and could not prevent is that I should have to undertake this move with the incompetent help in the way of secretaries which was all I could have at Ibstone in the conditions of Henry's last years. It was a vast move. I have thrown out half my books and there was nothing to do in the time—I could not face going on paying the huge wages bill I had at Ibstone a week longer than I needed, when I had no time to supervise the farm—except bring the other half and weed them out here, which has produced a kind of chaos. I have still thirty tea-chests in store at the Army & Navy—and what agony it is to break up one's library, I don't know how I shall go on reviewing. I have also too many pictures. Henry had a long and close friendship with a very nice old Polish-German painter, Katerina Wilzcynski,[12] an old dear, who was very kind to him. He must have bought twenty to thirty large drawings from her (she is a very good draughtsman, but enough is enough) and SHE KNOWS I HAVE THEM. What does A do? They clutter up my box-room and throw everything into disorder. I also have to sell off things gradually, such as I do want to sell and convey them to Sotheby's (things like Thomas Shotter Boys pictures of London)[13] after due consultation. . . .[14] I won't get this straight till summer. Oh, oh. . . .

private collection   typescript with autograph signature

[1] Strindberg's problems began with childhood poverty. He was prosecuted for blasphemy concerning the bitter stories of *Married* (1884–1886), had a succession of unhappy marriages, and felt persecuted when he experienced difficulty in having his plays produced.

[2] Dachine Rainer, recipient of a 1968 letter.

[3] Giovanni Battista Piranesi (1720–1778), Italian draftsman, printmaker, and architect whose large prints often accurately depict classical Roman architecture.

[4] A long paragraph concerning her dissatisfaction with Wells's will has been omitted.

[5] Vanessa Redgrave (1937–), English actress named best actress at the 1968 Cannes Film Festival for her role as Isadora Duncan.

[6] John Ruskin (1819–1900), English critic and art historian who admired J. M. W. Turner and defended the Pre-Raphaelites. His major works include the multivolume *Modern Painters* (1834–1860), *The Stones of Venice* (1851–1853), and *Sesame and Lilies* (1865, 1871). His marriage to Euphemia Chalmers Gray (1847–1854) ended when she divorced him on grounds of impotence.

[7] Philip Roth (1933–), American novelist whose works reflect upon his Jewish background. West is referring to *Portnoy's Complaint* (1969), which contains Alexander Portnoy's scandalous confessions to a psychiatrist.

[8] Lily West's sister Alexandra became the second wife of Arthur Schlesinger, Jr.

[9] Nonwords used by typesetters for practice. *Etaoin shrdlu* (note spelling) represents the commonest letters in English, in descending order of frequency in use.

[10] Ken Kesey (1935–), American novelist known for *One Flew Over the Cuckoo's Nest* (1962) and *Sometimes a Great Notion* (1962). Tom Wolfe's *Electric Kool-Aid Acid Test* (1968) describes the exploits of the Merry Pranksters, a group led by Kesey in the mid-1960s.

[11] A letter to Anthony (17 June 1969, private collection) suggests that the carpets and embroidery and Piranesi prints were sent to Anthony, while the first editions and Wyndham Lewis portfolio were sent to Sotheby's, for sale in which West acted as her son's agent.

[12] Wilczynski had her earliest successes in Berlin during the 1920s. A winner of the Prix de Rome (1930), she moved to London in 1939. Henry Andrews edited Wilczynski's *Homage to Greece* (Macmillan, 1964), an interpretive study incorporating fantasy. The book also includes the work of English travelers to Greece and translations from classical authors.

[13] Thomas Shotter Boys (1803–1874), *Original Views of London as It Is: Drawn from Nature Expressly for this Work and Lithographed by Thomas Shotter Boys*.

[14] Complaints about her secretary have been omitted from the postscript.

To: Edmund and Vita[1] West

Galeana 501
Cuernavaca
Morelos
Mexico
14 December [1969?]

Dear Vita and Em,

I should have written long before, but I have been writing at a great rate, and this is so welcome after a time of frustration that I let the thing rip. When I got to Mexico City to stay with my old friend Romney Brent I found myself in a right hole. He was remote and had turned into the old Spanish bachelor that appears in so many Spanish novels, (he is a Spanish Mexican, right name Larralde) and he was not interested in anything. He played crossword puzzles after his morning coffee, went to the supermarkets, slept in the afternoon and had a family reunion in the evening with his aged sisters and we played scrabble all the evening. The apartment was miles out in a lovely suburb, it is true, lovely in a quiet way with funny things like an old racécourse that had been built over with lots of houses like opera sets, which had little brightlýpainted houses in between in which a lovely Jewish colony lived, old people with the finest faces and wrinkles like faults in ivory. But I couldn't get anywhere, boy, boy, do I mean anywhere, not a museum nearer than two and a half miles and no taxis except by telephoning to a rank, which meant that while I could get places I couldn't get back. From one search of photographs in an Art Museum I had to walk about three and a half miles in the blinding heat. The buses are lovely when you get in, full of people with the most wonderful Asian faces, and all, all with lovely hands, but I never knew which bus to take. The Mexican family which had been terribly good to me when I was there with Henry had suddenly disap-peared—I thought they were Commies at the time, and I think they must have been, there was a mystery, and I couldn't therefore trace my wonderful English-speaking driver. Romney Brent's family drove me crazy, they were midńineteenthćentury (this Spanish typewriter coughs out an accent when I want a hyphen, I suppose it's all this saying Ole), anti-clericals, told funny stories all the time about Saint Joseph and while I do not root for him this still is not news, and I found it fantastic not to be allowed to go into a church or even look at the facade without derision. I could not get up to travel agents in the hotels, so Romney led me to a travel-agent, Mexican, female, beautiful, incompetent (odd here, where most people are competent in a way) who slightly distorted our trip to the ruins in Yucatan. Which was nevertheless gorgeous. Palenque, even in the dripping rain, was a series of dream-palaces, and the journey there runs through cattlećountry and the cattle are lovely humped Cebus, and we crossed three wonderful rivers, unlike any rivers I have ever seen, wide and swinging round curves with groves on the shores, every time you shift on the bridge there is another view. We stayed in a nice hotel in a little place called Villa Hermosa which was run by a Syrian, and there you got the most superb fourćourse dinners for a dollar and a half. We went on to a Spanish colonial town called Merida where the girls in the beauty parlour chattered Mayan, and it was the greatest fun to sit in the square as the twilight fell and there was a wonderful Renaissance palace which had belonged to an ancient family that had made a fortune in the nineties in hemp and had refurnished from Paris, woe, woe. The guide pointed to an awful Spode meatdish, the kind with channels for the gravy, and said to the people he was showing round, "This lady is English see if she knows what is this." I said, "Spode." He then showed me a very ugly Wedgwood plaque and I said, "Wedgwood," He turned to the people and says "This lady evidently comes from a refined home, she recognizes our treasures." I then identified some Baccarat glass, and he asked me if I had a title, and see how I made a good man happy, of course I was able to say I had. The ruins in Yucatan are simply lovely, much more so than I had supposed. They are a lovely pie-crust colour, and some are extremely beautiful in themselves, more so than you would suspect from the photographs. I have never seen simple decoration, variations on checkerboard stuff, which were so uplifting, you really felt delighted. There was lovely sunshine and no mosquitoes, and by the ruins there are wonderful Anglo-Indian sort of hotels, with palm patios and big swimming-pools, and passable food (very good food in the towns). The idiot beauty travel agent did me out of two days treks from Chichen-Itza, which I would have loved to do. One of the lovely things about the ruins is that when you have climbed the buildings (not that I did the big steep pyramids, I felt I would fall down and do Granny's trick of breaking a pelvis but I got up the lesser ones) you look down on the lay-out and it is framed in a green sea of tree-tops going right on to the horizon. It is so pleasant, could you pull about the process of life so that someday we would all go down there in a vacation of yours which had been nicely timed for November. I love the people, they keep so cheerful and derisive and independent on ghastly land, the opposition party is not Left but pro-Catholic and anti-Establishment because the anti-Catholic semi-Left Wing broke up the haciendas and gave it in small plots to the Indians, and the Indians can't make a living; and nobody thought this funny but me. Also there was talk of a faked election the Establishment Government got 90% of the votes, nobody believed this, they challenged the poll, desolation because this prolonged the operation of a law forbidding alcoholic drinks to be served during an election. This went on and on, everybody was angry

then saw the joke, and laughed at themselves, and at one hotel we were
served in our bedrooms with huge free drinks (rum cocktails.) "Only one,"
they said, with a grin, "but you won't want another." They were huge. The
women are utterly marvellous, they keep the children healthy and clean, and
themselves clean and not slatternly, and all the water is fetched I don't know
how it would not be so, the only water in this accursed land (why did the
Mayans build a civilisation there) comes from waterholes.

Why I am pouring this out I don't know, as I intend to arrive amongst you
on December 29. I will go to Dorset,[2] I think. I have a party on December 30,
but nothing else, and will have a few days before I go to Emanie [Arling]
Phillips ⟨before I⟩ and would like to see you. I am staying with Kit and Thew
Wright,[3] who thought me tired and dispirited {by my return to Mexico City}
and have nursed me like a couple of mothers, and I have sat in a lovely garden
and been waited on paw and paw and fed with delicious food and they have
asked in inhabitants of this beautiful place, or rather pretty place with a
beautiful climate and from this garden the most exquisite view of Popocate-
petl, which is as good as Fuyi Yama when you know it. The people are to my
mind very odd, but what is distressing is that the young Americans who have
settled here (on inherited money, arts and crafts, easy happy lives) have only
conversation about how awful the United States is and how rotten everybody
is. {The U. S. A. is the only country of which it is true that the vast majority
of its inhabitants have no conversation except expressions of hatred for their
own people.}[4] I have brought up your names and occupations several times
in a very nasty spirit, suggesting you are *there*, and they are *here*. Two people
came in who had been in Europe in the thirties ⟨and⟩ during the worst of the
Hitler time, two nice elderly men, and they spoke with horror [of] a Hitler
massacre they had been close to, and an American painter woman said,
"Well, the world is uglier now." "How?" I asked, remembering that Henry
might have had his head cut off. "Oh, Vietńam," they said, "and Nixon.
How I *pray* for Vietńam to end, so that those people will be out on a limb.
There will, of course, still be the Negroes, but suppose that gets settled.
Thank God you are doing something useful. Sometimes, when the guests
have gone, and I listen to Thew and Kit talking, and they are your sort of
people, they can think and know things and have sense, I wish there were not
such a variation in human beings, but I suppose the higher forms would
never have developed unless there had been an elasticity of production which

produces the lower forms as well. Such pleasant times I am having with them. My book on Mexico[5] is turning into a life of Henry—there is a connection, but have an easy mind, the connection is real, I am not just wandering—and I see my way {through the short book}, just because these people are petting me and letting me sit in their garden and write and giving me luscious meals. Yesterday they gave me a superb day, they drove me out to a restaurant outside the town where we lunched in the open air (onion soup and chopped chicken in fried tortillas better than any food you could get in New York outside the great restaurants) in the company of a spider monkey, a creature that stands up as tall as a ten year old child and then sits down and folds itself up to the bulk of a flute-case. It had great personality, its name was Sandra, and it had a filmstar air. We went on to Tepotzlan, a village among volcanic mountains with lots of woodland, masses of trees with huge white flowers, and came on the village children in bright clothes chanting the Lord's Prayer in Spanish {very gaily as if it was an infant's drinking song} at the behest of a beautiful old nun (in lay costume of course) outside a superb old cathedral, not great architecture, but cosey, in a sort of runaway park, everything lovely and shabby, and things like the flowers and the children's dresses so strong in colour and so well-done by pure chance. We came home by a crimson sunset. Something seems to be triumphing over the barrenness of this country all the time, though *what* barrenness.

I will be seeing you soon. Keep a date or two for me, if the holidays permit it. I should be going home (flying, there isn't a boat, which disappoints me) about January 14. I have a lot to do in London, and can finish my short book there. But I don't know why I make such remarks when I am going to see you, I hope.

I may as well say now, however, that I dread seeing Anthony in New York but certainly will, but want to talk to you two about something that rather bewilders me about what I ought to do in a matter concerning Anthony. I was worried by that curious dinner at his apartment. What distresses me is his air of complete selfsatisfaction which may be a cover-up but may not but in any case makes him so difficult to talk to. And my God I see what you meant about the furniture. When I think of the tide of money that has swept towards Anthony and has been seen no more I can't understand it. Which is partly what I want to talk to you about. I just mention this because I get tired and have a block about talking about what really worries me.

Think of yur mum, Christmassing (because of Caro [West (Duah)], who didn't ought to) with Dachine [Rainer] in her appalling house, which is the supreme example of that architectural style, Early Uncomfortable.

Much love,

Rac

Rebecca West Collection   typescript with autograph additions
University of Tulsa

[1] Edmund's first wife.
[2] Home of Kitty, Edmund's mother.
[3] See letter to Kit Freund, whose second husband was Thew, 24 October 1944.
[4] West's handwritten marginal note.
[5] This never appeared.

To: Emanie Arling [Phillips]   48 Kingston House North
                                                Prince's Gate, S.W. 7.
                                                [October 1971]

My dear Emanie,

I sympathise with you over the fall—I don't think there is anything worse than finding that your body is determined to get you into trouble, like a mean enemy and not part of yourself at all. I would have written to you long ago to say what I felt but I have been through the wars. I had a virus infection in the middle of October and did not seem to get over it. I had a number of things to depress me at the time—for one thing, I have a cataract in my left eye and though they tell me I may never need to have it [out] I have my doubts—and I have a bone wrong on my right foot which needs an operation here and now—but slowly it has dawned on me that there is something else wrong and the doctor came in after I had had Kitty two days to stay—and she packs more into two days than most people could in a month—and I was feeling all sorts of queer aches and pains and contractions (of my eyes for one thing) and he told me that there is something wrong with my heart, and I go to a specialist on Thursday. He said he did not think it was serious but it needs some sort of attention. As I haven't been able to work for two months I am really glad to hear that there is something wrong and that I am not just falling to pieces. I shall be out of commission I think for a month or two.

I haven't written to you for so long that I forget when I did. In September I went with my sister Lettie, who talked all the time, for a tour in the South of Ireland, to see the homes and tombs of my ancestors.[1] I loved it, I felt so much at home in that rich and varied countryside. We drove for miles between hedges of crimson fuchsias, and the hydrangeas are varicoloured and huge, and the antiquities are wonderful—on a hillside we found some wonderful eighth century crosses, just like the Byzantine ones, and we came too on a third century fort, which was curiously like the Indian temples in New Mexico. I felt slightly exasperated at the amount of money my ancestors had spent on the ungrateful people of Ireland, one of them woke up one morning in his castle at Tralee, and bethought himself that the town would be more prosperous if the river was by the town and not a mile away, so he just moved it, with money that might have been mine. It is odd how ill-informed people are—we met lots of American tourists who said about the North of Ireland, "Why do you English send troops into Ulster?" and we did think they might have known that Ulster has chosen to be in the Commonwealth and is Protestant and they asked for the troops to save them from the bullets of Roman Catholic Irish who [expect?] Ulster to be a part of Eire.[2] These Americans were all Liberals, and I do think that liberalism is the great factory of misinformation in the world. The situation really is horrible. In Dublin (where I ended up at a PEN congress) the people didn't care about the English troops being killed, they didn't care about the Protestants being killed, they didn't care about their own Catholics being killed—it was all just a lark. The PEN congress was awful. I was driven by the self-satisfaction of the Behind-the-Iron-Curtain delegates who yammered about ideologies (proving that Brecht[3] was sustained throughout life by the consciousness that he was ideologically sound) that I was driven to make a Woman's Lib speech asking where male ideologies had got us if people were behaving as they do in Belfast. Not a paper reported it. I was so sick of the situation that when I was one of the twelve people asked to meet de Valera[4] I went off and spent the afternoon in the National Gallery.

I wish I could see you. All my love to you, and Christmas wishes. I hope my Christmas card reached you in time.

Rebecca

Rebecca West Collection   typescript
University of Tulsa

[1] West's letter on the Irish trip to Edmund and Vita West (29 September 1971, University of Tulsa) included more family information:

The lively little 18th century house where my father was born has been completely gutted by a prosperous dentist who has been able to express his aesthetic self, but the very nice house where the last Sir Henry Denny to live in Kerry lived . . . has been bought by a Washington lawyer who has returned there, and it reveals itself as a most beautiful small house, Ballyseed House (where my cousins lived and from which my grandfather and grandmother were married) is a lousy hotel but a most amusing house—it is a [beige?] Regency house, and leeside it approximates a Tudor palace two storeys high. The Blaner-hassetts built the house in 1832, the Palace was then solely ruins about 4 ft high. They built up to two storeys high and put turrets on—as a screen for the stables. The funny thing about Ireland is that there are lots of houses—large and small—which have been allowed just to fall down through sheer neglect. There are agricultural cottages quite near my grandfather's shooting-lodge, but when my grandfather married out nobody went to live there and the roof just fell in, and it is a ruin (a lively little house, doll-sized). It really is a strange feeling—it's as if one was on a Western frontier in U. S. A. and the extending forces had not gone on to California and the Pacific but had retired. There was some hope for us, I thought, in the way that the Fairfields and the Dennys and the Rowans and the rest of our family did do useful things in this wild place—they had built harbours and canals and roads. But it was hateful now—only sometimes something dangerous showed—I got out of the car when we were in a lovely little village called Smeen, and there were boys in the road scuffling and playing with pistols. A woman grinned at me and said happily, "The lads are playing they're [in] Belfast."

[2] In a letter to Dorothy Thompson (21 November 1938, Yale University), West offered comparable explanations of partition.

[3] Bertolt Brecht (1898–1956), German poet and playwright initially influenced by Expressionism, who later helped develop the concept of epic theater. His plays written in exile during World War II reflected an anti-Nazi spirit. Even though he was a committed Marxist, his plays found popularity in the West. Among Brecht's well-known works are *The Threepenny Opera* (1928), *Mother Courage and Her Children* (1939), and *The Caucasian Chalk Circle* (1944–1945).

[4] Eamon de Valera (1882–1975), longtime prime minister of Ireland (Eire) (1937–1948, 1951–1954, and 1957–1959); also president (1959–1973). He was spared execution as a participant in the Easter Rising of 1916 because his mother was American. In 1926 he founded the extreme republican Fianna Fáil Party, which voted to sever all ties with Britain.

To: The Editor, The *Times Literary Supplement*[1]   21 April 1972

Sir,—The historians of the future should cherish the reply of your reviewer to Mr Bromley's strictures on his notice of *The Embattled Mountain* (October 22, 1971). It is characteristic of the anti-Mihajlovič[2] campaign in the crisp, judicial manner in which it retails inaccurate information.

The reviewer is incorrect in saying that the case for Mihajlovič rests on a "Mihajlovič myth which came into being in Britain and the United States in the last months of 1941 and in 1942." In 1936 I went to speak for the British Council in Yugoslavia and among the places I visited was a Military College at Nish; and there three officers spoke to me of Drazha Mihajlovič as a leading anti-Nazi spirit in the Army. The next year I was twice shown, once by a member in the Serb Peasant Party, and once by a well-known writer and teacher named Anica Sevic-Rebac,[3] copies of a memorandum on guerrilla warfare as a means of resisting the inevitable attack which Nazi Germany was certain to make on Yugoslavia. The author was given as Drazha Mihajlovič; and his name was known as a professional soldier of merit and an anti-Nazi among Embassy staffs in Belgrade.

For this reason, as soon as Yugoslavia came into the war, I enquired from the Foreign Office as to what Mihajlovič was doing. I was told, not over weeks but over months, by Foreign Office officials that he had got into the field and was performing a useful function, with British assistance. I remember going into the Ivy to have dinner with a friend and passing a table where Sir Orme Sargent[4] was sitting. He rose and shook hands and said that I might be interested to hear that they had very satisfactory news of what Mihajlovič was doing.

Your reviewer says, with the portentousness of Proust's Monsieur Norpois, that "the strength of the Chetnik movement and the importance of Mihajlovič as a leader were exaggerated beyond any semblance of reality by the Yugoslav government in exile for their own purpose of internal and external policy." In fact the Yugoslav Government officials never ceased to warn me not to exaggerate the strength of the Chetnik movement and once, the Prime Minister, Dr Jovanovič, said to me, "All that we can promise is that when the time comes to throw the Germans out of our country Drazha will be there with a disciplined force trained to fight over a terrain they know as your armies cannot." This cannot be regarded as a sinister device of the Yugoslav Government-in-exile, as it was what all Foreign Office and War office officials at that time declared they hoped Mihajlovič would do.

I should be surprised if there were any documents,[5] as your reviewer alleges there are, which really prove anything about Mihajlovič's "collaboration" and "unwillingness to fight." I know, because I was shown a number of them both in Great Britain and America, after the war. There were a number of messages from Britons who were in camp with Tito which, evidently, anxious to please, gave the impression that Tito was walking on the water and waiting till tomorrow to perform the miracle of the loaves and fishes. There were also messages from Britons in the Mihajlović camp which were laudatory of him but which explained that Mihajlović was reluctant to follow the policy the British were suggesting to him. But this was indeed instantly recognisable as idiotic. The British were suggesting that Mihajlović should engage in acts of sabotage such as blowing up railway lines and making hit-and-run attacks on the German troops. Mihajlović saw no sense in blowing up railway lines which the Germans could repair in a couple of days while their comrades conscientiously burned the nearest villages and shot the inhabitants. He could do something in that line of sabotage, he said, but not much without running the risk of eroding his forces and turning the local populations against him. Mihajlović's attitude was that his business clearly lay in establishing a network of guerrilla fighters over the countryside which could master the terrain and its obstacles and be ready to act as not only a fighting but an intelligence force when the Allies came to drive the Germans out of the Balkans.

This was horse sense, particularly as the British let him suppose they were going to land in Yugoslavia. And I am amazed by the effrontery of your reviewer in saying that "most British officers associated with Mihajlović" disapproved of his policy and, when they honoured him, honoured him only as a man. This was not my impression. I particularly recollect a conversation with Colonel Charles Clarke, who was at least as impressive a witness[6] as Mr Deakin,[7] in which he said that Mihajlović's policy was right and sound, and showed a proper recognition of the difficulties of a guerrilla army keeping on good terms with populations which they must weary with requisitions and put in danger of reprisals, as in Bulgarian Macedonia.

To satisfy myself that my impression of Mihajlović's conduct was correct, I sought out in 1949 the German who had been Political Officer in Yugoslavia, then a resident in Bavaria. He was a reliable witness, for he was a remarkable man, strongly anti-Nazi, who had proved the genuineness of his convictions before the war by rendering a valuable service to the Allies. He declared that he knew of no occasion on which Mihajlović had aided the Nazi troops. But I quite understand what your reviewer means when he alleges that the idea that Mihajlović was a collaborator and that he was guilty of "a persistent refusal to fight the Axis" were concepts during the war. They were indeed. I remember them being most eloquently expressed by Guy

Burgess. He asked me if I had heard the terrible news that Mihajlovič was a traitor.[8]

I write this letter without any real hope that the truth will prevail. I do not think it can.[9] But I am revolted by the continuance of the anti-Mihajlovič campaign. The situation was quite simple. Churchill one day came to the decision that he could please Stalin by giving him Yugoslavia, and therefore he backed Tito. His decision could be smelt in the London air as soon as he had made it. A great lady said to me one day, "I understand you know something about Yugoslav affairs. Can you tell me how I can get my son sent out to Tito? I'm told it's the thing for a young man to do if he wants to get on." This was by no means England's finest hour.

So a nation which had fought for centuries for its independence from the Turkish Empire was suddenly informed by the Allies that because of a mission carried out in their country, by Mr Deakin, who was then a history don, thirty years of age, they were to be forcibly converted from a non-communist state to a communist state. This was an insolent and tyrannous proceeding, and fatuous. I doubt if it has ever done us a halfpennyworth of good, and at this moment the state of the Mediterranean suggests that it may cost us a great deal. But it was done, and I can understand that the doing was made easier by letting Mihajlovič get shot. But need interested parties go on spitting on his dead body? I write, as I say, in no great hope that the truth will prevail.[10] But I feel obliged to describe the situation as it appeared to me over the years of observation.

REBECCA WEST

[1] Published in the *TLS,* 21 April 1972, 448–49.

[2] The *Times* substituted this spelling for West's preferred "Mihailovitch," which occurs throughout a very similar letter in carbon typescript in the Rebecca West Collection, University of Tulsa.

[3] See letter to Henry Andrews, 22 April 1936, for note on Šević-Rebac.

[4] Sir Orme Sargent, British deputy undersecretary for foreign affairs. He was among the minority who felt that it was in the long-term interest of Britain to support Mihailovitch and his Chetnik followers, and tried to maintain relations with him as late as November 1943.

[5] The typescript has "There are no documents."

[6] West has again tempered her draft, which read, "a man of far higher calibre and wider experience than Mr Deakin."

[7] Carl William Deakin, British intelligence officer, previously an Oxford history don, who reported that Tito and his Partisans had superior strength and that Mihailovitch was a collaborator with Hitler. This swayed Churchill's allegiance toward Tito. Deakin parachuted

into Yugoslavia (27 May 1943) to obtain supposed firsthand information but, according to David Martin, relied heavily on the Partisans (see Martin's *Web of Disinformation*). Deakin's book *The Embattled Mountain* gave rise to this exchange.

[8] West is savoring the fact that Burgess was later convicted of treason.

[9] This sentence was added in the final version.

[10] The draft ends more forcefully, starting from this point: "But I want to take my stand with Mihailovitch, for the same reason that, when I have been somewhere very dirty, I want to have a bath. But that is not a feeling with which either your reviewer or Mr Deakin will understand."

To: Gip Wells

48 Kingston House North
Prince's Gate S.W. 7
21 May 1973

Dear Gip,

We were mistaken about the MacKenzies.[1] They led me to understand—but I think they may have done this without a clear notion of what they were doing—that they were writing a critical study of H. G.'s work backed by some biographical detail. There is mighty little about his work and it is an attempt at biography, no more than that, at *the* biography. They cannot write *any* biography, because they just can't, as it turns out (the whole picture is highly conventional) and the only person who can write *the* biography is Gordon Ray. Besides the material you send him, he has collected a lot more, and he is the only person who has seen the 800 letters of H. G.'s I deposited in the Benicke [*sic*] (is that it?) Library at Yale.

But worse than this, they have sold the book for serialization to the *Sunday Times,* to be issued in three parts, on the three first Sundays of June, under the title, "The Sexual Torment of H. G. Wells."

This has absolutely stunned me. They wrote to me some time ago ⟨asking me to⟩ {telling me the} *Sunday Times* was going to serialise it, but having a critical work in mind I thought that it would be on the literary page. I had made arrangements to call Lambert, and I want to ask him very gently if he can get the title changed, pointing out that I really had not given the MacKenzies permission with such a publication in mind, and asking him if an alteration can be made in one paragraph in the book. I am afraid this is all I can see in the way of remedies.

About Anthony. He behaved very well throughout the whole of his daughter's illness. But I think he is very unhappy from all I hear. He has the same wife whom you dined with in New York, but she and the children, I gather, don't like London. I have asked him to come and see me, and I *hope* to get the whole thing sewn up, but this is Christian-Sciencing. It is very kind of you to say that you would greatly like to talk with him. His life is of course centred in the Wells family, which I cannot say has been an unmixed blessing, but still is a tribute to H. G. and your own kindness to him, and Frank's. I made an odd discovery the other day. I turned up in an old folder some letters written to me from a sanatorium in Norfolk by Anthony, at a time when his conversation was quite remarkably intelligent. It suddenly struck me that he had then suffered from what it is now fashionable to call dyslexia. I have not been reading the *Reader's Digest,* I have had rather a lot to do with this disorder because I had a god-daughter who suffers from it and a niece's husband who works on it in East End schools; and really his notes are very peculiar, on any other hypothesis. He must have snapped out of it in adolescence, and indeed I can remember when he suddenly did start reading and writing, with great fluency. I have just watched my god-daughter's elder sister do that same thing after having been almost a handicapped child. Anyway Anthony has lived a most uncomfortable life, and though he has made mine equally uncomfortable, and perhaps more so, I now bear no grudge.

I will be communicating with you about the *Sunday Times* before you go, I am simply going to go very softly, and I don't think it is worth telling the MacKenzies what I think of them. (I don't really think they know what they have done.)

I did not know your son was a doctor, I suppose you know that Em [Edmund West] has done very well at Lennox Hill and is going into practice at Stonington, where there is a good hospital.

Yours ever,
Rebecca

H. G. Wells Archive University of Illinois	Typescript with autograph signature
Rebecca West Collection University of Tulsa	carbon typescript

[1] Norman and Jean Mackenzie, authors of *The Life of H. G. Wells: Time Traveller* (1974), published in the United States as *H. G. Wells: A Biography* (1973).

To: Arthur Crook[1]   48 Kingston House North
                                            Prince's Gate, S.W. 7
                                            24 December 1973

My dear Arthur,

I could not believe my eyes, and I am staggered by your bravery; and I am also quite tearful with gratitude. I have forced my way into recognition of a sort, but I am treated as a witch, somebody to be shunned. My books (particularly when they were being reviewed in the *T. L. S.*, let me say) have always been treated as if they were maleficent spells. Bowra[2] was a man with a certain amount of intellectual honour, but he was a coward, more sensitive to the danger of doing what was not done by the best people than becomes any forked radish. Through the years we used to meet, and it amused and terrified me to see how amused and terrified he was whenever he liked anything I said. He was saying to himself, "No, the safer thing is to wait till sundown and go with the other village boys to burn down the cottage." I do admire you for having challenged this habit of the English intelligentsia.

This is not to say that I have not had recognition and kindness, from the people who mattered to me—such as Professor Hutchinson of Yale. But there have been moments when I really felt as if I were being pelted out of the village with my broom-stick. This is partly, as you say, a matter of interstices. That just could not be helped. It is a wonder I have written any books at all. From 1942, Anthony has been a perpetual source of misery and humiliation to me, and there has never been any way of placating him. Which is the worse because till then he had been a charming and companionable son. What happened to him when he was twenty-eight I cannot guess. Five years after my marriage to Henry, who was a much more brilliant person than people realised and could give me entertainment as well as steady love, {he} showed the first signs of brain damage, and after a short respite this went on and on and on till he was an ⟨xxx⟩ intractable case of cerebral arteriosclerosis. This meant not only that he was difficult to deal with, it meant I was enmeshed in the affairs and daily routine of a highly unsuccessful farm, which was his only form of recreation after he had [to] leave banking. I have had to struggle to get *anything* done.

I was also handicapped because you are right, I do care above all for reality. What chance did that give me in a world dominated by Eliot, who did not care for reality, who only cared to give out passes that certified the holder to be respectful to reality. I couldn't bear him or his work. The dominant factor in him was ambition, which is the enemy ⟨for⟩ of reality— ambitious people don't wait to be classified by reality. The cultural England he made seems to me like that cynical building, is it Centre Point or High Point,[3] which looms against the sky and should be sheltering the homeless and shelters no one. I don't feel that anybody in English literature has cared for reality since Yeats.

I don't belong to a world where E. M. Forster, a self-indulgent old liberal with hardly a brain in his head, could be taken as a national symbol of moral power. I am too good for the world of modern literature, and the way I come off so badly is that I know that I am not good enough for *my* world. I fall short and I fall short and only in parts of *The Birds Fall Down* have I ever felt that I was coming near what I wanted to do.

I am sorry you don't like more of my fiction. I think perhaps you are doing me an injustice because I seem to myself the only person who has written about certain people nobody else described. Waugh has described rich people who were bestial, or mediocre, but in *The Thinking Reed* I was writing about people who were rich *but* not bestial *but* in many ways trivial. One of the characters is a life-like portrait of Antoine Bibesco. The only other person who has written about them was Nancy Mitford,[4] and while I couldn't for the life of me have written *Don't Tell Albert*, she was the sort of mutt who would fall in love with a Parisian meteque,[5] while I was [not] and it gave me a certain advantage. As for *The Fountain Overflows*, you are quite wrong.[6] When my sister Winifred and I were young, we were full of such ideas about childhood, which was a subject constantly discussed, as serfs might discuss serfdom while fond of their masters, and I can assure you that the book understates the musical preoccupations of the household. I don't think a single line of the children's conversation could not have taken place, and many of them did take place. The incident of Cordelia and the violin-playing was literally true; Cordelia was the infant prodigy violinist sister of a famous English pianist dead long since, and they were our neighbours. But nobody else has written about such people. You are penalising me for keeping an unconventional eye. It seems to me now a source for pride that all my books are different. I was looking at something fresh each time. I don't think I should be judged as failing because what I saw was not the same as people without my experience do not recognise as familiar. But again I am not with my age. All Graham Greene's books are the same, and are the same as Mauriac's books except for a more intense slyness. All Iris Murdoch's[7] books are the same (and very entertaining that book is) but there is the same vision of a world grotesquely caricatured, and the caricature corrected by an ethical simplicism. I have not established my pattern, but did not want to, it would distress me to write another *Birds Fall Down*.

Let me remind you that Balzac and Dostoevsky did not keep on writing the same books, though Tolstoy did, but then he is not an artist, he is a preacher. And how vastly admired. I remember a German saying to ⟨him⟩ me, it is all the little touches I admired. Like the sentence, "The little children went into the wood and looked for mushrooms, uttering little cries when they found them." Now, that's an empty sentence, and a novel should have no empty sentences. I mean that seriously, because if there are empty sentences the reader falls into the same attention deeply stained by inattention which comes to congregations listening to preachers; and a novel is a matter of catching the attention to listen to something new and important. I meant *The Thinking Reed* and *The Fountain Overflows* to do that, I think.

By the way, in your mention of *The Fountain Overflows,* you accept a modern canon which I think quite inacceptable: that one should not write about exceptionally gifted people. I see no sense in that at all. Scientists do not refrain from investigating the habits of the dolphin because it is the most intelligent of the big-brained sea beasts.

This is not an indictment but a happy argument. You can be wrong as you like about me, it is all most enjoyable. But I really don't understand why you used that awful drawing. It is such a bad drawing—the relations between the shapes are ghastly—such as the streamers floating out to the actual angle at the right base of the whatever. Also the artist has apparently thought that my hearing-aids are part of the lobes of my ears. If you had asked me to draw myself I could have done a better job. (The two black shapes in the

[fore]ground look, as an unkind friend has remarked, like two toy rabbits trying to treat me as a nursing mother. But let that pass.

All love and Christmas wishes, and so much gratitude

Your devoted Rebecca

private collection   typescript with autograph signature and insertions

[1] Editor of the *Times Literary Supplement* (*TLS*).

[2] Sir Cecil Maurice Bowra (1898–1971), Oxford scholar and critic known for his wit and hospitality. His scholarly interests range from Greek translations to modern criticism. He wrote *The Heritage of Symbolism* (1943) and *The Creative Experiment* (1949).

[3] Centrepoint, infamous London tower building centrally located in the West End, where Oxford Street, New Oxford Street, Charing Cross Road, and Tottenham Court Road intersect. Owing to tax law, Centrepoint was more profitable to its owner if it was not rented; hence, squatters took up residence there.

[4] Nancy Freeman Mitford (1904–1973), English novelist and historical biographer who wrote for the *Sunday Times*. She offers witty treatments of the British upper class and is best known for *The Pursuit of Love* (1945) and *Noblesse Oblige: An Enquiry into the Identifiable Characteristics of the English Aristocracy* (1956).

[5] *Métèque*, French for "alien."

[6] Crook did not find the children's mature talk in *The Fountain Overflows* credible.

[7] Iris Murdoch (1919–1999) Irish-born novelist, poet, philosopher, literary critic, and playwright. Her existentially conceived protagonists typically go through a process discovering a pattern for survival that must be deconstructed by the reader. Her many novels include *Under the Net* (1954), *The Severed Head* (1961), *The Sea, The Sea* (1978), and *The Good Apprentice* (1985).

To: Arthur Schlesinger, Jr.   48 Kingston House North
Personal and confidential   Prince's Gate, S.W. 7.
                                               8 October 1974

My dear Dr Schlesinger—or Arthur, if I may make so bold,

I write to ask you a favour—but I shall quite understand if you refuse it.[1]

I shall be 82 on my next birthday. I have no idea how much money I shall leave. I had better explain my position, as you may have heard vague reports. My husband had no money when I married him, beyond his salary, and he had a number of debts due to the ⟨embezzlement⟩ {mishandling} of the family funds by trustees. When he died he left a certain amount (not much, as he was a "name" at Lloyds) and I am handing it over {to his family and friends}— I have already handed over some of it and will hand over the rest when the

Inland Revenue lets go of it. I want to make it clear that there is nothing more to come from this source, which I always intended to go to his family.

For myself, I have looked after my earnings carefully, and I used part of my capital to buy an annuity. Of what remains—I exchanged my house in the country for a flat in London, and I have confidence that so long as the private ownership of the house property continues it will be worth some money. I have some investments (not many) and some good pictures, bought in my youth. If Healy[2] goes ahead with his wealth tax these will expose me to new taxation and little will be left; but it is just possible that the axe may not fall, in which case there will be something left.

I have, as you may know, already settled something on the children of Anthony and his first wife—indeed I did this many years ago, and the joint settlement amounted until the recent crash to something around £30,000. They also will receive £10,000 apiece from insurance policies. I really do not think there is much need to do anything more for them, as their mother [Kitty West] is not only a person of substantial inheritance and she has also been given by Anthony all the funds H. G. intended for his support. I understand that your sister-in-law [Lily West] has an amount of capital from her mother which will guarantee the future of herself and her children. I ⟨?⟩ have therefore left as an overriding obligation which I cannot disregard, my concern for Anthony.

I have not succeeded in getting on easy terms with Anthony since he came back to England. This is partly my fault. Your sister in law and Anthony asked me to go up to their house for drinks, but this was, for reasons your sister-in-law probably did not appreciate, an extremely gloomy occasion for me. I was so disappointed that I failed to follow it up, but really could not have done so if I had wished, as I had to undergo a number of depressing cancer tests and my sight suddenly got much worse (as you may guess from this letter.)

It is my intention to divide whatever I can rescue between my nephew and niece [Norman Macleod and Alison Selford], who have been very good to me, and devote the residue (except for a few trifling legacies) to Anthony. The trouble is that I do not think that looking after money is one of his talents. I am wondering if you would consent to act as a trustee in cooperation with my London solicitors, Glen Slaghton & Gay.

I think you will understand the anxiety which makes me put forward such a preposterous suggestion. I shall quite understand if you dismiss it as just that. I should be gratified if you could top your dismay by naming someone who you thought would be willing to take on such a job. I really have very little hopes of anything coming of this letter—but what can I do?

Will you give my best regards to your wife who I always remember for her gay kindness—and accept all my good wishes yourself.

Yours sincerely,
Rebecca West

I am so uneasy about this letter, which seems to me quite an imposition on my part, that I opened it again and reread it, but really I feel I must send it. I am 82 and I am in various ways not well. I wrote to Anthony (when he was in [Alence?]) this summer—warning him in advance about Ray's book and other things—and I have had no answer. I am extremely distressed about him. I understand he published a book on some French writers and it was not reviewed, and I cannot think how that could be. Please do not inform him of my cancer as this seems to irritate him greatly.

private collection   manuscript

¹ He politely declined.
² Denis Healey (1917–), English politician, spokesman for the Labour Party. He served as chancellor of the Exchequer.

To: The Editor, *Harper's* Magazine   48 Kingston House North
                                           Prince's Gate, S.W. 7
                                           11 January 1975

Sir,

In your issue of { January} you have published a review of Professor Gordon Ray's book, "H. G. Wells and Rebecca West," by my son, Anthony West.

I would be glad if you would allow me to correct two serious errors out of the many in the review ⟨xxx⟩, and a minor error.

First: I told Professor Ray and he has repeated the statement in this book that in my childhood and my early youth my family were extremely poor. My son alleges that this statement is not true.

He writes:

My grandmother, Mrs. Fairfield, was always able to keep up a genteel, middle class establishment, to employ servants, to send her children to good private schools and to put her eldest daughter through medical school. When she died she was living in a pleasant house in the Hampstead Garden Suburb, a locale impossible to associate with penury, and she was able to leave her youngest daughter a legacy of £5,000 at a time when the pound was still worth five dollars and had six to eight times its present purchasing power. This "virtual poverty" as Professor Ray chooses to call it can only have been symbolic . . .

This picture is wholly untrue. My father was a victim of a number of financial misfortunes, of which some were his fault but most not, and my mother found herself in middle age facing the world with three daughters to educate and an income of something under three hundred pounds a year, supplemented by a small allowance from a former pupil to whom she had taught music. Her first act was to park her children and go on tour as the pianist of the Singing Evangelists, Torrey and Alexander, and she took several other such jobs before she settled down as a copy-typist, an occupation which she continued to practise after we moved to Edinburgh.

She was not "able to send her children to good private schools." We sent ourselves. With the aid of her preparation, my sister Winifred was at Cheltenham on a scholarship, and I took ⟨several⟩ {some} bursaries at George Watson's College. My mother did not "put her eldest daughter through medical college." Andrew Carnegie[1] of Pittsburgh did that. My sister Letitia was one of the many doctors who got their training free from this munificent endowment of the Scottish Universities. During the whole of this time my family and myself ate the cheapest food, wore the cheapest dresses, and had the most spartan holidays. At no time could our ill-provided home have been described as "a genteel, middle-class establishment."

As for the pleasant house my mother owned, it was indeed in Hampstead Garden Suburb, but it is startling to hear this described as "a locale which it is impossible to associate with penury." It is a large housing estate, designed by early Progressives at the beginning of this century, in which there are houses of every size. Ours was one of the tiniest, and my mother acquired it when she had educated all of us and my two elder sisters were out on the world and earning respectable salaries. As for the legacy of £5,000, this consisted in large of money she had inherited from four relatives in her last years.

It is not surprising that my son would be in error over all this. He is now sixty, and his grandmother died when he was seven; and he had not visited her house for at least a year before she died. From my own knowledge I am aware that he has never handled any papers which would enlighten him on the financial affairs of his grandmother.

The minor error concerns what seems like the sinful luxury of my domestic arrangements during the first World War. My son has noted that in 1914–1915 I employed a cook and a housemaid as well as a nurse; and that in 1915–1916 I employed a cook and housemaid and a companion-housekeeper as well as a nurse; and he concludes that I was a pampered young woman who had no reason to complain. But absolutely no conclusions can be drawn from these facts. All they mean is that in 1914–1915 I spent some months in a furnished house in the country which had been taken by friends who had promised the owners, who were justifiably nervous about their exceptionally well furnished and fitted house, that I would employ domestic staff of the kind then universally recognized as proper for such a house; and that in 1915–1916 I moved from there to a large uncomfortable and isolated villa. But my son and his nurse and myself were not the sole occupants of this villa, I shared it with a family of five which included two children under three. They were obliged to leave after a short time, upon which I found myself, with my child and my nurse, alone with a staff engaged to look after a household of seven people, in a house without central heating, two miles from the nearest shops, with no telephone and no car or any conveyance, or even public transport. As soon as possible I left and moved into a small modern house more conveniently sited. My actions throughout these situations were purely neutral, the most predictable responses to the pressures of necessity, and it is not possible to use them to discredit me.

Such misrepresentations can however be dismissed easily enough because they can be checked by recourse to material proof. The more dangerous misrepresentations are those which relate to actions and speeches and feelings, and an extremely painful example of this is the second important error I have mentioned.

My son writes:

Jane Wells, who had initially licensed my father's affair with my mother on the clear understanding that it would be no more than that had changed her mind when she felt that my mother was urging her claim to a central position in her husband's life and making increasingly heavy demands on her resources. She let her friends know that she felt that my mother was behaving badly by breaking the rules of the game they had agreed to play and that she resented it. . . .

I do not believe that Jane Wells, a reticent and dignified woman, gossiped to her friends about her husband's love affairs. Nobody has ever made such an allegation before. Some of her friends, it is true, invented spiteful stories about me, but nobody ever suggested that she inspired them and indeed they continued long after her death. I have never expressed indignation at Jane Wells' complaints about me to her friends, because this is the first I ever heard of them, and I believe the allegation to be false. It is therefore quite untrue that Professor Ray in his book shows signs of sharing my indignation.

I do not think that my son ever met Jane Wells but if he did he can hardly have gained much enlightenment about her emotional life. She died when he was thirteen.

Yours sincerely,
Rebecca West

Rebecca West Collection
Yale University

typescript copy with autograph signature and corrections

[1] Andrew Carnegie (1835–1919), the Scottish-born American steel magnate began to endow educational institutions and libraries after he sold Carnegie Steel Company (1901).

To: The Trustees
   The Beinecke Library
   Yale University

48 Kingston House North
Prince's Gate, London, S.W. 7
May 1975

Dear Sirs,

I have by my will given you all my private papers and would like to express my pleasure in the way they had been dealt with by the patient and intelligent Miss Wynne.[1] I do not wish anyone except Professor and Mrs.

Hutchinson, or Dr. Gordon Ray and Miss Wynne to have access to these papers until the death of my son, Anthony West. I made this proviso with a definite purpose. My son has published and repeated many stories about myself, my family, and various persons connected with me which are complete fabrications. Many of these can be detected as fabrications by reference to these papers. But I do not wish them to be accessible until after my son's death, because if he could see them he would be able to fabricate stories which were congruous with the circumstances disclosed, and there would be no way of detecting them. I therefore ask that if, after his death, it appears that any person is seeking to perpetuate or add to his fabrications, the librarians should use their discretion in dealing with this nuisance, by withholding permission to see them. But I am sure I can rely on your own good sense and kind feeling.

Yours sincerely,

Rebecca West Collection   carbon typescript
University of Tulsa

[1] Marjorie Wynne, research librarian at the Beinecke Rare Book and Manuscript Library, Yale University.

To: Michael Denison[1]   48 Kingston House North
                                              Prince's Gate, S.W. 7
                                              4 June 1975

My dear Michael,

I was watching you last night and enjoying every minute of it. I marvelled that Whitey[2] could keep up with the Niagara flow of African energy, and Whitey certainly did, although I quailed to think what the two matinée days must be like. I loved your Macmillan look and voice and there is a line I shall always treasure—"I am the registrar"—which is perfect Aide-de-camp in its delivery. At every moment you were perfection. I also, from the second row, thought I saw signs you were enjoying the show as much as I was—what miracles they are, miracles of loveliness, miracles of skill, miracles of grotesquerie, and what *industry,* what perfectionist passion there is behind it. The Mikado has the presence of Chaliapin,[3] he roars for all the bull bisons that ever were created (and what a voice). And that Tit-willow song is marvellous, so absolutely right, and ungreasy, if you know what I mean.

I know it's no use trying to see you when you're both in such successes, but I imagine these will go on for a long time, so I won't even say I hope to see you soon. But some day I hope we'll meet again, and meantime much love to you both.[4]

Yours ever,

Rebecca

What a chancy business you're in! There you are, in what might have seemed a most unlikely milieu, doing a lovely piece of work part of a lovely whole. I saw Paul Scofield[5] the other day playing Prospero—the island being converted to a pool hall with Ariel standing in the gallery and wearing tight pants and looking like the caretaker,—and I suppose Scofield like myself could never have thought that any production of the *Tempest* would work out that way—anyway his spirit died.

Denison and Gray papers   manuscript
Boston University

[1] Michael Denison, Oxford-educated actor, married to actress Dulcie Gray in 1939. They are the married couple with the longest partnership on the London stage and have performed together or separately in more than one hundred plays and films. Ibsen, Shaw, and Wilde are their favored playwrights. Born in Kuala Lumpur, Dulcie Gray has twenty-four published books to her credit, including *Baby Face,* set in South Africa, which West read en route to that country. Michael Denison's *Double Act* includes reminiscences of West, as does his account of Noël Coward, written for the *Dictionary of National Biography.* Denison and Gray entertained West regularly at their country home, on the last occasion introducing the delighted West to the Queen Mother; they were also regulars at her birthday parties at the Empress Hotel in her final years. Denison read a humorous selection from *Black Lamb and Grey Falcon* at her memorial service.

[2] West had attended *Black Mikado,* a rendition of Gilbert and Sullivan's work in which Denison was the only performer who was not black. Denison played Pooh-Bah as Harold Macmillan.

[3] Fyodor Chaliapin, famous Russian operatic bass soloist.

[4] Gray was discouraged from writing West's biography for interesting reasons:

I do not feel that this is really much loss to you, for it seems to me that it is going to be an extremely niggling and tiresome job. To cope with my writing career, my biographer will have to go through the files of countless periodicals. They will also have to visit America for my personal and my business correspondence, which is all filed at the Beinecke Library at Yale. This is most awkward for English people, partly because Yale is such a detestable

climate for most of the year, partly because it is such an immense collection. The reason
that I had to send it over to America was that the British Museum was so rude to me when I
offered the collection to them. {You} ⟨Yale⟩ have also got a peculiar hazard in connection
with my family affairs in that the Wells family are extraordinarily quarrelsome and disagreeable, and they seem remarkably hearty for their ages. So is Anthony. (letter to Dulcie
Gray, 1 February 1982, Boston University)
[5] Paul Scofield (1922–), British actor who distinguished himself in Shakespearean roles and
as Sir Thomas More in *A Man for All Seasons* (1960).

To: Alison Selford   21 July 1975
My dear Alison,
    Herewith some notes on the family.[1]
    (1) Uncle Alec's unkindness to my mother did not lie in refusing her
financial help. He had not much money, partly for the reason that he had
gone to the Royal Academy of Music some time early in the eighties and
stayed there for literally forty years, and they put his salary up hardly at all—
and he had to entertain a great deal. His capacity for work outside his official
duties was severely limited by his wife's hypochondria. He actually left about
£20,000, and his daughter Mamie not unnaturally had to dip into her
capital before she died, and left Ian something like £9,000.[2]
    Uncle Alec was a mean man, but his unkindness to my mother related not
to that but to his unpleasantness. When my mother returned from Australia
he simply refused to have anything to do with her. He had all the other
members of the family to his house, but not my mother or any of our family,
and he did not even send us Christmas cards. My mother could not discover
the reason for this. He may have feared that she would ask him for financial
help, but I rather think that his wife, who was a very beautiful and quite
fiendish woman, the daughter of a gardener whom he had met because she
came to sing in his choir when he was in charge of the music at St. George's,
Edinburgh, may have disliked my mother. In any case his conduct to my
mother was unpardonable, and when my mother asked him to come and
visit her on her death bed he refused to come on the ground that it would
have upset her too much.[3] He came to the funeral, but left without asking us
if he could do anything.
    (About Ian's inheritance; do not believe anything your mother told you
about this. Ian inherited the money because Uncle Alec directed Mamie to
leave it to him, as he was the only male in the family. . . .[4]

(2) I don't think Lettie's lack of interest in my grandfather's family—the Mackenzies and the Campbells—was due to snobbery, as much as the fact that little is known, and that is often of a very unpleasant nature. My grandmother, whose Christian name[5] I can't remember, was a Campbell related somehow to the Duke of Argyll's family. There was a custom in the old families that the head of the family (or a deputy) called once a year on all the relations within a certain (quite wide) degree. This comes into the Dilke case,[6] by the way. When I was little the deputy was an unmarried daughter of the Duke named Lady Victoria Campbell, and she called every year on my grandmother and her sister who lived with her, Grand-aunt Isabelle. Also when I was in my late twenties I knew Joan Campbell, an unusually rich Campbell, the niece of one of the later Dukes, and she on hearing this got the archivist of the Argyll family to look it up, for the reason she wanted to encourage her sister who feared there had never been an intelligent Campbell and was having or had had children, and she said that the archivist confirmed there was a relationship—which went back to the mid-eighteenth century! But when my grandmother ran away with the musician Alexander Mackenzie her family cut her off completely, and when she was left a widow with five children, her husband having died in his thirties, they gave her no help.[7] Her sister, Isabelle, then left her parents' house and went to the aid of her sister, and they cut her off too. Her parents were quite rich. (Ian has a very nice picture of the wife). To make the story more extraordinary, my grandmother took in Jessie Watson Campbell and her sister,[8] who were the children of a worthless cousin who deserted them when his wife died in childbirth, and went off to Australia, unable, he said, to face life owing to his grief at the death of his wife. None of the rich Watsons did anything about these children. The darling Jessie Campbell you must know all about. The other sister was supposed to have gone to the bad, but I don't think she did anything worse than marry [a] vaudeville actor and go to America with him and die in Chicago. [You w]ill understand that neither my grandmother or Aunt Isabelle (Easy—and what an inappropriate name, she was anything but) cared to talk about their own family. Her parents were textile manufacturers in the Galasheels or Peebles district, and they probably had quite interesting connections, but I don't think anybody knows who they were. They have been related to the Scotch ancestors of Henry!

The Mackenzies were peasants who had been musicians for five generations—one got into a town band and was taken up by a local grandee and encouraged to be a professional musician—I suppose in the mid-eighteenth century, and they advanced to the summit in Alec. My grandfather was obviously a great charmer, and had immense talent. Everybody seems to have loved and admired him. On his side we had two cousins called Mackenzie— and one was a coal engineer, Joe Mackenzie, and did the design for the roof of Paddington station, which is a beautiful construction. He had an idea that presently people would want to live in flats and built several blocks in Hammersmith and Turnham Green, and nobody wanted them, and he died a poor man. He was married to a woman with gypsy blood in her called Pennycuick, and they had five children—they were bold, vulgar people, in a curious way gipsy like, but they were warmed hearted and hospitable and I enjoyed staying with them. There was also Ian Mackenzie, who was head traveller to the paper firm of Spicers, and not at all a person to be despised, it was then quite a heavy job, he would now be called the sales manager, and he was a superb flautist—and he was one of the most nauseating of human beings, mean, undignified, loathsome. I did him pretty well in *The Fountain Overflows*. His wife was a darling, and so was one of his daughters, Marjorie, an angel (ill-rewarded by Heaven), but they had another daughter, Dorothy, who married a South African, and was worthy of her father in all respects. The Mackenzies also had cousins called the Dukes. We are descended from either Jessie or Arabella Duke, whose nephew became Lord Mayor of London after quite a distinguished career—starting in the navy—he was secretary to an Admiral. He married at 70 and had three daughters—all of whom married well, one into the Elphinstone family—and a son, who made an unhappy marriage and left no legitimate heir. I met him when he was middle aged in 1916, and thought him ravishing—enchanting in every way. He was not unlike Bobby.

(3) About my grandfather.[9] I don't know what the truth was. Your uncle Arthur once mentioned in my presence when I was 7 or 8 when his daughter [gap] said that she had sat next to the Duke of Albany at some dinner party "I hope he knew you were his cousin." The Duke of Albany was the youngest son of Queen Victoria. I often heard my mother calming Uncle Arthur, when he abused his mother for having, when she became a widow, refused to go on accepting an allowance from Queen Victoria, which had been her husband's main source of income, on conscientious grounds. This all sounds

like a child's dream, but I am sure it really happened. Uncle Arthur's complaint—as uttered to me in later years—was that Charles and Digby had both been destined for expensive regiments and Arthur and Edward for the Civil Service, and this would have been proper, during their father's life time, but impossible afterwards when there was no money, after their father's death, and that their mother had done nothing about this. When I asked *why* there was no money after my [grand] father's death, I was answered evasively. I was told that it was because he had had the income from the marriage settlement on his first marriage (which was to Frances Crosbie, a cousin of the Duke of Wellington) until his death, then it had gone back to the Crosbies. But it was not *that* large a marriage settlement, and certainly didn't cover his expenses.[10]

If we examine his history it really is odd. He was born in 1798, and was supposed to have been one of the numerous family (larger than is indicated on the pedigree) of Fairfield, who was in the [gap]. He was christened Charles George Augustus and he became an officer in the Coldstream Guards, and when he had got his Majority he, as was usual, left the Army and went to Ireland. He went to Kerry where he was immediately made High Sheriff of the County for a year, which is *utterly* mysterious. He was also supposed to have been made a land agent on the Mount Venus estate belonging to Lord Pembroke—the explanation being that he was a brother officer of Lord Pembroke—but he never was. He lived in Fitzwilliam Square and had a house (but I don't know where) in Kerry. Lettie says he hadn't but he is described in several places as of a parish in Kerry now unidentifiable. The Lord Pembroke of the day was a lunatic and lived abroad and the dates make it doubtful if the two men ever met—but the representatives of the Pembrokes constantly did things in connection with our grandfather, and parts of the Pembroke property were transferred to my grandfather. It is also odd that he should have been allowed to marry a Crosbie girl of this particular branch—her sister married a Barcley Drummond of the banking family, and they were quite heiresses. My grandfather was an extremely good and sweet man, devoted to [hi]s family, and was engaged in a great many charitable and [publ]ic activities. The extraordinary thing is that my [grand]father had no relations with his supposed brothers and sisters. My father and uncles never met them. I asked my Uncle Arthur about them and he said he had never met one of them. This is the more odd because the family were extremely close to the Crosbie family (the relatives of my grandfather's first wife) and the Rowans and Dennys (the relatives of my grandfather's second wife).

There is really no solution to this mystery. My grandfather was not connected with the Pembroke family. I have asked Lady Pembroke and she says that this was not so, he was confided to the family care when he came over to Ireland, and that is the first time he was heard of. (This was because of the Pembroke leases we hold). I have often wondered if my grandfather was the son of Caroline Fairfield, the daughter of [gap], who was married to a paranoic lunatic of a pathetic kind called Edward Tynewell Brydges, a clergyman, the brother of Sir Egerton Brydges, who got the wretched man to become "the Chandos claimant" and claim the barony of Chandos, which was extinct. The claim was pure nonsense, and Sir Egerton, who was very, *very* mad, forged some documents. But the claim nearly got through the House of Lords and was voted for by two of the Royal Dukes, the brothers of George IV and it was widely said that this was due to the fact that one or both had been her lovers. But there was also a rumour of a third Duke who did not vote in the House of Lords but was associated with her, the Duke of Cumberland, the one who was falsely believed to have murdered his valet. I think this is the candidate I would prefer if it were true she had had a love affair within the Royal family. But if the dates given are correct it seems doubtful, for she died in 1818, and is supposed to have been then 37, which would make her 17 at the time of our grandfather's birth, and this seems most improbable. She was also suspected of having a love affair with her cousin, Charles Small Pybus, who was M. P. for Dover and a pet of Pitt, a remarkably brilliant man who died at 41. But she seems to have been an intensely unhappy woman who lived a hell of a life with her lunatic husband, and her lunatic brothers-in-law, Sir Egerton and a horde of tiresome in-laws, including Madame Lefroy who was so afraid lest her son Tom Lefroy married Jane Austen. I would have guessed she had a dreary time. But certainly somebody protected Egerton Brydges who might well have gone to jug. Her cousin might have protected him but couldn't, I think, have got the Royal Dukes to vote for him in the House of Lords. There is, by the way, something very odd in the way that when my father got his commission in the Prince Consort's Own, he was sent for by Queen Victoria who had a long private audience with him.

I have no idea what is the truth behind this story. But it was ghastly for my father. He found himself and Digby doomed to go into the Army with no private income. He went into the pet regiment of Queen Victoria (the Prince Consort's Own) and did extremely well as a ballistics specialist and rifle instructor, but couldn't make ends meet. His brother Digby transferred to the Indian Army and anyway married a rich girl, Miss Hoare, I think of Stourhead, and died of cholera. Edward Fairfield found himself entering the Colonial Office as a second-class clerk but was sent into the Legal department and became one of the Colonial Office own house lawyers, and was very well looked after by various important people in London—he had a very satisfactory life—till he was ruined by Chamberlain. Arthur was a bookish eccentric and got himself out of the Board of Trade by writing a facetious letter which was reprinted in an Irish paper.

My father was stationed in Canada, was sent to the Civil War as an observer, went back to England, left the Army, went back to America, and in Virginia, where he had met a family who had taken a great liking to him, and got a job running a saw-mill, which was quite a considerable job. He then married a Miss Allison, who had a son, she was of a snobbish and I should judge tiresome family. He then developed a great desire to go West, and went, and was disconcerted when his wife refused to go with him and divorced him. Later his wife was left some money and had to change her name back to Allison to get it.[11] He was quite a long time in the West and became a mine manager, and was happy as that, but had two friends who got killed in a buggy accident, leaving a son who was still a school-boy. My father was now in his forties and had become more and more interested in political science and decided to take the boy back to his grandparents in Australia and go back eventually to England. Now there begins a divergence of opinion. Letty thinks he went back to England and then went to Australia, and that he met my mother on the boat going out; and that he was going to Australia because he had got a job as a cartoonist on one of the Melbourne papers, and lost it when he got there because he could not draw. I thought they had met on a boat that was going between one port to another in Australia, and I remember my mother saying she had seen him with the boy on the boat and had thought they were father and son, and had only found in Australia that they were no relation and my father was unmarried. My mother had gone out to Australia because she had had a nervous breakdown after she had had a shock because her hair was set alight by a falling candle at the Heinemann's house, and I think there was more to it. I think she had had a broken engagement. She had gone to Australia rather than anywhere else because she had a brother, John, out there, who, by all accounts, could have revived the nervous breakdown. He was a very eccentric musician. My mother and father married after six weeks or so. Then my father got a job on the Melbourne *Argus* and did well, but got into trouble by prophesying a bank crash, which annoyed the owners of the paper and its more influential readers. So he was sacked (the bank crash took place shortly afterwards) and went home with his wife and two children. I don't think his future on returning was so much to his discredit. He assumed, as one does, that the country would not have changed since he left it, and that jobs would be easy to get. He did an English letter for the Australian paper under a pseudonym and presently got a job in an anti Socialist society, headed by Lord Wemyss,[12] as speaker and organiser. He was getting the pay of a young man, a neophyte in journalism and I do see he had considerable difficulties. If you can imagine anybody trying to break into Fleet Street at the age of forty plus who had been out of the country for many years, you can imagine his position. Also it was very hard luck on him that Uncle Edward, who was very fond of him and helped him all he could, died in the mid-nineties. There is no doubt that my father was far from being an ideal husband and father, but at the same time he had his great difficulties. And it is not true at all that he had abandoned his family.[13] He must have known that if he had come back my mother would have taken him in, and he was simply not going to be a trouble to us all any longer.

(4) I cannot exaggerate what harm was done to the family by the connection with Aunt Sophy . . . .[14]

(5) We had really a number of pleasant relatives. Uncle Arthur was extremely pleasant and good with children. Uncle Edward must have been a kind and good and highly intelligent man. As for their mother, Mrs. Fairfield, remember that many Irish people of her class and kind were Plymouth Brethren—it was a sense of guilt, operating after the Famine. Our grandfather by all accounts was angelic. On my mother's side, her sister Jessie (Ian's grandmother), was extremely nice, and so was Jessie Campbell. All the men, I must admit, were unpleasant, except my grandfather, Alec Mackenzie, who seems to have been much loved. The Dukes, as I say, seemed fascinating, to

judge by the one specimen I met. And Marjorie Mackenzie (Marjorie Ver-
noe) was a darling. Aunt Sophy was one of the wickedest people I have ever
known, and I cannot think of one redeeming feature in her character. But
she was not a relative. We have been tormented by circumstance, and that is
our real trouble, rather than our genes.

Blessings

Rebecca West Collection   carbon typescript
University of Tulsa

[1] See family tree. Most of West's note 4, on Aunt Sophie, is omitted. There are gaps in the
carbon, perhaps where erasures were made, or space was left to fill in later. Some words in the
torn off lower left corner have been conjectured.

[2] Alison Selford disagrees with this financial assessment and asserts that "Uncle Alec was
rolling in money."

[3] West may have slipped in typing this recollection. According to Alison Selford, the family
story was that he reacted, "No, there's no point; it would only upset me."

[4] The remainder of this paragraph, concerning various family finances, is omitted.

[5] Janet, though she was always called Jessie.

[6] Sir Charles Dilke (1843–1911), English liberal M.P. whose political fortunes declined after
he was named corespondent in a divorce case in which Mrs. Virginia Crawford confessed that
Dilke had taken her to one side of his bed and the maid to the other. Both Lettie and Rebecca
knew Mrs. Crawford later. Rebecca thought she had lied. Lettie refrained from asking, but
doubted her charges.

[7] Alison Selford corrects this account with the information that the banns for this marriage
were called in church for three weeks beforehand; hence they had not exactly run away
together. She also suspects that West's great-grandfather set up his daughter's lace shop.

[8] Alison Selford makes the correction that they were the daughters of James Watson Campbell, Janet's elder brother.

[9] There was a family legend that Major Charles George Fairfield was the illegitimate son of
royalty and that hence special privilege came his way.

[10] Alison Selford supposes that the greatest loss was the country home.

[11] No papers documenting this marriage have been found.

[12] Francis Wemyss-Charteris-Douglas (1818–1914), Scottish Conservative M.P. (1841–1846
and 1847–1883). He founded the Liberty and Property Defence League (1882) to advocate
individualism over socialism.

[13] West struggled over this, but most of the family say that he indeed abandoned them.

[14] West writes at length and in extremely negative terms about Aunt Sophy, whom she
blames for misinforming and misleading Lettie, Sophy's favorite among the three Fairfield
sisters. See letter to Norman Macleod, 25 November 1958, for more on Aunt Sophie and
Lettie.

To: Victoria Glendinning[1]   48 Kingston House North
                                                     Prince's Gate, S.W. 7
                                                     21 November 1975

Dear Victoria,

I heard a rumor yesterday that you had been signed up by Weidenfeld for a book consisting of three studies of women writers—Gloria Manning,[2] Rosamund Lehmann, and myself. I want to make it plain that if this is so I couldn't assist you. The biography I have in mind for myself wouldn't fit into such a frame. For one thing, there would be quite a lot of space devoted to such things for example as my relations with Emma Goldman, and with the *New Statesman,* and with the rise of Titoism during the war. So I would be glad to hear from you whether the description of the book I have heard is accurate—in which case I wouldn't want to give you any more material of the sort I've been giving you—not because I don't realise you have every right to write such a book if you want to (and indeed I would of course be very pleased that you should write such an essay on me)—but it isn't the kind of book I want written.

                                        Yours ever,
                                        Rebecca West

Rebecca West Collection   photocopy of manuscript
University of Tulsa

[1] Victoria Glendinning (1937–), English biographer. In addition to *Rebecca West: A Life* (1987), she has written biographies of Elizabeth Bowen, Edith Sitwell, Vita Sackville-West, Jonathan Swift, and Anthony Trollope.
[2] By Gloria Manning, West might mean Olivia Manning (1908–1980), English-born, Irish-reared novelist, critic, and writer of radio scripts. Her works include *The Wind Changes* (1937) and her Balkan (1960–1965) and Lavant (1977–1980) trilogies.

To: Tony Redd[1]   48 Kingston House North
                                                  Prince's Gate, S.W. 7

Dear Tony,   [December 1976]

I send this off *too late* but I have been much impeded—my poor sister [Letitia Fairfield] of 91 had a stroke and with her mind and speech quite unaffected lost the power of her right arm and her right leg—and it was a question of finding her a permanent home, a nursing-home, and this proved an insuperable difficulty till suddenly I remembered she had been a doctor with the R. A. F. in the first war and the RAF is taking her in, with some fanfare, as she is by now a romantic relic. It really is quite picturesque—for she loved being in the R. A. F. I hope you've been well and prospering. I think Saul Bellow's *To Jerusalem and Back* not specially illuminating about Jerusalem, but what a gorgeous Commonplace Book, to use an old fashioned term. And something about it that recalls Coleridge (bits of *Biographia Literaria* I love.) He is strangely well-read. Write and tell me how you are. Sir Henry d'Avigon Goldsmid[2] has just died—I grieve it, he was so nice to me— he was long an M. P., being a wealthy bullion merchant, and was the authority on gold in the House of Commons, the only man whose speeches on currency filled the House and he wrote excellent reviews of modern French books in the *T. L. S.* when it was an anonymous publication.

All my regards to you and your dear Professor Sharp.

Rebecca

private collection   manuscript post card

[1] Tony Redd teaches English at the Citadel in Charleston, S.C., and wrote "Rebecca West: Master of Reality" (1972) as his dissertation. She liked the copy he sent her in 1974 and in 1975 requested another copy for a "young Italian lady" who was writing her thesis. He became West's frequent lunch and dinner companion when he was in London.
[2] Henry Joseph d'Avigon-Goldsmid (1909–1976), bullion broker, a Conservative M.P. (1955–1974), and president of the Jewish Colonization Association.

To: Terence de ere White[1]

48 Kingston House North
Prince's Gate, S.W. 7
15 December 1976

My dear Terence,

First, what a lovely card. The most beautiful we have had. And what a sad message.[2] It is so odd that sexual love, which does not work, should not have been scrapped by the species in the course of evolution, like other uselessnesses. All this sense that one must be always in the company of the beloved or suffer ⟨thirst⟩ {hunger} worse than hunger, it would be useful and delightful, if only circumstances were adapted to it. They aren't, and the result is hell. I am at present in a good deal of pain. I have a broken bone in my knee that was put into a position where it did no harm, about ten years ago or more, and it has cut loose again, and it can't be operated on because there is now a risk of thrombosis. I cannot have even a manipulation for ten days and in the meantime I am liable to attacks of sheer agony. In one of these I suddenly thought, "I'd rather be like this than going through what Terence is enduring." It's no good saying I'm sorry. What good does that do, what good can anything do unless it comes from Victoria? And the awful thing is that this is not an insane attitude. Victoria is one of the most wonderful human beings I have ever met—so romantic, without being silly for one moment, it is hardly to be believed. I suppose, with some anguish, that you both will go on as you are. I wish I could help, but the space ship we are on has no lifebuoys—I can only send you my friendship and affection.

I wasted my youth, spending seven years out of the ten I lived with H. G. in trying to get away from him. The only deep love I felt in my thirties was broken to pieces with a hammer for the horrible reason that the man I loved [Beaverbrook] believed quite wrongly that I had detected an extremely guilty secret in his life. He was right in thinking that if I had, I would have been horrified. I was left with the feeling I had been deserted, which was not a thing I could take well after my ten years' servitude. My husband would have bee[n] a wonderful companion if he hadn't gone down with a disease of the central nervous system complicated by a blow on the head by a German rifle (accidental) only a few years after our marriage. I rather think Victoria makes your score better than mine! And I'm glad it should be so.

I must say you struck me on your visit as not at all boring, only (to be bracketed together) sad and amusing. I can well imagine that London seems threatening. The people are all packed away in their houses and the effect is rather like the library of Sir Montague Norman,[3] where all the books were put on shelves in bays behind wood panels. There is no indication of human character in the streets.

I send you my, alas, ineffectual blessings.

Yours ever,
Rebecca.

I hope to find you in my drawing room again.

private collection   manuscript

[1] Terence de Vere White (1912–1994), Irish lawyer, author, and literary editor of the *Irish Times* (1961–1977). His nonfiction includes *The Parents of Oscar Wilde* (1967) and *The Anglo-Irish* (1972). Among his novels are *An Affair with the Moon* (1959), *Prenez Garde* (1961), *The March Hare* (1970), and *Chat Show* (1987).

[2] White's relationship with Victoria Glendinning, whom he eventually married, had broken off.

[3] Montague Collett Norman (1971–1950), English banker, governor of the Bank of England.

To: Jane Marcus

Dame Rebecca West, D.B.E.
48 Kingston House North
Prince's Gate, S.W. 7
4 August 1977

Alas, dear Jane, I can't type. Among the difficulties of my sight after a cataract operation is that I can't wear bifocals, and can't see the keys and the roller of a typewriter at one and the same time; (and my secretary is at this moment ill, quite ill, alas, for she is a dear, and enchanting creature). So my gift of typing, which I have cultivated ever since I was 9 years old and had mumps in the same room as a typewriter is at the moment useless, and I fear will be forever. All I can do at the moment is to tell you that Mrs Pankhurst[1] was profoundly influenced by Henri de Rochefort[2] and her visits to his family, and she had a French style about her. (See the photographs of the Lumière brothers.) Very respectably, and I would have said really not very sharply sexed, more the Mother type who doesn't eat Father but doesn't ⟨x⟩ {notice} him much. Certainly I remember that as a flapper dogs body at W. S. P. U. offices one was told never to expect Mrs P. or C. P. [Christabel Pankhurst] in the position of being alone in a room with a man. I have no doubt Keir Hardie[3] made a pass at her, he was a great ⟨x⟩ one for the girls, but I'm sure Mrs P would not have responded. Mrs P and C. P. lived at home and in their offices with continual surveillance, John Kennedy could not have been active in such circumstances. Let me answer later about your very kind ⟨x⟩ {suggestion} about the feminist articles. I am *wildly* occupied.

R. W.

Apologies for my brevity—but I am just having to settle a contract with the B. B. C. & must do it now.[4]

private collection   manuscript postcard

[1] See letter to Letitia Fairfield (1909) for notes on Emmeline and Christabel Pankhurst.

[2] Victor-Henri, Marquis de Rochefort-Lucay (1830–1913), French polemical journalist who in his youth supported the Paris Commune and socialism but wrote for the conservative and nationalist press in his final years. Mrs. Pankhurst attended school with his daughter in France.

[3] Keir James Hardie (1856–1915), Scottish socialist and labor leader, largely responsible for the founding of the Scottish Labour Party (1888) and the Independent Labour Party (1893). He was particularly close to Mrs. Pankhurst's left-wing daughter Sylvia.

[4] West's postscript is written at the top of the first side of the card. The contract related to the filming of a five-part serial of West's novel *The Birds Fall Down,* on which she reported to Marcus in subsequent letters.

To: Michael Sissons[1]   4 April 1978
My dear Michael,

Thank you for your letter and the particulars which seems to me an extraordinarily favourable contract. I can't believe it isn't madly so. All my gratitude to you for putting this through.

About Jane Marcus; let her have what she needs out of the advance. In fact, I would like particulars as to the situation of the permission fees. Unless there is some grisly twist to it, I would like to give this up. She seems to be going through hell, or several hells, most gallantly and I would very cheerfully give her what I suppose I must be careful to call the lionesses share. I think all these liberated ladies are delightful.

> With many thanks,
> Yours sincerely,
> Dame Rebecca West
> D. B. E.

Rebecca West Collection   carbon typescript
University of Tulsa

[1] Sissons worked (and works) as West's literary agent at Peters, Fraser & Dunlop.

To: Alan Maclean Esq,   48 Kingston House North
 Macmillans,   Prince's Gate, S.W. 7
 4 Little Essex St,   12 October 1978
 London W.C. 2

My dear Alan,

The Orel book[1] is most peculiar. It is wholly malicious and tried to cover up the malice by occasional flattering adjectives. It has hardly a correct fact in it. He is illiterate and judges me by the standards of an ill-informed man. He makes no mention of various important fields of my work. He represents me as being uneducated and as acquiring knowledge on the subjects which I write about only when I begin the actual writing. He has done no research beyond getting some clippings out of a local library: when he quotes from authors who have referred to me he tampers with the facts.

There are three main currents in the book which are unpardonable. One relates to my family. He gets every fact about them wrong, and the chronology is wrong so that the story makes no sense. On his addled facts he constructs a long attack on my father, alleging he is guilty of all the same things that I ascribed to the father, Piers Aubrey, in *The Fountain Overflows.* I have said that I have borrowed some of my father's amusing idiosyncrasies for Piers Aubrey, but I have always made it clear he did not share his less attractive characteristics, and I would not myself have mentioned my father in connection with Piers Aubrey. Not satisfied with this, Professor Orel finally turns on my quite blameless mother and accuses her of ill-treatment of my father. All this is nonsense. I am writing out separately the details of this idiocy, and sending you copies of the typed sheets relating to this matter.

The second current in the book relates to one part of my professional life. Professor Orel twice and at length alludes to my career as a reporter, which I have followed in England and America first of all because during the early years of Anthony's life, I badly needed the money, and continued at intervals during my life, largely for the interest of seeing exciting events. I wrote at the speed common among reporters sixty-five years ago when I learned my craft. (Largely from a man called J. M. Kennedy of the *Daily Telegraph,* assistant to the famous Dr Dillon). Professor Orel asserts that this work was scamped and hasty. He reprints an account of a law-suit that was brought against myself and the *Sunday Times* concerning an article I had written for them on a tour in South Africa, as if it substantiated this claim. This was totally inaccurate, it was a peculiar legal action. {The *Sunday Times* did not defend the action so I could not defend myself. You know the situation. See enclosed papers.} The five articles were written at a leisurely pace over a period of nearly three months (except a short account of the attempted assassination of Verwood at which I happened to be present, which was written in haste). Professor Orel also suggested that these articles were never published in book form because they were scamped work. They were not published because I was not at all keen to return to South Africa, and what I had written amounted to only about a third of a book. I will send you copies of the sheets containing these allegations of Professor Orel, with my comments.

There are frequent attempts to rob my work of any sort of dignity. He says of my *St. Augustine* (which I chose to write for Peter Davies when he asked me to contribute to a series of historical short biographies) as a "publisher's assignment" and definitely states (several times) that I had not known anything about St Augustine until I came to what he calls this "publishers assignment." After my father died one of my guardians was a Jesuit priest called Father Matthew Power, and I read my first St. Augustine when I was fourteen years old, and have never stopped reading patristic literature ever since. Professor Orel's remarks about all my work are impertinent, and I enclose a separate sheet on that. (He thinks among other things that the Greek Orthodox Church is the official Church of Russia and of Serbia and Macedonia.)

Professor Orel makes no mention of my years of activity as a director of *Time and Tide*, or my relationship with the *Daily Telegraph* which started nearly fifty years ago.

These are some of my objections. I would also like to mention Professor Orel's unfounded allegations about my attitude to H. G. Wells, which he confidently ascribes to Gordon Ray's book[2] but cannot be found there.

I frankly find all this extraordinary.

Yours sincerely,

Rebecca West

Incidentally Orel gives a catalogue, which he describes as a "rogues gallery," of people of Fascist sympathies whom I mentioned in the *Meaning of Treason*. A number of them have never been prosecuted for an illegal act.

Rebecca West Collection
University of Tulsa

typescript with autograph signature,
insertion and postscript

[1] Harold Orel, *The Literary Achievement of Rebecca West* (1986).
[2] *H. G. Wells and Rebecca West* (1974).

To: Anne McBurney   48 Kingston House North
                                     Prince's Gate, S.W. 7
                                     [October 1978]

My dear Anne,

I have just received the proofs of a book on myself written by the English professor of a large Middle Western University.[1] . . . On and on he goes through my books, exhibiting ignorance on a large number of subjects, and finally comes to a climax at the end of his chapter on *Black Lamb and Grey Falcon* with a rebuke to me for not having given conversionary values (into sterling) for Yugoslav currency—in a book published in 1941!—and another rebuke ⟨before⟩ for not giving the statistics of the parts that up to World War II (it should of course be World War I) were the Austro-Hungarian Empire. This would have presented peculiar difficulties. The statistics of Balkan Austro Hungaria were always uncomprehensible. Bosnia and Herzegovina were peculiarly difficult, they used masses of obsolete currency, including lots of Maria Theresa Dollars, and the inhabitants spoke six dialects of Turkish and three of Serbo-Croat. But when I checked up on the spot I found these statistics had another little [problem?]—⟨they⟩ {the} papers had nearly all been buried in the First World War. The rebuke is made with a superb air of academic authority. The whole book is honeycombed with examples of ignorance of a geographical and historical kind. I have come across example after example of this {sort of thing} in the last fifty years, and it's getting worse.

I thought this might interest you and amuse you and perhaps suggest that I'm not as silly as you thought! I will now go on to tell you the unhappy story of my life in recent months. Caro [Duah], who has had two mental breakdowns in the last five years, suddenly arrived in England, about to have a baby and, poor child, very dotty. She had not told her mother she was going to have a baby because she felt she was too worthless and incapable to be a mother. Deep, deep depression. But she arrived in superb physical shape—and then collapsed. I can't tell you the awfulness. Which Kitty at 70, recently operated on for [an] arthritic hip, has had to cope with. Anthony rang me up a lot at first, in great need of consolation, but he has—I don't mean to put it unkindly but it is true—he has {now} lost interest. I had a heartrending but *not* complaining conversation with Kitty ⟨yester⟩ {two} days ago. She finds the baby (who is a very large and handsome boy) heavy to lift and carry. But it is going back to the mother, who is improving. How I wish Caro hadn't gone to Girton. She should have been kept quiet. . . . What is so awful now is that she left her husband behind in Ghana because he had to finish some work—he visited a lab where a product of the farm was being turned into soap, a root (I think) full of safogen, and a flask exploded and he was injured and had to go to hospital in Accra. Life is hopelessly chaotic in Ghana ⟨till⟩ {since} the coup d'etat so everything is against travelling and communication—but we hope he'll get back soon. We are keeping all this as much as possible to ourselves. It is all a frightful mess. Anthony (of whom Caro is very fond) insists on going back to America (for good, they have sold their house) in about a fortnight's time. The money I settled on the children has not been properly looked after—just left at the bank and drawn on when Em [Edmund West] and Caro are in England—but even so it amounts to about £19,000 each. Both Caro and Em have spoken of it to me as being too small a sum to bother about. But there is plenty of money about. Now let me change the subject—though I can assure you that won't get us to an agreeable subject. My sister Lettie, throughout her life demanded more and more from me, and the last time I saw her demanded that I increase her allowance—so that she could leave more to ⟨my⟩ {our} nephew and niece. I explained that I really couldn't do this. (It afterwards turned out that to give her what she had had over many years out of my highly taxed income had cost {me} £24,000+.) When she died it turned out that she left about £35,000 (I don't know how she did[n't] leave more) and a flat which was sold for £20,000+. I had carefully told her that she must see to it that she left more to Bobbie [Norman Macleod] than to Alison—as I had given Alison [Selford] £12,000—and their {shares} should be equallised. It turned out she had not done this. She had left ½ the value of the flat and all the rest of the estate minus £1000 to Alison, and ½ the value of the flat to Bobbi, with £1000. Alison is now, with my £12,000 and her earnings for historical novels and her £25,000 from Lettie's estate worth about £50,000—Bobbie's salary has been frozen for 5 years and he is desperately poor. (He has 3 children half through their education) and in finding out the situation I have felt compelled to insure his life for £20,000 and give him an allowance of £500. This all seems so damned funny, when I think of Lettie's saintly and worried look. I don't know about the saintly look but it seems to me that the worried look by rights belongs to me.

Ibstone House has been resold to a charming and bizarre couple, the son of the famous [?] Enthover, who wouldn't go into the family business of Insurance, and went into stock management and has made a packet, and the daughter of a South African millionaire who married into the Wills tobacco fortune and later into the Douglas Home family.[2] They came to see me to look at photographs of the house and I liked them very much. Six dogs, and I think four horses and one child as yet.

Much love,
Rac.

Nobody knows what Lettie spent her large income on.

private collection   manuscript

[1] Her description of faults she finds with Orel's manuscript, also described above, has been omitted.

[2] The family included playwright William Douglas-Home (1912–1992) and the prime minister (1963–1964) Sir Alec Douglas-Home (1903–1995).

To: Kitty West   48 Kingston House North
                                        Prince's Gate, S.W. 7
                                        15 November 1978

My dear Kitty,

I must congratulate you on carrying out the ambitious plan of giving young Barnabas[1] a suitable introduction to society. I could not think how you could go through it, you must be so tired. But you looked very gay and I admired your spirit. Barnabas is a lovely baby—it may be the partiality of a great grandmother but I thought I had never seen a more ravishing creature—not only handsome but so intelligent and obviously sensible.

I see you must be wanting to make plans, and if you think you would care to discuss any part of them I would like to do so. I can meet you anywhere if you don't want to come here, and if you want quiet to talk. I can dine anywhere, for though I am much handicapped I still have energy to a certain degree. And you might like a change of scene. But you suggest anything you like.

It was nice seeing your friends—and everything looked beautifully unperturbed.

Yours ever,

Rac[2]

Rebecca West Collection   manuscript
University of Tulsa

[1] West's great-grandson, son of Caro and Osei Duah.
[2] Brief postscript is partially illegible.

To: Caroline West Duah   48 Kingston House North
                                                Prince's Gate, S.W. 7
                                                4 December 197[8]

My dear Caro and Osei,

I am so sorry that there dosn't seem much prospect of seeing you again before you go, but I hope you'll be back again. The Barnabas baby is so beautiful that you ought to take him on tour so that more and more people see how lovely he is. He not only looks so healthy and as if he was really "enjoying" good health, he is so beautifully carved, so to speak. I think you must both be bursting with pride.[1]

If you could sometimes let me know how you are I should be glad and grateful.

All my love,

Rac

private collection   manuscript

[1] West described the baby to Jane Marcus as "a most beautiful little Black Prince, or rather Bronze Prince—a lovely little creature, perfect even to a melodious cry" (27 January 1969, private collection).

To: Caroline West Duah   48 Kingston House North
                                                 Prince's Gate, S.W. 7
                                                 5 March 1979

My dear Caro

    I am so sorry.[1]

    I dearly love you and I hope you will get better soon. I am writing a brief letter not because I can't think of lots I would like to say to you, but because I don't want to tire you.[2]

                    Your affectionate Grandmama,
                    Rac.

personal collection   manuscript

[1] Over the death of Caro's son, Barnabas. West gave her reaction to Merlin Holland (25 March 1979, private collection): "My life has been ⟨x⟩ {entirely} ravaged by a catastrophe, the climax of a drama that began 6 years ago and came to a climax a month ago. My very good looking but strange granddaughter who married a very pleasant Ghanese Negro about 7 years ago . . . {and} after a sickening series of shocks lasting all summer she produced a beautiful and healthy and charming little boy. They returned to Ghana. The baby is now dead. . . . I am in a state of continual distress and can't get out of it."

[2] West did keep up an encouraging correspondence with Caro, as shown in the following letter (29 August 1979, private collection):

I have had your long and interesting letter and rejoice to see you bubbling with so many interests. To say nothing of the cat (of whose anatomy Osei and his camera have given me a most puzzling view!) I am glad he cares about photography. I cannot photograph any more. I am so apt to drop my camera, and I press it terribly. I am so glad I have my own record of Mexico. . . .

I have not thanked you for your poem which I find most interesting in its thought and accomplished in its execution. The sense of light and colour and your interpretation of their meaning is beautiful—and I think your admiration for Gerard Manley Hopkins has taught you a lot, though you've kept your own literary personality. Your account of your life and the help people are giving you make me feel you are getting well very fast.

To: Mark Boxer[1] Esq.
Weidenfeld & Nicolson   10 March 1980
My dear Mark,

    Thank you for your letter of March 5th which I have been studying with great interest over the weekend.

    I would like to get to work on the introduction fairly soon. I will ask you I think for a little further research on the various people that are concerned. I am not sure that it is wise to make the book a survey of 1900 in England, France, Italy, America and so on. You might if you concentrate on England get as big a sale as if you get a book that sprawls all over the place. Remember that France has not much interest in its recent past and Germany and Italy have even less.

The Boer War I think I can do on my own, in fact the difficulty is I think I know too much about that. I would be glad if you will tell me whether there is not a book on Faberge[2] which has most of the gen [sic] in it. Faberge had a number of English and French people working for him.

I think the idea of the pictures with anthology material underneath is a very good one.[3]

I will get to work on a skeleton of the introduction during the coming fortnight or three weeks, unless I fall dead or become temporarily insane! Then we can get on with that. There are things that interest me extremely. I have been reading through the old people's biographies in the *National Dictionary of Biography,* who were alive in 1900 and one of the most curious things is that while English men spoke European languages very badly, and many of them not at all, English young men who went out to the Orient showed an astonishing gift for acquiring Oriental languages. They also lived to great ages so that my impression is correct that I moved through a world peppered with old gentlemen who knew any number of Oriental languages and lived to a vast age. The vast age is rather interesting because it suggests that the tropics suited people in those days.

I am sure your royalty payments will be alright and if they were not, I would trust my dear Pat Kavanagh[4] to chase you round and round the flat in Ripon House until you fell dead.

As for the pictures, it occurs to me that there was a unique figure among the musicians in Victorian England and that was Parry of "Blest Sirens."[5] He wrote an oratorio about the most painful incident in holy writ while living a life of gorgeous luxury. He married a lady, one of the Herberts of Lea. He was a nob himself and he kept his own yacht and was a light of the Royal Yacht Squadron. When he died he was writing a book which was going to prove that all was for the best in this best of all possible worlds, which I think was {a} funny thing for a man to do whose greatest work was an oratorio on the subject of Judith and Holofernes.[6]

I will be grubbing away at this and will send you something?
With many thanks for all your doing.

Dame Rebecca West

Rebecca West Collection   carbon typescript
University of Tulsa

[1] Mark Boxer (1931–1988), English editor and (as "Marc") cartoonist for the *Times,* the *Guardian,* and the *Daily Telegraph.* He edited the *Sunday Times Magazine* (1962–1965) and was director and then assistant editor of the *Sunday Times* (1964–1979). He was a director with Weidenfeld and Nicolson (1980–1983) when West's *1900* was produced, and briefly the editor-in-chief of *Vogue* (1987–1988).

[2] Peter Carl Fabergé (1846–1920), Russian jewelry maker, best known for the ornamental Easter eggs exchanged by royalty. West includes two illustrations and an explanation of Fabergé products and mentions their large number of employees in *1900* (158).

[3] In a letter (15 July 1980), West gives a progress report, still mindful of the use of illustrations: "I have now got my piece written to the extent of a description of the change in political life, a passage about tarts which gives you a chance to use a Toulouse Lautrec type of illustration and the early part of the Boer War."

[4] Kavanagh was a literary agent at A. D. Peters.

[5] Sir (Charles) Hubert Parry (1848–1918), English composer, author, and teacher, influential in the late nineteenth-century revival of English music. His works include *Blest Pair of Sirens* (1887), the oratorios *Judith* (1888), *Job* (1892), and *King Saul* (1894), and the song "Jerusalem" (1916). *1900* reproduces a drawing of Parry, complete with caption.

[6] Judith beheaded the Assyrian general Holofernes, who was directing an assault on Palestine, as he lay in drunken sleep in his tent.

To: Motley Deakin[1]   21 April 1980
Dear Professor Deakin

I am most grateful to you for giving so much of your time and attention to my work, and for treating me so sympathetically, but I must explain that your publisher's letter came at the most inconvenient time. I am halfway through a short historical book I have to finish in a few weeks' time [*1900*], and I want to get back to my book on the lives of my father and mother. I am eighty-seven, and have difficulty with my sight, and my secretary is away on holiday, and I have a considerable amount of business to do. Most of the errors I have found in your proofs are due to your lack of knowledge about my life and European widows, and I wish you had written to me and asked for the information which you lacked, it would have been easier for both of us.

I find it difficult to understand why you and the nun (and another writer whose name I cannot remember) thought I had written *War Nurse*. And I cannot understand why you think that Graham Greene[2] ever brought a libel action against me. I can understand that you did not understand why I apologised to Roy Campbell[3] if I had not libelled him, but I can assure you that had he sued me for libel he would not have won the case, for the reason that I had taken what was considered reasonable care to ascertain that the list on which his name appeared as a member of the Partist Union of Fascists was accurate, and that he had admitted in that he was, though not a member of the P. U. F., a follower of the Spanish Fascists. (You may remember his "Flowering Rifle.") I apologized because I respected his gifts, and I am glad I did, for he modified his beliefs before his tragic death. I have been found guilty of libel once in my life, but this action was brought against me as a result of an action committed in another country, and I think you would have been as astounded as I was.[4]

I think it a pity that, owing to your ignorance of my circumstances, you have represented my comments on Germans under the Hitler regime as prejudiced, on the grounds that I failed to distinguish between the Nazis and the decent German people, and for that reason I came to conclusions not so well judged as that of Mrs Abbey Mann. If you knew anything about me you would know these comments are wide of the mark. I do not think that even allowing for your period at Heidelberg, you can have quite the knowledge of German life that I have, for you would see that I have always been able to distinguish between the Nazis and the decent German people. My mother's family were professional musicians and were mostly educated in Germany, and had as many German as British friends. I married a man who was born of a family which, although it had always preserved its British nationality, had many German connections because they had property in a part of Denmark which was annexed by Germany in 1865. He himself was brought up in Hamburg from the time he was eight until he was twelve, was at Oxford in 1913 but had to go to Germany to help his widowed mother wind up some business, and was unable to get back to England in time to avoid being interned in the German civilian prison camp at Ruhleben. When he had returned to Oxford and got his degree, he joined a private banking firm, which did some German and Austrian business. I married him in 1930, and for some years went with him to Berlin once every two months and to

Vienna once every three months, and visited his remaining relations in Bremen, Berlin, Hamburg and Dresden, all of whom were thoroughly decent German people, who for not one moment could have been confused with the few who had made the mistake of adopting the Nazi faith and later committed suicide. My husband did all he could to help them before the war, during the war, and after the war, and until his death in 196[8] and I am at this moment in touch with a number of them. I do not know what gave you the idea that my visits to Germany were simply the performance of assignments accepted by me mechanically as part of my employment.

You seem, by the way, not quite to understand the kind of journalist and writer I am. This explains your curious assumptions as to my knowledge of American literature. You judge this by the American books I have reviewed which do not exhaust my knowledge of American literature. I have nearly always written for serious newspapers which run a book page, where the literary editors make up the page with care and choose the authors to review certain sorts of books. My literary editors sent me the books you mentioned, but these do not represent my sum total of my knowledge of American literature, which began early with St Nicholas. For years I was reading Henry James when many of his countrymen neglected him, and I am a devoted reader of Nathaniel Hawthorne and G. W. Cable[5] and the whole cannon [sic] of H M Melville's whale ridden work which had far too much prominence. As to your reproach concerning my neglect of the depression, one of the four stories in *The Harsh Voice* [is] all [that] subject. (You are mistaken in think I was influenced by Scott Fitzgerald, whom I do not admire.)

I might also point out that your criticism of *Black Lamb and Grey Falcon* on the grounds that it is a mixture of travelogues and historical writing ignores the special difficulties of the area. Anybody who writes of Rome or Greece or Egypt need not describe the Coliseum or the Parthenon or the Pyramids; for centuries people have been visiting them. But very few people have visited the terrain north of Greece stretching up towards the Danube. This was partly because of I. M. R. [O.][6] I could not, for example, convince the reader of the importance of the medieval Serbian empire if I did not describe such of its achievements as their churches and their frescoes. This made the book technically difficult to get done. It took me five years, and I went over the track it describes three times.

I would also wish that you had taken the trouble to learn something about my personal life. You get much of the chronology wrong, which makes for misunderstandings. But I must thank you for the restraint with which you deal with it. But what embarrasses me is that you do not seem to have any sort of idea of what sort of life I have led. You seem to suggest that you feel uncertain of my status because you are not sure how intimate I was with the Bloomsbury Group. I could not have admired Virginia Woolf more as a writer and I was very fond of Clive Bell.[7] But I cannot say I found the company of this group very entertaining. They had a very limited experience and I don't think anybody would deny that my husband and I lived a much more interesting life than they did. I may be prejudiced on this matter by the fact that any demented lady, even if a genius, is a difficult neighbour in the country;[8] and that she was for a summer, when she was really unpardonable. The friends my husband and I dearly loved (we did not see them often, but always with great pleasure) were H. A. L. Fisher[9] and Lewis Namier.[10] We cast our nets widely; but were very busy. I wrote no book for twenty years but not because of any temperamental defect but because my husband was struck down by a disease of the central nervous system which moved very slowly and our rather difficult country house (and farm) were the only place where he was at ease; and to arrange this was certainly not much for me to do for him.

I hope you are not offended by this letter. I am actually too tired and too anxious to return to this work I must finish to express fully just why I find your study of my work quite wide of the mark. I do regret that I cannot enlarge on this, but you may be able to read my notes on the margins of your proofs, which I am returning in another envelope. I regret that you have made it necessary for these notes to be so many and so often frivolous in character. I do not know why you imagine that I have exaggerated the talent and training up of my mother as a pianist to satisfy some strange psychological need of my own. I can assure you that my mother's brother when he was the Principal of the Royal Academy of Music[11] used from time to time [to] send his best pupils to my mother's house so that she could play certain works (chiefly by Brahms, Schubert and Schumann) played as they should be. I also, to go to the other end of my story, do not understand why you take so little interest in the critical work I have done in the *Sunday Telegraph* for more than twenty years as one of the two principal reviewers, the other being Nigel Dennis.[12] I do not so much object to the line of criticism of my work as to the fact that you have not troubled yourself to acquaint yourself with the amount of work I have done or the degree of diligence I brought to the preparation of that work.

Yours sincerely,
Dame Rebecca West

Rebecca West Collection   carbon of typescript
University of Tulsa

[1] Motley Deakin, American professor at the University of Florida and author of *Rebecca West* (1980).

[2] Deakin may have been thinking of Evelyn Waugh, who threatened a libel action, as described in the letter of [November 1956].

[3] Roy Campbell (1901–1957), South African–born English poet who fought with Franco in the Spanish Civil War and resided for much of his life in Spain, France, and Portugal, where he took up both fishing and bullfighting. His works include *The Flaming Terrapin* (1924), *The Wayzgoose* (1928), and *Flowering Reeds* (1933). West accused him of being a member of the Partist Union of Fascists. He wrote a letter of protest that made her hair "curl with terror" (letter to Winifred Macleod, 12 December 1949, private collection). He died in an automobile crash.

[4] West was sued by Judge Alexander Angus Kennedy for misreporting his identity in her *Sunday Times* articles. See letter to John and Jane Gunther, 28 February 1961.

[5] G. W. (George Washington) Cable (1844–1925) American novelist who focused on Creole Louisiana in works such as *Old Creole Days* (1879) and *The Grandissimes* (1880).

[6] Internal Macedonian Revolutionary Organization, Balkan revolutionaries organized in the nineteenth century to combat the Ottoman Empire, later advocates of Macedonian independence, prone to terrorism.

[7] Clive Bell (1881–1964), English art critic who married Woolf's older sister Vanessa Stephen. Together with Roger Fry he organized the second Post impressionist exhibition in London (1910). His theory of "significant form" is espoused in *Art* (1914) and *Since Cézanne* (1922).

[8] West was not far from the Woolfs at Monk's House when she rented Old Possingworth Manor, Sussex, in 1939.

[9] H. A. L. Fisher (1865–1940), English historian and Warden of New College, Oxford (1925–1940).

[10] Sir Lewis Bernstein Namier (1888–1960), Polish-born British historian at Manchester University (1929–1953) whose specialty was eighteenth-century British Parliamentary history. A Zionist, he helped World War II refugees. Rebecca and Henry appreciated his talents as a brilliant conversationalist.

[11] Uncle Alec. Alexander Campbell Mackenzie (1847–1935), British composer associated with the late nineteenth-century revival of British music. He headed the Royal Academy of Music (1888–1924).

[12] Nigel Dennis (1912–1989), English novelist, playwright, and critic who also reviewed for the *New Republic* and *Time*. His capacity for absurdity and witty critique of human conduct is demonstrated in the novel *Cards of Identity* (1955), which had a stage version.

To: Mary and Gordon Haight[1]   48 Kingston House North
                                                 Prince's Gate, S.W. 7
                                                 [29 June 1982]

My dear ⟨Gordon⟩ {Mary} and Gordon (forgive a very untidy letter)

Thank you for the photographs of the said Mary, Madame de Pompadour and me (in the order of their importance). I remember that visit very well because Henry had not long to live and was immensely cheered up by the presence of you two.

These are indeed dreadful times. When the Falkland Islands[2] horror dropped into our laps it was a nightmare—not for a moment did any of us expect Argentina would add to its own troubles and ours in this extraordinary way.—and don't think we went into it without foreseeing what the reckoning ⟨of⟩ would be. And don't think that Mrs Thatcher didn't too. She and I are mutually allergic—We haven't a word to say to each other—but I am quite sure (having known a great friend of hers, for one thing, Airey Neave[3] who was blown to pieces in his car a year or so ago)—I am quite sure, I repeat, that she has none of Milner's[4] vast capacity for doing the wrong thing at the worst time. She is a sensible and utterly courageous woman, and every Tory I detest is fiercely in opposition to her—notably a man I cannot stand called Pym.[5] I haven't the faintest desire to spend five minutes with her, but I am quite sure she has all the most necessary qualities for high office. Now, I am sure, people loved to spend hours with Milner, but he had no tie with the efficient of the earth except that he could mimic the way they might behave. (When we three meet again I must tell you how it is I have such strong feelings about all people connected with the South African War. It may interest you as an example of how children do not forget what is said in front of them, even at a very early age). Among the things I wish I could forget as an advanced octogenarian is what is going on in the Near East. How heartily I agree with you.

Thank you for your kind words about *1900*. I agree with you about the superiority of the *Ambassadors* in everything except its lack of the sustained fervor which makes *The Golden Bowl* such a winged book—it seems to fly like an angel. But I am like you, I don't really believe in the importance of any of the four main characters. By the way I don't think it was any deep fault or unorthodoxy in James that makes for the dark shadows.[6] I think it was his curious penchant for people who were rich and kept good company and were thoroughly unpleasant and malicious and devious. I knew one very well—a man with a double barrelled name, something Smith or Smith something[7]—and he belonged to an old family and also to a Legion of the Damned but was not immoral but simply shadowy. He spent far too much time with people like that. I've always wondered how he adapted himself to conversation with them and with Joseph Conrad, who always struck him as a good and pleasant man.

It is baleful weather—you left at the right time—the rain came down in buckets when I went to the country for six days lately. Come back in the autumn when this present misery (said to be due to one of your earthquakes' erupting) [is over]. And in the meantime let me thank you for those lovely photographs and my revived memory of the visit.

Much affection,

Rebecca

How Lawrence hit the nail on the head quite often. It is true that it was George Eliot who made what goes on inside the head and the body important. She did it much better than James Joyce.

uncat. ms. Vault 390   manuscript
Yale University

[1] Gordon Haight (1901–1985), American literary scholar at Yale University. He is best known for his work on George Eliot which includes an edition of her letters and a biography.

[2] In response to the Argentine invasion of the tiny islands, a British crown colony off the South American coast, in April 1982, the British landed, forcing surrender of the Argentine troops on June 14.

[3] Airey Neave (1916–1979), English intelligence officer and Conservative M.P. who helped topple Edward Heath to make way for Margaret Thatcher as prime minister. He was killed by an IRA bomb. West met him at the Nuremberg war tribunal, later the subject of one of his books (1978). His World War II escape from the Colditz Prison is described in *They Have Their Exits* (1953).

[4] Perhaps Alfred, first Viscount Milner (1854–1925), English statesman and staunch imperialist. Much of his career was spent in South Africa, where he was high commissioner and governor of the Cape Colony, Transvaal, and Orange River Colony. His intransigence may have set the stage for the Boer War.

[5] Francis Pym (1922–), English politician, a defense minister for Margaret Thatcher, who became foreign secretary after the Falklands War. He was thought of as her potential successor.

[6] West had instructed her editor at Viking Mark Boxer to replace the her statement that "it can hardly be doubted today that Henry James was homosexual, sometimes achieving his

desires in reality and sometimes in fantasy" with: "It can hardly be doubted today that Henry James had a fantasy life that sometimes contravened convention, and that some of his male companions were of the same slightly fantastic breed, but on this he preserved the strictest silence. He even spoke with bitterest contempt of Oscar Wilde." Her reasoning was, "I do not care to be censorious where I do not feel it" (24 August 1981, University of Tulsa).

⁷A. John Hugh-Smith (1881–1964), English banker and gourmet, a classmate of Percy Lubbock at Cambridge and one of Edith Wharton's inner circle. James took an interest in him after they met at the Mount, Wharton's home, in 1910.

To: Gordon and Mary Haight

NO NECESSITY TO READ THIS. I JUST FEEL I WOULD LIKE TO TALK TO MY
FRIENDS THE HAIGHTS   48 Kingston House North
                                                            Prince's Gate, S.W. 7
                                                            [5 August 1982]

My dear Gordon and Mary,

I rather blench at what you will think of a Provence that has ⟨hem⟩ run a hem ⟨x⟩ {along} the Mediterranean littoral consisting of ghastly apartment houses. The market at Antibes is not to be spoiled but nearly everything else has been spoiled there, and inland, though much is not spoiled, at any moment one is faced with the fact that too many people, just by being too many people, become lethal. It is a curious thing how unprotected France has proved to be. I go to Amiens every ten years, thinking it has one of the most beautiful cathedrals in the world, but every time I visit it I am horrified to see how the town has been destroyed. There used to be nightingales singing not ten minutes of the Cathedral, in the garden of an old municipal building. But this is just the worst of living long—one sees that time is the enemy of nightingales as well as one's own knee joints and is disappointed.

But please do not fall into the generous error of thinking that Ulster is our Vietnam. This really is to simplify the tragedy too much. There was a plebiscite, and it was agreed the populations would stand by it, and poor devils, they found they would not stand by it. They just couldn't. And then we were faced with the horrible fact that there is no reason to suppose that every problem has a solution. This one has none. And that it hasn't is giving some people heartaches and other people dreadful joy. I certainly don't forget that a connection of mine (mentioned in [Fraud?]) was shot by English troops when he was driving down to an English camp to secure the release of some tenants of his who had been arrested by mistake. But this does not blind me to the fact that not all problems do not have a solution.

I had such a curious experience yesterday. I was taken out for a day's [drive?] by Alan Maclean (of Macmillan's) and his delightful wife Robin and their 14 year old son and Stanley Olsen[1]—to go to Ely Cathedral. We started in a morning of intense heat which was quite agreeable, and we lunched at Ely in glorious sunshine, in a garden. We then spent a happy time in the Cathedral until a storm broke over it that was incredible. It was not only the thunder and lightning, the whole cathedral seemed enclosed in a cascade of rain—rushing down the windows and ⟨spalling⟩{pelting} them with hail—all accompanied by a beautiful choir practice. After an hour more we decided we could not stay there forever and walked out to the car (under an avenue of trees!) and drove out of town in a ⟨distant⟩ [?] of [??] where there was no daylight—it was pitch dark, and as it was only about 4.30 there were no lights anywhere except at {road} junctions. It stopped ⟨outside London⟩ {about an hour} outside London, and there is nothing in the papers this morning about it though it must have destroyed a great deal of cereal crops and fruit—and the point of this anecdote is that Mrs Thatcher has the worst luck in the world. The fiends are always prescribing her with a new calamity!

Yours with much affection,

Rebecca

uncat. ms. vault file 390   manuscript
Yale University

---

[1] Stanley Olsen (1947–1989), American biographer who settled in London in 1969 and met West when he consulted with her about *Elinor Wylie: A Life Apart* (1978). He became a trusted friend, sharing her love of gossip and good food. West commissioned him to write her long biography, though he died before progressing very far with it.

Bibliography

Briggs, Austin. "Rebecca West vs. James Joyce, Samuel Beckett, and William Carlos Williams." In *Joyce in the Hibernian Metropolis: Essays,* ed. Morris Beja and David Norris. Columbus: Ohio State University Press, 1995.

Cowles, Fleur. *She Made Friends and Kept Them: An Anecdotal Memoir.* New York: Harper Collins, 1996.

Denison, Michael. *Double Act.* London: M. Joseph, 1985.

Ferguson, Moira. "Feminine Manicheanism: Rebecca West's Unique Fusion." *Minnesota Review* 15: 53–60.

Frankau, Pamela. *A Letter from R*b*cc* W*st.* Edinburgh: Tragaura Press, 1986.

Fromm, Gloria G. "Rebecca West: The Fictions of Fact and the Facts of Fiction," *New Criterion* 9 (1991): 45–53.

Glendinning, Victoria. *Rebecca West: Artist and Thinker.* London: Weidenfeld & Nicolson, 1987.

Hutchinson, G. E. "The Dome." In *The Itinerant Ivory Tower: Scientific and Literary Essays,* 241–55. New Haven: Yale University Press, 1953.

———. *A Preliminary List of the Writings of Rebecca West, 1912–51.* New Haven: Yale University Press, 1947.

Hynes, Samuel. "Introduction: In Communion with Reality." In *The Essential Rebecca West,* ix–xviii. Harmondsworth: Penguin, 1978.

Joyce, James. *Finnegans Wake.* New York: Viking, 1939.

Martin, David. *Ally Betrayed: The Uncensored Story of Tito and Mihailovitch.* New York: Prentice Hall, 1946.

———. *The Web of Disinformation: Churchill's Yugoslav Blunder,* San Diego: Harcourt Brace Jovanovich, 1990.

Orel, Harold. *The Literary Achievement of Rebecca West.* London: Macmillan, 1986.

Ray, Gordon N. *H. G. Wells and Rebecca West.* New Haven: Yale University Press, 1974.

Rollyson, Carl. *The Literary Legacy of Rebecca West.* San Francisco: International Scholars Publications, 1998.

———. *Rebecca West: A Saga of the Century.* London: Hodder and Stoughton, 1995.

Scott, Bonnie Kime. *The Gender of Modernism.* Bloomington: Indiana University Press, 1990.

———. *Refiguring Modernism.* 2 vols. Bloomington: Indiana University Press, 1995.

———. "The Strange Necessity of Rebecca West." In *Women Reading Women's Writing,* ed. Sue Roe, 263–86. Brighton: Harvester, 1987.

Thomas, Sue. "Rebecca West's Second Thoughts on Feminism." *Genders* 13 (Spring 1992): 90–107.

Untermeyer, Louis. *Bygones: The Recollections of Louis Untermeyer.* New York: Harcourt, Brace & World, 1965.

Weldon, Fay. *Rebecca West.* Harmondsworth: Penguin, 1985.

Wells, H. G. *The Correspondence of H. G. Wells.* Ed. David C. Smith. 4 vols. London: Pickering & Chatto, 1998.

——. *Experiment in Autobiography: Discoveries and Conclusions of a Very Ordinary Brain (Since 1866).* London: Gollancz, 1966.

West, Anthony. *H. G. Wells: Aspects of a Life.* London: Hutchinson, 1984.

——. *Heritage.* New York: Random House, 1955; London: Secker and Warburg, 1984.

West, Rebecca. *Arnold Bennett Himself.* New York: John Day, 1931.

——. *Cousin Rosamund.* New York: Viking Penguin, 1986.

——. *Ending in Earnest: A Literary Log.* New York: Doubleday Doran, 1931.

——. *The Essential Rebecca West.* 1977. Reprint, Harmondsworth: Penguin, 1983.

——. *Family Memories.* Ed., Faith Evans. London: Virago, 1987.

——. *The Fountain Overflows.* Harmondsworth: Penguin, 1987.

——. "The 'Freewoman.'" In *The Gender of Modernism,* ed. Bonnie Kime Scott, 573–77.

——. *Harriet Hume.* London: Virago, 1980.

——. *Henry James.* London: Nesbit, 1916.

——. "High Fountain of Genius." In *The Gender of Modernism,* ed. Bonnie Kime Scott, 592–96.

——. "Imagisme." *New Freewoman* 1 (1913): 86–87.

——. *The Judge.* 1922. London: Virago, 1980.

——. *A Letter to a Grandfather.* London: Hogarth Press, 1933.

——. *The Meaning of Treason.* New York: Viking, 1947.

——. "Mr Setty and Mr Hume." In *The Essential Rebecca West,* 260–319.

——. *1900.* New York: Viking, 1982.

——. *The Only Poet and Short Stories.* Ed. Antonia Till. London: Virago, 1992.

——. *Rebecca West: A Celebration.* New York: Viking, 1977.

——. *St. Augustine.* London: Peter Davies, 1933.

——. "Spinster to the Rescue." In *The Gender of Modernism,* ed. Bonnie Kime Scott, 577–80.

——. *The Strange Necessity.* London: Virago, 1987.

——. *Sunflower.* London: Virago, 1986.

——. *A Train of Powder.* London: Macmillan, 1955; Virago, 1984.

[West, Rebecca]. *War Nurse: The True Story of a Woman Who Lived, Loved, and Suffered on the Western Front.* New York: Cosmopolitan Book Corporation, 1930.

——. "What Is Mr. T. S. Eliot's Authority as a Critic?" In *The Gender of Modernism,* ed. Bonnie Kime Scott, 591–92.

——. *The Young Rebecca: Writings of Rebecca West, 1911–1917.* Ed. Jane Marcus. London: Virago, 1983.

Woolf, Virginia. *The Diary of Virginia Woolf.* 5 vols. Ed. Anne Olivier Bell. San Diego: Harcourt Brace Jovanovich, 1977–1984.

——. *The Letters of Virginia Woolf.* 6 vols. Ed. Nigel Nicolson and Joanne Trautmann. San Diego: Harcourt Brace Jovanovich, 1975–1980.

——. *A Room of One's Own.* 1929. Reprint, San Diego: Harcourt Brace Jovanovich, 1957.

Index